*Magic,*
*Witchcraft, and Ghosts*
*in the Greek and Roman Worlds*

DANIEL OGDEN

# Magic,
# Witchcraft, and Ghosts
# in the Greek and Roman Worlds

A SOURCEBOOK

OXFORD
UNIVERSITY PRESS
2002

# OXFORD
#### UNIVERSITY PRESS

Oxford   New York
Auckland   Bangkok   Buenos Aires   Cape Town   Chennai
Dar es Salaam   Delhi   Hong Kong   Istanbul   Karachi   Kolkata
Kuala Lumpur   Madrid   Melbourne   Mexico City   Mumbai   Nairobi
São Paulo   Shanghai   Singapore   Taipei   Tokyo   Toronto

and an associated company in Berlin

Published by Oxford University Press, Inc.
198 Madison Avenue, New York, New York 10016

www.oup.com

Oxford is a registered trademark of Oxford University Press

Library of Congress Cataloging-in-Publication Data
Ogden, Daniel.
Magic, witchcraft, and ghosts in the Greek and Roman worlds : a sourcebook / Daniel Ogden.
p. cm.
Includes bibliographical references and index.
ISBN 0-19-513575-X; ISBN 0-19-515123-2 (pbk.)
1. Magic, Greek.  2. Magic, Roman.  I. Title.
BF1591.O335   2002
133.4′0938—dc21     2001036667

9 8 7 6 5 4 3 2 1
Printed in the United States of America
on acid-free paper

# Acknowledgments

Thanks to my colleague Byron Harries for his moral support and help of different kinds with a number of the more obscure literary texts in this collection, to my colleague Stephen Mitchell for Apphia, and to Professsor David Bain of Manchester University for help with the text of *Cyranides*. I am particularly indebted to my friends Rena Georgiou and Panos Vassiliu for their help in securing figure 12.1 for me. Once again deep gratitude goes to Dr. Simon Price and Dr. Peter Derow of Oxford University for their continuing support. Thanks also to my editors at Oxford University Press, Ms. Susie Chang and Ms. Elissa Morris. I dedicate the book to my parents.

University of Wales Institute of                                    *D. O.*
Classics and Ancient History and
University of Wales, Swansea

# Contents

# Abbreviations

## ABBREVIATIONS FOR CORPORA OF MAGICAL DOCUMENTS

| | |
|---|---|
| CT | Gager 1992 |
| DT | Audollent 1904 |
| DTA | Wünsch 1897 |
| PDM | Betz 1992 |
| PGM | Preisendanz and Henrichs 1973–74 |
| SGD | Jordan 1985c |
| Suppl.Mag. | Daniel and Maltomini 1990–92 |
| Tab. Sulis | Tomlin 1988 |

## OTHER ABBREVIATIONS

| | |
|---|---|
| AAA | Athens Annals of Archaeology |
| AfO | Archiv für Orientforschung |
| AJA | American Journal of Archaeology |
| AJP | American Journal of Philology |
| AM | Mitteilungen des deutschn archäologischen Instituts. Athenische Abteiliung |
| ANRW | Aufstieg und Niedergang der römischen Welt |
| Arch.Eph. | Ἀρχαιολογικὴ Ἐφημερίς |
| ARW | Archiv für Religionswissenschaft |
| ASG | Abhandlungen der Sächsichen Gesellschaften. Philologisch-historische Klasse |
| BCH | Bulletin de correspondance hellénique |
| BICS | Bulletin of the Institute of Classical Studies |
| BJ | Bonner Jahrbucher |
| BO | Biblotheca Orientalis |
| BSA | Annual of the British School at Athens |
| CA | Classical Antiquity |
| CCC | Civiltà classica e cristiana |
| CIL | Corpus Inscriptionum Latinarum, consilio et auctoritate Academiae litterarum regiae Borussicae editum. 16 + yols. Berlin. 1863– |
| CJ | Classical Journal |
| C&M | Classica et Mediaevalia |
| CP | Classical Philology |
| CPG | Leutsch 1839–51 |
| CQ | Classical Quarterly |
| CR | Classical Review |
| CRAI | Comptes-rendus de séances de l'Académie des Inscriptions et Belles Lettres |
| CW | Classical World |
| DK | H. Diels and W. Krantz, eds. 1952. Die Fragmente der Vorsokratiker. 6th ed. Berlin |
| EMC/CV | Echos du monde classique/Classical views |

| | |
|---|---|
| ENS | *École normale supérieure* |
| EPRO | *Études préliminaires aux religions orientales dans l'empire romaine* |
| FGH | F. Jacoby, ed. 1923–58. *Die Fragmente der griechischer Historiker.* 15 vols. Berlin |
| GRBS | *Greek, Roman and Byzantine Studies* |
| HSCP | *Harvard Studies in Classical Philology* |
| HTR | *Harvard Theological Review* |
| IG | *Inscriptiones Graecae* 1903–. Berlin |
| ILS | H. Dessau, 1892–1916. *Inscriptiones Latinae selectae.* Berlin. |
| JbAC | *Jahrbuch für Antike und Christentum* |
| JHS | *Journal of Hellenic Studies* |
| JNES | *Journal of Near-Eastern Studies* |
| JOAI | *Jahreshefte des österreichischen archäologischen Instituts in Wien* |
| JRA | *Journal of Roman Archaeology* |
| JWCI | *Journal of the Warburg and Courtauld Institutes* |
| LCM | *Liverpool Classical Monthly* |
| LIMC | *Lexicon Iconographicum Mythologiae Classicae* |
| LS | C. T. Lewis and C. Short, eds. 1879. *A Latin Dictionary.* Oxford |
| MÉFRA | *Mélanges d'archéologie et d'histoire de l'École française de Rome* |
| MGH | *Monumenta Germaniae Historica.* 15 vols. 1877–1919 |
| NJKlA | *Neue Jahrbücher für das klassische Altertum* |
| OMRL | *Oudheidkundige Mededelingen uit het Rijksmuseum van Oudheden te Leiden* |
| PBSR | *Proceedings of the British School at Rome* |
| PCPS | *Proceedings of the Cambridge Philological Society* |
| PG | J-P. Migne, ed. 1857–66. *Patrologiae cursus completus. Series Graeca.* Paris |
| PL | J-P. Migne, ed. 1841–64. *Patrologiae cursus completus. Series Latina.* Paris |
| PO | *Patrologia Orientalis* 1903–. Paris |
| PP | *Parola del Passato* |
| QUCC | *Quaderni urbinati di cultura classica* |
| RAC | *Reallexikon für Antike und Christentum* |
| RE | Pauly et al. 1893– |
| REA | *Revue des études anciennes* |
| REG | *Revue des études grecques* |
| REL | *Revue des études latines* |
| RGVV | *Religionsgeschichtliche Versuche und Vorarbeiten* |
| RhM | *Rheinisches Museum für Philologie* |
| RHR | *Revue de l'histoire des religions* |
| RIB | R. G. Collingwood, 1965–. *The Roman inscriptions of Britain.* Sundry volumes. Oxford |
| RP | *Revue de philologie* |
| RSO | *Rivista degli studi orientali* |
| SEG | *Supplementum Epigraphicum Graecum.* 1923–. Leiden |
| SIFC | *Studi italiani di filologia classica* |
| SO | *Symbolae Osloenses* |
| Syl.[3] | W. Dittenberger, ed. 1915–24. *Sylloge inscriptionum graecarum.* 3rd ed. 4 vols. Leipzig |
| TAPA | *Transactions of the American Philological Association* |
| TrGF | Snell, B., R. Kannicht, and S. Radt, ed. 1971–. *Tragicorum Graecorum Fragmenta.* 4+ vols. Göttingen |
| VC | *Vigiliae Christianae* |
| WS | *Wiener Studien* |
| ZPE | *Zeitschrift für Papyrologie und Epigraphik* |

*Magic,*
*Witchcraft, and Ghosts*
*in the Greek and Roman Worlds*

# 1
# *Introduction*

## THE AIM OF THIS BOOK

The aim of this book is to provide a selection of sources in translation for magic and ghosts in Graeco-Roman antiquity that does the following:

- Provides a very full account of the rich representations of sorcerers and witches and their rites in ancient literature.
- Provides a good range of the ghost stories and other sources for ghosts and ideas about them from ancient literature.
- Provides a useful selection from the many hundreds of curse tablets from antiquity, which can be striking in their language and their goals, including a number of recently deciphered ones of great importance. Texts bearing upon the closely related phenomenon of voodoo dolls are also represented.
- Provides a similarly useful selection of amulet texts.
- Provides a meaningful selection of recipes and spells from the often daunting corpus of the Greek magical papyri.
- Attempts to expose such connections as there are between the documentary evidence for magic and its representation in high literature, and to do the same for ghosts.
- Selects and presents sources with an eye to important developments in the new scholarship on these subjects.
- Exploits pre-Christian and especially archaic and classical Greek evidence to the full, without neglecting the later period.
- Presents this material in a fashion that is readily accessible to undergraduates and interested amateurs (whether approaching the material from an interest in ancient social history or from a more general one in the so-called occult).
- Allows the material, so far as possible, to "speak for itself," through careful sequencing of passages and through heavy use of cross-referencing.
- Gives clearly and systematically for all passages their chief significance, their authorship (or provenance), their citation, their date of composition, and their original language.
- Provides all sources in original translations. Particular care has been taken in the selection of text-editions for the magical documents.
- Includes a substantial, up-to-date, guide to further reading.

In the last decade there has been an explosion in interest in ancient magic and the related field of ghosts among scholars of classical antiquity. This has generated new insights into these inherently fascinating subjects and, beyond this, into the broader social history of the ancient world. The new interest has been combined with an eagerness to widen the accessibility of the challenging source material on which the subjects depend, as is exemplified in the work of Hans Dieter Betz, David Jordan, Christopher Faraone, John Gager, Fritz Graf, Sarah Johnston, and their collaborators (see the bibliography). Such work has understandably given rise to a proliferation of undergraduate courses on ancient magic throughout United States and United Kingdom universities. But these courses have been hampered by the lack of a single-volume sourcebook that meets all the desirable criteria listed above, the need this volume aspires to fill.

The closest thing to such a sourcebook already available is Georg Luck's *Arcana Mundi* (1985), a title he translates as *Secrets of the Universe*. This book, compiled before the appearance of what we may call the "new scholarship" of ancient magic, remains a hugely important achievement. It can, however, be a difficult volume for a beginner to find his or her way around. It spreads its purview very wide, with the texts it classes as "magic" only occupying a single chapter out of six (large chapters are devoted to more specialized and late-antique-centered subjects such as astrology and alchemy). The documentary evidence for magic and ghosts is weakly represented. Space is given only to a few of the Greek magical papyri, while the curse tablets, the object of the most exciting developments in scholarship over the last decade, are almost entirely neglected, as are amulets. For the documentary material one must depend on more specialized sourcebooks. John Gager's *Curse Tablets and Binding Spells from the Ancient World* (1992) is extremely useful but is inevitably limited to the genre it serves. The same is true of Hans Dieter Betz's *Greek Magical Papyri in Translation* (2nd ed., 1992), which provides comprehensive translations of the fundamental corpus of the Greek magical papyri. This large volume, which has room for only sparing fragments of exegesis, is scarcely less baffling to novice students of the papyri than their Greek originals are. For obvious reasons, a number of the texts translated here overlap with those to be found in these three books, but there are also many that will be found in none of them, and indeed some texts of considerable importance that are not, to my knowledge, available in English, such as the major piece with which I close the volume, Libanius's speech *Against the Lying Mage*, **300**.

## THE PARAMETERS OF THE BOOK AND ITS STRUCTURE

The passages collected here translate literary and documentary texts written in Greek or Latin (occasionally both) produced throughout the Graeco-Roman world between the beginning of the Greek archaic period, 776 B.C., and the end of the Roman Empire, 476 A.D. (with a few run-overs). The primary focus is on magic in its pagan context; Christian sources are included where they shed important light on this, but there has been no systematic attempt to cover Christianity's reception of magic. A particular attempt has been made to give heavy coverage to material from the earlier end of this period, that from archaic and classical Greece.

The definition of "magic" is famously problematic, and authors of books on the subject usually feel the need for many pages of philosophical reflection on the issue in their introductions. It is obviously desirable that a sourcebook, particularly one designed to be used by undergraduates, among others, should avoid the expression of any dogmatic view on the matter and leave its readers to make up their own minds on it. At the same time, it would be naïve to suppose that such a book could be compiled in the first place without any criteria of selection of material, and these criteria must proceed from, or lead to, some sort of definition of magic, however inexplicit, inchoate, or half-baked. The primary criterion I have in fact adopted for the selection of passages for this book is that of relevance to the subject matter of recent scholarly books on antiquity with such words as "magic" in their titles. I am aware that this will appear to be a disappointing sleight of hand to many of a philosophical bent, but it would have been pedagogically irresponsible to take any other course of action. Some recent discussions on the definitional problems of magic in ancient context can be found in *A Guide to Further Reading* I.8.

It would also be naïve to suppose, running commentaries aside, that the source passages, once selected, could be grouped and sequenced within the book without the entailing of a series of arguments about the configuration of ancient magic. If there is one overriding argument implicit in the book, it is, as the title itself indicates, the contention of the centrality of ghosts to ancient magic: they were not its only motor, but it is fair to say that they were its chief one. The importance of the role of ghosts in ancient magic has particularly come to the fore in recent work on curse tablets. The chapterization of the book has been developed to take this importance into account. Otherwise the book has been structured at chapter level in accordance with a number of overlapping categories: in part in accordance with sorcerer type (shamans, mages, Egyptians, neo-Pythagoreans, witches, etc.); in part in accordance with type of magical document (literary account, curse tablet, voodoo dolls, papyrus recipes [these being concentrated in chapter 11], amulets, and laws); in part in accordance with type of magical activity (necromancy, cursing, erotic attraction, etc.). Heavy cross-referencing between the passages reproduced extends the range of each chapter. Cross-referencing has also been used to draw together groups of passages united by themes unaddressed at chapter or subsection level. In this way one can quickly assemble passages relevant to the goddess Hecate, for example, or to healing magic, or to the technique of snake-blasting. Where particularly desirable, chronological factors have also been used in sequencing. Some of the sourcebook's focal subjects are treated in considerable detail, with the reproduction of series of passages on similar themes, in order to afford the reader opportunities for a greater depth of engagement. The advantages of such opportunities, in my opinion, outweigh the corollary retraction in the range of subjects covered.

The book begins with a series of chapters, 2–7, on sorcerer types, focusing first on men, then on women. These chapters include many narratives of a particularly appealing and accessible nature and so afford a relatively congenial entry into the study of ancient magic. Chapter 2 looks at the earlier home-grown Greek sorcerers of various kinds. First, consideration is given to the Pythagorean-inspired traditions of a group of men that supposedly flourished in the archaic period, whom we now call the Greek "shamans." These men had a number of miraculous capacities, many of which proceeded from their abilities to detach their souls from bodies during life. In the classical period a range of largely hostile sources constructs for us, under such terms as *goêtes* ("sorcerers") and *magoi* ("mages"), an impression of a nebulous group of supposedly fraudulent and beggarly magical professionals who concerned themselves with such things as the curing of illness, the manufacture of curse tablets, and the well-being of the soul in the afterlife. Among these a subgroup of "evocators" (*psuchagôgoi*) is identifiable. Also in the classical period is found the phenomenon of the "ventriloquists" (*engastrimuthoi*, etc.), men or women with prophetic demons in their stomachs that use their hosts as mouthpieces. But already too in the classical period the Greeks were beginning to project the idea of the male sorcerer onto alien races, primarily Oriental ones, and many of the most exciting portraits of male practitioners in the Graeco-Roman tradition belong in this category. The developing trend in the representation of male sorcerers as Median or Persian mages, as Babylonian Chaldaeans, and as Egyptians is the subject of chapter 3. Chapter 4 looks in greater depth at three sorcerers from the first and second centuries A.D. for whom substantial and developed literary portraits survive. Two of these, Apollonius of Tyana and Alexander of Abonouteichos, were neo-Pythagoreans and revived the work of the shamans. The first is known primarily from the positive portrait of Philostratus; the second is known almost exclusively from the extremely hostile portrait of Lucian. These two pieces accordingly constitute a useful antithesis. Also included here is a substantial portrait of Simon Magus, supposedly the great rival of Saint Peter. Our accounts of him may be almost entirely fictional.

Chapter 5 turns to the women—to witches, the representation of whom in the Graeco-Roman tradition is almost entirely fictive. First are a series of portraits, some of them extended, of the two great witches of Greek mythology, the kindred Medea and Circe. The tales about these women, already well established in the Archaic period, bestow a full range of powers upon them. Chapter 6 looks at other witches and witch-like women in Greek (and related Latin) literature, such as Deianeira, the wife of Heracles. Chapter 7 is devoted to the Latin response to such imaginary witches, first in poetry, in which witch figures became commonplace, and second in novels. The Romans liked to imagine their witches as altogether more bloodthirsty, gruesome, and morbid figures. Readers who prefer their magic in "Gothic" style should turn straight to the sections given to Horace's Canidia, Lucan's Erictho, and Apuleius's Meroe.

Ghosts and cadaverous material play an important role in the unlovely craft of the Latin witches, which leads conveniently to consideration of ghosts and the dead in their own right in chapter 8. The categories of dead most likely to be restless, and therefore to manifest themselves as ghosts or to haunt, were those who died before their time (*aôroi*), those who died by violence (*biaiothanatoi*), those, particularly girls, who died before marriage (*agamoi*), and those who were denied due burial after death (*ataphoi*). It was the restless dead who lent themselves most easily to exploitation for magical purposes. Much of this chapter is devoted to the laying of ghosts, and in this connection some entertaining stories about haunted houses survive. Attention is also given to the (Jewish-influenced) evidence for the expulsion of possessing ghosts from individuals. The souls of young boys could be so valued for magical operations that they could, in popular imagination at any rate, even be "manufactured" for the purpose. The supposed purity of the soul of the living boy in any case gave it a privileged position in attempts to communicate with ghosts and other powers. Finally this chapter looks briefly at werewolves, which were sometimes regarded as a kind of ghost.

The most direct use of ghosts for magical purposes was for necromancy, a term I use here in its original sense to mean "divination from the dead," and this forms the subject of chapter 9. Ghosts could be evocated for divination either at oracles of the dead or at tombs. The existence of the former seems to be attested already in Homer's *Odyssey*. The Roman period sees the emergence of a new variety of necromancy alongside the evocation method, that of the reanimation of corpses. The roots of this form of divination in reality are difficult to fathom but may have been connected with skull necromancy. Other varieties of magical divination, some of them not entirely unconnected with ghosts, are also considered here.

Another important magical use for ghosts, directly or indirectly, was in the execution of binding spells (*katadesmoi* or *defixiones*). These form the principal subject of chapter 10. The main themes of these fascinating texts are now conventionally classified under five headings: legal curses, competition curses, trade curses, erotic curses, and the slightly distinctive "prayers for justice." All these varieties are exemplified here, apart from the erotic one, which is dealt with in the next chapter. Included with our treatment of binding spells are also some passages on the "evil eye," another variety of cursing, which, however, did not always proceed from intention.

Chapter 11 is devoted to erotic magic. Apart from being the subject of many of the more striking curse tablets, it is a particularly popular theme in the Greek magical papyri, which are given prominence here, and it is very often the chief concern of the witches in the literary portraits of them. It is also a subject of interest within the continually expanding field of ancient gender studies. Here consideration is given to the two principal varieties of erotic magic, curses of separation and curses of attraction, and to some of the paraphernalia particularly associated with the latter, the drawing-down of the moon, the *iunx* or "wryneck," and the *hippomanes* or "horse-madness" plant, gland, or secretion. This is also the place to consider some magical techniques ancillary to erotic magic, namely, those offering contraception or procuring abortion.

The next chapter, 12, turns to another category of magical document, *kolossoi* or voodoo dolls and similar magical images, and to the literary sources that bear upon them. These intriguing artifacts, it seems, preceded curse tablets, to which they are closely related and the functions of which they share for the most part. In chapter 13 consideration is given to a final category of magical document, amulets, and again the literary sources that bear upon them. Amulets afforded many forms of protection to their wearers and in particular were often curative or exorcistic. Many of them bestowed erotic attractiveness or general favor.

Finally, chapter 14 looks at some of the evidence for legislation against magic; this is surprisingly meager for Greek culture but more plentiful for Roman. The book closes with two forensic speeches on magical subjects. Apuleius's *Apology* is a defense against a series of charges of magical practice, chiefly erotic magic. Libanius's speech *Against the Lying Mage* is a fictitious speech based on an imaginary premise. Both speeches are interesting for the logical tricks they play with the concept of magic in a legal context.

## THE PRESENTATION OF SOURCES AND THE COMMENTARIES

Every attempt has been made to present the sources in as clear a way as possible. Not only are these distributed across fourteen chapters, but they also participate in a continuous numerical series. Each source's serial number is followed by essential information about it: its main significance, its formal reference, its original language, and its date of production (which, it should be noted, is not necessarily the same as the events referred to in it).

The translated source follows at once, without further introductory material, for the sake of immediacy. Care has been taken in the case of the documentary sources to base the translation on the best available published editions, since the difficulties of decipherment and interpretation can lead to significant variations between them. The editions used for the literary sources are usually listed in alphabetical order of ancient author or of corpus in the list of texts in the bibliography; occasionally, for some more obscure sources, direct reference is made in the heading (using the format of author and date) to items of scholarship listed in the works cited section of the bibliography. The translations printed here are all my own, but I do not disguise the fact that some previously published translations, particularly those offered by the editors of the more difficult and obscure documentary sources, have been of influence. I do not confront the reader with the niceties of textual disputes, except on the rare occasions where these have a particular bearing upon magical issues. The style of some of the documentary sources is less exquisite than that expected from the heights of classical literature, and this will sometimes be apparent in the translations provided. Round brackets in the translations, (. . .), are used merely in punctuation of the original text. Square brackets, [. . .], enclose the translator's brief explanatory material or the original word translated, with Greek terms transliterated. In particular, they supply the words used for such things as "sorcerers," "witches," and "sorcery," usually with the exceptions of *magos* and its derivatives, which go conveniently into "mage" and its derivatives, and *daimôn* and its derivatives, which go conveniently into "demon" and its derivatives. Angle brackets, <. . .>, are used, infrequently, to indicate significant editorial supplements to the ancient texts as preserved.

The translated source is then followed by a commentary or exegesis. The commentaries are of varying length, depending on the intrinsic importance of their source and on its strategic role within the sourcebook. The commentaries seek to shed light on major obscurities in the sources, to provide germane background information, and, above all, to draw attention to the source's relationship with the other sources in the volume. The frequent cross-references to such other sources utilize their serial number in bold type. Occasionally direct reference is made, in conventional format, to texts not included in the volume. There has not been room to explain every last obscurity in the cases of some of the richer and more complex texts, but I have not taken this as a ground for exclusion. Nonclassicists who want to know more about ancient authors and institutions represented here only by name are referred in the first instance to N. S. R. Hornblower and A. J. Spawforth's *Oxford Classical Dictionary* (3rd ed., Oxford, 1996), a categorical improvement on that work's earlier editions. For mythological references, M. C. Howatson's *Oxford Companion to Classical Literature* (Oxford, 1989) may be of use. Places are most conveniently located with the maps in *The Barrington Atlas of the Greek and Roman World*, edited by R. J. Talbert (Princeton, 2000).

# 2
# *Greek Sorcerers*

## SHAMANS

The earliest variety of indigenous male sorcerer attested for the Greek world is the "shaman." This term is commonly applied to a linked series of figures celebrated in the Pythagorean and Orphic traditions. They flourished, supposedly, in the archaic period. The notices of Herodotus and the fragments of Empedocles demonstrate that the notion of the shaman-type had at any rate already become established by the early classical period. No doubt it was much older. The modern term "shaman" is derived from the Tungus medicine man of that name. He detaches his soul from his body in an ecstatic trance. This detached soul then speaks with the gods in their own language and cures the sick by retrieving their souls from the land of the dead or by defeating death-bringing demons in battle. He also attracts animals to the hunt with his music and by defeating the gods that preside over them with his soul. The Greek shamans are similarly characterized by the ability to manipulate their own souls, be it by detaching them temporarily from their bodies and sending them on voyages of discovery, suspending them from life, reincarnating them, or "bilocating." The principal figures in the series, with their supposed *floruits*, are as follows:

| | |
|---|---|
| Orpheus: | mythical era |
| Trophonius: | mythical era |
| Aristeas of Proconessus: | early seventh century B.C. |
| Hermotimus of Clazomenae: | seventh century B.C.? |
| Epimenides of Cnossus or Phaestus: | ca. 600 B.C. |
| Pythagoras of Samos: | 530s–520s B.C. |
| Abaris the Hyperborean: | sixth century B.C.? |
| Zalmoxis of the Thracian Getae: | sixth century B.C.? |
| Empedocles of Acragas: | ca. 485–35 B.C. |

A number of further themes recur in the representations of the shamans: extended retreats into underground chambers (a symbolic death and descent to the underworld, from which they return with enlightenment); divination; control of the elements; association with the cult of Hyperborean Apollo; dismissal of pollution and pestilence. For another possible archaic shaman see **140**; for later Greek "shamans" see **57–64**.

## 1  Pythagoras finds wisdom in the underworld

iii B.C. (Hermippus);
iii A.D. (Diogenes
Laertius)

Diogenes Laertius 8.41;
Hermippus of Smyrna
*FGH* 1026 F24

Greek

And Hermippus has something else to say about Pythagoras. For he relates that when he was in Italy he made a little chamber under the ground and told his mother to write down what happened on a tablet, indicating the time at which things took place, and to send them down to him until he came up again. This his mother did. After a time Pythagoras came up again emaciated and skeletal. He went into the assembly and claimed that he had come from Hades, and he read out to the people what had happened. They were beguiled by his words and wept and wailed. They believed that he was divine, and even handed their wives over to him, thinking that they would learn something from him. They became known as the *Pythagoricae*. This is what Hermippus says.

HERMIPPUS OF SMYRNA, AN IMPORTANT FIGURE in the history of Greek biography, worked in the third century B.C. (see also **45**). This is a rationalizing account of the shamanic practice of mapping descent into underground chambers and emergence therefrom onto the sequence of death, edification in the underworld, and return to life. Burkert (1972:155–9) suggests that the mother who slips Pythagoras notes is in particular a rationalization of his instruction in the underworld by the mother-goddess Demeter.

## 2  Pythagoras, Egyptian crypts, Chaldaeans, and mages

iii A.D.

Diogenes Laertius 8.3

Greek

He was in Egypt when Polycrates introduced him to Amasis by letter. He learned the language of the Egyptians, as Antiphon says in his book on *Men excelling in virtue*, and he associated with Chaldaeans and mages. And then in Crete he went down into the Idaean cave with Epimenides, and in Egypt he also descended into crypts [*aduta*]. He learned the secrets of the gods. Then he returned to Samos, and, finding his homeland under the tyranny of Polycrates, departed to Croton in Italy. There he laid down laws for the Greeks in Italy and he and he was held in high regard, along with his pupils. There were almost three hundred of them, and they governed the state in the best way, so that the constitution more or less was a true "aristocracy" [*aristokrateia*, literally "rule by the best"].

THIS PASSAGE DEMONSTRATES THE EXTENT TO which the shamans came to be perceived as sorcerers among sorcerers. It makes a general principle out of Pythagoras's descent into underground chambers for some sort of mystery-initiation. In this practice it associates him both with other Greek shamans, in particular Epimenides and his Idaean cave (**9**), and with Egyptian sorcerers and their crypts (**53–4**). But he is also said to have derived learning from the other great sorcerer races, those of the Orient (**43, 45**).

## 3  Pythagoras's range of miracles

Mid–iv B.C.

Aristotle *On the
Pythagoreans* F191
Rose; Apollonius
*Historiae Mirabiles* 6

Greek

Pythagoras the son of Mnesarchus came after these men. First he worked on mathematics and numbers, but later on he involved himself also in Pherecydes's miracle-mongering. When a cargo ship was coming to harbor at Metapontum and those at hand were praying that it should come in safely on account of its freight, Pythagoras, who was standing by, said "Then you will see a dead body sailing the boat!" And again in Caulonia, as Aristotle says. <The same Aristotle> tells many stories about Pythagoras. He tells that Pythagoras killed a snake of deadly bite in Etruria by biting it himself. He prophesied the dispute that arose among the Pythagoreans. So he disappeared to Metapontum seen by no one. And while he was crossing a river at Cosa with other men he heard it address him in a loud and superhuman voice, "Hail, Pythagoras." Those with him were terrified. Once he appeared in Croton and Metapontum on the same day and at the same hour. Once he was sitting in the theatre, and as he stood up, Aristotle says, he accidentally revealed that his thigh was golden to those sitting next to him. Other marvelous things are told of him too, but since it is not my intention merely to recycle material I shall end my discussion here.

THIS PASSAGE SUMMARIZES PYTHAGORAS'S extraordinary abilities; Lucian could apply the term "sorcery" to them (*goêteia*; *Bion Prasis* 2). Among these abilities bilocation is of particular interest; see **5**, where, however, the bilocation is said to have taken place between Metapontum and Tauromenium. The neo-Pythagorean Apollonius of Tyana similarly manifested himself simultaneously at Ephesus and Thurii (**58**). Pherecydes of Syros, whose supposed *floruit* was the mid–sixth century B.C., was a traveling miracle-worker. He speculated on the origins of the cosmos and was a proponent of the immortality of the soul. He is said to have been the first writer of Greek prose. For snake-blasting see **49**, with commentary.

## 4   Pythagoras, Salmoxis, and underworld mysteries

420s B.C.

Herodotus 4.94–6

Greek

**94.** [The Thracian Getae] hold themselves immortal in the following way. They do not believe that they die, but that after "death" they go to join the demon Salmoxis. Some of them call this same power "Beleïzis." Every five years they choose one from among themselves by lot and send him as a messenger to Salmoxis, giving him instructions as to what they need on each occasion. They send him to Salmoxis in the following way. Some of them are organized to hold up three spears. Others take hold of the man being sent to Salmoxis by his hands and feet, swing him round and throw him up into the air and onto the points of the spears. If he dies from being impaled, the god is held to be propitious to them. But if he does not die, they blame the messenger himself and say he is a worthless man, and then they proceed to send another messenger. The instructions are given to him while he is still alive. These same Thracians shoot arrows up toward heaven at thunder and lightening and threaten their god. They believe there to be no god other than their own. **95.** As I learn from the Greeks who inhabit the Hellespont and Pontus, this Salmoxis was once a man and was a slave in Samos, and he was owned by Pythagoras the son of Mnesarchus. He subsequently gained his freedom and acquired a great deal of money, after which he returned to his native land. The Thracians lived miserable lives and were rather witless, so Salmoxis, who was familiar with the Ionian lifestyle and a culture richer than that to be found in Thrace (he had after all associated with Greeks and among these Pythagoras, who was not the feeblest intellectual), constructed a men's chamber. In this he entertained the chief of the townsmen and feasted them well. He taught them that neither he nor those that drank with him nor their descendants would die. Rather, they would come to a place where they would live forever and have all good things. While he was doing and saying these things, he was constructing an underground chamber. When he had completed it, he disappeared from the Thracians' sight and, descending below into the underground chamber, he lived there for three years. They missed him and mourned for him as dead. In the fourth year he appeared again to the Thracians, and this is how they came to believe his claims. **96.** This is what they say he did. I myself neither disbelieve nor indeed place a great deal of belief in the stories about this man and his underground chamber, but I think that Salmoxis lived many years before Pythagoras. As to whether Salmoxis was a man or is some local god of the Getae, I leave the question open.

SALMOXIS (OR ZALMOXIS) IS ALSO HERE BROUGHT into an (admittedly problematic) association with Pythagoras. The imagery of underworld-descent and initiation underlie these details. For Salmoxis see further **44, 299**.

## 5   Pythagoras's golden thigh; Abaris's flight on his arrow

iii A.D.

Porphyry *Life of Pythagoras* 28–9

Greek

**28.** It is commonly spoken of that Pythagoras showed his golden thigh to Abaris the Hyperborean after the latter had conjectured that he was Hyperborean Apollo, whose priest he was, thus confirming the truth of it. It is also known that when a ship was putting in to port and his friends were praying that its cargo should be theirs Pythagoras said, "Then you will have a corpse," and the ship duly arrived with a corpse on board. A great many tales even more marvelous and divine have been told about the man, either similar to these in nature or compatible with them. In brief, there is no one of whom more achievements or more extraordinary achievements have been suspected. **29.** He is recorded as making infallible predictions of earthquakes and as promptly averting pestilences and fierce winds. He checked hailstorms and calmed the waters of rivers and seas so that his companions could enjoy a gentle passage over them. Empedocles, Epimenides, and Abaris shared similar abilities and often accomplished such things. Their poems testify clearly to this. Also, Empedocles acquired the title "wind-warder" [*alexanemos*], Epimenides "purifier" [*kathartês*], and Abaris "air-traveler," because he rode on an arrow given him by Hyperborean Apollo and crossed rivers and seas and inaccessible places, traveling somehow through the air. Some supposed that Pythagoras had exercised the same power when he conversed with his companions in both Metapontum and Tauromenium on the same day.

HERE THE STRONG LINK IS MADE BETWEEN Abaris, Pythagoras, and other shamans. Nor is the figure of Aristeas far away: the Hyperboreans were one of the remote northern peoples his soul had visited, and he had returned to promote Apollo (**7**). Pythagoras is compared with Abaris, Empedocles, and Epimenides specifically in his ability to avert pestilences and control elements. The latter was a commonplace of the literary sorcerer's and the witch's repertoire (**91–107**). Abaris's journey through the air on a (presumably feathered) arrow represents the flight of his detached soul, just as Aristeas's flying soul was visualized as a bird (**6**). With Abaris should be compared also Lucian's "Hyperborean mage," who, among his other abilities, could similarly fly through the air (**244**).

## 6   Pythagoras's reincarnation and the soul-projection of Aristeas of Proconessus

ii A.D.

Maximus of Tyre 10.2

Greek

Pythagoras the Samian was the first of the Greeks to dare claim that his body would not die, but that his soul would fly up and go off, immortal and unaging. And indeed he said that it had existed before coming into him. People believed this assertion, and that he had been on the earth before in another body. He had been Euphorbus the Trojan at that time. This was why they believed him. He came to the temple of Athena, where there were many dedications of all sorts. Among them was a shield of Phrygian shape, faded with age. He said that he recognized the shield and that the man that had killed him in battle in Ilium at that time had taken it from him. The locals were amazed. They took the dedication down and on it was the legend: "Menelaus dedicates this to Pallas Athene, having taken it from Euphorbus." If you want, I'll relate another story too for you. The body of a man of Proconnesus would lie there breathing, albeit indistinctly and in a fashion close to death. His soul would escape from his body and wander through the ether like a bird, observing everything beneath, land, sea, rivers, cities, peoples, their experiences and the natural world. Then it would enter into his body again and set it back on its feet, as if it were making use of an instrument, and it would recount the various things it had seen and heard among the various peoples.

FOR MAXIMUS, AS FOR OTHERS, THE ASSOCIATION between reincarnation and soul-projection was an obvious one, as was the bond between Pythagoras and Aristeas.

## 7 Aristeas of Proconnesus: Soul-projection, metempsychosis, and bilocation

420s B.C.

Herodotus 4.13–6

Greek

**13.** The Proconessian poet Aristeas, son of Cay-strobius, said that he was possessed by Apollo [*phoibolamptos*] and came to the Issedones, and that beyond the Issedones lived the one-eyed Arimaspians, and beyond these the gold-guarding griffins, and beyond these again the Hyperboreans, the last people before the sea. He said that all these peoples apart from the Hyperboreans were forever attacking their neighbors, and that the Arimaspians started it. The Issedones were being expelled from their territory by the Arimaspians, the Scythians from theirs by the Issedones, and that the Cimmerians who live on the southern sea [i.e., the Black Sea] abandoned their territory under pressure from the Scythians. Thus Aristeas too disagrees with the Scythians about this land.

**14.** I have told where the Aristeas that said these things came from. Now I shall tell the story I heard about him in Proconnesus and Cyzicus. They tell that Aristeas, from one of Proconnesus's best families, went into a fuller's in the city and dropped dead. The fuller shut up shop and went off to inform the dead man's relatives. The news of Aristeas's death spread throughout the city, but it was disputed by a man of Cyzicus who had just come from the city of Artace. He said that he had met Aristeas heading for Cyzicus and had had a conversation with him. His denial was strenuous. Meanwhile, the dead man's relatives arrived at the fuller's with the appropriate accoutrements to perform the funeral. When the room was opened up there was no Aristeas to be seen, dead or alive. Seven years later he rematerialized in Proconessus and composed the poem that is now known by the Greeks as the *Arimaspeia*, only to disappear again as soon as he was done. **15.** This is the story one hears in these two cities, but I know for sure what happened to the Metapontines in Italy two hundred and forty years after Aristeas's second disappearance, as I discovered by making calculations in Proconnessus and Metapontum. The Metapontines tell that Aristeas made an actual appearance in their country and bade them establish an altar for Apollo and to erect by its side a statue bearing the legend "Aristeas of Proconessus." For, he explained, they were the only people in Italy to whose land Apollo had come, and that he himself, who was now Aristeas, had attended him. But at the time he had attended him, he had been a crow. After saying this he disappeared. The Metapontines sent to Delphi and asked the god what this manifestation/ghost [*phasma*] of the person was, and the Pythia bade them obey it and told them that they would benefit from doing so. On receipt of this response they carried out the instructions. And there now stands a statue bearing the legend "Aristeas" beside the actual effigy of Apollo. Laurels surround it, in the marketplace. No more need be said of Aristeas.

**16.** No one really knows for sure about the land currently at issue. I haven't been able to interrogate anyone who claims to have seen it for himself. And not even Aristeas, whom I mentioned just above, claimed in his poems to have gone beyond the Issedones, but he described the peoples to their north on the basis of hearsay alone, and explained that he had his information from the Issedones. But I shall lay everything out as accurately as possible and covering the furthest distance possible.

Comparison with other shaman stories indicates that the Proconessus-Cyzicus narration (14) has been conflated from two or three different tales:

1. A tale in which Aristeas performed bilocation, as Pythagoras could (3).
2. A tale in which Aristeas's soul could temporarily leave his body as dead and wander at will before returning to it and reanimating it (see 6).
3. A tale in which Aristeas dematerialized completely before rematerializing again after an extended interval (as in 15).

Aristeas was evidently supposed to have made his journey to the fantastic lands north of the Black Sea by means of soul-projection. The term *phoibolamptos* apparently describes the ecstatic condition in which this was achieved. The more cynical might observe that Aristeas's island of Proconessus, situated in the Propontis, was an obvious collection point for travelers' lore about the lands around the Black Sea. Aristeas's reappearance is undated, but even if recent at the time of Herodotus's writing, it puts his original lifetime back in the early seventh century. He was to be referred to by Strabo as a sorcerer (*goês*) *par excellence* (C589 F16). For Aristeas's detached soul as a bird see **5, 6**; the crow was sacred to Apollo. For the Pythagorean connection with Metapontum see **3**.

## 8   Hermotimus of Clazomenae: Soul-projection

ii B.C.

Apollonius *Historiae Mirabiles* 3

Greek

The following sort of thing is reported of Hermotimus of Clazomenae. They say his soul would wander from his body and stay away for many years. Visiting places, it would predict what was going to happen, for example torrential rains or droughts, and in addition earthquakes and pestilences and the suchlike. His body would just lie there, and after an interval his soul would return to it, as if to its shell, and arouse it. He did this frequently, and whenever he was about to go on his travels he gave his wife the order that no one, citizen or anyone, should touch his body. But some people came into the house, prevailed upon his wife and observed Hermotimus lying on the floor naked and motionless. They brought fire and burned him, in the belief that, when the soul came back and no longer had anything to reenter, he would be completely deprived of life. This is exactly what happened. The people of Clazomenae honor Hermotimus even to this day and have a temple to him. Women may not enter it for the reason above [i.e., the wife's betrayal].

See clearchus's account of the drawing-out of a boy's soul with a stick (**133**).

## 9 Epimenides purifies Athens after the murder of the Cylonians

vi B.C. (Xenophanes);
iv B.C. (Theopompus);
ii A.D. (Phlegon);
iii A.D. (Diogenes)

Diogenes Laertius
1.109–112, incorporating
Theopompus *FGH* 115
F67a, Phlegon of Tralles
*FGH* 257 F38,
Xenophanes *DK* 21 B20

Greek

**109.** According to Theopompus [*FGH* 115 F67a] and many others Epimenides's father was Phaestius, but others say he was Dosias or Agesarchus. He was Cretan by birth, from Cnossus, although he changed his appearance by growing his hair long. One day his father sent him to the farm to look for a sheep. Around midday he left the road and went to sleep in a cave for fifty-seven years. After this he got up and continued to look for the sheep, thinking he had only been asleep for a little while. Since he could not find it, he came to the farm, where found everything altered, and the property now belonging to someone else. He returned to the town in a state of incomprehension. He entered his own house and found inside it people who asked him who he was. Eventually he found his younger brother, who was by that time now an old man, and learned the whole truth from him. **110.** He became known among the Greeks and was taken to be exceptionally favored by the gods.

At that time the Athenians were in the grip of a pestilence. The Pythia prophesied that they should purify the city. They sent Nicias the son of Niceratus to Crete with a ship, to call in Epimenides. He came in the forty-sixth Olympiad [595–2 B.C.], purified their city, and put an end to the pestilence in the following fashion. He took black sheep and white ones and led them onto the Areopagus. From there he let them wander wherever they wanted, instructing their followers to sacrifice each sheep to the deity at hand, wherever it should cast itself down. In this way the blight was abated. As a result even still in these days it is possible to find nameless altars around the demes of Attica that are memorials to the propitiation performed at that time. Some writers say that he declared the cause of the pestilence to be the Cylonian pollution, and that he indicated how to dismiss it. For this reason two young men, Cratinus and Ctesibius, went to their deaths and the city was delivered from its disaster. **111.** The Athenians decreed that he be given a talent in reward and a ship to take him home to Crete, but he would not accept the money. Instead, he made a treaty of friendship and alliance between the peoples of Cnossus and Athens.

He died soon after his return home, at the age of 157, as Phlegon says in his book *On the Long-lived* [*FGH* 257 F38]. But the Cretans say that he lived one year short of three hundred. Xenophanes of Colophon says that he heard that he lived to the age of 154 [DK 21 B 20]. He wrote poems *On the Birth of the Curetes and Corybantes* and a *Theogony*, five thousand lines, and *The Construction of the Argo* and *Jason's Voyage to Colchis*, six thousand lines. **112.** In prose he wrote *On Sacrifices*, *The Constitution of Crete*, and *Minos and Rhadamanthys*, four thousand lines. He founded the temple of the Semnai goddesses in Athens, as Lobon of Argos says in his *On Poets*. He is said to have been the first to have purified houses and fields and founded temples. There are some who say that he didn't go to sleep, but that he went into retreat for a certain period while he concerned himself with root-cutting.

THIS IS THE GRANDEST OF ALL THE underworld/underground-chamber stories attaching to the shamans. Perhaps the works attributed to Epimenides on the underworld judges Minos and Rhadamanthys were supposed to convey the mysteries he had learned in that place. His long sleep and extended life can be compared with the lengthy disappearance of Aristeas before his rematerialization (7). His un-Cretan long hair was also a Pythagorean trait. The alternative tale, in accordance with which Epimenides withdrew from society to study root-cutting, associates him with a more conventional variety of sorcery (see 67).

The tale of Epimenides' purification of Athens after the pollution caused by the Alcmaeonid slaughter of the supporters of the would-be tyrant Cylon (for which see Plutarch *Solon* 12) is of particular interest. The technique employed is very similar to that said to have been used by evocators to track down the corpses of restless ghosts for propitiation (**30**). Epimenides' solution seems therefore to have been one of ghost-laying, an entirely appropriate approach for the shamans with their interests in soul-manipulation. The altars may have been dedicated to the Semnai goddesses, who were also supposedly honored by Epimenides with a temple of their own. These obscure beings appear to have been some sort of demons of vengeance for the dead, related or comparable to Eumenides and Erinyes.

## SORCERERS, MAGES, BEGGAR-PRIESTS, AND (ORPHIC) INITIATORS

A series of important texts in the classical period, the ideas of which are reflected in later sources too, string together series of terms around the notion of a variety of male professional: sorcerer (*goês*), mage (*magos*), beggar-priest (*agurtês*), diviner (*mantis*), (Orphic) initiator, and charlatan. Such men are in particular attributed with manipulations of souls, purifications, the use of incantations, and the manufacture of binding spells. Most of the allusions to them are ostensibly "external" and hostile, although some may, on closer scrutiny, be less "external" than they would like to think (see **13, 14**, with commentaries). But the one obviously "internal" text in this series, the Orphic commentary (**18**), is evidently making similar connections, albeit without the negative connotations. These texts focus on the Greek world. It is unclear, already from the time of Heraclitus, whether the term "mage" need carry a specifically Oriental significance, but it does not obviously do so in the texts collected here. Texts in which this term does carry a clear Oriental significance are collected chiefly at **36–48**. The term *agurtês*, originally denoting a beggar-priest specifically of Cybele, may also have carried some Oriental connotations.

## 10　Night-wanderers, mages, bacchants, Lenaeans, and mystery-initiates

Ca. 500 B.C.
(Heraclitus);
Later ii A.D.
(Clement)

Heraclitus DK 12b F14;
F87 Marcovich;
Clement of Alexandria
*Protrepticus* 22

Greek

For whom does Heraclitus of Ephesus make this prophecy? "Night-wanderers [*nuktipoloi*], mages, bacchants, Lenaeans [*lênai*], mystery-initiates": for these he makes threats about what they will suffer after death, for these he prophesies fire. "For they are initiated into men's customary mysteries in unhallowed fashion."

AN EARLY AND IMPORTANT BUT ENIGMATIC reference to mages, if genuinely Heraclitan. I assume here that it is. The tone appears to be hostile. The three terms "bacchants, Lenaeans, mystery-initiates" are most easily taken as referring to initiates into Orphic mysteries, in which a key, if largely obscure, role was played by Dionysus, the god honored by bacchants and Lenaeans (see **87, 282**). The association of mages with these terms suggests that they too were thought to undergo initiation and claim arcane knowledge. The term "Night-wanderers" (similarly applied to bacchants at Euripides *Ion* 718) can also be applied to ghosts (see **25**) and may suggest involvement with them here.

## 11   Oedipus abuses the seer Tiresias as a mage

Later v B.C.

Sophocles *Oedipus Tyrannus* 380–403

Greek

Oedipus: O wealth and kingship and triumph in the battle of life's arts, how great the envy you have allowed to accrue for me, if it is for the sake of this office, which I did not ask for but which the city gave me as a gift, that trusty Creon, who was my friend from the start, secretly stalks me and is eager to cast me out. For he has suborned this mage [*magos*; i.e., Teiresias], a stitcher of devices, a deceitful beggar-priest [*agurtês*], who can see only profit, but has a blind art. Come, tell me, how can you be a percipient diviner [*mantis*]? How was it that you did not utter something to deliver these citizens when the song-stitching dog [i.e., the Sphinx] was here? Her riddle was not going to be solvable by just anyone, but true prophecy was required. It became all too clear that you had no prophetic knowledge either from the birds or from any of the gods. But I came along, ignorant Oedipus, and I stopped her. I hit home with pure intelligence, not with anything I learned from the birds. This is the person you are trying to cast out, in hopes of becoming right-hand man at Creon's throne. You and the contriver of this plot will regret, I think, your attempt to expel me as polluted. If you did not have the look of an old man, a beating would have taught you how presumptuous you are.

TIRESIAS IS A RESPECTED AND TRUTHFUL SEER, but here he is abused by Oedipus, under pressure, with a constellation of associations that will become commonplace in Greek culture, if they are not so already. He is a mage, a prophet and a beggar-priest; he is a deceitful charlatan without real power; he is motivated purely by financial profit and self-interest; he claims arcane sources of knowledge but understands less than an ordinary person of intelligence. Many of these themes are still to be found in Libanius's fourth-century A.D. speech against the lying mage (**300**). Mages (*magoi*) are also briefly referred to at Euripides *Orestes* 1496–8 (of 412 B.C.), where a Phrygian slave wonders whether the sudden disappearance of Helen was caused by spells (*pharmaka*) or the devices of mages.

## 12   Gorgias the sophist on magic and rhetoric

Later v B.C.

Gorgias *Encomium of Helen* 10

Greek

Come now, let me progress from one argument to another. Divinely inspired incantations made through the medium of words induce pleasure and dismiss pain. The power of the incantation engages with the soul's understanding and bewitches [*ethelxe*] and persuades it and alters it by sorcery [*goêteia*]. An art of magic [*mageia*] and an art of sorcery have both been discovered: these are mistakes of the soul and deceptions of the understanding.

GORGIAS, THE PUPIL OF EMPEDOCLES (**5**), explains the persuasive power of words in rhetoric as akin to their power in magical incantation. It is not clear whether "mistakes of the soul" and "deceptions of the understanding" are intended to correlate to "magic" and "sorcery" either respectively or chiastically and so construct an (obscure) distinction between the two. Gorgias praises rhetoric; his attitude to the magic and sorcery with which he compares it is less clear, even though he views deceit as integral to them. Contrast the negative views later expressed by Plato and others toward magic and rhetoric alike (**17, 75, 102, 299, 300**; see also Aeschines 3.137).

## 13  Hippocrates attacks the mages' cure for epilepsy

v–iv B.C.

Hippocrates *On the Sacred Disease* 1.10–46

Greek

**10.** I think that the first people to have projected this disease [epilepsy] as "sacred" were men like those who are now mages [*magoi*] and purifiers [*kathartai*] and beggar-priests [*agurtai*] and vagrant-charlatans [*alazones*]. These people purport to be extremely reverent of the gods and to know something more than the rest of us. **11.** They use the divine to hide behind and to cloak the fact that they have nothing to apply to the disease and bring relief. So that their ignorance should not become manifest, they promoted the belief that this disease was sacred. **12.** They added further appropriate arguments to render their method of healing safe for themselves. They applied purifications [*katharmoi*] and incantations [*epaoidai*] and told people to refrain from bathing and many foods unsuitable for the sick to eat: [**13.**] among fish they banned red mullet, black-tail, grey mullet, and eel (for these are the most hazardous); [**14.**] among meats goat, venison, pork and dog (for these are the meats that upset the stomach most); [**15.**] among poultry cock, pigeon, the *otis*-bird and all those birds considered to be least indigestible; [**16.**] among vegetables mint, garlic, and onions (their sharpness is deleterious for a sick man). **17.** They also forbade the wearing of a black cloak (for black is deathly), [**18.**] the lying on or wearing of goatskin, [**19.**] the placing of foot upon foot or hand upon hand (for this is shackling). **20.** These measures they establish because of the divine nature of the disease, as if they know something more. And they talk of other causes too, so that if the sick man becomes well again, they may claim a reputation for cleverness, but that if he dies, their defense can be based on safe ground and they can have the excuse that it is not they themselves who are responsible, but the gods. **21.** If they have given their patient no drug [*pharmakon*] to eat or drink and if they have not soaked him in baths, they cannot be thought responsible. **22.** I think that none of the inland Libyans could enjoy good health, because they lie on goat skins and eat goat meat, since they have no blanket or cloak or shoe that is not derived from the goat. For they have no herds other than of goats. **23.** If the consumption of these and their application to the body causes and fosters disease while abstinence from them heals and cures it, the god can no longer be held responsible, and purifications offer no help. Rather it is the foods that cure and harm, and the effect of the divine disappears.

**24.** Thus I think those who try to cure these diseases in this way believe them to be neither sacred nor divine. **25.** For where the diseases can be dislodged by purifications and therapy of this kind, what is to prevent them being inflicted on and made to attack men through the use of corresponding techniques? So the cause is no longer divine, but human. **26.** For the man who is capable of banishing such an illness through exhaustive purifications [*perikathairôn*] and magic [*mageuôn*] is equally capable of inflicting it by using complementary techniques. By this argument too the prospect of a divine effect is abolished. **27.** With such claims and contrivances they pretend to know something more and they deceive men by giving them sacred purifications, and most of their talk is directed to the divine and to supernatural powers. **28.** But I think their talk does not demonstrate their piety, as they believe, but rather their impiety, claiming as it does that the gods do not exist, while their supposed piety and their devotion to the divine is impious and unholy. I will show you why.

**29.** They claim to know how to draw down the moon, make the sun disappear, create bad weather and good, rains and droughts, render the sea impassable and the land sterile, and all the other things like this. Those skilled in these things say that such effects are achievable through the performance of rites or some other cleverness or practice. **30.** But they seem to me impious, to believe that the gods do not exist and that they have no power, and I think there is no extreme action that they would forbear to undertake, since the gods hold no terror for them. **31.** For if a man will draw down the moon by magic [*mageuôn*] and sacrifice, make the sun disappear and create bad weather and good, I for my part would not consider any of this divine, but human, if the power of the divine is defeated and enslaved by human cleverness. **32.** But perhaps it is not so. Perhaps it is just that men trying to make a living invent all manner of things and make elaborate claims, especially with regard to this disease, and stick the blame for each form of the disease on a god. For they do not blame just one, but several gods for these things. **33.** If the sick mimic a goat and bellow, or if they have spasms on the right side, they say the mother of the gods is responsible. **34.** If he shrieks loudly they compare him to a horse and say that Poseidon is responsible. **35.** If a patient makes his stool, as often happens to those under the compulsion of disease, the god is named as Enodia. **36.** If the stools come frequently and are rather thin, as in the case of birds, Apollo Nomios is responsible. **37.** If he has foam coming out of his mouth and he kicks out with his feet, Ares gets the blame. **38.** If the patient is attended by fears, terrors, and madnesses in the night, jumps up out his bed and flees outside, they call these the attacks of Hecate or the onslaughts of ghosts [*hêrôes*]. **39.** They make use of purifications [*katharmoi*] and incantations [*epaoidai*] and so do a thing that is quite unholy and ungodly, as it seems to me. **40.** For they purify those who are in the grip of a disease with blood and other such things as if they were subject to pollution [*miasma*] or avenging ghosts [*alastores*], or were bewitched [*pepharmagmenoi*] by men, or had done some unholy deed. **41.** They should do the opposite to these men: they should sacrifice, pray, and bring them into temples and supplicate the gods. **42.** Yet they do none of these things, but just purify them. Some of the purifications [*katharmôn*] they bury in the earth, some they throw into the sea, and some they carry off to the mountains, where no one will touch them or tread on them. **43.** But they ought to take them into temples and return them to the god, if the god is indeed responsible. **44.** But I don't believe that the human body is polluted by a god, when it is so corrupt and the divine is so holy. But if the body happens to have been polluted or made to suffer by some third party, I believe that it would be purified and made holy by the god rather than polluted by him. **45.** The divine is what purifies and makes holy the greatest and most unholy of our errors and the dirt that attaches to us as a result. **46.** We ourselves mark out boundaries for the temples and sanctuaries of the gods, so that no one should cross them if he is not pure. When we enter them we are sprinkled, not in the belief that we are being polluted, but so that we may be cleansed of any prior pollution we have. This is what I think about purifications.

WHETHER THE HISTORICAL HIPPOCRATES WROTE any one of the words attributed to him in his corpus remains unclear, but it is generally accepted that *On the Sacred Disease* is one of the earlier works in the tradition. The dismissal of epilepsy was to become a commonplace of the magical repertoire (see **47, 51, 85,** and, with commentary, **134**).

In this polemical preface the author strings together a series of attributes for his rivals:

- They are mages
- They are beggar-priests (*agurtai*)
- They are initiates (the phrase "know something more" recurs)
- Charlatanry
- Venality
- Amorality
- Purification

- Compulsion over the gods
- Ghost aversion
- Incantation
- Healing magic
- Drawing down the moon and astronomical control
- Defense against the magic of others

This series of terms is comparable to that constructed by Plato (see **14–16** with commentaries), and seems to expand the associations already apparent in the Heraclitus fragment (**10**).

To the casual observer, the author may not have seemed so different from the mages himself, and the dispute may well have seemed one internal to a trade. Thus, for example, he goes on, after this passage, to make dietary prescriptions of his own that strongly resemble those he abuses the mages for making. For the tendency to cast professional rivals as mages see **14, 62, 65, 92, 94, 295**. However, the author is persuasive in singling out apparent contradictions in his rivals' attitudes to the divine. They claim control over it (see also **45, 47, 96**) but, when their healing magic fails, make the excuse that the infliction of the disease is ultimately and unalterably due to the will of the gods.

Of particular interest is the notion that those who dismiss disease by magic can also inflict it by magic (25–6). Magical operatives are thus shown to be dangerously amoral. This parallels Plato's implicit indication that those who lay ghosts are also those who rouse them to make mischief. For the drawing-down of the moon see **214–23**.

## 14　Plato against the sorcerers (1): Beggar-priests, prophets, spell-binders, Orphics, initiators

Earlier iv B.C.

Plato *Republic* 364b–e

Greek

Beggar-priests [*agurtai*] and prophets [*manteis*] go to the doors of the rich and persuade them that they have the power, acquired from the gods by sacrifices [*thusiais*] and incantations [*epôidais*], to cure with pleasures and festivals any wrong done by the man himself or his ancestors, and that they will harm an enemy, a just man or an unjust man alike, for a small fee, if a man wishes it, since they persuade the gods, as they say, to serve them, by certain charms [*epagô-gais*] and bindings [*katadesmois*]. And they bring in [*epagontai*] the poets as witnesses to all these claims. Some give out that vice is easy:

It is easy to choose vice in abundance. The road is even and nearby. But the gods put sweat in the way of virtue [Hesiod *Works and Days* 87–9]

and a long and steep road. Others call Homer as a witness to the deception of the gods by men, since he too said:

The gods themselves too can be persuaded by prayer, and men can change their will by praying with sacrifices and soothing vows and libation and the savour of meat, whenever one oversteps the mark and errs. [Homer *Iliad* 9.497–501, altered]

And they provide a hubbub of books of Musaeus and Orpheus, the children of the Moon and the Muses, as they say, in accordance with which they perform sacrifices, and persuade not only individuals but also cities, that there are deliverances from and purifications of injustices through sacrifices and childish pleasures while still alive, and that there are the same things for the dead too, which they call "rites" [*teletai*], which deliver us from the bad things in that world, while terrible things are in store for those who have not sacrificed.

THIS IS THE FIRST OF A GROUP OF FOUR passages in which Plato constructs negative images of sorcerers in allusive fashion. The similarities between the details of the passages and the attitudes that inform them are sufficient to indicate that Plato has the same phenomenon in mind in each. The attributes of his sorcerer "amalgam" are remarkably similar to those grouped together by Hippocrates in **13**. Some may have been keener to make distinctions between the categories of operatives that Plato is happy to collapse, although the *Derveni* commentary (**18**) suggests that Orphic initiates at any rate may have perceived a kinship with mages for themselves. The attributes of Plato's amalgam may be summarized:

- They are sorcerers (*goêteia* and *manganeia*)
- They are beggar-priests (*agurtai*)
- They are initiates into mysteries
- They offer initiation into mysteries
- They use Orphic books
- They are persuasive but charlatan
- Venality
- Amorality

- Charms (*epagôgai*)
- Purifications of individuals and cities
- Compulsion over the gods
- Evocation and ghost-laying
- Binding-spells (*katadesmoi*)
- Incantations
- Prayer and sacrifice
- Prophecy

The association between mystery-initiation, ghost-evocation, spell-binding, and deceitful persuasion, all of which involve the manipulation of souls in one form or another, is superficially plausible.

As in the case of the Hippocratic text (**13**), the casual observer could have found in Plato's own work many of the qualities he attributes to sorcerers: charlatan persuasion, attempts to manipulate souls, revelation of underworld secrets, the challenge to conventional morality, the guidance of books (see, above all, his *Phaedo*). And his master Socrates had been explicitly seen as a beggarly evocator (**26**). For Plato, as for Hippocrates, "sorcery" distinguishes the modus operandi of his competitors. These competitors may well have felt the same way about Plato. Other observers may have seen both alike as sorcerers jostling for position within their characteristically competitive profession. Pliny, indeed, was indeed to include Plato in his history of magic (**45**).

## 15 Plato against the sorcerers (2): Punishment prescribed for evocators

Earlier iv B.C.

Plato *Laws* 909a–d

Greek

But let us address those who take up the wild belief that the gods do not care or are placable, those who, in contempt for men, charm the souls [*psuchagôgousi*] of many of the living, by alleging that they charm the souls [*psuchagôgein*] of the dead. They undertake to persuade the gods, through the practice of sorceries [*goêteuontes*] with sacrifices and prayers and spells, and try to destroy root and branch individuals and entire houses for the sake of money. The court should punish one judged guilty of these things with confinement in the inland prison; no free person should approach him, but slaves should be used to provide him with the ration of food decided by the guardians of the law. When the convict dies, he should be cast outside the boundaries unburied. If any free person colludes in burying him, he is to be liable to an accusation of impiety by anyone who wishes to make it. If he leaves behind children good enough for the city, those in charge of orphans shall take them in hand from the day of their father's conviction, as being orphaned, and treat them no worse than others.

PLATO MAKES A PLAY ON THE TERM *psuchagôgeô*. He uses it in both its basic, apparently original sense of "evocate" and in its metaphorical sense of "bamboozle," which became the term's predominant usage in Greek literature. The harshness of the punishment prescribed for those offering evocation seems more appropriate to operatives genuinely exercising this power than to mere charlatans.

The association of the *goêt-* root with words for evocation or soul-charming (*psuchagôgein*, etc.) is highly significant: see **36** and **48**, especially, and **25–31** for evocators in general. The use of the *goêt-* root here in this series of Platonic passages, which seemingly corresponds tightly with the Hippocratic passage (**13**), also suggests that *goêtes* and *magoi* (mages) were already perceived as more or less equivalent terms. This conclusion matches Gorgias's and Herodotus's adjacent use of the two terms (**12, 41**).

## 16    Plato against the sorcerers (3): Spell-binding and persuasion

Earlier iv B.C.

Plato *Laws* 933a-b and e

Greek

a. [A type of "poisoning," *pharmakeia*, distinct from the physical sort:] The other kind of poisoning, which operates through sorceries [*manganeiai*], incantations [*epoidai*], and so-called bindings [*katadeseis*], persuades those who are bold enough to attempt harm with them that they can in fact achieve something of this sort, and persuades others that more than anything they are being harmed by those who have this power.

With phenomena of this sort it is not very easy either to know the truth, or to persuade others of it if one does know it. b. It is not worthwhile for us to try to tell the souls of men who mistrust each other, if ever they see molded wax figures at doors or at crossroads or in some cases on the tombs of their ancestors, to ignore all such things, if we do not ourselves have a clear opinion about them. . . . e. And if a man appears to be like one causing harm by bindings [*katadeseis*] or charms [*epagôgai*] or certain incantations [*epôidai*] or any "poisoning" of this sort whatsoever, whether he is a diviner [*mantis*] or interpreter of portents [*teratoskopos*], he is to be executed. But whoever is convicted of poisoning without prophecy [*mantikê*] is to be punished in the same way as one convicted of ordinary poisoning. In this case too let the court assess the punishment or recompense they feel appropriate.

PLATO AGAIN HARPS ON THE ROLE OF DECEITFUL persuasion in sorcery. Sorcerers deceive their clients and their victims alike. The information that wax voodoo dolls might be displayed at doors, crossroads, or tombs is valuable and suggests to modern minds a plausible explanation as to how they may have, in effect, "worked" (for voodoo dolls see **236–47** and for binding spells more generally see **168–84, 197–213**). In confronting one's victim with a doll, presumably one additional to one "activated" within a tomb, and so on, one let him know that the curse had been made and started his own powers of suggestion against him.

### 17 Plato against the sorcerers (4): Sophist-sorcerers

Earlier iv B.C.

Plato *Statesman* 291B.C.

Greek

**Eleatic visitor:** Yes, for it is from ignorance that people find things strange. I myself have just had this experience. I suddenly failed to recognize, on seeing them, that band which devotes itself to the city's affairs.

**Young Socrates:** Which band is that?

**Eleatic visitor:** The band which of all sophists is the greatest sorcerer [*goêta*] and most skilled in sorcery. This band must be distinguished from genuine statesmen and people of kingly stature, even though this is very difficult to do, if we are to see clearly what we are after.

LIKE GORGIAS, PLATO SEES AN ASSOCIATION between sophists and sorcerers, but for him both terms are wholly negative. He makes the same association twice elsewhere in passing (*Euthydemus* 288b and *Sophist* 234c). As for Gorgias (**12**), the association is promoted by the perception of sorcerers as persuasive deceivers.

### 18 Fragments of a commentary on an Orphic poem: Mages, initiates, and souls

iv B.C.

*Derveni papyrus* cols. 6, 10

Greek

**6.** . . . prayers and sacrifices propitiate the souls, and the incantation of the mages has the power to remove obstructing demons. Obstructing demons are the enemies of souls. This is why mages make sacrifice, as if paying a penalty. They pour water and milk over the victims, and from these liquids they also make full libations. They sacrifice unnumbered and many-bossed cakes, because the souls are also unnumbered. Initiates [*mustai*] make first sacrifices to the Eumenides just as mages do. For Eumenides are souls. For this reason. . . .

**10.** . . . all those people who have performed sacred rites in the cities have seen them. I am less surprised that these people do not understand, for it is not possible to listen to and comprehend what is being said at the same time. But all those people who seek understanding from one who makes the sacred his craft should be wondered at and pitied. I say "wondered at" because they think they will receive knowledge before they perform their rites, but they depart after performing them, before they know anything and without having asked again, supposing that they know something of what they have seen or learned. And I say "pitied" because it is not sufficient for them to have spent their money too soon, but they also have to depart in want of knowledge too. Before they perform their sacred rites they hope that they will know, but when they have performed them they depart deprived even of hope . . .

IN THE FIRST OF THESE FRAGMENTS the Orphic commentator apparently sees the "mages" as in some way of kindred spirit, and perceives links between their activities and the Orphic rites of initiation in which he considers himself well versed. So here we apparently have an "internal" view of a group of operatives not dissimilar to that for which Hippocrates and Plato provide (misleadingly?) "external" ones. The deliverance of souls from obstructing demons presumably speeds their journey to a blessed place in the afterlife, and is a goal of initiation. At any rate it is clear that some sort of soul manipulation is envisaged. The second fragment seems to be a dig at the commentator's rivals, those "who make the sacred [their] craft," and to provide a further example of competition within trade. The point appears to be that their clients are fools because they hand their money over to them all too quickly in exchange for an enlightenment that they are unable to provide: the venality argument (see **13, 14,** with commentaries) with a slightly different spin. For Orpheus and Orphics, see also **19–21, 44, 45, 71, 159.** The ostensibly plain statement that the Eumenides are ghosts is held to be problematic (see *A Guide to Further Reading* 2.3).

## 19   Philip, the beggarly Orphic initiator

i–ii A.D.

Plutarch *Moralia* 224ef (*Spartan Sayings*)

Greek

Philip the Orphic initiator [*Orpheotelestês*], who was wholly beggarly, was claiming that people who were initiated by him brought their lives to a fortunate end. [Leotychidas the son of Ariston] responded, "So why, fool, do you not die without delay, so that you may at once stop having to bewail your misfortune and penury?"

HERE THE STEREOTYPE OF BEGGARLINESS IS attributed to another, no doubt fictional, Orphic initiator. It seems to have been commonplace to scoff at magical operatives claiming great powers by confronting them with the paradox of their penury (see **300**).

## 20   Orpheus the initiator, sorcerer, beggar-priest, and prophet

Late i B.C.

Strabo C333 F18

Greek

At the foot of Olympus lies the city of Dium. The village of Pimpleia is its neighbor. There they say Orpheus the Ciconian lived. A sorcerer [*goês*], he first lived the life of a beggar priest [*agurteuôn*] by means of music and divination [*mantikê*] and the celebration the secret rites of mystery-initiation. Later on he began to think more highly of himself and acquired for himself a troop of disciples and a degree of power. Some people accepted him willingly, but others suspected that he was plotting violence against them and clubbed together and killed him. Near here too is Leibethra.

THE ROLE OF THE ORPHIC INITIATOR, OR something akin to that of Plato's sorcerer amalgam, is projected backward in this rationalizing account of the life of the mythical Orpheus: the roles of Orphic—devotee, initiator, sorcerer, beggar-priest, and prophet are drawn together. In the famous version of Orpheus's myth he descended to the underworld in order to retrieve his dead wife Eurydice from it but failed (Virgil *Georgics* 4.453–525; Ovid *Metamorphoses* 10.1–63). It is likely, however, that in the original version of his myth he was successful, and that the myth served as a paradigm for the Orphic ability to penetrate the mysteries of the underworld and reveal them in the world of the living, and to manipulate the souls of the dead.

## 21   The Dactyls: Initiators, instructors of Orpheus, sorcerers, metal-workers, and creators of amulets

i B.C.

Diodorus 5.64

Greek

The first of these Cretan gods handed down in tradition were the so-called Idaean Dactyls, who lived in the area around Mount Ida in Crete. One tradition tells that they were a hundred in number, but another one says that there were ten of them and this is how they got their name, because they were equivalent in number to the fingers [*daktuloi*] on the hands. But some record, Ephorus among them, that the Idaean Dactyls were born on the Mount Ida that is in Phrygia but crossed over into Europe with Mygdon. They also say that they were sorcerers, that they practiced incantations [*epôidai*] and initiation-rites and mysteries, and that, spending time in Samothrace, they amazed the inhabitants of the island to an extraordinary degree with these. This was the time at which Orpheus too, who had an outstanding ability in poetry and song, became their pupil, and became the first to make initiation rites and mysteries known to the Greeks.

Anyway, tradition tells that the Idaean Dactyls in Crete, in the region of the Apteraeans, around so-called Berecynthus, discovered the use of fire, the nature of bronze and iron, and the process for preparing them. Regarded as having shown the way in great boons for humankind, they received divine worship. They record that one of them was called Heracles. With an outstanding reputation he was able to found the Olympic Games. People of subsequent generations attributed the foundation of the Games to the son of Alcmene because he had the same name. As proof of this they say that the custom persists even to this day in accordance with which many women derive their incantations and their manufacture of amulets from this god, in the belief that he was a sorcerer [goês] and practiced rites of initiation, and that these are highly uncharacteristic of the Heracles that was born of Alcmene.

THIS MYTHICAL RACE OF SORCERERS AND initiators, said even to have initiated Orpheus himself, is also credited with the invention of metalwork and, appropriately, the invention of (metal) amulets (see **248–77**). Hephaestus, the metal-working god, was himself credited with magical powers (note his animated golden serving-girls at Homer *Iliad* 18.417–20), powers embodied in his twisted feet.

## 22  The Telchines (1): Their metalwork

i B.C.

Diodorus 5.55

Greek

The so-called Telchines were the first to inhabit the island named Rhodes. These were sons of Sea, as it is handed down in myth, and the myth also says that they reared Poseidon, together with Capheira the daughter of Ocean, and that Rhea had entrusted the baby to them. They discovered some techniques and were the introducers of other useful things into the human sphere. They are said to have been the first to make statues of the gods, and some of the ancient effigies derive their name from them. Thus the Lindians have an Apollo called "Telchinian," the Ialysians a Hera and nymphs called "Telchinian," and the Cameirans likewise a Hera. It is said that these men were sorcerers [goêtes] and that they could induce clouds and rains and hailstorms whenever they wanted, and similarly bring on snows. They say that they did this just like the mages do. They could shift their own shapes, and they were envious [phthoneroi] in the teaching of their techniques.

THE TELCHINES ARE IN SOME WAYS doublets of the Dactyls, as mythical inventors of metal-working. They too are appropriately visualized as sorcerers, compared to mages, and credited as such with the abilities to control the elements and to shift shape. For their envious evil eye see **23**.

## 23  The Telchines (2): Their evil eye

Late i B.C.

Strabo C654

Greek

Rhodes used to be called Ophioussa and Stadia, and later Telchinis, after the Telchines that occupied the island. Some say that they are evil-eye-ers [baskanoi] and sorcerers [goêtes], who pour the waters of the Styx with sulphur [or: with envy] to destroy plants and animals. Others say, to the contrary, that, because they excelled in their crafts, they were evil-eye-ed [baskanthênai] by competing craftsmen and were consequently branded with this ill repute. They say that they came first from Crete to Cyprus, and then moved on to Rhodes. They were the first to work iron and bronze, and they made Cronus's sickle for him.

AS OFTEN, THERE IS AMBIVALENCE AS to whether sorcerers are generators or victims of the envious evil eye (for which see **192–6**), but the Telchines did usually have the name of the archetypal generators of it: see **22** and, famously, Callimachus *Aetia* F1. We should almost certainly read Meinecke's conjecture of "with envy" (*phthonôi*; compare *phthoneroi* in **22**) instead of the barely intelligible "with sulphur" (*theiôi*) of the manuscripts.

## 24  A (male) Thessalian sorcerer

**Amphitruo:** By Pollux, I'll have my revenge today on that Thessalian sorcerer [*veneficus*] that has turned my family's wits upside down!

Ca. 189 B.C.

Plautus *Amphitruo*
1043–4

Latin

THE GREEK SOURCE FOR THIS LATIN adaptation remains unidentified. The (female) Thessalian witch was a commonplace of ancient literature. A male Thessalian sorcerer is something of a novelty, but see **27, 161**.

# EVOCATORS (*PSUCHAGÔGOI*)

"Evocators" is used here in its technical meaning, that of people who call up the souls of the dead. It translates the Greek term *psuchagôgoi*, literally "soul-drawers." For Plato's hostile remarks on evocators see **15**.

## 25  Lakeside evocators instruct Odysseus in the evocation of souls

**F273 Chorus of Evocators:** We, the race that <lives> around the lake, do honor to Hermes as our ancestor.

Earlier v B.C.

Aeschylus *Psuchagogoi*
F273, F273a, F275 *TrGF*

Greek

**F273a Chorus of Evocators:** Come now, guest-friend, take up your stance on the grassy sacred enclosure of the fearful lake. Slash the gullet of the neck, and let the blood of this sacrificial victim flow into the murky depths of the reeds as a drink for the lifeless. Call upon primeval Earth and chthonic Hermes, escort of the dead, and ask chthonic Zeus to send up the swarm of night-wanderers from the mouths of the river, from which this melancholy off-flow water, unfit for washing hands, is sent up by Stygian springs.

**F275 Ghost of Tiresias:** For a heron, flying from up above, will strike you with its dung, the evacuation of its belly. From this a spine of a marine creature [i.e., probably, a roach] will turn your sparse-haired head septic.

AESCHYLUS'S FRAGMENTARY TRAGEDY, RETELLING Homer's account of Odysseus's consultation of the ghost of Tiresias (**144**), constitutes the earliest extant reference to evocators. The consultation happens beside and through the medium of a lake that is connected to the waters of the underworld and so provides passage for the ghosts. Many take the lake to be Avernus, near Cumae, in Italian Campania, a lake famous for necromancy and one that certainly in later times was identified as the site of Odysseus's consultation (see **153** and, for evocators there, **154**), but there is no compelling reason why the site should not be identical with the one used in the *Odyssey*, namely, the "Acherusian" lake on the Acheron in Thesprotia (see **150**). Here the evocators attached to the lake instruct Odysseus in the evocation of ghosts, taking over the role of Homer's Circe. The ghosts are to be summoned with a drink of re-vivifying blood poured directly into the lake. The sacrificial animal we may assume to have been a black ram, as usual in necromantic consultations. Prayers are to be made to the Earth that contains the ghosts and to chthonic Zeus, that is, Hades, lord of the dead, to allow their temporary release. Hermes is called on, in his traditional role as the escort of the souls of the newly dead to the underworld, to escort the souls, extraordinarily, in the other direction (see Homer *Odyssey* 24.1–14). And as transporters of souls up from the underworld and back down to it again, the evocators appropriately conceptualize themselves as descendants of Hermes. The prophecy delivered to Odysseus by the ghost of Tiresias addresses, as often in ancient scenes of necromantic consultation, the death of the consulter himself (see **155, 157**).

## 26 A comic representation of Socrates as an evocator

414 B.C.

Aristophanes *Birds*
1553–64

Greek

Chorus of Birds: Beside the Shadow-feet [*Skiapodes*] there is a lake (unfit for washing in) where (unwashed) Socrates evocates souls. Thither came Pisander asking to see the "spirit" that had deserted him while he was alive. He had a camel-heifer to sacrifice. He cut its throat, just like Odysseus, and then went off. And then there came up for him from below, for the slaughtered blood of the camel, Chaerephon the bat.

THIS COMPLEX PASSAGE PARODIES AESCHYLUS'S *Psuchagogoi* (**25**). The term *aloutos* is ambivalent: it is semantically and syntactically applicable both to the lake, as "unfit for washing in," thus recalling Aeschylus's description of it, and, mockingly, to Socrates himself, as "unwashed." The Shadow-feet are a comic reworking of the Cimmerians, the shadowy people of the Land of Night who live beside the oracle of the dead in Homer's *Odyssey* (**144**; see also **153–4**), with a hint of Herodotean-style ethnology thrown in (compare **7**). The camel-heifer is a bizarre comic substitution for the expected black ram. Pisander is mocked by means of an equivocation in the word *psuchê*, meaning "spirit" in both the sense of "courage" and the sense of "soul/ghost." The coward comes in search of his "courage," but flees in an all-too-predictable act of cowardice at the prospect of the "ghost's" appearance. Socrates and his associate Chaerephon are mocked as corpse- or ghost-like ascetic Pythagoreans (compare **1–9, 57–64, 115**) and therefore quite suited to things necromantic. Socrates and Chaerephon had been represented by Aristophanes as associates in the "Thinking House" of his *Clouds*, and in that play Chaerephon had been described as "half-dead" (504). The souls of the dead are conceptualized as bats by Homer (*Odyssey* 24.6). It remains unclear whether Chaerephon was actually alive or dead in 414: the passage would be all the more pointed if he were in fact still alive. The implied similarity between the death-like evocator and the object of his evocation is intriguing.

## 27 Thessalian evocators and the laying of the ghost of Pausanias

438 B.C. (Euripides);
i/ii A.D. (Plutarch);
Hellenistic-Byzantine
(Scholium)

Euripides *Alcestis*
1127–8 with scholium,
including Plutarch
*Homeric Studies* F1
Bernardakis

Greek

Admetus: Make sure this [i.e., the apparition of my wife Alcestis] is not a ghost of the dead!

Heracles: You did not make your guest-friend here into an evocator [*psuchagôgos*]!

*Scholium ad loc.:* There are some evocators [*psuchagôgoi*], sorcerers [*goêtes*] in Thessaly being so termed, who summon up and drive out ghosts. In fact the Spartans sent for these, when the ghost of Pausanias was frightening away people who tried to approach the temple of Athene of the Bronze House, as Plutarch says in his *Homeric Studies*.

IN EURIPIDES' PROSATYRIC *ALCESTIS*, HERACLES, who had dragged up Cerberus from the underworld, has repaid his host Admetus's hospitality by restoring his recently dead wife, Alcestis, to life. He had wrestled Thanatos, "Death," for her as he came to collect her from her tomb. Heracles presents her to Admetus again in this scene. If Heracles had brought back merely the ghost, as Admetus fears, as opposed to the living body of the woman, he would have done the job of an evocator. For the recovery of a wife from the underworld, see **20**, with commentary.

The ancient commentary does little to elucidate the passage but provides an interesting identification of some sort between *psuchagôgoi* and *goêtes* (see **15** for the association between *psuchagôgoi* and *goêtes*; see also **36**). The term *psuchagôgos* does not appear, as the commentary may imply, to have been specifically Thessalian (compare **24** for a male Thessalian sorcerer). Of particular interest is the assertion that evocators both raise and lay ghosts. As we see in **28** and **29** ghosts could often be raised paradoxically in order to be laid once and for all.

The Spartan regent Pausanias, victor of Plataea and the man who, alongside the Athenian Themistocles, was responsible for the repulsion of the Persian invasion of 480/79 B.C., was a decade later accused of treating with the Persians and with the Spartan helots (serfs), and starved to death in the temple of Athene of the Bronze House or "Chalkioikos" in violation of his supplication. Hence his ghost haunted. As it stands this scholium perhaps implies that the evocators who were used to lay the ghost of Pausanias came from Thessaly, but Plutarch himself says otherwise (**152**).

## 28   Pausanias the regent consults the evocators of Phigalia

ii A.D.

Pausanias (periegetes)
3.17

Greek

Beside the altar of Athene Chalkioikos stand two statues of the Pausanias that led the Greeks at Plataea. I will not relate his adventures to people already familiar with them. The accounts of earlier writers are sufficiently accurate. It will be enough for me to add a gloss to what they say. I heard from a man of Byzantium that Pausanias was discovered in his plotting and was the only suppliant of Chalkioikos to fail to secure immunity for no other reason than that he could not wash out the pollution of a murder. For when he was based at the Hellespont with the Spartan navy and the navies of the allies, he developed a passion for a virgin of Byzantium. At nightfall Cleonice—for this was the girl's name—was brought to him by officers detailed to do so. Pausanias was asleep at this time, but he was roused by the noise. For as she made her way toward him she accidentally knocked over a lighted lamp. Pausanias was in a perpetual state of restless anxiety because of his guilty conscience for betraying Greece. So he leapt up at once and struck the girl with his Persian sword. Pausanias could not escape the pollution that arose from this, although he supplicated and received purifications of all sorts from Zeus Phuxios and even went to Phigalia in Arcadia to the evocators. But, understandably, he paid the penalty to Cleonice and the god. The Spartans, carrying out Delphi's command, made the effigies from bronze and honor Epidotes, explaining that Epidotes averted the anger of Hikesios/the-attacking-ghost over Pausanias.

THE TALE OF THE GHOST OF Cleonice forms a diptych with that of the regent Pausanias's own ghost: he kills Cleonice and is hounded by her ghost, which he must then propitiate (with his own death, as becomes apparent). His ghost then hounds his Spartan killers and must be propitiated in turn (see **27, 29, 152**). Other versions of the Cleonice tale locate Pausanias's evocation of her at the Heracleia Pontica oracle of the dead (**151**), a more convenient site for one based in Byzantium.

As for the act of ghost-laying, the association made between the evocators' calling up of ghosts for placation and the purification of pollution is valuable; compare 9. The term *hikesios* in the final sentence is usually read as an epithet abbreviating "Zeus Hikesios," that is, "Zeus of Suppliants." This is hard to believe, since Epidotes was also an aspect of Zeus (Pausanias [peregetes] 3.17). The term is more likely to be the noun denoting "attacking ghost" found in the Cyrenean ghost-laying prescriptions (**124**) and to refer directly to the angry ghost of Pausanias.

## 29 The ghost of Pausanias the regent is laid with the dedication of two bronze effigies of him

Late v B.C.

Thucydides 1.134

Greek

When Pausanias was on the point of giving up the ghost [*apopsuchein*] in the chamber [of the temple of Athene Chalkioikos], the Spartans realized this and brought him out of the shrine still just about breathing, but as soon as he was brought out he died. They were going to throw him into the Caeadas crevasse, where they throw criminals, but then they decided to put him in the ground somewhere nearby. Later on the god in Delphi responded to the Spartans that they should transfer Pausanias's burial to the place in which he died (and he now lies in the forecourt of the precinct [of Athene of the Bronze House], as inscriptions testify in writing), and that, since what they had done constituted a pollution, they should repay to Athene of the Bronze House two bodies in exchange for one. And so they made two bronze statues and dedicated them as in place of Pausanias.

THE RATIONALIZING THUCYDIDES CONTRIVES TO TELL the story of the ghost of Pausanias (for which see **27, 28**) without mention either of the ghost or of its evocators. It is clear, however, that a haunting ghost and evocators were already part of the tradition. The dedication of double effigies is a known technique of ghost-laying: see **124**. Thucydides' reference to the dismissed plan to throw the body of Pausanias down the Caeadas crevasse is apparently a tribute to a countertradition, found in other sources, according to which Pausanias's body was indeed hurled down this crevasse without due rites of burial. Such a deprivation of burial rites (compare **110, 112–3**) would have unsettled the ghost and entailed the resort to evocators (see **30**).

## 30 How evocators locate the corpse of a restless ghost, and the methods used to settle the ghost

x A.D.

*Suda* s.v. [*peri*] *psuchagôgias* (evocation)

Greek

They accomplish certain sorceries with regard to the dead. For whenever they come to the places from where the people who ask them in want them to drive away the ghosts, they come to where those to be subjected to evocation are dead. However, they do not immediately find the exact place, but track it down in the following fashion. They bring along with them a black sheep, taking hold of it either by one of its horns or by its front feet, and they lead it around standing on its other feet. It follows the dragging very readily. But whenever it comes to the place where the man or woman in question lies buried, there the sheep casts itself down. When this happens, they remove the sheep, burn it in holocaust and then, together with certain elaborate sacrifices and spells, they mark off and walk around the place and they listen to the ghosts as they speak and ask the reasons for their anger. Antoninus the emperor of the Romans evocated concerning his father Commodus.

THE BYZANTINE LEXICOGRAPHER'S DESCRIPTION OF THE ghost-laying procedure, though stilted, is largely self-explanatory. In order to placate a haunting ghost, its body must first be "found" by an elaborate technique. If the ghost was restless for being deprived of due burial (compare **110, 112–3**), this technique could locate its (doubtless unmarked) grave (compare **27–9**, with commentaries). Or it could be used to locate a marked grave and so identify a ghost restless for some other reason. It may have been considered therapeutic and mollifyingly considerate to let the ghost speak even in cases where the cause of its distress was apparent. But sometimes it will have been necessary to learn in precisely what manner an apparently satisfactory burial had been defective (compare **150**). Interestingly, the text does not go on to say what we might have expected, namely, that the inadequately buried body, once found, could be dug up for proper (re-)burial (compare **115**): reality was not permitted, therefore, to compromise the success of the location technique.

For purificatory and protective wheeling movements in necromancy, around tombs, corpses or pits, see **56, 71, 109, 123, 125, 148, 157,** and **300**; see also **57, 141**. Behind the phrase "burn it in holocaust" I conjecture *katakausantes* for the manuscript's nonsensical *katakrypsantes* ("hide completely"). Holocaust sacrifice is the inevitable fate of black sheep offered to the dead (e.g., **144**). The reference to Antoninus and "his father Commodus" is problematic: it is most easily understood to refer to a consultation by Caracalla (formally, M. Aurelius Severus Antoninus, who reigned 198–217 A.D.) of his predecessor (but not his father) Commodus (reigned 180–92 A.D.).

## 31 The Dodona oracle consulted over the employment of an evocator

To Zeus of the place and to Dione. They shouldn't use Dorios the evocator [*psuchagôgos*], should they?

iv B.C.?

Christidis et al. 1999, no. 5.

Greek

QUESTIONS WERE SUBMITTED TO THE ORACLE of Zeus at Dodona on lead tablets, many of which survive. This intriguing consultation-question, addressed to Zeus and his usual wife at Dodona, stands alone. Is the consulter's basic concern whether evocation should or should not be employed, or is it the choice of actual evocator? It is tempting to associate Dorios the evocator with the other great oracle of Thesprotia, the Acheron oracle of the dead (**144, 150**). The sanction of a respected oracle of a heavenly deity is sought for the practice of evocation.

## VENTRILOQUISTS

The term "ventriloquist" is not used here in its usual modern signification of a shabby entertainer who throws his voice into a sinister dummy but in its original one, that of a person whose stomach is inhabited by a ghost or demon that speaks through his mouth. For further passages on ventriloquism see **112, 129**. For mechanisms more akin to those used by entertainer-ventriloquists see **64, 160**.

## 32 Eurycles, the possessing, prophetic demon (1)

Now, people, pay attention, if you like frank advice. The poet now wants to censure his

424 B.C. (Aristophanes); Hellenistic-Byzantine (scholia)

Aristophanes *Wasps* 1015–22, with scholia

Greek

audience. For he says that he is the victim of an undeserved wrong after conferring many benefits upon them. Initially he did not do this openly, but secretly, by helping other poets. In imitation of the prophetic method of Eurycles, he entered their stomachs and poured out lots of comedy. But after this he openly ventured out on his own, in chariots drawn by his own Muses rather than other people's.

*Scholiast R:* Eurycles was a prophet who manifested himself through others, so he says, "Just as Eurycles gave to others, so did I."

*Scholiast Lh:* This Eurycles was called a ventriloquist [*engastrimuthos*], since he prophesied to the Athenians through the demon he had inside him. . . . Hence all prophets were called ventriloquists [*engastritai*] and Eurycleids [i.e., "Descendants of Eurycles"], after Eurycles, who had been the first to do this.

ARISTOPHANES' ANALOGY FOR THE PROCESS BY which he came to put his own name to his comedies after writing them for others speaks for itself. There is no need to suppose that the Eurycles in question, famous to Aristophanes and his audience, was contemporary; he may well have belonged to myth. Both Aristophanes and Plato (**33**) make it clear that the original Eurycles was a possessing demon, not a host. The confusion in Scholiast *Lh* here, in the Platonic scholiasts, and in the *Suda* (**34**) may derive from the fact that the name, alongside "Eurycleid," did in time come to be applied generally to the hosts of this variety of demon (**35**).

## 33   Eurycles, the possessing, prophetic demon (2)

Earlier iv B.C. (Plato);
Hellenistic-Byzantine (scholium)

Plato *Sophist* 252c,
with scholium

Greek

**Eleatic visitor:** [Those who forbid us to call things by other names] do not need people to confute them, for they go round all the time with their enemy and opponent in their own house, as it is said, speaking from inside, just as if they were carrying round the bizarre Eurycles.

*Scholium ad loc.:* Eurycles was the name proverbially given to those who prophesied to their own misfortune. For Eurycles was believed to have a demon in his stomach, which inspired him to speak about the future. Hence he was also called a ventriloquist [*engastrimuthos*]. He met a bad end when one day he made someone a prediction they did not like. . . . A kind of prophet is called a Eurycles after him.

THE SCHOLIUM CONTINUES WITH THE MATERIAL found in the *Suda* (**34**). Once again Eurycles affords a useful analogy. The opponents of predication cannot help but disprove their own contentions about language with every sentence they utter. The scholiast's story of Eurycles's bad end looks suspiciously like an overinterpretation of Plato's analogy.

## 34   A collection of ancient sources for ventriloquism

v B.C. (Sophocles);
iii B.C. (Philochorus);
x A.D. (*Suda*)

*Suda* s.v. *engastrimuthos* (ventriloquist), including Sophocles *Aichmalotides* F59 *TrGF* and Philochorus *FGH* 328 F78

Greek

**Ventriloquist** [*engastrimuthos*]: belly-prophet [*engastrimantis*]. Some people now call this a "Python," Sophocles uses the word "chest-prophet" [*sternomantis*] and Plato the philosopher "Eurycles," after a prophet of this sort called Eurycles. Aristophanes says in the *Wasps* "in imitation of the prophetic method of Eurycles." Philochorus says in the third book of his *On Divination* that women too are ventriloquists. These called up the souls of the dead. Saul used one of these, who called up the soul of the prophet Samuel.

SOPHOCLES' UNDATED USE OF THE TERM *sternomantis* may have preceded Aristophanes' mention of Eurycles. It is clear that Philochorus spoke of women ventriloquists. It is less clear that he also said that they called up the souls of the dead; the notion that they did may be an extrapolation from the application of the term *engastrimuthos* to the witch of Endor in the Septuagint (1 Samuel 28.3–25) and derived Greek accounts.

## 35  Ventriloquists, mages, mystery-initiators, and evocators

ii A.D.

Iamblichus (novelist)
*Babyloniaka* at Photius
*Bibliotheca* 75b

Greek

Iamblichus lays out categories of magic: the mage of locusts, the mage of lions and the mage of mice. Accordingly, he says that the mys-teries derive their name from mice [i.e., *mus*] (for the magic of mice is the first kind). And he speaks of a mage of hail, a mage of snakes and also of necromancy and a ventrilo-quist. He says that the Greeks call a ventriloquist "Eurycles" but the Babylonians "Sacchouras."

THIS INTRIGUING IF IN PART OBSCURE passage serves to bind ventriloquism into the familiar notions surrounding the sorcerer-figure: mages, mystery-initiation, and necromantic evocation. The Oriental contextualization of these phenomena is explicit. For Babylonian sorcerers see **49** (where snakes are burst) and **50**. The use of magic to control the elements is commonplace; see **5, 41, 97–103** and note in particular the amulet against hail at **268**.

# 3
# Alien
# Sorcerers

## PERSIAN MAGES

A large proportion of the male sorcerers in the Graeco-Roman literary tradition are strongly characterized as deriving from the lands of the ancient civilizations of the Near East and Egypt and as manipulating the wisdom of these civilizations. The frequent representation of sorcerers as Orientals and Egyptians in the extant texts is perhaps best explained as an example of the Greek tendency to "invent the barbarian," that is, to project attributes regarded as undesirable or bizarre among free Greeks onto alien peoples. It should not be taken to document directly the impact of these peoples on the development of Greek magical culture. From the classical period on the Greeks tended to identify the Persians as the fount of alien magical wisdom, and their projection of magic onto other Oriental races tended to be secondary to this. Yet the *Odyssey*, with all its magic, including some Egyptian, must have reached its final form long before the Greeks had even heard of the Persians (Cyrus acceded to the throne ca. 557 B.C.).

The terms "mage," "Median," "Persian," "Babylonian," "Chaldaean," and "Syrian" tend to function almost interchangeably in the following texts. The key to these identifications or associations lies in the Persian empire. The mages (Greek *magos*; Old Persian *makuš*) were the professional wise men of the Persian empire, whose expertise was by no means confined to religious matters. When the Persians first made their impact on the Greeks, they had already subsumed the Medes and had taken Babylon within their empire. The Chaldaeans were a series of tribal groups among the Babylonians. The Greeks came to associate them with astronomy and astrology in particular and with magic in general, but there is no indication that they had any such significance for the Babylonians themselves. Other Eastern peoples were added to the mix at a later stage. "Syrians" were perhaps added in the Seleucid period. The Seleucid kings took over much of the territory of the former Persian empire but were based in Syria. The A.D. period added Armenians (in the figure of Nero's Armenian mage, Tiridates, **45**) and even Arabs (in the figure of Lucian's amulet-monger, **275**). Arabs no doubt recommended themselves for these purposes as being both remote and in a sense conveniently poised between the Orient and Egypt. For another Oriental mage see **148**.

If the Graeco-Roman texts, despite appearances, do not *document* any transfer of magical culture from the Near East to Greece, this is not to say that no such transfer occurred. It is a cornerstone assumption of many scholars that it did, either during the Mycenean period (ca. 1500–1000 B.C.) or, as most prefer, the so-called Orientalizing period (the eighth century B.C.). In particular, it has become commonplace to adduce Assyrian-Babylonian evidence from around the time of the Orientalizing period in discussions of early Greek magic. The transfer is held to have occurred primarily through the medium of itinerant religious technicians. (See *A Guide to Further Reading* 2.2 and 3.4.)

## 36   Atossa and the Persian elders (mages?) call up the ghost of Darius

472 B.C.

Aeschylus *Persians* 598–708

Greek

**Atossa:** Friends, whoever has experienced difficult times knows that whenever a wave of troubles comes upon mortals it is usual to fear everything, but that whenever fortune flows well, it is usual to believe that it will continue blowing their way forever. For me now all the fearful things before my eyes seem to represent the hostile purposes of the gods. In my ears resounds a clamor that is far from healing. This is how the shock of my troubles frightens my mind. For this reason I have come here again before the house on foot, without chariot and without the luxury of former times, bringing propitiatory full libations to my son's father, things which soothe the dead, white milk, good to drink, from an unyoked cow, the secretion of the flower-processing bee, gleaming honey, offerings of water from a virgin spring, and an unmixed drink from its mother in the field, this restorative from an ancient vine. The fragrant fruit of the light olive tree, which always luxuriates in leaves, is here too, as are woven garlands of flowers, children of the earth that bears everything. But, my friends, sing hymns in support of these libations to the dead below, and call up the demon Darius, while I pour these honors to the gods below into the thirsty earth.

**Chorus of Persian elders:** Royal woman, revered by the Persians, send the libations into the chambers of the earth, and we will ask the senders of the dead beneath the earth with hymns to be well disposed to us. But, holy chthonic powers, Earth, Hermes, and king of the dead below [i.e., Hades], send up from below a soul into the light. For if he knows any further cure for our ills, he alone of mortals could tell us how to bring an end to them. Does my blessed godlike king heed at all the clear [*or* unclear], barbarian, manifold, perpetual, ill-sounding words I utter, or shall I cry out sounds of misery and distress? Does he hear me from below? Earth, and the other leaders of those in the earth, grant that the much-vaunted demon, the Susa-born god of the Persians, should come from your home. Send up above the one like no other that Persian earth has covered. The man was dear, dear is his barrow, for dear are the personal qualities that are covered there. Aidoneus [i.e., Hades, again], you who send shades up, Aidoneus, may you let our divine lord Darian come up. *Ee.* For he never destroyed men with the folly of destructive wars, but was called godlike in counsel by the Persians, and a godlike counselor he was, since he governed the army well. *Ee.* Suzerain ancient suzerain, set out, come here, come to the very pinnacle of the barrow, raising the saffron-dyed sandal on your foot and revealing the peak of your royal tiara. Come, father Darian, doer of no harm. *Oi.* Appear, master of our master, to hear our new griefs. For a Stygian mist hangs over us, since the entire cohort of youths has perished now. Come father Darian, doer of no harm. *Oi. Aiai, aiai.* You were much mourned when you died. Why are these things possible, possible? . . . double mistake concerning your [?—text corrupt]. . . . The triremes are quite lost to all the land: the ships are not ships, they are not ships.

**Ghost of Darius:** Trusty men among trusty men, with whom I grew up, noble

Persians, under what difficulty does the city labor? The earth groans, is beaten and stamped upon. I am alarmed because I see my wife near the tomb. I received her full libations propitiously. You stand beside my tomb and raise the dirge and call me forth pitifully by shrieking out with evocating noises of grief [*psuchagôgois . . . goois*]. The way out of the underworld is not an easy one, not least because the gods under the earth are better at receiving than at letting go. However, I have come because of my power among them. Make haste, so that I shall not be blamed for tarrying. What is this new evil that weighs heavily upon the Persians?

**Chorus of Persian elders:** I am too awestruck to look at you, I am too awestruck to speak before you, because of my former fear of you.

**Ghost of Darius:** But since I came from below specifically in response to your noises of mourning [*goois*], do not spin out what you must say, but speak concisely and make your point, forgetting any awe of me.

**Chorus of Persian elders:** I fear to do what you ask, I fear to talk before you, and to say words it is hard to say to friends.

**Ghost of Darius:** Well, since the ancient fear in your heart stands in your way, noble, well-born woman, sharer of my bed, stop crying and lamenting and speak to me plainly. Mortal men tend to be subject to mortal woes. Many ills come upon men from the sea, and many from the land, if a life runs to any length.

ATOSSA, THE WIDOW OF KING DARIUS and mother of the current king, Xerxes, is prompted by fearful dreams to make offerings to her dead husband. The chorus of Persian elders then call the ghost up, which duly appears atop its barrow. The ghost goes on to deliver prophecies of the doom of Xerxes' expedition against Greece.

This is an important and controversial text in the history of the developing Greek conception of the mages. Is the chorus of Persian elders here supposed to represent or recall Persian mages, even though the term is not used? The negative view predominates in modern scholarship, but the positive one has much to recommend it. Some sort of association between mages and necromancy in the classical period is implied in passages **10** and **14–20**, and specifically Oriental mages are directly attributed with necromancy in two other pre-Hellenistic sources (**41–2**). This is the second document of necromantic practice in the Graeco-Roman tradition after Homer's *Odyssey* (**144**). The offerings made to the ghost do not include the usual blood sacrifice. Either it was not essential, or it was impractical for or inappropriate to the stage; for another evocation without blood sacrifice see **59**. The application of the term *psuchagôgos*, "evocating," to the chorus's wailing grief (*goois*), which is also explicitly said to have brought the ghost up, is noteworthy: see **25–31** and, with commentary, **48**.

Difficulties attend the phrase "clear [*or* unclear], barbarian, manifold, perpetual, ill-sounding words." The Greek may be construed, perhaps designedly so, with either significance. The term "barbarian" connotes foreignness of tongue primarily and savagery only secondarily. The Persians apply the term to themselves elsewhere in this play, as if speaking from a Greek perspective. But in this particular context, and with the "unclear" reading, the term may also suggest the use of *voces magicae*, exotic polysyllables without immediate meaning (**174**), to call the ghost up. Aeschylus may have thought "Darian" the true Persian form of the king's name, but it is hardly closer than "Darius" to *Darayavaus*.

## 37   The incest of the mages (1); the antiquity of their tradition

v B.C.

Xanthus of Lydia *FGH* 765 F31–2

Greek

F31. Xanthus says in his book entitled *Magica* "The mages have sex with their mothers," and he says that it is customary for them to have sex with their daughters and sisters too, and that the women were held in common. Such unions were not forced or secret, but were readily consented to by both parties, whenever one man wanted to marry the woman of another.

F32. Xanthus of Lydia says that there was a span of six thousand years from Zoroaster to Xerxes' crossing into Greece. He says that after him there was a succession of many mages, men called Ostanes, Astrampsychus, Gobryas, and Pazates, right up until Alexander's destruction of the Persians.

THIS EARLY TRACE OF THE NOTION of the antiquity of the mage tradition is subsequently found in full-blown form in Pliny's *Natural History* (45). Xanthus's contemporary Herodotus readily ascribes the practice of free love to races inhabiting the margins of the known world.

## 38   The incest of the Persian mages (2)

55 B.C.

Catullus 90

Latin

Let there be born a mage from the unspeakable union of Gellius with his mother, and let him learn Persian soothsaying. For a mage should be born from mother and son (if there is any truth in the impious religion of the Persians), so that the son may worship the gods with a welcome incantation [*carmine*], melting the rich fat-skin in the flame.

## 39   Media: Astyages and the mages; dream-interpretation

420s B.C.

Herodotus 1.101, 107–8, 120, 128

Greek

1.101. Anyway, Deioces brought the Median race together into one nation and ruled them. This is the number of the tribes of the Medes: Bousai, Paretakenoi, Strouchates, Arizantoi, Boudioi, and Magoi [i.e., Mages].

1.107. Astyages had a daughter, whom he named Mandane. In his sleep he saw her make so much water that she flooded his entire city, and the whole of Asia was deluged too. He communicated the dream to the dream-interpreters among the mages and when he heard what they had to say he was terrified. Afterward, when Mandane was of an age to be given to a husband, he did not give her to wife to any of the Medes worthy of him, in fear of the vision, but he gave her to a Persian, whose name was Cambyses. He found him to be of good house and refined disposition, but considered him to be far below even a middle-ranking Mede. 108. So Mandane took up married life with Cambyses. In the first year of the marriage Astyages saw another vision. He saw a vine grow from his daughter's genitals, and this vine covered all Asia. After seeing this he communicated it again to the dream-interpreters. He summoned his daughter, who was now with child, from the Persians. When she arrived he kept her under guard with the intention of killing the child she bore. For the dream-interpreters of the mages had interpreted the vision as indicating that his daughter's offspring would rule in his place.

[Cyrus survives, is reared in secret, and plays at being king with other boys before his continued existence comes to Astyages' notice.]

1.120. In his deliberations about Cyrus Astyages summoned those of the mages who had interpreted his dream in this way. When they arrived he asked them how they had interpreted the vision. They repeated what they had said before, namely that the child must become king if he survived and did not die first. He responded to them with these words: "The child lives and survives. He was living in the country where the boys from his village made him king. He did every last thing that real kings do. For he distributed the posts of bodyguards and door-keepers and messengers and everything else, and ruled them. What do you think is the significance of this?" The mages replied, "If the child survives and has become king without contrivance, take heart from this and be of good cheer. For he will not rule a second, further time. Some of our prophecies are fulfilled in small events, and dream predictions can be brought to perfect realization in trivialities." Astyages answered with the following words: "I too, mages, am very much of the same opinion, that the dream has been fulfilled now that the boy has been named king, and that the lad no longer constitutes any threat. Even so, reflect well and advise me of the safest course of action for my house . . . and for yourselves." The mages replied, "It is of great importance for us ourselves that your rule should continue successfully. Otherwise, if the rule passes on to this boy, who is a Persian, it becomes estranged from us, and we, as Medes, are become slaves and considered of no account by the Persians, since we are aliens to them. But so long as you, our fellow countryman, remain established as king, we enjoy a share of power, and receive great honors from you. Accordingly we must by all means take precautions on behalf of you and your rule. If we could now see any cause for alarm, we would be forecasting it all to you. But now that the dream has come to a trivial conclusion, we ourselves take heart and we bid you do the same. Send this child out of your sight to the Persians and his parents."

[Cyrus, grown to manhood, has destroyed the Median army.]

1.128. As soon as Astyages learned that the Median army had been shattered so shamefully, he uttered threats against Cyrus: "Not even so will he get away with it scot-free." This much he said first, and then he proceeded to impale the dream-interpreters of the mages, who had induced him to release Cyrus. Then he armed the remnants of the Medes in the city, the young and the old. He marched them out, joined battle with the Persians, and was defeated. Astyages himself was taken alive, but he lost the army of Medes he had led.

CYRUS CONQUERED MEDIA IN 550 B.C. Herodotus is the only source to assert the Median origin of the mages. He may be right, but the claim may be based on nothing more substantial than the Greek folk etymology that derived the name of the Medes from Medea (**40**). The Persians could themselves perceive mages as frauds: Darius so describes the mage that became the "false Smerdis" in the Behistun inscription (see also Herodotus 3.61–78). The notion that dream-prophecies cannot be fulfilled and thereby diverted by contrivance is striking.

## 40   Media: Medea and the Medes

420s B.C.

Herodotus 7.62

Greek

Everybody used to call [the Medes] Arians, but after Colchian Medea arrived among these Arians from Athens, they too changed their name. This is what the Medes say of themselves.

THIS FOLK-ETYMOLOGY AT ANY RATE serves to unify traditions relating to male and female magical practitioners at a relatively early stage. For the relationship between Medea and the Medes see also **66**.

## 41   Persia: Xerxes and the mages

420s B.C.

Herodotus 7.43, 113–4, 191

Greek

**7.43.** When Xerxes had come to this river [Scamander], he went up to the Pergamos, the citadel of Troy, being desirous of seeing it. When he had seen it and learned all about it, he sacrificed a thousand oxen to Ilian Athene, while the mages poured full libations to the heroes. Because they had done this terror fell upon the encamped army during the night.

**7.113–4.** The mages sacrificed white horses into the river [Strymon] and obtained good omens. After applying this and many other charms in addition to the river [*pharmakeusantes*], they passed over it at the Edonian city of Ennea Hodoi, finding the Strymon to be bridged at that point. On learning that the place was called Ennea Hodoi ["Nine Ways"] they buried alive there that number of boys and girls, children of the locals. It is a Persian custom to bury people alive, for I am told that Amestris too, the wife of Xerxes, when she was an old woman, buried twice seven children of distinguished Persians to give thanks on her own behalf to the god said to be under the earth.

**7.191.** The storm continued for three days. At last the mages made sacrifices to the dead [*entoma*] and sang an incantation [*kataeidontes*] to appease the wind with the help of sorcerers [*goêsi*]. They also sacrificed to Thetis and the Nereids and stopped it on the fourth day. Otherwise, the storm may have abated of its own accord and without compulsion.

HERODOTUS ATTRIBUTES THE MAGES WITH THE abilities to manipulate the dead and to control the elements. The army evidently fell into panic in the night on the plain of Troy because it believed that the mages had called up with their offerings the ghosts of the dead heroes of the Trojan war buried there. These ghosts were particularly vigorous and ever ready to manifest themselves, as we learn from Philostratus's *Heroicus* and from his account of Apollonius's necromancy of the ghost of Achilles there (**59**). If Herodotus tells the story indirectly, this is due to his frequent reticence about the divine and the supernatural. The mages are implied to manipulate the dead also in the process of calming the storm.

The reading of *goêsi* and the interpretation of the word are disputed. If it is correctly read and interpreted, it suggests that for Herodotus mages (*magoi*) and sorcerers (*goêtes*) were distinct categories, albeit very closely allied.

## 42   Mages offer to call up the ghost of a dead girlfriend

Ca. 326 B.C. (Python); ii/iii A.D. (Athenaeus)

Athenaeus 595e–596a, including Python *Agen*, *TrGF* 91 F1

Greek

This is indicated too by the writer of the satyr play *Agen*, which Python of Catana or Byzantium or perhaps even the king [Alexander the Great] himself produced at the Hydaspes river during the Dionysia. The play was produced when Harpalus had already fled to the sea and revolted. He mentions Pythionice as already dead, and Glycera as being by his side and as the origin of the accusation that the Athenians took bribes from Harpalus. This is a passage from the play:

> There is, where this reed grows, a birdless lake. Here on the left is the famous temple of the prostitute, which Pallides built before condemning himself to flight through his actions. It was there that some mages of the barbarians saw him in a wretched condition and persuaded him that they would raise up the ghost of Pythionice.

He called Harpalus Pallides here.

ALEXANDER THE GREAT'S ROGUE TREASURER BECAME notorious for the extravagances lavished on his girlfriends in life and in death. The magnificent memorials he constructed for the same Pythionice in Athens and at Babylon caused outrage. The text of the opening of the quoted fragment of the comic *Agen* is uncertain, but it is at least clear that the mages' plan was to call up the ghost at a "birdless" lake, a lake of the type familiarly used in necromancy (compare **25–6, 144, 153–4**). The site here is Babylon, which perhaps indicates that the mages are already being identified with the Chaldaeans associated with that city (see **49**).

## 43  Persian mages, Pythagoras, Numa and lecanomancy

early v A.D.
(Augustine); i B.C.
(Varro)

Augustine *City of God*
7.35, citing Varro

Latin

Even Numa himself, to whom no prophet was sent by god, nor any holy angel, was compelled to perform hydromancy [water-divination] to see images of gods in water, or rather the deceptions of demons, by whom he was told what sacred rites and observances he should establish. Varro again says that this variety of divination was brought over from the Persians, and he reports that it was employed both by Numa himself and subsequently by the philosopher Pythagoras. He tells that when blood is used the dead too are summoned up, and says that this is called necromancy [*nekuomanteia*] in Greek. Whether it is called hydromancy or necromancy, it is the technique in which the dead appear to give prophecies. They themselves can look to the crafts by which these things are achieved. For I do not wish to assert that these crafts used to be prohibited by law in the actual cities of the various peoples and punished by the severest of laws even before the arrival of our Savior. I repeat, I do not wish to say this, for such things may well have been allowed then. But at any rate it was by these crafts that Numa Pompilius learned those sacred rites, the details of which he published, while concealing their significance, so much did he himself fear what he had learned. When books explaining their significance were brought to light, the senate burned them. So why, I ask, does Varro give some other interpretations of the significance of those sacred rites, interpretations making appeal to nature? If this had been the significance of those books, the senate would not then have burned them, or they would also similarly have burned the books that Varro wrote to Caesar, the *pontifex maximus*, and then published. They burned the books because Numa drew and transported water with which to perform hydromancy. This is the reason he is said to have married the nymph Egeria, as explained in the aforementioned book of Varro. In this way actual events tend to be turned into myths, with a sprinkling of lies. Anyway, it was through the medium of this hydromancy that that most inquisitive of Roman kings learned the sacred rites which the priests were to have in their books, and the significances of them, which he wanted no one to know apart from himself. So he wrote down the significances in a separate place, and made them die with him, as one might say, when he made sure they were removed from human knowledge and buried. So, either the disgusting and harmful desires of the demons were recorded in them, with the result that the whole of the city's theology would have appeared detestable to such men, even though they had taken up so many things to be ashamed of in the rites themselves; or, all those whom practically all peoples of the various races had believed to be immortal gods over such long ages were revealed as nothing other than dead men. Such rites delighted the demons that had inveigled themselves into being worshiped in the place of these actual dead men, whom they had made people think were gods, through the evidence of some false miracles. But by the hidden providence of the true God it was brought about that the demons were made to bestow favor on their friend Numa Pompilius through the crafts associated with hydromancy, and were allowed to tell him everything, except to warn him to burn the books before he died as opposed to merely burying them. Nor were they able to prevent their discovery either by the plough which turned them up or by the pen of Varro, the means by which the story of these events was passed down to the awareness of the current generation. For they cannot bring about that which they are not permitted to. They are given permission by the lofty and just judgment of the highest God, which is made in accordance with the just deserts of those who either are merely afflicted by the demons or are even made subject to them and deceived by them. We can understand how dangerous or how far removed from the worship of the true divinity these books were judged to be from the fact that the senate preferred to burn the writings Numa had hidden, than to live in fear of what he had feared, even though he could not dare to burn them. So, let the man who is not content to live a pious life seek an eternal life through such rites. But the man who does not want any association with evil demons should have no fear of the harmful superstition with which they are worshiped, but should recognize the true religion with which they are brought into the light and conquered.

VARRO, ROME'S GREATEST SCHOLAR AND POLYMATH, associated Persian mages, Pythagoras (see **2**), and the Roman magical tradition. Numa traditionally reigned 715–673 B.C. The attribution of hydromancy, lecanomancy (for which see **163–4**, with commentaries), and necromancy (for which see **144–62**) to the mages is comparable to that found in **44–5**. Varro appears to have held that water-lecanomancy was powered by gods or demons but that blood-lecanomancy was powered by ghosts. Augustine's notions are more complex: both are powered by demons masquerading as dead men masquerading as gods. For magic and the law see **278–98**.

## 44 Persian mages and Greek shamans in the context of international divination

Late i B.C.

Strabo C762

Greek

Whether true or not, men had trusted in and believed these things. This was the reason that prophets were held in honor, to such an extent that they were held worthy of kingship, insofar as they published to us the commands and corrections of the gods, both as living men and after their deaths. Tiresias is an example of this:

> Upon whom, even after death, Persephone bestowed a mind, so that he alone could have wits, while the others, mere shades, just flit about. [Homer *Odyssey* 10.494–5]

Like this too are Amphiaraus, Trophonius, Orpheus, Musaeus, and the god of the Getae, who was once Zalmoxis, one of the Pythagoreans, and, in our own generation, Decaeneus, prophet to Byrebistas. The Bosporeni have their Achaicarus, the Indians their gymnosophists, the Persians their mages and necromancers [*nekuomanteis*] and furthermore their so-called lecanomancers [*lecanomanteis*] and hydromancers [*hydromanteis*], the Assyrians their Chaldaeans, and the Romans their Etruscan horoscope-mongers [*hôroskopoi*]. Moses too was such a man, as were his successors. They started well but got worse.

THIS TEXT USEFULLY ASSOCIATES DIVINERS OF the Greek shaman variety with Persian mages, "Assyrian" Chaldaeans and others. No doubt the terms "necromancers," "lecanomancers," and "hydromancers" are intended to amplify the term "mages" rather than to be differentiated from them as further varieties of Persian diviner (see **45**). For Orpheus and Zalmoxis/Salmoxis see **4, 18–21**. For Moses see **45**.

## 45   The tradition and lore of the mages

i A.D.

Pliny *Natural History*
30.1–20

Latin

**1.** I have repeatedly been exposing the emptiness of the claims made by the mages in the foregoing part of this work, whenever this was demanded by the case and the theme, and I go on to reveal it again now. The subject is one among few requiring further development, for the very reason that this most fraudulent of crafts has exercised the greatest power all over the world for many centuries. It is no wonder that it has been so influential, since it alone has encompassed three other crafts that exercise the strongest control over the human mind and incorporated them into itself. **2.** No one will doubt that it first came to birth in medicine, and that it was gradually introduced in healthful guise as if a higher and more holy form of that craft, and that it added the power of religion, to which even today the human race is quite blind, to promises that were so agreeable and desirable and, in order to acquire this too, mixed in the craft of astrology, since everyone is keen to know his future and believes that it is found most truthfully in the heavens. Thus magic held man's senses in a triple bond and grew to such a height that today it prevails over most of the world and in the East gives orders to kings of kings.

**3.** Without doubt magic was first invented over there in Persia by Zoroaster, as writers agree. But it is not established whether there was just one man of this name or whether there was another one afterward too. Eudoxus, who wanted magic to be understood as the most distinguished and useful among philosophical sects, asserted that this Zoroaster lived six thousand years before the death of Plato, and Aristotle follows him in this. **4.** Hermippus, who wrote about the whole craft in a very careful way, compiled abstracts for and commentaries on the two million verses written by Zoroaster [*FGH* 1026 F57]. He reported that he [Zoroaster or Hermippus?] had been instructed by Azonaces, and that the man himself had lived five thousand years before the Trojan war. The thing that is particularly amazing is that the memory of the craft should have survived over such a long period, despite the fact that it was not preserved by any intervening commentaries or, moreover, any distinguished line of successors. **5.** For how many of us have even heard of those who are just names and for whom no monuments survive, such as Apusorus and Zaratus the Medes, Marmarus and Arabantiphocus the Babylonians or Tarmoendas the Assyrian? However, what is most amazing is the fact that Homer kept so quiet about that craft in the case of Trojan war, while at the same time so much of his work on the wanderings of Odysseus was derived from the craft. Indeed the whole work is composed of nothing else, **[6.]** if indeed the mages wish Proteus and the songs of the Sirens to be understood in this way, and this is by all means to be the only subject of the episodes of Circe and the evocation of the dead. Nor has anyone subsequently explained how magic came to Telmessus, a most religious city, or when it crossed to the older women of Thessaly, whose name has long been proverbial in our world, even though magic was alien to the race, which at the time of the Trojan war at any rate was content with the medicines of Chiron and the thunder of Mars, god of war, alone. **7.** I find it amazing that the reputation for magic was so strongly attached to the people of Achilles that Menander, who remains unrivaled in the precision if his writing, gave the title *Thessalian Woman* to his play about the deceits of women who draw down the moon. I would be inclined to believe that Orpheus was the first to introduce magic to the neighboring Thessalians, and that such a superstition on his part derived from medicine, had not all the whole of Thrace, his home, been completely ignorant of the magical craft. **8.** As far as I can discover, the first man to have written an extant treatise on magic was Osthanes, who accompanied the Persian king Xerxes in his invasion of Greece.

He scattered, as it were, the seeds of the hideous craft along the way, infecting the world with it wherever they passed. More scrupulous scholars date another Zoroaster, Zoroaster of Proconessus, shortly prior to Osthanes. What is certain is that it was this Osthanes above all who worked the Greek peoples up to a ravening hunger, not a mere keenness, for that discipline. And yet I note that the highest literary distinction and repute have been sought from this discipline, in virtually all times since antiquity. **9.** Certainly Pythagoras, Empedocles, Democritus, and Plato sailed abroad to learn it, in periods of self-imposed exile rather than mere visits. On their return they expounded it and included it among mysteries. Democritus promoted the work of Apollobeches of Coptus and Dardanus from Phoenicia, after he had sought out the latter's books in his tomb. The books he himself published were based on their teachings. It is more amazing than anything else in life that anyone accepted these books and that they were passed down in memory. They are so completely lacking in plausibility and rectitude that even those who approve of other parts of his oeuvre deny that these works are genuine. **10.** But this is all in vain, for it is well known that it was Democritus who was primarily responsible for planting this sweetness in the minds of men. And this too is a thing full of wonder, that both of these crafts flourished side by side and at the same time, I mean medicine and magic. While Hippocrates promoted the former, Democritus promoted the latter. This was around the time of the Peloponnesian war in Greece, which began [431 B.C.] in the 300th year from the foundation of our city [753 B.C.!]. **11.** There is another magical tradition too, deriving from Moses, Jannes and Iotapes, and the Jews, but this was many thousands of years after Zoroaster. The Cyprian magical tradition is all the more recent. A second Osthanes added no small influence to magic in the time of Alexander the Great. He had the honor of accompanying Alexander and clearly wandered over the whole earth, as no one could doubt.

**12.** Traces of magic still survive, to be sure, among the Italian tribes too, in our Twelve Tables and other pieces of evidence, which I laid out in an earlier book [28.17]. At long last in the 657th year of the city, in the consulship of Gnaeus Cornelius Lentulus and Publius Licinius Crassus [97 B.C.] the senate passed a resolution banning human sacrifice. Up until that time hideous rites had been celebrated openly.

**13.** Certainly magic was everywhere in the Gallic provinces, and this was true even within living memory. For it was in the principate of Tiberius Caesar that their druids and prophets and healers of this type were abolished. But why should I make mention of this when the craft has even crossed the ocean and passed to the ends of the inhabitable portions of the earth? The Britain of today performs the rites of magic in manic fashion and with such elaborate ceremonies that you would think it was they who had given magic to the Persians. Peoples are agreed in their attachment to magic the whole world over, for all that they may be at war with each other or be unaware of each others' existence. It is difficult to overestimate the debt owed to the Romans, who did away with these terrible rites, in which it was an act of piety to kill a man, and indeed very good for you then to eat him.

**14.** The varieties of magic are several, according to Osthanes. He claims to divine from water, balls, air, stars, lamps, bowls, and axes and in many other ways, and he claims also to hold conversations with ghosts and the dead below. In our own era the emperor Nero discovered all these claims to be empty and false. Indeed his devotion to magic outstripped even his devotion to the lyre and the songs of tragedy. The greatness of his fortune in the human sphere developed desires in the deep flaws of his mind. His first ambition was to give commands to the gods. He had no nobler aims. No one ever supported any other craft more strongly.

**15.** To the pursuit of this end were devoted no shortage of money, power, inquiring intellect, or anything that the world allowed. Nero's abandonment of the craft is a huge and indisputable proof that it is bogus. Would that he had consulted the dead below and any of the gods about his suspicions rather than entrusting the inquiries to brothels and prostitutes. Any rites, however alien and wild, would have been gentler than his thoughts. With all too much cruelty did he fill our city with ghosts.

**16.** The mages have a number of excuses at their disposal, such as the claim that the powers do not obey those with freckles and are not seen by them. Was this perhaps the difficulty in his case? But there was nothing wrong with his limbs. It was freely available to him to pick out fixed days. It was easy to get hold of sheep pure black in color. And he was very keen on human sacrifice. The mage Tiridates had come to him when the triumph was celebrated over his land of Armenia, and in so doing had heavily burdened the provinces. **17.** He had refused to sail, since they do not think it holy to spit in the seas or to contaminate them with other mortal necessities. He had brought mages with him, and he had initiated Nero into their meals. But even though Nero gave him his kingdom, he could not acquire this craft from him. For this reason we should be persuaded that magic is abominable, vain, and empty. Although it contains certain ghosts of truth, it is the powers of poisoning [*veneficas*] that are powerful here, not magical ones. **18.** Someone may ask what lies the old mages told, in view of the fact that when we were young we saw Apion, by trade a grammarian, proclaim that the herb dog-head [*cynocephalia*], which was called the "Osiris-herb" [*osiritis*] in Egypt, enabled divination and was proof against all poisonings [*veneficia*], but that one died if one pulled it up whole. He also proclaimed that he had evocated ghosts in order to ask Homer about the land of his birth and his parents. However, he did not dare to tell the reply he claimed to have received.

**19.** A particular proof of the emptiness of their claims should be noted: of all animals they hold moles in the greatest awe, this even though they have been penalized by nature in so many ways. Not only are they always blind, but even then they are buried in other darkness besides and resemble the entombed. They trust the entrails of no other creature more than these. Nor do they judge any other creature to have a greater religious efficaciousness. Accordingly, if one consumes its heart, freshly excised and still palpitating, they promise that one will gain the ability to divine the outcome of current projects. **20.** They claim that toothache is cured by the attachment of a tooth removed from the living mole. I shall supply their other tenets concerning this creature in the appropriate places. None of their claims will be found more plausible than the one that holds that moles combat the bite of the shrew mouse, since earth compacted by a wheel also combats it, as I have said.

BOOKS 20–32 OF THE ELDER PLINY'S *Natural History* are devoted to medicines. These books bristle with discussions of cures promoted by the mages (see **47**). Pliny's attitude to their claims is usually—though not always—one of scoffing contempt for cheats and frauds. But the sheer amount of text devoted to them may indicate a greater level of respect for them than is explicitly acknowledged. The opening section of Book 30 contains his valuable history of magic and his more programmatic statements about the mages.

Where did Pliny get his information about the beliefs of the mages from? Dickie (1999) has recently argued that he draws on Pythagorean collections of magical lore. Such collections can be traced back through Anaxilaus of Larissa (see **288**), Apion the grammarian, who wrote a book *On Mages*, and

Nigidius Figulus (see **137**) to Bolus of Mendes, a Hellenized Egyptian whose *floruit* was probably the second century B.C. and who wrote treatises on magic pseudonymously ascribed to Democritus. For further manifestations of the mage tradition see **37, 46, 112**.

Pliny contends that magic grew out of medicine and then incorporated into itself elements of religion and astrology (2). This is the start of a debate that continues to rage, with historians of ancient magic arguing still about the relationships between magic and religion and magic and science. In focusing on astrology here (see also 14) Pliny foregrounds the role of divination within magic, as the Romans tended to do; see **283–98** for Roman attitudes and **55**, with commentary, for astrology. Eudoxus of Cnidus (3), however, saw magic rather as part of philosophy. This was not an absurd association, when one bears in mind Pythagoreanism's affinities with magic (**1–9, 57–64**; see also **14, 286, 299**).

Eudoxus (408–355 B.C.) studied under Plato, among others, and in Egypt. He founded a school in Cyzicus. He was survived by Plato, and so is unlikely to have been the source of the information that Zoroaster lived six thousand years before the latter's death. Aristotle is said to have followed Eudoxus's views here (3). The ancient biographies of him report that he wrote an *On Magic*, but this was probably apocryphal. Hermippus of Smyrna (4) lived in the third century B.C. (see **1**); the embedded fragment is one of three that survive from his work *On Mages* (*FGH* 1026 F56–8). The Latin leaves it ambiguous as to whether Azonaces (some manuscripts have Agonaces) was the tutor of Zoroaster or of Hermippus, but context makes the former more likely.

One of the most important aspects of this discussion is its explicit unification within the same category—whatever that category is—of figures of very different varieties (5–13). Compared, explicitly or implicitly, to the mages (of Persia, Media, Babylon, Assyria, and even Armenia, all closely identified [5, 16]) are: Circe, the Sirens, Proteus, Thessalian witches, Carian Telmessus (known for various forms of divination), Orpheus, Pythagoras, Empedocles, and Democritus, as well as Jewish, Cypriot (Cyprus is identified as a particular home for magic in later sources), Latin, and Gallic sorcerers. For all that magic spread over the entire world, it is presented as fundamentally external and antithetical to Roman culture (13).

The rationalization of conflicting claims in the tradition twice leads to the differentiation of originally single figures into plural ones. "Zoroaster" (3) and "Zaratus" (5) are both alike transcriptions of the Zend Zara(t)hustra, and Pliny further suggests that there may have been two Zoroasters (9), with a more recent one hailing from Proconessus, home of Aristeas (**6–7**). Ost(h)anes (the manuscripts of Pliny and other sources are divided between the two forms) is similarly differentiated into an early classical one, Xerxes' associate (8), and an early Hellenistic one (11); it is difficult to identify this second Ostanes with the son of the great one who appears in **46**. The development of the great Osthanes into the key figure that introduced the wisdom of the mages to the Greek world evidently occurred after Herodotus, who features him without mention of magic or magery. For Osthanes see also **161, 202, 232, 299**.

The Egyptian background to "Democritus," that is, Bolus of Mendes, becomes clear in his promotion of "Apollobeches of Coptus" (otherwise unknown) and his discovery of Dardanus's books in his tomb, for all that he is described as Phoenician (9). This was a well-established theme in (Graeco-) Egyptian lore: see **46** and **53**, with commentaries. The name Dardanus appears to have been applied to a disparate range of magical figures, including the Dardanus that the Greek magical papyri know as a founder of mysteries and the Biblical Darda(la): see further **112, 127, 249–50, 299**. The blending of figures from the Jewish tradition into the magical mix (Moses, Jannes, and Iotapes, 11) also speaks of Egypt. Hellenistic Alexandria was home to a large Hellenized Jewish population

The treatment of Nero's adventures in magic is particularly valuable (14–17). The notion that magic could compel the gods was a common one: see **13, 14, 96, 300**. Accordingly, it well suits the projection of Nero as megalomaniac that he should be represented as turning to it. Pliny's use of the case of Nero to disprove the efficacy of magic is a persuasive one: if even he could not get it to work, with all the world's resources at his command, and with complete freedom from moral restraint, how could anyone else?

The explanation of the efficaciousness of the mole in divination (19) makes appeal to necromancy. The mole resembles a dead man in his tomb. For Circe (6), see **72, 144**. For Thessalian witches (6), see **96–107**. For drawing down the moon (7) see **214–23**. For the opposition of Hippocrates (10) to the mages see **13**. For lychnomancy and lecanomancy (14) see **163–6**. For the twelve tables (12) see **280**.

## 46    The ghost of Ostanes is called up by Pseudo-Democritus and his own son, also Ostanes, to reveal the secrets of alchemy

i A.D.?

[Democritus] *Physica et Mystica* II p 42, 21 Berthelot (Bidez and Cumont 1938:2:317–8)

Greek

After learning these things from the teacher I mentioned earlier [i.e., the great Ostanes], and having come to understand the diversity of matter, I tried to find a way to transmute natures. Since our teacher was dead, and we had not yet completed our education, but were still engaged in the understanding of matter, I ventured to bring him from Hades, as they call it. Setting my hand to this, I summoned him at once and said, "Will you provide me with gifts in return for what I have done for you?" He made no reply. I beseeched him repeatedly, and asked him how to transmute natures. He told me it was difficult to speak, because the demon did not allow him. All he would say was: "The books are in the shrine." I turned back to the shrine and began to see if I could avail myself of these books. For he had not mentioned them to me in life, and he died intestate. Some say he used poison to separate his soul from the body; but his son says that he died suddenly while feasting. Before death he had contrived to reveal the books to his son alone, since he had come to maturity. None of us knew anything of these books. We searched, but we found nothing. We expended a great deal of labor in the attempt to fuse or blend essences and natures. Some time after we had given up trying to join matter, there was a festival and we were all feasting in the shrine. When we were in the temple building, a pillar split open of its own accord. We could see nothing in it. But Ostanes [i.e., the son] said that his father's books were deposited in it. He brought them out to plain sight. We huddled over them and were surprised to see that we had not been leaving anything out. However, we found this useful phrase everywhere, "Nature delights in nature; nature conquers nature; nature dominates nature." We were amazed that he had crystallized all his writings in this brief phrase.

THIS FRAGMENT, DERIVING FROM THE FOUNDING work of ancient alchemy, concludes with a crystalization of the craft's underlying principles of sympathy, antipathy, and neutralization. The date of the text is uncertain, as is its relationship to the work of Bolus of Mendes. Other testimonia for the great Ostanes' revelation to Democritus (collected by Bidez and Cumont 1938, vol. 2) add nothing to the necromantic episode here but make it clear that the shrine in question was in Memphis in Egypt. Hence the two great magical cultures, Persia and Egypt, are brought together (see 96). For the notion of two Ostaneses see 45. Presumably the great Ostanes had revealed the existence alone of the (already hidden) books to his son but not their contents.

This tale's themes are found refracted in a number of Graeco-Egyptian contexts. The association of Egyptian books, incomplete education, ambitious but failed experimentation with technology, Egypt, revelation in a crypt, and the manifestation of a ghost is also found in the preface of Thessalus of Tralles (53; see also 54, 148). It is similarly told that Bitys/Bitos found a book of Thoth-Hermes in a sanctuary at Sais (Iamblichus *On the Mysteries* 8.5 and 10.7; Zosimus *On Apparatus and Furnaces* Greek fragments 230–5 Jackson; see 161). The erotic spell at 213 claims to hail from a book of Hermes found in an inner chamber at Heliopolis. In addition, the Ptolemaic Demotic-Egyptian tale of Prince Khamwas tells how he discovered a book of Thoth-Hermes in the tomb of Naneferkaptah, and of his encounter with his reanimated mummy and the ghost of his wife Ahwere there (*Setne i = Cairo Museum Papyrus* no. 30646, translated at Lichtheim 1973–80, 3:125–38). For further magical books, compare the formularies among the Greek magical papyri and see 43, 45, 115. See further 253 for the discovery of revelations on a Syriac stele.

## 47    The mages and the uses of the hyena

i A.D.

Pliny *Natural History* 28.92–106

Latin

92. Of all animals the mages accord the deepest admiration to the hyena, inasmuch as they have attributed magical skills to it too and specifically the ability to deprive men of their minds and draw them to itself. We have already dealt with its annual change of sex and other aspects of its portentous nature [8.105]. Now we shall review the medical resources it provides. 93. Panthers above all are said to be terrified of it, so much so that they do not even attempt to stand their ground, nor do they attack a man carrying an object made from its skin. There is an amazing claim that if the pelts of both creatures are hung up back-to-back, the panther's hairs fall off. When it is being hunted, it veers rightward in order to seize the course of the hunter and put him in front. If the creature manages to do this, the hunter loses his mind and can even fall off his horse. But if it twists rather leftward, this is an indication that it is failing and that it will be swiftly captured. Also, it is more easily caught if the hunter ties seven knots each into his belt and into the whip with which he directs the horse. 94. Then, so deviously evasive is the empty craft of the mages, they require that the creature be caught when the moon is traversing the constellation of Gemini, and that virtually every last hair be kept safe. The skin that was on its head, if tied on, cures headache. The gall, smeared on the forehead, cures eye inflammation. Or, to cure this once and for all, one should make a decoction of the gall with three ladles of Attic honey and an ounce of saffron. This is also a way to cure dimness of sight and cataracts. 95. If the medicine is allowed to mature, it induces clear vision more effectively, but it must be kept in a copper container. The same medicine cures also eye ulcers, eye scabs, and growths and scars on the eyes. But glaucoma is cured by anointing the eyes with the juices of the fresh roasted liver mixed with honey, with the foam skimmed off. The hyena's teeth assuage toothache when brought into contact, or when worn as amulets in corresponding order. They also cure pains in the shoulders and arms. The teeth of the same creature, if taken from the left side

of its muzzle, bound up in sheepskin or goatskin, cure severe stomach aches, the lungs, taken in food, cure coeliac pains, [96.] and their ashes, smeared on with olive oil, cure belly pain. Painful sinews are soothed by the marrow from its backbone, made into a paste with old olive oil and gall. Quartan ague is soothed by three tastes of its liver before the attack is due. The ash from the creature's backbone soothes gout, if mixed with the tongue and right flipper of the seal and bull's gall. All these things should be cooked up together and smeared onto a hyena skin. Hyena gall is beneficial for the same disease, combined with the Assos stone. **97.** Those suffering from trembling, spasms, nervousness, and heart palpitations should eat part of the hyena's heart, cooked, with the remainder of the organ mixed with its brain and smeared on. This mixture removes hair, when smeared on, as does the pure gall. If you do not want any of them to grow back, they must be torn out first. Unnecessary eyelashes can be removed in the same way. Meat from the hyena's loins should be eaten for pains in the loins, and it should be smeared on in a mixture with olive oil. Barrenness in women is cured by its eye, taken in food with liquorice root and anise. The method promises conception within three days. **98.** One of its large teeth, tied on as an amulet with thread, is said to be helpful against the terrors of the night and the fear of ghosts. They bid us fumigate the raving mad with one eye and to hang the other one on the person's chest, together with kidney fat or liver or skin. The white flesh from a hyena's breast, together with seven of its hairs, and a stag's penis, bound up in the skin of a gazelle and hung from a woman's neck, preserve her from miscarriage. **99.** The hyena's genitals, taken in honey, stimulate desire for the sex corresponding to the organs, even when men detest sex with women. Indeed, harmony is maintained throughout the house if one keeps in it the same genital organ and a vertebra from the backbone with some skin still sticking to it. Hence they call this spinal vertebra "the knot of Atlas." It is the first vertebra. They hold it among the cures for epilepsy too. **100.** They claim that snakes are put to flight by the burning fat of the hyena. The jawbone, ground up in anise and taken in food, calms down shivering fits. A fumigation with the same mixture induces periods in women. So bogus are their claims that they assert that if a tooth from the upper right part of the muzzle is tied to one's arm, the blows of the spears one throws will never go astray. The palate of the same creature, desiccated and warmed with Egyptian comfrey, and refreshed in the mouth three times, cures halitosis and mouth ulcers. Those who keep the creature's tongue in their shoe under their foot are not barked at by dogs. **101.** The left part of the brain, smeared on the nostrils, gives relief from serious diseases in men and animals. The skin of the forehead affords protection against the evil eye [*fascinationes*]. The meat from the neck, if eaten or if desiccated and drunk, relieves pain in the loins. Sinew pain is to be fumigated by sinews from the back and the shoulders. Hairs taken from the muzzle, if brought into contact with women's lips, constitute an erotic charm. The liver, given in a drink to the patient, heals gripes and bladder stones. **102.** The heart, taken in food or drink, soothes all the body's pains, the spleen soothes spleens, the caul, mixed with olive oil, soothes inflamed ulcers, the bone marrow soothes sinew pain and restores tired sinews. The sinews of the kidneys, drunk in wine with incense, restore fertility taken away by witchcraft/ poisoning [*veneficium*]. The womb, mixed with the skin of the sweet pomegranate, given in drink, is helpful for the womb of women. Women struggling in labor, fumigated with the fat from the loins, give birth immediately. Marrow from the back, worn as an amulet, gives help against empty hallucinations. The sexual organ from the males gives relief to those suffering from spasms, [103.] when used for fumigation, and it similarly helps bleary eyes. The feet, kept by, are helpful for ruptures and against inflammations; one touches the affected part with them: the left feet for the right side, the right for the left. The left foot, passed over a woman in the course of giving birth, is fatal, but she gives birth easily if the right foot is applied. The membrane which held the gall, drunk in wine or taken in food, helps heartburn. The bladder, drunk in wine, helps against urinary incontinence. The urine which is found in the bladder, [**104.**] with the addition of oil, sesame, and honey, relieves long-time acidity in the stomach when drunk. The first and the eighth ribs, if used in fumigation, are healthful for ruptures. The bones from the spine are healthful for women giving birth. The blood, taken together with pearl barley, is healthful for gripes. If the doorposts are touched all over with this same blood, the craft of the mages is thwarted. They cannot summon gods or hold converse with them, whether the attempt is made with lamps or with a bowl, with water or with a globe, or by some other means. If the meat is eaten, it is efficacious against the bites of a rabid dog, and the liver is more efficacious still. The flesh or bones of a man, found in the stomach of a killed hyena, are helpful for gout when used in fumigation. **105.** If nails are found among these parts, the death of one of the capturers is indicated. Feces or bones passed as the animal is killed are powerful against magical attack. Excrement found in the bowels, when dried, is powerful against dysentery. Drunk or smeared all over the body together with goose fat, it helps those who have been harmed by evil potions. But for those bitten by a dog the fat should be smeared on, and they should lie on the skin for aid. On the other hand, if you are pasted with a decoction of the ash of the left pastern-bone and the blood of the weasel, you will be hated by all. **106.** This can be done also with a decoction of the eye. Their most emphatic recommendation is the use of the end part of the intestinal tube against the unfair behavior of leaders and rulers, and for success in elections and law-courts and the winning of suits, provided that one carries it with one. If a man looks upon a woman while wearing the anus of the same creature as an amulet on his left arm, it acts as an erotic charm of such immediate power that she follows him at once. The ashes of the hairs from the same body part, mixed with olive oil and smeared onto men of reprehensibly decadent lifestyle, makes them adopt not merely a modest but actually an austere mode of conduct.

THIS IS ONE OF PLINY'S MORE extensive investigations of the magical uses of a particular animal. For the use of animal parts in amulets see also **253, 266**. For the hyena's change of sex (92), see also Ovid *Metamorphoses* 15.408–10. For conception, fertility, and abortion magic (97–103) see **233–5**. The "knot of Atlas" (99) is so called because as the topmost vertebra it supports the skull, as Atlas supports the globe. For epilepsy see **13**. For erotic attraction magic (99, 101, 106) see **204–32**. For snake dismissal (100) see **49**. For magic against magic (101–2, 104) see **269–70**. For the compulsion of the gods (104) see **13, 14, 96, 300**. For legal curses (106) see **168–72, 237**.

## 48 Byzantine distinctions of the varieties of magic; the derivation of the term *goês*

x A.D.

*Suda* s.v. *goêteia* (sorcery)

Greek

Sorcery [*goêteia*]: magic [*mageia*]. Sorcery and magic and witchcraft/poisoning [*pharmakeia*] are different things. They were the inventions of the Medes and the Persians. Magic is the invocation of beneficent demons to achieve a good goal, as with the miracles of Apollonius of Tyana. The term "sorcery" is applied to the raising of the dead by invocation, and the term is derived from the wailing [*gooi*] and the laments that are performed at tombs. The term "witchcraft/poisoning" is used whenever some deadly drug is made into a potion and given to someone by mouth. Magic and astrology were begun by the Magousaioi. For the Persians were called Magog by the natives.

THE NAME "MAGOUSAIOI" IS ITSELF DERIVED from the Semitic version of *makuš*. The Medes and Persians are presented as the inventors of all varieties alike of magic, the distinctions between which are overschematic and not borne out by ancient usage. The *Suda* seems to read *pharmakeia* as signifying "poisoning" almost to the exclusion of "witchcraft," while the claim that *mageia* was only used for good magic does not survive casual scrutiny. Nor was the term *goêteia*, as used in ancient sources, confined to the raising of the dead, but the *Suda* is in fact right about the etymology. So the *goês*-sorcerer was indeed *in origin* likely to have been concerned with the manipulation of the ghosts of the dead through wailing, be this for purposes of laying or raising or both. For uses of the *goêt-* root in particular association with the manipulation of the dead, see **15, 36**.

## CHALDAEANS AND SYRIANS

**49** **A Chaldaean Babylonian revives a snake-bite victim and blasts snakes**

ii A.D.

Lucian *Philopseudes* 11–3

Greek

11. "Forget him," said Ion. "I'll tell you an amazing story. It took place when I was a lad, just about fourteen years old. Someone came with news for my father that Midas the vine-dresser, a generally strong and hard-working slave, had been bitten by a viper at around noon, and was lying there with his leg already going rotten. For as he had been tying up the vine tendrils and winding them around the props, the creature had crept up on him and bitten him on his big toe. Then it had slipped off again and shot down its hole, while he was left to wail, dying from the pain. This was the news, and then we saw Midas himself being carried in on a stretcher by his fellow slaves, his whole body swollen and livid. He looked clammy, and he was only just still breathing. My father was upset, but a friend who happened to be present said, 'Don't worry. For I'll go after a Babylonian fellow, one of the Chaldaeans, as they say, right away, and he will cure your man.' To make a long story short, the Babylonian came and set Midas back on his feet by driving the poison out of his body with an incantation. Also, he tied a rock he had chipped off a virgin's tombstone to his foot. You may think this a rather ordinary achievement. Even so, Midas himself picked up the stretcher on which he had been brought and went off straight back to the farm. That was the power of the incantation and the piece of tombstone. And the Babylonian did other things too that were truly marvelous. 12. He went out to the farm at dawn, recited seven sacred names from an old book, and purified the place with a torch, encircling it three times. He called out all the reptiles within its boundaries. There came as if drawn to the incantation many snakes, asps, vipers, horned snakes, darting snakes, common toads, and puff-toads. Only one old snake was left behind, unable to crawl out or too deaf to hear the command. The mage said someone was missing, and chose out the youngest snake and sent it with a message, and shortly that snake too arrived. When they were all assembled, the Babylonian blew upon them all. At once they were all burned up by the blast, and we looked on in amazement." 13. "Tell me, Ion," I said, "did the young snake that took the message lead the snake of, as you say, advanced age back by the hand, or did the old snake have a stick with which to support himself?"

IN THE *PHILOPSEUDES* (EXCERPTED ALSO at **51, 54, 115, 244, 275**) Lucian presents a series of supposedly incredible tales on the themes of ghosts and magic, ostensibly to be scoffed at, but their entertaining nature suggests a more complex attitude on the author's part. Lucian gives us another Chaldaean Babylonian, this time an expert in necromancy, in the figure of the Mithrobarzanes who escorts his Menippus down into the underworld (**148**). Theocritus had perhaps had a Chaldaean in mind when he referred to the "Assyrian" who had taught Simaetha the power of evil herbs (**89**); for Chaldaeans as "Assyrian" see **44**. See further **2, 42, 44, 286, 291–2, 294**, including some of the copious evidence for the repeated expulsions of "Chaldaeans" from Rome.

The revival of Midas has affinities both with healing (see **13, 256–66**) and with reanimation (**155–62**), since the victim's flesh has already mortified. The fragment of the virgin's tombstone is evidently a mechanism for bringing to bear on the wound the action of a ghost in the key categories of dead-before-her-time and unmarried (see **110, 112, 181**). This is a particularly vivid account of the commonplace ancient magical activity of snake-bursting or -blasting (see **3, 35, 47, 55, 66, 68, 69, 90, 96, 220** and, for the snake-bursting Marsi, Pliny 28.28). The seven sacred names were no doubt *voces magicae* (compare **174**). For the purificatory circle see **30** with commentary.

## 50   An old Chaldaean revives a dead girl

Later ii A.D.

Iamblichus (novelist)
*Babyloniaka* at Photius
*Bibliotheca* 74b

Greek

They flee away from there, and come across a girl being taken out to burial, and they run up to watch. An old Chaldaean arrives and halts the burial with the claim that the girl is still breathing. And it is shown to be so. He predicts also to Rhodanes that he will be a hero.

RHODANES IS THE NOVEL'S HERO. IN restoring a person from death the Chaldaean performs a similar trick to that of Lucian's (**49**). An almost identical tale is told of Apollonius (**61**).

## 51   A "Syrian from Palestine" exorcises ghosts and epilepsy demons

ii A.D.

Lucian *Philopseudes* 16

Greek

"You're making a fool of yourself," said Ion, "by disbelieving everything. Now I would like to ask you what you have to say about those who deliver the possessed [*daimonôntes*] from their fears, by so clearly singing the ghosts [*phasmata*] out of them. But you don't need to take my word for it—everybody knows the Syrian from Palestine who's such an expert at this. He takes anyone who falls down at the sight of the moon, twists their eyes and foams at the mouth and sets them on their feet again and sends them off sound in mind, delivering them from their affliction for a large fee. Whenever he stands over them as they lie afflicted and asks from whence they have come into the body, the sick man himself makes no response, but the demon answers, speaking in Greek or in the language of its country of origin, and explains how and when it entered the person. The Syrian adjures it to leave, and if it does not obey, he drives it out with threats. I saw one leaving: it was black and smoky in color." "I'm not surprised that you should see such things, Ion," said I, "since you can also see the actual forms which your spiritual father Plato reveals, whereas we only have a dim perception of them, short-sighted as we are."

THE BLACK AND SMOKY NATURE OF the demon probably signifies that it was a ghost, since they were often conceptualized in this way in antiquity; see **115, 135, 140**. The form of the possession depicted here partly resembles the more positive form of possession experienced by ventriloquists (**32–5**), in that the demon speaks with the voice of its host. For the magical dismissal of epilepsy, a particular concern of sorcerers, see **13**, with commentary. Is the large fee demanded an index of the Syrian's abilities or of his venality?

The exorcism is accomplished by the familiar method: the possessing power is compelled to confess its identity and origin (see **57, 127–32**). Most ancient exorcism narratives have a Jewish context, and this is found here in the Syrian's association with Palestine. Indeed Ovid attributes the celebration of the seventh-day Sabbath to the "Syrian from Palestine" and thereby seems to use this term specifically to mean "Jewish" (*Ars Amatoria* 1.416). The use of the two-stage technique is a familiar one in ancient magic: a relatively polite request is first made, but this goes unheeded; this is then followed by compulsive threats, which provoke an instant reaction (see **155**, with commentary).

## 52 Courtesans use a Syrian witch for an attraction spell

ii A.D.

Lucian *Dialogues of Courtesans* 288–9

Greek

**Bacchis:** Dear girl, there is an extremely useful witch [*pharmakis*], Syrian in race, her flesh still young and firm. She once reconciled my Phanias with me when he too was angry without good cause, just as your Charinos is with you now, this after four whole months, when I had already given up hope. He came back again to me, drawn by her incantations.

**Melitta:** What was her price, if you still recall?

**Bacchis:** She doesn't take a large fee, Melitta, just a drachma and a loaf of bread. But you need to add also, along with the salt, seven obols, sulphur, and a torch. The old woman takes these, and one must also mix a bowl of wine for her to drink all by herself. You'll also need one of the man's own possessions, clothes, boots, some hairs, or some such thing.

**Melitta:** I've got his boots.

**Bacchis:** She hangs these up on a peg and fumigates them with the sulphur, meanwhile sprinkling some of the salt over the fire. She intones both your names, his and yours. Then she brings forth a magic wheel [*rhombos*] from her garment, sets it spinning, and utters an incantation of foreign and terrifying names with a tripping tongue. That's what she did then. And not long after Phanias, despite the reproach of his colleagues and despite the fact that Phoebis, with whom he was living, begged him at length to stay, came back to me, drawn mainly by the power of the incantation. Also, she taught me this spell to engender in him a hatred [*misêthron*] for Phoebis. I had to watch out for her footprints, whenever she left any, rub them out, and place my right foot over the trace of her left one, my left one over her right one, and recite "I have trodden on you and I am on top of you." And I did as she said.

**Melitta:** Do not delay, Bacchis, please don't, Bacchis, but call the Syrian right away. And you, Acis, prepare the bread and the sulphur and everything else for the incantation.

THE WITCH IS EVIDENTLY ADEPT NOT only at the magic of *erôs*, or sexual seduction, the main subject here, but also at the magic of *philia*, or the retention of affection, to use Faraone's taxonomy (1999a). It may be noteworthy that the women planning to avail themselves of her services are courtesans: for Faraone the use of seduction magic was the usual preserve of men or those in a "structurally male" role, as he holds courtesans to have been. The witch's spell of attraction over Phanias is combined with a spell of separation against his existing woman, Phoebis, the imagery of which is self-explanatory (see **197–203**). For the elements of the witch's seduction magic, notably her use of the victim's "stuff" (*ousia*) and her magic wheel (*rhombos*), see **204–13, 224–9**. For anger-subduing spells and their role in erotic magic see **114**. The terrifying names are doubtless supposed to be *voces magicae* (see **174**). For a supposedly historical example of a Syrian witch see **181**. The witch is not venal, but she is evidently fond of drink, and is reminiscent of the drunken bawd-witches of Latin elegy (**100–103**). Why are we told that the witch's flesh is still young and firm? Evidently the expectation is that such a woman should be a hag; see **91–2**. Perhaps she has used magic to preserve her youth.

## EGYPTIANS

The notion that there was a special association between magic and Egypt is already found in the seventh-century B.C. *Odyssey* (**74**), but it came to thrive particularly in Graeco-Roman literature in the A.D. period, reflecting in part, no doubt, the culture of the Graeco-Egyptian magical papyri. In particular, it was held that, just like the Greek shamans, the Egyptians derived their wisdom from protracted sojourns in underground chambers or inner crypts. Accordingly, Pythagoras was said to have acquired his wisdom by descending into Egyptian crypts as well as receiving instruction from Chaldaeans and mages (**2**). The relevant Egyptian experts are typically presented as "priests." For further Egyptian sorcerer-priests see **90, 105, 127, 184**. For an Egyptian witch see **157**.

## 53   Thessalus is taught the secrets of medicine by Asclepiusin an Egyptian crypt

i–iv A.D.

[Thessalus of Tralles]
*De virtutibus herbarum*
1–28 Friedrich

Greek/Latin

**1.** Even though many men, Caesar Augustus [i.e., Nero], have tried in their lives to pass on a large body of marvelous information, no one has been able to bring his promises to fulfillment because fate's darkness clouds the perception. I believe that I alone of all men from the beginning of our epoch have achieved something that is marvelous and understood by few. **2.** I embarked on a project that went beyond the measure of human nature, and after many ordeals and hazards I brought it to a proper conclusion. **3.** For I studied grammar in Asia and, outstripping everyone there, I persisted until I should get some benefit from the field. **4.** Then I sailed to the highly desirable city of Alexandria with a great deal of money and studied with the most accomplished men of letters. I won praise from all for my perseverance and insight. **5.** I went continually to the schools of the methodist physicians, for I was extraordinarily keen on this field. **6.** When it was time to return home, my medical studies progressing suitably, I went round the libraries in search of the material I needed. I found a book of Nechepso containing twenty-four treatments for the entire body for every condition, organized in accordance with the zodiac, and exploiting stones and plants. I was amazed at the marvels the book promised. This was, as it seems, the empty delusion of royal folly. **7.** I made the "sun's disk" of which he spoke in admiration, and the rest of his powerful accoutrements, but I failed in all my attempts to cure conditions. **8.** The deception was harsher to me than death itself, and I was consumed by grief. For I had placed premature trust in these writings and had written of their effectiveness even to my parents as if I had already made proof of it, and I had promised them that I was on my way home. **9.** Anyway, I could no longer remain in Alexandria because of the ridicule of my fellow physicians. Success is peculiarly envied. **10.** But I had no eagerness to go back home either, now that I had failed to live up to my promises, so I wandered round Egypt, driven on by my restless soul, seeking to make good some part of my premature claim, or to relinquish the remainder of my life to death if I could not do so. **11.** My soul was always keen [text corrupt here] to have converse with the gods, and I was continually stretching my hands up to heaven and beseeching the gods to give me, through manifestations in dreams or divine inspiration, something with which I could proudly and cheerfully return to Alexandria and my homeland.

**12.** So I came to Diospolis [i.e., Egyptian Thebes], Egypt's most ancient city and the location of many temples, and settled there. For it had learned and aged chief priests who were expert in manifold fields of knowledge. **13.** As time went on and my friendship with them grew stronger, I inquired whether any magical power was preserved, but I had to condemn most of them for making claims reminiscent of my own premature enthusiasm. **14.** One man alone did not disappoint me. He inspired trust through his self-confidence and the measure of his years. He promised to show me for myself the power of lecanomancy. **15.** I urged him to come for a walk with me in the deserted parts of the city, without revealing my motives. **16.** So we went off to a most peaceful grove, where I immediately fell to the ground and, weeping, grabbed hold of the chief priest's feet. **17.** He was taken aback by this unexpected sight and asked why I was doing it. I told him that he had the power of life and death over me. For I just had to converse with a god. If I did not achieve my desire, I told him, I was going to kill myself. **18.** He brought me to my feet and consoled me with the most soothing words. He promised to do this for me gladly, and he bade me be pure for three days. **19.** I was overjoyed at the chief priest's promises, kissed his right hand and thanked him with tears gushing like a fountain. For it is the nature of unexpected joy to provoke more tears even than grief does. **20.** We returned from the grove and set about my purification. Because of my anticipation the days passed like years. **21.** At dawn on the third day I went to the chief priest and greeted him humbly.

He had prepared a pure chamber and everything else for the encounter. The chief priest had me bring along pen and paper, as I was in any case inclined to do, to note down whatever words I had to. **22.** The chief priest asked me whether I wished to converse with the ghost of some dead person or with a god, and I told him I wanted to talk with Asclepius. It would be the ultimate benefaction if he could arrange for me to converse with the god one-to-one. **23.** He was not pleased about this (as I could tell from his appearance), but even so he undertook to bring it about. He shut me into the chamber and bade me sit down opposite the throne, in which the god would take his seat. He produced the god through a series of secret names, went out and shut the door again. **24.** As I sat there my body and my soul became feeble because of the marvelous nature of the sight. Human words could not convey accurately his appearance or the beauty of the clothes he wore. He raised his right hand and began to speak. **25.** "Thessalus, you are blessed for receiving this honor from a god. As time goes on and your successes are known, people will worship you as a god. So be confident and ask what you want, as I will gladly provide all the answers." **26.** I could only just comprehend the words, for I was absolutely amazed and my mind was preoccupied with gazing at the form of the god. Even so, I asked him why I had failed in my attempt to use the powers of Nechepso. To this the god replied, [**27.**] "King Nechepso was very sensible, and endowed with all virtues, but he received none of the things you seek to learn from the voice of a god. But these excellent qualities allowed him to observe the affinities of stones and plants, and he was aware of the times at which and the places in which the plants had to be picked. **28.** For everything waxes and wanes in due season under the influence of the stars. The divine spirit is composed of the smallest of particles and pervades all existence and in particular those places in which the stellar influences fall upon the structure of the universe."

GREEK AND LATIN ACCOUNTS OF THE original text survive. This translation is based on the Greek BH text, but some obscurities have been resolved with reference to the Latin M version.

Pliny describes the huge impact that the real Thessalus's methodist doctrines had in the age of Nero. Crowds would attend him when he walked abroad. He is said to have railed against the doctrines of all ages of medicine in frenzied fashion and to have described himself as "vanquisher of doctors" on his own monument on the Appian Way (Pliny *Natural history* 29.8–9).

Here the writer posing as Thessalus presents as revealed mysteries the medicinal discoveries that he will lay out in his work on the power of plants. The sealed inner chamber, the meeting with the god, and the suggestion of a ghostly environment help in this projection. The narrative has much in common with a number of others: see **46**, with commentary. "Thessalus" makes strong associations between lecanomancy and necromancy (see **43, 163**). Indeed, where the Greek version has "power of lecanomancy" (14), the Latin version at the corresponding point has "necromancy in a crypt," in anticipation of the forthcoming episode. A coincidence obtains between this narrative and a fragment from a Greek novel in which a person expecting an encounter with Asclepius is instead confronted with a ghost (*P.Oxy.* 416; see Stephens and Winkler 1995, 409–15). The priest apparently uses *voces magicae* in calling up the god (see **174**). For the desire for a direct one-to-one encounter, or *sustasis*, with a deity in magical context, see **55**. Nechepso was the fictional author of a late Hellenistic astrological treatise.

## 54  The sorcerer's apprentice

ii A.D.

Lucian *Philopseudes*
33–6

Greek

[Eucrates speaks:] "I'll tell you another story, one in which I was a participant, not one I heard from someone else. When you hear this, Tychiades, perhaps even you will be persuaded of the truth of the narrative. I was in Egypt at the time. I was still a young man, and had been sent there by my father for my education. I was eager to sail up to Coptus and from there to go to the statue of Memnon to hear the marvelous sound it makes before the rising sun. The common experience is to hear some meaningless voice from it, but Memnon actually gave me a prophecy, opening his mouth to utter seven words. If it were not irrelevant, I would have told you the words. **34.** We happened to be accompanied on the voyage up the Nile by a man of Memphis, one of the sacred scribes. His wisdom was marvelous and he had had the full Egyptian training. It was said that he had lived underground for twenty-three years in crypts [*aduta*] while being trained in magic [*mageuein*] by Isis."

"You're speaking of Pancrates", said Arignotus, "He was my teacher: a holy man, always shaven, thoughtful, speaking his Greek with a heavy accent, long and thin, snub-nosed, with protruding lips and rather skinny legs." "Yes, that's Pancrates!" Eucrates said. "At first I didn't know who he was, but when I saw him performing all sorts of miracles every time we put to, most notably riding on crocodiles and swimming with the animals, while they fawned on him and wagged their tails, I realized that he was a holy man, and by being nice to him I became a friend and comrade by gradual and imperceptible stages. As a result, he shared all his secrets with me.

"Eventually he persuaded me to leave all my servants behind in Memphis, and to accompany him, the two of us on our own. For, he explained, we would not want for attendants. This is how we lived thenceforth. **35.** Whenever we came to an inn, he would take the wooden bar from the door or the broom or even the pestle, dress it in a cloak, utter some incantation [*epôidê*] over it and make it walk. Everyone else would think it was human. It would go off and pump water, buy provisions and prepare them, and in all respects be a perfect servant and attendant for us. Then, when he no longer required its services, he would speak another incantation over it and make the broom a broom again or the pestle a pestle again.

"I was eager to acquire this power, but I had no way of learning this from him, for he was jealous of it [*ebaskaine*], although openly generous with everything else. But then one day I secretly eavesdropped on the incantation—it consisted of three syllables—by lurking in the dark. He then went off to the market after giving the pestle its instructions. **36.** The next day, while he was again looking after some business in the market, I took the pestle and dressed it up in the same way, spoke the syllables over it, and bade it fetch water. When it had filled an amphora and brought it back, "Stop," I said, "fetch water no more, but be a pestle again." But it now refused to obey me, and kept on fetching water, until it had flooded our house with water by its continual drawing. I did not know what to do, for I was terrified that Pancrates would return and be angry, which is in fact what ensued. I took an axe and chopped the pestle in half. But they, each of the two parts, took up amphoras and began fetching water, and I now had two servants instead of one. Meanwhile Pancrates returned to the scene. He realized what had happened and returned the servants to wood, just as they had been before the incantation, but then he had abandoned me before I realized it, and I do not know where he went off to after disappearing."

"So now," said Dinomachus, "do you know how to do that, to make a man out of a pestle?"

"Yes indeed", he said, "Well—half of it. For I still cannot return it to its former state, once it has become a water-carrier. But if I perform the spell now our house will be deluged as water is continuously drawn into it."

THE THEMATIC CORRESPONDENCES WITH THESSALUS'S introduction are clear; see **46**, with commentary, and **53**. The name "Pancrates" means "All-powerful." It is typical of Egyptian priests to be completely shaven; see **55, 105**. His taming of wild animals, to render them fawning, recalls Circe's (**72**). For the manufacture of magical assistants from inanimate objects see **65, 244**. Fundamental to the tale is Pancrates' jealous protection of his craft. Jealousy and envy are often the accompaniment of ancient sorcery; see **192–6, 295, 300**. The sounding statue of Memnon is described by Pausanias (1.42). Here it utters seven words: a magical number of particular appeal to Lucian in this text (compare **49**). The narrative is of course the ultimate source of Mickey Mouse's finest hour (*Fantasia*).

## 55 Nectanebo, the last pharaoh, seduces Olympias and sires Alexander the Great

iii A.D.

Pseudo-Callisthenes
*Alexander Romance*
1–7, 12

Greek (and Armenian)

1. The Egyptians are very wise, descended as they are from the gods. They it was that took the measurement of the Earth, tamed the waves of the sea, traversed the river Nile, invented astronomy, and gave the world the force of speech, the discovery of magical power. For they say that Nectanebo, the very last of the pharaohs of Egypt, gained mastery over all peoples by magical power. By speech he could subject all the elements of the universe to himself. For if a cloud of war had suddenly come upon him, he did not

bother with the army-camp, processions of arms, the sharpening of steel or engines of war, but he would retreat into his palace, take a bronze bowl, fill it with rain water, and mold some little boats and little human figures out of wax, put them in the bowl, and recite a spell while waving an ebony wand. He would call upon the angels and upon Ammon, the god of Libya. So it was that he would destroy and prevail over the enemies that attacked him, with lecanomancy of this sort and by <sinking> the boats.

**2.** So the kingdom held firm because of the man's great expertise, but after a lapse of time one of the men the Romans call *exploratores*, and the Greeks "spies," came to the pharaoh and spoke as follows: "Greatest Nectanebo, abandon your peaceful lifestyle and take thought! For no small cloud of enemies, tens of thousands of them, are on the attack. There are Scythians, Arabs, Oxydraces, Iberians, Chinese, Caucones, Lapates, Bosporoi, Agroi, Zalboi, Chaldaeans, Mesopotamians, Agriophagoi, Euonymitai, and all the great races of the East. They come with an unnumbered army, tens of thousands of men, keen to capture your Egypt." So said the general, but Nectanebo just laughed and said, "You are to be congratulated on the vigilance with which you keep the watch assigned to you, but you spoke like a coward, not a soldier. For power does not manifest itself in numbers, but in application. A single spell can repel many, grasping hosts in a good hand." So he spoke, and dismissed him.

**3.** Nectanebo returned to his palace and bade all leave him. Once alone he set up his bowl and filled it with water. He tossed the little boats up into the bowl, raised his wand in his hand, and used his powerful spell. Then he gazed into the bowl and saw the gods of the Egyptians steering the boats of the barbarian enemies. Accordingly he conjectured that the pharaoh of the Egyptians had now been betrayed by the blessed gods. So he shaved his head and beard to avoid being recognized, pocketed as much gold as he could carry, and left Egypt through Pelusium. After wandering through the lands of many peoples he arrived at Pella in Macedonia. He donned a linen tunic of the sort worn by an Egyptian prophet and astrologer and set up stall in public, offering divinations to all comers.

After Nectanebo's disappearance from Egypt, the Egyptians asked the forefather of their gods, Hephaestus, what had become of the pharaoh of Egypt. He gave them an oracle that told them to consult the unseen god of the Sinopium, who prophesied to them as follows: "The powerful, strong, elderly, lord pharaoh will come again after a time, now a young man, after casting off his old appearance and traversing the world, to the plain of Egypt, giving us the subjection of our enemies." This was the oracle given. They could not solve its riddle, but they inscribed the lines on the base of Nectanebo's statue so that they could be borne in mind, in case the oracle should one day be fulfilled.

**4.** In Macedonia Nectanebo became so universally renowned for his perfect divinations that Olympias, no less, conceived the desire for a divination from him and summoned him while Philip happened to be out of the country, engaged in warfare. He presented himself at the palace and saw that her beauty surpassed that of the moon. He was in any case susceptible to women, but now he charged up his mind with erotic desire, extended his hand, hailed her, and said, "Greetings, Queen of the Macedonians." He did not deign to address her as "mistress," bearing in mind his own royal status. Olympias said, "Greetings, most excellent astrologer, come to me and take a seat." When he had sat, Olympias said, "You are a truthful Egyptian diviner." Nectanebo replied, "That is what those that have made trial of me say." She said, "What form of divination do you utilize in making your truthful pronouncements?" He replied, "That is a good question, O Queen, for there are many varieties of divination to choose from. There are dream-interpreters, omen-interpreters, augurs, prophets, Ammon-prophets, nativity-casters, mages, and astrologers. Although I draw on all these methods, as a supreme prophet of the Egyptian school, I am basically a mage and an astrologer." As he spoke he looked at her keenly. She noted this and asked, "For what reason, supreme prophet, did you look at me so intently?" Nectanebo said, "Because I remembered an oracle, Queen. For I was once told by my own gods that it was fated for me to give a divination to a queen and for my predictions to be found truthful."

As he said this he produced a precious royal tablet, the form of which cannot be conveyed in words. Three bands separated its ivory, ebony, gold, and silver sections. On its first circle it had the thirty-six decans, on the second the twelve zodiacal signs, on the middle one the sun and the moon. He put it on a stool. Then he opened a small box, this too of ivory, and emptied from it the seven stars and the nativity-ascendant sign, made from eight stones. . . . He arranged them and illuminated this little heaven by placing them in a small circle. He added a sun made from rock crystal, a moon made from adamant, a Mars of hematite, a Mercury of emerald, a Saturn of serpentine, and the nativity-ascendant sign of white marble. He said, "Tell me, Queen, the year, month, day and hour of your birth." She told him, and Nectanebo charted his own birth and that of Olympias, to see if their stars were in a favorable conjunction. Once he saw that they were, he said, "What do you want to hear about, Queen?" She said, "I want to learn about Philip. I hear rumor that after the war he will cast me off and marry another woman." Nectanebo said, "The rumor of a current separation is false, for this is in fact destined to happen at a later point. However, as an Egyptian prophet and mage I can be of service to you in many ways, whenever you have need of me in such a matter. As for the present, it is fated, according to the birth you laid down as your own, that you should have sex with a god come to earth and be impregnated by him. It is fated that you should bear a child that will avenge you for the wrongs done you by Philip." She replied, "Who is the god with whom you tell me to sleep?" He said, "The horned, wealth-bringing Ammon." She said, "How old is he, young or middle-aged? And what type of man is he?" He replied, "He is middle-aged, his hair is gray and he has a ram's horns on his forehead. You will have a dream and you will see the god making love to you." Olympias said "When?" He replied, "Not long—today. So I exhort you to prepare yourself like a queen. For he will embrace you this night in a dream." She said, "If I see this, I shall honor you not as a prophet or a mage, but as a god."

**5.** After this conversation, Nectanebo left the palace. Without delay he ran out into the wilderness and picked some plants suitable for the sending of dreams.

<[*Insertion from the Armenian manuscript*:] He made a decoction of these. Then he modeled a female body out of wax and wrote Olympias's name on the effigy. He made a little bed also from wax and laid the doll of Olympias on it. He kindled a lamp, threw the plant juice into it and invoked with oaths the demons made for this purpose, with the result that he put images into Olympias's mind.>

By these means he bewitched Olympias's sleep and generated for her a dream of the action he desired, with the result that Olympias actually saw Ammon embrace her and sleep with her in a dream. Then he rose up from the bed and said, "Woman, you have your avenger coming into being in your womb."

**6.** Olympias rose from her sleep. She was amazed by the way in which these experiences had coincided with Nectanebo's prediction, and sent for the astrologer. She said to him, "I saw the god of whom you spoke, and he slept with me, just like a blessed god. So I now want to have sex with him while awake, and during the day. You will know how to achieve this. I'm surprised if you do not." He replied, "I know everything. But since you confirm that you wish to have sex with him in your waking state, we need to give this some thought. A dream is one thing, a direct, waking experience is another. I think I should take a room adjacent to your bed-chamber, so that, should the god come to you, you may not be seized by fear, be-cause I will be helping you out with my incantations. For when the god comes to you he will first manifest himself in the form of a snake, slithering on the ground and hissing. Then he will transform himself into horned Ammon, then into strong Heracles, and then into Dionysus the thyrsus-keeper. Then, as he embraces you, the god will manifest himself in human form, with my looks." Olympias said, "Good, prophet. Take the bedchamber. Whenever I see the god, in my waking state, and I learn that I have been impregnated by him, I will reward you in queenly fashion, and I shall declare that you also are father of my son." He said, "I forewarned you about the hissing of the snake, so that you might not be frightened by the monster but be gentle and fearless with it."

<[*Insertion from the Armenian manuscript*:] And the next morning she gave him a bedchamber adjacent to her own. He made ready the softest ram's fleece, with its horns on its forehead, a scepter, and a white cloak. Then he took a snake and rendered it tame and harmless. He had it crawl from his hands and raise itself up. It entered Olympias's bedroom. She was not afraid to see it, for she had been expect-ing it. She ordered her attendants to retire to their own quarters and lay down on the bed. She covered her face but from the corner of her eye she watched him ap-proach, in the form that she had seen him in the dream. He put down his palm scepter, climbed on the bed, turned Olympias to him and had sex with her.>

**7.** All that had been predicted took place. The queen was not afraid, but en-dured the divine transformations of the gods with courage. Getting up once again from her bed, he patted her belly and said, "Be strong, my invincible, unbeatable seed!" With this he left to go to his own room. Henceforth this sort of thing be-came usual, with the queen delighted to be embraced by a snake, Ammon, Hera-cles, and all-divine Dionysus.

So her belly conceived a child. She called Nectanebo and said, "Prophet, what am I to do if Philip returns and finds me pregnant?" He replied, "Do not panic, Queen. Ammon the three-formed god will help you in this, showing him a dream, with the result that you will remain blameless with him." So it was that Olympias went astray, sleeping with a human adulterer in the belief that he was a god, al-though he was indeed pharaoh of Egypt.

**12.** When the pregnancy came to term Olympias sat on the birthing stool for safety and began her labor. Nectanebo attended her. He measured the heavenly courses of the stars in relation to the turning of the zodiacal cycle, and said, "Get up briefly from the stool and walk around a bit. For Scorpio is in the ascendant. The all-shining sun, seeing the team of four ethereal horses going backward, will by all means turn one born at this hour away from heaven. Control yourself, august lady, for the ascendancy of this star. For Cancer is in the ascendant. His own twin chil-dren schemed against Cronos. They castrated him to the belly and . . . [?: text unintelligible as preserved] to Poseidon, ruler of the sea, and Pluto below. . . . At this hour you will give birth to a eunuch. Hold on briefly for this hour. For the horned Moon has left the highest point of heaven with her bull-drawn chariot and come down to earth, to embrace the beautiful cowherd Endymion. So . . . burned by flame, he dies. Not even thus is the . . . birth propitious. For Venus, who loves the bedroom, the mother of Eros the archer, will destroy Adonis, the driver of swine. A child born in this hour takes the gleam of the women of Byblos and rouses disturbance around himself . . . and the anger of the lion Mars. For he loves horses and is keen on war, but at this point was shown by the Sun, unarmed and naked, in his bed of adultery. Hence, the child produced at this hour will be despised. Wait also for this star of Mercury to pass, Queen, the goat-horned one beside the ill-named one. In this way you will produce a distraught, argumentative man of much learning . . . your own son. At this hour you will produce a monster. Sit down just now, Queen, on the stool that bestows blessing, and make yourself comfortable. Increase the frequency and strength of your contractions. For Jupiter, who loves maidens and who gave birth to Bacchic Dionysus from his thigh, is in midheaven and the sky is clear, and becomes the Aries-Ammon, over Aquarius and Pisces, and makes an Egyptian man king and ruler of the universe. Produce the child at this hour!" As he said this the baby fell to the ground, there was a flash of lightening, a peal of thunder, and an earthquake, so that the whole universe was shaken.

THE *ALEXANDER ROMANCE,* WHICH, BY GENRE, belongs with the ancient novel, has a complex, multilingual, open recension. The earliest version accessible to us is one that circulated in the third century A.D. The two most useful accounts of this version are a Greek codex of the eleventh century A.D. in Paris, which, however, represents it in abbreviated form, and an Armenian translation of the fifth century A.D. The English translation given here is based on the text of the codex as edited by Kroll but incorporates supplements from the Armenian text as indicated in Kroll's notes. The *Romance* is transmitted pseudonymously under the name of Alexander's historian, Callisthenes.

The purpose of the *Romance*'s opening episode is to portray Alexander's conquest of Egypt as a restoration of the rightful Egyptian heir to the throne, hence this contrived tale to make Alexander the son of the last pharaoh, Nectanebo II, that is, Nekht-hor-heb (reigned 349–41 B.C.). In the excluded section (8–11) Nectanebo sends a dream to Philip by means of a sea-hawk, which a Babylonian interprets for him as indicating that Olympias has been impregnated by Ammon. On Philip's return, Nectanebo provides further "proof" of the divine source of Olympias's impregnation by transforming himself into a gigantic snake, kissing her, then transforming himself afresh into an eagle and flying off. Subsequently to the portion translated, Nectanebo is killed by the twelve-year-old Alexander, who throws him down a pit, out of contempt for astrology. As he dies, Nectanebo reveals to Alexander and Olympias that he is the boy's father (14).

Nectanebo is attributed with a range of magical abilities, including, indeed, control of the universe. It is curious that he should claim to be, qua Egyptian, primarily a mage, but this again exemplifies the tendency to merge the traditions of the two great magical cultures (see **46**). His skills in various forms of divination are harped upon, particularly astrology. His comical attempts to control the point at which Olympias is delivered of her child take the precepts of astrology to their logical conclusion. It was in the Roman period that divination came to be seen as the greater part of magic. For astrology, see **45, 53, 56, 96, 214–23, 286**.

The *Romance* is keen on voodoo dolls but twice here amalgamates their use with other varieties of magic in seemingly awkward and artificial ways (see **91, 244**). This may in part reflect the fact that our text of the *Romance* is itself an amalgamation of variant versions. Nectanebo's bowl spells combine the binding and analogical magic of voodoo dolls with the divinatory magic of lecanomancy (for rainwater in lecanomancy see **163**). The use of the "Olympias" voodoo doll in the dream-sending spell seems rather to belong to the erotic magic that the context leads us to expect: see **244–6**. There is a hint of lychnomancy here too: see **165–6**. For the desire for a direct, one-to-one encounter with a deity or *sustasis* in a magical context (6) see **53**.

## 56   The two varieties of Egyptian wisdom

iv A.D.

Heliodorus *Aethiopica*
3.16

Greek

Before dawn had properly broken, there was a banging on the inner door of the courtyard, and I heard someone calling "Boy!" The servant asked who was knocking at the door and what the person wanted. The caller replied, "Say that I am Theagenes the Thessalian." I was delighted when the young man was announced to me, and I bade the servant call him in. I saw that the inception of the plans I had in hand was giving itself to me on a plate. I reckoned that he had heard at the drinking party that I was Egyptian and a prophet, and had come to ask me to help him in a love affair. I supposed that he was making the same mistake as the many, who, in ignorance, are tricked into thinking that the wisdom of the Egyptians is all one and the same. One is common and, as it were, creeps over the ground. It attends ghosts and circles around the bodies of the dead. It clings to plants and relies on incantations. Neither does it result in any good, nor does it confer any good on those that use it. For the most part it slips itself up, although it occasionally achieves some miserable, trivial successes. It can make that which does not exist appear to do so, and it can cheat people of their hopes. It is an inventor of lawless activities and the servant of licentious pleasures. But the other wisdom, my child, the true one, of which this first variety is a corrupted version, masquerading under the same name, is one practiced by priests and the prophetic caste from childhood. It looks up toward heaven, it associates with the gods and participates in their nature. It tracks the movements of the stars and so derives the benefit of knowledge of the future. It has nothing to do with these earthly evils but it devotes itself to all that leads to good and that is helpful to man.

THE SPEAKER IS THE EGYPTIAN PRIEST Calasiris. Here the tendency to identify Egyptian priests with sorcerers is acknowledged, even if objected to. This passage has strong links with Heliodorus's subsequent narrative of the old woman of Bessa (**157**), where the same contrast between the two varieties of Egyptian wisdom is realized, respectively, in the figures of the witch and Calasiris. The portrayal of the witch there salutes all the attributes of the common wisdom described here: she digs a pit in the ground, she calls up a ghost into a dead body, and she makes use of plants and incantations. She certainly slips herself up, for the reanimation she brings about results in her own death, and her success in the operation is thus rendered trivial. The positive form of Egyptian wisdom belongs to the priests and the prophets and is based in astrology; see **55**. For erotic magic in an Egyptian context, see **55** again and **206–13, 239–40, 245–6**.

# 4

# *The Rivals of Jesus*

## APOLLONIUS OF TYANA

Apollonius of Tyana (in Cappadocia) and Alexander of Abonouteichos (in Paphlagonia) were both neo-Pythagoreans, and the miraculous feats attributed to them can, accordingly, be seen to follow in the tradition of those attributed to Pythagoras himself and the "shamans" (see **1–9**). Alexander was pupil to a pupil of Apollonius. For each a substantial ancient biography survives, and these conveniently form an antithetical pair: Philostratus's biography of Apollonius is positive and admiring, if highly fictionalized and ironic; Lucian's of Alexander is hostile and contemptuous.

Apollonius's life was approximately coterminous with the first century A.D. As a neo-Pythagorean he rejected wine, marriage, and meat and in particular devoted himself to the condemnation of blood sacrifice. His appearance was the familiar Pythagorean one: he went unshod, grew hair and beard long, and wore only linen. Appropriately, he could remember a previous incarnation. He lived for a time in the temple of Asclepius at Aegae in Cilicia (Alexander was to share his interest in this god), where he cured the sick. He gave his inheritance up to his relatives and urged others to give their money to the poor. He spent five years touring Asia Minor, but in complete silence, and went on to visit Persia, India, and Egypt. He was arrested by Nero and Domitian but talked himself back to liberty on both occasions, and died under Nerva, with whom he was on good terms. His body rose into heaven, but he manifested himself after death to doubters in the afterlife. Temples were set up for him all over Asia Minor.

The correspondences between his life and work and those of Christ are striking. They were almost exact contemporaries; they both preached against blood sacrifice; they both healed the sick; they both advocated alms for the poor; they both brushed with the Roman authorities; they both ascended into heaven; they both manifested themselves after their deaths. And some of the miracles ascribed to Apollonius, as set out hereafter, will seem familiar to readers of the *New Testament*. These similarities did not go unnoticed in antiquity. In the early fourth century Hierocles wrote his comparison of the two, putting them on a par. Eusebius was stung into writing a rebuttal. Hierocles' text does not survive independently, but Eusebius's reply quotes much from it and summarizes the rest, as can be seen from the excerpts.

## 57 Apollonius exorcises a pederastic ghost from the boy it loves, cures the sick, and prescribes for sterilization

After 217 A.D.

Philostratus *Life of Apollonius* 3.38–9

Greek

**38.** In the midst of these discussions the messenger came before the sages bringing some Indians who were asking for deliverance. He brought in a woman who was making supplication on behalf of her son, whom she said was sixteen years old, but had been possessed for two years. The character of the demon was that of a dissembler and liar. One of the sages asked her what her reason was for saying this, and she said, "My son is very attractive and the demon is in love with him, and so will not allow him to keep his mind, or to go to school or to archery class, or even to be at home, but it drives him out to the desert. The boy does not even have his own voice, but he speaks in a deep and hollow voice, like a man. He looks with eyes other than his own. I weep about this and rend my cheeks and chide him as far as it is reasonable to do so, but he does not know me. So I decided to make my way here. Indeed I decided to do this last year, but the demon revealed himself, using my child as a medium, and said that he was the ghost of a man who had once died in war. On death he had been in love with his wife, but when his wife insulted their bed by marrying another man on the third day after his death, he came to hate love for women and so had transferred himself and his affections into this boy. He promised, if I did not slander him to you, that he would bestow many good and fine qualities on the boy. I put up with this for a while, but he has been fobbing me off for a long time and he is now in sole charge of my house. He has no moderate or honest intentions." The sage asked again if the boy was nearby. She said he was not, although she had done much to get him to come. "But the demon threatens me with cliff-tops and deep pits and says he will kill my son, if I bring him to justice here." "Don't worry," said the sage, "for he will not kill him when he has read this." With this he drew a letter from his robe and gave it to the woman. The letter was addressed to the ghost and contained terrifying threats.

**39.** A lame man came too. He was now thirty years old, and an accomplished hunter of lions. A lion had jumped on him and he had damaged his hip in the fall, with the result that he walked with a limp. Their hands massaged his buttock, and the young man set off again with a straight gait. Another man had lost his eyes and went off with all the light restored to them. Another man had lost the strength in his hand, but went off with full control over it. A woman had had seven difficult labors. Her husband made a petition on her behalf and she was cured in the following way. He instructed the husband, whenever his wife was giving birth, to take a live hare in his robe into the room in which the birth was taking place. He was to walk round her and at the same time release the hare. In this case the womb would be passed out together with the child, unless the hare was immediately taken outside.

L. FLAVIUS PHILOSTRATUS, FROM A LEMNIAN FAMILY of sophistic Philostrati, was, as he claims, first commissioned to write the *Life of Apollonius* by Julia Domna, wife of the emperor Septimius Severus.

This episode (which takes place during Apollonius's trip to India) has something in common with that in **60**, in that the ghost-culprit is in love with its victim. The ghost's claim that it would bestow fine qualities on the boy, though fraudulent, was not absurd. The education and improvement of a boy's soul is presented as the ideal goal of a pederastic relationship in Plato's *Symposium*. In speaking with its own voice through the boy's mouth, the possessing ghost behaves like the demons that inhabited the ventriloquists (**32–5**). As having been a warrior and as having died by violence, it belongs in one of the familiar categories of restlessness (see **110, 112**). The imperious tone is de rigeur in addressing possessing ghosts and demons (see **51, 127–32**). In curing the sick Apollonius advertises his devotion to Asclepius, but the combination of exorcism and healing miracles is particularly comparable to Jesus's repertoire (**128**). For sterilization, see **82, 234**.

## 58  Apollonius orders the stoning of a plague-demon at Ephesus

after 217 A.D.

Philostratus *Life of Apollonius* 4.10

Greek

When the plague fell upon the Ephesians, and no defense against it could be found, they sent to Apollonius, and made him their doctor for the disease. He thought that this was a trip he could not put off, but on saying "Let us go" he was already in Ephesus. I think he did the same thing as Pythagoras, who contrived to be at once in both Thurii and Metapontum. Apollonius assembled the Ephesians and said, "Do not worry, for I will put an end to the disease this day." Saying this, he led all the people into the theatre, where the statue of the Averter is now sited. There he found what appeared to be an old beggar contriving to squint. He carried a wallet and morsel of bread in it. He was dressed in rags and had a squalid face. Apollonius grouped the Ephesians around the beggar and said, "Collect as many stones as you can and throw them at this enemy of the gods." The Ephesians were taken aback by this instruction, and thought it terrible to kill a stranger in such an unfortunate condition. The beggar himself was beseeching Apollonius and begging for pity, but Apollonius was insistent and urged the Ephesians to get on with the job and not to let the man go. When some of the people began to pelt him with stones, the man who had been pretending to be squinting suddenly looked up at them and showed that his eyes were full of fire. The Ephesians then recognized that he was a demon and so they stoned him to death so thoroughly that they built up a heap of stones over him. Apollonius waited a little and then asked them to remove the stones and see what creature they had killed. When they got down to what they thought was the man they had stoned, he had disappeared, but they saw a dog resembling the Molossian breed in form, but the greatest lion in size. It had been crushed by the stones and was spitting foam from the side of its mouth, as if rabid. The statue of the Averter, that is, Heracles, is set up in the place in which the apparition [*phasma*] was pelted to death.

IN EPHESUS'S HOUR OF NEED, APOLLONIUS flies or "teleports" there instantaneously. Evidently this is a variety of soul-projection, and it securely locates Apollonius in the shaman tradition, as Philostratus is aware (see **5–8**). He teleports also at 8.12, where, however, it is made clear that the materialized form of Apollonius is substantial.

The stoning of an individual to deliver a city from pestilence was an ancient "scapegoating" (in Greek, *pharmakeia*) technique. In the final sentence the victim is referred to as a *phasma*, which may, but need not, indicate that it was a ghost; the translation is accordingly left ambiguous. But the demon evidently had shape-shifting abilities, like the ghost in **115**; see also the werewolf-ghost in **140**. And the burying of it under rocks is comparable to the ghost-laying technique in **125**.

## 59   Apollonius calls up the ghost of Achilles at his barrow on the Trojan plain

After 217 A.D.

Philostratus *Life of Apollonius* 4.11, 16

Greek

**11.** He came to Ilium. Full of all the traditions about the Achaeans, he went to visit their tombs. He gave many speeches over them, and made many bloodless and pure sacrifices. He bade his companions go to the ship, and said that he himself would spend the night on Achilles' mound. His companions were afraid (for in fact the Dioscorids and the Phaidimoi and all that crowd were already accompanying Apollonius), and they said that Achilles still manifested himself in terrifying form. This was actually what the inhabitants of Ilium believed about him.

**16.** The others too asked to hear the story, and were very keen to hear him speak. "It was not by digging a pit as Odysseus did, or by evocating ghosts [*psuchagôgêsas*] with the blood of sheep, that I managed to speak with Achilles, but by using the prayers that the Indians claim to use for their heroes. 'Achilles,' I said, 'Most men say that you are dead, but I do not agree with their reasoning, nor did Pythagoras, the originator of my wisdom. If we are right, show us your own form, for you would benefit much from my eyes, if you were to use them as witnesses of your continued existence.' At that there was an earth tremor around the barrow, and a young man, five cubits high, sprung out of it, wearing a Thessalian cloak. He did not give the appearance of being pretentious, as some think he was. He was an impressive sight, and he gleamed still. I don't think his beauty has yet met with the praise it deserves, even though Homer had much to say about it. Rather, it was inexpressible and could not be appropriately represented in hymns of praise, but could only be underrepresented by them. As I watched him he grew to twice the size I said he was, and more than this. Anyway, he seemed to me to be twelve cubits tall upon reaching his full height, and his beauty increased in line with his height. He said he never cut his hair, but kept it intact for the river Spercheios, for this was the first river with which he had been intimate. The first down was upon his cheeks. He addressed me and said, 'I'm glad to have come across you, for I have long been in need of a man of your sort. For a long time now the Thessalians have been neglecting offerings to me. I do not think it appropriate to become angry yet, for if I do become angry they will perish more utterly than the Greeks ever did here. Rather, I offer them a reasonable piece of advice. They should not be contemptuous of tradition, nor show themselves to be worse than the Trojans here, who make public sacrifices to me and make first offerings to me from seasonal fruits, even though I killed so many of their men. They also lay down suppliant branches and ask for peace from me, which I will not give them. They foreswore themselves to me, and for this reason Ilium shall never recover its former appearance, nor attain the greatness achieved by many cities formerly destroyed, but they shall live in it in no better condition than if they were captured yesterday. In order, then, that I may not bring the Thessalians to the same pass, make an embassy to their state about the matters of which I have spoken.' 'I shall make the embassy,' I said, 'For the goal of the embassy will be to prevent them from perishing. But I want something of you, Achilles.' 'I know,' he said, 'for you are clearly going to ask about the Trojan war. Ask me five questions of your own choosing and the Fates' approval.' [Achilles duly answers five questions from Apollonius.] After saying this, and finishing with the words about the young man from Paros, he disappeared in a middling bolt of lightening, for the cockerels were already beginning to sing."

APOLLONIUS CANNOT USE THE BLOOD of a sheep to call up the ghost of Achilles, for as a Pythagorean he preaches against blood sacrifice (and, as often in the *Life*, Pythagoras is explicitly saluted here). The Indian prayer, doubtless acquired on his Indian sojourn (see **57, 62**), is conceived of as a substitute for it. However, although the sacrifice of a black sheep was usually central to rites of evocation of the dead (see **25, 144, 148**), it was perhaps not essential. In Aeschylus's *Persians* the ghost of Darius is evocated without blood sacrifice (**36** with commentary), and indeed the manifestation of that ghost may have been modeled on the manifestation of the ghost of the same Achilles atop his barrow in earlier tragedies. As usual, the evocation takes place during the course of the night and ends with it. It is further implied (**11**) that Apollonius encountered the ghost through incubation, the normal means of encountering ghosts (see **149**).

Philostratus has a great deal of interest to say about the restless ghosts of the warriors of the Trojan war, all of course dead by violence, and of their various manifestations on the Trojan plain in his *Heroicus*. In that text we learn that Homer himself had similarly called up the ghost of Odysseus to learn all about the Trojan war, before composing his epics. As a ghost called up in necromancy, Odysseus was bound to speak the truth, and so he exacted from Homer the undertaking not to include the details his disgraceful treatment of Palamedes, "the young man from Paros," in his work (*Heroicus* 43, pp.194-5 Kayser). Achilles' ghost is becoming still more restless for the neglect of offerings at his tomb. This variety of restlessness is comparable to that caused by inadequate burial or the complete deprivation of it (for which see **110, 112**). For outsized ghosts see Pliny the Younger *Letters* 7.27, telling of the apparition of a giant woman, and **275**.

## 60  Apollonius unmasks and defeats a female "vampire"

After 217 A.D.

Philostratus *Life of Apollonius* 4.25

Greek

It happened that at that time one Demetrius was studying philosophy in Corinth. He had taken up into his system all the strength of the Cynic doctrine. Later on Favorinus was to make repeated generous mentions of him in his own writings. His relationship toward Apollonius was comparable to that they say Antisthenes adopted toward the wisdom of Socrates, for he followed him about in his eagerness to learn and applied himself to his writings, and he directed toward Apollonius the most respected of his associates. Among these was the Lycian Menippus, twenty-five years of age, quite sensible enough, and with a body so finely toned that he gave the appearance of being a beautiful gentleman athlete. Many thought that a foreign woman was in love with him, a woman who in turn seemed beautiful and quite gentle. She also claimed to be rich. But all this was completely false, a complete deception. When he had been walking unaccompanied down the road to Cenchreae, a ghost [*phasma*] met him, materialized in the form of a woman, clung to his hand, and claimed that she had been in love with him for a long time, that she was Phoenician, and that she lived in one of the Corinthian suburbs, using the name of one or other of them. "When you arrive there during the evening," she said, "I will be singing a song for you, and I'll give you wine, the like of which you have never drunk before. There will be no competitor for my love to give you any trouble, but I shall live with you, a beautiful woman with a beautiful man." The young man was enticed by these words. He was strong in all other aspects of the philosophical life, but could not resist sex. So he went to see her in the evening and thenceforth paid constant visits to her, as if to a catamite, not yet perceiving that she was a ghost. Apollonius eyed up Menippus as a sculptor would do, drew a sketch of him, watched him, and came to a conclusion about him. "You are a beautiful man, and you are pursued by beautiful women, but you are warming a snake on your bosom, and it is a snake that warms you." Menippus was taken aback. "Because your woman," Apollonius continued, "is not marriageable. And why? Do you believe that she loves you?" "Yes, by Zeus," he said, "since she behaves toward me like a woman in love." "Would you marry her?" "Yes, for it is a delightful thing to marry a woman who loves you." So Apollonius asked "When's the wedding?" "I'm burning to do it," he said, "—perhaps tomorrow." So Apollonius waited for the drinking party, and then stood over the guests once they had come, saying, "Where is the gentle lady for whose sake you have come?" "Here," said Menippus, and began to rise from his couch with a blush. "To which of the two of you does the silver, the gold and all the other finery with which the drinking room has been decorated belong?" "To the woman," said Menippus, "for this is all I own," and he pointed to his rough philosopher's garment. "Do you know about the gardens of Tantalus," said Apollonius, "which exist and do not exist at the same time?" "Yes, we know about them from Homer [*Odyssey* 11.582–92]," they replied, "for we have yet to go down to Hades." "You must believe these decorations too to be such, for they are not substantial, but merely appear to be so. So that you may accept what I say, the good bride is one of the *empousai*, which many consider to be *lamiai* and bogies. These female creatures fall in love, and they crave for sex, but most of all for human flesh, and they use sex to ensnare the men upon whom they wish to feed." "Shut up," she said, "and get out." She pretended to be repulsed by what she heard, and I supposed she jeered at the philosophers, to the effect that they were always talking rubbish. But then the golden cups and the pretended silver were shown to be made of air, everything flew from sight, and the wine-pourers and the cooks and all the servants disappeared after their unmasking by Apollonius. The ghost pretended to cry and asked him not to subject her to torture or to compel her to admit what she was. However, Apollonius was insistent and would not release her. She admitted that she was an *empousa* and that she was feeding Menippus fat with pleasures as a prelude to eating his body. For it was her practice to feed upon beautiful young bodies, since their blood was pure. I have had to tell this story at length because it happens to be the best known of all the Apollonius stories, for a great many people are familiar with it, inasmuch as it occurred in the middle of the Greek mainland. However, they have only had access to a summary version, to the effect that he once captured a *lamia* in Corinth, but they do not yet know what her purpose was and that he acted to protect Menippus. My version of the story comes from Damis and his writings.

THIS TALE HAS MUCH IN COMMON with that of the ghost of Philinnion (**119**, with commentary). Ghosts of young women, of which this may be one, were the most bitter of all the varieties of the restless dead, usually for having missed out on marriage, sex, and motherhood. Accordingly, they were dangerously vindictive (see Johnston 1999a, especially 161–202). The original meaning of *empousa* was perhaps "(female) obstructing ghost"; the name may have been derived from the practice of such ghosts of impeding the journeys of other ghosts to the underworld. The original meaning of *lamia* seems to have been, more appropriately for this context, "(female) devourer." Such ghosts usually specialized in attacking children, and were supposedly named for a mortal archetype who had killed her own children and/or those of other women. The ghost's condition is poignant. Her love and her desire for her fiancé are genuine, but it remains her destiny to devour him. For Apollonius's pupil Damis see **62**.

## 61 Apollonius raises a girl from the dead

After 217 A.D.

Philostratus *Life of Apollonius* 4.45

Greek

Here is another of Apollonius's miracles. A girl appeared to have died at the time of her marriage. The bridegroom was attending the bier, shouting out all that one would after a marriage left uncompleted. Rome grieved with him, for the girl belonged to a family of consular rank. Apollonius, happening on their misfortune, said, "Set the bier down. I will put an end to your tears over the girl." At that he asked her name. Most people thought that he would make a speech, an elegy to provoke lamentation. But all he did was lay hold of her and say a few obscure words over her, and he woke the girl up from what everyone thought was death. The girl spoke and returned to the house of her father, just like Alcestis when restored to life by Heracles. The girl's relatives gave him 150,000 sesterces, but he declared that he gave it freely to the girl as a dowry. One could not say whether he noticed a spark of life in her, which had eluded those who had been tending to her—for it is said that Zeus was drizzling, but that vapor was rising from her face—or whether he warmed up and restored a life that had been extinguished. This is not my view alone, but also that of the observers.

THE OBSCURE WORDS APOLLONIUS UTTERS ARE presumably *voces magicae* (see 174). On the assumption that this was indeed a miracle, soul manipulation was presumably involved. Apollonius retrieved the girl's soul and reinserted it into her body. His transfer of his reward money to the girl signifies both his rejection of the material and his humanity. For reanimation, see 50, 105, 155, 157; for Heracles and Alcestis, see 27. One is reminded of Jesus' raising of Lazarus (John 11.1–44).

## 62 Hierocles' comparison of Apollonius and Jesus condemned

Early iv A.D.

Eusebius of Caesarea
*Against Hierocles* 2, 27

Greek

2. [Hierocles] is admiring and approving of Apollonius, and claims that he performed his miracles not with the tricks of sorcery [*goêteia*], but with certain divine and ineffable wisdom. He claims too that they were truly performed in the fashion in which he happened to believe they were, and maintains this without proof. Hear what he says, and I quote him verbatim: "They prattle out their exaltations of Jesus all over the place, with the claim that he made the blind see and performed miracles of this sort." Then he says some other things before adding, "However, let us consider how much better and more intelligent our understanding of such things is, and let us consider our ideas about virtuous men." After this he passes over Aristeas of Proconessus and Pythagoras as too ancient and continues, "But in the age of our forefathers, during the principate of Nero, came the floruit of Apollonius of Tyana. From the time when he was still just a young boy and served as priest to Asclepius, who loves mortal men, in Aegae in Cilicia, he accomplished a great many miracles. I shall pass over the bulk of them and make mention of just a few." Then he begins with the first and catalogues his amazing acts, after which he adds the following words: "For what reason did I bring this subject up? So that you may be able to compare and contrast our accurate and solid judgment on each point with the gullibility of the Christians. For we consider a man who has done such things not a god, but a man that is pleasing to the gods. But they proclaim Jesus a god on the basis of a few wonders." After a few more words he adds to this the following claim: "This too is worth thinking about. Peter and Paul and others of their ilk have exaggerated Jesus' exploits. These men were liars, they were uneducated and they were sorcerers [*goêtes*]. But the exploits of Apollonius are recorded by Maximus of Aegae, Damis the philosopher, who went about with him, and Philostratus of Athens. These men were highly educated, they had a respect

for the truth based on their love of humanity, and they wanted to publicize the actions of a man who was noble and dear to the gods." These are the verbatim words of Hierocles, who wrote the treatise *The Lover of Truth* [*Philalêthês*] against us.

27. He adds the following words, and I quote: "What has been said makes it clear that he made predictions of this sort under the influence of a demon, and that the argument of those who consider him a sorcerer [*goês*] is unsound. But let us consider this too. I hold sorcerers to be the most unfortunate of men. Some of them turn their hand to the torturing of ghosts, others to savage sacrifices, others again to incantations and anointings. In doing this they claim to alter fate. But Apollonius followed the ordinances of the Fates, and he predicted that it was inevitable that they would be fulfilled. He made his predictions not through sorcery, but from the revelations of the gods. When he was with the Indians and saw their tripods and wine-jars and all the other things I said used to come in of their own accord, he did not ask how these tricks were done, nor did he want to find out. He praised them, but he did not think it appropriate to copy them."

Hierocles' project was to cut Jesus down to size: his miracles were comparable to Apollonius', yet Apollonius was not for that reason considered a god. (He did, however, acquire a posthumous cult of his own.) The reference to Aristeas and Pythagoras indicates that Hierocles saw Apollonius as within the shaman tradition (see **1–9**). Hierocles evidently made source-criticism too a part of his case (mistakenly so, if we follow Bowie 1978).

Hierocles explicitly contrasted Apollonius with a sorcerer (*goês*) while applying precisely this designation to Jesus' disciples. We are reminded again that individuals seldom see themselves or their own as sorcerers but project their rivals as such (see **13, 14**). And there were indeed those who saw Apollonius himself as a sorcerer, for good or ill: Dio Cassius 78.18.4, Philostratus *Life of Apollonius* 8.19 (both using *goês*), and *PGM* XIa 1–40 (a spell for the manufacture of a demon assistant calling itself "The Old Serving Woman of Apollonius of Tyana"). Despite what is said here, Apollonius was not always immune to the charms of Indian sorcery (**59**). A useful characterization of the activities typical of a sorcerer is provided: the torturing of ghosts (for cursing or divination), the making of savage sacrifices, incantations, and anointings.

## 63  Origen rejects Celsus's comparison of Jesus to a sorcerer

*Ca.* 249 A.D.

Origen *Contra Celsum* 1.68

Greek

And at once he equates [the miracles of Jesus] with the acts of sorcerers [*goêtes*], since they undertake to perform somewhat miraculous feats, and with the achievements of the disciples of the Egyptians, those who sell their sacred learning for a few obols in the middle of the market, expel demons from people, blow diseases away and call up the souls of dead heroes.

Hierocles (**62**) was not the only pagan to see Jesus as a sorcerer. The middle Platonist Celsus had written his attack on Jesus ca. 176 A.D., the *Alêthês logos,* or *True Doctrine,* a title that doubtless inspired that of Hierocles' piece. Celsus in turn had subsequently received this corresponding attack from the learned eunuch Origen, which became the most important work of Christian apologetic. Indeed Eusebius explicitly sees himself as following in Origen's footsteps (*Against Hierocles* 1). As with Hierocles, our access to Celsus's work is now primarily through its representation in the Christian attack on it. The summary of the points of comparison made by Celsus serves to demonstrate the superficial plausibility of the case to the pagan mind. Note that the stereotype of the sorcerer implied by these remarks—beggarliness, use of sacred texts, exorcisms, purifications, and ghost-manipulations—corresponds closely to the Platonic amalgam (14–7).

## ALEXANDER OF ABONOUTEICHOS

**64 The rise of Alexander**

ii A.D.

Lucian *Alexander/False Prophet* 9–18, 26

Greek

**9.** From that point Alexander and Cocconas began to decide on first the location and second the form their scheme should take, and how they should start it off. Cocconas thought Calchedon an opportune and fertile place, neighboring Thrace and Bithynia, not far from Asia [i.e., the Roman province of that name] or Galatia and all the peoples who lived further inland. But Alexander chose in preference his own homeland, since, as he rightly said, they needed dense and foolish people whom they could take in for the inception of a scheme of such a kind. He said that the Paphlagonians that lived above Abonouteichos were of just this sort, most of them being superstitious and rich. Someone only had to appear before them with a flautist or a tambourine-player or cymbal-player, "fortune-telling with a sieve," as the proverb says, and they would all immediately gape at him open-mouthed and look upon him as a heavenly god.

**10.** They had a minor dispute over this, but Alexander eventually had his way. They came to Calchedon—for even so they thought the city had its use—and buried some bronze tablets in the temple of Asclepius, the most ancient temple of the Calchedonians. The tablets said that Asclepius and his father Apollo would soon move to Pontus and live in Abonouteichos. These tablets were conveniently "discovered" and their message accordingly was easily disseminated across all Bithynia and Pontus, and especially in Abonouteichos. The Abonouteichians voted at once to erect a temple and in no time they were at work on digging the foundations. At that point Cocconas was left in Calchedon to compose ambiguous, ambivalent, contorted, and indirect oracles. He died a little later, bitten by a viper, I believe. **11.** Anyway, it was Alexander who was sent into Anobouteichos first. He had already grown his hair long and let it hang loose. He wore a tunic of white and purple, and threw a white cloak over it. He carried a scimitar like Perseus, from whom he claimed descent on the maternal side. And even though those accursed Paphlagonians knew that both his parents were obscure and wretched, they believed the oracle that said:

> This man you see, dear to Phoebus, is descended from Perseus, the divine Alexander, who has inherited the blood of Podaleirios.

So, it seems, Podaleirios had such a lusty and woman-obsessed constitution that his state of arousal brought him all the way from Tricce to Paphlagonia for Alexander's mother.

Now an oracle had been found, supposedly given out in earlier times by the Sibyl:

> By the shore of the Euxine sea near Sinope, there will be a prophet beside a Bastion, in the days of the Romans. Beginning with the first unit [one: = "A"], and with threefold tens [thirty: = "L"] he will display five further units [five: = "E"] and a triple score [sixty: = "X"], sharing the four-wheeled name of a defending man [*andros alex-êtêros*; compare *Alex-andros*].

**12.** Alexander invaded his homeland after so long away with a great deal of drama. He was a distinguished celebrity. Sometimes he feigned madness and filled his mouth with foam. This was easy for him: he did it simply by masticating the root of the dyers' plant, soapwort. To the Paphlagonians even the foam seemed something divine and fearful. Long in advance they had made ready a linen snake head with a rather human appearance. It was painted up, and looked very real. It opened its mouth and shut it again through the action of horse hairs. And a tongue like the black forked one of a snake would dart out of its mouth. This too was controlled by horse hairs. The snake from Pella too had already been prepared and was being kept at home, ready to make its appearance before the Paphlagonians and join Alexander on stage when the time was right, nay, destined to become the star of the show.

**13.** It was now time to begin. This was his plan. He went by night to the foundations of the temple that they had recently been digging. A pool of water had formed in them, either draining there from the ground or fallen from the sky. In this pool he stored away a goose egg, which he had emptied out. It concealed within a newborn snake. He stuffed this into a corner of the mud and went off back home again. In the morning he leaped forth into the marketplace, naked apart from the loincloth round his genitals, this too of gold, with the scimitar in his hand. He shook his loose hair like the frenzied beggar-priests of Cybele. He climbed up onto a high altar and addressed the people. He called the city blessed for being on the point of receiving a manifestation of the god. The people present—for virtually the entire city had come running to the marketplace, together with the women, old men, and children—stood amazed, prayed, and abased themselves before him. He uttered some meaningless words, perhaps Hebrew or Phoenician, and turned the heads of men who did not know what he was saying, except this alone, that he mixed Apollo and Asclepius into everything he said. **14.** Then he ran to the site on which the temple was to stand. He went to the hole that had been dug and the spring of the oracle that had been used hitherto and waded into the water singing loud hymns to Asclepius and Apollo. He called on the god to come to the city, with good fortune. Then he asked for a bowl. Someone passed one to him, and he easily slipped it under the egg in which he had shut the god and dredged it up with water and mud. He had sealed the cap back onto the egg with white wax and white lead. He took it into his hands and claimed that he now had Asclepius. They gazed at the proceedings with rapt attention, greatly amazed already by the discovery of the egg in the water. He broke the egg out into the palm of his hand and received that snake's baby. When the bystanders saw it moving and coiling around his fingers, they immediately raised a shout, welcomed the god, and called the city blessed. Each of them, mouths open, began to fill themselves up with prayers, asking him for treasures, riches, health, and the other good things. But Alexander quickly rushed back home again, taking the newborn Asclepius with him, "born twice, while other men are born just once" [Homer *Odyssey* 12.22], and borne not by Coronis, by Zeus, or even by a crow, but by a goose. The entire people attended, all inspired and maddened by their hopes.

**15.** He waited at home for some days in anticipation of what did actually come to pass: in no time at all, as the story circulated, vast hordes of Paphlagonians converged upon his house. The city was fit to burst with people who had had their brains and hearts removed and no longer resembled grain-eating men, and differed from sheep in form alone. At this point he took his seat on a couch in a small room, got himself up in divine clothing, and took that Asclepius of Pella to his bosom. As I said, this snake was very large and very beautiful. He wound the body of the snake round his neck and let its considerable tail hang down. This was so big that it trailed into his lap and on over the floor. The head alone he concealed under his armpit (it would put up with everything). He would display the linen head on one side of his beard, as if it was by all means part of the snake you could see.

16. So, envisage a little room, not very well lit, and not letting in enough daylight, and a crowd of human flotsam, excited, already bedazzled, and elated with expectation. It was only to be expected that when they entered they found what they saw miraculous. Within the space of a few days that little snake had become such a big one, and that too humanoid and domesticated. They were quickly hustled toward the exit and, before they could get a good look at it, were driven out by the press of those who were forever coming in from the opposite side. For another doorway had been driven through the wall opposite the entrance to provide an exit. It is said that the Macedonians did something like this with Alexander at Babylon when he was ill. He was very poorly, and his men surrounded the royal quarters and longed to see him and address him for the last time. The accursed fellow is said to have put on this display not just once but repeatedly. He was particularly keen to do it when rich men were new in town.

17. In this respect, my dear Celsus, we must be honest, we should forgive those Paphlagonians and men of Pontus, dense and uneducated people as they are, if they were deceived when they touched the snake. Alexander offered anyone who liked the opportunity to do this. They could just see its head in murky light opening and shutting its mouth. This trick really needed a Democritus or even Epicurus himself or Metrodorus or someone else with a mind able to steel itself against such things. Such a man could disbelieve it and guess how it was done or, even if he could not discover this, could nonetheless be certain from the start that the thing was a complete fraud and impossibility and that trickery [*manganeia*] lurked behind it.

18. Gradually Bithynia, Galatia, and Thrace flooded to his house, as each visitor spread the news and claimed, as you might expect, that he had seen the god being born and had later touched him when, after just a brief interval, he had grown to be huge and to resemble a man in the face. In the wake of this came the painted plaques and the statuettes, some of bronze, some of silver, and the god was given a name. He was called Glycon after some divine instruction in meter. For Alexander cried out, "I am Glycon, third blood of Zeus, a light to men!"

26. As I said before, he repeatedly displayed the snake to people who asked to see it. He did not exhibit the whole thing, but just the tail and the main body, but he kept the head out of sight in his armpit. But he wished to amaze the crowd still further, so he promised to give them the god speaking, giving oracles himself directly and without an interpreter. Then, without much difficulty, he fitted together a series of cranes' windpipes and strung them through the lifelike head he had made. Someone else would then shout down the tube from outside, and this is how he would answer the questions put to him, with the sound emerging through the linen Asclepius. These oracles were called "given by direct voice." They were not given to all, nor were they given willy-nilly, but only to those in fine purple-bordered clothes, to the rich, or to those giving large benefactions.

LUCIAN'S HOSTILE ACCOUNT OF THE CAREER of his contemporary is the only significant literary source for it, but the cult that Alexander inspired is attested also in inscriptions and by images of Glycon, in models and on coins, for which see the plates in Victor (1997).

Like Apollonius, Alexander begins his career under the patronage of Asclepius (see the preface to **57**). Podaleirios (11) was a mythical son of Asclepius and, like his father, a healer; it may be implied that Alexander claimed that his mother had been impregnated by the hero in epiphany. The name of Coronis, the traditional mother of Asclepius, derives from *korônê*, "crow," hence Lucian's play on words (14).

The narrative of Alexander's supposedly fraudulent career, as engagingly laid out here, is for the most part self-explanatory. He presented himself as the privileged interpreter of the prophecies of Asclepius as embodied in the semihumanoid snake Glycon. Coins tell us that Glycon was supposedly born under Antoninus Pius (reigned 138–61 A.D.). Statuettes of the creature portray him as a snake with human hair, compatibly with Lucian's description. Initiates into the cult of Sabazius could supposedly pass snakes through their breasts, and Alexander may have appropriated this imagery (see Clement of Alexandria *Protrepticus* 1.2.16). The trick alleged to lie behind the snake's voice (26) is identical to that behind a variety of supposedly fraudulent skull-necromancies exposed by Hippolytus (**160**). Whereas Apollonius's affinities with Christ could subsequently be appreciated by pagans and even by some Christians, Alexander explicitly set himself against Christians. He developed mysteries for Glycon from which he banned them, alongside Epicureans (Lucian *Alexander* 38; compare 25). Epigraphy reveals that the cult of Glycon flourished around the Black Sea and in the Balkans through the third century A.D.

Alexander began his career, we are told, in the guise of a beggar-priest, an *agurtês* (*mêtri ageirontes*, 13; compare *mêtragurtês*) and in this respect salutes the model of the sorcerer projected by Hippocrates and Plato (**13, 14**; see **19–20**). His long hair and his sometime disdain for clothing is Pythagorean. The golden loincloth was perhaps a tribute to Pythagoras's golden thigh (**3, 5**), an attribute which Alexander was also to claim for himself (Lucian *Alexander* 40). In asking for the bowl with which he was able to dredge up Asclepius/Glycon's egg, Alexander presumably presented himself as performing lecanomancy with the water in the temple foundations (14; see **163-4**).

# SIMON MAGUS

**65**  **Simon Magus: His rise and his claims**

ii–iv A.D.

Pseudo-Clement of
Rome *Recognitions* 2.5,
7–15, 3.73 (at *PG*
1:1157–1474)

Latin (translated from
Greek)

**Book 2:5.** When Peter had said this to us, Niceta asked to be permitted to say something to him. Peter graciously granted the request. "I beseech you," he said, "my lord Peter, to give heed to me in my anxiety for you. I am afraid that you may give the impression of being beaten in your contest with Simon. For it often happens that the defender of truth is not continuously successful, when the audience is prejudiced in someone's favor, or when they don't have any great concern for the better opinion. But, all this aside, Simon himself is the most powerful of speakers, nurtured all his life on the art of dialectic and little syllogistic snares. More serious than this though is the fact that he is well practiced in the art of magic. This is why am frightened lest, strongly fortified on all sides as he is, he may be thought to be championing the truth through false claims by those who do not know him. Nor in fact would we ourselves have been able to escape him and be converted to the Lord, had we not realized that he was a deceiver and a mage while we were his helpers and shared in his errors."

**7.** [Aquila speaks:] "This Simon was the son of Antoninus and Rachel. His race was Samaritan and he came from the town of the Gethones. He was a mage by trade, but had an excellent education in the Greek liberal arts. He was so eager for glory and opportunities for superhuman ostentation that he wished to be held to be an outstanding power, over and above God the creator, and to be thought Christ, and to be called the Stander. He uses this name as if to suggest that he is impervious to dissolution, and he claims that his flesh has been structured by the power of his divinity in such a way that it can survive forever. This is why he is called the Stander, as if subject in no way to decomposition.

**8.** "After John the Baptist had been killed, as you yourself know too, Dositheus had embarked upon his heresy along with thirty other of the Baptist's leading disciples, and one woman by the name of Luna ["Moon"]. These thirty men accordingly seem to have been set up to correspond to the number of days in the moon's cycle. This Simon was eager to acquire distinction for evil. He accosted Dositheus, feigned friendship, and begged him to appoint him as a substitute as soon as any of the thirty died. For they were not allowed to exceed the established number, nor to bring into it anyone unknown or not yet proven. Hence the rest of the disciples were eager to become worthy of the position and of inclusion within the number, and to be pleasing in all regards in accordance with the institutes of their sect. It is the goal of each one of those who seek inclusion within the number to be able to appear worthy to take the place of the dead man, whenever one of them, as I said, dies. So, when a place did become available within the number, Dositheus brought Simon into it, after he had pleaded with him for it at length.

**9.** "But not long afterward Simon fell in love with the woman they called Luna, and he told us all about it, as his friends. He told us that he was a mage, that he was in love with Luna, and that he did not wish to enjoy her in a disreputable way, desirous of repute as he was. He was waiting patiently, he said, until he could experience her in an honorable way. This he could do if we would conspire with him and help him to achieve all he wished. But he also promised to give us a reward for this service: we would be graced with the highest honors and would be held to be gods by men. But there was a condition: 'Bestow the leadership of the cult upon me, Simon, who am able to display many signs and portents by magic craft, through which I can establish either my own repute or that of our sect. For I can make myself invisible to those who wish to capture me, and I can reveal myself openly again when I wish to be seen. If I wish to escape I can tunnel through mountains and pass through rocks as if they were mud. If I were to throw myself headlong down from a high mountain, I would be carried down to the earth unharmed, as if carried in a vehicle. If I am bound I release myself, and render those that threw the bonds on me bound in turn. Confined in prison, I will make bolted doors open of their own accord. I will bring statues to life, in such a way that they will be thought by those that see them to be men. I will make new trees spring up from the earth at once, and produce instant shrubbery. I will throw myself into a fire, but I will not burn. I transform my face so that I am not recognized, but I can have two faces and show them to men. I will make myself into a sheep or a goat, I will bring beards out on the chins of little boys, I will travel into the air by flying, I will display vast quantities of gold, I will make men into kings and cast them down again. I will be prayed to as God. I will receive divine honors from states, so that men will dedicate a statue to me, and worship me and revere me as if I am God. Why need I go on? Whatever I want to do, I will be able to. For I have already achieved a great deal to test my abilities. To make the point,' he said, 'when my mother Rachel commanded me to go out to the farm to reap, I saw a sickle someone had put down, and I ordered it to go and reap, and it reaped ten times as much as the other reapers. I have already produced many new shrubs from the earth and made them thrive. I have made them appear in the blink of an eye. I successfully tunneled through the nearest mountain.'

**10.** "But when he began to speak about sprouting the shrubs and tunneling through the mountain, I was baffled, since he wanted to deceive even us, whom he seemed to want to impress and seemed to trust. For we knew that these things he was claiming to have done himself recently were really done of old by our ancestors. Although we heard these wicked claims from him, and others worse than these, even so we followed him in his crimes, and let others be tricked by him. We told many lies on his behalf. And this was before he had fulfilled any of his promises, with the result that even though he had yet to achieve anything, some people were already considering him God.

**11.** "In the meantime, and from the beginning, once he was included among the thirty disciples of Dositheus, he began to criticize Dositheus himself, as if his teaching was not whole or complete. This was, he said, done from ignorance rather than malice. But when Dositheus realized that he was being criticized by Simon, he became frightened that his reputation might become overcast among those who thought him himself to be the Stander. When they assembled, as usual at the school, he became frenzied and snatched up a rod and began to beat Simon. But all of a sudden the rod appeared to pass through his body as if through smoke. Dositheus was devastated by this. He said to him, 'Tell me, whether you are the Stander, so that I may worship you.' On Simon's response, 'I am,' Dositheus saw that he himself was not the Stander, and fell down and worshiped Simon, and ceded his leadership to him. He ordered the whole group of the thirty to obey him, removed himself to the rank that Simon had occupied, and soon after this he died.

**12.** "So, after the death of Dositheus Simon took Luna. He is still going around with her now, as you see, deceiving the crowds and claiming that he himself constitutes some sort of power, which is above God the creator, and that this Luna he has by his side has been drawn down from the skies above. He contends that she is wisdom, and the universal mother. The Greeks and the barbarians, in their conflict over her, were able to see a partial image of her, but they were completely ignorant of her in her true form, that is, as the woman who lived with him who was first of all men and the sole God. By publishing such claims and others similar to them in elaborate processions of words he deceived many. But I should also mention something I myself remember seeing. When his Luna was once on some tower, a huge crowd assembled to see her and surrounded the tower on all sides. But she was seen to bend forward and look down upon all the people through all the windows of the tower. He did many other marvelous things and continues to do them, so that men are amazed at them and think that he himself is God on high.

**13.** "Niceta and I once asked him how these things could be achieved with the craft of magic, and what the nature of this craft was. Simon began to explain it to us, since we were his intimates, in the following way: 'I have summoned up with unutterable conjurations the soul of a pure boy who was killed with violence, and made him my assistant. It is through this soul that everything I order is accomplished.' I asked, 'Is it possible for a soul to do these things?' He replied, 'I want you to understand this: a man's soul takes second place after God, once released from the darkness of its own body. As soon as it is free it possesses foreknowledge, and this is the reason it is evocated for necromancy.' And I replied, 'So why do the souls of the murdered not take revenge upon their killers?' He replied, 'Do you not recall what I just said, namely that the soul takes possession of foreknowledge on leaving the body?' 'Yes,' I said. 'Therefore,' he said, 'when it leaves the body, it immediately foresees that there will be a judgment, and that everybody will pay the penalty for the sins he has committed here. This is the reason they decline to take revenge upon their killers, because they themselves are still enduring tortures for the sins which they had committed here, and they are aware that heavier punishments await their killers in their judgment. But above and beyond all this, they are not allowed to go out or to do anything by the angels set over them.' I replied, 'If the angels don't allow them to come here or do what they want, how can the souls obey the mage evocating them?' 'They do not give special permission to those souls that are willing to come, but when the presiding angels are constrained by their superior, they have an excuse in the compulsion exerted upon them by us who conjure them, so that they do allow out the souls we evocate. For they commit no sin if subject to violent compulsion. Rather, we are the sinners, who inflict compulsion upon them.' At this Niceta, no longer able to contain himself, responded in a way I was about to do myself (although I wanted first to inquire further about some individual points). But, as I said, Niceta got in first: 'And do you,' he said, 'not fear the day of judgment, since you do violence to angels, evocate souls, deceive men, and are rewarded with divine honor from men? And how are you going to persuade us that there will be no judgment, as some of the Jews acknowledge, and that souls are not immortal, which many believe, when you see them with your very own eyes, and receive from them the assertion of divine judgment?'

14. "When he said this, Simon turned pale. However, after a short while he gathered his wits, and replied as follows: 'Do not think,' he said, 'that I am a man like you. I am not a mage, nor a lover of Luna, nor a son of Antonius. For before my mother Rachel had congress with him, she conceived me while still a virgin, since it was in my power to be either small or great, and to appear as a man among men. So it is in order to test you that I have taken you as my first friends, so that I may set you first in my heavenly and unutterable places, when I have proved you. I have made the false claim of being human, to test you more clearly, to see if you preserve your affection for me intact.' On hearing this, I decided that he was pathetic, but even so I retained some respect for his nerve, and I blushed for him. At the same time I was frightened that he might do us some harm. I nodded to Niceta, indicating that he should continue the pretence with me for a little while, and I said to Simon, 'Please do not be angry at us, who are only corruptible men, incorruptible God. Rather, receive our affection and our mind, wishing as it does to know who God is. For we did not yet know who you were, nor did we realize that you were the very one we were seeking.'

15. "As we ran through these words and others like them, trying to look sincere about them, that most conceited fellow believed we were deceived, and, buoyed up all the more by this, added, 'I look upon you benignly now, for the affection you exhibit toward me, God, for you loved me even when you did not know who I was, and, although seeking me, did not realize that you had found me. But I don't want you to doubt that this is really what it is to be God, when one can become small or great, if one wishes, for I could appear to men in any form. Now I will begin to reveal to you what is true. Using my power I once turned air into water, and the water again into blood, and solidifying the blood, I formed a new human being, a boy, and I produced a much better piece of work than God the creator. For he only made a man from earth, but I did something harder in making one from air. And I dissolved him again and returned him to the air. However I set a likeness and painted image of him in my bedroom, to be a proof and memento of my work.'

We understood that in this he was speaking of the boy killed by violence whose soul he was exploiting for the services he wanted."

**Book 3:73.** But in those days a letter was sent by the brothers who had gone in advance, the subject of which was Simon's crimes. It described how he was deceiving crowds from city to city and lambasting Peter for one thing or another, so that when he eventually arrived, no one was prepared to listen to him. For Simon claimed that Peter was a mage and without God, harmful, devious, without real skill and promising the impossible. Peter claimed that the dead would be resurrected, which was, Simon said, impossible. "But if anyone wishes to confute Peter, he foils the attack with hidden ambushes, carried out by his team. For this reason," he said, "I too, even though I had overcome him and triumphed, fled in fear of ambush, lest he should destroy me with his evil enchantments [*maleficia*], or organize my death through ambush." They revealed that he was based at Tripolis.

THE *RECOGNITIONS* WERE COMPOSED IN GREEK between and the second and fourth century A.D. They are now preserved only in Latin, translated by Rufinus (fourth century A.D.), and Syriac. They were a derivative, alongside the *Homilies*, of a lost *Clementine Romance*. Clement of Rome himself, the principal subject and supposed author, flourished at the end of the first century A.D. For further texts on Simon, see: Acts 8.9–24; Acts of St. Peter; Justin Martyr *Apologies* 26.1–3 and *Dialogue with Trypho* 120; Irenaeus *Adversus haereses* 1.23.1–2 and 24.1–2; Epiphanius *Adversus haereses* 6.21; Hippolytus *Refutations* 6.3–20; Pseudo-Clement of Rome *Recognitions* 2.20–3.48, *Homilies* 3.30–58 and 16–19. For another reference to Simon see **112**.

The Samaritan Simon, who may have been entirely fictional, was introduced to Christian teaching by the apostle Philip, according to tradition. Peter rebuked him when he attempted to buy his miraculous powers from him (Acts 8.18–25; hence "simony"). Simon went on to develop his own sect, the "Simonians." As a Samaritan Simon does not derive from a land particularly associated with magic in the Graeco-Roman tradition, for all that it is Middle Eastern.

Simon's tenets were as follows. He himself was the supreme God. Luna is elsewhere known as Helena and is said to have been a Phoenician prostitute saved by Simon from a Tyrian brothel. For Simon Helena was his own Thought (*Ennoia*); she had created the intermediate powers of the angels and archangels, who had in turn created the world but then enviously shut *Ennoia* herself into her human body. Simon had descended to the earth in order to free Helena and all mankind from the intermediate powers. He too projected himself as Father, Son, and Holy Spirit and as virgin-born (see 14). He evidently adapted the gospel to suit himself. Christian writers repeatedly identify the performance of miracles and free love as characteristic of his priests. Christian heresiologists came to regard Simon as the founder of the heresy of gnosticism. The battle between Peter and Simon culminated in a contest of powers before Nero. Peter won this when he broke Simon's flying spell and sent him crashing to earth. He did not recover from his injuries. His resurrection, promised for three days after his death, failed to materialize.

My frequent generalization bears repetition: sorcery is often the defining characteristic of one's rivals (compare **13, 14**); here Simon is projected as the rival of Peter and hence as "Mage." The corollary of this is that Simon in turn denied that he was himself a mage (2.14) while reciprocally accusing Peter of being one (3.73). *Pari passu*, Simon is accused of using tricky rhetoric and sorcery hand-in-hand (2.5), and he in turn makes a comparable accusation of his own against Peter (3.73). For the old association between magic and rhetoric see **12**, with commentary. The lively narrative of the rise of Simon as a cynical, dedicated and conscience-free charlatan (2.7–12) is comparable to Lucian's narrative of the rise of Alexander (**64**).

Much of Simon's art can be understood in terms of soul- or ghost-manipulation. Simon is represented as claiming that the principal motor of his sorcery is the ghost of a boy, untimely dead and dead by violence, that he has made into a demonic assistant (2.13; see **92, 136–8**). This boy he had himself, it appears, made out of thin air (2.15). Simon appeals to Platonic notions of the percipience and power of the soul unencumbered by the things of the body (2.13; see **133**), and in so doing provides an important explanation for the working of necromancy. These same ideas also provide a convenient explanation as to how sorcerers can create ghosts for themselves to use by human sacrifice and then go on to exploit these ghosts for themselves, without being attacked by them. A number of Simon's miraculous claims can be associated with soul-projection: his ability to disappear and reappear, and his ability to pass through solid objects, his ability to fly (9), his ability to let objects pass through himself (2.11); see **1–9**.

Once again, the compulsion of the gods or the higher powers is taken as a characteristic of magic (13). Simon's claim to have animated a sickle and sent it out to do its work alone (9) is comparable to Lucian's sorcerer's apprentice and his animated pestle (**54**). Simon's close involvement with Luna, "Moon," is used to associate him with the commonplace activity of ancient sorcery of drawing down the moon (especially 2.12, see **214–23**).

# 5

# *Medea and Circe*

Female sorcerers, or "witches," are far more prominent than their male counterparts in mainstream classical literature, which is not to say that women were more inclined than men to turn to sorcery in reality. Two related, all-round witch figures above all flourished in Greek myth and Greek and Latin literature, Medea and Circe. Both of them are very ancient figures and were developed in the early epics. No early epic account of Medea survives, although there is perhaps a very dim reflection of such an account in the Hellenistic *Argonautica* of Apollonius of Rhodes. Circe, however, features prominently in the *Odyssey*.

## MEDEA

For Medea see also **40, 89, 92, 97–8, 104, 224.**

### 66   A rationalized account of Medea's career

i B.C.

Diodorus 4.45-6, 48, 50–2, 54–6

Greek

45. They say that there were two sons of Helios [Sun], Aeetes and Perses. Of these Aeetes was king of Colchis, and the other brother king of the Tauric Chersonnese. Both of them stood out for their cruelty. Perses had a daughter, Hecate, and she excelled her father in her brazen lawlessness. She was fond of the hunt, and when her luck therein failed she would turn her bow upon men instead of beasts. She was a keen contriver of mixtures of deadly drugs [*pharmaka*], and she discovered the so-called aconite. She tested the powers of each drug by mixing it into the food given to strangers. In this way she developed a great experience. First of all she destroyed her father with a drug and so took over his throne, then she founded a temple of Artemis and had strangers that put in sacrificed to the goddess. Hence she acquired a name for cruelty. After this she married Aeetes and gave birth to two daughters, Circe and Medea, and also a son Aigialeus. Circe too devoted herself to understanding drugs of all sorts, and discovered all kinds of qualities and unbelievable powers of roots. She had been taught a great deal by her mother Hecate, but she discovered far more by her own research, so that her own knowledge was unsurpassed by her mother's. She was given in marriage to the king of the Sarmatians, whom some call Scythians. First she killed her husband with drugs, and after this, succeeding to his throne, she exercised much cruel violence upon her subjects. For this reason she was thrown out of her queenship and, according to some mythographers, fled to Ocean. She occupied a deserted island in it with some women who had fled with her and set herself up there. But according to some historians, she abandoned Pontus and settled on that Italian headland which is still called "Circaeum" after her.

**46.** They report that Medea learned all the powers of drugs from her mother and her sister, but her own inclination was the opposite. For she continually saved the strangers that put in from dangers. Sometimes she did this by begging and pleading with her father for the salvation of those who were sentenced to die. Sometimes she herself released them from prison and provided safe passage for the unfortunate men. For Aeetes, spurred on in part by his own cruelty, and in part by his wife, accepted the custom of killing strangers. But since Medea was always working against her parents' project, they say that Aeetes began to suspect that his daughter was plotting against him, and so set guards to attend her. Medea escaped from them and fled to the precinct of Helios that lay by the sea. At this point the Argonauts, traveling from the Tauric Chersonnese, sailed into Colchis by night and to the aforementioned precinct. There they came across Medea as she wandered on the shore, and, learning from her of the custom of killing strangers, explained their own scheme to her. They also learned from her about the danger to which she was subject from her father, because of her piety toward strangers. It became clear that they had common interests. Medea promised to help them until they completed their proposed contest, while Jason swore oaths that he would marry her and keep her as his partner for the whole of his life. After this the Argonauts posted guards on the ship and set off with Medea under cover of night to get the golden fleece. It would be appropriate to expound the details of this, so that no matter of relevance to the subject before us should be unknown.

**48.** They report that Medea led the Argonauts to the precinct of Ares, which was seventy stades from the city. The city was called Sybaris and it contained the royal palace of the Colchians. She approached the closed gates during the night and addressed the guards in the Taurian dialect. The soldiers opened the gates readily, as they would for a princess. They say that the Argonauts rushed in, swords drawn, and killed many of the barbarians. They chased the rest, who were taken aback by the unexpected attack, out of the precinct, collected the fleece, and rushed back to the ship in all haste. In a similar fashion Medea too killed with her drugs the unsleeping snake, which, according to myth, coiled round the fleece, and went down to the sea with Jason. The escaping Taurians ["Bull-men"] brought news of the attack that had occurred to the king.

**50.** While they [the Argonauts] were in this state of confusion it is said that Medea promised to kill Pelias by her own abilities and hand over the palace to the chiefs without any danger. They were all astonished by the claim and asked her to explain the nature of her scheme to them. She said that she brought with her many drugs with strange powers which had been discovered by her mother Hecate and her sister Circe. She had never used them to destroy people before, but she would now use them to take easy vengeance on those who deserved punishment. She laid out the details of her attack to the chiefs, and she promised that she would send a signal from the palace to them on the vantage point above the sea, with smoke if by day, with fire if by night.

**51.** She prepared a hollow effigy of Artemis and hid within it all sorts of powerful drugs. She also anointed her own hair with certain powerful agents and made it gray, and she filled her face and body with wrinkles, with the result that those who saw her thought she was by all means an old woman. Finally she took up the goddess that had been designed to terrify the general populace into superstitious terror and entered the city at dawn. She took on divine frenzy and the crowds rushed through the streets and converged upon her. She urged them all to receive the goddess in pious fashion, for she had come to them from the Hyperboreans to bestow good fortune on the entire city and their king. They all abased themselves before the goddess and honored her with sacrifices and, in short, the whole city joined Medea in her divine frenzy. She entered the palace and inflicted superstitious terror upon Pelias. Through her strange powers she brought his daughters to such a state of bewilderment that they believed the goddess herself was present and bestowing good fortune on the king's house. For Medea told them Artemis had driven through the air on a chariot drawn by snakes and had flown over many parts of the inhabited world, and that she had chosen out the most pious of all kings to establish herself and for eternal honors. The goddess had, she said, commanded her to use certain powers to take Pelias's old age from him and make his body completely young, and to give him many other gifts as well, so that his life could be a blessed one dear to the gods. The king was astonished by these unexpected words. Medea promised that she would at once afford proof of her claims on her own body. She told one of the daughters of Pelias to fetch pure water, and the girl immediately fulfilled her request. They say that she then shut herself into a little room and washed her whole body, rinsing away the effects of the drugs. When she had returned to her former condition and shown herself to the king she amazed all the onlookers and seemed to have transformed her old age into the youth of a girl and an eye-catching beauty by the will of the gods. She also used some drugs to make phantom snakes appear, on which, she said, the goddess had ridden through the air from the Hyperboreans to come to visit Pelias. Medea's achievements seemed to be beyond the nature of a human, and the king gave her warm welcome and, in short, believed that she was speaking truthfully. They say that she spoke one-to-one with Pelias and urged him to tell his daughters to cooperate with her and do whatever she ordered them to. For it was fitting that the body of the king should receive its benefaction from the gods tended not by the hands of slaves but by the hands of his children. So Pelias expressly told his daughters to do whatever Medea commanded them to in respect of their father's body, and the girls were ready to do what was bidden of them.

**52.** When night had fallen and Pelias had gone to sleep Medea told them that they must boil Pelias's body in a cauldron. The girls were averse to the proposal, so she devised a second proof of her claims. They kept in the house a very old ram, and Medea proposed to the girls that she should first boil this and make it a lamb all over again. The girls agreed, and they say that Medea took the body of the ram apart limb from limb and boiled it, and then, deceiving them with some drugs, drew the image of a lamb out of the cauldron. The girls were astonished by this and believed they had full proof of Medea's promise and so carried out her commands. They all struck their father and killed him, apart from Alcestis, who held back from her father because of her greater piety. After this they say Medea stood back from cutting up the body or boiling it. Pretending that she must first pray to the moon, she told the girls to mount with lamps to the top of the palace roof, but she herself spent a lot of time reciting a long prayer in the Colchian language, so making an opportunity for the attackers.

**54.** They say that Jason resided in Corinth and lived with Medea for ten years. He fathered children by her, the eldest two being twins, Thessalus and Alcimenes. The third, Tisander, was much younger than these. They report that at this time Medea was highly favored by her husband not only because she excelled in beauty, but also because she was endowed with self-restraint and the other virtues. After this, as time ever more diminished her physical attractiveness, it is said that Jason fell in love with Glauce the daughter of Creon and wooed the girl. When her father had agreed and had appointed a wedding day, they say that Jason at first tried to persuade Medea to withdraw voluntarily from their marriage. For, he said, it was not because he disdained Medea's society that he wished to marry her, but because he was keen to make the royal house the kin to their children. His wife became angry and invoked the gods that had been witness to their oaths. They say that Jason held the vows in contempt and married the king's daughter. Medea was banished from the city, and was given one day by Creon to prepare for her exile. She entered the palace under cover of night after altering her appearance with drugs. She set fire to the building, using a little root, which had been discovered by her sister Circe. It had the quality of being difficult to extinguish once set alight. The palace was suddenly aflame. Jason quickly leaped out of it, but Glauce and Creon were cut off by the fire and perished. Some historians say that Medea's sons took gifts to the bride smeared with drugs, and that when Glauce accepted them and put them on she met with disaster, and that her father, who came running to help, also died when he touched her body. Medea's first projects were successful, and she did not hold back from taking revenge on Jason. For she became so enraged, envious, and cruel that, since he had escaped the danger in which his wife had perished, she embroiled him in catastrophe by slaughtering the children they had between them. One of her sons managed to escape, but she sacrificed the others and fled from Corinth while it was still the middle of the night with her most trusty women attendants. She managed to get to Heracles in Thebes. Heracles had been an arbitrator of agreements among the Colchians and had promised to help her if these agreements were compromised to her disadvantage.

**55.** In the meantime everyone thought Jason had had his just deserts in being deprived of his children and his wife. For this reason, and because he could not endure such a great catastrophe, he killed himself. The Corinthians were dismayed by this terrible reversal, and were particularly at a loss as to how they should bury the children. Therefore they sent to Delphi to ask the god how to dispose of the children's bodies. The Pythia bade them bury them in the precinct of Hera and to confer heroic honors upon them.

They say that Medea found Heracles in Thebes in the grip of madness and fresh from the killing of his sons. She cured him with drugs [*pharmaka*]. But Eurystheus was imposing his orders on Heracles, and she gave up hope of receiving help from him at that time. She fled on to Athens, to the house of Aegeus, son of Pandion. Here, as some say, she married Aegeus and gave birth to Medus, who subsequently became king of Media. And some say that Hippotes, the son of Creon, demanded she be tried, but that she was absolved of the charges. After this, when Theseus had returned from Troezen to Athens, she was charged with poisoning/witchcraft [*pharmakeia*] and fled the city. Aegeus gave her a guard to escort her to whichever country she wished, and she journeyed to Phoenicia. From there she traveled to the inland part of Asia and married one of the distinguished kings, to whom she bore the son Medus. After the death of his father this son inherited the kingdom. He was admired for his bravery, and named the peoples Medes after himself.

**56.** In general a varied and contradictory story about Medea has been circulated because of the strange tastes of the tragedians. And some, wishing to curry favor with the Athenians, say that she conceived Medus by Aegeus and made her way safely to Colchis. At around this time Aeetes, who had been forcibly expelled from his kingdom by his brother Perses, recovered his rule, after Medea's son Medus had killed Perses. After this Medus, taking charge of an army, traversed much of Asia above Pontus and took control of the land called Media after him. But in my opinion there is no need to record all the claims the mythographers have made about

Medea, and it would take too long to do so. So I will confine myself to laying out the remainder of the story of the Argonauts.

DIODORUS'S ACCOUNT DRAWS ON THAT OF the rationalizing and euhemerist early Hellenistic mythographer Dionysius Scytobrachion, a contemporary of Apollonius of Rhodes. It draws together many of the ideas that had been attached to Circe and Medea in the course of the developing tradition, and so is a useful place to start in laying out the tales associated with them. The rationalized elements are for the most part implicitly acknowledged; others will become apparent by comparison with the following excerpts in this section.

Hecate (for whom see **275**, with commentary), the favored goddess of witches, is reduced to a historical queen (45). As a goddess she came to be considered an aspect of Artemis; but here as a historicized figure she is represented rather as a devotee of her, as is Medea herself (50). Medea also claims devotion to the moon (52), the third aspect of Artemis-Hecate.

Here Hecate is presented as the discoverer of herbal drugs, *pharmaka*, and this is consequently the specialization of her daughters also. Medea's magic is entirely worked through the medium of drugs. It is with these that: she heals (48); she transforms her own appearance and becomes a crone (51 and 54); she inflicts madness (51) and, complimentarily, dismisses it (55); she (supposedly) rejuvenates Pelias in a boiling cauldron (51–2); she makes phantom snakes and a phantom lamb (51–2); she burns up Glauce's wedding-dress or burns down the palace of Creon (54; compare Euripides *Medea* 1136–1230).

The tale of Medea's "animated statue" of Artemis (50) should be compared with the myth of the Spartans Astrabacus and Alopecus. They were similarly driven mad on their discovery of a statue of Artemis Orthia (Pausanias 3.16). The famous Trojan horse may be construed as another hollow talisman designed to capture a city (see Faraone 1992c, 94–112). The Greek magical papyri give recipes for the manufacture of hollow figures into which further magical material can be inserted (see **242**, with commentary). In whipping up divine frenzy Medea resembles a bacchant (see **87, 282**).

Medea is, importantly, bound in with traditions of male sorcery. She is the granddaughter and niece of Perses ("Persian"; 45, 56) and the mother of the Medus ("Median"; 55–6), named for her, through whom she is explicitly said to have engendered the Median race (see **40**); (an interpolation in?) Hesiod already gives her a son Medeios at *Theogony* 1001. She also poses as a Hyperborean (not too great a stretch for one from the Black Sea), and in so doing salutes the shaman tradition of Aristeas and Abaris (51; see **5–7, 244**). Diodorus is, furthermore, keen to emphasise Medea's links with the home of female witchcraft in the Greek world, Thessaly (50), and she is also said to be the mother to Thessalus ("Thessalian"; 54). For Thessalian witches see **96, 104–5, 107, 214–23**. Medea's prayer to the moon (52) hints at her ability to draw it down (compare **214–33**).

## 67   Medea and her root-cutters

Later v B.C.

Sophocles *Rhizotomoi*
F534–6 *TrGF*

Greek

F534 (Macrobius *Saturnalia* 5.19.8): In the *Root-cutters* Sophocles describes how Medea crops evil plants while turning away, so that the power of their noxious smell will not kill her, and drains the juice of the plants into bronze jars. She crops the actual plants with sickles also made from bronze. These are Sophocles's lines:

> She covers her eyes with her hand and collects up the white-clouded juice that drips from the cut in bronze jars.

Shortly afterward he continues:

> The covered chests conceal cut roots, which this woman reaped, naked, with bronze sickles, while crying out and howling.

**F535 (Scholium on Apollonius Rhodius *Argonautica* 3.1214):** Hecate is crowned with an oak branch and snakes. In the *Root-cutters* Sophocles has the chorus say:

> Lord sun and holy fire, sword of Hecate of the roads, which she carries over Olympus as she attends and as she traverses the sacred crossroads of the land, crowned with oak and the woven coils of snakes, falling on her shoulders.

**F536 (Hesychius s.v. "melted" [*aistôsas*]):** Sophocles in *Root-cutters* says:

> After he had melted a doll [*koros*] with fire.

THE SUBJECT OF THE TRAGEDY IS thought to have been Medea's murder of Pelias. The "root-cutters" who gave their name to the play would have been the chorus. F535 seems to confirm that this chorus was made up of Medea's witch-attendants. Plant-drug magic was evidently their speciality. For the aversion of the eyes while cutting animal throats in sacrifice see **144**. It is common for Medea and other witches to perform their rites with their clothing untied (see **69, 91, 98**), but Sophocles takes the notion to an extreme here. The rationalization of this may have been that one performing binding magic should not herself be bound. F536 is intriguing. The subject of the melting is masculine and cannot therefore be Medea. It is unclear whether this referred to erotic magic or to an oath-taking ceremony (see **236**).

## 68  Medea aids the Argonauts

Ca. 270–45 B.C.

Apollonius of Rhodes
*Argonautica* 3.475–80,
528–33, 1026–62,
1191–1224, 1246–67,
4.123–66, 445–81,
1636–93

Greek

**Book 3: 475.** [Argus speaks:] "Son of Aeson, you will scorn the cunning advice I am about to give you. But in a bad situation everything must be tried. You yourself have heard from me in the past that there is a girl that practices witchcraft [*pharmassein*] under the instruction of Hecate, daughter of Perses. If we can persuade her to help us, you will, I think, have no more fear of being defeated in the contest."

**528.** [Argus speaks:] "A girl was reared in the house of Aeetes, whom the goddess Hecate taught to be the greatest exploiter of the drugs [*pharmaka*] that grow on the dry land and in the full-flowing water. With these drugs she extinguishes the blast of the unwearied flame. With these she at once stays the noisy course of rivers, and binds the stars and the paths of the sacred moon."

**1026.** [Medea addresses Jason:] "Pay attention now, so that I can devise help for you. When you come and my father gives you the destructive teeth from the jaws of the snake to sow, wait then for the precise midpoint of the night. Bathe in the streams of the unwearied river, then alone, apart from the others, and in dark clothing, dig a round pit. Jugulate a female sheep over it, and sacrifice it whole. Heap up a fire at the pit. Then appease Hecate, the only child of Perses, making libations of the hive-produce of bees from a cup. Then, whenever you have carefully propitiated the goddess, retreat back from the fire. Let not the noise of feet cause you to turn back, nor the barking of dogs, lest you should vitiate the rites and prevent yourself from returning to your companions in good condition. At dawn make a solution of the drug, strip off, and smear it over your body like oil. There will be boundless might in you and great strength. You will think yourself equal to the immortal gods rather than to other men. In addition to your actual spear, sprinkle your shield and sword with it. Then the spear-points of the earth-born men will not be able to cut through you, nor the irresistible darting flame of the destructive bulls. But you will not have these powers for long, but just for the day. Even so, do not shy back from the contest. I will give you another piece of helpful advice too. When you have yoked the strong bulls, and driven the plough through all the difficult fallow land with your manly hands, the Giants will now grow up in the furrows as you sow the snake's teeth in the dark soil. At that point immediately, if you see them rise from the fallow land in vast numbers, secretly throw a large stone. They will then destroy each other over it, like ravening dogs over their food. Make haste and rush into the battle yourself too. By doing this you will carry the fleece far from Aea to Greece. In any case, go somewhere dear or pleasing to you, when you have departed."

1191. Far off in the west the Sun was entering the dark earth, beyond the re-motest hills of the Ethiopians. Night was yoking up her horses. The heroes were making their pallet-beds ready beside the ship's cables. But as soon as the stars of Helice, the shiny Bear, had set, and the heaven's ether had grown silent, Jason made for a deserted place, like a furtive thief, with all the things he needed. For he had already taken care of all the details during the day. Argus came and brought a female sheep and milk from the flock. These things he brought from the ship. But when he saw a place that was off the beaten track, under a calm sky and in a pure meadow, he first of all washed his soft body there and made himself pure with water from the divine river. He put on a dark robe, which the Lemnian Hypsipyle had formerly given him, a memento of their frequent sex. Then he dug a pit in the ground, a cubit in diameter, and piled up the firewood. He cut the sheep's throat and laid it out well over the top. He set light to the wood, inserting a flame underneath, and over the sacrifice he poured mingled libations. He called upon Brimo-Hecate to be his helper in the contests. After invoking her he retreated. The terrible goddess heard him from the depth of her lair and came to accept the sacrifice of the son of Aeson. Around her head dreadful snakes intertwined with oak twigs. The boundless light of torches flashed. Around her the underworld dogs gave voice to sharp howls. All the meadows quaked at her step. The nymphs of the marsh and the nymphs of the rivers shrieked out, as did all that wheeled around that meadow of Amarantian Phasis. Fear gripped the son of Aeson, but even so his feet carried him out of danger without him turning around, until he found his way back to his companions. Already Dawn, child of the morning, was rising and casting her light above snowy Caucasus.

1246. In the meantime, following Medea's instructions, Jason made a solution of the drugs and sprinkled his shield, his stout spear, and his sword with it. Around him his companions tested the weapons with all their might. They could not bend the spear even a little, but it withstood them in its seasoned state and remained un-broken, just as it was, in their hands. Yet Idas, son of Aphareus, violently angry at them, struck the spear near the butt-end with his great sword, but the blade, beaten back, jumped up like a hammer from an anvil. The heroes shouted out in joy, buoyed up by their hopes for success in the contest. And Jason sprinkled himself. A terrible strength entered him, inexpressible and unshakeable. On both sides his hands moved quickly as they began to burst with all strength. As when a war horse, eager for battle, whinnies, leaps, and beats the ground, but lifts up his neck and pricks up his ears with pride, so the son of Aeson exulted in the strength of his limbs. He kept throwing his feet into the air this way and that, shaking his bronze shield and his ashen spear in his hands. You would have thought that winter lightening, darting forth from the dark ether, was repeatedly shooting from clouds, when they bring their blackest rain.

**Book 4:123.** Jason and Medea came down the path to the sacred grove in search of the giant oak, over which the fleece had been cast, like a cloud that glows red under the fiery rays of the rising sun. But the snake, watching out with his sleepless eyes, stretched out his long neck to meet them as they came and gave out a monstrous hiss. The long riverbanks and the vast grove reverberated around them. This was heard by the inhabitants of the Colchian land who lived a long way from Titanian Aea, by the debouch of the Lycus, which splits off from the roaring river Araxes and mixes its sacred stream with the Phasis. They combine their streams into one and debouch into the Caucasian sea. New mothers woke in fear and, distressed, threw their hands round their baby children, who were sleeping in the crooks of their arms, and who shook at the hiss. As unnumbered circles of sooty smoke coil upward above smoldering wood and one ever rises quickly on top of another, ascending upward from below in spirals, so then did that huge creature gather its unnumbered coils, covered over with dry scales. The girl came before its eyes as it coiled. In a sweet voice she invoked Sleep, highest of the gods, to help her in bewitching the monster. She cried out to the night-wandering queen, the underworld goddess, to look kindly upon her project. The son of Aeson followed her, scared, but the snake was already bewitched by her song and was unfolding its long spiraling spine and straightening its countless circles, just as a black wave, silent and without noise, rolls over a calm sea. Even so, it raised its terrible head aloft and was eager to enfold the pair of them in its ruinous jaws. But she sprinkled his eyes with a fresh-cut sprig of juniper, dunking unmixed drugs into her potage and singing spells. Round about the intense smell of the drug cast sleep. It laid down and rested its jaw just where it was. Its endless coils were unfurled a long way behind through the wood of many trees. Then, as the girl instructed him, he seized the golden fleece from the oak. But she stood her ground and smeared the head of the creature with her drug, until Jason himself bade her return to his ship, and she left the shady grove of Ares.

**445.** Reckless love, a great pain, a hateful thing for human beings. From you derive, in tumultuous fashion, destructive strifes, lamentations and wails, and other boundless agonies on top of these. Rise up, demon, and take up arms against the children of enemies, just as you once cast hateful madness into the mind of Medea. For how did she subdue Apsyrtus in evil death when he came to her? That is the next part of my song. When they had left her by agreement on the island of Artemis, the two parties beached their ships separately. Jason settled himself in ambush for Apsyrtus and then again for his comrades. But Apsyrtus, tricked by the terrible promises, swiftly crossed over the swell of the sea in his ship and landed on the sacred island under the dark night. He went to face his sister on her own and to try to speak to her, as a delicate child makes trial of a winter storm, through which not even vigorous men pass, to contrive some trick against strangers. The pair of them agreed all details with each other. Immediately the son of Aeson leaped out from his thickly covered ambush and raised his naked sword with his hand. The girl quickly turned her eyes back, covering herself with her linen veil, so that she should not see her brother struck and murdered. Just as an ox-butcher strikes a great stout-horned bull, Jason found his mark and struck him down near the temple which the Brygi, who dwelt on the mainland across the water, once built for Artemis. He fell on his knee in its front chamber. The hero cupped in both his hands the black blood from the wound, as he breathed out his life – his last act. He stained red Medea's shiny white veil and dress as she shied away. The all-conquering pitiless Fury with a sharp sideways look saw what sort of murderous act they had perpetrated. The hero, the son of Aeson, chopped off the dead man's extremities. Three times he licked up some of the blood from the murder, and three times he spat the polluted material from his teeth. This is the right thing for murderers to do to propitiate killings by trickery. He hid the wet corpse in the earth. Those bones still lie there now in the midst of the Apsyrtian men.

1636. From Carpathus they were destined to cross over to Crete, which stands above other islands in the sea. Bronze Talos prevented them from fastening their hawsers to the land by breaking off rocks from a stout crag, when they were come to the Dictaean harbor to moor. He was of bronze stock, one of the men born from ash trees, the last survivor of the demigods. The son of Cronos had given him to Europa to be a guard for the island. Three times a day he would run round the island on his brazen feet. In all the rest of his body and limbs he was made from bronze and could not be broken. But on his ankle he had a bloody vein below the tendon. This was covered by a fine membrane, upon which depended his life and death. The men, although overcome with misery, thrust the ship off from shore with the oars in dread. They would gloomily have taken themselves far from Crete, suffering both from their thirst and their pains, had not Medea said to them as they shrank back: "Listen to me, for I think that I am the only one who can overcome this man for you, whoever he is, even if his entire body is made of bronze, so long as his life is not also inexhaustible. But be willing to keep the ship here beyond the reach of the stones, until he falls to me." So she spoke, and they pressed on their oars to withdraw the ship from the reach of the missiles, waiting to see what unexpected piece of cunning she would execute. She held the fold of her purple dress up to her cheeks on either side and went up on the deck. The son of Aeson took her hand in his and escorted her through the rowing benches. Then with songs she propitiated and called on the soul-devouring Deaths, the fast dogs of Hades, which whirl through all the air and pounce on the living. Beseeching these she invoked them three times with songs and three times with prayers. Turning her mind evil, she bewitched the sight of bronze Talos with hating eyes. She gnashed baneful anger against him, and sent out destructive phantoms in her vehement rage. Father Zeus, great amazement blows through my mind, to think that baneful doom meets us not just through diseases and wounds, but can even crush us across a great distance. So Talos, even though he was made of bronze, fell before the power of Medea of the many drugs. As he was levering up heavy rocks to prevent them from reaching a mooring, he scratched his ankle on a sharply pointed rock. The ichor flowed out of him like molten lead. Not much longer was he able to maintain his stand on the projecting crag. But he resembled some monstrously tall pine in the mountains, which the lumberjacks have left half cut through with their sharp axes before returning from the wood. First of all it shudders in the night, but then later it is broken from its stump and collapses. So too Talos for some time swayed this way and that on his untiring feet, but then, when his strength was gone, he fell down with a great crash. The heroes camped on Crete for that dark night. Afterward, as dawn was brightening, they founded a temple to Minoan Athene. They drew water and embarked, so that they could first of all row past the peak of Salmone.

APOLLONIUS WAS LIBRARIAN OF THE GREAT Ptolemaic library of Alexandria ca. 270–45 B.C., during which time he composed the *Argonautica*, the most important extant work of Hellenistic literature. The context of these particular passages is readily understood from the Diodorus excerpt (**66**).

Drugs are once more here presented as the basis of Medea's power and underpin all her magical achievements except for the destruction of Talos. Among the various abilities attributed to her are the commonplace ones of ancient witchcraft, namely the ability to control elements, landscape, moon, and stars (3.528–33; compare **97–103, 214–33**). For control over snakes see **49**.

The rites by which Medea instructs Jason to call up Hecate (3.1026–62, 1191–1224) strongly resemble the traditional rites of evocation for ghosts and are evidently modeled on them (see **144**). Jason must not look back on Hecate during the rite. It is implied that the goddess will damage or destroy him if he does; or perhaps the terrible sight of her alone is harmful. But it is also implied that the magic will thus be vitiated. This may be because it will send Hecate back to the underworld. According to the well-known version of his myth, Orpheus sent his wife Eurydice back into the underworld by looking back at her as she came (see **20**). For Hecate's arrival from an underworld hole (3.1191–1224) and her appearance see **275**.

For the destruction of Talos Medea uses the "evil eye" (4.1636–93; see **192–6**). It may be significant that the evil eye could be particularly associated with the attempts of metal-workers to blight each others' products (**22–3**; see also **178**). Talos shares his unique noninvincible heel with Achilles. Ichôr flows through the veins of the divine in place of blood.

For the mutilation (*maschalismos*) of Apsyrtus's body (4.445–81) see **122**. Much of Apollonius's material is recycled in the late-first-century A.D. Latin *Argonautica* of Valerius Flaccus (books 5–8), but that text includes little of further magical interest

## 69  Medea's rejuvenations

8 A.D.

Ovid *Metamorphoses*
7.159–351

Latin

**159.** The Haemonian [i.e., Thessalian] mothers brought thanks-offerings for the safe return of their sons, as did their aged fathers, and with fire they melted piles of incense. A sacrificial victim, its horns plated with gold, repaid their vow. But Aeson was absent from the congratulations, for he was now quite close to death and worn out by his old years. The son of Aeson spoke: "My wife, to whom I admit I owe my safety, you have already given me everything, and the sum of good services is beyond belief. Even so, if your spells have the power— but is there anything they cannot do?—take some of my years and give the ones you have taken to my father." He could not hold back his tears. She was moved by the piety of Jason's request, and the thought of her own abandoned father Aeetes came into her mind, with its different attitude. However, she disclosed no such feelings, but said, "What crime comes from your mouth, husband! Do you think then that I can reassign a span of your life to another? Hecate would not allow it, and what you seek is unfair, but, Jason, I will try to give you a gift greater than the one you seek. I shall attempt to renew the long life of my father-in-law not with your years but with my own craft. I only pray that the three-formed goddess will help me and come to give her blessing to our immense enterprise."

**179.** It was three nights short of the point at which the horns of the moon come together fully and complete the disc. When the moon shone at its fullest and looked over the earth with an unbroken face, Medea left the building dressed in untied clothes, bare of foot, and with her hair flowing loose over her shoulders. She wandered unaccompanied through the dumb silences of the middle of the night. Deep peace had relaxed men, birds, and beasts. No murmur came from the hedges. The motionless leaves were quiet, the misty air was quiet. The stars alone twinkled. Medea reached her arms up to them and turned herself around three times. Three times she wetted her hair with water drawn from a river, and she opened her mouth to howl three times over. She lowered her knees onto the hard earth and said, "Night, trustiest keeper of my secrets, and stars who, together with the moon, follow on from the fires of the daylight, and you, Hecate of the three heads, who know all about my designs and come to help the incantations and the craft of the mages, and Earth, who furnish mages with powerful herbs, and Breezes, Winds, Mountains, Rivers, and Lakes, and all the gods of the groves and all the gods of the night, be present to help me! By your help, when I have wished it, rivers have flowed backward to their sources, to the amazement of their banks. I calm tumultuous seas, and make calm ones tumultuous with an incantation. I dispel clouds and assemble them, I drive off winds and summon them. I burst the jaws of snakes with the words of my incantations. I move living rocks and oak trees, tearing them up from the ground in which they lie, and entire forests too. I command mountains to shake, the earth to bellow and ghosts to come forth from their tombs. You too, Moon, I draw down, even though the Temesaean bronze cymbals try to reduce your toils. Also, the chariot of my grandfather the Sun grows pale at my incantation, as does the Dawn at my drugs. You rendered ineffectual for me the flames of the bulls, and you yoked their necks, which refused to carry loads, with the hooked plough. You inflicted wild civil war on the snake-born and lulled the snake that guarded the golden fleece to unfamiliar sleep and sent the gold to the Greek cities after tricking its protector. Now I need juices, through which a renewed old age may return to the flower of youth and recover its first years. And you will supply them! For the stars have not flashed to no purpose, nor is it to no purpose that the chariot, drawn on the necks of flying snakes, is here." The chariot had arrived, sent down from the ether. Medea boarded it at once. She stroked the harnessed necks of the snakes with her hands, and jerked the light reins. She was snatched up into the air and looked down on Thessalian Tempe below. She directed the snakes toward specific places and surveyed the plants grown by Ossa, by lofty Pelion, by Othrys, by Pindus, and by Olympus, greater than Pindus. Of the ones she chose, some she plucked up root and all, others she cut with the curve of a brazen sickle. She found many suitable plants on the banks of the Eridanus, many too on those of the Amphrysus, nor did you escape, Enipeus. Yes, and the Peneus and the currents of the Spercheus made their contribution, as did rush-filled banks of the Boebe. At Euboean Anthedon she picked a life-giving herb, which was not yet famous for transforming the body of Glaucus. And now the ninth day and the ninth night had witnessed her wandering over all the fields with the aid of the chariot and the wings of the snakes, when she returned. The snakes had been touched by the scent alone of the plants, but even so they sloughed off the skin of their old years.

238. On arrival she stopped short of the threshold doors. Covered by the sky alone, she avoided contact with men and set up two altars of turf, the one on the right to Hecate, that on the left to Youth. She wreathed these with sacred boughs and forest wood. Nearby she scooped out two trenches in the earth and made sacrifice, plunging her knife into the throat of a black ram, and drenched the open trenches with the blood. Then she poured on top beakers of flowing wine, and further beakers of warm milk. At the same time she poured forth words and called on

the chthonic powers. She asked the king of the shades and his snatched wife not to be too quick to steal the old man's soul from his limbs. When she had placated them with prayers and a protracted droning, she gave the command that the worn-out body of Aeson should be brought forth into the breezes. She relaxed him into a deep sleep with an incantation and laid his body out, as if it were a corpse, on a bed of herbs. She ordered the son of Aeson to retreat to a distance, and her helpers similarly, and told them to avert their uninitiated eyes from the secret rites. They scattered, as ordered, while Medea, her hair unbound, danced around the flaming altars like a bacchant. She dipped her multiply split torches in the black ditch of blood, and, when they were thus steeped, set light to them on the two altars. She purified the old man three times with fire, three times with water, and three times with sulphur. In the meantime a powerful substance was seething in its bronze cauldron, set over the fire. It boiled up and grew white with swelling foam. In this she infused roots cut in the Haemonian valley, seeds, flowers, and black juices. She threw in stones sought from the furthest part of the Orient and sands which the ebbing sea of Ocean washed. She added frosts collected under the all-night moon, the notorious wings of the screech owl, together with its flesh, and the entrails of the shape-shifting wolf, which changes its wild-animal form into a man. Also in there was the scaly skin of the small Cinyphian water snake and the liver of a long-living stag. On top of these she added the head and beak of a crow that had endured for nine generations. With these and a thousand other substances without name the barbarian woman prepared her more-than-human scheme. She stirred all these things together with a long dry branch from a gentle olive and blended the lower part into the upper. Lo! As the old stick was turned about in the hot bronze it first became green and then soon after was clothed in leaves, and suddenly it was loaded with heavy olives. And wherever the fire threw foam out of the hollow bronze vessel and hot drops fell to the earth, the ground grew green and flowers and soft grasses sprung up. As soon as she saw this, Medea drew her sword and opened the old man's throat. She let the old gore drain out and refilled his body with the juices. Aeson drank these up, taking them in either through his mouth or through the wound. His beard and his hair laid aside their whiteness and took back their black color. His emaciation was driven off and put to flight, and off went his pallor and decay. His hollow wrinkles were filled out as his body was built up. His limbs extended exuberantly. Aeson was amazed as he recognized his body from forty years before.

294. Dionysus had seen this astonishing trick from on high. It occurred to him that young years could be restored to his nurses and he received this favor from the Colchian woman.

297. Medea's tricks were not over. The Phasian feigned a bogus hatred toward her husband and fled as a suppliant to Pelias's threshold. His daughters received her, for he himself was heavy with age. In a short space of time the cunning Colchian captivated them with her lying pretense of friendship. While she told them that, among the greatest of her good offices, she had removed Aeson's decay and tarried over this detail, the maiden daughters of Pelias were inspired with the hope that their own father could grow young again with similar craft. They asked Medea to do it, and to name her price without limit. She kept silent for a while and pretended to hesitate. She kept the girls in suspense about her response by pretending to ponder seriously. At last, on undertaking to do it, she said, "So that you may be more confident in this service I offer, let the oldest flock-leader among your sheep become a lamb by my drugs."

312. Straightaway a worn-out wool-bearer of unnumbered years was dragged

in, horns curling around its hollow temples. She stabbed its hanging throat with her Haemonian knife and stained the iron with its meager blood. The witch [*venefica*] plunged the animal's limbs and the strong juices together in the hollow bronze. This shrank the limbs of its body and burned away its horns, and with its horns its years. A feeble bleating was heard from the midst of the cauldron, and at once a lamb jumped out before them as they were still marveling at the bleating. It ran off in a frolic to look for some milk-laden udders. The daughters of Pelias stood astonished. Now that Medea had proved her ability to make good her promises, they pressed her all the more keenly. The Sun had three times unyoked his horses after they had plunged into the Spanish sea. And the shining stars were twinkling on a fourth night, when the deceitful daughter of Aeetes set pure water over a vigorous fire, and herbs without power. Deathlike sleep now had the king, his body relaxed, in its grasp, and with the king his guards. This had been produced by Medea's incantations and the power of her magical tongue. As bidden, Pelias's daughters entered his room with the Colchian and surrounded his bed. "Why do you hesitate and do nothing?" she said. "Draw swords and drain out his old blood, so that I may fill his veins with young blood. The life and age of your father is in your hands. If you have any respect for him, and you do not cherish vain hopes, do this duty for your father and drive out his old age with weapons and let the corrupted blood with a blow of the sword." At these exhortations, each of the girls was impious in proportion with her piety and criminal in avoidance of criminality. But none of them could watch the blows they dealt. They averted their eyes and, turned away, dealt blind wounds with their cruel right hands. He, drenched in blood, nonetheless raised his body on an elbow and, half mangled, tried to rise from his bed. He stretched out his pale arms in the midst of all those swords. "What are you doing, daughters? Who gives you weapons to kill your father?" So he spoke. Their spirits and their hands fell. Although he wanted to say more the Colchian made away with his throat together with his words and plunged his lacerated body into the seething waters. If she had not risen into the breezes with her winged snakes, she would not have escaped punishment.

THE PRECEDING LINES (98–158) CONTAIN AN account of the magical help given by Medea to Jason in Colchis, which runs roughly parallel to Apollonius's narrative (68). The succeeding lines (351–424) detail Medea's flight and tell of her murder of Glauce and of her own children in Corinth. Her attempt to poison Theseus with aconite is thwarted, and she escapes in magical clouds.

Ovid provides the most elaborate extant account of Medea's magical rejuvenations. It seems that the cauldron method (the one deliberately perverted in the case of Pelias) was the one traditionally used by Medea. The method Ovid has her use here to rejuvenate Aeson is strikingly similar to that we subsequently find Lucan's Erictho using to reanimate a corpse for necromancy (155). Since Ovid's Aeson-rejuvenation comprises much material typical of necromantic evocation, it is likely that both he and Lucan alike are drawing inspiration from a now lost reanimation sequence or tradition. The accidental rejuvenation of the flying snakes that draw Medea's chariot is a comic touch (179–237). Elsewhere Medea is said also to have rejuvenated Jason himself (Halm-Tisserant 1993, 235–7, 243–7), as well as the nurses of Dionysus (just hinted at here, 294–6). Drugs once again are presented as at the heart of Medea's arts. The centerpiece of her magical preparations is her extensive journey with her dragon-chariot to collect them (179–237); it is precisely the withholding of drugs from the cauldron in which Pelias is boiled that vitiates the magic (312–51).

Medea identifies her craft here with that of the mages (179–237) and presents Hecate as ministering equally to them. As often, magical rites are presented as restricted to an initiated group (238–93). Sorcerers, even those with genuine abilities, are often projected as deceitful, and Medea exemplifies this phenomenon well in the Pelias episode. The commonplaces of a witch's control of elements, landscape, and stars are rehearsed (179–237; see **97–103**). So too is that of drawing down the moon (see **214–23**). For the avoidance of human contact in the course of purification before a magical rites (238–93) see **53, 148**. For werewolves (238–93) see **139–43**.

## 70 Medea destroys Talos

i–ii A.D.

[Apollodorus] *Bibliotheca* 1.9.26

Greek

From there they put out to sea but were prevented from coming to land in Crete by Talos. Some say that he was of the race of bronze, others that he was a gift to Minos from Hephaestus. He was a man of bronze, although some say that he was a bull. He had one vein, which stretched down from his neck to his ankles. A bronze plug stopped the vein at its end. Talos guarded the island by running around it three times a day. When at that time he saw the Argo putting to, he pelted it with stones. He was tricked and killed by Medea. Some say that she inflicted a madness on him through drugs [*pharmaka*]. But others say that she promised to make him immortal and took the plug out. All his ichor [divine blood] flowed out and he died. Others again say that he died when Poeas shot him in the ankle.

APOLLODORUS SPEAKS OF MEDEA AT *BIBLIOTHECA* 1.9.23–8 and *Epitome* 1.5–6. The *Bibliotheca* narrative on the whole shadows those of Euripides' *Medea* and Apollonius's *Argonautica*. The differences, however, between Apollodorus's account of the Talos episode and that of Apollonius are self-evident. There is no explicit mention of the evil eye here. The methods attributed to her correspond with those she is said to have used in other contexts. The infliction of madness resembles the method used to overthrow the palace of Pelias (**66**); the draining of the ichor as part of a bogus immortalization procedure resembles the draining of the blood of Pelias as part of a bogus rejuvenation procedure (**69**). (It remains an oddity that ichor was itself normally the blood of immortality.)

## 71 Medea as aide to Orpheus

iv A.D. or later

*Orphic Argonautica* 887–1021

Greek

**887.** When Medea had secretly quit the house of Aeetes and arrived at our ship, we then tried to work out the easiest way to go and take the golden fleece from its sacred oak. We thought about it in our minds, but none of us realized that the task was hopeless. For great is the challenge that attends all heroes, and the nadir of our troubles became apparent. For before the house of Aeetes and fast river a terribly high enclosure, some fifty-four feet high, confronted us. It was defended by towers and well-polished blocks of iron and crowned by seven parapets in a circle. In it there were three gigantic gates fitted with bronze. A wall ran atop them, decorated with golden battlements. At one of the gateposts was a statue of the far-seeing lady, brandishing flashing fire. The Colchians worship her as Artemis of the Gates, rushing among the noise of the chase, terrible for men to see and terrible for them to hear, unless one has come to rites of initiation and purificatory sacrifices. All these purifications were kept hidden by the initiating priestess, Medea of the terrible bed, together with the girls of

Cyta. No mortal entered within by that route, stepping over the threshold, whether a man of the city or a stranger, for the terrible goddess prevented them by all means, the queen that breathes madness into her fiery-eyed dogs. In the furthest recess of the enclosure was a sacred grove, shaded by flourishing trees. In it there were many laurels and cornels and tall plane trees. Within this the grass was carpeted with low-growing plants with powerful roots. Famous asphodel, pretty maidenhair, rushes, galingale, delicate verbena, sage, hedge-mustard, purple honeysuckle, healing cassidony, flourishing field basil, mandrake, hulwort, in addition fluffy dittany, fragrant saffron, nose-smart, there too lion-foot, greenbrier, camomile, black poppy, *alcua*, all-heal, white hellebore, aconite, and many other noxious plants grew from the earth. In the middle a stout oak tree with heaven-high trunk spread its branches out over much of the grove. On it hung, spread out over a long branch, the golden fleece, over which watched a terrible snake, a monster deadly to mortals, which cannot be described. For it was decked with golden scales and it wound up around the trunk in its huge coils. It tended the tomb of chthonic Zeus as it guarded the fleece. Untiring but without sleep, it scrutinized its surroundings with gray eyes, rolling its shameless gaze this way and that.

**934.** But when we heard the true situation regarding Mounychian Hecate [i.e., Artemis] and the snake's guard, for Medea explained everything to us clearly, we sought an unexpected way to accomplish the woeful task, namely to propitiate and sway Artemis the Huntress and approach the monstrous beast, so that we could steal the fleece and return to our homeland. Then Mopsus, who knew about these things because of his prophetic abilities, urged the other heroes to beseech me and to give me the job of propitiating Artemis and of bewitching the overweening beast. So they stood around me and begged me. But I commanded the son of Aeson, and these two strong fellows, Castor the horse-tamer and Pollux the good boxer, to accomplish the task together with Mopsus the son of Ampyx. Alone of the others, Medea accompanied me.

**950.** When I arrived at the enclosure and the divine abode I dug a triangular pit in some flat ground. I quickly fetched some logs of juniper, dry cedar, prickly box-thorn and much-lamenting black poplars, and I made a pyre of them in the pit. Knowledgeable Medea brought many drugs [*pharmaka*], taking them from the coffers of an incense-laden crypt. At once I fashioned figures from barley meal [text briefly corrupt]. I threw them onto the pyre and slaughtered three all-black puppies as a sacrifice to the dead. With their blood I mixed copper sulphate, soapwort, a sprig of safflower, and in addition odorless fleawort, red alkanet, and bronze-plant. Then I filled the bellies of the puppies with this and placed them on the logs. I mixed the bowels with water and poured it round the pit. Dressed as I was in a dark mantle I sounded bronze cymbals and made my prayer. The Furies readily gave heed, breaking forth from the caverns of the cheerless abyss, Tisiphone, Allecto, and divine Megaira, brandishing the flame of death in their dry pine torches. At once the pit was kindled, and the deadly fire crackled. The dirty flame sent its smoke high. At once, on the far side of the fire, the cruel Fearful Ones assembled themselves. One could not bear to look upon them. One of them had a body of iron. Mortals call her Pandora. With her came a shape-shifter, who could be seen to have three heads, a deadly monster that could not be described, Hecate, child of Tartarus. A horse with a long mane leaped from her left shoulder. On her left shoulder one could see a dog with maddened face. In the middle was a snake of wild form. With both hands she held well-hilted swords. They wheeled around the pit in circles, this way and that, Pandora and Hecate. The Poinai leaped with them. Suddenly the wooden guardian statue of Artemis dropped its pine torches to the ground and raised its eyes to heaven. Her attendant dogs fawned. The bolts of the silver bars were loosed and the beautiful doors of the thick, strong wall flew open, and the mighty grove within was revealed.

**988.** I crossed the threshold. Then Medea, the daughter of Aeetes, the glorious son of Aeson and the Tyndarids, hurried across too, and Mopsus followed along. But when we could see the lovely oak nearby and the plinth of Zeus of Visitors and the altar base, then the snake, his head wound underneath his broad coils, spun around and raised his head and fearful jaws. He emitted a deadly hiss. The boundless ether resounded. The trees cracked, shaken from the bottom of their roots. The shaded grove cried out. My companions and I were seized by trembling. Alone among us Medea kept an unflinching heart in her breast. For she had picked with her hands cuttings of baneful roots. Then I matched my divine voice, resounding deeply, to my lyre, plucking its lowest-pitched string, and sent an unuttered word from silent lips. I invoked Sleep, lord of the gods and of all men, to come and bewitch the might of the strong snake. He heeded me at once and came to the land of Cyta. Sending to sleep tribes of ephemeral men, powerful blasts of winds, waves of the sea, springs of ever-flowing waters, streams of rivers, beasts, and birds, and bringing stillness to everything that lived and moved, he traveled by the power of his golden wings. He came to the land of the hard Colchians. A deep sleep suddenly descended on the eyes of the monstrous snake, like death. He laid out his long neck, his head drowsy under the weight of its scales. Medea of the dreadful destiny marveled to see it. She encouraged the glorious son of Aeson and sent him to seize the golden fleece quickly from the trunk. Jason heard her and did not disobey, but he took up the vast fleece and came to the ship. The Minyan heroes were overjoyed, and lifted their hands to the immortal gods, who inhabit wide heaven.

THE FOURTH-CENTURY A.D. OR LATER *Orphic Argonautica* presents itself as an autobiographical retelling of the Argonaut myth by Orpheus himself. The pattern of events resembles that of Apollonius's poem, but the narrator pads his part. Here he virtually usurps Medea's role. The fact that this could happen at any rate serves to demonstrate that in late antiquity associations of some sort could be perceived between the work of witches and that of Orphics.

Medea's magical expertise is presented here in terms of her initiation into a cult of Artemis-Hecate. The cult is associated with an enclosure in which the plant-drugs that form the basis of her powers flourish (887–953; see 950–87).

The rite Orpheus directs (950–87) to open the doors of the sacred enclosure corresponds to that with which Apollonius's Jason activates his invincibility ointment (**68**). Like that rite, it has strongly necromantic overtones, and it corresponds in particular with the reanimation rite of Heliodorus's old woman of Bessa, with its grain-meal doll (**157**). The triangular shape of the pit is a novelty; as we see from Apollonius such pits were usually round. Black puppies play a role partially corresponding to that of the familiar black sheep, but puppy sacrifice is often found in the magical papyri and curse tablets. They are particularly appropriate to Hecate, who is attended by dogs (**275**) or indeed, as here, actually incorporates one. For the insertion of magical material into sacrificial creatures see **103**. For circular movements around the pit see **30**, with commentary.

# CIRCE

For Circe see also **66, 80, 94, 144.**

## 72    Circe, Greek literature's first witch, and Odysseus

vii B.C. or earlier

Homer *Odyssey*
10.133–405 and
569–74

Greek

**133.** We sailed on from there grieved in heart, glad to escape from death ourselves, but having lost dear companions. We arrived at the island of Aeaea. There lived Circe of the beautiful tresses, a terrible goddess, endowed with speech. She was the full sister of Aeetes of the destructive mind. Both were born of the Sun that shines on mortals and from their mother Perse, the daughter sired by Ocean. We beached the ship in a harbor suitable for vessels, in silence. We were guided by some god. Then we disembarked and lay there for two days and two nights devouring our hearts with sleep and agonies alike. But when Dawn of the beautiful tresses accomplished the third day, then I took my spear and my sharp sword and swiftly went up from the ship to a place from which I could survey the island, to see if I could see signs of human habitation or hear voices. So I climbed up and stood on a craggy vantage-point. I saw smoke rising from the land of broad roads. It came from the halls of Circe, which I could see through the thick shrubbery and wood. Then I pondered in my heart and mind whether to go and investigate, since I saw the smoke of fire. As I deliberated about this I decided that it was better to go first to my swift ship and the shore of the sea, to give dinner to my comrades, and then to send someone else to investigate. But when, on my way, I came close to the curving-ended ship, one of the gods took pity on me, alone as I was, and sent a great high-horned stag right into my path. He had come down from its pasture in the wood to the river to drink. For the might of the sun oppressed him. As he broke cover I struck him in the middle back on the spine. The bronze spear pierced him all the way through, and he fell down in the dust with a bellow, and his soul flew off. I put my foot against him and drew the bronze spear from the wound. I laid it aside on the ground. I pulled up brushwood and withies and wove a plaited rope a furlong in length and bound the great beast's feet together. Then I went to the black ship carrying him across my back and leaning on my spear, since he was too big to carry on my shoulder with one hand. For the creature was huge. I threw him down before the ship. I encouraged my comrades with gentle words, standing by each man:

**174.** "My dear men, we will not yet go down to the house of Hades, grieved as we are, before the fated day comes upon us. But come, while there is food and drink in the swift ship, let us turn our thoughts to eating, and let us not be worn down by hunger."

**178.** So I spoke, and they swiftly followed my advice. They unveiled their heads and stood in awe at the stag on the shore of the unharvested sea. For the creature was huge. When they had had enough of gazing at him with their eyes, they washed their hands and prepared a glorious meal. In this way then we sat all day long until sunset dining on unlimited flesh and sweet wine. When the sun had set and darkness had come upon us, we went to sleep on the seashore. When rosy-fingered dawn, child of the morning, appeared, I called a meeting and spoke to them all:

**190.** "Hear my words, my comrades who suffer much. My friends, we do not know where the west is or where the east is, where the sun that shines on mortals goes under the ground, and where it rises up. Let us quickly consider whether any course of action will be available to us. I don't think there is. For I went up to a craggy vantage-point and saw that this land is an island, around which the boundless sea is wreathed. The island is low-lying. With my eyes I saw smoke in the middle of it through the thick oaks and woods."

**198.** So I spoke, and their dear hearts were broken, for they remembered the actions of the Laestrygonian Antiphates, and the violence of the man-eating Cyclops. They wailed shrilly and cried heavy tears. But there was no profit in their mourning.

**203.** But I counted off all my well-greaved companions into two groups, and I gave both groups a leader. I led one, and godlike Eurylochus the other. We quickly shook lots in a helmet fitted with bronze. Out jumped the lot of great-hearted Eurylochus. He set out, and with him twenty-two companions, weeping. They left us behind, and we were wailing too. In the glens they found the house of Circe, built with polished stones, in a sheltered place. Around it were wolves of the mountain and lions, which Circe herself had enchanted, for she had given them evil drugs [*pharmaka*]. But they did not attack the men, but stood on their hind legs and wagged their tails. As when dogs fawn on their master as he comes from dinner, for he always brings them tid-bits to cheer their heart, in this way the strong-clawed wolves and lions fawned on them. But they took fear, when they saw the dreadful wild animals. They stopped in the gatehouse of the goddess of beautiful tresses, and they heard Circe singing within in a lovely voice. She was going back and forth at her immortal loom, making the sort of fine, subtle, and glorious fabrics that goddesses do. Polites, leader of men, was the first to speak. He was the dearest and best of my comrades.

**226.** "My friends, someone within is going back and forth at a great loom and singing a beautiful song, and all the floor resounds. She is either a goddess or a woman. Let us shout out to her right away."

**229.** So he spoke, and they shouted out and called to her. She quickly came out, opened her shining doors and invited them in. They followed her in altogether in their ignorance. But Eurylochus stayed back, suspecting a trick. She took them in and sat them down on chairs and thrones, and for them she mixed cheese, grain, and pale honey with Pramnian wine. She blended baleful drugs into the food, so that they should forget their homeland completely. But when she had given it to them and they had drunk it down, she immediately struck them with her wand and shut them into pigsties. They had the heads, voices, bristles, and bodies of pigs, but their minds remained unchanged and just as they were before. Thus they were penned up weeping, and before them Circe threw down varieties of acorn and cornel fruit to eat, the sorts of thing usually eaten by pigs that lie on the ground.

**244.** Eurylochus came straight back to the swift black ship with news of his comrades and their cruel fate. He could not utter a word, much as he longed to, stricken in heart with great pain. His eyes were full of tears, and his heart knew grief. But when we put questions to him in our astonishment, then he told us of the fate of the other companions:

**251.** "As you bade us, we went through the oak woods, glorious Odysseus, and we found the beautiful house in the glens made with polished stones, in a sheltered place. There someone was going back and forth at a great loom and singing shrilly, either a goddess or a woman. They shouted out and called to her. She came out immediately, opened the shining doors and invited them in. They all followed her inside in their ignorance, but I stayed back, suspecting a trick. And they all disappeared, and none of them reemerged, although I sat there and watched for them for a long time."

**261.** So he spoke, but I threw my silver-nailed sword over my shoulder, a great bronze one, and put my bow around me. I bade him take me back the same way. But he grabbed hold of my knees with both hands and besought me, and, groaning, addressed winged words to me:

**266.** "Do not make me go there against my will, nursling of Zeus, but leave me here. For I know that neither will you come back, nor will you bring back any other of your companions. But let us escape quickly with these men, for we still have the chance to avoid our evil day."

**270.** So he spoke, but I answered him and said, "Eurylochus, you stay here in this place, eating and drinking by the hollow black ship, but I will go, for stern necessity is upon me."

**274.** So I spoke and went inland from the ship and the sea. But when, as I made my way, I was about to come to the great house in the glens of Circe of the many spells [or: drugs—*polupharmakos*], Hermes of the golden wand met me as I approached it. He was in the guise of a young man growing his first beard, the time of youth when they are most charming. He grabbed my hand, addressed me by name, and spoke:

**281.** "My poor man, where are you going alone through the hills, in ignorance of the country? Your comrades are penned up like pigs in close sties in Circe's house. Do you come here to set them free? I tell you that you will not return, but remain there just like the others. But, come, I will free you from your difficulties and save you. Take this. Go to Circe's house with this good drug, which will keep the evil day from your head. And I will tell you all the deadly tricks of Circe. She will make you a potage, and throw drugs into the food. But even so, she will not be able to bewitch you, for the good drug I will give you will prevent her from doing so. I will explain the details. Whenever Circe strikes you with her long wand, at that point draw your sharp sword from your thigh and rush on Circe, as if you intend to kill her. She will be frightened and bid you go to bed with her. Do not then refuse the goddess' bed, so that she will free your companions and give you hospitality. But bid her swear a great oath by the blessed gods not to devise any other evil woe for you yourself, lest she make you cowardly and unmanly when you have taken your clothes off."

**302.** So spoke the slayer of Argos and gave me the drug, pulling it up from the ground, and he showed me the nature of it. It was black in the root, but its flower was like milk. The gods call it *môlu*. It is difficult for mortal men to dig up, but the gods can do everything. Then Hermes went off through the wooded island to high Olympus, but I went to the house of Circe. My heart was greatly troubled as I went. I stopped at the doors of the goddess of the beautiful tresses. I stood there and shouted out, and the goddess heard my voice. She quickly came out, opened the shining doors, and invited me in. I followed her, grieved in heart. She took me in and sat me on a beautiful throne, skillfully wrought with silver nails. Under my feet was a footstool. She made a potage for me to drink in a golden cup, and she put a drug into it, plotting evil in her heart. She gave it to me and I drank it down, but it did not bewitch me. She struck me with her wand and spoke to me, addressing me by name: "Go now to the pigsty, and lie with your other comrades."

**322.** So she spoke, but I drew the sharp sword from my thigh and rushed upon Circe as if I intended to kill her. She cried out aloud, ducked under the blade, grabbed my knees, and, groaning, addressed winged words to me:

**325.** "What man are you, and where do you come from? Where are your city and parents? I am amazed that you were not bewitched after drinking my drugs. For no other man has been able to resist these drugs, if he has drunk them and taken them past the fence of his teeth. But you have a mind in your breast that cannot be charmed. I am sure that you are Odysseus of the many wiles. He of the golden wand, the slayer of Argos, was always telling me that he would come, on his return from Troy in his black ship. But come now, put your sword in its scabbard, and let us climb upon my bed, so that we may learn to trust each other by joining with each other in sex and love."

**336.** So she spoke, but I answered her and said, "Circe, how can you bid me be gentle toward you, when you have made pigs of my companions in your hall. Now you have me myself here, and, plotting trickery, you bid me go to your bedroom and climb upon your bed, so that you may make me a coward and unmanly when I have taken my clothes off. I could not consent to climb upon your bed, unless you would be prepared, goddess, to swear a great oath that you will not contrive some other evil woe against me."

**345.** So I spoke, and she immediately swore that she would not, as I asked her to. But when she had sworn and completed the oath, then I climbed upon Circe's very lovely bed.

**348.** In the meantime her maids were at work in the hall. There were four of them, and they did her housework. They were the children of the springs and the groves and the sacred rivers that flow into the sea. The first of them threw beautiful rugs over the thrones, purple on top, but underneath she put linen. The second set silver tables before the thrones and laid golden baskets on them. The third one mixed honied sweet wine in a silver bowl, and distributed golden cups. The fourth one brought water and kindled a roaring fire under a large tripod-cauldron. The water was warmed. But when the water had boiled in this flashing bronze, she sat me in a bathing-tub and washed me with water from the great tripod-cauldron, blending it until it was just right. She poured the water down over my head and shoulders until she had taken the heart-devouring tiredness from my limbs. But when she had bathed me and anointed me well with oil, she threw round me a beautiful cloak and tunic. She brought me into the hall and sat me on a beautiful throne, skillfully wrought with silver nails. Under my feet was a footstool. A maid brought water for me to wash my hands and poured it over them from a beautiful golden ewer and into a silver bowl. Beside me she set a polished table. The estimable housekeeper brought bread and set it beside me, and added much food, helping me generously to what she had. She bade me eat. But I could not bring myself to do so. I sat there in distraction, and my heart had foreboding of bad things.

**375.** When Circe saw that I was just sitting there without touching the food, and that I was deeply aggrieved, she stood by me and addressed winged words to me.

**378.** "Odysseus, whyever do you sit there like a man without voice and devouring your heart? Why don't you touch the food and drink? Do you think it's another trick? You have no need to fear, for I have already sworn a strong oath that I will not trick you again."

**382.** So she spoke, and I answered her and said, "Circe, what decent man could endure to turn to food and drink before liberating his companions and seeing them again with his own eyes? But if you are serious in bidding me drink and eat, free them, so that I can see my trusty companions with my own eyes."

**388.** So I spoke, and Circe went out of the hall, rod in hand, and opened the gates of the sty. She drove out my companions, who looked like nine-year-old pigs. They stood ranged before her, and she went among them and anointed each of them with another drug. The bristles, which had been caused to grow by that accursed drug that lady Circe had given them, fell from their limbs. They became men again, and younger than they had been, and much more attractive and tall to look at. They recognized me and held onto my hand. They all turned to passionate lament, and the house reverberated terribly, and even the goddess had pity.

**400.** The divine goddess stood beside me and spoke to me. "Son of Laertes, descendant of Zeus, Odysseus of the many schemes, go now to your swift ship and the shore of the sea. First, drag your ship up onto the land, and put your goods and all your ship's tackle away in caves. Then come back yourself and bring your trusty comrades."

**569.** But while we were coming to our swift ship and the shore of the sea, grieving and shedding heavy tears, Circe in the meantime made her own way and tethered a ram and a black ewe beside the ship, easily slipping past us. For who could see with his own eyes a god going to and fro, if the god did not wish it?

THE HOMERIC EPICS ARE TRADITIONAL, ORAL, formulaic productions, generated through hundreds and probably thousands of years of bardic composition. They are thought to have reached the form in which they have come down to us in the seventh century B.C. The Homeric portrayal of Circe is of great importance, for it may be considered the first extant portrait of a witch in Greek literature. The usual terms for "witch" in Greek, *pharmakis* and *pharmakeutria*, both based on *pharmaka*, the "drugs" and/or "spells" that formed the witch's stock-in-trade, are only attested later. Circe is, however, described as "of many drugs" (*polu-pharmakos*, 274–80) and is repeatedly said to use *pharmaka*. The hesitating description "goddess or woman" may suggest the notion of a mortal woman with supernatural powers, although Circe is also defined as a goddess without qualification. Close reading expands the range of powers with which Circe is explicitly attributed here:

- She transforms men into pigs (229–43) and back into men again (388–99). The first is achieved by a drugged potion, wand, and command/spell. The second is achieved by ointment. Circe's bewitching of the lions and wolves around her house need only have been to tame them (203–25), but the supposition that they too are transformed sailors is an easy one and seems to have been made by Apollodorus, who has Circe change Odysseus's companions into pigs, lions, wolves, and asses (*Epitome* 7.14–18). Apollonius of Rhodes, however, fills Circe's island with beings made up from the jumbled body parts of different creatures, à la *Island of Dr. Moreau* (*Argonautica* 4.659–72). He may have taken inspiration from representations of Circe in art, where her victims are portrayed as part men, part pig, in order to convey the narrative of transformation (*LIMC*, Circe, nos. 5–26). Do the Homeric animals fawn upon the visitors to appeal for help? To warn them of the fate that awaits them? To express their longing for their own lost human form? Particular poignancy is added to Odysseus's killing and consumption of the great stag that presents itself to him if we imagine that it was once a correspondingly stout human warrior (133–73). For magical transformations into animals see **107**, and for transformations into wolves in particular, see **139–43**.

- She rejuvenates Odysseus's men as she returns them to human form, again with the ointment (388–99). While this *need* not be a reference specifically to magical activity in a Homeric context (compare *Odyssey* 6.229–35), the prominence of magical rejuvenation in the traditions relating to Circe's sister Medea (**69**) invites us to read it as such.

- She can either render herself invisible or send her soul flying through the air, like the shamans (569–74; see **5–8**).

- It is implied that Circe is capable of erotic magic. Odysseus must make her swear not to make him "cowardly and unmanly" once he has taken his clothes off (281–301, 325–35). Faraone has recently observed that women's love magic against men was perceived as feminizing (1999a). Circe's doublet in the *Odyssey*, the nymph Calypso, has the power to keep Odysseus sleeping with her on her island indefinitely, even though he still loves and longs for his wife Penelope (**73**). With their welcoming singing (203–25, for Circe's), Circe and Calypso resemble in turn Homer's Sirens, who entrance sailors with their song and trap them on their barren island, where they waste away (*Odyssey* 12.37–54 and 165–200; see **75**). Later on, Apuleius's Meroe was to enslave Socrates and reduce him to beggary by having sex with him once (**104**). For Circe's association with erotic magic see **80**.

- She is also an expert in necromancy: she instructs Odysseus in the performance of it, provides him with supplies for it, and may even indirectly preside over his consultation, for which see **144**.

Odysseus also employs magic against Circe. The *môlu* given to him by Hermes protects him from her attempt to turn him into a pig (281–301). It is unclear whether he is to ingest it as an antidote, or whether he is to wear it as a protective talisman or phylactery (for the wearing of plants in this fashion, see **253, 266**). Apollodorus has Odysseus throw the *môlu* into the potage to neutralize it before drinking. Theophrastus (fourth to third centuries B.C.) identified *môlu* as garlic (*Historia Plantarum* 9.15.7). It seems unlikely that Odysseus could have inflicted physical harm on Circe with his sword (322–24), any more than he could have done on the ghosts (see **144**), so the significance of this too here may be talismanic. At any rate, we may have here the earliest example of the magical "arms race" and competition between sorcerers in the Greek world.

Early Greek notions of witchcraft are not the only influence on the portayal of Circe in the *Odyssey*. Aspects of her representation here correspond with episodes in wider folktales and with the Siduri episode in the Mesopotamian *Epic of Gilgamesh* (tablet 10).

For Polites (203–25) see **140**, with commentary.

---

## 73   Sisters of Circe (1): Calypso

vii B.C. or earlier

Homer *Odyssey*
1.11–19, 5.151–8

Greek

**1.11–19.** All the others who escaped the absolute destruction of Troy were at home, and were finished with the war and the sea. But Odysseus alone, longing for his return and his wife, did the lady nymph and noble goddess Calypso detain in her hollow caves, desiring him to be her husband. But when, as the years came round, that one arrived in which the gods had decreed that he should come home to Ithaca, not even then was he done with struggles, and that too with his own friends.

**5.151–8.** She found Odysseus sitting on the shore. His eyes were never dry of tears. His sweet life was melting away as he grieved about returning, since the nymph did not please him any longer. To be sure, he would spend the night beside her under compulsion in her hollow caves: she was willing, but he was not. By day he would sit on the rocks and the shore, buffeting his heart by crying, groaning, and grieving. He would gaze out over the unharvested sea, and his tears would flow.

CALYPSO, ANOTHER BEAUTIFUL, SUPERNATURAL WOMAN, WHO also detains Odysseus on her island, is a doublet of Circe in this traditional poem, and there are many points of contact in the portrayals of the two. At 5.16 Athene says that Odysseus is kept on the island for lack of a boat, but Odysseus has no need a boat to escape in the end. Perhaps the easiest explanation therefore of Odysseus's detention on Calypso's island is that he is the victim of an erotic spell, which compels him to have (joyless) sex with her while still loving his wife Penelope.

## 74   Sisters of Circe (2): Helen

vii B.C. or earlier

Homer *Odyssey*
4.219–39

Greek

Then Helen, born of Zeus, thought of other things. Immediately she threw a drug [*pharmakon*] into the wine from which they were drinking, a drug to free them from pain and to soothe them, and to make them forget all their troubles. Whoever swallowed it, when it was mixed into a wine bowl, could not drop a tear down his cheeks for a day, not even if his mother and father were to die, not even if they were to kill his brother and dear son with bronze before him, and he were to see it with his own eyes. Such were the clever drugs that the daughter of Zeus possessed, which the Egyptian Polydamna had given her, the wife of Thon. The corn-giving earth brings forth many drugs in Egypt, many of them good when used in mixtures, but many of them baneful. Each of them is a healer with a knowledge superior to that of other men. For they are of the race of Paean. But when she had put the drug in the wine and had bidden the wine be poured, she again responded to them with words and said:

"Menelaus, son of Atreus, nursling of Zeus, and you here, sons of noble men. At different times the god Zeus gives good to one man and evil to another. For everything is within his power. But now sit in the hall and feast, and enjoy stories. For I will tell you a suitable one."

ONCE AGAIN THE WITCH'S POWER IS based in plant-drugs. This passage is important for a number of reasons. First, it recognizes that magic used for good and magic used for bad are two sides of the same coin. Second, it identifies magic with Egypt in particular already at this early stage, an identification that was developed fully by the Greeks many centuries later; see **53–6, 105, 157**. It is also the first explicit connection of magic with healing (see **14, 45, 256–66**) and with the inducing of forgetting (see **207**). *Polydamna* means "much-subduing."

## 75   Sisters of Circe (3): the Sirens . . . and Pericles

Early iv B.C.

Xenophon *Memorabilia*
2.6.10–3

Greek

10. Socrates: They say that there are incantations, which those who know them sing against whomever they wish to make friends of them, and they also say that there are love-potions [*philtra*], which those who know them employ against whomever they wish, to make themselves loved by them.

11. Critobulus: Where could we learn these?

Socrates: Have you heard the incantation the Sirens made against Odysseus in Homer? It begins more or less like this: "Come hither, much praised Odysseus, great glory of the Achaeans."

**Critobulus:** Did the Sirens sing this incantation against other men too, Socrates, and keep hold of them, so that their incantation-victims did not leave them and return home?

**12. Socrates:** No, they only used their incantations against those who were ambitious for the glory of virtue.

**Critobulus:** You seem to be saying that one must employ incantations against each individual of such a kind that he will not think the person giving praise is making fun of him when he hears them.

**Socrates:** Yes, for he would become more hostile toward people and drive away them from himself, if one were to praise him as beautiful and tall and strong, when he knew that he was small, ugly, and weak.

**Critobulus:** Do you know any other incantations?

**13. Socrates:** No, but I heard that Pericles knew many. He used to sing them against the city and make it love him.

**Critobulus:** So how did Themistocles make the city love him?

**Socrates:** By Zeus, it was not by incantations, but he fastened an amulet [*periapsas*] around the city.

THE PRINCIPAL INTEREST OF THIS EXCHANGE, which plays with a series of magical conceits, lies in Socrates' presentation of the song of the famous Sirens as an example of an erotic-magical incantation. The Sirens do indeed play a similar structural role in the *Odyssey* to that of the more obviously witchlike figures of Circe and Calypso (**72–3**, with commentary). Women above and birds below, they charm passing sailors onto their barren island with their irresistible song. The sailors cannot then pull themselves away, and so they waste away there, and their island is piled high with moldering bones. Odysseus blocks his men's ears with wax as they sail past, but has himself lashed to the mast so that he can listen without danger to himself. The claim that the Sirens only used their powers against the ambitious is Xenophon's conceit. Pericles' rhetoric is compared to magical incantation in a salute to the familiar notion of rhetoric as magic (see **12**). For a further magical association of Pericles see **259**. The protective "amulet" that Themistocles placed around the city of Athens consisted of a city wall, a new harbor, and a vastly expanded fleet.

# 6
# *Witches in Greek Literature*


## THE DEIANEIRA TRADITION

For Deianeira see also 94 (importantly).

### 76   Deianeira kills Heracles with a bogus love potion

i B.C.

Diodorus 4.36 and 38

Greek

**36.** While he was making his way Heracles arrived at the river Evenus and came across the centaur Nessus ferrying people across the river for a fee. He ferried Deianeira across the river first, fell in love with her because of her beauty, and so tried to rape her. But she shouted out to her husband and Heracles shot the centaur. Nessus, in the midst of congress and dying almost at once because of the severity of the blow, told Deianeira that he would give her a love potion [*philtron*] to prevent Heracles from desiring sex with any other women. He urged her to take the semen that he had dropped on the ground, blend it into olive oil and the blood that dripped from the arrow, and smear it over Heracles' tunic. Nessus expired at once after giving this advice to Deianeira. She followed his instructions, collected up his semen and put it in a jar, dipped the arrow into it, and kept the jar secret from Heracles. He crossed the river.

**38.** Heracles planned to make sacrifice at Cenaeum. He sent his servant Lichas to his wife Deianeira in Trachis. He had been entrusted with the order to fetch the tunic and cloak he usually wore for sacrifices. Deianeira learned from Lichas of Heracles's love for Iole. She wished to have more love herself, so she smeared the tunic with the love potion [*philtron*] given her by the centaur, to his destruction. In ignorance of this Lichas took the clothing to the sacrifice. Heracles put on the smeared tunic. The effect of the corrupting drug was gradual, but he met with great disaster. For the arrow had been armed with the adder's poison. And so as the tunic destroyed his body's flesh with its heat Heracles, in the utmost pain, killed his servant Lichas, disbanded his army, and returned to Trachis. Ever more oppressed by the sickness, Heracles sent Licymnius and Iolaus to Delphi to ask Apollo what he should do about it. But Deianeira was overwhelmed by the magnitude of Heracles' disaster and, feeling guilty about it, ended her life with a noose.

DIODORUS GIVES A SUMMARY ACCOUNT OF the myth of Deianeira, Heracles, and Nessus (see Sophocles's dramatic take on this tale in *Trachiniae*, especially 531–87, 672–707, 750–93). This myth constitutes what may be considered an archetype for a recurring magical narrative type in the Greek world in which a woman attempting to use a love potion to retain the affection of a man accidentally poisons him instead. Further instances of this narrative type are laid out in **77–81** and **114**. The erotic force of semen is self-evident.

## 77 Daughters of Deianeira (1): The wicked stepmother and the concubine of Philoneos

430–11 B.C.

Antiphon 1.14–20

Greek

**14.** Our house had an upper story, and Philoneos used to occupy it when he was in town; a fine and upstanding man, and a friend of our father. Philoneos had a concubine, whom he was planning to station in a brothel. So my brother's mother made a friend of her. **15.** When she learned of how she was to be maltreated by Philoneos, she sent for her. When she came, she told her that she herself was also maltreated by our father. She told her that if she was willing to follow her instructions, she had the wherewithal to make Philoneos love her and make my father love herself. Her part, she said, had been the making of this discovery; the concubine's part was to do the job. **16.** So she asked the concubine if she was willing to do what she said, and she immediately promised to do so, I believe. Later on Philoneos happened to have a sacrifice to perform to Household Zeus. At the time my father was about to sail for Naxos. Philoneos thought it a nice idea to join my father on the journey and escort him as far as Piraeus, since he was his friend, offer sacrifice with him, and feast him. **17.** Now Philoneos's concubine came with us for the sacrifice. When they had come to Piraeus, naturally, they made the sacrifice. After the sacrifice, this person deliberated as to how she was to give them the drug [*pharmakon*], whether, that is, before or after dinner. She decided as a result of her deliberations that it was better to give it to them after dinner, and in this she was also following the instructions of this "Clytemnestra." **18.** To give you all the other details about the dinner would require an account too long for me to relate and for you to listen to. But in the remainder of my account I will try to explain to you how the drug was administered, as briefly as I can. When they had finished their meal, the one of them sacrificing to Household Zeus and entertaining the other, and this other one planning to sail and dining with his friend, they made libations and put incense on the altar, for their own safety. **19.** Philoneos's concubine poured the wine into their cups for the libation as they made prayers that were destined not to be accomplished, gentlemen, and she poured in the drug. At this point she thought she was doing something clever, and gave more of it to Philoneos, no doubt on the assumption that if she gave him more, Philoneos would love her more. For she did not yet know that she was being deceived by my stepmother, and only realized it when she was already in the midst of the horror. She poured less of the drug for my father. **20.** When they had poured their libation, they took hold of their own killer and gulped down their final drink. Philoneos died at once and without delay, but our father succumbed to a sickness, from which he eventually died twenty days later. For this the woman that carried out the instructions and physically did the deed got the punishment she deserved, although she was not at all responsible: she was tortured on the wheel and handed over to the public executioner. But she that was responsible and that actually dreamed up the crime will get her punishment, with the gods' will and yours.

ANTIPHON'S FORENSIC SPEECH APPEARS TO HAVE been a fictional one designed for show purposes. This is indicated by (among other things) the correspondence of the events narrated with the Deianeira myth, and by the traditional folktale role assigned to the stepmother. The mythical atmosphere is enhanced by the allusion to the unnamed stepmother as "Clytemnestra"; she had famously butchered her husband, as told in Aeschylus's *Agamemnon*. Evidently the concubine was unfamiliar with the notion that love potions were dilute poisons (Faraone 1999a), or she would not have been tempted to increase its effectiveness through an extra large dose. While the speaker is somewhat sympathetic toward the concubine, he does not doubt that she was properly executed for her actions; see **78–9**.

## 78   Daughters of Deianeira (2): "Deianeiras" should be forgiven

ii B.C.

Pseudo-Aristotle *Magna Moralia* 1188b

Greek

They say that a woman once gave someone a love potion [*philtron*] to drink, and that the man was consequently killed by it. So she was tried before the Areopagus court. But they let her off precisely because she had not acted with malice aforethought. For she had given the potion out of love, but failed in her project. Therefore, the killing was judged involuntary, because she had given him the potion without the intention of killing him.

THE COURT THAT SUPPOSEDLY HEARD THIS charge, the Areopagus in Athens, would have been the court that would have heard the charges against Philoneos's concubine, **77**, but here it is said to have fallen the other way.

## 79   Daughters of Deianeira (3): "Deianeiras" should not be forgiven

iv A.D.

St. Basil of Caesarea *Letters* 188.8

Greek

However, even if someone concocts a magical drug [*periergon pharmakon*] for some other purpose, but kills with it, we consider such a deed to be intentional. For women are always doing this. They try to induce men to love them with their incantations [*epaoidai*] and binding spells [*katadesmoi*] and they give them drugs that defy their intentions. The deeds of such killers do not match their purpose. Even so, they are classified in the category of premeditated murderers because of the magical [*periergon*] and forbidden nature of their practice. Similarly, women who supply abortifacient drugs are also murderesses, as are those that take the destructive, child-killing drugs from them. So much for this subject.

BASIL TAKES THE SEVERE VIEW IN the "Deianeira" debate, which had evidently become a commonplace. For binding spells see **168–84, 197–213**; for abortifacients see **82, 233–4**.

## 80   Daughters of Deianeira (4): The principle that love potions destroy the mind

i/ii A.D.

Plutarch *Advice to Bride and Groom, Moralia* 139a

Greek

If one goes fishing with poison, one quickly captures and easily lands the fish, but the poison renders the fish inedible and disgusting. In the same way those women who devise love potions [*philtra*] and sorceries [*goêteiai*] against their husbands and control them through pleasure share their lives with bewildered, mindless, and ruined men. For the men enchanted by Circe were of no benefit to her, nor did she use them for anything after transforming them into pigs and asses, but she cherished a surpassing love for Odysseus, who retained his mind and shared her life in prudent fashion.

THE NOTION THAT WOMEN USED LOVE potions of deleterious effect on their men in the context of existing relationships was evidently widespread. The Circe analogy implies that her animal transformations were the results of failed love potions; this is not something that emerges easily from the Homeric text, **72**. It is of interest that women's magical activity should be embraced under the term *goêteia*.

## 81  Daughters of Deianeira (5): Caesonia turns her husband, the emperor Caligula, mad with a love potion

Early ii A.D.

Suetonius *Caligula* 50

Latin

[Caligula] had himself realized that his mind was not very healthy and from time to time considered going on retreat to clear his brain. He is believed to have been given a love potion by his wife Caesonia, but it turned him mad. He was tormented by sleeplessness. He could not get more than three hours' rest in a night, and even then these would be troubled, as he was terrorized by outlandish apparitions. For example, he once imagined that he was holding conversation with a vision of the sea.

AS WITH PLUTARCH'S GENERALIZATION, A LOVE potion administered to an existing partner turns him mad, here via sleeplessness. Love spells did indeed often seek to work by torturing their victims with sleeplessness: see **200, 207, 209, 211.** Further passages of interest on the "daughters of Deianeira" theme include: Polyaenus *Stategemata* 8.38, Plutarch *Moralia* 256c, and Quintilian *Institutio* 9.2.105.

## SOME MINOR WITCHES

## 82  Andromache is accused of procuring magical abortions

Ca. 425 B.C.

Euripides *Andromache* 29–35, 155–60, 205-8, 355–60

Greek

**29. Andromache:** But since my master married the Spartan Hermione and rejected his slave bed, I have been the constant victim of troublemaking by her. For she says that I am making her childless and hateful to her husband with secret drugs [*pharmaka*], and that I wish to thrust her out of her marriage and to be mistress of the house myself in her place.

**155. Hermione [to Andromache]:** But you, a slave-woman, won by the spear, want to throw me out of my house and take control of it. I am hated by my husband because of your drugs. You are destroying my womb and making it barren. For the soul of an Asiatic woman is clever at this kind of thing. But I will foil you.

**205. Andromache [to Hermione]:** It is not because of my drugs that your husband hates you, but because you are unpleasant to him. I'll tell you a love potion [*philtron*]: it is not beauty but good character that delights one's lover.

**355. Andromache [to Menelaus]:** If I am bewitching [*pharmakeuô*] your daughter [Hermione], and making her miscarry her babies, as she herself claims, I will not resist but will actively seek to be tried before your son-in-law [Neoptolemus], nor shall I throw myself upon altars in supplication. Because if I am causing the childlessness, I am doing every bit as much harm to him.

LOVE-RELATED MAGIC—OR THE ALLEGATION of it—is found here in a competitive context, as often. Such contexts may well have produced more (groundless) allegations of magic than instances of its actual practice. As with Deianeira and Iole, the rival women of one man, Neoptolemus's wife Hermione and his concubine Andromache jostle for position. In this case affection is competed for by means not of desire but of childbearing. Drugs are, as usual, the supposed means of women's magic. Andromache's Asiatic origin is adduced in support of the case for witchcraft. One is to think of the Colchian Medea or perhaps the Persian mages. For magically procured abortions see **57, 79, 233–4.**

## 83  An imaginary and confused love spell

428 B.C.

Euripides *Hippolytus*
476–81 and 507–18

Greek

**476. Nurse [to Phaedra]:** You're in love, so endure it. This is the will of a god. Since you are sick with love, turn the disease to your advantage. There are incantations and bewitching words. A drug [*pharmakon*] will be found for this disease. Men would be slow to find solutions, if we women didn't.

**507. Nurse:** You should not be erring thus, but since you do, take my advice. This will be the next best thing you can do for me. I have in the house a bewitching love charm [*philtron*]. I have just thought of it. It will deliver you from this disease without disgrace and without a damaged mind, if you are not a coward about it. We need to get a token from the man you desire, either a lock of his hair or a piece of his clothing, and from these two things unite a single joy.

**Phaedra:** Is the drug to be used as a lotion or to be drunk?

**Nurse:** I don't know. You should be interested in a good outcome, rather than in the mechanics of it.

**Phaedra:** I fear that you seem all too clever.

PHAEDRA IS SICK WITH AN ILLICIT love for her stepson Hippolytus in this tragedy. The love charm of which her sympathetic nurse speaks does not exist but is part of a ruse. Her plan is rather to declare her mistress's love to Hippolytus and thus bring the couple together. Hence her ambiguity about the love charm's mechanics. A *philtron* is normally a potion, but I preserve the ambiguity here by rendering it as "love charm." At any rate it is drug-based, as usual in women's magic. The notion that Phaedra is to be made to cease from her sickness seems to speak of a separation spell (compare **197–203**). But the need for some "stuff" (*ousia*) of Hippolytus suggests rather that an attraction spell is envisaged (see **204–13**). Whose mind might or might not be damaged? In context it seems to be Phaedra's, but it was traditionally men's minds that were damaged by love magic (**80**).

## 84  A "woman mage" confuted in court

Traditional

Aesop *Fable* 56 Perry,
*The Woman Mage*

Greek

A woman mage kept claiming to be able to placate divine anger with incantations. She performed a lot of these and did well for herself. Because of this some men brought a charge against her of making religious innovations and took her to court. As a result of their accusation they had her condemned to death. Someone saw her being taken away from the courtroom and said, "You poor woman. You claimed to be able to avert the anger of the demons, so how was it that you could not even work your persuasion upon mere mortals?" One could employ this tale against a fantasizing woman who promises great achievements but is shown to be incapable of even moderate ones.

AESOP WAS A MYTHICAL FIGURE. The tales ascribed to him are already cited in archaic texts such as those of Hesiod and Archilochus. This particular tale is preserved only in the Byzantine prose collections, but may be rather more ancient in essence. It is curious that a woman should be defined as a mage, and this phrasing may be relatively late. For the scoffing challenge to the magical practitioner brought to court to use his powers to extricate himself from his predicament see **300**.

## 85    Theoris the Lemnian witch (1)

Ca. 330 B.C.

Demosthenes 25
[*Against Aristogiton*]
79–80

Greek

**79.** You put to death the accursed Theoris, the Lemnian, the witch [*pharmakis*], the woman herself, and all her family. The reason for this was her drugs [*pharmaka*]. **80.** This man got these drugs of hers and her incantations from her maid, the woman who gave all the information about her at the time of her trial. For she was the mother of this evil-eye-er [*baskanos*]. Now he plays magical tricks [*manganeuei*] and cheats and claims that he cures epileptics [*epilêptoi*], while he himself is caught [*epilêptos*] in wickedness of every kind. So this is the man, this scapegoat, this pestilence, who is to save the defendant. One would be more inclined to shun him on sight as an evil omen than to wish to speak to him.

IT IS SUPPOSED THAT MAGICAL EXPERTISE is passed on from mistress to maid and from mother to son; for transmission of the craft see also **103**. Women's magic is again presented as based on drugs. For the magical curing of epilepsy see **13**.

## 86    Theoris the Lemnian witch (2)

iv/iii B.C.

Philochorus *FGH* 328
F60; Harpocration s.v.
*Theôris*

Greek

Theoris: Demosthenes, in the speech against Aristogiton, if genuine. Theoris was a diviner [*mantis*], and she was executed for impiety [*asebeia*], as Philochorus says in his sixth book.

THEORIS IS TERMED A *MANTIS*, "DIVINER," which was one of the words found in the Platonic amalgam of terms associated with sorcery; see **14–7**. Plutarch *Demosthenes* 14, by contrast, says that Theoris the "priestess" (*hiereia*) was executed for teaching slaves to deceive their masters, and that Demosthenes prosecuted. For magic and the law see **278–300**.

## 87    Olympias turns Arrhidaeus into an idiot with drugs

Early ii A.D.

Plutarch *Alexander* 77

Greek

Arrhidaeus was born of a common woman of no account, Philinna. He had lost his wits through some disease. This had not come upon him naturally or of its own accord. Rather, they say that when he was a boy his graceful and noble character had shone out, but that Olympias had then damaged and destroyed his mind with drugs.

ARRHIDAEUS, SON OF PHILIP II OF MACEDON by a rival wife, the Thessalian Philinna (compare **261**), was a potential threat to the succession of Olympias's son Alexander (III, the Great), hence this preemptive strike. For Olympias's magical associations see **55**. Olympias was also, famously, a devotee of Orphism (compare **20–1, 71**) and Bacchism, and handled snakes: Plutarch *Alexander* 2.

## SIMAETHA AND HER TRADITION

One of the most famous and distinctive descriptions of magical practice in ancient literature is the monologue composed as an *Idyll* by the Hellenistic poet Theocritus for Simaetha as she performs erotic magic to recover her supposedly errant lover Delphis. It is reproduced here together with a text from which it may be derived (**88**) and a text derived from it (**90**).

## 88   Women claiming to drive out the goddess?

v B.C.

Sophron at Page 1942,
no. 73

Greek

"Put [*plural*] the table down as it is. Take a salt lump in the hand and put bay leaves around your ears. Now, go to the hearth and sit down there. You [*singular*] there! Give me the double-edged blade. Bring the dog over here. Where is the bitumen?"

"Here."

"Hold the torch and the incense. Come [*plural*] now, let all the doors be open! You watch from where you are, and extinguish the firebrand, as it is. Give me silence now, while I box for the women here. Lady, you have come to receive your meal and your blameless gifts."

THE MAIN SPEAKER IN THIS FRAGMENT from a mime manages a rite and gives general orders to plural people (initiates?) and more direct orders to a singular assistant. The language used tells us that the people include men, but there is evidently among them a group of women. There is no direct indication of the sex of the main speaker or the assistant, but there are several reasons for thinking them both female. First, the tone and style of the piece strongly resembles Theocritus's Simaetha poem (**89**). Second, the main speaker seems to identify herself with the group of women for whom she will "box." Third, it is possible that this fragment is to be identified with the mime of Sophron, of which Athenaeus preserves the title *Women Who Claim That They Drive out the Goddess* (*Deipnosophistae* 480b). In the surviving passage it appears that the goddess is summoned rather than expelled, but, as with ghosts, the summoning-up may be a prelude to the driving-out; see **30**. Theophrastus's Superstitious Man (*Characters* 16) "obsessively purifies the house all the time, claiming it to have been put under a spell [*epagôgê*] by Hecate."

Sophron's *Women Who Claim* was probably a major influence both on Theocritus's Simaetha poem and on Virgil's closely related Amaryllis poem, **90**. Sophron's poem included the line "Where is my pitch? What are you looking at, Thestylis?" (F5 Kock), remodeled by Theocritus in the first line of his Simaetha poem, and the line "a dog barking loudly before the house" (F6 Kock), remodeled by Virgil at the end of his Amaryllis poem.

The salt and the bay leaves are apotropaic. The table at the hearth may be the focus of the rite, as opposed to a separate altar; the hearth is evidently within an (initially) closed chamber. The curious phrase repeated twice, "as it is," may have a magical-formulaic role. The goddess addressed as "Lady" is likely to be Hecate (for whom see **275**, with commentary), in view of the magical context and the sacrifice of the dog with the double-edged blade.

## 89   Simaetha's erotic magic to recover the errant Delphis

270s B.C.

Theocritus *Idyll* 2, *The Witch* [*Pharmakeutria*]

Greek

Where did I put my bay leaves? Fetch them, Thestylis. Where are my love potions [*philtra*]? Garland the bowl with crimson sheep's wool, so that I may bind [*katadêsomai*] my dear man, who is unkind to me. The miserable man has not even visited me for eleven days, nor does he know whether I am alive or dead. Nor has he knocked at my door, the hateful one. Eros and Aphrodite have gone off, taking his flighty mind with them. I'll go to Timagetus's wrestling gym tomorrow to see him, and I'll reproach him for his treatment of me. But now I will bind him with sacrifices. Moon, shine brightly. For I shall sing gently to you, goddess, and to chthonic Hecate, at whom even the dogs tremble as she comes across the tombs of the dead and the black blood. Welcome, frightful Hecate, and accompany me to the completion of my task. Render these drugs no less powerful that those of Circe, Medea, or blonde Perimede.

*Wryneck* [*iunx*], *draw this man to my house.*

First, barley-grains disintegrate in the fire. But sprinkle them on, Thestylis. Poor woman, have you lost your mind? Sprinkle them, and while you do it say this: "I sprinkle the bones of Delphis."

*Wryneck, draw this man to my house.*

Delphis has caused me pain. I burn this bay leaf against Delphis. And as this bay leaf is set alight, crackles loudly in the flames, and quickly blazes up, leaving no ash for us to see, so may Delphis too shrivel his flesh in the flames.

*Wryneck, draw this man to my house.*

Now I will sacrifice the bran. You, Artemis, could move even the adamant in Hades and anything else difficult to shift. Thestylis, the dogs howl in the city. The goddess is at the crossroads. Sound the bronze as quickly as possible.

*Wryneck, draw this man to my house.*

See, the sea is silent, silent the breezes. But the pain within my breast is not silent. I am ablaze over him who has made me a wretched, wicked, despicable nonvirgin, instead of a wife.

*Wryneck, draw this man to my house.*

As I melt this wax doll with the help of the goddess, so may Delphis of Myndos at once be melted by love. And as by the power of Aphrodite this bronze bull-roarer [*rhombos*] whirls round, so may he whirl round at my door.

*Wryneck, draw this man to my house.*

Three times I libate, and three times, lady, I make this utterance. Whether a woman lies beside him or a man, may he forget the person as utterly as they say Theseus once forgot fair-tressed Ariadne on Dia.

*Wryneck, draw this man to my house.*

Hippomanes is a plant from Arcadia. All the swift mares and the foals rave on the hills for it. May I see Delphis in this condition, and may he come to this house like a madman from his shining wrestling gym.

*Wryneck, draw this man to my house.*

Delphis lost this bit of cloth from his cloak. I pluck it apart and cast it into the fierce fire. Oh, grievous Eros, why have you drunk all the black blood from my skin, sticking to me like some leech of the marsh?

*Wryneck, draw this man to my house.*

I will powder a lizard and take him an evil drink tomorrow. Thestylis, take now these herbs and knead them above his threshold while it is still night, and say the while, in a mutter, "I knead the bones of Delphis."

*Wryneck, draw this man to my house.*

I am alone now. From what point shall I bewail my love? From what point am I to begin? Who inflicted this suffering on me? When our Anaxo, daughter of Eubulus, went to the grove of Artemis as a basket-carrier, many wild animals went in procession around the goddess at that time, including a lioness.

*Observe the origin of my love, lady Moon.*

And Theumaridas's Thracian nurse, of blessed memory, lived close to my door. She begged and pleaded with me to watch the procession. I, doomed as I was, went with her trailing a tunic of linen and wearing Clearista's dress.

*Observe the origin of my love, lady Moon.*

When I was halfway down the road, at Lycon's house, I saw Delphis and Eudamippus on their way together. The down on their chins was more golden than helichryse, and their breasts gleamed much more than you do, Moon, since they had just come from the beautiful efforts of the gym.

*Observe the origin of my love, lady Moon.*

As I saw, so I went crazy, so the heart of this poor woman was stricken with fire, and my beauty began to melt. I no longer paid attention to the festival, nor do I know how I got back home again, but a feverish illness shook my frame, and I lay on my bed for ten days and ten nights.

*Observe the origin of my love, lady Moon.*

My skin often came to resemble yellow fustic, and my hair was coming out of my head. My bones and skin alone were left. To whose did I not go? Was there any old woman, adept at incantations, whose house I neglected? But the problem was a serious one, and time was running out fast.

*Observe the origin of my love, lady Moon.*

I confessed the truth of the matter to my slave-girl in the following words: "Come, Thestylis, find me a way to combat this difficult sickness. The Myndian completely occupies my poor heart. But go and watch out for him at Timagetus's wrestling gym. For that is his haunt, and he likes to sit there."

*Observe the origin of my love, lady Moon.*

"Whenever you learn that he is on his own, nod to him subtly and tell him 'Simaetha asks for you,' and escort him here." That is what I said. She went on her way and brought the glossy-skinned Delphis to my house. As soon as I realized he was stepping over my threshold with light foot . . .

*Observe the origin of my love, lady Moon.*

. . .  my whole body grew colder than snow. Sweat rose on my brow like damp dew. I could not say anything, not even as much as children burbling in their sleep say to their dear mother, but my beautiful skin grew rigid all over, like a doll.

*Observe the origin of my love, lady Moon.*

He glanced at me, this unloving man, and then fixed his eyes on the ground. He sat down on my couch and, sitting there, said his piece: "Indeed, Simaetha, your invitation to your house preceded my arrival at it by the same short interval by which I beat the graceful Philinus in a race the other day" . . .

*Observe the origin of my love, lady Moon.*

. . .  "For I would have come, yes I would, by sweet Eros, as soon as it was night, with two or three friends. I would have brought with me in my clothes some apples of Dionysus. On my head I would have had white poplar, the sacred shoot of Heracles, wound all round a purple band" . . .

*Observe the origin of my love, lady Moon.*

. . .  "And, if you had welcomed me in, that would have been lovely (for in fact I am known for being nimble and beautiful among all the bachelors), and I would have been able to sleep, if only I had kissed your beautiful mouth. But if you had rejected me and sent me off, and your door had been shut with a bar, then by all means axes and torches would have been brought against you" . . .

*Observe the origin of my love, lady Moon.*

. . .  "But as it is, I think, I owe thanks first to the Cyprian goddess, and after the Cyprian to you in the second place, who have rescued me half burnt from the fire, woman, by inviting me to your house like this. Eros often lights a more intense fire than Hephaestus of Lipara" . . .

*Observe the origin of my love, lady Moon.*

. . .  "With his evil madnesses Eros frightens a virgin from her bedroom and a bride into leaving her husband's bed, still warm." This is what he said. And I, all too easy to persuade, took him by the hand and laid him down on my soft bed. In no time skin was warmed on skin, and our faces were hotter than before, and we whispered sweetly. So as not to draw out too long a story, dear Moon, the greatest act was done, and we both met our desire. He found no fault with me until yesterday, nor did I with him. But the mother of Philista, our flute-player, and of Melixo came to me today, when the horses were running to the heaven conveying rosy Dawn from Ocean. Among the many things she said, she told me that Delphis was in love. Whether it is desire for a woman or a man that grips him, she said she did not know for sure, but this much she did know: he kept toasting Eros with unmixed wine and in the end he ran off, and he said he would cover the person's house with garlands. This is what the visitor told me, and she is truthful. For before he would visit me three and four times a day, and he would often leave his Dorian oil-flask at my house. But I have not even set eyes on him now for eleven days. Has he not found some other source of pleasure, and has he not forgotten me? But now I shall bind him with love-potions [*philtra*]. If he continues to cause me pain, by the Fates, he will knock at the gate of Hades. I keep drugs [*pharmaka*], I tell you, of such evil power in a box. I learned of them from an Assyrian stranger, mistress. Goodbye, lady, turn your horses toward Ocean. I will continue to endure my desire just as I have been doing. Goodbye, Moon of the shining throne, goodbye, you other stars, attendants of quiet Night's chariot.

THEOCRITUS WORKED AT THE COURT OF Ptolemy II Philadelphus in Alexandria, although the use of the names Delphis and Philinus suggest that the setting of this *Idyll* is Cos.

The highly literary nature of this touching portrait of a girl's insecurity is self-evident. It almost certainly does not set out to "document" a particular, complete, and unified magical rite as practiced. Rather, it appears to weave together a series of different love-magic practices that would seldom have been employed all together. The plethora of magical methods used and Simaetha's apparent confidence in the issuing of instructions to her slave-girl Thestylis give the impression that she is as accomplished witch, but she sees herself as no more than an amateur and consults greater professionals. Before the beginning of the affair with Delphis she had herself turned to old women with knowledge of incantations in order to rid herself of her love for him, although evidently without success. She had also acquired some of her drugs from an "Assyrian" stranger, no doubt equivalent to a Babylonian Chaldaean; compare **49–50**. The transfer of magical expertise between genders is relatively rare in Graeco-Roman literature, but the Assyrian here finds his counterpart in the Egyptian Moeris in Virgil's adaptation of this poem, **90**; see also **85**.

Simaetha uses both erotic-attraction magic to bring Delphis back and erotic-separation magic to make him forget any potential rival. As to attraction magic, Simaetha combines two projects, according to the typology of Faraone (1999a): that of *philia* magic, magic used by a woman to retain the affection of her existing partner; and that of *erôs* magic, the magic of sexual seduction. Faraone holds that *erôs* magic was normally practiced by men against women; Simaetha's use of it here accordingly indicates that she is "structurally male" and so a courtesan. The last claim is reductive, sits ill with Simaetha's remarks about her lost virginity and desired marriage, and, if true, deprives the poem of much of its poignancy.

As to separation magic (in the stanza beginning "three times I libate"), note the exhaustive-dichotomies phrase familiar from the curse tablets, "whether man or woman"; see **124, 169, 185–6, 197**. The adduced paradigm of Theseus's forgetting of Ariadne functions as a *historiola*, a paradigmatic mini-narrative corresponding to the situation at hand, with the desired denouement; compare **260–1**.

Some or all of the magic employed is explicitly conceived of as binding magic (*katadêsomai*); compare **168–84, 197–213**. The incantatory repetition characteristic of curse tablets and the Greek magical papyri is here represented in repeated refrains.

Much of the magic is of a simple, sympathetic nature. Delphis is to be consumed with a fiery passion for Simaetha just as the barley, the bay leaf, the bran, the wax, and the cloak fragment are burned or melted. This burning and melting is precisely the effect of the love Delphis himself had claimed to experience for Simaetha (stanza beginning "But as it is . . .") and of Simaetha's own love for Delphis (stanza beginning "as I saw . . ."). We may be confident that the wax was molded into the form of a voodoo doll (see **236, 238–9, 243, 245–6**). The fragment of Delphis's clothing acts as a lock of his hair would have done, as his *ousia*, his "stuff" or "essence." The burning of the cloth is not merely sympathetic in effect but also *pars pro toto* or "part for whole" magic, the notion being that the operation effected on part of Delphis is magically transferred to his whole. The kneading of the herbs to the accompanying statement that the bones of Delphis are being kneaded is also an act of sympathetic magic. The beloved's threshold is a significant place for the deposition of magical material against them: see **90, 103, 204**.

It is in the context of this poem above all that the debate over the meanings of the terms *iunx* and *rhombos* rages; see **224–9** for discussion. Difficulties surround *hippomanes* too, a commonplace of literary erotic magic, but conceptualized both as a plant, as here, and as a gland: see **230–2**.

Delphis is also to be attacked separately with a love potion on the next day. This will contain powdered lizards, these creatures being ever-popular magical ingredients (see **247**). This is evidently a dangerous substance, and it is not therefore surprising that Simaetha also claims the power to kill with drugs, as we learn toward the end. The proximity between love-potions and poisons is again evident (compare **76-81**).

There is a hint of love-magic on Delphis's part too. The apples he would have brought with him on his revel-rout would have enabled him to perform "apple-spells" on Simaetha. One pelted one's beloved with soft fruit; her acceptance of the fruit, knowing or otherwise, secured her love; compare **213**. It was precisely "apples of Dionysus" that enabled Hippomenes to win the love of Atalanta (Philetas F18 Powell).

The bay leaf is apotropaic (see **88**), as is wool and the color crimson, as well as the sounding of the bronze, which deters the ghosts and demons that fear bronze and iron, at the goddess's approach; compare **144**. The presence of the bowl may indicate that lecanomancy is involved; see **163–4**.

It is a commonplace of literary portraits of witches to compare them with the great mythical archetypes of Circe and Medea. Perimede is in fact a variant form of Medea's name, although the names are used in conjunction here apparently to differentiate two figures. This may be a knowing joke on Theocritus's part. For Hecate, here identified, as often, with Selene, the Moon, and with Artemis, see **275**, with commentary.

## 90    Amaryllis's (?) erotic magic to recover the errant Daphnis

39 B.C.

Virgil *Eclogue* 8.64–109

Latin

Bring out the water, and deck these altar-offerings with a soft band. Burn the rich sacred herbs and the male incense, so that I may try to turn away with magical rites my partner's cautious mood. Nothing is missing except the spells.

*Bring Daphnis home, my spells, bring him from the city.*

Spells can even bring the moon down from the sky. It was by spells that Circe transformed the companions of Odysseus, and it is by incantation that the cold snake is burst in the meadows.

*Bring Daphnis home, my spells, bring him from the city.*

First I tie around you these three threads of threefold colors. I draw your image three times around the altar-offerings. The god delights in the uneven number.

*Bring Daphnis home, my spells, bring him from the city.*

Amaryllis, tie the three colors into three knots. Amaryllis, tie them now and say the while, "I tie the bonds of Venus."

*Bring Daphnis home, my spells, bring him from the city.*

As this clay grows hard and as this wax melts in one and the same fire, so may Daphnis melt in his love for me. Scatter the meal, and burn the crackling bay leaves with pitch. Wicked Daphnis burns me, so I burn these bay leaves against Daphnis.

*Bring Daphnis home, my spells, bring him from the city.*

May Daphnis be seized by such a love as when a heifer, tired out by searching for a bullock through the groves and the deep woods, collapses in despair on the green sedge beside a stream of water, and does not think to go home even though it is late in the night . . . may such a love seize Daphnis, and may I not be bothered to assuage it.

*Bring Daphnis home, my spells, bring him from the city.*

That treacherous man once left me these spoils, pledges of himself which were dear to me. On my threshold, Earth, I entrust them to you. These pledges owe me Daphnis.

*Bring Daphnis home, my spells, bring him from the city.*

These herbs and these poisons, picked in Pontus, were given to me by Moeris himself (they grow in profusion in Pontus). By their power I often saw Moeris change into a wolf and hide himself in the woods, and I often saw him use them to rouse ghosts from the bottom of their tombs, and spirit sown crops away into another field.

*Bring Daphnis home, my spells, bring him from the city.*

Take out the ashes, Amaryllis, and throw them over your head into a flowing stream, and do not look behind you. With these I shall attack Daphnis. He cares nothing for gods or spells.

*Bring Daphnis home, my spells, bring him from the city.*

Look, while I am slow to carry it out the ashes have kindled the altar-offerings with trembling flames of their own accord. May this be a good omen! It certainly means something, and Hylax is barking at the threshold. Do I believe it? Or do people in love fashion dreams for themselves?

*Halt, my spells, halt now: Daphnis is coming from the city.*

THE INDEBTEDNESS OF THIS POEM TO Theocritus's work (89) is self-evident, and typified by the alteration of "Delphis" to "Daphnis" and the parallelism between the slave-girls Amaryllis and Thestylis (although some hold that Amaryllis is the name of the speaker). The major difference is the happy end-ing. The welcoming bark of the family dog replaces the terrifying baying of Hecate's hounds; compare **88**.

Again sympathetic magic plays a major role, with the "burning" of Daphnis. It seems that Daphnis's love-gifts are exploited as a source of his "stuff."

Perhaps a pair of voodoo dolls is used: this is the implication of "clay hardens and wax melts," these two substances both being used for voodoo dolls. A pair of voodoo dolls of different substances (this time clay and wool) is used by Horace's Canidia and Sagana (**91**; see also **239**). It has been suggested that the hardening of the clay is intended to induce a sympathetic hardening in Daphnis's loins.

The magical number three was exploited by Simaetha. Here it is manifested in the three groups of three colored twisted threads (red, white, and black, according to the commentator Servius) and their knots, and in the number of times the voodoo doll that represents Daphnis is drawn around the altar. The threads are used explicitly to "bind" Daphnis; for magical threads see **254**, with commentary.

For drawing down the moon, see **214–23**. For snake-bursting see **49**. For werewolves, see **139–43**. For the evocation of ghosts, see **144–8**. For the charming away of crops, see **280–1**.

Like Simaetha, this speaker too compares herself knowingly to Circe; the reference to the herbs of Pontus indirectly salutes Medea, whose home city of Colchis is on the Black Sea. Moeris is the Hellenized name of an Egyptian pharaoh, and is probably used here to suggest an Egyptian sorcerer. He takes on the role of Simaetha's Assyrian; Virgil swings from one magical race to the other.

# 7

## *Witches in Latin Literature*

### CANIDIA AND ERICTHO

The *Epodes* and *Satires* are Horace's earliest books of poems. Both were complete by 30 B.C. Within these a cycle is devoted to the horrid witch Canidia and her colleagues. Passing mentions of her in poems beyond those printed here use her name as a byword for poisoning: *Epodes* 3, where Horace compares garlic to her poisons; *Satires* 2.1.48, where Canidia threatens people she does not like with the poison of Albucius; and *Satires* 2.8.95, where Fundanius runs from an elaborate feast as if Canidia had breathed over it. Many of the commonplace themes attributed to Canidia and to Lucan's Erictho are tabulated at the beginning of the next section.

### 91 Canidia and Sagana perform necromancy and erotic magic

Ca. 30 B.C.

Horace *Satires* 1.8

Latin

I used to be a fig-tree stump, a useless bit of wood. The carpenter did not know whether to make me into a bench or a Priapus, but decided I would be better as the god. Hence, a god I am, the greatest terror to thieves and birds. My right hand wards off the robbers, as does the red stake that sticks out from my rude groin. The reed fixed into my head frightens off the pesky birds and prevents them from settling in the new gardens. In former times, when corpses were thrown out of their narrow cells, a fellow slave would pay someone to carry them here in a cheap box. This place was a common tomb to the unfortunate masses, for Pantolabus the jester, and for Nomentanus the spendthrift. An inscription gave it a thousand feet against the road, and a width of three hundred feet, and stipulated that it should not be handed down to an heir. One can live on the salubrious Esquiline now and go for walks on the sunny rampart, whereas until recently one could only look gloomily on a field disfigured by white bones. It is not so much the thieves and the wild animals accustomed to disturb the place that concern and bother me, so much as the women who try to twist human minds about with spells and poisons [venena]. I just cannot put an end to these women or stop them collecting bones and destructive herbs, once the wandering moon brings out her comely face.

I myself have seen Canidia coming with her black dress girt up, feet bare and hair unbound, howling together with the elder Sagana. One shuddered to look at either of them, because of their pallor. They began to dig up the earth with their fingernails and tear apart a dark lamb with their teeth. The blood was poured into a pit, so that they could call forth from it ghosts from the underworld to give them answers. There was a woolen doll, and another one made from wax. The woolen one was larger, so that it could restrain the smaller one with punish-

ments. The wax doll held the pose of a suppliant, as if it were about to be executed in slave fashion. One of the women called on Hecate, the other on cruel Tisiphone. You could see snakes and underworld dogs wandering about and the
moon blushing red and hiding behind the great tombs, lest she witness these
things. If I tell a lie, may crows drop their white crap on my head, may Julius come
to piss and shit on me, and so too the feeble Pedatia and the thief Voranus. Why
should I go through all the details? Why should I tell you how the ghosts held
a conversation with Sagana, making mournful, shrill noises; how they secretly hid
a wolf's beard together with a tooth from a variegated snake in the ground; how
the fire flared up higher because of the wax image, and how I shuddered at the
voices and actions of the two Furies, although this witness did not go unavenged?
For I split my fig-wood buttocks and farted as loud as an exploding bladder. They
ran off to the city. You could have seen Canidia's teeth, Sagana's tall wig, and their
herbs and enchanted bonds fall from their arms. You would have laughed long and
hard.

A WOODEN STATUE OF THE ITHYPHALLIC god Priapus speaks. He stands in the
Esquiline gardens, which are laid out over the former paupers' cemetery. This
mass of bones, inadequately buried, offered a rich fund of ghosts ripe for
magical exploitation and was a magnet for witches; compare 113. The presence of the bodies or their ghosts is also seen to encourage the growth of
herbs with magical powers.

The rites performed blend evocation necromancy and erotic-attraction
magic. It is unclear how coherent and unified the women's activities are intended to be; if they are intended to cohere, then we must assume that they
call up the ghosts in order to instruct them to carry out the erotic spell. Evocation necromancy and erotic-attraction magic are loosely associated also in
the work of Lucian's Hyperborean mage (244).

Elsewhere in ancient literature necromantic pits are dug with a sword and
sheep are sacrificed with the same object (see 144). It is a mark of their bes-
tiality that the women use their bare hands for both activities; as we see from
92, Canidia keeps her thumbnail untrimmed. The conversation with the dead
is made up of familiar noises: howling on the part of the witches, shrill
screeching from the ghosts. Like the ghosts with which they converse, the
women are pallid. As usual, the witches invoke their underworld patron
Hecate (for whom see 275), and, as often, she is accompanied by Tisiphone,
one of the Furies (Erinyes). Witches are often portrayed as "unbound" to a
greater or lesser extent in the performance of magical rites; here Canidia's
hair is said to be loose; see 67.

The use of doll-pairs was common in erotic-attraction magic (e.g., 90).
Sometimes their configuration could express the act of coercion, as here and
as in 239, and sometimes it could express the desired result with the two
dolls bound together in a tight embrace, a configuration known as a *symplegma* or "entwined group." A number of examples of these *symplegmata*
have been found. Wax dolls are commonly mentioned and often symbolically
melted, as here (see 89–90, 236). Wax dolls and woolen dolls are mentioned
together (albeit not as pairs) by Ovid too (99), perhaps in tribute to this
poem. The "enchanted bonds" dropped by the departing witches are evidently materials for binding magic. In having the moon dip behind tomb-
stones for shame Horace indirectly alludes to the topos familiar in the con-

text of witches and erotic magic, that of the drawing-down of the moon (see **214-23**).

The attempts of both women to perform erotic magic are revealed as pathetic or even distasteful in the final lines, where we learn that they are old hags. Canidia ("Gray-hair") leaves her false teeth behind, Sagana (her name an extended form of *saga*, "wise woman" or "witch") an old-fashioned wig; as we seem to learn from the following poem, **92**, she kept her real hair short to accommodate it (see Mankin 1995 ad loc.).

## 92 Canidia, Sagana, Veia, and Folia murder a boy to make a love potion

Ca. 30 B.C.

Horace *Epodes* 5

Latin

"Oh gods, whichever of you rule the earth and the human race from the sky! What is this uproar? Why are all your murderous faces turned upon me? By your children, if Lucina came to help your honest birth when called, by this glorious but useless purple robe, I beg you, by Jupiter who is bound to condemn all this, why do you look at me like a stepmother or a beast I have struck with iron?" The boy made this complaint with trembling lips and stood there, his distinguished clothes snatched away, a youthful body, of the sort that could have softened the impious hearts of the Thracians. Canidia, small vipers entwined in the unkempt hair on her head, ordered wild fig trees, torn up from graves, funereal cypresses, eggs pasted with the blood of the foul frog, a feather of the nocturnal screech owl, herbs which Iolcus and Iberia, fertile in poisons, export, and bones snatched from the mouth of a ravening dog to be burned in Colchian flames. Sagana, dressed for action, sprinkled waters of Avernus all over the house. Her hair bristled, like a sea urchin with its spikes, or a Laurentian boar. Veia, impeded in no way by conscience, scooped out the earth with a hard mattock, grunting at the toil, so that the boy, buried in it, might die at the sight of a feast changed twice or three times over the long day, pushing his face toward it and resembling swimmers who seem to hang their bodies from the surface of the water by their chin. This was so that his moistureless marrow and dried liver could form a love-potion, when once his pupils had melted away, fixed on the forbidden food. Folia of Ariminum, with her masculine sex drive, was there too, or so idle Naples believed, and every town round about. She enchants the stars with Thessalian voice and snatches the moon down from the sky. Here, Canidia, gnawing at her untrimmed thumbnail with blue tooth—what did she say, or what keep silent? "Entirely faithful witnesses to my actions, Night, and Diana, who rule the silence when my secret rites are performed, come to our aid now, now, now turn your anger and power upon enemy houses. While wild animals lie hidden in the frightening woods, weary with sweet sleep, let the dogs of the Subura bark at the old adulterer, so that all may laugh at him. He is soaked in nard better than any made by my hands. What goes on? Why do the dread poisons of barbarian Medea have no effect, the poisons with which she avenged herself on her haughty rival, the daughter of great Creon, before fleeing, when the dress, a gift steeped in corruption, carried the new bride away in a blaze? And yet no herb, no root lying hidden in rough places has escaped me. Does he lie on a drugged bed and forget all my rivals? Ah! He walks abroad, delivered by the spell of a more knowledgeable witch [*venefica*]. I will not use the familiar potions. Varus, you will weep at length and run back to me. Your mind will not return to me summoned merely by Marsian spells. I am preparing something stronger. I shall administer a stronger drink to you in your haughtiness. The sky will settle down beneath the sea, with the earth stretched out atop both of them, before you can avoid burning with love for me like pitch with its black fire." In response the boy no longer tried, as before, to placate the impious women with gentle words. He hesitated as to how he should break the silence, before unleashing Thyestian imprecations: "Enchantments have the power to throw righteousness and wickedness into turmoil, but they cannot change human destiny. I will chase you with Furies. A dreadful curse is expiated by no sacrificial victim. Indeed, when you order me to die and I expire, I shall rush upon you in the night, as frenzy itself. A ghost, I shall attack your face with curving nails—ghosts have this power—and sitting on your restless hearts I will deprive you of sleep by terror. A crowd will pelt you with rocks from all sides and from street to street, and smash you to pulp, you disgusting crones. After that wolves will scatter your unburied limbs, as will the birds of the Esquiline. This is a sight that will meet my parents, destined as they are, alas, to survive me."

THE FOUR WITCHES HAVE TAKEN A rich boy captive and are killing him to manufacture ingredients for a love potion, erotic magic once again being the hags' concern. In the secrecy of an inner court he is buried, naked, up to his neck and starved to death while food is wafted before him just out of reach of his lips. The notion is to imbue his innards, notably his liver and bone marrow, with an intense sense of longing as he dies. This feeling of longing will transfer itself, in an erotic register, to the object of Canidia's love, Varus, when, rendered cannibal, he consumes this material. For child sacrifice in magic see **93, 136–8**. For love potions more generally see **76–81**. Canidia expresses the wish that Varus, the object of her love, should "forget" her rivals, as common in erotic magic (see **75, 104, 207**). For the notion that women performing the magic of erotic seduction are "structurally male," see **89**, with commentary. As usual, the desire to be instilled in the beloved is compared to burning fire. Canidia is shown to project her enemies and rivals as sorcerers themselves: compare **13–4, 94**. For magic at war with magic, see **269–70**.

Canidia presides over an elaborate series of sacrifices of outlandish magical ingredients. For similar lists of ingredients, compare **69, 155–6**. Those deprived of burial were said to be cast out for the dogs (or, in Canidia's own case, the wolves) and the birds; bones snatched from the mouth of a ravening dog are therefore strongly marked as unburied, and they constitute a particularly effective mechanism for the exploitation of the restless ghosts; see **108, 110, 112**.

The curse of a dying person was held to be especially fearful, for it would be directly and vigorously enacted by the released ghost (as well as any Furies acting for it). Hence the terrible effect of the curse Dido lays upon Aeneas as she commits suicide (Virgil *Aeneid* 4.504–21, 607–65). Canidia and her colleagues therefore have much to fear from the boy's words. We are not, however, explicitly told that the boy dies.

Underworld imagery abounds. For the waters of Avernus and its ghosts see **153–4**; the water, than which none could be more impure, is sprinkled for purification in a magical inversion. The vipers that adorn Canidia's hair give her the appearance of a Fury.

The Marsi were supposedly one of Italy's own magical races. They claimed descent from Circe and Odysseus, and specialized in snake-charming (compare **9**) and divination; see Pliny *Natural History* 7.15 and Aulus Gellius 16.11.1.

## 93   Epitaph of a child snatched by witches

Ca. 20s A.D.

*CIL* vi 19747; Bücheler
1895–97: vol. 2, no.
987

Latin

Iucundus, the slave of Livia the wife of Drusus Caesar, son of Gryphus and Vitalis. As I grew towards my fourth year I was seized and killed, when I had the potential to be sweet for my mother and father. I was snatched by a witch's hand [*saga manus*], ever cruel so long as it remains on the earth and does harm with its craft. Parents, guard your children well, lest grief of this magnitude should implant itself in your breast.

LIVIA JULIA, THAT IS LIVILLA, MARRIED Drusus the son of Tiberius before 18 A.D. and died in 31 A.D. This inscription is taken as independent testimony that the sort of practice described by Horace did or at any rate was believed to take place, but one wonders how familiar Livilla would have been with the work of the previous emperor's poet. Livilla was herself put to death for supposedly having poisoned her husband, in 23 A.D. (Suetonius *Tiberius* 62, etc.).

## 94   Canidia scorns Horace's recantation

Ca. 30 B.C.

Horace *Epodes* 17

Latin

**Horace:** Now at last do I yield before your science, which works after all. As a suppliant I implore you, by the kingdom of Persephone, by the unutterable names of Diana, and by your books of powerful spells, to dislodge the stars from the sky and call them down. Canidia, at long last put an end to your sacred incantations and spin, spin your swift wheel backward. Telephus prevailed upon the grandson of Nereus [Achilles], against whom he had arrogantly arrayed his columns of Mysians and against whom he had hurled sharp weapons. The Trojan matrons were able to give due mourning to Hector, the killer, after he had been given over to the wild birds and dogs, after King Priam left the city walls and went forth, alas, to the feet of willful Achilles. Odysseus's rowers, subject as they were to so much toil, sloughed off their bristly limbs from their hardened skins, with Circe's assent. Then their minds and their voices slipped back, as did their familiar dignity to their faces. I have paid sufficient penalty and indeed more to you, who are loved so much by sailors and pedlars. My youth is gone, as is my bashful complexion. I am left as just bones clothed in yellow skin. My hair is white because of your scents. No rest I take relieves me from toil. Night presses the day hard, and day night, and I cannot relax my tight-drawn lungs to draw breath. I am beaten, so I now believe, in my unfortunate condition, what I had previously denied, that Sabine spells burn the breast and that heads are burst apart by Marsian incantations. What more do you want? Oh, sea and earth, I burn more than Hercules did when he was steeped in the black gore of Nessus and than the seething yellow flame in Etna in Sicily. Does your workshop glow hot with poisons [*venena*] until the point at which I am carried on the noxious winds as dry ash? What end do you have in store for me, or what price to pay? Tell me. I will pay the penalty in good faith, and I am ready to expiate myself, whether you demand this be done with a hundred bullocks, or whether you will want to be celebrated by my lying lyre: "You chaste woman, you honest woman, you will walk through the stars, a golden star yourself." Castor was upset when Helen was defamed, as was the brother of great Castor. But they were persuaded by prayer to restore to the poet [Stesichorus] the eyes of which they had deprived him. You too, for you have the power, deliver me from my madness. You are not a shabby person from squalid parents, nor are you a crone who knows how to scatter nine-day-old dust on poor men's tombs. You have a welcoming heart and clean hands. Pactumeius was the fruit of your womb, and it was your blood the midwife washed from the reddened sheets, however brave you were to leap out of bed for a woman in labor.

**Canidia:** Why do you pour prayers upon bolted ears? Winter Neptune does not pound with his white swell rocks that are more deaf to sailors stripped of their ships. Are you to have publicized and mocked, scot-free, the rites of Cotytto, the sacred practice of free love? Are you, the high priest of Esquiline sorcery [*venefi-cium*] to have filled the city with my name, with impunity? Of what benefit was it that Paelignian crones grew rich or mixed a faster poison? But death awaits you, a slower one than that for which you will pray. Your thankless, wretched life is to be extended to this end, so that you may continue to be available for torture. The father of treacherous Pelops longs for peace, so too Tantalus, ever deprived of the generous feast, and Prometheus, whose crimes devoted him to the bird. Sisyphus longs to rest his rock on the mountaintop. The laws of Jupiter forbid it. At one point you will wish to jump down from high towers, at another to open up your breast with a Noric sword. In vain will you tie a noose round your neck in your misery at grinding agony. Then I shall ride as a horseman on your enemy shoulders, and the crowd will yield to my arrogance. Or am I, who can animate wax effigies, as you yourself know from interfering, I, who can snatch the moon down from the sky by my incantations, I, who can raise up the cremated dead, I, who can blend love potions, am I to weep for my craft not encompassing your death?

HORACE SINGS A PALINODE OR RECANTATION for his former abuse of Canidia, just as Stesichorus had sung a palinode for his abuse of Helen. He presents himself specifically as having cast doubt on Canidia's magical abilities in the context of this abuse (such doubts are not evident in his other Canidia poems). One can reconstruct the other terms of the abuse Horace had supposedly cast against Canidia by reading his ironic compliments to her backward. One of his accusations had been that her "son" was a changeling. The victim now of her erotic magic (always Canidia's chief concern in the major poems), Horace begs for pardon and concedes her abilities. Canidia remains implacable, and resolved to torture him to death.

Horace's description of the state of his distress seems to express the experience of one suffering under a binding spell: notably, his lungs are "tight-drawn" (compare **184**); he also suffers from the burning, sleeplessness, and madness that erotic binding spells typically inflict (see **200, 204, 207–9, 224, 230–2, 239-40, 244**). The comparison of the burning of desire with that of the burning of Heracles emphasizes the proximity of Nessus's blood to an erotic charm (**76**). Horace does not explicitly say for whom he feels this desire, but Canidia is not shown elsewhere to work her erotic magic in anyone's interest but her own. For Canidia's use of wax dolls for erotic magic, see **91**; for the animation of voodoo dolls, see **244**.

Canidia projects her enemy Horace as a competing sorcerer; again we note that sorcery is, as so often, the attribute of one's rivals; see **13, 269–70**. The attribution of spell-books to a female professional is noteworthy. For the Sabine Marsi, see **92**, with commentary; the Paelignians are perhaps magical through association with them. Cotytto (or Cotys) was a Thracian goddess of love and war.

An ancient commentary on this text is given at **227**.

## 95   Canidia as the Neopolitan Gratidia

Ca. v A.D.

Pseudo-Acro on Horace

*Satires* 1.8.24

Latin

On *Satires* 1.8.24: "Canidia" stands for Gratidia the Neapolitan perfume-seller, whom Horace is always harassing as a witch [*venefica*].

ACRO'S COMMENTARY ON *EPODES* 3.8 and 5.1 carries similar material, as does Porphyrio's on *Epodes* 3.7 and 5.43 and *Satires* 1.8.13. Acro defines Canidia also as *malefica* and a *maga*. The device alluded to is the one familiar from amatory poetry, whereby the name of the "real" subject is replaced with one that is metrically equivalent (hence Catullus's poems to Clodia as "Lesbia"). Whether there ever was any such Gratidia remains doubtful.

## 96    Erictho and the witches of Thessaly

65 A.D.

Lucan *Pharsalia*
6.413–587

Latin

**413.** When the commanders had pitched camp here in the land cursed by fate, all were disturbed by presentiment of the war that was imminent. The grim point of final resolution was obviously about to come. Death was now moving closer. Degenerate minds trembled and contemplated the bad outcome. A few steeled themselves for the uncertain result and joined hope with fear. In the midst of this helpless crowd was Sextus, the unworthy offspring of his father Magnus. He was subsequently, in exile, to pollute the waves of Scylla, and as a Sicilian pirate vitiated his father's naval triumphs. His fear goaded him on to learn the course of his destiny. He could not bear to wait and was sick with fretting about everything that was to come. He did not consult the tripods of Delos or the caves of the Pythia. He had no interest in asking about the sounds of Jupiter's bronze at Dodona, provider of man's earliest nurture, or asking who could discover fates through entrails, who could interpret the flight of birds, who could observe the lightening in the sky, or who could investigate the stars with the Assyrian discipline. He had no interest in any method which, albeit arcane, was lawful. He was acquainted with the mysteries of the cruel mages, rites despised by the gods above, and with altars made grim with funereal sacrifices. He placed his confidence in the ghosts and in Hades. It was obvious to this pitiful man that the gods above knew too little.

**434.** The very place in which he found himself gave succor to his cruel frenzy, as did the walls of the Thessalian witches, which neighbored his camp. No monstrous fantasy surpasses them. Theirs is the power of the incredible. Indeed, the Thessalian earth brings forth deleterious herbs on its crags and stones which respond to the secret and deadly incantations of mages. Many plants grow there which will constrain the gods, and the Colchian visitor picked in the area the herbs she had not brought with her. The Thessalians' impious spells catch the ears of the heavenly gods, which are deaf to the prayers of so many peoples, so many races. Their voice alone ascends through the recesses of the ether and carries their words of compulsion to the unwilling power. No concern for the heaven or the revolving sky distracts the power from such a spell. When their unutterable drone has touched the stars, then, even though Persian Babylon and mysterious Memphis should unlock every sacred chamber of their ancient mages, the Thessalian woman will draw the gods above away from others' altars. By the spell of Thessalian women love flows into hard hearts, contrary to destiny, and austere old men burn with the flames of unlawful desire. Their powers are not restricted to harmful potions or the *hippomanes*, stolen from the mare, the succulent gland that grows on a foal's forehead, the pledge that its mother will love it. A mind, even when not corrupted by a poisonous drink, can be overcome with incantations. Couples who cannot be bound to each other by the contract of the marriage bed or the power of a lovely form are dragged together by the magical twisting of threads. The natural progression of the day is halted. Night is postponed while the day is prolonged and tarries. The ether disobeys its law. Once their spell is heard, the earth slows its revolution. Jupiter, driving the poles round on their swift hinges, is amazed that they do not move. Sometimes they fill up the whole world with rain and cover the hot sun over with clouds, and the sky thunders without Jupiter's knowledge. By the same spells they disperse the broad, damp mists and the loose locks of the clouds. The winds have fallen but the sea swells. Or, contrariwise, the sea is forbidden to react to storms and remains at peace while the South Wind squalls, and the sails that carry the ship swell against the wind. The torrent of water is fixed in its path and hangs from the sheer crag, and the river runs in a direction other than its former downward one. The summer stops bringing up the Nile, the Meander sends its waters straight, the Arar speeds along the tarrying Rhone. Mountains lower their peaks and smooth out their ridges. Olympus looks up to its clouds. The Scythian snows melt away without sun in the cold of winter. The spell of the Thessalian women drives back Tethys, the Tide, who is impelled by the moon-star, and defends the shore against her. The globe shakes the axis of its stable weight and, with its balance upset, the earth totters. By the force of an incantation the heavy bulk of the earth, great as it is, is parted and affords a view through itself of the revolving heaven. Every animal that is capable of inflicting death and was born to harm is terrified of the Thessalian craft and furnishes it with its deadly mechanisms. Greedy tigers and lions of noble anger fawn on the women and lick them. For them the snake unravels its chilly coils and stretches out in the frosty field. Vipers in their knots are split apart and reassembled. The serpent falls dead when blown upon with human poison. Why are the gods so anxious to obey their incantations and their herbs, and why do they fear to ignore them? The terms of what agreement constrain them? Is it compulsory for them to obey, or does it please them to do so? Do the Thessalians earn this service through some unrecognized piety? Or does their strength lie in implicit threats? Do they have power directly over all the gods, or do their imperious spells address one particular god, who can turn on the world the compulsion to which he himself is subject? By these Thessalians stars were first brought down from the revolving sky, and the bright moon, beset by the dreadful spells of their words, grew pale and blazed with black and earthly fires, as if the earth separated her from her brother's light and blocked off the heavenly fires with its shadows. Such are the toils the moon suffers, brought down by incantation, until she deposits her foam on the plants close below.

**507.** Wild Erictho had condemned as too pious these wicked rites, these criminal practices of a dreadful race. She had directed her corrupt craft toward new rites. For her it was a crime to put her deathly head under a roof of the city or the protection of household gods. She inhabited abandoned graves and took over tombs after driving out the shades. She was welcome to the gods of Erebus. Neither the gods nor her still-living state forbade her from hearing the assemblies of the silent dead or knowing the Stygian houses and the secrets of buried Dis. The impious woman's visage exhibited a foul and wasted decay. Her horrible face was burdened by a Stygian pallor and uncombed locks. It was unknown to the bright sky. But if a rainstorm and black clouds remove the stars, then the Thessalian emerges from the bare graves and tries to capture the lightenings of the night. She burns up the seeds of a fertile cornfield by treading on them, and by breathing she destroys breezes that were not formerly death-bringing. She does not pray to the gods; she does not call on the aid of any power with a hymn of supplication; she has no knowledge of favorable entrails. She delights in laying funereal fires on altars, together with the incense she has stolen from the lighted pyre. The gods concede to her every criminal prayer at her first asking, and they dread to hear the second spell. She buries in the tomb souls that are still living and governing their limbs, while death comes, despite itself, upon those to whom the fates still owe years of life. She turns the cortege around and brings the funeral back from the tomb. The corpses escape death. She snatches from the middle of pyres the smoking ashes of the young, together with their burning bones. She collects the very torch that the parents held, the remains of the funereal bier, fluttering about in black smoke, the clothes as they dissolve into cinders, and the ashes that smell of burnt limbs. But when the corpses are preserved in stone coffins, through the action of which their innermost moisture is drained and the bodies dry out, the corruption of the marrow drawn off, then she greedily exercises her cruelty on all the limbs. She plunges her hands into the eyes and delights to have dug out the frozen balls. She gnaws at the pale nails of the dried-out hand. She breaks with her jaws the noose and its harmful knots. She plucks at the hanging corpse and scrapes off crosses. She tears at guts beaten upon by rainstorms and bone marrow roasted in the rays of the sun. She takes the iron nail that pierces the hands, the corrupt black matter that runs over the limbs, and the congealed slime. She hangs off muscles that are resistant to her bite. And, should a body be lying on exposed ground, she takes up her position beside it before the wild beasts and the carrion birds arrive. She has no wish to harvest the limbs with a knife or her own hands. Rather, she waits for the wolves to bite it so that she can snatch the pieces from their unmoistened jaws. Her hands do not hesitate to slaughter, if living blood is required, of the kind that is the first to burst forth when a throat is opened, and her funereal tables demand entrails still aquiver. Babies are dragged out from a slashed-open belly, not the way nature intended, to be laid upon hot altars. Whenever she needs cruel and brazen shades, she herself manufactures the ghosts. Every human death is of some use to her. She tears the blooming cheek from the body of a young man. She cuts the lock with her left hand from the dying adolescent. Often too, at the funeral of a relation the dreadful Thessalian presses herself upon his limbs, dear to her as they are, and, while fixing kisses upon them, hacks bits off his head. With her teeth she releases the mouth, frozen shut, and, biting the end of the tongue that sticks fast in the dry throat, pours mutterings between the chill lips and sends secret and criminal orders down to the Stygian ghosts.

569. Local talk betrayed the woman to Pompey. Night was high in the sky, the time at which Titan, the Sun, draws on midday on the underside of our earth. Pompey made his way through the abandoned fields. His usual retinue, reliable for wickedness, wandered around the broken barrows and tombs, and caught sight of her in the distance, sitting on a precipitous crag, at the point where Haemus swoops down and stretches out its Pharsalian ridge. She was testing out words unknown to the mages and to the gods of magic, and was formulating a spell for a new purpose. For she was frightened that Mars, War, might stray into another part of the world, and that the Thessalian land might be deprived of so much slaughter. So the witch [*venefica*] defiled Philippi with her incantations, sprinkled it with her juices and forbade it to send the war on, so that she could have all those deaths to herself and could make use of the blood of the world. She had hopes of hacking bits off the corpses of slain kings, of carrying off the ashes of the western race together with the bones of its nobles, and of bringing such powerful ghosts under her control. This was her one great anxiety: what part could she snatch from the corpse of Magnus, what limbs of Caesar's could she steal?

LUCAN'S PORTRAIT OF ERICTHO IS THE most elaborate, overblown, and gloriously horrible portrait of a witch in classical literature, and the most striking account of Thessalian witchcraft in general. Erictho is introduced to perform a reanimation-necromancy for Sextus Pompey, son of Pompey the Great, to predict the outcome of the civil war against Julius Caesar, in which they are engaged and which, as Sextus learns, they are destined to lose. The narration of this reanimation (155) is preceded by this protracted introduction devoted to both the woman herself and her context within the wider world of Thessalian witchcraft.

Thessalian witches are, to some extent, aligned here with the standard alien-sorcerer types (434–506): Egyptians (Memphis), Persians, and Babylonians, the last two types being conflated (see 36–56). If Lucan is happy to conflate Persians and Babylonians in his own voice, his Sextus was perhaps keener to make the distinction: he admires Persian mages but scorns "the Assyrian discipline," by which astrology is clearly meant, the characteristic activity of the Babylonian Chaldaeans. Romans generally identified astrology with magic, but Sextus classes it with the pious forms of divination that he scorns (413–33).

Much attention is given to the various means by which Erictho collects body parts for exploitation in her magical rites (507–68); compare the contents of Pamphile's workshop at 107. For the significance of snatching human body parts from the mouths of wolves, see 92. The notion that witches tear fetuses from wombs for their rites is probably a refraction of the secretive work of female abortionists; compare 233–4. Erictho's spell to detain the war in her own area, so that she can avail herself of body-part supplies, is a humorous inversion of an established variety of spell for the aversion of war; see 55.

Constraint of the gods is seen as a prime characteristic of Thessalian witchcraft (434–68). Lucan further speculates as to the mechanism of this control. The notions that the witches use threats against the gods and employ an even greater god of their own against them is realized in the subsequent narration of Erictho's reanimation.

Lucan introduces scientific theory in an incongruous and humorous way. He combines the traditional notion that witches can open up the underworld with the theory that the earth is a globe. The witches are so powerful that they pierce the earth right through and so can look down the hole at the heavens on the other side (434–506). The drawing-down of the moon is here knowingly and wryly described in terms of an eclipse; compare 218, 220. The foam deposited by the moon was gathered and used for love-potions; see 222.

For blasting snakes by blowing on them, see 49. For love potions assimilated to poisons, see 76–81. For *hippomanes*, here conceptualized as the gland, see 230–2. For magical threads, see 90.

## THE WITCH-THEME IN LATIN POETRY

A notable topos of Latin poetry is the thumbnail sketch of the witch. These sketches, particularly prominent in elegy, recycle a syndrome of commonplace themes (of course, not all the elements of it are present in all cases). For further similar sketches see 69, 90. Such themes are more conveniently tabulated here than repeatedly adverted in the several commentaries that follow:

- The witches' Thessalian origin; see also 24, 45, 96, 155, 161, 214, 261.

- Erotic magic, their primary concern, in its various manifestations.

- Constraint of the gods.
- Control of the landscape and of the sea. Rivers are sent back to their sources. Mountains are leveled. Forests walk.
- Control of the elements, winds, clouds, rain, sunshine; see also **5, 13, 22, 35**.
- Crop-charming from one field into another; see also **280–1**.
- Control of the motion of the heavenly bodies, which sometimes entails control of night and day. The sun can also be turned pale.
- The drawing-down of the moon for erotic purposes, the most significant aspect of control of the heavenly bodies. It can also be turned blood red; see also **214–23**.
- The opening up of the earth and the evocation of the dead; see also **144–54**.
- The saluting of the mythical witch-archetypes Circe and Medea, either as individuals or as a pair; see also **66–75**.
- The patronage of Hecate; see also **275**, with commentary.
- The gathering of noxious herbs and of human bones for magic, the latter often snatched from the mouths of wolves; see also **107**.
- Shape-shifting, usually into wolves; see also **139–43**.

A subgroup of such sketches, confined to love elegy, combines the witch-figure with that of the drunken bawd, who corrupts the lover-poet's girl and throws obstacles between them.

**97 Tibullus's tame witch**

Ca. 27 B.C.

Tibullus *Elegies* 1.2.42–66

Latin

Nor will your husband, however, believe this person [a witness to Tibullus's illicit affair with Delia], as a reliable witch [*saga*] has promised me, with the help of her magical services. I have seen her draw down the stars from the sky. I have seen her turn around the course of a river with her incantation. She cleaves the ground with her spell, brings forth ghosts from tombs, and calls down bones from warm pyres. Sometimes she holds fast the underworld hordes with a magical screech; sometimes she sprinkles them with milk and bids them retreat. When it pleases her, she dispels clouds from a gloomy sky; when it pleases her, she induces snow on a summer day. She alone is said to possess Medea's evil herbs, she alone to tame the wild dogs of Hecate. She composed a spell for me by which you could deceive him. Sing it three times, and spit after each of the three singings. Then he will not be able to believe anyone who tells him about us. He won't even believe himself, if he sees us in our soft bed with his own eyes. But you must keep away from other men, for he will see everything else. About me alone will he perceive nothing. What should I believe? For as a matter of fact this same witch said she could deliver me of my loves, by incantations or herbs. She purified me with torches and on a cloudless night sacrificed black victims to the gods of magic. I prayed not that love should be completely gone, but that it should be reciprocal. I would not wish to be able to live without you.

FOR ONCE THE WITCH IS ON the side of the poet-lover rather than that of his girl. For husband-blinding spells, see **101**. Control of the ghosts in evocation can be a problem (see **144**); this is the only text to suggest that they can be dismissed by the scattering of milk.

## 98  Medea in a thumbnail sketch

Before 2 B.C.

Ovid *Heroides* 6.83–94

Latin

It is not because of her beauty or her good deeds that you find Medea pleasing, but she knows incantations and she culls dreadful plants with her enchanted sickle. She works hard to draw the struggling moon down from its path and to bury the horses of the sun in darkness. She reins back waters and brings rivers to a halt in their descent. She transports woods and rocks, as if alive, from their place. She wanders amid tombs, ungirt, her hair in disarray, and gathers the pick of the bones from warm pyres. She places binding spells [*devovet*] on people from afar, molds voodoo dolls out of wax, and pushes fine needles into their pathetic livers. She does other things it would have been better for me not to know. Love should be acquired through character and beauty. It is wrong that it should be sought through herbs.

THIS PORTRAIT OF MEDEA (SEE **66–71**) is comparable to other thumbnail sketches of witches in Latin poetry. For her prowling around cemeteries, compare **91, 96**; for binding spells, see **168–84, 197–213**; for voodoo dolls, see **236–47**; for Medea's ungirt and unbound state as she performs her rites, see **67**.

## 99  A witch inflicts impotence with a drug or a voodoo doll

Ca. 16 B.C.

Ovid *Amores*
3.7.27–36, 73–84

Latin

**27.** Did my limbs grow heavy, bound [*devota*] by a Thessalian drug? Was I damaged by a spell and herbs? Or did a witch bind [*defixit*] my name with red wax and drive fine needles through the middle of my liver? Harmed by an incantation Ceres, Corn, shrivels on her fruitless stalks. When a spring is harmed by incantation, its waters dry up. Acorns fall from oaks and the bewitched grape falls from the vine. Apples drop without being touched. Why shouldn't my muscle too fail under the influence of magical crafts? Perhaps this is why I have lost sensation in it.

**73.** My girlfriend did not disdain to try to rouse it with the gentle application of her hand. But once she saw that there was nothing she could do to make it rise and that it lay as flaccid as if she wasn't there, "Why are you trifling with me?" she said, "Who told you to lay yourself in my bed if you didn't want to perform, crazy man? Either some Circean witch [*venefica*] is binding you by piercing wool, or you come to me after wearing yourself out by having sex with someone else." Without delay she put on her tunic, without fastening it, and jumped out of the bed. Her bare feet were so pretty as they tripped along. She concealed my disgrace by drawing water for a bath, to prevent her maids realizing that she had gone untouched.

OVID AND HIS GIRL FANCY THAT a Thessalian witch has inflicted a binding curse on him (see **197–203**) by means of a voodoo doll of red wax or of wool, into which she has inserted pins. For dolls in general, see **236–47**, and **239–40** in particular for piercing. For the association between wax dolls and woolen ones, see **91**, a poem perhaps alluded to here. The use of voodoo dolls in erotic contexts is normally for attraction rather than separation or the infliction of impotence (a Boeotian curse-text inscribed on what is apparently a flattened voodoo doll, the "Gingerbread-man," may be an exception: see Gager 1992, 86–7). However, comparison with the following excerpt from Tibullus may indicate that the doll has been used to attract Ovid to a third party (the witch herself?) so that he can find no pleasure with any other woman. Magic could also cure impotence: see **254**.

## 100 Drunken bawd-witches (1): Tibullus's curse

Ca. 27 B.C.

Tibullus 1.5.39–59

Latin

I often have another woman in my arms, but at the threshold of love's joys Venus has recalled my mistress Delia to my mind and abandoned me. The woman has said I'm under a curse [*devotus*] as she leaves. The shame of it! She tells the story that my lady knows evil crafts. But she doesn't use herbs to achieve her effects. My girl binds me with her face, her gentle arms, and her blonde hair, like Thetis of the sea, the Nereid that once reined a dolphin and rode it to Thessalian Peleus. That has been my undoing. A rich lover is now on the scene: a cunning bawd works toward my destruction. May she eat bloody feasts and with gory mouth drink joyless cups full of gall. May ghosts ever flit about her complaining of their fates and may the screech owl call from her roof. May starvation goad her to madness and send her searching for herbs on graves and bones abandoned by fierce wolves. May she run bare-groined and howling through the city, and may she be chased from the crossroads by a rough pack of dogs. It will happen. So indicates the god. The lover has his gods, and Venus can be cruel when she is unjustly neglected. But, Delia, cast the instructions of that greedy witch aside at once.

TIBULLUS'S GIRL HAD SUGGESTED THAT DELIA had put him under a binding-curse of attraction to herself (compare **204–13**), so that he could take no pleasure in other women. Note the contrived reference to Thessaly. But Delia is now under the influence of a bawd that Tibullus implies to be a witch. He in turn inflicts a curse on the bawd. Hunger is to drive her to eat the noxious herbs and gnaw at the bones that she collects for her magical purposes. She is to be harried by the ghosts she evocates. In place of her beloved wine, she is to drink only cups of gall. For bones taken from the mouths of wolves or dogs, see **92**.

## 101 Drunken bawd-witches (2): Propertius's curse against Acanthis

Ca. 16 B.C.

Propertius 4.5.1–18, 63–78

Latin

1. Bawd, may the ground cover over your tomb with brambles, and may your shade go thirsty—the last thing you want! May your ashes' ghost find no peace, and may avenging Cerberus terrify your foul bones, howling with hunger.

She knew how to break down even Hippolytus's resistance to Venus and, ever the worst bird of omen for a harmonious lover's bed, could compel even Penelope to disregard rumors of her husband and marry lusty Antinous. If she wished, loadstone could fail to attract iron, and the bird could be a stepmother to the chicks in her nest. And if she brought Colline herbs to the trench, things standing solid would be dissolved into running water. She was bold enough to bewitch the moon and impose her orders on it, and to change her form into that of the nocturnal wolf, so that she could, by her craft, blind keenly watchful husbands. With her nail she tore out the eyes of crows—they did not deserve this—and asked the screech owls about my blood. She gathered hippomanes, the seed of the pregnant mare, to use against me.

[Propertius relates at length how the bawd-witch Acanthis instructed his girl to wring gifts from him and to take competing lovers.]

63. While Acanthis manipulated my girlfriend's mind with this advice, you could count my bones beneath my stretched skin. But, queen Venus, accept this ring-dove, its throat cut in sacrifice before your altar, in repayment. I saw the final cough rise in her wrinkled neck, and the bloody spittle coming through the gaps in her

teeth. I saw her breathe out her foul spirit into her father's old rough blankets. Her hearth went cold, and a chill fell on her dilapidated shack. Her funeral's pomp consisted of the filthy, faded turban she had once stolen, tied over her thinning hair, and the dog that was always awake to cause me misery when I tried to slip the bolt secretly with my thumb. May the bawd's tomb be an old amphora with a broken neck! May you jostle it with your vigorous growth, fig tree. If you are a lover, break this tomb with rough stones, and with the stones hurl words of cursing!

Another curse against a bawd-witch, this time after her death. An *acanthis* is, appropriately, a little finch that lives in thistles. In life Acanthis had, in particular, the abilities to inflict and suppress love, and thus exercise her influence over Propertius's beloved. As usual, she had the power to draw down the moon. For the blinding of husbands see **97**. For *hippomanes* see **230–2**. Here Propertius appears to be knowingly vague as to whether the *hippomanes* is a plant or a gland. The significance of bringing Colline herbs to the trench is obscure. It may refer to the destruction of city walls. Cerberus will worry Acanthis's bones, just as dogs would worry the bones she had herself exploited for her magic; compare **92**.

## 102  Drunken bawd-witches (2): Ovid's curse against Dipsas

Ca. 16 B.C.

Ovid *Amores* 1.8.1–20, 105–14

Latin

**1.** There is this (listen up, if you want to learn about a bawd!), there is this old woman called Dipsas. Her name is a significant one: she has never seen roseate-horsed Dawn, the mother of black Memnon, in a state of sobriety. She knows the craft of magic and Aeaean incantations. By her craft she turns flowing waters back to their source. She knows all too well the powers of the herb, the threads twisted by the spinning *rhombos*-wheel, and the secretion of the mare in love. At her wish, clouds crowd over the entire heaven; at her wish, the daylight shines in a clear sky. If you believe it, I have seen the stars dripping with blood. The face of the moon was deep red with blood. I suspect that she shape-shifts and flits about among the shades of the night and that her old body is covered with feathers. This is what I suspect, and this is what they say. Also, double pupils flash from her eyes, and the beams shine from twin circles. She calls forth great-grandfathers and the great-grandfathers of great-grandfathers from their ancient tombs and cleaves open the solid ground with a protracted incantation. This woman set herself the task of violating the chastity of my girl's bedroom. It must be said, her tongue does have a destructive eloquence.

[Dipsas tempts Corinna to abandon Ovid for rich rivals. She addresses her.]

**105.** "If you follow this advice of mine, culled as it is from long experience, and if the winds and the breezes do not carry my words off, you will often have cause to praise me while I live, and, when I am dead, to pray that my bones lie at peace." She was continuing, when my shadow gave me away. I could scarcely keep my hands from ripping apart her thin white hair, her eyes, tearful from the wine, and her wrinkled cheeks. May the gods deprive you of a home and give you an impoverished old age, long winters, and eternal thirst!

This poem is evidently closely related to Propertius's Acanthis poem, **101**, although the chronological priority is disputed. Dipsas is appropriately named for Greek *dipsa*, "thirst." Here the bawd-witch anticipates her girl's blessings after her death, rather than the poet-lover's cursing. For the *rhombos* see **224–9**. For the *hippomanes* see **230–2**. For Dipsas's double pupils, associated with the evil eye, see **192–6**. For her corrupting eloquence and its association with magic compare **12**. For her thin white hair compare **91**, with commentary.

## 103  Drunken bawd-witches (4): An old woman passes on her skills to girls

Ca. 8 A.D.

Ovid *Fasti* 2.572–83

Latin

See! An old woman of many years sits among the girls. She will perform the rites of Tacita, "the Silent One," although she scarcely keeps silent herself. With three of her fingers she places three pieces of incense under a threshold, exploiting the secret run a mouse has made for itself. Then she binds enchanted threads together with dark lead and turns seven black beans over in her mouth. She roasts on a fire the sewn-up fish head, which she has sealed with pitch and pierced with a bronze needle. She also drips wine over it. She drinks the leftovers of the wine with her companions, but she herself drinks the greater part. As she leaves she proclaims, "We have bound the tongues of our enemies and hostile mouths." With that the old woman goes off drunk. Straightaway you will ask me, "What is this goddess, 'Mute'?"

HERE THE WITCH'S DRUNKENNESS IS MOCKED. She is not explicitly said to be a bawd, but her role in the instruction of young girls may present her as one (see Pseudo-Demosthenes [i.e. Apollodorus] 59.18–20). This passage is important for presenting us with a vignette of the transmission of magical expertise from one generation of women to another; compare **85**. The spell described is evidently one of tongue-binding (see **168–72**). It makes use of lead tablets and of a symbolically silenced animal. So too Libanius was to have his tongue bound by means a decapitated chameleon, its mouth closed with its foot (**247**). The context of the old woman's activity is the Feralia, the festival of the dead. Ovid goes on to explain (to line 616) that Muta Tacita had once been an all-too-chattersome naiad, Lara (from La-la, from *lalein*). She chattered indiscreetly about Jupiter's love for Juturna, and so he tore the tongue from her mouth, and then ordered Hermes to take her down to live with the ghosts as a "nymph of the underworld marsh." On the way he had sex with her, and she bore the *La-res Compitales*, the public guardians of the city. The appeal to Muta Tacita for tongue-binding is intriguingly confirmed by a Latin curse tablet addressed to her, asking her to silence Quartus and send him scurrying about like a mouse (Gager 1992, 252, with references).

For the insertion of incense under the threshold, compare Simaetha's kneading of herbs over the threshold of her beloved (**89**) and the insertion of erotic curse tablets under the virgin's threshold at **204**. For the importance of the number three see **90**. For magical threads see **254**.

## WITCHES IN THE LATIN NOVELS

The *Metamorphoses* or *Golden Ass* of Apuleius (ca. 125–170? A.D.), is the only fully extant Latin novel. Lucius narrates in the first person his accidental transformation into an ass and his eventual deliverance from this state by the goddess Isis. It is "picaresque" in style and contains a number of engagingly narrated and exciting episodes involving Thessalian witches. Apuleius was born and lived in Roman North Africa, although he was educated at Athens and Rome. Since there is no mention of the novel in his *Apology* (**134, 158, 242, 299**) of 158–9 A.D., it is usually assumed that it was written subsequently. For a further excerpt from the novel see **114**.

## 104    The Thessalians Meroe and Panthia reanimate Socrates

Later ii A.D.

Apuleius *Metamorphoses* 1.5–19

Latin

**5.** Let me begin my telling you my town and my name. I'm Aristomenes, from Aegium. My business, you are to know, consists of traversing Thessaly, Aetolia, and Boeotia in all directions with supplies for innkeepers: honey, cheese, that sort of thing. Once I learned that fresh, fine cheese was on sale for quite a good price at Hypata, the first city of all Thessaly. I raced there to buy it all up. But, as usually happens, I set out under ill omen, and my hopes of profit came to nothing. For on the day before my arrival Lupus the wholesale dealer had bought it all. So, exhausted by my fruitless rush, I had begun to walk to the bathhouse as the evening star was beginning to rise.

**6.** See! There was Socrates, my old comrade. He sat on the ground, only half-dressed by his ragged cloak. He was so yellow that I almost failed to recognize him. He was pitifully disfigured in his scrawniness, and he looked like the unfortunate dregs of society that beg for money at the crossroads. Although I knew him well and he was so close to me, I accosted him with some doubt in my mind, since he was so much changed. "My friend Socrates," I said, "What's going on? What a sight you are! What an outrage! In your home you have already been wept over and lamented as dead and legal guardians have been appointed over your children by the ruling of the province's judge. Your wife has completed the due funerary rites and wrecked her looks with her mourning and protracted grief. Her eyes are all cried out, almost to the point of blindness. She is now being urged by her parents to cheer the house's misfortune with the delight of a new match. And I find you here, looking just like a ghost. This is a disgrace for us!"

"Aristomenes," he replied, "You should inform yourself of fortune's slippery twists, its unpredictable attacks and its reversals, now this way, now that." As he spoke he covered his face, which had been blushing with shame for some time, with the collection of sewn-together patches that was his cloak. As he did so he exposed the rest of his body from his navel to his genitals. With that I could not bear the pitiful sight of his destitution any further. I took his hand and tried to pull him up.

**7.** But he would not budge. From under the covering of his head he said, "Leave me, let fortune take further pleasure in the trophy she has set up."

I managed to make him come with me. At once I took off one of the two things I had on and hurriedly clothed him, or, perhaps I should just say, covered him. Without delay I gave him over to the baths and furnished him myself with the wherewithal for oiling down and drying off. At the expense of no little effort I rubbed a mountain of filth off him. When this was all sorted out, I propped the exhausted man up and brought him to an inn. This was no easy task, for I was tired out myself. I put him to bed to aid his recovery, stuffed him with food, helped him to relax by giving him a drink, and chatted to him to soothe him. Then we fell readily into pleasant conversation. We joked and even exercised our wit. We were hesitantly embarking upon banter, when he drew a tortured sigh from the bottom of his heart, and wildly beat his forehead with his right hand. "I am done for," he began. "It was while I was looking for a good time at a famous gladiator show that I fell into this mess. As you know of course, I went off to make some money in Macedonia. After nine months of hard work there I was coming back rather better off. Just before I reached Larissa, where I was going to catch the show en route, I was mugged in an out-of-the-way valley, which was full of holes for ambushes, by some brutal bandits. Everything was taken off me, but at least I escaped with my life. In this state of absolute destitution I turned to an innkeeper, Meroe. She was an old woman but quite pretty. I told her the story of my protracted travels, my keen journey home, and my pitiful mugging. She began by treating me with exceptional kindness. She gave me a wonderful free meal and then, roused by desire, took me into her bed. The minute I went to bed with her I was undone. By that single bout of sex I trapped myself into this protracted and pestilential relationship. I even gave up to her the clothes those kind muggers had let me keep to cover myself up with, and the pittance I earned by carrying sacks while I still had my strength, until my good wife and bad fortune brought me to the condition you witnessed a little earlier."

8. "By Pollux," I said, "You deserve the extremities of hardship, if, that is, there is anything beyond the condition you were lately in, for preferring sexual pleasure and a wrinkled strumpet to your home and children."

But he put his index finger to his mouth and, shocked and confounded, said "Quiet! Quiet!" He looked about to check that he could speak securely. "Be careful what you say about this woman of divine properties, lest you bring some harm upon yourself for not moderating your tongue." "What do you mean?" I said. "What sort of woman is this powerful queen who yet remains an innkeeper?"

"She is a witch [saga]," he said, "and has divine powers that enable her to bring down the sky, suspend the earth, turn flowing water solid, dissolve mountains, raise ghosts, bring down the gods, extinguish the stars, and throw Tartarus open to the light."

"I beg you," I said, "dispense with the tragic curtain, bundle up the backcloth, and tell me the tale in plain language."

"Would you like," he said, "to hear one or two, or even more, of the things she's done? Making people fall passionately in love with her, not just the people round about, but even Indians, Ethiopians (both varieties, west bank and east bank), and Antipodeans, no less—this is an easy thing for her craft, a simple trifle. But hear what she has achieved before multiple witnesses.

9. "With a single word she changed a lover into a wild beaver, because he had strayed with another woman, because when the creature fears it is about to be captured by its hunters it gets away by biting off its genitals. She wanted this to happen to him, because he had had sex with another. She had an innkeeper neighbor, who, for that reason, was a competitor, so she transformed him into a frog. Now the old man swims about in a pot of his own wine, hovers in the dregs at the bottom and croaks polite greetings to his former customers. Then there was the lawyer. She transformed him into a ram because he opposed her in court. Now he pleads his cases in this form. A lover's wife came out with a witty bit of abuse for her. She had a bun in the oven. Meroe sealed off her womb and deprived her of the ability to bring the child forth, condemning her to an eternal pregnancy. According to everyone's reckoning the poor little woman has now been carrying the burden for eight years and is so distended that she looks as if she is about to produce an elephant.

10. "She kept doing these things and many were getting hurt. Public outrage grew and a decree was passed that the severest punishment, that of stoning, be inflicted upon her the next day. She undermined this plan with the power of her spells. The famous Medea had prevailed upon Creon to give her the grace of one little day and had then used it to burn up his whole house and his daughter, together with the old man himself, with the flames that shot out of the girl's crown. Meroe did something similar. She made some binding spells [devotionibus] over a pit, exploiting ghosts, as she recently told me after getting drunk, and she shut everyone up in their own homes with the secret power of demons [numina]. The result was that bolts could not be broken, doors could not be torn out of their

hinge-sockets, and party-walls could not even be dug through, for a whole two days. By that time they had all persuaded each other and, shouting out as with one voice, swore the most solemn of oaths to the effect not only that they would not move a hand against her themselves but also that if anyone had any other ideas, they would protect her. And so, duly mollified, she released the whole town. But in the dead of night she spirited away the man who had organized that meeting together with his whole house, walls, floor, and all its foundations, sealed up just as it was, to another town a hundred miles away. This town was on the very top of a rough mountain and so waterless. And since the dense development of the place by its inhabitants left no room for their new guest, she threw the house down in front of the gate and went off."

**11.** "You're telling me some amazing things, Socrates, and cruel things too. What you say has given me some needling concerns—or rather it impales me with terror—that that old woman may be exploiting the service of some demon in similar fashion to learn of our conversation. So let's go early to bed and get some rest and then, once sleep has unburdened us of our exhaustion, let's escape before dawn and get as far away from her as we can."

"I was still making the case when the good Socrates, suffering from the effects of wine-bibbing, for which he was out of practice, and from his long weariness, had already fallen asleep and was snoring quite soundly. But I shut the door, made the bolts fast, and pushed my pallet-bed tight up behind the hinge, and laid myself upon it. To start with I was awake for quite a while because of my fear. Then, at around the third watch [i.e., midnight] I managed to shut my eyes for a bit. I had only just got off the sleep when the doors suddenly flew open with greater force that you would have thought robbers could muster. Indeed they were actually broken open, torn right out of their hinge-sockets and flung onto the floor. My pallet-bed, which was an insubstantial thing anyway, rotten and with one leg too short, was also flung forward by the strength of the force used. I was thrown out of it, but it landed back on top of me upside down, and covered me and hid me.

**12.** Then I realized that some feelings by nature express themselves through their opposites. For just as tears are often the product of joy, so in that state of excessive terror, I could not contain a laugh at the thought that I had been transformed from Aristomenes into a tortoise. Down there in the dirt, I looked out sideways to see what was going on, shrewdly shielded by my bed. I saw two rather old women. One was carrying a bright lamp, the other a sponge and an unsheathed sword. With this paraphernalia they stood over Socrates, who was still fast asleep. The one with the sword spoke first: "Panthia, my sister, this is my sweet Endymion, this is my Ganymede, the one who mocked my youthful innocence night and day, the one who disdained my love and not only slanders me with abuse but is even planning to run away. No doubt I, like Calypso, shall be deserted by my cunning Odysseus and weep for my eternal solitude." Then she stretched out her right hand and indicated me to her Panthia. "And here is his wise adviser Aristomenes, who was the instigator of this escape and now, on the point of death, lies on his face under his bed and takes all this in. He thinks he's going to get away with insulting me scot-free. I'll ensure that he'll one day—no, very soon—but no, right away—repent of the wit he was displaying before, and of his current nosiness."

**13.** As soon as I heard that I was pitifully soaked in cold sweat, and my heart thumped so much that the bed actually picked up the vibration and started to shake over my back. Good lady Panthia spoke: "Well then, sister, do we tear this one apart first, like bacchants, or do we tie up his genitals and lop them off?"

To this Meroe responded—for at that point I actually realized that her name fitted with Socrates's stories—"No, let this one at least live, so that he can heap up a bit of earth over the body of this little wretch." She pushed Socrates' head to one side and plunged the whole sword into the left side of his neck, right up to the hilt. She carefully applied a leather bottle to his neck and carefully caught up the blood that welled out, so that there was not a drop to be seen anywhere. I saw this with my own eyes. Because, I believe, the good lady Meroe did not wish to depart in any way from sacrificial observance, she stuck her right hand into the wound and, delving down to his innards, probed about and pulled my poor companion's heart out. With that Socrates brought forth a noise, or rather an indistinct screech, through the wound in his throat that the sword had hacked open and gurgled out his last breath. Panthia used the sponge to stop up the wound at its widest point and said, "Now, sponge, born in the sea, cross not over a river!" With this proclamation they came away, took the bed off me between the two of them, straddled over my face and evacuated their bladders, until they had soaked me in their foul urine.

**14.** They had just stepped through the doorway when the doors leaped back into position, undamaged. The hinge-axles slotted back into their sockets, the bars returned to the posts, and the bolts ran back to do their locking. But I stayed just as I was, still sprawling on the ground, lifeless, naked, cold, and drenched in urine, like a newborn baby just out of the womb. No, rather, I was half-dead and already outliving myself, as my own posthumous child, or at any rate I was a candidate for the waiting cross. "What will happen to me, when they find him with his throat cut in the morning? Who will think my true story seems true? 'At least you could have been calling out for help, if such a big man as you could not stand up against a woman. A man's throat is cut before your very eyes and you don't make a murmur? Why didn't the robbers kill you too? Why, in their cruelty and bloodthirstiness, did they spare a witness to their crime and informer? So, since you have escaped death, return there now!'"

I went through this in my mind over and over, and night became day. The best course of action seemed to be to sneak out secretly before first light and get on the road, albeit with legs a-tremble. I took up my bag, put the key in, and drew back the bolts. But those solid, reliable doors, which had opened up all by themselves in the night, could now only be made to open at the cost of much time and effort, and I had to put the key in again and again.

**15.** "Oy you, where are you?," I said, "Open up the inn doors. I want to leave before it gets light."

The porter was asleep on the floor behind the entrance to the inn. He was still only half awake. "What's the matter?," he said. "Don't you realize that the roads are infested with muggers? What are you doing traveling by night? Even if you're feeling guilty about some crime and want to get yourself killed, my head isn't made out of a gourd! I have no wish to die on your behalf!"

"It will soon be light," I said. "Anyway, what can muggers steal from an absolutely destitute traveler? Don't you realize, idiot, than a naked man cannot be stripped even by ten wrestlers?"

At this he languidly rolled onto his other side, still half asleep. "How can I be sure that you haven't cut the throat of your fellow wayfarer, the man you came in late with, and are now looking to protect yourself by flight?" At that moment, I recall, the earth opened up beneath me, and I looked down into the depths of Tartarus, and in it there was Cerberus eager to gobble me down. I reflected that it was not out of pity that the good lady Meroe had spared my throat. Rather, it was out of cruelty that she had postponed my death for the cross.

**16.** So I returned to the bedroom and started to think how I could kill myself quickly. Fortune provided me with no lethal weapon apart from my bed. "Now, bed," I said, "so dear to my heart, provide me with a secure weapon as I hasten to the shades below. You have been my partner in so many ordeals. You know, you witnessed, the events of the night. You are the only witness I can call to my innocence, in my defense." With this I set to pulling out the rope with which it was strung. I threw one end of the rope round the window sill, which stuck out on both sides, and tied it off. The other end I made into a solid knot. Then I climbed up on the bed, got myself to a height from which I could kill myself, stuck my head through the noose and put it round my neck. With one foot I kicked out the support, so that the force of my weight would draw the rope tight around my throat and shut off my ability to breathe. All at once the rope, which was in any case old and rotten, snapped, and I fell down from on high on top of Socrates (he was lying beside me), and rolled onto the floor with him.

**17.** At the same time the porter burst in and bellowed "Where are you, you who were all too hasty in the middle of the night and are now wrapped up in your sheets and snoring?"

At this Socrates, roused either by my falling on him or by that man's ugly shouting, got up first and said, "All these innkeepers are deservedly hated by their guests. For by bursting in at this ungodly hour (intent on stealing something, no doubt) this interfering man has woken me from deep sleep with all his noise, and that too when I'm so worn out!"

I got up, bright-eyed and bushy-tailed, full of unexpected delight. "See, faithful porter, here is my friend, my father, my brother, whom you accused me of murdering during the night, in your cups." As I spoke I embraced Socrates and showered him with kisses. But he was repulsed by the stink of the filthy substance those bogie-women [*lamiae*] had drenched me in, and thrust me back. "Get off me!" he said. "You smell like a public toilet." Then, more kindly, he began to ask the reasons for the smell.

Poor me, I made up some stupid joke on the spot and changed the subject. I put my hand on him and said, "Let's go and make the most of an early start." I took up my bag and, the bill paid, we were on our way.

**18.** We had covered some distance and now the world was being illumined by sunrise. I carefully tried to scrutinize the part of my friend's throat where I'd seen the sword go in. "You're raving," I said to myself. "You were deep in your cups and had a bizarre dream. See, Socrates is safe, sound, and unharmed. Where's the wound? Where's the sponge? Where, indeed, is the scar, which went so deep, and is so new?" To Socrates I said, "Our trusty doctors are right when they say that people have cruel and disturbing dreams when distended by food and drink. I wasn't as restrained as I should have been with my imbibing last evening, and the terrible night displayed dreadful, murderous visions before me. They were so convincing that I still believe that I've been bespattered and defiled with the blood of a man."

At this Socrates smiled and said, "But it's urine you're soaked with, not blood! But I too saw myself jugulated in a dream. I felt a pain here in my throat and I thought my heart was being pulled out. Even now my breath is failing, my knees are knocking, and I'm reeling on my feet. I have to eat something to recover my breath."

"See," I said, "I have some breakfast ready for you here." As I spoke I took my knapsack off my shoulder, and hurriedly offered him some bread and cheese. "Let's sit down beside that plane tree," I said.

**19.** With that I myself took some of the same. I watched him tuck into his food voraciously, and I saw him begin to fail, as he became scrawnier still and as pale as boxwood. His complexion deteriorated so much that in my fear the vision of those nocturnal Furies appeared before me once again, and the first piece of bread I'd eaten, even though quite small, stuck in the middle of my throat, and I could not get it down or bring it up. My fear grew all the greater because there were so few wayfarers around. For who would believe that one of two traveling companions could be killed without the other one being the killer? But when Socrates had chomped through enough food, he was seized by an unbearable thirst. He had, after all, greedily gulped down a healthy helping of excellent cheese. Not far from the roots of the plane tree there dawdled a small stream, as calm as a pond, and looking like silver or glass. "See," I said, "refresh yourself with the milky water from this spring." He rose to his feet and found a place where the bank had an even edge. Then he got down on his knees and brought himself close to the water in his eagerness to get a drink. He had hardly touched the water's surface with the tips of his lips, when his throat-wound yawned open and deep, and the sponge suddenly bounced out of it, followed by just a bit of blood. Then his lifeless corpse almost fell headlong into the river, but I managed to hold onto one of his feet and, with an effort, drag him back up the bank. Once there, I wept over the poor little man, as much as I could under the circumstances, and covered him with the sandy earth. He will lie forever beside that river. I was shaking and absolutely terrified for myself. I made my escape by remote and deserted routes. As if I were myself guilty of killing a man, I left my country and my home behind and chose a life of exile. I live in Aetolia now, where I have made a new marriage.

ONE OF THE MOST CHILLING ASPECTS of Aristomenes' tale is the sense of humor that underpins the witches' cruelty. Meroe is, as we would expect, attributed with the commonplaces of witchcraft (8 and 10; compare **97–103**). Like the bawd-witches, she is inclined to drunkenness (10). The major witch sequences of this novel all involve animal-transformations, consonantly with its central theme. Here we learn that Meroe can transform men into beavers, frogs, rams (9), and, metaphorically at any rate, tortoises (12). She is explicitly attributed with the performance of binding magic through the exploitation of ghosts (10). Indeed she can bind in a very literal way: she can bind a womb shut (9; compare **82, 233–5**); she can bind an entire town into its houses (10); and she can bind Aristomenes into his hotel room (14). Her use of magic in competitive contexts is also suggestive of the culture of binding curses, in that she uses her powers to resolve conflicts of trade, law, and love (9), the three principal categories into which curse tablets fall; see **168–84, 197–213**.

As becomes clear in the course of the narrative, Socrates is indeed killed in bed by the women (13, 19). His subsequent actions after his "awakening" must therefore be ascribed to magical reanimation (see **155–62**). The mechanism that brings this about can only be the sponge and the incantation.

One distinctive attribute of Meroe's powers is the range over which she can exercise them. Love is her primary concern, as usual with the witches of the Latin tradition, and she can make even remote races fall in love with her (8). She can send houses flying off to far places (10). She can hear speech across great distances, particularly when it is slanderous, with the aid of a demon (8, 11, 12). Slander is in fact something to which she is particularly sensitive, and she is also shown to punish it. Sorcerers generally fear slander (see **300**), a thing partly akin to the evil eye (**192–6**) and which they themselves exploited as a deleterious magical technique (see **211, 234**).

It is a recurring theme of ancient literature that men who encounter witches do not return home. As Socrates makes clear (6–7), Meroe only had to sleep with him once to have him enslaved, so as never to return home. Odysseus was threatened with a similar fate at the hands of Circe, Calypso (of whose precedent Meroe is aware, 12), and the Sirens (**72–3, 75**). Here the narrator Aristomenes, in terror after his encounter with the witches, resolves never to return home again (19). Later in the novel we learn that Thelyphron was also kept by shame from returning home after his encounter with Thessalian witches (**105**). And Lucius's own encounter with the trainee witch Photis (**107**) makes him give up thoughts of returning home.

For Meroe's advanced age (7, 12) compare **91–2, 102**. For scoffing at the grandiose claims of magical professionals by confronting them with the lowliness of their station (8), see **19, 300**. For lamias (17) see **60**.

## 105   Thessalian witches, the Egyptian Zatchlas, and the reanimation of the Thelyphrons

Later ii A.D.

Apuleius
*Metamorphoses* 2.21–30

Latin

**21.** So Thelyphron made a pile of coverlets and leaned on his elbow to prop himself up on the couch. He stretched out his right hand and shaped it in the orators' style. He folded in the bottom two fingers, pointed the top two forward, and projected his unsheathed thumb upward. He rose gently as he began:

When I was a ward I set out from Miletus for the Olympic Games. I also wanted to come to this part of the famous province, so I toured all round Thessaly and arrived in Larissa. But my arrival was attended by the dark birds of ill omen. My money for the road was running out, so I went around the whole town in search of ways to relieve my poverty. Then I caught sight of a tall old man in the middle of the forum. He was standing on a stone and making a loud proclamation: if anyone was willing to watch over a dead man, offers would be heard. I addressed one of the passersby: "What's this I find? Are the dead in the habit of running away around here?"

"Shush!," he replied, "for you are just a boy and a complete stranger here. So you don't realize that you are in Thessaly, and that this is a place where witches [*sagae mulieres*] everywhere nibble bits off the faces of corpses, to use as magical supplies."

**22.** To this I said, "Tell me please, what does this watching of the dead consist of?"

"In the first place," he replied, "one must remain wide awake the whole night long. One must focus one's eyes continuously on the corpse, straining them and not allowing them to blink. One must never divert one's gaze, or even glance to the side, because those hateful women can skin-shift into any animal and sneak in secretly in new guise. They could easily better even of the eyes of the Sun, or of Justice. For they take on the forms of birds, or again of dogs and mice, and even of flies. Then, with their awful spells, they bury the watchers in sleep. No one could begin to estimate the number of ruses these evil women devise to service their lust. But no more than four or, perhaps, six gold pieces are offered in reward for this job, as deathly as it is. And oh yes!—the thing I almost left out: if a watcher does not return the copse in one piece the next morning, he is forced to repair any part of the corpse that has been chopped off or mutilated by having it cut from his own face."

**23.** In the light of this I worked up my courage and approached the herald at once. "You can stop shouting now," I said. "You have a watcher here, all present and correct. What's the reward?" "A thousand sesterces will be set aside for you," he said. "But I say, young man, be sure to guard the corpse properly against those wicked Harpies: it is that of the son of one of the town's first families." "You're speaking to me of irrelevancies," I said, "and complete trivialities. You're looking at a man of iron, a man who does not sleep, a man indeed more sharp-sighted than Lynceus or Argos, a man who is just one big eye!"

I had hardly finished. At once he led me through the city to a house. Its main doors were shut, but he ushered me in through a little door round the back. He took me into a shadowy room, its window-shutters closed. There he showed me the weeping wife swathed in black. He approached her and said, "This man has been hired to watch over your husband faithfully." She parted the strands of hair that hung before her face and revealed a face that was pretty even in grief. She looked at me. "I beg you," she said, "do your job as vigilantly as possible." "Don't worry," said I, "just get an appropriate gratuity ready."

**24.** The agreement made, she got up and took me into another bedroom. There lay the corpse, covered in bright linen. Seven witnesses were brought in. She unveiled the corpse with her hand and wept over it protractedly. Then she took an oath from all present and scrupulously exhibited each part of the corpse, while a secretary carefully made formal notes on tablets. "See," she said, "nose complete, eyes undamaged, ears safe, lips whole, chin sound. Good men of the city, bear witness to this." With this, the tablets were sealed and she made to go.

But I said, "Mistress, order them to provide me with all the things I'll need." "And what are those?," she said. "A large lamp," I said, "together with enough oil to keep it lit until daylight, hot water, pitchers of wine, a cup, and a dish heaped up with left-over food." She shook her head and said, "Off with you, fool. You seek to dine in this house of mourning and look to share our food, when there has been no sight of smoke in the place for so many days! Are you under the impression that you have come here to revel? Why don't you rather put on a show of mourning and tears, in keeping with the place?" With this she looked back to a maid and said, "Myrrhine, give him a lamp and oil quickly, shut the watcher in the bedroom, and leave him to it right away."

**25.** So I was left alone to comfort the corpse. I gave my eyes a rubbing and armed them for the night watch. I calmed my mind by singing, through twilight, evening, then bedtime, and finally the depth of the night. I was sinking under an increasing burden of fear, when suddenly a weasel crept in and stood opposite me. It directed a piercing stare toward me. I was disconcerted by the extraordinary self-confidence of this tiny animal. Eventually I said to it, "Off with you, dirty creature, go and hide with the mice you resemble! Otherwise, you will soon feel my might. Off with you!" It turned tail and disappeared at once from the room. But all of a sudden a profound sleep suddenly plunged me to the depth of an abyss. I slept so fast that not even Apollo of Delphi himself could easily have told which of the two of us lying there was the more dead. So lifeless was I, and so much in need of a watcher in turn, that I may as well not have been there.

**26.** The crowing of the crested race was just sounding the cessation of the night when at last I awoke and in abject terror ran to the corpse. I brought the light up to it, uncovered its face and scrutinized each part of it. Everything was there! Then the poor wife burst in, weeping and anxious, together with the witnesses I had met the day before. At once she threw herself over the body and smothered it with kisses. Then, by the light of the lamp, she checked everything. She turned, called for the steward Philodespotus, and told him to pay the good watcher his reward, without delay. The money was produced at once. "We are deeply grateful to you, young man, and, by Hercules, we shall henceforth number you among our friends for your conscientious service to us."

I was overjoyed at this unexpected profit, and distracted by the shiny gold pieces, which I turned over and over in my hand. "On the contrary, mistress," I said, "think of me as one of your servants, and whenever you need my services, don't hesitate to tell me."

I had hardly finished speaking when at once the household, cursing the bad omen I had uttered, snatched up what they could to use as weapons and attacked me. One punched my jaw with his fists, another jabbed my shoulders with his elbows, another again dug into my sides with open hands. They kicked out at me with their feet, pulled my hair, and tore my clothes. And so, torn to shreds like Pentheus, the arrogant Aonian youth, or Orpheus, the tuneful Pimpleian prophet, I was bustled out of the house.

**27.** As I composed myself in the adjacent street I recognized all too late that my remark had been improvident and ill-omened. I accepted that I had deserved all the blows I had received and more. At this point the dead man had just been brought out of the house for the final weeping and mourning. Since he was from the top drawer, he was being carried through the forum with all the pomp of a public funeral, in the traditional fashion. Then a grief-stricken old man ran up, dressed all in black, weeping and tearing out his venerable white hair. He seized hold of the bier with both hands, and spoke out in a strained voice, which was, however, continually interrupted by sobbing. "I implore you by your good faith, men of the city, and by your sense of public duty, come to the aid of your murdered citizen and exact strict revenge for the ultimate crime upon this wicked, criminal woman! It was she and no other who poisoned this unfortunate young man, my sister's son, to please his cuckold and to plunder his estate."

The old man kept voicing these pitiful complaints to each of us individually. In the meantime, the crowd began to turn nasty and to incline to believe the accusation because of its plausibility. They called out for fire, looked for stones, and urged the little boys to kill the woman. With appropriate crocodile tears she invoked all the gods as solemnly as she could, and disowned a crime so great.

**28.** The old man then responded, "Let us look to divine providence for a decision as to the truth. Here I have Zatchlas, a leading Egyptian prophet, who has already agreed with me, for a large sum, to bring back the ghost from the world below for a short time and to reanimate the corpse." With this he produced before us a young man dressed in linen and with palm-leaf sandals on his feet. His head was shaven bald. The old man showered his hands with kisses and held onto his knees. "Have pity on us, priest," he said, "have pity on us. By the stars of heaven, by the powers of the world below, by the elements of nature, by the silences of the night, by the inner sanctuaries of Coptus, by the rising of the Nile, by the mysteries of Memphis, by the rattles of Pharus, grant a brief loan of the sun and pour a bit of light into eyes sealed for ever. We do not oppose fate, nor do we deny the earth its right, but we ask for a tiny span of life to give us the comfort of vengeance."

The prophet was prevailed on by this and laid a sprig of a certain herb on the corpse's mouth and another on his breast. Then he faced east and prayed silently to the majesty of the rising sun. By this awesome show he brought his audience to the eager expectation of a miracle.

**29.** I shoved my way into the crowd and took up position on a raised rock just behind the bier and took the fascinating scene in with my eyes. First the dead man's chest swelled out, then an artery throbbed in jolts, and finally his body was suffused by his soul. The corpse rose, and the young man gave voice: "Why, I beg you, do you restore me to the functions of life, albeit a life so brief, when I have already drunk from Lethe and am swimming in the Stygian waters? Stop now, I pray, stop, and leave me to my peace."

These were the words that emanated from the corpse, but the prophet said, more fervently, "Why won't you tell the people all the details and shed light on the mystery of your death? Or don't you believe that I have the power to invoke the Furies with my spells, or that I have the power to have your weary limbs tortured?"

The corpse responded from his bier and addressed himself to the people, groaning from the bottom of his heart: "I was killed by the evil crafts of my new bride, the victim of a poison drink. I made over my warm bed to her adulterous lover."

Then his excellent wife, bold as ever, impiously challenged her husband as he demonstrated her guilt and began to argue with him. The people fell in tumult, and divided into opposite camps, one group insisting that the wicked woman should at once be buried alive together with the body of her husband, the other insisting that no faith should be placed in the lies of a corpse.

**30.** But what the young man had to say next put an end to the delaying. For again he drew out a deep groan and said, "I will give it you, I will give you clear proof that I speak pure truth, and, moreover, I shall tell you something that no one knows or has divined." Then he pointed me out with his finger. "For while this shrewd watcher was attentively guarding my body, some old-women witches [*cantatrices*] threatened my remains. To this end they repeatedly shifted shape, but in vain, because they could not get the better of his zealous diligence. In the end they threw a mist of sleep over him and buried him in deep oblivion. Then they summoned me by my name until my slow joints and cold limbs began to strain to comply with their magical art, struggling heavily. But since this man was actually alive, and merely dead with sleep, and because he is my namesake, he rose unknowingly in response to his name and walked automatically like a lifeless ghost. The doors to the bedroom had been locked tight, but he suffered the butchery in my place with first his nose and then his ears being cut off through a hole. To tidy up after their trick, they molded some wax into the shape of his chopped-off ears, fitted them onto him in exact fashion, and got him a nose like his own. And now the poor man stands here, after winning not a reward for work but compensation for mutilation."

I was petrified by these words and made to test my face. I put my hand to my nose and grasped it. It came off. I felt my ears. They fell away. The people pointed at me with their fingers and nodded at me, and there was an outbreak of laughter. Drenched in cold sweat, I escaped between the feet of those around me. In this mutilated and ridiculous state I could not take myself back home again, but I have concealed the wounds to my ears by growing my hair long on both sides. For decency's sake I have covered the ugly scar of my nose with this tightly fitted piece of linen.

THIS LIVELY TALE BLENDS THE SINISTER with the humorous. For a witch's collection of magical supplies (21 etc.) see **107**. It is curious that the witches should make life difficult for themselves by attempting to cut off Thelyphron's facial parts from outside the room and through a chink in the wall (30), when they can and indeed already have entered the room in animal form. No doubt Apuleius banishes them from the room at this point in order to explain their mistake. It is unlikely that the witches would have considered the body parts of the living Thelyphron an acceptable substitute for those of the dead one: their possession and manipulation would not give them control over any ghost. Wax is an appropriate material from which to make the prostheses, since it was commonly used to make the voodoo dolls that stood for entire fleshly bodies (see **89–90, 99, 236, 238, 239, 243, 245–6**). Since the widow is revealed to have poisoned her husband (29), and since there was a generally close association between witchcraft and poisoning (see **76–81**), we may assume that she is herself a witch. It remains unclear whether she participates in the mutilation of her own husband, or is indeed to be identified with the witch who transforms herself into the sleep-casting weasel (25; compare 22, 30). For shape-shifting see **115, 139–43**. For sleep-casting (22, 25, 30) see **66, 68, 71**. Once again the witches' magical powers, whatever their sort, are employed primarily in the service of love (22; see **97–103**).

For Egyptian sorcerers (28) see **53–6**. As here, they are usually portrayed as priests in their own terms. Zatchlas's appearance, bald head and linen garment, is typical of the Greek notion of an Egyptian priest (compare Herodotus 2.37). Egyptian sorcerers are inseparable from their inner sanctuaries (**46, 53–4**), and Zatchlas is appealed to in the name of them.

Of all the supplies the living Thelyphron requests for his watch, only the lamp is provided (24). Ghosts (we must assume that one comes to reanimate the dead Thelyphron) are often found in association with lamps (compare **115**), whether this is simply because they belong in the night when one sees with a lamp, because they are seen in the flickering and shadowing of the lamp, or because of an association with lychnomancy (see **165–6**).

For Zatchlas's reanimation (28), compare **155–7**, where the key features that this particular reanimation narrative shares with the others in the Graeco-Roman tradition are reviewed. The Sun, a favorite god of the Greek magical papyri (see **189**), is an awkward god to appeal to for necromancy, which typically takes place in the dead of night. Hence the compromise of performing the divination at dawn. Lethe (29) was the spring of "Forgetting" from which all souls were held to drink on entry to the underworld. It is unclear how, having drunk from this, the ghost can remember the circumstances of its death. The people debate the likely truthfulness of the ghost and its corpse, but in general necromancy had the name of the most reliable form of prophecy (see **96**). For the supplying of "proof" by a ghost in necromancy see also **150**.

For Orpheus (26) see **19–20, 71**.

## 106  Witches steal the body of a dead boy

Ca. 66 A.D.

Petronius *Satyricon* 63

Latin

I myself will tell you a tale to make you shudder: an ass upon the roof-tiles. When I still had my hair long (for from being a boy I led a life of "Chian" luxury), our master's favorite boy died. He was a pearl, and delightful in every respect. While his pitiful mother was mourning over him, and many of us were feeling miserable about it, the witches [*strigae*] suddenly started to screech. You would have thought it was a dog chasing a hare. We had at that time a Cappadocian slave, tall, quite daring, and strong. He boldly drew his sword and ran out of the door, carefully binding up his left hand in place of a shield. He ran one of the women through the middle, round about here—gods preserve the part of my body I indicate. We heard a groan, but—honestly, I won't lie—we did not actually see them. Our great hulk of a man returned within and threw himself down on the bed. His whole body was black and blue, as if he'd been beaten with whips (this was obviously because an evil hand had touched him.) We shut the door and returned to what we were doing, but, when his mother embraced the body of her son, as she touched it she realized that it was just a tiny thing made of straw. It had no heart or guts, nothing. You see, the witches had stolen the boy and left a straw doll in his place. I beg you to believe it. Wise women do exist, night-women do exist, and what is up, they can make down. But that hulking man never properly recovered after this adventure, and indeed he went mad and died a few days later.

THE AUTHOR IS ALMOST certainly to be identified with the courtier whom Nero compelled to suicide in 66 A.D., Petronius Arbiter. Only a fraction of this massive novel survives, the brilliant *Dinner of Trimalchio*, from which this extract derives, constituting its most substantial fragment. It is the freedman Trimalchio himself who narrates this tale to his guests, following on directly from Niceros's werewolf story (141). From the coincidence in theme between this tale and that of 105, we may assume that the witch on the hunt for body parts was part of the stock-in-trade of the Latin novel.

The witches here evidently have the power of invisibility and are able to use this to beat the Cappadocian; see 72, 274, 276–7. His ensuing madness and death may indicate that they also do something more sinister to him. The explanation of his bruising, here enclosed in round brackets, is thought to be an interpolation into the original text. The narrative leaves us uncertain as to what the witches actually do with the dead boy: they may take him whole and simply substitute a staw doll, or they may hollow him out, remove his organs, and leave the remnants stuffed with straw, in line with the use of wax prostheses to replace the stolen parts in the Apuleius tale (105). The witches' ability to make "what is up . . . down" may be a reference to the drawing-down of the moon, see 214–23.

## 107 The Thessalian witch Pamphile and her transformations

Later ii A.D.

Apuleius
*Metamorphoses* 3.15–25

Latin

15. Photis cheered up again. "Allow me first," she said, "please, to lock the bedroom doors carefully, in case I commit some great crime by talking loosely, profanely, and indiscreetly." With this she pushed in the bolts and firmly engaged the hook. Then she returned to me, embraced me round the neck with both arms and spoke in a subdued and barely audible voice: "I am frightened and just full of fear to uncover the secrets of this house and to reveal my mistress's arcane mysteries. But I think you will be more discreet than I, in view of your learning. Not only were you born into a noble family, not only do you have great character, but you have been initiated into many cults and you can be trusted not to divulge such sacred rites. So, whatever I commit to the holy inner sanctum of your heart, be sure to keep it shut in that enclosure, please, and repay the openness of my revelation with the rigor of your silence. The love I feel for you drives me to divulge to you things that I am the only mortal to know. I'm going to tell you now all about the setup of our house, and my mistress's marvelous secret spells, by which she makes the ghosts her servants, by which she throws the stars into disorder, by which she forces her will upon the gods, and by which the elements are brought under her power. She depends most on the power of this craft when she has taken a shine to some young man with a good body. And, indeed, this happens to her all the time.

16. "At the moment she is passionately in love with a very attractive lad from Boeotia, and she is feverishly employing all the resources and mechanisms of her craft against him. I heard her this evening, with my own ears, I say, I heard her threatening the Sun. Because it was not departing from the sky quickly enough and

making way for night soon enough, the time at which she can perform the charms of her magic, she threatened to bury it in a misty cloud and continual darkness. Yesterday, on her way back from the baths, she caught sight of him by chance sitting in the barber's. She told me to steal some of his hair secretly. It lay on the ground where it had fallen after being cut off. But the barber found me as I was carefully and stealthily gathering it up and, because we are in any case notorious throughout the town for our evil techniques, he grabbed hold of me and shouted at me meanly: 'You are the lowest of the low! Is there no end to your constant theft of choice young men's hair? If you do not now put an end to this criminal activity, nothing shall stop me hauling you before the magistrates!' He matched his actions to his words. He stuck his hand down my dress and felt around, and angrily pulled out from between my breasts the locks I had already managed to hide there. I was in anguish. Bearing in mind what my mistress is like, and that she usually becomes furious over failures like this and gives me a savage beating, I began planning to run away, but I abandoned the idea when I thought of you.

17. "But as I came away from there in misery at the prospect of returning with absolutely nothing, I noticed a man trimming some goatskin bags with scissors. I saw that they were tightly sealed and inflated and hanging up, and that their hair lay on the floor. The hair was yellow and in this respect very similar to that of the young Boeotian man. So I scooped up an amount of it and gave it to my mistress, concealing the truth. As night began, before you brought yourself back from dinner, my lady Pamphile, by now having lost her mind, went up onto a shingled terrace on the other side of the house. It is open and exposed to the winds and affords views in all directions, especially the east. She frequents this place secretly, since it is so useful for her magical crafts. First she organized her laboratory of death with her usual equipment. It was full of every sort of spice, metal tablets with undecipherable inscriptions, and preserved pieces of shipwrecks, and it included an array of quite a few parts from mourned and even from buried corpses. Here there were noses and fingers, there nails from the crucified, flesh still clinging to them. Elsewhere she kept the gore of the slain and mutilated skulls twisted from the jaws of wild animals.

18. "Then she made incantations over some palpitating entrails and made libations with a range of liquids, water from a spring, cow's milk, mountain honey, and also with honey-wine. Then she plaited the hairs together and laid them on the hot coals to burn, together with a range of scents. Then, all at once, the bodies to which the hairs that were smoking and whistling in the fire belonged acquired human animation through the irresistible power of her magical craft and the hidden force exerted by the deities she had put under constraint. They felt, they heard, they walked, and followed the scent of the hair they had shed. Instead of the young Boeotian man it was they who were throwing themselves against our doors in their eagerness to get in. That was when you came along, soaked in booze and misled by the sudden darkness of the night. You boldly drew your sword and armed yourself like the crazy Ajax. But whereas he attacked live sheep and butchered whole flocks of them, you were far braver, for you took the breath out of three inflated goatskins. So you laid the enemy low without shedding blood, and now I embrace not a killer of men but a killer of bags."

19. Photis's witty speech made me laugh, and I responded with some joking of my own: "So now I can count this as my first heroic action, on the pattern of the twelve labors of Hercules, comparing the three slaughtered bags to the triple body of Geryon or the three heads of Cerberus. But if you want me to forgive you from the bottom of my heart for this misdemeanor, through which you plunged me into

so much trouble, grant me a thing for which I plead in my sincerest prayers. Let me observe your mistress when she is employing this divine craft, when she is calling on the gods and, at all costs, when she is shape-shifting. For I burn to witness magic with my own eyes, although you yourself do not seem to me to be a novice in these things, or to lack experience of them. I know it well and am proof of the fact. Hitherto I have always scorned the embrace of women, but now you have me in your power like a bondman or a bought slave, albeit not an unwilling one, with your flashing eyes, blushing cheeks, glossy hair, French kissing, and sweet-scented breasts. I am no longer homesick, and I am no longer preparing to return there. The only thing that matters now is spending the night with you."

20. "Lucius," she replied, "how I wish I could give you what you want, but, her difficult personality aside, she always buries herself in solitude and makes sure she is completely alone before she performs secret rites of this sort. But satisfying your request is more important to me than my own safety. I'll watch out for a suitable opportunity and carefully organize it for you. Just promise me, as I said to begin with, that you won't breathe a word about such an important thing."

As we talked like this our desire for each other warmed up our passion and our limbs. We tore off all our clothes, and in this state of complete nakedness held a revel in honor of Venus. When I was worn out Photis kindly let me have sex with her as if she was a boy. When we could no longer keep our eyes open, after staying awake so long, sleep poured over them and held onto them well into the next day.

21. We passed several nights in this kind of pleasure until one day Photis ran up to me quivering with excitement. She told me that her mistress, since she was having no success in consummating her love with her other techniques, was going to grow feathers and become a bird during the following night and fly down to the man she desired. Accordingly, she bade me prepare myself carefully to watch this great spectacle. Then, around the first watch of the night, she led me herself up to that upper room. We tiptoed quietly. She told me to watch what went on through a crack in the door. This is what I saw.

First Pamphile divested herself of all her clothes. She opened a casket and took a few little boxes from it. She took the top off one of these and scooped some lotion out of it. For a while she worked it between her palms and then she smeared herself all over with it, from the ends of her toenails to the hairs on the top of her head. She had a mysterious conversation with her lamp and set her limbs fluttering. As they gently flowed, soft down sprung from them, and strong feathers grew. Her nose grew hard and became hooked, and her toenails curved round into talons. An owl was made of Pamphile. With this she issued a mournful screech and, testing herself, jumped up from the ground, a little higher each time. Then she pulled herself aloft and flew out of the house, using the full power of her wings.

22. She had shifted shape of her own accord and by the exercise of her powerful techniques. But I, even though the victim of no incantation, was rooted to the floor with amazement at the miracle that had been achieved before my eyes, so that I seemed to be anything but Lucius. I was out of my mind and distracted to insanity. It was like a waking dream. I kept rubbing my eyes, and tried to discover whether I was actually awake. At last I came back to earth. I grabbed Photis's hand and put it to my eyes. "I beg you," I said, "while the opportunity presents itself, give me a great and distinctive token of your love. Get me some of the lotion from that same box, I beg you by your little breasts, my honey. Keep me as your slave forever by conferring upon me a benefaction I can never repay. Make me stand beside you like a winged Cupid beside his Venus."

"What are you saying?" she said, "You're a tricky fox, lover-boy! Do you want me to hack into my own legs with an axe? I can hardly preserve you, in your un-armed state, from the Thessalian she-wolves. Where will I look for you if you have wings? When will I see you?"

**23.** "May the gods in heaven keep me from that crime," I said. "Even though I flew all across the sky, borne aloft on the wings of an eagle, and became the trusty messenger of Jupiter on high and the happy bearer of his arms, still I would fly straight home to my nest after such a noble flight. I swear by that sweet knot in your hair, with which you have bound my spirit, that I prefer no other woman to Photis. Now this notion too comes to mind. When once I have anointed myself and put on the guise of this kind of bird, I will have to keep well away from all the houses. For what a beautiful and delightful lover the women will find in an owl! What of the fact that we see that, when these birds of the night enter a house, they are assiduously captured and fixed to the door, so as to dispel through torture the threat of doom that their ill-omened flight brings upon the household? But—a thing I almost forgot to ask about – by what utterance or action shall I slough off these feathers and return to being Lucius again?"

"There is no need to be concerned about this," she said. "For my mistress has shown me the various substances which can return such creatures to human form. You should not think she did this out of any kindness, but so that I could be ready for her upon her return with the remedy to restore her. See what tiny, common-or-garden herbs produce so great an effect: put a little anise in spring water, together with laurel leaves, and apply externally and internally."

**24.** She repeated this over and over and, with great trepidation, sneaked into the room and took a box from the casket. First I hugged the box to me and smoth-ered it with kisses. I prayed that it bless me with a happy flight. I quickly tore all my clothes off, then keenly thrust my hand into the box and drew out a large blob of lotion, which I rubbed over every limb of my body. Next, I hung out my arms and flapped them one after the other, and tried to make myself into a bird. But there was no down, and there were no feathers. Rather, as was clear to see, my hair thickened into bristles, and my tender skin hardened into leather. All the fingers on the ends of my hands reduced in number and coalesced into undivided hooves. A large tail was produced from the base of my spine. By now my face was huge, my mouth long, my nostrils gaped and my lips hung down. At the same time my ears shot up high and grew shaggy. There was not one good thing about this pitiful transformation, except that my genitals increased in size, although I was no longer in a position to embrace Photis. Without the means to help myself, I looked over all my body and saw that I was not a bird but an ass. Although minded to complain about what Photis had done, I no longer had the human ability to speak or gesticu-late, so I did the only thing I could, which was to droop my lower lip, look at her askance with tearful eyes, and reproach her silently.

As soon as she saw what I had become, she slapped her head hard and shouted, "Ah me, I've had it! I got it wrong because of my nerves and through working too quickly. I mistook the box, because they look the same. It's a good job that the remedy for restoring your form is quick to hand. For you only need to nib-ble some roses to lose your ass-shape and return immediately to being my Lucius again. I wish I had made us some garlands this evening, as I usually do, so that you would not have to hold on even for one night. But at first dawn I'll rush out and get the antidote for you."

PAMPHILE IS GIVEN SOME OF THE commonplace powers of a Thessalian, such as constraint of the gods (15, 18) and control of the heavenly bodies (16). She seems to direct her amazing range of powers to the Thessalian's usual end, the achievement of love (15, 21, etc.). Her directly erotic magic seeks to inflame the Boeotian youth with desire for her through the sympathetic burning of his hair (18). As the barber indicates, the theft of locks of hair to serve as "stuff" in erotic attraction magic is a common occurrence in Thessaly (16). The summary of Pamphile's powers (15) indicates the centrality of ghost manipulation to the witches' magic. Her magical rites are presented as akin to mysteries; Photis's words to Lucius evoke the imagery of an inner sanctuary appropriate to such things (15, 20). And in his eagerness to have such "mysteries" explained to him Lucius resembles Thessalus (53).

The description of Pamphile's witch's laboratory (17) is of particular interest. The metal tablets with indecipherable inscriptions are evidently curse tablets with *voces magicae* and perverted forms of writing (see 168–84). Shipwreck material is of value for its connection with those lost at sea and therefore forever unburied and restless; see 211. Like Pamphile, Lucan's Erictho too sought material from the corpses of criminals (96). For the value of wolf-worried corpse parts, see 92.

For shape-shifting see 115, with commentary. In Pamphile's shape-shifting magic (21-4) an external lotion is used to effect the transformation to an animal, and an ingested substance effects the transformation back to human. This is the reverse of Circe's transformation magic (72). The nature of the contribution of Pamphile's lamp to the transformation process here is obscure (21); elsewhere we are told that she uses it for lychnomancy (165).

# 8

# *Ghosts*

## THE UNTIMELY DEAD AND THE DEAD BY VIOLENCE

Ghosts that were wont to manifest themselves, and ghosts that were relatively active and therefore convenient for magical exploitation, tended to belong to one of the following (often overlapping) categories of the "restless" dead. It is unclear at what point this (in any case shifting) categorization was developed, although it appears to be latent already in Homer (**144**).

1. *Aôroi*: "those dead before their time." Those cheated of their full stint of life bitterly stayed back to haunt the land of the living of which they had been deprived. In theory anyone who died of anything other than of natural causes in old age could generate a ghost restless qua *aôros*, although as a class *aôroi* tended to be conceptualized primarily as the ghosts of children or babies.
2. *Bi(ai)othanatoi*: "those dead by violence." These included the battle-dead and executed criminals, although murder victims and suicides provided the bitterest ghosts in this class.
3. *Agamoi*: "those dead before marriage." Both male and female ghosts could be assigned this category, although the female ones were regarded as particularly bitter, insofar as marriage and the motherhood consequent upon it were a woman's defining rights in antiquity.
4. *Ataphoi*: "those deprived of burial." Whatever the circumstances of death, a ghost could not achieve rest without the due funeral rights. These were importantly distinct from the mere insertion of the corpse into a hole in the ground, and indeed the concealment of a dead body in precisely this way is often presented as the chief obstacle to the peace of its soul.

**108**  **The ghost of Patroclus**

vii B.C. or earlier

Homer *Iliad* 23.62–76

Greek

Sleep poured around him in sweetness, seized Achilles and released the concerns of his heart. For he had worn out his glorious limbs by chasing Hector to windy Ilium. The ghost of unfortunate Patroclus came upon him, resembling the living man in all things, in stature, in his beautiful eyes, and in his voice, and it was dressed in clothes resembling his. The soul stood over his head and spoke to him: "You sleep, but you have forgotten me, Achilles! You cared for me when I was alive, but not now I'm dead. Bury me as quickly as possible, so that

I may pass through the gates of Hades. The souls ward me back a distance, the ghosts of the dead, and they do not yet allow me to mingle with them beyond the river, but in this condition I wander about the broad-gated house of Hades. Give me your hand, I beg you through my tears. For I shall not come again from Hades, when you have given me the fire that is my due."

ACHILLES ENCOUNTERS THE GHOST OF PATROCLUS in what seems to have been the usual way of encountering ghosts in antiquity, namely, through sleep; see **149**. Preparations are under way for a magnificent and fitting funeral for the great warrior, but the ghost no longer cares about this. All it wants are the basic rites so that it can achieve peace and join the other ghosts. In antiquity there were a great many conflicting conceptualizations of the physical relationship between the world of the living and that of the dead, and of the internal organization of the latter. Here the dead seem to be separated from the land of the living by an (unnamed) river and the ghost itself does not seem to know whether it is in Hades. In the *Odyssey* Odysseus travels to the world of the dead by crossing one river, Oceanus, and then walking to the confluence of three more, Acheron, Cocytus, and Pyriphlegethon (**144**). For an ancient discussion of this passsage see **112**.

## 109 Ghosts hover around their tombs

Earlier iv B.C.

Plato *Phaedo* 81c–d

Greek

[Socrates addresses Cebes.] "But I think it [a soul excessively devoted to the things of the body] is shot through with a corporeal element. The company of and the communion with the body ingrains this element, on account of the soul's constant association with the body and its devotion to it."

"Yes."

"One must imagine this corporeal element to be burdensome, heavy, earthy, and visible. The sort of soul that has it is weighed down and drawn back to the realm of the visible, in fear of the unseen [*aïdous*] and of Hades [*Haïdou*], as it is said, and rolls [*kulindoumenē*] around gravestones and tombs, around which in fact some shadowy manifestations of souls are seen, such as are the ghosts that souls of this kind produce, souls that have not been purely released, but still participate in the realm of the visible, and for that reason are seen."

"Yes, that is likely, Socrates."

"Likely it is, Cebes. And it is likely that they are not at all the souls of the good, but the souls of the bad, that are compelled to wander about such places paying the penalty for their former nurturing, which was an evil one. And they wander around until they are once again imprisoned in a body because of their desire for the corporeal part that ever accompanies them. As you would expect, they are bound into characters of the sort that they happened to have prepared themselves for in life."

"What sort of characters do you mean, Socates?"

"For example, those who have devoted themselves to gluttony, rough sex, and drunkenness and have not scrupulously avoided these things are likely to enter into donkeys and similar beasts. Don't you agree?"

"Yes, what you say is likely."

"Whereas those who have privileged injustice, tyranny, and robbery are likely to enter into wolves, hawks, and kites. Or where else do we think such souls go?"

"Into such animals, of course," said Cebes.

THE PYTHAGOREAN BACKGROUND TO THE NOTIONS of reincarnation and of the virtuous practicing the separation of the soul in life is evident. Indeed Socrates' interlocutor, Cebes, is explicitly portrayed as a Pythagorean (see **1–9**). The notion of ghosts hanging around graves is founded in popular belief (see also **297**), but the precise degree of Plato's manipulation of this belief is, as often, difficult to gauge. In general such ghosts are likely to have been held to derive from the dead-before-their-time, who tarried on earth to the extent of a full life-span (compare **110, 112**), or from those whose burial had been imperfect. The motion of the ghosts around the graves is described in similar terms to those used of sorcerers and evocators when engaged in their manipulation (compare **30**).

## 110    Categories of the restless dead debarred from Hades proper

19 B.C.

Virgil *Aeneid* 6.325–30, 426–443

Latin

**325.** [On the near side of the Styx, the Sibyl speaks:] All the crowd you see here is destitute and unburied. This is Charon, the ferryman. These, whom he transports over the wave, are the buried. He may not carry the souls across the awful banks and the rumbling waters before their bones have found peace in a resting place. They wander over and flit about these shores for a hundred years. Only then are they admitted to the pools they have longed for and can revisit them.

**426.** [On the far side of the Styx:] At once he heard voices, a great squalling and the weeping souls of children, deprived of sweet life on the very threshold of it. The black day had snatched them from the breast, stolen them away, and plunged them in bitter death. Adjacent to them were those who had been condemned to death on a false charge. These dwelling-places are not given without lot or judge. Minos is on the bench, and shakes the lot. He summons the court of the silent dead and listens to men's lives and the charges based on them. The next region is occupied by the sad folk who innocently accomplished their death with their own hand and, in hatred of the light, forfeited their lives. How they would be willing now to endure poverty and hard toil in the air above! But divine law stands in the way, and the sad marsh with its revolting water binds them, and the interposed Styx pens them in nine times over.

Not far from here the Fields of Mourning are to be seen, extending on all sides. This is what they call them. Here obscure paths and a surrounding myrtle grove conceal those whom hard love devoured with its cruel wasting. Even in death their love remains with them.

FOR VIRGIL ALL CATEGORIES OF THE restless dead remain liminal. The unburied are confined to the living-side bank of the Styx for a hundred years before they may cross (**325–30**). A hundred years symbolically represents the full span of a human life; one might have thought such a delay more fitting for the untimely dead, in view of Tertullian's remarks (**112**). But these reside rather on the dead-side bank (**426–43**), although still outside the underworld proper. They are divided into two main groups, according to whether or not they died by violence. Those who did not are characterized as wailing babies. The group that died by violence is then further subdivided into four: those unjustly executed, general suicides, love-suicides, and (following on from the quoted excerpt) the battle-dead.

## 111 A taxonomy of ghosts

Later ii A.D.

Apuleius *De deo Socratis* 15

Latin

Another variety of "demon" consists of the human soul that abandons its body when it has finished its services in life. I note that in the old Latin language these used to be termed *lemures*. Now, to some of these *lemures* was allotted the care of their descendants. These occupy houses with a propitious and peaceful attitude, and they are called *Lares* of the family. But others, because of their misdeeds in life, are punished with a kind of exile, namely, with the denial of a home and with undirected wanderings. They can only be harmless terrors to good men, but they are dangerous to bad men. People usually call these *larvae*. When it is unclear what category of ghost one is dealing with, whether it is one of the *Lares* or the *larvae*, one uses the term *Di Manes*. No doubt the addition of the term "gods" [*di*] here is honorific, because it is only applied to those among the demons who have conducted their life with justice and wisdom, who have subsequently been awarded temples and rites by men as being divine powers, and who are in receipt of observances from the people. Examples of these are Amphiaraus in Boeotia, Mopsus in Africa, Osiris in Egypt. Every people has their own, but all worship Asclepius.

APULEIUS'S CHARACTERIZATIONS OF *DI MANES* AS a general and honorific term for all ghosts, of *Lares* as a term for benign protectors of households, and of *larvae* as a term for bad and dangerous ghosts accord well enough with the usages of other authors. His characterization of *lemures*, however, does not. These too are generally conceived of as a bad and dangerous subcategory, like *larvae*; see, especially, Ovid *Fasti* 5.419–92.

## 112 The untimely dead and the dead-by-violence

Ca. 200 A.D.

Tertullian *De Anima* 56–7 (edited)

Latin

56. It was held that the unburied were not accepted into the underworld until they had received the due rites. We learn this from Homer's Patroclus, who demands burial from Achilles in his dreams, since he could not otherwise approach the entrance to the underworld, as the shades of the buried were keeping him far away from it [*Iliad* 23.72]. We recognize, however, that Homer's creativity here exceeds poetic license. His concern for the due burial of the dead was equaled by his censure of the delay in accomplishment, which is so harmful to souls. . . . And they say that souls that experience death before their time wander about until they complete the remainder of the period for which they would have lived if they had not died early.

57. Either it is excellent to be kept here with the "untimely dead" [*ahori: aôroi*] or it is awful to be kept here with the "dead-by-violence" [*biaeothanati: biaiothanatoi*], to employ the terms now voiced by the source of such beliefs, namely magic—Ostanes, Typhon, Dardanus, Damigeron, Nectabis, and Berenice. A famous text promises to evocate even souls that have been laid to rest at their proper age, even souls separated from their bodies by a just death, and even souls dispatched with prompt burial. What then shall we say of magic? The same as almost everyone: that it is deceit. But the nature of its deceit is apparent only to Christians, because we know the superhuman powers of evil, by virtue of an awareness developed through opposition to them, not, of course, through association with them. Our dealings with this multifarious pestilence of the human race, this deviser of all error, this destroyer of salvation and soul alike, are not to invite it in but to overpower it and expel it. So too the nature of magic is apparent to us. It is of course a second idolatry, in which demons pretend that they are dead people, just as in the

case of idolatry proper, demons pretend that they are gods. And why not? For the "gods" too are dead. And so the untimely dead and the dead-by-violence are actually invoked on the principle that it seems credible that those souls in particular that a cruel and untimely death has violently and unfairly wrenched from life should contribute to violence and unfairness, as if in retaliation for their injury. But demons work under the cover of these souls, particularly those demons that were within them when they were still alive and that had driven them to deaths of this sort. For we have actually suggested that almost every man has his own demon, and many are aware that premature or violent deaths are effected by the work of these demons, although people impute them to chance. Unless I am deceived, we can prove by facts the deceit perpetrated by evil spirits that conceal themselves in the characters of the dead. Thus, in exorcisms a spirit sometimes declares that it is one of its host's ancestors, sometimes a gladiator or a beast-fighter, or otherwise even a god. In doing this it makes it its chief concern to exclude the truth we declare, so that we may not find it easy to believe that all souls are gathered into the underworld, and so that they may interfere with our belief in the day of judgment and the resurrection. Even so the demon, after attempting to trick the spectators, is overwhelmed by the impact of divine grace and confesses the truth against its will. So too in that other variety of magic, which is held to tear out of the underworld souls already at rest and display them to view, the power of deceit is no different, but it is obviously more effective, since an apparition is made manifest, a body being attached to it. And it is no great achievement to evade the outer eyes of a man whose mental insight is easily blinded. The snakes that came from the magicians' staffs did indeed appear as solid bodies to Pharaoh and the Egyptians [Exodus 7.10]. But the truth of Moses gobbled up their lies. The mages Simon and Elymas tried many tricks of this sort against the apostles, but the blindness with which they were afflicted did not emanate from trickery. What is new about an unclean spirit mimicking the truth? See, even today, the audacity of the disciples of this same heretic Simon is so great that they promise to bring even the souls of prophets from the underworld. And I believe that they make this promise because they can achieve it—through a lie. For all that time ago the ventriloquist [*pythonicus*] spirit was allowed to feign the soul of Samuel, when Saul consulted the dead, after consulting God. But let us not come to a pass where we believe that the soul of any saint, still less that of a prophet, can be evocated by a demon. We are taught that "Satan himself is transfigured into an angel of light," rather more into a man of light, and that in the end he will declare that he is God, and that he will bring forth portentous signs, "to overthrow, if it were possible, the chosen." The demon did not exactly hesitate then to declare that he was a prophet of God, and this to Saul in particular, within whom it was itself lodging. So, you should not think that one person produced the apparition and another one consulted it, but that the same spirit, in both the false prophet and in the apostate, easily accomplished the lie it had made them believe. Because of this spirit, Saul's treasurehouse was in his heart, but God certainly wasn't. And so Saul saw the spirit that masqueraded as Samuel by the agency of this same spirit, which had made him believe that he would see Samuel, because he was led to believe by the spirit he saw. But it could be objected that the dead are often seen in nocturnal apparitions for a reason. For the Nasamones take their personal oracles by tarrying on the graves of their ancestors, as Heraclides, Nymphodorus, and Herodotus [4.172] wrote, and the Celts spend the night at the tombs of their brave men for the same reason, as Nicander tells us [F117 Gow and Schofield]. However, we do not experience the dead in dreams any more truthfully than we experience the living in them, but we regard the dead in dreams in the same way as the living and indeed everything seen in dreams. For things are not true simply because they seem to be so, but because they are fulfilled. Faith in dreams is declared in accordance with their outcome, not their appearance. Moreover the Lord, speaking through Abraham, established it well enough that the way out of the underworld lies open for no soul at all, in the parable of the poor man at peace and the rich man in lamentation. He said that no messenger could be dispatched back from there to tell us about the organization of the underworld [Luke 16.26]. On this occasion at any rate one might have thought that it could have been allowed, to bring about belief in Moses and the prophets. But even if the virtue of God has called certain souls back into their bodies as proof of his rights, there will never, just because of that, be anything in common between God's faith and the brazen arrogance of mages, the deceit of dreams, and the license of poets. There are cases of actual resurrection, when God's virtue, working through the prophets or Christ or the apostles, restores souls to bodies. In these cases it is inevitable, because of the solid, physical, and fulfilled truth of the resurrected body, that the shape of truth is such as to make you judge every incorporeal manifestation of the dead to be mere trickery.

TERTULLIAN'S EXCLUSION OF MAGIC FROM CHRISTIANITY and his association of it with evil demons anticipates later Christian approaches to the subject.

By attributing the development of the standard categorizations of the restless dead to Ostanes and others, Tertullian demonstrates the importance of such concepts for ghost-manipulation in magic. As a Christian, Tertullian knows that on death all souls alike are gathered directly into the underworld to await the day of judgment, and that none of them tarry on the surface or can return to it. Hence, the supposed ghosts or souls of the restless dead exploited in magic are, he argues, not what they seem. Rather, they are usually the masquerading personal demons of the respective dead, evil in nature, and responsible for their unhappy deaths in the first place. It is unclear whether the demon at work in the witch of Endor's supposed evocation of Samuel, which took up residence in Saul and in the witch herself, was the demon of the dead Samuel; compare **34**. The "famous text" promising difficult varieties of evocation is unidentifiable. For the notion of magic as deceit, see **14–7**. For the performance of necromancy by sleeping on the grave of a dead person see **59**.

The list of great magicians and sorcerers associated with the doctrine of the restless dead blends the oriental with the Egyptian. For Ostanes and Dardanus, see **45**; Nectabis is an alternate form of Nectanebo, for whom see **55**; for Simon (Magus) see **65**. Seth-Typhon is the familiar underworld god of the Graeco-Egyptian magical papyri. Damigeron was the supposed author of a Hellenistic Greek treatise on the magical powers of stones, which survives to us in Latin translation (for which see Halleux and Schamp 1985). Elymas was the Jewish sorcerer blinded by Paul (Acts 13.6–12).

For demons masquerading as dead people see **43**. For exorcism see **127–32**; it is implicit here that the demon is forced, as usual, to confess its identity in the course of the exorcism. For necromancy see **144–62**.

## 113  The ghosts of the Marathon battlefield

ii A.D.
Pausanias 1.32.4–5
Greek

[At the site of the battle of Marathon:] All night long there one can hear the sound of horses neighing and men at war. It has never been good for anyone to go there in the deliberate attempt to get a clear look, but the anger of the demons is not directed against those who find themselves there accidentally and for some other reason.

These demons receive worship from the Marathonians, who identify them as the heroes who died in the battle. They also worship Marathon, after whom the town is named, and Heracles, claiming to have been the first among the Greeks to consider Heracles a god. They say that there was a man in the battle line, a peasant to judge from his appearance and equipment. This man slew many of the barbarians with a plowshare, but was nowhere to be seen after the battle. The Athenians asked the god about him, but they received no reply, other than the instruction to give honor to Echetlas as a hero. They have made a trophy from white stone. The Athenians claim that they gave the Medes due burial, it being universal religious practice to conceal bodies in the earth, but I could find no trace of a tomb. There was neither any barrow nor any other marker there to be seen, but they evidently took them and threw them carelessly into a pit.

AT THE FAMOUS BATTLE OF MARATHON in 490 B.C. the Athenians and Plataeans heroically thwarted the first Persian attempt to invade the Greek mainland. The ghosts that continued to haunt the battlefield will have done so as dead-by-violence, and perhaps also, if Persian, as deprived of due burial. The archaeological investigation of the site has neatly confirmed Pausanias's suspicion about the disposal of the Persian dead. The notion that the ghosts should be able to and should choose to discriminate between innocent travelers and curious spectators is intriguing. The fate that met the curious was presumably death; see **114–6**. Echetlas would appear to have been a ghost already at the point of helping his Greek comrades in the battle. Given his—at one level—solid and vigorous form, he should perhaps be considered a "revenant"; see **119**.

## 114   A witch sends the ghost of a dead woman to accomplish a murder

Later ii A.D.

Apuleius *Metamorphoses* 9.29–31 (edited)

Latin

**29.** She [the miller's wife] reverted to type and was incited to turn back to the skills that are women's own. She painstakingly sought out some old crone, who was held to be able to accomplish absolutely anything through binding curses and witchcraft. She prevailed on her with many prayers, and stuffed her to the gills with large quantities of money. She asked for one of two results, either that her husband should be pacified, and that she should be reconciled with him, or, if she could not do that, that at any rate a ghost or some dreadful demon be sent to do violence to him and destroy him. Then the witch [*saga*], able as she was to compel divine powers, opened a skirmish with just the basic weapons of her evil trade. She tried to redirect the husband's mind from its deep feelings of offence toward love. The plan did not work as she had intended. She became angry with the powers, and was impelled to her task now not only by the promised profit of her payment, but also by the contempt of the powers for her. Now she began to threaten the life itself of the unfortunate husband, and sent the ghost of a woman killed by violence to kill him.

**30.** At around the middle of the day a woman suddenly appeared in the mill, disfigured by the sort of extreme misery affected by defendants in court. She was only semiclothed, by a pitiful piece of patchwork. Her feet were bare and uncovered. She was yellow like boxwood and foully emaciated. Her unkempt hair was partially grey and caked in the ashes that had been scattered over it. It hung down and covered most of her face. In this state as she was, she reassuringly put her hand on the miller, as if she wished to share something with him in secret. She drew him aside to his room and, with the door put to, stayed there for an awfully long time. But when the workers had processed all the grain that they had to hand, and a further supply inevitably had to be sought, the boys came to the room and called on their master and asked for new supplies for their work. They shouted out repeatedly and frequently, but no master responded to them. They began to beat more vigorously on the door. It had been carefully bolted, and so they began to suspect that something rather serious and rather bad was afoot. With a stout shove they pushed out or broke the hinge and at last opened a way in for themselves. There was no sign of the woman, but their master was there to be seen hanging by a noose from a beam and already dead. They took the noose from his neck and lowered him down amid the keenest wailings and lamentations, and looked after his final wash. When the wake had been duly performed they gave him over to burial, with a packed crowd in attendance.

**31.** On the following day his daughter came running from the next town, to which she had formerly moved upon marriage. In misery she shook her unbound hair and from time to time beat her breasts. She knew everything that had happened, even though no one had told her of the house's misfortune. The tearful visage of her father had brought itself before her as she slept, his neck still bound by the noose, and revealed the entirety of her stepmother's crime. He told her about her adultery and sorcery, and how he had been bewitched with a ghost and had gone down to the underworld.

IN THIS FURTHER PASSAGE FROM APULEIUS'S *Metamorphoses* the miller has found his wife's boy-lover in the house, buggered him, and thrown him out. The wife now seeks to make her situation with her husband tolerable again.

The action takes place at an unnamed location in Thessaly, and the witch is therefore apparently yet another Thessalian one. The brief description given to her is not incompatible with the representations of witches in Latin poetry, and her venality in particular is reminiscent of its bawd-witches (see **100–103**). Like Apuleius's other witches, Meroe and Pamphile (**104, 107**), this one is explicitly attributed with the power of binding magic. The two goals the miller's wife seeks, the pacification and reconciliation of her husband, or his death, are, in magical terms, not as distinct as may first appear, when we recall the tradition of fatal love-potions administered by Deianeira and her like (**76–81**) and when we bear in mind Faraone's insight that such love-potions were often held to work specifically by calming anger (1999a); see **52**. The pattern of a failed attempt to prevail upon the demonic powers, followed by a redoubled attempt that is successful, is a familiar one (see **155**), but the change of magical goal between attempts is novel.

The appearance of the ghost is evidently that of a living woman of a kind: she is taken for such by the miller. However, she has a yellowness and emaciation one might associate with a corpse; her face is perhaps shrouded by her unkempt hair to conceal a more obviously corpse-like or ghost-like face. She is portrayed as in mourning either because of the general association between mourning and death or, more specifically, because she mourns her own death, untimely and violent as it was. The ghost's resentment at this renders it restless and exploitable for magical purposes. Her sudden appearance and her mysterious disappearance from a locked room suggest intangibility (compare **144**), but the fact that she can touch the miller with her hand suggests the opposite (compare **119**). How did she kill the miller? With the superior physical strength that tangible revenant ghosts sometimes display (e.g., Phlegon of Tralles *Mirabilia* 2)? Or did she terrify him into suicide? Or was mere contact with the dead woman sufficient in itself to pass on the state of death, as in **113, 116, 157, 161, 163**, with one ghost creating another? After his own violent death the miller's ghost proceeds to appear to his daughter. As often with appearing ghosts, the means of the manifestation is a dream and the subject of its utterance is none other than the circumstances of its own death, and complaints about it (compare **144**).

## HAUNTED HOUSES

### 115    Arignotus the Pythagorean exorcises a haunted house

ii A.D.

Lucian *Philopseudes* 30–1

Greek

"But," said Arignotus, "if ever you go to Corinth, ask where the house of Eubatides is, and when it is pointed out to you, beside the Cherry Trees, go into it and tell Tibeios the janitor that you want to see where Arignotus the Pythagorean dug up the ghost, drove it out, and made the house fit for living in thereafter."

"What happened, Arignotus?" asked Eucrates.

"The house had long been rendered uninhabitable," said Arignotus, "by its terrors. If anyone occupied it he was immediately frightened out of his wits and fled from it, chased out by some terrifying, panic-instilling ghost. So it was by now falling in and the roof was in disrepair, and there was absolutely no one to be bold enough to enter it. When I heard this, I took up my books (for I have very many Egyptian books on this kind of thing) and went to the house at around bedtime. My host tried to discourage me, and fell just short of physically restraining me when he learned where I was heading, which was into foreseeable trouble, as far as he was concerned. I picked up my lamp and went in on my own. I put my light down in the biggest room, sat on the floor, and began to read peacefully. The ghost materialized in attack. He thought he was up against an average fellow and expected me to flee in terror like the others. He was squalid, he had long hair and was blacker than the dark. He stood opposite and put me to the test. He attacked me on all sides, in case he could beat me on one, and transformed himself now into a dog, now into a bull, and now into a lion. But I mobilized my most blood-curdling spell, one in the Egyptian language, drove him into the corner of the dark room, and laid him with the charm. I made a note of the place at which he went down, and then took my rest for the remainder of the night. By morning all were in despair and thinking that they would find me a dead man, like the others. But, against all expectation, I emerged from the house and went to Eubatides with the happy news that he could now live in a house purified and empty of terrors. So I took him along, together with a large number of the others, who wanted to come with us because of the marvel. I brought them to the place where I had seen the ghost go down and I told them to get forks and spades and to dig. When they'd done that they found buried there, some six feet under, a moldy corpse, with its bones alone in place. So they took it out of the ground and gave it proper burial, and from that time the house ceased to be troubled by ghosts."

THE BEST ATTESTED TRADITIONAL "HAUNTED HOUSE" story from antiquity is found in three examples. Before Lucian it had been told first in Latin by Plautus (**116**) and Pliny the Younger (*Letters* 7.27.5–11, ca. 102 A.D.). But the tale is evidently Greek in origin, as its setting indicates, and Plautus's *Mostellaria* was an adaptation of a Greek play entitled *Phasma*, probably by Philemon. The three versions of the tale are interestingly analyzed by Deborah Felton (1999).

As a Pythagorean Arignotus is particularly well suited to the manipulation of ghosts and souls (compare 1–9). The physical description of the ghost is comparable to Apuleius's description of the female ghost sent to kill the miller (114). But it is also remarkably similar to the Pythagorean himself, with its long hair and its squalid appearance (*Philopseudes* 29), and the two are therefore accordingly implied to be akin.

The Egyptian books from which Arignotus sustains himself are doubtless supposed to be akin to the formularies of Graeco-Egyptian magical papyri (e.g., 132, 135, 156, 161–3, 166–7, 189, 208–9, 211–3, 235, 239, 243, 245–6, 261, 277); for Egyptian magical books see 46, 53. As often a lamp is associated with the materialization of a ghost (compare 105, 116, 165–6). The ghost's shape-shifting is reminiscent of Proteus's attempts to evade Menelaus (Homer *Odyssey* 4.454–91).

Pliny's version for the most part runs quite tightly parallel to this account but omits some features and includes others. The school of his philosopher-hero, Athenodorus, goes unspecified. His ghost wears iron chains, which it rattles menacingly, and its body, when found, is also wearing them. Such chains have become a familiar attribute of the ghost in the Western tradition but are somewhat of a curiosity in ancient terms, since ghosts were held to be terrified of iron in general and its clanking in particular (see 144, 244). Pliny's ghost is also portrayed as beckoning to the philosopher with its finger. This appears to be a narrative misdirection; the reader is supposed to think that it is beckoning the philosopher down to the underworld (compare 116). In fact, it just wants to take him to the site where its bones lie.

## 116   A tricky slave keeps his returning master from his house by manufacturing a ghost story

iv–iii B.C. (Philemon);
ca. 200 B.C. (Plautus)

Plautus *Mostellaria*
446–531

Latin, adapted from
Greek

Tranio: O Theopropides, my master, hello! I'm glad that you've come back safe and sound. Have you kept well all this time?

Theopropides: Indeed, as you see.

Tranio: Excellent!

Theopropides: What are you up to? Are you mad?

Tranio: Why do say that?

Theopropides: Because here you are walking around outside! There isn't a soul on watch in the house, and there is no one to open the door and no one to answer it. I almost broke these two doors by beating on them!

Tranio: Oh no! Did you touch this house?

Theopropides: Why shouldn't I have touched it? Indeed, as I say, I almost broke the doors by beating on them.

Tranio: So you did touch them?

Theopropides: I touched them, I tell you, and I beat upon them.

Tranio: Agh!

Theopropides: What's the matter?

Tranio: That was an unfortunate thing to do.

Theopropides: What's the problem?

Tranio: I can't express how terrible and unfortunate a thing it is you have done.

Theopropides: What are you saying now?

Tranio: Flee, I beg you, and get away from the house! Get over here, get over here, where I am! You did touch the doors?

Theopropides: How could I beat on the door without touching it?

Tranio: By Hercules, you've destroyed . . .

**Theopropides:** Who on earth?

**Tranio:** . . . all your family!

**Theopropides:** May all gods and goddesses make you and your omen . . .

**Tranio:** I fear you can't cleanse yourself or your people of the pollution.

**Theopropides:** For what reason? What sudden novelty are you inflicting on me now?

**Tranio:** Hey now, tell those two fellows to get away from there!

**Theopropides:** Get back!

**Tranio:** Don't touch the house! You too touch the earth!

**Theopropides:** I beg you by Hercules, tell me what all this is about!

**Tranio:** It's because it's been seven months since anyone set foot inside this house, when once we got out of it.

**Theopropides:** Tell me! Why so?

**Tranio:** Look about you. Is there anyone to overhear our conversation?

**Theopropides:** It's quite safe.

**Tranio:** Look again!

**Theopropides:** There isn't anyone. Now tell me!

**Tranio:** It's a capital crime!

**Theopropides:** What is? I don't really understand.

**Tranio:** A crime, I say, was committed long ago, an old and ancient crime.

**Theopropides:** An old one?

**Tranio:** Yes, and we have now discovered it.

**Theopropides:** What sort of a crime are you speaking of? Or who did it? Tell me.

**Tranio:** A host seized his guest and slaughtered him—that man, I'm inclined to believe, who sold you this house.

**Theopropides:** Slaughtered?

**Tranio:** Yes, and he took his guest's gold and stuck his body in the ground, right here inside the house—his guest!

**Theopropides:** What makes you think all this happened?

**Tranio:** I'll tell you. Listen! When your son had been dining out, and he had come back home from the dinner, we all went off to bed. We fell sound asleep. By chance, I had forgotten to put the light out. And then he suddenly shouted out at the top of his voice.

**Theopropides:** Who did? My son?

**Tranio:** Shhh! Be quiet. Just listen. He said a dead man had come to him in his sleep.

**Theopropides:** This is in his sleep, is it?

**Tranio:** Yes. But just listen. He said that this dead man had spoken to him as follows . . .

**Theopropides:** In his sleep?

**Tranio:** It is surprising that he didn't speak to him while he was awake . . . since he had been killed sixty years ago! Sometimes you can be really stupid, Theopropides.

**Theopropides:** I'm being quiet now.

**Tranio:** But see what the dead man said to him: "I am Diapontius, a guest from across the sea. This is where I live. This house has been allocated to me to live in. For Orcus refused to admit me to Acheron, because I died before my time. My trust was betrayed. My host slaughtered me and secretly stuck me in the ground inside this house without due burial, all for my gold, the wicked man! Now get out of here. This is a cursed house, an unholy place to live." If I had a year I'd be hard pressed to tell you all the strange things that have happened here. Shhh!

Theopropides: What's the matter, then?

Tranio: The door made a noise! Was he the one that knocked on it?

Theopropides: I don't have even a drop of blood! The dead are calling me to Acheron alive!

Tranio: I'm done for. Those people in the house will spoil my drama this day! I'm petrified he'll catch me out!

Theopropides: What are you saying to yourself?

Tranio: Get back from the door! Flee, by Hercules, I beg you!

Theopropides: Where am I to flee to? You flee too!

Tranio: I'm not afraid. I have peace with the dead.

Voice from within: Hey, Tranio!

Tranio: You won't call for me, if you are wise. I've done nothing to deserve it, and I didn't knock on those doors.

Voice from within: Please . . .

Tranio: Don't say a word!

Theopropides: Explain why you've stopped speaking to me.

Tranio: Take yourself off!

Theopropides: What's got into you, Tranio? To whom are you speaking?

Tranio: Oh! Was it you that had called me? So may the gods love me, I thought that that dead man wanted my soul because you'd knocked on the door. But you—are you still standing here and taking no notice of what I tell you?

Theopropides: What am I to do?

Tranio: Don't look back, just flee, and cover your head.

Theopropides: Why aren't you fleeing?

Tranio: I have peace with the dead.

Theopropides: Yes, I know. But what about just now? Why were you so panic-stricken?

Tranio: Don't concern yourself about me, I say. I'll look out for myself. But you, just as you were doing, flee, as fast as you can, and call on Hercules!

Theopropides: Hercules, I call upon you!

Tranio: As do I, to give you a heap of trouble this day, old man! Immortal gods, look after me! What a nasty piece of work I've got through today!

IN THIS COMEDY THE YOUNG MASTER is carousing in the house with courtesans when his father Theopropides unexpectedly returns. The tricky slave Tranio devises a plan to keep him away from the house until the coast is clear. The story he invents is constructed out of a traditional haunted-house story very similar to the one in **115**. It is this scene that gives the play its name, "The Haunted House." Tranio's tale gives a useful insight into the sort of sequence of events that might be imagined to have produced a haunting ghost.

Central to Tranio's conceit is the notion that contact of any sort with a ghost brings death upon one (compare **114**). It is sufficient merely to have touched a haunted house. Theopropides fears that for this alone the ghost will call his name and thus summon him "alive" down to the underworld (see commentary to **115**). Tranio asks Theopropides to touch the earth in order to cleanse himself of this ghostly contact.

The ghost explains that it wanders on the surface still and cannot enter the underworld because it died before its time. It is implied that it must consequently stay behind to fulfil a normal span (see **112**). One might have thought that it ought already to have done this, since its death was over sixty years before, but Tranio is hardly concerned with such details (he is careless too in selecting the name "Diapontius" for his ghost of a "guest from across the sea," since it actually means "from across the sea"). But the ghost also emphatically belongs in the "unburied" category. The important distinction between due burial and mere insertion into the ground is clearly made here.

## 117 At Megara a ghost appears proleptically before returning to seek revenge and due burial

44 B.C.

Cicero On *Divination* 1.57

Latin

Two Arcadian companions hit the road together and came to Megara. One of them went to stay with an innkeeper, the other with a friend. After a meal they took to their beds. Just after he had retired for the night the man who was staying with his friend saw a vision of the other companion in his dreams, in which he begged him to come help, because the innkeeper was plotting to murder him. His first reaction was to wake in terror at the dream, but then he gathered his wits, concluded that the vision was nugatory, and went back to sleep. As he slept on he saw another vision in which the same man begged him that he should not suffer his death to go unavenged, since he had not come to help him while still alive. After killing him, he said, the innkeeper had thrown his body on the back of a cart and covered it with dung. He asked him to bring himself to the town gate in the morning before the cart could leave the place. This dream disturbed him, and so he confronted the driver at the gate and asked him what was in the cart. He fled in terror, the dead man was pulled out of the dung, all was revealed, and the innkeeper paid the penalty.

ALTHOUGH NOT A HAUNTED-HOUSE STORY, this tale has much in common with those above, **115–6**. For the danger of inns compare **104**. Here the ghost's motives for its second appearance are clear: revenge on its killer and the securing of due burial. But the first, "proleptic" appearance of he ghost, prior to its person's actual death, is remarkable. The ghost was directly experienced in sleep—the usual way, it seems, of experiencing ghosts in antiquity (see **116, 149**). A version of this tale is also to be found at Aelian F82 Domingo-Forasté.

## 118 A young man falls in love with the ghost of a beautiful girl haunting his house

Late iv B.C. (Menander);

iv A.D. (Donatus)

Menander *Phasma*, fragment at Körte, 1 p.134; Donatus on Terence *Eunuch* 9.3

Latin (summarizing Greek)

*Ghost* is the name of one Menander's plays. A young man acquires a stepmother. She had once fallen and conceived a daughter. She has had her brought up in secret and has installed her secretly in the house next door. Without letting anyone know, she maintains the following practice. She has dug a hole through the partywall between her husband's house and that of the neighbor, in such a way that she can pretend that the place is a niche-shrine. She decks it out with garlands and a bough of good fortune and worships at it frequently, so calling her daughter to her. The young man notices her doing this, and is stricken with terror upon seeing the beautiful girl for the first time, as if he had seen some supernatural power. It is from this that the play gets the title *Ghost*. Thereafter, bit by bit, the truth emerges, and he develops a burning passion for the girl so strong that marriage is the only cure that can be found. The play concludes with the wedding, in accordance with the convenience of mother and daughter, the prayers of the lover, and the consent of his father.

THE CONTRIVED PLOT OF THIS LOST New Comedy plays with the theme of a youth falling in love with a beautiful young woman ghost, which can be seen also in **119** and **60**.

## 119 The ghost of the girl Philinnion returns to sleep with the lodger

Ca. 140 A.D.

Phlegon of Tralles
*Mirabilia* 1

Greek

[The nurse] came to the door of the guestroom and by lamplight saw the girl sitting beside Machates. The sight was so amazing that she could not remain there any longer, but she ran to the girl's mother. Shouting at the top of her voice, "Charito! Demostratus!" She asked them to get up and to come with her to see their daughter for themselves. For, she said, she had materialized alive and was with the guest, by some divine will, in the guestroom. The unexpected report struck panic into Charito's soul as soon as she heard it. She felt faint because of the enormity of the news and the excitement of the nurse. Then, after a moment, she started thinking about her daughter and wept. Finally, she accused the old woman of having lost her mind, and ordered her out of her presence at once. The nurse reproached her in turn and, speaking without restraint, said that she retained her wits and was of sound mind, but that she was not the one who was too timid to see her own daughter. At long last Charito, in part at the nurse's behest, and in part because she wanted to know what had gone on, came to the door of the guestroom. But because a considerable time had now elapsed, it being a couple of hours since the nurse had brought the news, she arrived too late. So it happened that they were already asleep. The mother craned her neck and thought that she recognized her daughter's clothes and general appearance, but she had no way of ascertaining the truth and so thought that she should keep quiet. She hoped that if she got up early she could catch the girl, or, if she was too late, interrogate Machates about everything. For he would never lie when asked about a matter of such importance. So, she said nothing and went off. By dawn it happened that the girl had slipped away unnoticed, perhaps by chance, or perhaps by the will of the gods. When Charito came to the room she was angry with the young man because the girl had got away, but she told Machates the whole story from the beginning, embraced his knees, and demanded that he tell her the truth, hiding nothing. The young man felt uncomfortable to begin with, and was upset, but eventually he vouchsafed to her the girl's name: Philinnion. He told her how she had first come to him and how great her desire for him was, and he explained that she had said that she was coming to him without her parents' knowledge. To help her believe him he opened his trunk and took out the things the girl had left behind, the golden ring he had been given by her and the bra she had left the night before. When Charito saw such significant tokens, she cried out and tore her own clothes and her cloak. She threw the hairnet from her head, fell to the ground, clasped the tokens to her breast, and started to grieve all over again. When the guest saw what was happening and that all were overcome with emotion and lamenting, as if only just now preparing to bury the girl, he became troubled and begged them to stop. He promised that if she came to him again he would show the girl to her. She took him at his word, urged him to observe his promise to her scrupulously, and left him. Night came on and it was that hour at which Philinnion was accustomed to visit him. They all kept a lookout in their eagerness to learn of her arrival, and she came. She entered the room at her usual time and sat down on the bed. Machates pretended that nothing had changed, but he wanted to investigate the affair, although he did not really believe what he had been told. He wished to find out whether the woman he was consorting with, the one who so assiduously visited him at the same time each night, and who dined and drank with him, was dead. He was dubious of the claims that they were making, and believed that some grave-robbers had dug into their girl's tomb and sold her clothing and her gold jewelry to his girl's father. Anyway, because he wanted to know the truth, he secretly dispatched the slaves to call them. Demostratus and Charito arrived at once. When they saw her they were at first speechless and terrified by the unexpected sight, but then they shouted out aloud and embraced their daughter. Then Philinnion said this to them: "Mother and father, it is unfair of you to have begrudged me spending three days with the guest in my father's house. I was causing nobody any trouble. As a result of this you will grieve afresh, because of your interference, and I shall return to my appointed place. For it was by the will of the gods that I came here." So much did she say before dying at once, and her body was stretched out on the bed for all to see. Her mother and father threw themselves upon her. The house was filled with uproar and lamentation because of the disaster. The events were irreversible as well as incredible. The rumor of them quickly spread through the city and was reported back to me. For that night I kept back the crowds that were flocking to the house, taking precautions that there should be no disturbance with a story of this sort being spread abroad. The theatre was already full by early dawn. The whole affair was laid out. It was resolved that we should first go to the tomb, open it up, and find out whether the body was on its bier or whether we would find the place empty. It was not yet six months since the girl had died. When we had opened up the vault into which all her relatives were put on death, we saw the bodies lying on the other biers, or the bones in the case of those that had died long ago. But in the case alone of the bier on which Philinnion had been laid out and put to rest, we found lying on it the iron ring, which had belonged to the guest, and the gold-plated cup, which she had been given by Machates on the first of their days. Amazed and terrified we proceeded immediately to the guestroom in Demostratus's house to find out whether the dead girl was really to be seen there. We saw her lying on the ground, and then we all gathered into the assembly. What had happened was grave and difficult to believe. There was vehement uproar in the assembly and almost no one could give a judgment about the happenings. The first to stand up was Hyllus. He is not only regarded as the best prophet in our city, but he is also considered to be a clever augur, and he has exercised his craft generally with exceptional insight. He bade us burn the girl outside the city limits, since no good could come of her being buried within the limits again, and to propitiate Chthonic Hermes and the Eumenides. Everyone should then be purified. They should cleanse the temples and perform the customary rites of the chthonic deities. He spoke privately to me about the king and what had happened. He told me to make sacrifices to Hermes, Zeus of Guests, and Ares, and not to skimp in the performance of these. After he had made these revelations we carried out his orders. But the guest Machates, whom the ghost visited, committed suicide from despair. If you resolve to write about this to the king, notify me too, so that I can send you one of the men who investigated the details. Best wishes.

THE BEGINNING OF PHLEGON'S NARRATIVE IS lost, but its outline is preserved by Proclus (*Commentary on Plato's Republic*, pp. 115–6 Kroll; fifth century A.D.). From this we learn that the setting is Amphipolis during the reign of Philip (II, presumably; he ruled 359–36 B.C. and acquired Amphipolis in 357) and that Philinnion was newly wed upon her death. Her desire for love and sex had evidently been aroused. Phlegon's tale is cast in the form of a report by a governor of Amphipolis to one of Philip's more immediate staff, and Proclus indicates that the letter may have been in the name of a Hipparchus or an Arrhidaeus.

Philinnion is evidently far more tangible than the ghosts of Homer's *Nekuia* (**144**), tangible enough indeed to make love to the living Machates.

Her manifestation evidently makes use of her body. She should accordingly be considered a "revenant". An even more tangible revenant is described in the second of Phlegon's *Mirabilia*.

The implication of Philinnion's claims prior to her second death are perhaps that, if left to her own devices, and not spied upon by her parents, she may in time have been fully and permanently restored to life. We are reminded of the way Orpheus lost his chance to restore his wife Eurydice to life as he walked her out of the underworld by looking back at her too soon; see **20**, with commentary.

Phlegon's tale was the model for Goethe's *Bride of Corinth*, which transforms the sympathetic Philinnion into a deceitful vampire who is frustrated in her attempt to devour the guest. Such a sinister reading of the original tale may be less inappropriate than initially appears. First, it bears a general similarity to Philostratus's tale of Apollonius's exposure of the Empusa-bride in Corinth (**60**), who was precisely planning to devour her man. Second, the tale does after all result in the guest's death, albeit through a broken heart. But, as already shown, death often results merely from contact with ghosts (**114, 116, 157**). Philinnion may have loved Machates as genuinely as the Empusa loved her bridegroom, but both men may nonetheless have been destined for death.

For an interesting discussion of this text, with special reference to its folklore context as well as its *Nachleben*, see Hansen 1996.

## GHOST-LAYING

For ghost laying see also **0, 25 31, 17, 68, 149–54**.

### 120 Odysseus calls the souls of his dead companions into cenotaphs

vii B.C. or earlier

(Homer); Hellenistic-Byzantine (Scholium)

Homer *Odyssey* 9.62–6, with scholium *ad loc.*

Greek

We sailed on from there, grieved in heart, but glad to have escaped death ourselves. We had lost some dear comrades. Nor did I allow our rounded ships to travel any further before I had called three times on each of the unfortunate companions who had died on the plain, slain by the Cicones.

**Scholium:** For they used to think that they had to call those who died in a foreign land, to transport them back to their fatherland. Similarly, the Athenians made cenotaphs for those who died at sea and set them beside the shore. They called their names three times, and this was how they came back.

ODYSSEUS HAS HAD TO LEAVE HIS men where they fell in a raid against the Cicones and so does not have their bodies available for burial. His solution is to set up cenotaphs and to draw their souls into them by calling their names three times over. The *scholium* allows us to understand how death at sea became regarded as a type of deprivation of burial *par excellence*.

### 121 Aeneas calls the soul of Deiphobus into a cenotaph

19 B.C.

Virgil *Aeneid* 6.494–510

Latin

And here he saw Priam's son Deiphobus, his whole body torn to pieces and his face cruelly mutilated, his face and both his hands, his temples stripped of the ears snatched from them, and his nose hacked off to leave a disgraceful wound. I almost failed to recognize him as he trembled and tried to cover his dreadful punishment. I addressed him first, with familiar words:

"Deiphobus, powerful in arms, descendant of the lofty blood of Teucer, who decided to exact such cruel punishment? Who was in a position to do it? I heard that on Troy's last night, exhausted by the wide-scale butchery of Pelasgians, you had collapsed on top of a twisted heap of slaughter. So after that I set up an empty tomb for you on the Rhoetean shore and called loudly on your ghost three times over. Your name and your weapons dwell in this place. But I was not able to find you yourself, my friend, and lay you in your ancestral land as I left."

The son of Priam replied to this: "You omitted nothing, my friend. You paid all due rites to the ghost of the dead Deiphobus."

THIS PASSAGE IS VIRGIL'S RESPONSE TO the Odyssey passage (120). Deiphobus had become Helen's lover (husband?) in Troy after Paris' death. His ghost goes on to explain that she had betrayed him to Odysseus as he and his men infiltrated the city, and they had killed him in their bed. It is not made clear whether the mutilation preceded, succeeded, or indeed constituted his killing: was it a form of *maschalismos* (see **122**)?

## 122   "Armpitting" (*maschalismos*): The mutilation of the corpses of the murdered to hobble their ghosts

x A.D.

*Suda* s.v. *maschalisthê-nai* (on "being armpitted")

Greek

Being armpitted: Men usually wipe their swords on the heads of the slain to avert the pollution of the killing. Or, to purify themselves, they would cut off the slain man's extremities and hang them around his armpit, so that, it is said, he would be too weak to avenge the murder. So too Apollonius says, "You cut the first pieces from the dead man." This of Jason [*Argonautica* 4.477]. Or, those engaged in civil war used to cut the extremities from the slain, cutting them off from all parts of the body, and fasten the pieces around them, stringing them together, as if they were thus depriving them of strength, so that they would not subsequently terrorize them. The corpses used to wear the extremities on their armpits. They called this process "being armpitted". Sophocles says, "Consider whether the dead man in the grave appears to receive these gifts propitiously from the woman who killed him, dishonored him, subjected him to armpitting like an enemy, and wiped off the bloodstains with his hair to clean her sword." This of Agamemnon [*Electra* 442–6].

THE EXTREMITIES REMOVED IN ARMPITTING WERE probably eyes, ears, nose, hands, feet, and genitals. The thinking behind it was evidently that a ghost and its powers were drawn directly from its corpse in its current state. Accordingly, if one hobbled the corpse, one hobbled the ghost. The ghost would hardly be left at peace, but it would no longer have the power to terrorize its murderer—a particularly cruel fate for it. Compare **68**, **121**.

## 123   Directions for the laying of attacking ghosts (1): Selinus

Ca. 460 B.C.

*Lex sacra* from Selinus (Jameson, Jordan, and Kotansky 1993, col. B)

Greek

If a person wants to purify himself from attacking ghosts [*elasteroi*], he is to call on the ghost wherever he wants and at whatever point in the year he wants and in whatever month he wants and on whatever day he wants and facing in whatever direction he wants. Then he is to be purified. He is to welcome the ghost and give it water for washing the hands, bread, and wine, and he is to give salt to this same ghost. He is to sacrifice a piglet to Zeus, to step back from it and turn in a circle [around it?]. He may then be addressed. He may eat and he may sleep wherever he wishes. If someone wants to be purified of the attacking ghost of someone outside his family or of a member of his family, one that manifests itself to his hearing or his vision, or any attacking ghost at all, he is to be purified in the same way as a murderer, when he is purified of his attacking ghost. Once he has sacrificed a full-grown victim on the public altar, he is to be pure. He is to mark off the [altar-?] boundary with salt, sprinkle [it in a water solution?] from a gold cup, and go away. Whenever someone needs to make sacrifice to an attacking ghost, he is to sacrifice as he does to the immortal gods. He is to jugulate the victim in such a way that the blood flows into the earth.

THE EXACT SIGNIFICANCE OF SOME PHRASES here remains obscure, and the translation seeks to reflect this. The nature of the *elasteroi* is disputed. The editors see them not as ghosts, as this translator does, but as avenging spirits acting on their behalf. Whatever their exact nature, the victims of the attacks are, as we would expect, either the ghosts' murderers or innocent third parties the ghosts seize on in their attempt to find peace. To be the victim of such attacks is to be polluted (murderers were commonly considered so); to be delivered from them is to be cleansed.

The making of peace with the ghost entails the sharing of a symbolic meal with it. Piglet sacrifice was a familiar means of pollution-purification. For the pouring of sacrificial blood into the earth for ghosts to drink, see **144**. The exact nature of the circular movements to be made remains obscure, but circular movements of some sort are common in the laying of ghosts (compare **30**). After the initial rites have been performed, the ghost may then, for the first time it seems, be addressed. This implies a scheme of action implicit in narratives of ghost placation, according to which the killer is first attacked by a terrifying ghost with which he cannot communicate and in response calls it up by rites of evocation in a form in which he can communicate with it and learn from it what he must do to placate it (see **124, 126, 151**).

## 124   Directions for the laying of attacking ghosts (2): Cyrene

Ca. 300 B.C.

Inscription from Cyrene: Solmsen and Fraenkel 1966, no. 39 B 27–39; *SEG* 9. no.72 lines 110–21

Greek

Rules for attacking ghosts [*hikesioi*]. An attacking ghost sent upon one: if ever an attacking ghost is sent against one's house, if one knows from whom it comes to attack one, one is to give name to him, proclaiming the name over three days. If he is dead in the earth, or dead in some other condition, if one knows his name, one is to proclaim the name. But if one does not know the name, one is to proclaim "O person, whether you are man or woman." He should make dolls [*kolossoi*], a male one and a female one, from wood or from clay, entertain them, and set before them helpings of all food. When you have performed the rites, take the dolls to an unworked forest and fix them there with their helpings.

THIS EARLY HELLENISTIC INSCRIPTION SUMMARIZES directives that are older, perhaps even archaic. Parker (1983) and Faraone (1991b), among others, understand this text to address the situation in which a ghost is sent against one by a sorcerer, as in the world of the curse tablets; see **168–84, 197–213, 237–41**. For them it is accordingly the sorcerer's name that one is to proclaim, whether he is dead or alive. I find it easier to believe that, despite references to the ghost as "being sent," sorcery is not primarily envisaged here. The envisaged situation is rather akin to that of the Selinus directives in **123**, which these instructions strongly resemble. This situation is one in which a restless ghost attacks either its killer or an innocent third party in an attempt to achieve peace. The phrase "from whom it comes to attack" is a way of describing the dead person who gave rise to the ghost. If one knows the name of this person and the derived ghost, one can proclaim it three times over, just as

Odysseus and Aeneas did (see **120–1**), to lay the ghost expeditiously. The difficulty comes when one does not know the ghost's name, whereupon one must resort to the doll procedure. Here one presumably calls the ghost into (the relevant one of) the doll(s), comes to terms with it by hosting a meal for it, and then removes it, still in its doll(s), to the wilderness, from where it will cause no more trouble. For the sequence of terrible uncommunicative encounter with a ghost followed by communicative ritual encounter see, again, **123**. Here male and female dolls, together with accompanying proclamation, are used to cover both bases, the gender of the ghost being unknown and unidentifiable. For the use of exhaustive dichotomies compare **89, 169, 185–6, 197**. Male-and-female doll pairs are used rather differently in the context of erotic magic; see **91, 99, 239**. For another inscription from Cyrene involving dolls see **236**.

## 125   A mage seals a friendly ghost into its tomb, to the dismay of its mother

Before iv A.D.

Pseudo-Quintilian
*Declamationes maiores*
10 resumé, 1, 7, 8–9,
15, 16, 19

Latin

*Resumé:* A case about mistreatment. A woman who saw her dead son in her dreams at night has indicted her husband. He brought in a magician and placed a spell upon the boy's tomb. The mother stopped seeing her son. She accuses her husband of mistreatment.

1. The ghost who came to her was not one she had deluded herself into imagining in her grief; no insubstantial vision disturbed her fragile sleep. She was not confronted in the night by a face covered in dismal cinders or a head sprinkled with ash, but her son came to her in his former shape, a young man of beautiful mien. Nor was he content just to be seen and watched, but, if you put any faith in the needs of the poor woman who was the only one to see him, he embraced her, kissed her, and lived the whole night. The mother lost much, if this actually happened to her, and hardly any less, if it only seemed to be happening. But now she measures out the empty darknesses of the long nights, her eyes full of tears, as she lies awake and bereft beside her sleeping husband. Now she frets about a soul confined in prison and the young man struggling against the magical iron. This most unfortunate of all mothers thinks her son something more than a mere shade, since it was possible to shut him in, and it is not just her own penalty and punishment that wears her down in her bereft state. She is all the more tortured by her fresh bereavement, because her son is not allowed to come to her even though he wants to: "Now the whole night long the ghost beats on the earth made to lie heavily upon it by barbarian incantation, and it is baffled at not being able to escape the tomb planted on top of it, when it could dispel the dead themselves. Poor boy! He has not just been shut in with words (for perhaps he could have got past them), but bonds of iron and tight knots have escorted him back to death. How unfortunate is he to be confined: he cannot even come to complain about it!"

7. So, this deviser of a second death at once calls in a mage behind the mother's back. The gods above are tortured by his grisly mutterings and words of power. The man was not brought in to summon ghosts and bring them up, or to make a shade come rushing to us from somewhere or other, evocated by night-time howlings. Rather, it seems, he was brought in because the grave was not pressing heavily enough upon the boy, and the weight of his barrow was too light. "My son," he

[the boy's father] said, "is not sufficiently dead. He still roams abroad when the stars shine in the night. When daylight is gone, he puts an end to his death, returns home, and terrorizes his mother in her sleep. Find something, find some bonds of words, pushing your craft and your energies to their limits. Great is your glory, if you can confine my son, who returns to his mother even from death." A deleterious spell is put around the tomb, and the urn is closed off with terrible words. Then for the first time the son becomes a corpse and shade.

8. Great, accordingly, are the chains on the ghosts; they tie even the most fleet and elusive apparition tightly to death and bind a soul like the body of a man accused. But I say that to confine an actual ghost with iron and stones, and to bind it down first with chains, in the way that one strengthens gates in war, and then too with bars is not only cruel but monstrous and criminal, especially if the man that does this believes that his son will perceive it. And now his poor mother thinks about those swords have gone down into his body and his limbs. 9. O cruel, heartless mage, contriver of our tears, would that you had not given such a demonstration of your powers! Although we are angry with you, we must cajole you: since it is you who shuts in the ghost, we have come to realize that you are the only one that can evoke it.

15. A man is brought in whose craft is the contravention of nature. As soon as he has muttered barbarian noises from his filthy mouth, the powers above grow pale, the powers below give heed, and the earth trembles, as those who speak from experience of such things say. A more absolute death took its stand beside the poor young man's tomb.

16. Thus you shut in your own son, just as harmful ghosts are usually recalled to the underworld, those ghosts that roam and hover around the sick and one's family's sad illnesses and which are trapped by healing magic. Had he lost his life in the executioner's noose? Had he driven a sword through his guts? Had he deliberately taken poison? Would he not withdraw except when shut in with a spell? When did he terrorize you or your house by manifesting himself in foul and deathly guise? Most heartless of fathers, you made an evil ghost of your son!

19. The powers of your craft torture the gods above and the ghosts below. You disturb the bottom of the cave and the deepest parts of the earth with your terrible night-time howling. Sometimes you call back the souls that are enslaved to you, at other times you confine them heartlessly and are deaf to entreaty. Now at last give heed to the prayers of the mother too.

THIS RHETORICAL EXERCISE IS BASED ON an (absurd) hypothetical situation. If the details of this case are to be taken with any degree of seriousness, we may begin by noting that the ghost, as that of a boy, is untimely dead; see **110, 112**. As a welcome, repeatedly returning, seemingly tangible ghost that stays with its loved one the whole night long, the boy's ghost resembles that of Philinnion (**119**). The father, however, portrays the ghost's returns as of the more familiar harassing and terrorizing mode.

The mage is explicitly attributed with the complementary abilities to raise and lay the dead. And once again, the laying of a ghost is associated with a circular motion ("spell . . . put around the tomb"); compare **30**. The means by which the ghost is bound into its grave is not entirely clear: there is one reference to the use of stones, another to the use of bars, numerous ones to the use of iron bands or chains, apparently knotted, and one reference, apparently, to swords being driven down into the grave, no doubt to pin the ghost down into it (compare the pinning of voodoo dolls and curse tablets, **173,**

239–40?). For ghosts' weakness before iron, see **244**. Also attributed to the mage are the magical commonplaces of the attempt to control the gods (see **14**) and the use of *voces magicae* (see **174**).

For other examples of this combination of magic and absurd hypothesis in the Pseudo-Quintilian declamations, see *Declamationes maiores* 14 and 15, which deal with potions of erotic separation, and *Declamationes minores* 385, where a pimp sues a young man for giving one of his prostitutes a successful love potion, with the result that she refuses to sleep with other clients.

## 126    Nero employs mages to settle the ghost of his murdered mother Agrippina

Early ii A.D.

Suetonius *Nero* 34

Latin

Nero did not know what else to do. When his mother's freedman, Lucius Agermus, came to deliver in joyous fashion the news that she was safe and sound, he had a dagger secretly thrown to the ground beside him, and ordered his arrest and confinement, on the pretext that he had been suborned to assassinate him. He then gave the command that his mother should be killed in such a way as to give the appearance that she had killed herself once detected. Authors in whom we may have confidence add more horrific details. They say that he ran to inspect the corpse of his dead mother, fondled her limbs, criticized some, praised others, and that he drank when thirst welled up. But he could not endure the guilty conscience arising from his crime either in the immediate aftermath of it or ever afterward, even though he was supported with the congratulations of the soldiery, the senate, and the people. He often confessed that he was haunted by the specter of his mother and by Furies' whips and burning torches. He actually went so far as to have the mages perform a rite and attempted to call up her ghost and beg off its anger. And when he was touring Greece he did not have the courage to participate in the Eleusinian mysteries. The Herald makes proclamation and debars the impious and wicked from initiation.

THE NARRATIVE TAKES UP FROM THE point at which Agrippina has survived Nero's attempt to murder her with a collapsible boat. The murder took place in 59 A.D. at Baiae, adjacent to lake Avernus: an unfortunate spot to choose if one wished to avoid ghostly retaliation (see **153–4**). The interest Nero takes in his dead mother's limbs hints at the incestuous relationship they are said to have had (Tacitus *Annals* 14.2–3 and 8 and Dio Cassius 61.11). According to the familiar scheme Nero is first harried by the ghost in a form with which he cannot communicate; but he then has it ritually evocated so that he may communicate with it (compare **123–4, 151**). Nero's fear of initiation into the Eleusinian mysteries may have had less to do with sacred law than the fact that initiation entailed a visit to the underworld (see Brown 1991). He would not want to put himself in the way of his mother's ghost or the Furies of his own accord. For Nero's association with mages, see also his use of the Armenian-king mage Tiridates (**45**), who is also mentioned by Suetonius himself at *Nero* 13.

## EXORCISM

▬▬▬▬▬▬▬▬

Sometimes ghosts had to be expelled not merely from places but actually from individuals of whom they had seized possession. A particularly clear example of this phenomenon is provided by Apollonius's exorcism of the ghost of a soldier from a boy (**57**). Often the possessing entity is referred to as a "demon" without much further definition; not all of them need be considered demons of the dead (*nekudaimones*) or ghosts as such. For other sources bearing upon the exorcism of individuals see **13, 51, 265–6**. Much of the richest evidence for exorcism of individuals in the Graeco-Roman world derives from or salutes the Judaeo-Christian tradition, and it is likely that the phenomenon as we know it was imported from Jewish culture. For a convenient discussion, see Kotansky (1995).

The Judaeo-Christian affiliation aside, exorcism sequences in ancient literature tend to conform to the following pattern:

- The demon is ordered out but does not initially obey.

- The demon is ordered out once more again, with terrible threats, and does obey.

- Often the demon is adjured in the name of a particularly powerful sorcerer; the following examples use the names of Solomon, Moses, and Jesus.

- The demon is made to confess its name and identity, and this act is often in itself tantamount to expulsion: confirming the presence of a demon is more than half the battle.

- The demon gives a physical token of its departure: either it is visible as it departs, usually in the form of a dark figure, or it is made to knock over an external object on its outward flight.

## 127 Eleazar uses the wisdom of Solomon to perform exorcism before Vespasian

93/4 A.D.

Josephus *Jewish Antiquities* 8.42–9

Greek

So great was the intelligence and wisdom that God bestowed on Solomon that he outstripped the abilities of the ancients. The Egyptians are said to surpass all men in their understanding, but even they were outstripped by Solomon, and not just by a small measure; rather, they were proven to fall far short of the king's intellect. He also outflanked and surpassed the wisdom of the men of his own age whom the Jews regarded as clever. I will include their names: Athanus, Haemanus, Chalceus, and Dardanus, the sons of Hemaon. He also composed books. These contained a thousand and five songs and three thousand parables and comparisons. For he provided a parable for every kind of tree from the hyssop to the cedar, and likewise for the birds and all the earthbound creatures, and the swimming ones and the flying ones. There was no aspect of nature of which he was ignorant, or which he passed by without examination, but he made a philosophical study of these in all cases and demonstrated a consummate knowledge of their characteristics. God permitted him to learn the craft of demon control, since it was a helpful and healing one for men. He composed incantations to relieve diseases and left behind him methods of exorcism for the expulsion of possessing demons in such a way that they never return. And this cure is very powerful still now in our own time. For I have observed Eleazar, one of our tribe, delivering men of the demons that possessed them before Vespasian, his sons, some tribunes, and many other soldiers. This was the method of the cure. He applied a ring to the demoniac's nose. This had under its seal one of the roots Solomon prescribed. As the victim smelled the ring, Eleazar drew the demon out down his nostrils. The victim collapsed at once. Then Eleazar adjured the demon never to return to him, invoking Solomon's name and speaking the incantations he had composed. Eleazar wanted to persuade his audience and prove to them that this power was his. So he would set up, at a short distance, either a cup or a footbath, filled with water, and command the demon to overturn it as it came out of the man, and let those watching know that it had abandoned him. As a result of this the intelligence and wisdom of Solomon was made manifest.

FOR THE REQUIREMENT THAT THE DEMON give physical proof of its departure, compare Philostratus *Life of Apollonius* 4.20. For Solomon as a magical figure see **131**. Josephus acknowledges Egypt as a major source of magical expertise; compare **53–6**. For Dardanus see **45**. For the ring and the plant material enclosed under its inset stone see **229, 253, 266, 276**.

## 128   Jesus exorcises the demons of Gerasa

i A.D.

Mark 5.1–20

Greek

They arrived at the far side of the lake, the land of the Gerasenes. As Jesus disembarked, he was immediately confronted by a man who emerged from the tombs. He was possessed by an unclean spirit. He lived among the tombs. No one could hold him in check with chains, for he had often been bound in fetters and chains, but he would just pull the chains apart and smash the fetters, and no one was strong enough to control him. All day long and all night long he sat among the tombs or on the mountains bawling and mutilating himself with stones. Espying Jesus from a distance he ran up and abased himself before him and, shouting out in a loud voice, said, "What business do we have, Jesus, son of the highest God? I implore you in the name of God, do not torture me." For Jesus was saying to him, "Unclean spirit, depart from this man." He asked him, "What is your name?" He replied, "My name is Legion, because we are many." He begged Jesus at length not to send them out of the land. A large herd of pigs was grazing there on the mountain. They begged him and said, "Send us into the pigs, so that we may enter them." He granted them this. The unclean spirits came out and went into the pigs and the herd rushed over the bank into the lake, around two thousand animals, and they were drowned in it. The swineherds ran off and reported the events in town and country. People came to see what had happened. They approached Jesus and saw the demoniac sitting there with clothes on and sound of mind, the man that had housed the legion, and they were frightened. The eye-witnesses told them all about what had been done to the demoniac and about the pigs. The people began to urge Jesus to leave their borders. As Jesus was boarding the boat the former demoniac begged to go with him. Jesus would not allow it, but said to him, "Return to your home and your family, and tell them how much the Lord has done for you and how he pitied you." He went off and began to spread the news of all that Jesus had done for him in the Decapolis, and everyone was amazed.

THIS IS PERHAPS THE BEST-KNOWN account of exorcism in the Western tradition. The demon's expulsion into a third party, which is then destroyed, is reminiscent of Jewish and Greek scapegoating practices; see **58**. This episode is narrated also at Luke 8.26–39. For other exorcisms by Jesus, see Matthew 4.23–5, 12.22–4, 15.29–31, 17.14–8, Mark 9.17–29, Luke 4.31–741 and 9.37–43. The following passage, **129**, documents another disgruntled local reaction to costly Christian exorcism.

## 129  Paul exorcises a ventriloquist at Philippi

i A.D.

Acts 16.16–24

Greek

It happened that when we were going to prayer a girl with a prophetic spirit [*puthôn*] met us. She provided her owners with a great deal of profit by prophesying. She attached herself to Paul and our group and cried out, saying, "These men are servants of the highest God, and they declare to you the road to salvation." She did this over many days. Paul was vexed by this and turned on the spirit and said, "I order you to depart from her in the name of Jesus Christ." It departed at once. When her owners saw that their hope of profit had departed they seized hold of Paul and Silas and dragged them to the officials in the marketplace. They brought them before the magistrates and said, "These men are throwing the city into turmoil. They are Jews and they promote customs that as Romans we cannot legally take up or practice." The crowd was against them. The magistrates tore off their clothes and gave the order for their thrashing. They subjected them to many blows and threw them into jail, and ordered the jailer to keep careful watch over them. On receipt of this order he threw them into the inner keep and locked their feet in the stocks.

AS WITH JESUS' DESTRUCTION OF THE pigs in the course of his exorcism of the "Legion" demons at Gerasa, Paul's exorcism of the prophetic demon is an expensive one for the locals and very much resented by them. This prophetic demon, a *puthôn*, is of the ventriloquists' variety (see **32–5**).

## 130  Right name, wrong exorcist

i A.D.

Acts 19.13–7

Greek

Some itinerant Jewish exorcists tried to use the name of the Lord Jesus on those possessed by evil spirits, saying "I adjure you in the name of the Jesus promoted by Paul." The seven sons of Sceva, the Jewish chief priest, were doing this. The evil spirit answered them and said, "I recognize Jesus and I know Paul. But who are you?" And the man possessed by the evil spirit leaped at them. He did them violence and trounced them completely, so that they fled from his house naked and wounded. This became known to all the Jews and Greeks that lived in Ephesus. Fear fell upon them all, and the name of the Lord Jesus was magnified.

JESUS' NAME IS USED AS A powerful one with which to expel the demon, as it is in the following Judaeo-Christian spell (**131**) and as Eleazar successfully uses that of Solomon (**127**). Here Jesus' power is endorsed even by an enemy, but the key message appears to be that one must have proper faith in Jesus to be able to use his name successfully.

## 131  A Judaeo-Christian-influenced exorcism spell

iv A.D.

PGM IV.3007–86

Greek

Validated recipe of Pibechis for use upon those possessed by demons. Take some oil made from unripe olives together with the plant *mastigia* and lotus fruit pulp and boil them with colorless marjoram, while saying: "IÔÊL ÔS SARTHIÔMI EMÔRI THEÔCHIPSOITH SITHEMEÔCH SÔTHÊ IÔÊ MIMIPSÔTHIÔÔPH PHERSÔTHI AEÊIOUÔ IÔÊ EÔ CHARI PHTHA, come out of (*insert name here*)." Do as usual. Inscribe the phylactery on a tin leaf: "IAÊÔ ABRAÔTHIÔCH PHTHA MESENPSINIAÔ PHEÔCH IAÊÔ CHARSOK." Fasten it around the sufferer. This is a terrifying thing for every demon, and he is frightened of it. Stand the sufferer opposite and perform the exorcism. This is the exorcism: "I adjure you by the god of the Hebrews, Jesus, IABA IAÊ ABRAÔTH AIA THÔTH ELE ELÔ AÊÔ EOU IIIBAECH ABARMAS IABARAOU ABELBEL LÔNA ABRA MAROIA BRAKIÔN, appearing in fire, who is in the middle of land, snow, and mist. TANNÊTIS. May your angel come down and be deaf to dissuasion. Let him assign to the demon that flits about the shape that God molded in his own holy paradise, because I pray to the holy god, AMMÔN IPSENTANCHÔ. (Use the formula.) I adjure you LABRIA IAKOUTH ABLANATHANALBA AKRAMM. (Use the formula.) AÔTH IATHABATHRA CHACH-THABRATHA CHAMUN CHEL ABRÔÔTH OUABRASILÔTH HALLÊLOU IELÔSAI IAÊL. I adjure you in the name of the one that was seen by Osrael in a shining column and in a day-time cloud and delivered his people from the Pharaoh and inflicted on Pharaoh the ten plagues because he would not listen to him. I adjure you, every demonic spirit, to give voice and tell of what kind you are, because I adjure you by the seal that Solomon set upon the tongue of Jeremiah, and he gave voice. You too give voice and tell of what kind you are, a demon dwelling in heaven or the air or on the earth or under the earth or in the underworld, or whether you are of the abyss or of the dry land or of the sea, give voice and tell of what sort you are, because I adjure you by the god that brings light and is invincible, the one who knows the contents of the hearts of all living creatures, the one who molded the human race from clay, the one who gathers the clouds from out of now-here and rains upon the earth and bestows his blessing upon its fruits, the one whom the entire heavenly host of angels and archangels praises. I adjure you in the name of the great god Sabaoth, through whom the river Jordan went into retreat, and the Red Sea, through which Israel passed [and which] became impassable, because I adjure you in the name of the one who invented the hundred and forty tongues and allotted them in accordance with his own orders. I adjure you in the name of the one who burned up the haughty giants with his thunderbolts, whom the heaven of heavens hymns, whom the cherubim's wings hymn. I adjure you in the name of the one who enclosed the sea with mountains or with a wall of sand and ordered it not to flow over it. And the abyss gave heed. You too give heed, every demonic spirit, because I adjure you in the name of the one who shakes together the four winds from the sacred eternities, the one who resembles the heaven, the sea, the clouds, the light-bringer, the invincible one. I adjure you by the one who dwells in pure Jerusalem, beside whom the unquenchable fire burns throughout all eternity, by his holy name, IAEÔ BAPHRENEMOUN (use the formula), before whom the Hell of fire trembles, around whom flames flare, before whom iron bursts apart, and whom every mountain fears from its foundations. I adjure you, every demonic spirit, by the overseer of the earth and the one who makes its foundations quake and the one who brought all things into existence from nothingness." And I adjure you, the one who take up this exorcism, not to eat pork. If you do not, every spirit and demon, of whatever kind it is, will be made subject to you. As you perform the exorcism, blow once on the possessed person, raising your breath from the tips of his feet up to his face, and the demon will be assigned. Guard your purity, for this spell is Hebraic and kept safe by pure men.

THE SPELL IS PREDOMINANTLY AND self-avowedly Judaeo-Christian in texture and contains many echoes of the language of the Septuagint. Despite this, it is attributed to the legendary Egyptian sorcerer Pibechis and includes some Egyptianizing names amongst its *voces magicae*. "Osrael" is a variant for "Israel." The "seal of Solomon" was a famous Jewish amulet; for Solomon, see **127**; for amulets, see **248–77**.

## 132 Exorcism spell from the "Eighth Book of Moses"

iv A.D.

PGM XIII.242–4

Greek

If you say the name to a man possessed by a demon while applying sulphur and bitumen to his nose, the demon will give voice at once and depart.

ANOTHER GRAECO-EGYPTIAN MAGICAL PAPYRUS attributes its wisdom to the Jewish tradition, with Moses being projected as an archetypal sorcerer. Brief as this spell is, it conveys the notion that a demon is expelled through being forced to confess its identity. The "name" is presumably that revealed to the magician by the god as the culmination of the ritual, instructions for which have preceded. See **127** for the nose in exorcism.

## THE EXPLOITATION OF BOYS' SOULS

## 133 A boy's soul is drawn out of his living body with a wand

iii B C

Clearchus of Soli On Sleep, F7–8 Wehrli

Greek

**F7.** Here is a proof that it is possible for the soul to leave the body and enter it again: the man in Clearchus who used a soul drawing wand [*psuchoulkos rhabdos*] on a sleeping lad and persuaded the great Aristotle, as Clearchus says in his books *On Sleep*, that the soul separates from the body and enters it again and treats it as a sort of hotel. For the man struck the boy with his wand and drew out his soul. Leading the soul some distance from the body with the stick, he demonstrated that the body remained motionless and was preserved unharmed and was unable to feel anything when pricked, as if it were dead. In the meantime the soul was at some remove from the body. But when the wand brought it back into association with the body and it reentered it the boy described everything in detail. As a result of this, Clearchus says, Aristotle and the other spectators of such scientific experiments came to believe that the soul was separable from the body. But the point I'm making, that the soul is able to leave the body and enter it again and make it breathe again after abandoning it, has long been demonstrated by the writings of the leaders of the Peripatos.

**F8.** In our own time some men have appeared to die and have been put in their tombs before returning to life. Some of them have been seen sitting on their tombs, others actually standing on them. Similarly in ages past Aristeas of Proconnesus, Hermotimus of Clazomenae, and Epimenides of Crete are reported to have rejoined the living after death. There is no need to go into detail.

CLEARCHUS WAS A LEARNED AND MUCH-TRAVELED pupil of Aristotle, founder of the Peripatos school. These fragments are both preserved in Proclus's commentary on Plato's *Republic* (2: p. 122, 2 and 2: p. 113, 19 Kroll). Boys were often exploited in magical divinations. Their supposedly purer souls were evidently felt to be less firmly mired in their bodies and worldly things and so more easily detachable, be it for soul-flights, as here, where the shaman-comparison is very appropriate (see **1–9**), or for magical observations, as in **163**, where the greater percipience of a detachable soul could be useful. It is likely that the boy here was put into a state we would recognize as hypnosis; see **134–5**. The use of boys in this fashion contextualizes the famous experiment of Plato's Socrates with a boy's soul (*Meno*). For ghosts appearing atop their tombs, see **36, 59**.

## 134   Apuleius and the boy Thallus: Divination or the expulsion of an epilepsy demon?

158–9 A.D.

Apuleius *Apology* 42-3

Latin

**42.** So they made up a story to play to the popular stereotype and said that I had bewitched some boy with an incantation in a secret place. I had made sure there were no witnesses apart from my few accomplices, and used a little altar and a lamp. He supposedly collapsed where he had been enchanted. When he came round he was out of his mind. They did not have the courage to take their lie to its logical conclusion. If they wanted to complete the story, they should have added that the same boy made many predictions from foreknowledge. For foreknowledge and divination are the prizes that magical incantations confer upon us. This amazing phenomenon with boys is guaranteed by the authority of educated men, not just popular superstition. I recall some things I read in the works of the philosopher Varro, a man of the most studied learning and erudition. He has a lot of this sort of material. Some people in Tralles made a magical inquiry about the outcome of the Mithridatic war. A boy stared at a likeness of Mercury in water and prophesied the future in a hundred and sixty verses. Similarly Fabius, after losing five hundred denarii, turned to Nigidius. By means of an incantation he compelled some boys to reveal where the purse had been buried, with part of the money, and how the rest of it had been spent. Marcus Cato the philosopher actually had one of the denarii. He admitted that it had been given to him by a footman as a donation to Apollo.

**43.** This, and more, is what I read about the practice of magic with boys in several authors. But I am in two minds as to whether to say that it can be done, or to deny it, although I follow Plato in the belief that certain divine powers occupy the middle ground between the gods and mortals, in terms of both their nature and their location, and that they control all the divinations and the amazing feats of the mages. I also hold the view that the human soul, especially the pure one of a boy, can be lulled to sleep, either by the enticement of a spell/singing [*carminum*] or by soothing aromas, and drawn out of its body to the extent that it is oblivious to the body's circumstances. As it is briefly liberated from awareness of its body it reverts to its own nature, which is of course immortal and divine, and in this way, as if asleep, it has foreknowledge of the future.

However, this is the situation. If any trust is to be placed in this foreknowledge, a boy selected to look into the future must, as I hear, be attractive and unharmed in body, quick of mind and articulate, either so that the divine power may lodge within him as a place worthy of itself, as if in a good house (if, that is, that divine power is brought within the body), or so that the soul itself, once roused, may be directed at once to its divine prescience, which it can recover easily, since it is innate and ready to hand and is not impaired or obscured by any forgetting. For, as Pythagoras used to say, Mercury must not be sculpted out of just any sort of wood.

In view of this, give me a name, please. Who was that healthy, perfect, clever, attractive boy that I considered worthy of initiation with a spell? But Thallus, whom you did name, needs a physician rather than a mage. For the poor boy is so devastated by epilepsy that he often collapses three or four times a day without any incantations, and wears out all his limbs with his convulsions. His face is ulcerous, his forehead and occiput are bashed up, he is dull of eye, gaping of nostril, and unsteady on his feet. He is the greatest of all mages, before whom Thallus has remained standing for any period. And so he often has to lie down, wilting from his illness or from weariness.

APULEIUS'S DEFENSE AGAINST THE CHARGES RELATING to his treatment of the boy Thallus is disingenuous (compare similarly **242, 299**), and not only for the deep knowledge of magical practices it evinces. The first paragraph here purports to address the specific accusation that he had used the boy for an observation in a lamp-divination and accordingly put him into a hypnotic trance; see **165–6**. He counters such a charge with the claim rather that Thallus was epileptic and had fallen down before him in a fit. Yet the expulsion of epilepsy demons from boys was itself just as much a typical activity of sorcerers as was divination, and we are left with the strong impression that Apuleius had been embarked on an enterprise of precisely this sort (see **14, 127–32**, with commentaries).

Apuleius provides us with some useful general remarks on the use of boys for divination. His stipulation that the boys used for magical divination must be attractive and perfect in body suggests that the manipulation of boys in this way may have fit well into the pederastic culture of Graeco-Roman antiquity (see also Justin Martyr *Apologies* 1.18). We have learned earlier in the speech that Apuleius has been writing erotic poems about boys (3–19).

The divination at Tralles appears to have combined the closely related scrying techniques of lecanomancy and catoptromancy; see the remarks before passage **163**. For the magical uses of images of Hermes/Mercury, including those by Apuleius himself, and the importance of such images being made from exceptional varieties of wood, see **242**. For Varro, compare **43, 45**. The writings of Nigidius Figulus (first century B.C.) no longer survive intact; see **137**. This Pythagorean appears to have been an important figure in the history of Roman magic. For Pythagoras himself see **1–6**.

### 135 One boy is used to observe the ghost (?) of another in divination

iii/iv A.D.

PGM VII.348–58

Greek

**Divination using a boy.** Lay him down on the floor and speak, and a dark-colored boy will appear before him. Spell: "I invoke you, dwellers in Chaos, Erebos, the abyss, and the earth, overseers of heaven and of the darkness, masters of the unseen, guardians of the hidden, leaders of those in the earth, managers of the infinite, earth-rulers, servants of the chasm, terrifying wrestlers, fear-messengers, powers of dark Erebos, compelling watchers, crag-rulers, heart-grievers, oppressive demons, iron-souls, BITHOURARA ASOUÊMARA . . . OTROUR MOURROUR APHLAU MANDRAROUROU SOU MARAROU, give me an oracle on the matter I investigate." Do the usual.

THE METHOD OF DIVINATION TO BE used is not directly expressed, but comparison with similar recipes (such as *PGM* V.1–53) suggests that the boy was to be used to observe a lamp and/or bowl divination (see **163–6**). The dark color of the appearing boy (compare **51, 115, 140**) and the underworld context of the powers that are appealed to suggest that he is a ghost. The ghost of a boy, useful for magical purposes as untimely dead and therefore restless, is perhaps thought to have a special affinity with the soul of the observing boy.

### 136 Apollonius of Tyana is accused of sacrificing a boy for divination

After 217 A.D.

Philostratus *Life of Apollonius* 7.11

Greek

7.11. [Demetrius speaks.] "Inasmuch as you are cleverer than the rest of us, a cleverer indictment has been found against you. Domitian wants to include you in the accusations for which he has exiled Nerva and his men."

"On what ground did he exile them?" said Apollonius.

"On the gravest charge that can currently be made, as the prosecutor thinks.

For he says that he has caught them rebelling against his rule, and that you incited the men to do this by, I think, cutting a boy."

"What do you mean? So that his rule might be destroyed by a eunuch?"

"No, that is not the charge trumped up against us. Rather, they say that you sacrificed a boy for divination, as is afforded by the guts of the young. Added to the indictment are accusations about your dress and lifestyle and the fact that some people worship you."

IT WAS HELD THAT A PARTICULARLY authoritative divination could be effected through boy-sacrifice. The victim's fully released soul, untimely dead, of course, could then be consulted in necromancy. Boys perhaps recommended themselves for this practice because of their use for observations in other varieties of divination. Whether or not such boy-sacrifice was ever put into practice, the idea of it was a useful stick with which to beat those one wished to accuse of magical practices. For boy sacrifice, see **92–3, 65, 137–8, 143, 241, 300** and, perhaps, **147**; for baby sacrifice, see **96**.

## 137   Cicero accuses Vatinius of sacrificing boys for necromancy

56 B.C.

Cicero *In Vatinium* 14

Latin

You [Vatinius], who are accustomed to call yourself a Pythagorean and to conceal behind the name of a most learned man your monstrous and barbarian customs, what crookedness of mind possessed you, what frenzy so great? You have undertaken unheard-of criminal rites. You are accustomed to call up the spirits of the dead. You are accustomed to make sacrifices to the ghosts of the dead with the entrails of boys.

THE SCHOLIAST COMMENTING ON THIS PASSAGE misidentifies the "most learned man," who is evidently Pythagoras, just mentioned, as Nigidius Figulus, for whom compare **45, 134**.

## 138   A plan to sacrifice an Ethiopian slave-boy in Beirut to enact an erotic attraction spell on a woman

Late v A.D.

Zacharius Scholasticus
*Life of Severus of Antioch*, PO, 2:57–9

Syriac

At that point it happened that some law students in Beirut had acquired a great reputation for magic. These were George, originally from Thessalonica, the first city of Illyricum, Chrysaoris of Tralles, a city in Asia, Asclepiodotus of Heliopolis, together with an Armenian and other individuals of this ilk. They were supported by John, surnamed Foulon, originally from Thebes in Egypt, and they never stopped devising impieties like the ones that follow. They collected magic books from everywhere and shared them with people who delighted in meddlesome schemes. Hence, everyone thought that they were going to accomplish an abominable murder. It was noised abroad besides that they were planning a sacrifice an Ethiopian slave belonging to the Theban in the circus by night. They wished, as they said, to conciliate the demon that was attached to them by this crime abhorrent to God and so get it to accomplish their project, as they supposed. Their general goal was to commit some kind of criminal act, and their immediate one was to bring a woman forcibly to the slave's master by erotic desire and the violence of demons. This woman lived in chastity and he was desperately in love with her. So they escorted this slave to the circus in the middle of the night, as if for some other end. But at the moment when they were about to commit this crime, God, who cares about the actions of men, had pity on this wretched slave and made some people pass by the place. Alarmed by their own boldness, as well as this unforeseen incident, they took flight, and the Ethiopian consequently took the opportunity to escape from their murderous hands, which were already in the course of putting him to death.

THE GREEK ORIGINAL OF THIS LIFE is lost, and it survives only in a Syriac translation. This English version is based on the French rendering of the Syriac in *PO*. For erotic magic, see **197–232**.

## WEREWOLVES

The relationship between werewolves and ghosts in antiquity is not easy to define. The Euthymus tale (**140**) appears to project werewolves as a subcategory of ghosts, and Petronius's tale (**141**) may do the same; at any rate it associates them with ghosts. But living sorcerers and witches could also transform themselves and others into wolves; see **90, 101–2, 144**. Compare also Medea's exploitation of werewolf body-parts (**69**) and witches' exploitation of wolf-worried bones (**92, 96, 101, 107**). Ghostly or magical associations are less obvious in the context of the rituals of Zeus Lycaeus. For more general ghostly shape-shifting see **115**.

**139**  **The Neuri become wolves**    These people [the Neuri] may well be sorcerers [*goētes*]. It is said by the Scythians and the Greeks living in Scythia that every year each of the Neuri at one point becomes a wolf for a few days, before returning to his previous form. They don't persuade me of it, but they certainly say it, and they swear to what they say.

420s B.C.

Herodotus 4.105

Greek

HERODOTUS CONVENIENTLY MAKES THE ASSOCIATION between lycanthropy and sorcery.

**140**  **Euthymus of Locri drives a werewolf into the sea**    When Euthymus returned to Italy he fought with the Hero. This was the background. They say that after the sack of Troy Odysseus was, in the course of his wanderings, brought to shore by the winds at several cities in Italy and Sicily, and in particular they say that he put in with his ships at Temesa. Anyway, one of his sailors got drunk there and raped a virgin. In punishment for this wrongdoing he was stoned to death by the locals. Odysseus thought no more about his loss and sailed off. However, the demon of the man that had been stoned let no opportunity pass but killed the Temesans indiscriminately and launched attacks on every age group. It came to the point that the Temesans were preparing to abandon Italy altogether, but the Pythia forbade them to do so. Rather, she bade them propitiate the Hero, enclose a precinct for him, build him a temple, and give him the fairest of Temesa's virgins as a bride each year. They carried out the god's behest and the ghost stopped terrorizing them. Now Euthymus came to Temesa, and it happened that the customary offering was being made to the ghost at that time. He inquired into the rites they were performing and conceived the desire to enter the temple and take a look at the virgin. When he saw her, his first reaction was pity for her, his second desire. The girl swore that she would marry him if he saved her, so Euthymus made his preparations and waited for the demon to arrive. He defeated the Hero in a battle, and (since he had driven it from the land) it disappeared and dove into the sea. Thereupon Euthymus had a glorious marriage and the people of the place were delivered from the ghost for evermore. I also heard a story of the following kind about Euthymus, to the effect that he lived to an extreme old age, es-

ii A.D.

Pausanias 6.6.7–11

Greek

caped death, and rather departed from the world of men in an alternative way. I heard from a man that had sailed there to trade that Temesa is still inhabited in my own time. That is just what I heard, but I know what follows because I happened across a painting. It was a copy of an ancient one. It showed a young man, Sybaris, and a river, Calabros, and a spring, Lyca. There was also a hero's shrine and the city of Temesa, and in the midst of these things was the ghost that Euthymus cast out. His skin was awfully black and he was utterly terrifying to see. His clothing was a wolfskin. The picture was inscribed, and gave him the name Lycas/Alibas ["Wolfy" or "Corpse"]. That is enough on this subject.

ALTHOUGH DEMONS COULD OFTEN TAKE ON animal shapes, the association of the wolf-form with ghostliness suggests that this tale is influenced by notions of werewolves. Euthymus's *floruit* was the early fifth century B.C. The giving of the fairest virgin to the Hero presumably did not in reality entail the girl's sacrifice but her temple-service for a year prior to marriage. The reading of the ghost's name is uncertain; the manuscripts imply *Lybas*, which would not be independently meaningful. The two usual conjectures would, in their different ways, both be appropriate. Blackness befits a ghost or demon; see **51, 115**, and, more generally, Winkler (1980). We learn elsewhere (Strabo C255) that the member of Odysseus's crew concerned was none other than Polites, he who witnessed Circe's animal transformations (**72**). For the defeated demon's disappearance into water compare **128**. There are intimations of shamanism in Pausanias's claim that Euthymus lived to an extreme old age and then departed from the realm of the living by a mechanism other than death (compare **5–8**). Aelian *Varia Historia* 8.18 tells that he disappeared into the river Caecinus.

## 141   A werewolf transformation

Ca. 66 A.D.

Petronius *Satyricon* 61–2

Latin

61. When I was still a slave, we lived in a narrow street. The house is now Gravilla's. There, by the will of the gods, I fell in love with the wife of Terentius the innkeeper. You knew Melissa of Tarentum, that gorgeous creature. But, by Hercules, I didn't love her just for her body or for sexual reasons, but because she had such a nice personality. If I asked her for anything, I was never refused. If she made tuppence, she gave me a penny. She kept my money for me, and never cheated me. Her husband met his end one day out on the estate. I did everything I could to get to her. People make themselves your friend when they're in need. By chance the master had set off on his way to Capua to deal with some odds and ends. I seized the opportunity and persuaded our guest to come with me to the fifth milestone. He was a soldier, as brave as Orcus. We shifted our butts just before dawn. The moon was shining like the midday sun. We arrived among the tombs. My man went for a pee against a gravestone. I held back, singing and counting the stones. Then, when I looked back at my companion, he had taken all his clothes off and laid them beside the road. I almost died of fright, and I stood there like a dead man. He peed a circle around his clothes and suddenly became a wolf. Don't think I'm joking. No one's inheritance is so valuable as to make me lie. But, as I'd begun to say, after he had become a wolf, he began to howl and ran into the woods. At first I didn't know where I was, but then I went to his clothes to pick them up. But they had turned to stone. Whoever died with fright, if I didn't then? But I drew my sword and hacked at the shades, until I arrived at my girlfriend's house. I was like a ghost when I got in, and almost bubbling out my final breath. My groin was awash with sweat, my eyes were dead, and I have still barely recovered from the experience. Melissa expressed amazement that

I'd walked there so late and said, "If you'd come earlier, at least you could have helped us. For a wolf got into the estate and among the flocks. He was draining the blood out of them like a butcher. But even if he got away, the last laugh was ours, for our slave managed to get a spear through his neck." When I heard this, I could not even think of sleep, but when it was fully light I ran off home like the robbed innkeeper. When I came to the place where the clothes had turned to stone, I found nothing but blood. But when I arrived home, my soldier was lying on his bed like an ox, and a doctor was attending to his neck. I realized that he was a werewolf/shape-shifter [*versipellis*], and I could not thereafter bring myself to break bread with him, not even if you had forced me on pain of death. Others can make up their own mind about this. But if I'm lying, may your guardian spirits exercise their wrath upon me.

THIS TALE IS TOLD BY THE freedman Niceros at Trimalchio's dinner party and immediately precedes Trimalchio's own tale of witches (**106**). Petronius (or his chief narrator, Encolpius) uses both tales to enthrall and entertain in their own right, but at the same time they serve to convey the gullibility and feeble-mindedness of their tellers. Petronius's (or Encolpius's) attitude toward them may therefore be compared to the attitude of Lucian (or that of his chief narrator, Tychiades) to the tales narrated by the diners of the *Philopseudes*. And like Trimalchio's witch story and a number of the stories in the *Philopseudes*, this one has the feel of a traditional folktale.

The transformation takes place under a full moon. Niceros's companion is presumably taken unawares when the transformation-urge comes upon him, although he has time to take the precaution of stripping and urinating around his clothing. The purpose of this seems to be to turn his clothes into stone, so that no one can make off with them. It is a commonplace of werewolf lore that the wolf must recover his clothes in order to effect the reverse transformation; see **143**. For the circular motion of the urination, compare **30**. Here again the werewolf is associated with ghosts: the transformation takes place in a cemetery (see **142**); Niceros "dies" of fright on witnessing the transformation; he flees from the sight of it by hacking at the ghosts with his sword (see **244**); and he arrives at his destination resembling a ghost. The "robbed innkeeper" metaphor alludes both to the proverbial thievishness of innkeepers; compare the behavior of the witch-innkeeper Meroe at **104**.

## 142  Marcellus Sidetes on medical lycanthropy

Earlier ii A.D.
(Marcellus); ca.
mid–vi A.D. (Aëtius)

Aëtius of Amida *Libri medicinales* 6.11

Greek

Marcellus on lycanthropy ["werewolfism"] or cynanthropy ["dogism"]. Men afflicted with the disease of so-called cyanthropy or lycanthropy go out by night in the month of February in imitation of wolves or dogs in all respects, and they tend to hang around tombs until daybreak. These are the symptoms that will allow you to recognize sufferers from this disease. They are pallid, their gaze is listless, their eyes are dry, and they cannot produce tears. You will observe that their eyes are sunken and their tongue is dry, and they are completely unable to put on weight. They feel thirsty, and their shins are covered in lacerations which cannot heal because they are continually falling down and being bitten by dogs. Such are their symptoms. One must recognize that lycanthropy is a form or melancholia. You will treat it by opening a vein at the time of its manifestation and draining the blood until the point of fainting. Then feed the patient with food conducive to good humors. He is to be given sweet baths. After that, using the whey of the milk, cleanse him over three days with the gourd-medicine of Rufus or Archigenes or Justus. Repeat this a second and third time after intervals. After the purifications one should use the antidote to viper bites. Take the other measures too prescribed earlier for melancholia. As evening arrives and the disease manifests itself apply to the head the lotions that usually induce sleep and anoint the nostrils with scents of this sort and opium. Occasionally supply sleep-inducing drinks too.

MARCELLUS SIDETES LIVED AND WORKED IN the reigns of Hadrian and Antoninus Pius. Even in this medical interpretation of werewolfism the association with ghosts is maintained; compare **141**.

## 143  Arcadian werewolf lore

i A.D.

Pliny *Natural History* 8.80–2

Latin

**80.** We should be confident in the belief that it is untrue that men are turned into wolves and restored again to their own form. Otherwise, we should believe everything that we have learned to be fabulous over all these centuries. All the same, we will indicate the origin of the popular superstition that werewolves [*versipelles*] are among those subject to a curse [*maledictis*]. **81.** Evanthes, by no means the most despicable of Greek writers, reports the Arcadian tradition that a man chosen by lot from the family of one Anthus is escorted to some marsh in the area. He hangs his clothes on an oak tree, swims across the marsh, goes off into the wilderness, is transformed into a wolf, and joins a pack with others of the same kind for nine years. If he has held himself back from human flesh in that time, he returns to the same marsh, swims back across it, and recovers his form, with nine years' aging added to his erstwhile guise. Also . . . he recovers the same clothing. **82.** The extent of Greek gullibility is amazing. No lie is so outrageous as to want witness. Similarly Scopas, recorder of the Olympic victors, reports that Demaenetus of Parrhasia, at the human sacrifice that the Arcadians were still then making to Zeus Lycaeus, tasted the entrails of the slaughtered boy and turned himself into a wolf. The same man was restored to human form in the tenth year afterward, underwent athletic training in boxing, and returned from Olympia a victor.

THIS MORE EXPLICIT ACCOUNT OF THE fate of the werewolves is read as refracting a rite of passage in which Arcadian youths were relegated to the territorial borders to patrol them, in an institution parallel to that of the Spartan *krypteia* and the Athenian *ephêbeia*. The myth of Dolon, who goes spying by night in a wolf-skin (Homer *Iliad* 10 and Pseudo-Euripides *Rhesus*), is also thought to reflect such an institution. But puzzles remain: nine years is too long a period of exclusion for such a ritual; nor are such rituals performed by individuals, but by age-classes.

Like Petronius's werewolf (**141**), Pliny's werewolves remove their clothes prior to transformation, symbolically divesting themselves of human attributes. These too subsequently seek to recover their clothes, although the (slightly corrupt) text does not as it stands make this a prerequisite of their reversion. Pliny's material can be shown, by comparison with Augustine *City of God* 18.17, to derive in the first instance from Varro. The ultimate Greek sources, Evanthes and Scopas (whose name some emend to Apollas), are otherwise unknown.

For boy-sacrifice see **136**, with commentary.

# 9
# Necromancy

For necromancy see also **25–31, 34, 36, 42, 44–6, 59, 65, 90, 112, 126, 291, 244.**

## EVOCATION

Ghost-evocation technology is first laid out in Homer's *Odyssey* (**144**) and remains fairly conservative throughout ancient literature. These are its main features:

- The rites take place at night (in Homer night becomes a place).
- The rites are focused around a pit and a fire.
- There are libations of honey-milk, wine, water, and sometimes olive oil, together with sprinkled barley. These are identical with normal, nonmagical, tributary tomb-side offerings to the dead. They are of a nourishing, soothing, and propitiatory nature.
- Black cattle (usually sheep) are sacrificed, their color saluting that of the underworld and of night. As usual with offerings directed toward the underworld, as opposed to heaven above, their carcasses are burned whole (in "holocaust"), not eaten.
- The blood from the jugulated throats of the cattle is allowed to drain into the pit for the ghosts to drink. This restores to them, temporarily, an element of corporeality, and so aids their communication with the living.
- Prayers are made to the ghosts and the underworld powers that reignb over them, in the latter case to secure the ghosts' temporary release.
- The ghosts arrive in a pressing host and must be managed with a sword, since they remain frightened of bronze and iron (see **244**).

---

## 144 Circe sends Odysseus to consult the ghost of Tiresias at the Acheron

vii B.C. or earlier

Homer *Odyssey*
10.488–540, 11.13–149
(edited)

Greek

**10.488.** So I spoke. The divine goddess Circe answered me at once, "Zeus-born son of Laertes, Odysseus of the many devices, please do not remain in my house if you do not want to. But, first, you must accomplish another journey and come to the house of Hades and dread Persephone, to consult the ghost of Theban Tiresias, the prophet who is blind, although his mind is sound. For to him alone did Persephone grant retention of his wits even after death. But the other dead just flit about as shadows."

**496.** So she spoke, but my dear heart was broken. I sat on the bed and wept, and my spirit did not want to go on living and seeing the light of the sun. But when I had sated myself of weeping and rolling about, I made reply to her: "Circe, who will guide me on this journey? No one has yet come to Hades in a black ship."

**503.** So I spoke, and the divine goddess answered me at once, "Zeus-born son of Laertes, Odysseus of the many devices, do not tarry beside your ship fretting about not having a guide. Put your mast up, spread your white sails, and then just sit. The north wind will carry it for you. But when you have crossed Ocean in your ship, you will find a fruitful shore and the groves of Persephone, tall poplars and fruit-shedding willows. Beach your ship there by deep-eddying Ocean, but proceed yourself to the dank house of Hades. There is a place where Pyriphlegethon and Cocytus, which is an off-flow from the water of the Styx, flow into the Acheron, and there is a rock and the confluence of two loud-roaring rivers. Draw near to this spot, hero, and, as I bid you, dig a pit a cubit wide this way and that. Around it pour a full libation to all the dead, first with honey-milk, then with sweet wine, and third with water. Sprinkle white barley on top. Pray at length to the powerless folk of the dead, and promise them that when you have come to Ithaca you will sacrifice to them in your palace your best barren heifer, and that you will heap up a pyre with offerings, and that you will sacrifice to Tiresias separately an all-black sheep, the outstanding one among your flocks. But when you have prayed to the glorious tribes of the dead, sacrifice a male sheep and a black ewe, twisting their heads down to Erebus, while turning back yourself, in longing for the streams of the river. At that point many ghosts of the dead will come up. Then rouse your men and give them the order to flay and burn the sheep that lie there jugulated by the pitiless bronze, and to pray to the gods, to strong Hades and dread Persephone. You must yourself draw your sharp sword from your thigh and sit there, and do not allow the powerless folk of the dead to approach the blood before you make inquiry of Tiresias. Then the prophet will come up at once, leader of peoples. He will tell you your route, the distances of your travels, and the nature of your return over the sea of fish."

**11.13.** The ship came to the far edge of deep-streaming Ocean. That is the location of the people and city of the Cimmerian men, buried in mist and cloud. Never does the shining sun look upon them with its rays, neither when he goes up to the starry heaven, nor when he turns back from heaven toward the earth. Rather, baneful night is spread over the unfortunate mortals. Here we came and beached the ship, and took the sheep out. Then we went on foot along the course of Ocean, until we came to the place that Circe had indicated. There Perimedes and Eurylochus held the victims. I drew my sharp sword from my thigh and dug a pit a cubit wide this way and that. Around it I poured a full libation to all the dead, first with honey-milk, then with sweet wine, and third with water. I sprinkled white barley on top. I prayed at length to the powerless folk of the dead, and promised them that when I came to Ithaca I would sacrifice to them in my palace my best barren heifer, and that I would heap up a pyre with offerings, and that I would sacrifice to Tiresias separately an all-black sheep, the outstanding one among my flocks. But when I had prayed to them, the tribes of the dead, with prayers and vows, I took the sheep and jugulated them over the pit, and their dark blood flowed. The ghosts of the dead assembled from Erebus, brides, bachelors, old men who had suffered much, tender maidens with their fresh grief, warriors wounded by bronze-tipped spears, men killed in battle with their bloodied armor. From all sides they crowded en masse round the pit with a terrible cry. Fear gripped me and turned me pale.

<*JA*> Then I roused my men and gave them the order to flay and burn the sheep that lay there jugulated by the pitiless bronze, and to pray to the gods, to strong Hades and dread Persephone. I myself drew my sharp sword from my thigh and sat there, and I did not allow the powerless folk of the dead to approach the blood before I made inquiry of Tiresias <*JA*>.

51. First came up the ghost of my comrade Elpenor, for he had not yet been buried under the earth of broad roads. We had left him unwept and unburied in Circe's palace, since other concerns were pressing upon us. I wept on seeing him and felt pity in my heart. I gave voice and spoke to him: "Elpenor, how did you come under the dark of the west? You beat me on foot, while I came with my black ship."

59. So I spoke, and he groaned and answered me. "Zeus-born son of Laertes, Odysseus of many devices, an evil demon and an excess of wine destroyed me. Lying in the palace of Circe I did not think to come back down by going to the tall ladder, but I fell straight down from the roof. My neck was broken and my soul came down to Hades. Now I beseech you by those left behind, those who aren't here now, by your wife and your father, who reared you when you were little, and by Telemachus, whom you left on his own in your palace. I know that when you leave the house of Hades here you will direct your well-made ship to the island of Aeaea. When you get there, lord, I bid you have thought for me. When you return do not leave me unwept and unburied, turning your back on me, lest I become a cause of the gods' anger against you. Rather, burn me with all my weapons, and heap up a barrow for me on the shore of the hoary sea, unfortunate man that I am, so that future generations too will learn of me. Do these things for me and fix my oar into the tomb, the one with which I used to row when I was alive and with my comrades."

79. So he spoke, and I said to him in reply, "Poor man, I shall do all this for you." We sat there exchanging miserable words, I on the one side holding my sword over the blood, while on the other side the ghost of my comrade had much to say.

84. There came up the ghost of my dead mother, Anticleia the daughter of the great-hearted Autolycus, whom I had left behind alive when I went to holy Ilium. I wept to see her and I pitied her in my heart. But even so I did not allow her to approach the blood, deeply grieved though I was, before I made inquiry of Tiresias.

90. Then there came up the ghost of Theban Tiresias with his golden scepter. He recognized me and addressed me: "Zeus-born son of Laertes, Odysseus of the many devices, why, poor man, have you left the light of the sun and come here to see the dead and the joyless place? But step back from the pit, so that I may drink and give you infallible information."

97. So he spoke, and I stepped back and fixed my silver-studded sword back into its scabbard. He drank the dark blood, and then the blameless prophet spoke to me: ". . . A death ever so gentle will come upon you from the sea, and it will slay you only when you are overcome by your old age, comfortable though it be. You will be surrounded by your people in fortunate condition. These infallible prophecies I declare to you. . . . Whichever of the dead you allow to approach the blood will speak infallibly to you. But if you begrudge it to anyone, he will retreat."

THESE EXCERPTS INTERLOCK WITH THOSE IN 72. Circe is the first necromantic witch of the classical tradition. Although she does not participate physically in Odysseus's evocation of the dead (as the Sibyl does in that of Aeneas at

*Aeneid* 6, or as Erictho does in that of Sextus Pompey, **155**), she masterminds it, provides him with full instructions for the journey and procedure, and even supplies him with the necessary sheep. When Odysseus subsequently returns to her island from the consultation, she already knows all that has passed between him and the ghosts. Had she been there in invisible form, since we know that she can pass through space unseen? Had she used an ability comparable to Meroe's to hear speech across vast distances (see **104**)? Or had Odysseus never really left her island at all?

Varied and contradictory ideas about the afterlife are found here. The notion that the dead inhabit the same level as the living, but separated from them by a river (see **108**), is embodied twice, in Odysseus's crossing of Ocean and in his meeting with the dead at the Acheron. But Homer's descriptions of the arrival of the ghosts, together with the ritual in which a blood-offering is poured into the ground, implies rather than they live in the earth below. The notion that the dead, Tiresias aside, are witless before drinking blood is imperfectly carried through: Ajax will be seen to recognize Odysseus even without drinking blood.

The description of the place at which Odysseus makes his consultation conforms well enough with the topography of Thesprotia for us to conclude that it reflects the historical oracle of the dead at the actual Acheron (**150**). The Cimmerians were a mythical race, although the name also became identified with that of a historical people in Asia Minor. Their role was to live in darkness beside underworld entrances (compare **153–4**), and they were parodied in Aristophanes's "Shadow-feet" (**26**).

Odysseus perhaps averts his gaze as he makes the sacrifice because ghosts do not like to be looked upon as they emerge from the underworld: Orpheus famously sent the ghost of his wife Eurydice flying back into the underworld when he looked upon her as she emerged (see **20**, with commentary). The flaying of the sheep may be more significant than first appears. In Apulia one consulted the ghosts of the dead prophets Calchas and Podalirius by sacrificing sheep to them, flaying them, and then performing incubation on their tomb on the fleece (Strabo C284 and Scholia to Pseudo-Lycophron *Alexandra* 1050; compare **149** for incubation). Similarly one consulted the prophet Amphiaraus, who had entered the underworld without actually dying, at his sanctuary at Oropus on the Boeotian-Attic border by sacrificing a sheep to him and performing incubation on the fleece in a purpose-built dormitory (Pausanias 1.34).

Why does Odysseus promise further sacrifices to the ghosts upon his return home? Circe could easily have provided these along with the sheep. Such a promise gives the ghosts a continuing incentive to cooperate with Odysseus once they have enjoyed their offerings and, perhaps more importantly, gives them an incentive to release him alive as opposed to dragging him back down to the underworld with them. Contact with ghosts in itself could often be fatal to the living (see **114, 115–16, 157**).

It is curious that Odysseus should only be told to pray to Hades and Persephone once the ghosts have actually arisen, since one would expect the object of the prayer to have been the ghosts' release. For subsequent dissatisfaction in antiquity with the verbal element of this rite, see **145**, next.

Julius Africanus remodels the Homeric text between the points indicated by "<JA>." After quoting *Odyssey* 11.34–43 in accordance with the canon, he continues as follows in the next passage, **145**.

## 145 A more explicitly magical incantation is interpolated into Homer's narrative

Ca. 230 A.D.

Julius Africanus *Kestoi* 18 (*PGM* XXIII)

Greek

But I drew my sharp sword from my thigh and sat there, and I did not allow the powerless folk of the dead to approach the blood. I said in reply [*sic*]:

(*Here Homer has explained what one has to do.*)

"O Rivers, Earth and you who punish whoever of the dead is forsworn, be witnesses and accomplish this spell for us. I have come to inquire how I may come to the land of Telemachus, whom I left on the bosom of his nurse, my child." Such was his outstanding spell.

(*Here Homer explains the spell that must be uttered.*)

"Hear me, propitious god, overseer, well-sired Anubis . . . [undecipherable verse 1] . . . come, Hermes, snatcher, come to me underworld Zeus, with your fair tresses, grant that this spell should work and accomplish it. Come here Hades and Earth, imperishable fire, Sun-Titan, come also Yahweh and Ptah and Phre [Ra], guardian of laws, and greatly honored Nephtho and very blessed Ablanatho, with belt of fiery snakes, earth-tearing, Isis-headed, Abraxas, demon celebrated for your cosmic name, director of the earth's axis and the star's dance and cold light of the Bears, come also for me Phren, outstripping all in self-control . . . [undecipherable verse 2] . . . and Birth and Passing-of-prime and beautifully burning Fire, come Isis of earth and heaven, you who control dreams and Sirius, who . . ." This is the invocation I made as I stood beside the pit. For well did I recall the instructions of Circe, who knows all the drugs that the broad earth grows. Then there came the great wave of lion-fighting Acheron, Cocytus, Lethe, and the greatest Pyriphlegethon, and a vast array of dead gathered around the pit. First came up the ghost of my comrade Elpenor.

Therefore, since this is so, either the poet himself passed in silence over the extra passage of the spell to preserve the tone of the narrative, or the Pisistratids excised it when they were making their recension of these verses, because they felt that it had been interpolated into the poem at this point. . . . I myself have restored it here as a rather valuable piece of epic creativity. You will find the whole section deposited in the archives of my home town, the colony of Aelia Capitolina [i.e., Jerusalem] in Palaestine and in Nysa in Caria, and, up to the thirteenth verse, in Rome at the Baths of Alexander and in the beautiful library of the Pantheon, which I myself assembled for Augustus [i.e., Severus Alexander].

LATER AGES WERE DISTURBED BY THE lack of an explicitly magical incantation in Homer's necromancy sequence, and this one was eventually interpolated into the text. This supplement, perhaps composed by Aristodemus of Nysa in the first century B.C. (as Robert supposed), is preserved in a fragment of the Christian Julius Africanus's *Kestoi*, or *Magical Embroideries*. The world of the interpolated incantation is very much that of the Greek magical papyri: appeal is made to Greek underworld deities, to the Sun, to Egyptian deities (Anubis, Ptah, Phre/Ra, Nephtho), to Jewish ones (Yahweh), and to the familiar demons of the papyri (Ablanatho and Abraxas/Abrasax; the latter's name is "cosmic" because the total numerical value of its constituent letters equals 365, the number of days in the year).

Africanus's speculations on the supposed suppression of the passage are of particular interest. They are founded on the notion that such magical material is incompatible with the tone of epic. Is this because the sort of magic implied by the passage is low-class? Charlatanry? Un-Greek? Pisistratus and his sons, tyrants of Athens continuously between 546 and 510 B.C., are traditionally said to have presided over the first recension and standardization of the Homeric poems. Africanus says that the Roman version of the text only included this material as far as the "thirteenth verse," but it is only after the thirteenth verse in Julius Africanus's quotation that the fully extraneous material begins!

The undecipherable verses read, according to Preisendanz's reconstructions: (1) "and hear me, wily one, hidden lover, lady-savior of Osiris"; (2) "I call you, Briareus, and Phrasios, and you, Ixion."

## 146 Empedocles brings the might of a dead man from Hades

Ca. 450 B.C.

Empedocles F101
Wright; F111 DK (Diogenes Laertius 8.59)

Greek

You will learn of all the drugs that are defenses against ills and against old age, since for you alone I shall accomplish all these things. You will stay the might of the tireless winds that rush over the land and destroy crops with their gusts, and then, if you wish, you will unleash again requiting blasts. After black rain you will bring a drought upon men in the fair season and, after the summer drought, you will create the streams that live in the ether and rear trees, and you will bring from Hades the might of a dead man.

IN THIS FRAGMENT EMPEDOCLES SEEMINGLY EITHER makes or reports a promise of powers. These appear to include the ability to evocate the ghost of a dead man and to make it work for one, perhaps even in cursing (see **168–84, 197–213**). Compare **45** and especially **5**, where Empedocles's wind-warding abilities are compared with those of the other shamans, Pythagoras, Abaris, and Epimenides; see also **97–103** for witches' control of the elements.

## 147 An epigram in the Ovidian style on the evocation of the ghost of Pompey with an impious human sacrifice

Ca. 50–80 A.D.

*Latin Anthology* no. 402
Shackleton-Bailey; no.
406 Riese; [Seneca]
*Epigram* 16 Baehrens

Latin

*On the rites of one evocating the ghosts of the Magni:*
The impious [*impius*] chief of an unspeakable religion, accustomed to learning the fates in advance through human entrails, laid the spasming guts of a free born breast in the flames and broke the ground with a magical incantation. He dared to draw Pompey from the Elysian fields. For shame! That (a) Magnus should look upon this rite! Stupid man, why do you seek Pompey among the shades of the underworld? His spirit could not be confined by the earth.

LITTLE IS CERTAIN ABOUT THIS PUZZLING epigram transmitted under Seneca's name in manuscripts. Its versification and vocabulary point to a composition in the ca. 50–80 A.D. period, which would be compatible with Senecan authorship, but they also indicate that it is Ovidian rather than Senecan in style. The Magnus evocated as a ghost is presumably the original Pompeius Magnus, Pompey the Great. The chief of the unspeakable religion is presumably his son, Sextus Pompey, the epithet "impious" ironically saluting his adopted surname, "Pious" (Pius). For Sextus's traditional association with necromancy in general and the evocation of the ghost of his father in particular see **96, 155**. The Magnus that will, for shame, look upon the rite could be either the evocator-son, or, more probably, the innocent evocated father as he rises to it. For human sacrifice see **136**, with commentary.

## 148 Menippus exploits necromancy to discover the secret of life

ii A.D.

Lucian *Menippus* 2, 6–10, 21–2

Greek

**2. Friend:** What are you saying? Have the people in the underworld passed a new resolution about the people here?

**Menippus:** Yes, by Zeus, lots of them. But it's not right to disclose them to everyone or to blurt out these secrets. I fear someone may indict us for impiety in the court of Rhadamanthys.

**Friend:** No, Menippus! Please, by Zeus, don't begrudge the tale to your friend. You'll be telling it to someone who knows how to be discreet, not least because I've been initiated into the mysteries.

**6. Menippus:** So, deceived in this hope too, I was even more dissatisfied, but I heartened myself a little with the consideration that in being foolish and going around in ignorance of the truth I shared the company of many "wise" men, men greatly celebrated for their insight. So one day, as I tossed and turned in my bed because of these concerns, I decided to go to Babylon and consult one of the mages, one of the disciples of Zoroaster and the upholders of his tradition. I heard that they could open the gates of Hades with rites and incantations, take down anyone they wanted, and send him back up to the surface again safely. So I thought it the best course to secure a descent from one of these men, to go to Tiresias the Boeotian and to find out from him, since he was a prophet and a wise man, what life was the best and the one that a sensible man would choose.

I leaped to my feet and made my way directly to Babylon, as quickly as I could. When I arrived I fell in with one of the Chaldaeans, a wise man whose skill amazed me. He had white hair and a long and venerable beard. His name was Mithro-barzanes. After much begging and supplicating I eventually prevailed on him to escort me in my descent for any price he named. **7.** The man took me into his care. First, for twenty-nine days from the start of the new moon, he took me down to the Euphrates to wash me at dawn, before the rising sun. He accompanied this with a protracted recitation, which I could not properly catch, since he spoke hurriedly and obscurely, like bad heralds at games. But he seemed to be calling on some demons. After the spell he would spit into my face three times and then he went back without looking at any of the people we met. Our food was nuts, our drink milk, honey-milk and the water of the Choaspes. We slept on the grass under the stars.

When I had been sufficiently prepared by this regimen, he took me to the river Tigris around midnight and purified me, cleansed me and consecrated me with a torch, a squill, and a number of other things, and at the same time muttered that incantation. Then he cast a spell over all my body and walked around me, so that I would not be harmed by the ghosts, and took me back home in that condition, having me walk backward. Thenceforth, we busied ourselves with the journey. **8.** He himself donned the dress of a mage, which strongly resembled Median garb, but he produced these things and got me up in them, the felt cap, the lion-skin, and also the lyre. He advised me, should anyone ask me my name, not to say Menippus, but Heracles or Odysseus or Orpheus.

**Friend:** To what end, Menippus? I don't understand the rationale of the getup or the names.

**Menippus:** This is quite clear and no secret at all. For, since these people had gone down to Hades alive before us, he thought that, if he made me resemble them, I could easily escape the detection of Aeacus, who guards the door, and pass within without hindrance as a familiar visitor. The idea was that they would wave me through because of the getup, as they do in the tragedies.

**9.** Anyway, daylight was just beginning to show, and we went down to the river and got on with putting out. He had prepared a boat, victims, honey-milk, and all the other things we needed for the rite. We stowed all the equipment away and then ourselves "went grieving, letting drop a healthy tear" [Homer *Odyssey* 11.5]. The river carried us a certain distance, and then we sailed into the marsh and the lake into which the Euphrates disappears. We crossed this and came to a deserted place, wooded and sunless. Here we disembarked and, Mithrobarzanes taking the lead, dug a pit, jugulated the sheep, and libated their blood around it. Meanwhile the mage, holding up his torch, shouted out at the top of his voice, using his subdued tone no longer, and invoked all the demons together, the Poenae, the Furies, "Hecate of the night and dread Persephone" [unidentifiable quotation], and he mixed in some meaningless foreign names and polysyllables.

**10.** At once the whole area shook and the ground was broken open by the spell. One could hear the barking of Cerberus in the distance, and everything looked dismal and gloomy: "Down below, Hades, lord of the underworld, was afraid" [Homer *Iliad* 20.61]. Most things could be seen—the lake, Pyriphlegethon, and the palace of Pluto. Even so, we went down through the hole and found Rhadamanthys all but dying from fright. Cerberus barked and became somewhat agitated, but I struck up a tune on my lyre and he was soon bewitched by the song. When we got to the lake, we almost didn't get across, for the ferry was already full to overflowing with lamentation. All the passengers were wounded, one in the leg, another in the head, a third with some other injury. I suppose they'd all come from some war. However, when the excellent Charon saw the lion-skin he thought I was Heracles, took me on board, ferried me across gladly, and showed us the path on the other side.

**21. Menippus:** This was what I had come for. I accosted Tiresias, told him everything, and begged him to tell me what sort of life he held to be the best. He laughed—a little old blind man, pallid, with a weak voice—"My son," he said, "I understand the reason for your confusion: you got it from the wise men who all think different things. But it is not right for me to speak to you, for it has been forbidden by Rhadamanthys." "No," I said, "father, please tell me and don't stand by and see me going round in life even blinder than you." He took me to one side and drew me far apart from the others. Then he gently leant into my ear and said, "The life of the ordinary man is the best. It is more prudent to give up speculation about the heavens and investigation into ends and beginnings, to spit on these wise syllogisms and consider this sort of thing nonsense. This is the only thing to pursue: make the best of your present situation, keep moving, laugh a lot, and don't take anything too seriously." "So he spoke and went back over the asphodel meadow" [compare Homer *Odyssey* 11.539].

**22.** It was late by this point. "Come now, Mithrobarzanes," I said, "Why are we tarrying and not going back to life?" He replied, "Courage, Menippus, for I'll show you a quick and easy path." He took me to a little place darker than elsewhere and pointed his finger at the dim, narrow ray of light, like the one that shines through a keyhole. "That," he said, "is the sanctuary of Trophonius, and is the place where people from Boeotia come down. Go up that way and you'll arrive in Greece directly." I was delighted by these words. I embraced the mage in farewell and, not without a struggle, somehow or other crawled up through the opening and arrived in Lebadeia.

MENIPPUS OF GADARA, THE SATIRICAL CYNIC philosopher who flourished ca. 300–250 B.C., was Lucian's favorite figure from literary history, and he wrote a number of comic dialogues based on his life (most of our knowledge of which derives from Diogenes Laertius 6.99–101) and work (which no longer survives in its own right). The *Menippus* or *Necromancy* aside, Lucian's other "Menippean" works are: *Dialogues of the Dead, Cataplus, Charon, Icaromenippus, Jupiter tragoedus, Jupiter confutatus, Deorum concilium, Convivium, Gallus, Vitarum auctio, Piscator, Fugitivi, Bis accusatus, Saturnalia,* and *Timon.*

In making Tiresias the focus of Menippus's quest, Lucian makes the *Odyssey* his first model, and he reminds the reader of this with frequent Homeric quotations. The advice Tiresias eventually gives is of course thoroughly Menippean. Menippus's guide, Mithrobarzanes, fits squarely into the tradition of the Oriental mage, as he is explicitly defined: he is both Babylonian and Chaldaean; he wears Median dress; his name is a Persianizing one, perhaps parodically so; and he draws his wisdom from Zoroaster (compare **36–48**).

Menippus's supplicatory approach to Mithrobarzanes for an ultimate revelation and the purifications to which he then subjects himself under his guidance closely resemble the experiences of Lucian's sorcerer's apprentice and Thessalus of Tralles with their respective Egyptian sorcerers (**53–4**). The imagery of mystery-initiation is very much in evidence, not inappropriately, inasmuch as mystery-initiation involved a (symbolic) descent to the underworld in which its secrets were revealed; see **1, 20-1, 157**. Hence, Menippus only feels able to impart his experience to his friend once he learns that he has himself been initiated (presumably into the Eleusinian mysteries). The elaborate preparatory purifications undergone by Menippus prior to descent accordingly resemble those given to initiates and to consulters of Trophonius, whose hole provides Menippus with his exit (see Pausanias 9.39); for purifications before magical rites see **53, 273**.

Menippus descends at the full moon, a favored occasion for necromancy. Mithrobarzanes's obscure appeals to demons as he purifies Menippus and again as he opens up the underworld are evidently *voces magicae* (see **174**). The circular movements he makes around Menippus to protect him from ghosts should be compared to the circular movements often made around ghosts by their evocators (compare **30**), which also perhaps erect a barrier around the ghosts to prevent them from causing harm. We may think that Heracles, Odysseus, and Orpheus were particularly desirable models for imitation less for their successful penetrations of the underworld than for the fact that they had subsequently emerged unscathed from it.

As a river disappearing into a marshy lake as it approaches the site of underworld access, Lucian's Babylonian Euphrates is clearly calqued upon the Thesprotian Acheron and its traditions. Lucian differentiates the underworld water into two: the marsh on the surface and a further lake below.

It is curious that Menippus should have to travel for months by land and sea to Babylon for his descent when he could after all have descended in Boeotia. More curious still is the fact that in less than a day's journey by foot through the underworld Menippus can cover the distance between Babylon and Boeotia. We are wrong if we think of the underworld as laid out directly beneath the surface world, like the basement of a house. It's dimensional relationship with the surface is evidently a complex one.

## ORACLES OF THE DEAD

### 149  Elysius of Terina and incubation-evocation

Early ii A.D.

Plutarch *Moralia*
109b–d (*Consolation to Apollonius*)

Greek

They tell the following sort of tale about the Italian Euthynous. He was the son of Elysius of Terina, who was first among people there in virtue, wealth, and reputation. He died suddenly from an uncertain cause. The thought that would have occurred to anyone else in the same circumstances occurred to Elysius: perhaps he had been killed by poisons. For he had been his only son, and he had a large estate and much money. He was at a loss as to how to test this possibility, so he arrived at some oracle of the dead [*psuchomanteion*]. He made the customary preliminary sacrifices, went to sleep, and saw the following vision. His own father seemed to stand by his side. Seeing him, he told him about his misfortune concerning his son, and he besought him and asked him to help in discovering the cause of his son's death. His father replied, "This is the reason I have come. Take from this one here what he brings you, and from this you will know everything you are grieving about." The one he pointed out was a young man who was following him, and he resembled Elysius's son in age and generation. He asked the boy who he was. He replied "I am the demon of your son." And thus he offered him a small written tablet. He unrolled it and saw these three lines written on it:

> Indeed the minds of men wander in folly. Euthynous lies in his destined death. It was not good for him himself to live, nor was it good for his parents.

COMPARISON WITH CICERO *TUSCULANS* 1.115 shows that this material derives from the early Hellenistic Crantor of Soli. This is the only ancient text to give a "realist" account of the means of experiencing ghosts at an oracle of the dead. For want of contradictory indications, we may assume that incubation was the usual method in all of them. For ghosts manifesting themselves in dreams, see **59, 108, 161, 166**. The rolled tablet resembles a curse tablet in form; see discussion before **168**.

### 150  The Acheron oracle of the dead: Periander and Melissa

420s B.C.

Herodotus 5.92

Greek

On one day Periander stripped all the women of Corinth on account of his wife Melissa. For he sent messengers to her, to Thesprotia, to the Acheron river, to the oracle of the dead [*nekuomanteion*], on the question of the deposit of a guest-friend. Melissa appeared and said that she would neither indicate nor declare where the deposit lay, for she was cold and naked. The clothes that had been buried with her were of no use to her because they had not been burned. As witness to the truth of these assertions stood the fact that Periander had thrown his loaves into a cold oven. The token was proof: he had had sex with Melissa's corpse. When these utterances were reported back to Periander, he at once issued an edict that all the women of Corinth should go out to the precinct of Hera. So they came out as to a festival in their finest adornments, but he posted his bodyguards in ambush and stripped them all alike, free and slave, piled their clothing up into a pit, and burned it with a prayer to Melissa. After doing this he sent to Melissa a second time and she told him where she had put the guest-friend's deposit.

PERIANDER WAS TYRANT OF CORINTH (ruled ca. 627–587). Comparative evidence for this traditional story-type helps to fill out context: Melissa had hidden the guest-friend's money but died taking the knowledge of its location with her (see Augustine *De cura gerunda pro mortuis* 13). Her ghost has seemingly not made trouble hitherto, but it takes the opportunity of its evocation to demand rectification of an inadequate burial (as precisely happens in **59**); it might also have demanded recompense for Periander's (accidental) killing of her (Herodotus 3.50–3). The ghost's token does not prove the truth of its claims as such; it comes closer to proving that the risen ghost does indeed belong to Melissa. We may suppose that Periander had actually preserved the body of Melissa (whose speaking name means "bee") in honey to have sex with it. This detail is found in the closely parallel traditions relating to Herod the Great and Mariamme. For the evocation of the ghost of a woman with whom one is erotically obsessed, see. **42**. For the Acheron oracle see also **31, 144**.

**151**    **The Heracleia Pontica oracle of the dead: Pausanias and Cleonice**

Early ii A.D.

Plutarch *Cimon* 6

Greek

It is told that Pausanias sent for a virgin of Byzantium, Cleonice by name, a girl of distinguished parents, in order to subject her to sexual disgrace. Her parents sent the girl out to him, under compulsion and in fear. She asked the men before the bedroom to remove the light, and she approached the bed in silence through the darkness. Pausanias was already asleep. But she stumbled into and accidentally overturned the lamp stand. He was disturbed by the noise and drew the dagger at his side, thinking that an enemy was coming against him. He struck the girl and dropped her to the ground. She died from the blow, and would not permit Pausanias to be at peace, but during the night she would visit him as a ghost in his sleep, and declare this hexameter in anger: "Go to justice; hubris is a very bad thing for men."

The allies took this outrage particularly badly, and, with Cimon, forced him out of the city. Chased out of Byzantium, and, hounded to distraction by the ghost, as it is said, he fled to the oracle of the dead [*nekuomanteion*] at Heracleia. He called up the ghost of Cleonice and tried to beg off her anger. She came before his vision and said that he would quickly be delivered from his troubles when he was in Sparta, making a riddle, as it seems, about the death that was awaiting him. Anyway, many tell this tale.

PAUSANIAS, THE SPARTAN REGENT AND VANQUISHER of the Persian invasion in at the battle of Plataea in 479 B.C., supposedly lost his mind while presiding over further operations against the Persians from the allied base of Byzantium.

The restless ghost hounds its killer. As often, the ghost manifests itself in two forms: first, a spontaneous and terrible one with which its victim cannot communicate; second, upon evocation, a more rational and communicative one. For this schema see **123–4, 126**. The ghost knows that return to Sparta will result in Pausanias's own death; only this, an eye for an eye, will give it satisfaction. For Pausanias's own death and its aftermath, see **27–9, 152**. Heracleia Pontica was a convenient oracle to turn to from Byzantium, an eastward voyage along the southern coast of the Black Sea. An alternate version of the Pausanias tradition sends him instead to the evocators of Phigalia, north of Sparta (**28**).

Plutarch tells this tale again in his *Moralia* (555c), where he supplies an alternative technical name for an oracle of the dead, *psuchopompeion*, literally "prophecy-place of souls" (compare **152**) and tells us that the ghost was called up "with propitiations and libations."

## 152  The Tainaron oracle of the dead: Corax and Archilochus; Italian evocators

Early ii A.D.

Plutarch *Moralia* 560ef;
Archilochus T141
Tarditi

Greek

The man who killed Archilochus in battle was called Callondes, as it seems, but he had Corax ["Crow"] as a nickname. At first he was thrown out by the Pythia as having killed a man who was sacred to the Muses, but then he had recourse to prayers and supplications, and attempted to justify himself with arguments. He was bidden to go to the house of Tettix ["Cicada"] to propitiate the soul of Archilochus. This was Tainaron. For they say that Tettix the Cretan came there with a fleet and founded a city and settled the area around the oracle of the dead [*psuchopompeion*]. In like manner, the Spartans received an oracle that they should propitiate the soul of Pausanias, so evocators [*psuchagôgoi*] were summoned from Italy. They made a sacrifice and drew the ghost away from the temple [of Athene of the Bronze House].

THE TALE OF CORAX AND ARCHILOCHUS is also recounted in the *Suda* (s.v. *Archilochos*; Aelian F83 Domingo-Forasté; Archilochus T170 Tarditi), where we learn that Corax's argument in justification was the equality of battle. Archilochus died ca. 652 B.C. The Aesop-like animal imagery implied by the speaking names here is curious. It may be of significance that the cicada carried strong associations with the underworld.

For Pausanias and the evocators, see **27–9, 151**. Here Plutarch directly and explicitly says that the evocators used to lay the ghost of Pausanias were brought from Italy, and there is no good reason to doubt this assertion. Perhaps they were based at the Avernus/Cumae oracle of the dead (see **153–4**). Nonetheless, it has been suggested by some that Plutarch's text should be emended to read not "from Italy" but "from Phigalia" (*ex Italias/ek Phigalias*), a town in Arcadia, since Pausanias had himself, according to one version, evocated the ghost the girl he had murdered, Cleonice, there (**28**). Others have suggested that Plutarch's text be emended to read "from Thessaly" (*ek Thessalias*) on the basis of the Euripides scholium (**27**).

## 153  The Avernus oracle of the dead: Ephorus and the Cimmerians

Late i B.C. (Strabo);
mid-iv B.C. (Ephorus)

Strabo C244–6, includ-
ing Ephorus *FGH* 70
F134a

Greek

[C244] Before me people used to tell the myth that the Homeric *Nekuia* episode took place in Avernus. And they tell us that there was an oracle of the dead there [*nekuomanteion*] there and that Odysseus came to it. The gulf of Avernus is deep close to shore and has a good entrance. It has the size and nature of a harbor, but it cannot be used as a harbor because the Gulf of Lucrinus lies in front of it, which is large and shallow. Avernus is shut in by steep beetling banks that overhang it from all sides except for the entrance. Now they have been worked hard and cultivated, but formerly they were covered over with a wild wood of black and impenetrable trees. These made the gulf into a home for shades, because of superstition. The locals used to tell another myth that birds that flew over the gulf fell into the water, because they were destroyed by gases that came off it, as in *ploutônia* [sanctuaries with mephitic emissions]. And they took this place for a *ploutônion*, and they believed that the Cimmerians lived there. Those who had sacrificed in advance and propitiated the underworld powers sailed into it. There were priests to guide one through the process, who managed the place under contract. There is a source there of drinkable water by the sea, but all kept back from this, considering it to be the water of the Styx. And the oracle is situated somewhere there. And they took the hot springs nearby, and the Acherusian lake, to be evidence of Pyriphlegethon.

Ephorus, assigning the place to the Cimmerians, says that they live in underground houses, which they call *argillai* [clay-houses], and that they visit each other through tunnels, and that they receive strangers visiting the oracle, which is situated a long way under the earth. He says that they live on the profits of the mines and the consulters of the oracle, and the king who decreed contributions to them. He says that there is an ancestral custom for those who live around the oracle, that they should never see the sun, but that they should only come out of their holes at night. It was for this reason, he says, that the poet said of them that "nor ever does the shining sun look on them." **[C245]** But, he says, these people were later destroyed by a king, when a divination did not succeed for him, although the oracle still remains, removed to another place.

These are the things people before me have said, but now that the woodland around Avernus has been cut down by Agrippa, and the land has been built up, and an underground tunnel has been cut from Avernus to Cumae, all those things have been shown to be mere myths. Cocceius, who made this tunnel and also the one to Naples from Dicaearchia near Baiae, perhaps followed the tale I have just told about the Cimmerians, possibly because he considered it traditional to the area that its roads should be through tunnels. The Gulf of Lucrinus broadens out until Baiae. It is divided from the open sea by an earthwork eight stades long and the breadth of a wagon road. They say that Heracles built this, when he was driving the cattle of Geryon. But it would allow waves over the top in storms, so that it was not easy to walk along, so Agrippa built it up further. It allows only light boats to enter. It is useless for mooring, but it provides a plentiful catch of oysters. And some say that this is actually the Acherusian lake, but Artemidorus says that Avernus itself is the Acherusian lake. They say that Baiae is named after Baios, one of the companions of Odysseus, and so too Misenum. Next come the headlands around Dicaearchia and the city itself. It was formerly a port-town of Cumae, situated on a bank, but during Hannibal's campaign the Romans colonized it and renamed it Puteoli after the wells [Latin *putei*]. But others say that they named it after the stench [Latin *puteo*] from the waters that occupy the whole area as far as Baiae and Cumae, because it is full of sulphur and fire and hot waters. Some say that the territory of Cumae was called Phlegra [Fiery] because of this and that it is the thunderbolt-inflicted wounds of the fallen giants that send up such projections of fire and water. . . . **[C246]** Immediately above the city lies the forum of Hephaestus, a plain shut in by very fiery banks, which have somewhat stinking vents everywhere. The plain is full of swept sulphur.

THE GREEKS HAD BEGUN TO LOCATE Odysseus's wanderings on the west coast of Italy from as early as the sixth century B.C. His underworld was found there in Lake Avernus, a flooded volcanic crater beside the sea in a district of fumaroles and hot springs. Strabo's remarks preserve traces of disputes about the mapping of the *Odyssey* onto the local topography. For Strabo and, it seems, for his source Ephorus, the age of the oracle was long past. An ancient king (of Cumae?) had destroyed it in its Avernus setting, and it had been transplanted elsewhere, to a place perhaps unknown. Myth too had made the Cimmerians, perpetual neighbors of the underworld, into a race of troglodyte managers of the oracle (compare **144**). These should be compared with the evocators (*psuchagôgoi*) into whose charge Maximus of Tyre gives the oracle (**154**). For Ephorus and Maximus alike the oracle had been based in a cave, like the Heracleia and Tainaron ones. However, there was clearly no sign of a suitable cave in the crater of Avernus in Ephorus's day. If there ever was an oracle of the dead in Avernus, it is more likely to have consisted of a lakeside precinct. In Strabo's own day Avernus was transformed into a naval base by Agrippa in pursuit of the war against Sextus Pompey (see **155**).

## 154 Evocators and the consultation procedure at the Avernus oracle of the dead

ii A.D.

Maximus of Tyre
*Dissertationes* 8.2

Greek

Somewhere in Italy, in Magna Graecia, at the so-called lake Aornos/Avernus there was an oracular cave and "evocator"-men [*andres psuchagôgoi*] were attendants of the cave. They took their name from their job. A man wanting an oracle would come to them, pray, sacrifice an animal, pour full libations, and call up the soul of any of his ancestors or friends. Then the ghost would confront him. It would be hard to see, and one could doubt that one was seeing it, but it would have the power of speech, and could deliver prophecies. After discussing what was asked of it, it would depart. I think Homer knew this oracle, since he sent Odysseus to it, but, with considerable poetic license, removed the place from our sea.

THIS PASSAGE CONSTITUTES THE MOST EXPLICIT association of evocators, *psuchagôgoi*, with oracles of the dead. It is also implied by the alternative versions of the tradition of Pausanias the regent and Cleonice, which send him variously to the oracle at Heracleia (**151**) and to the *psuchagôgoi* (**28**) of Phigalia to call up her ghost. Maximus's *psuchagôgoi* here strongly resemble Ephorus's Cimmerians in their role at Avernus. The apparently matter-of-fact summary of necromantic procedure does not actually tell us anything of the mechanics of the experiencing of the ghost.

## REANIMATION

Three major accounts of reanimation-necromancy survive from antiquity: that of Lucan's Erictho (**155**), that of Heliodorus's old woman of Bessa (**157**), and Apuleius's account of Zatchlas and Thelyphron (**105**). They share a number of features:

- Associations with Egypt: some of Erictho's magical ingredients are distinctively Egyptianizing; Zatchlas is an Egyptian priest; the old woman of Bessa is an Egyptian in Egypt.

- Associations with Thessaly: Erictho is a Thessalian witch; Zatchlas works in Thessaly. For the Egyptian-Thessalian association in the context of skull-necromancy see also **161**.

- The uprighting of the corpse. Before the corpse can be made to speak, it must first be stood upright to symbolize its return to life. Because the corpses are stiff with rigor mortis, they rise directly onto their feet without bending their limbs, as is particularly apparent from the Erictho episode. We have already seen how stiff the corpse of Thelyphron was when it failed to respond promptly to the witches' attempt to reanimate it, prior to Zatchlas's reanimation of it. See also **161**.

- Use of herbs: Erictho puts them in the potion she pumps into her corpse; Zatchlas lays sprigs on the chest (to restart breathing) and the mouth (to bestow speech) of his corpse; and the Bessa-woman uses laurel to crown her voodoo doll and flick blood into her fire.

- In all cases the ghost is angry and resentful at the disturbance of its peace. But in normal evocations ghosts can be keen to enjoy a brief return to life (e.g., **144**).

- Hence the need to threaten a second spell. In all cases the initial attempt to reanimate fails, but the reanimation is instantly accomplished on the threat of a second spell that will inflict underworld tortures. In a sense, the mere threat is itself a—or even the—second spell.

## 155 The Thessalian Erictho reanimates a dead soldier for Sextus Pompey

65 A.D.

Lucan *Pharsalia*
6.588–830

Latin

**588.** The degenerate son of Pompey spoke to her first. "Glory of the Thessalian women, able, as you are, to reveal fates to peoples and to derail the future, I beseech you, let me have sure knowledge of the result that the fortune of war makes ready. I am not the lowest of the Roman hoard, but the brilliant son of Magnus, destined to be master of the world or to inherit total doom. My mind is stricken with doubts and is in panic, but, however, is ready to endure quantifiable fears. Deprive chance of the ability to rush upon us suddenly and unexpectedly. Either torture the powers above or leave them aside and press the truth from the ghosts. Open up the house of Elysium, call death itself and compel him to confess to me whom he seeks from among us. This is not a trivial task. It is worth even your while to trouble to inquire which way the hazard of so great a destiny is inclining." The impious Thessalian was delighted that her reputation had preceded her and said in reply, "If you wanted to alter the minor details of Fate, it would be a straightforward thing to induce the gods to bring to pass the actions you desired. It is granted to the craft to insert delays when the stars have urged on the death of a single man with their rays. And, even though every star should have destined a man for old age, we break off his life in the middle of his years with our herbs. But when a series of causes and effects derives from the very origin of the world, and all destinies are put under strain if you wish to make any change, and the human race as a whole feels the impact, in this case—we, the Thessalian gaggle, admit it—Fortune is more powerful than we are. But if you are content merely to know outcomes in advance, many and easy are the ways to the truth that will lie open before us. The earth, the sky, chaos, the seas, the fields, and the Rhodopaean rocks will speak to us. But the obvious method, in view of the fact that there is such an abundance of fresh death around us, is to raise a single body from the Thessalian plains so that the mouth of a corpse only recently dead and still warm may make utterance with full voice. We will not have to cope with a deathly shade, its limbs dried up by the sun, squeaking indistinctly to our hearing."

**624.** So she spoke. She used her craft to redouble the darkness of the night. She shrouded her miserable head in a filthy mist and wandered amid the bodies of the dead soldiers, cast forth without burial. The wolves fled at once and the vultures too fled hungry, withdrawing their talons, as the Thessalian chose her prophet and, testing the innards, chill with death, came across the lobes of a hardened lung, firm and intact. She seeks a voice in the dead body. A question now hangs over the fates of many dead men: Who will she wish to call back to the world above? If she had attempted to raise up the complete armies, ranged against each other on the battlefield, and return them to war, the laws of Erebus would have allowed it, and the mighty monster would have drawn people up from Stygian Avernus to fight. Eventually a corpse was chosen, one with its throat cut, and brought. She put a hook into a deathly noose round its neck and dragged the pitiful corpse, destined to live again, over the crags and rocks. Dour Erictho stationed it under the high roof of the mountain cave she had dedicated to her rites.

**642.** There the ground fell steeply down, almost to the sightless caverns of Dis. It was pressed close by a colorless wood, its foliage drooping down. Yews, never raising their tops to the sky, impenetrable to the Sun, cut off its light. Within the cave is a morose darkness and gray mould, the product of protracted night. No light is shed except that which is manufactured with a spell. The air in the jaws of Tainaron is not as stifling as here. It is the dismal boundary between the hidden world and our own. It is such that the kings of Tartarus do not fear to let the dead pass to it. For, although the Thessalian prophetess does violence to the fates, it remains uncertain whether she is able to look upon the Stygian shades by virtue of drawing them up or by virtue of going down herself to them. She donned the particolored garb of the Fury. She scraped the hair back from her face to reveal it. She tied back her rough locks with bands of vipers. When she saw that the young companions were terrified and that Pompey himself was trembling, his face lifeless and his gaze frozen, she said, "Lay aside the terrors conceived in your fearful mind. Any moment now life will be restored anew in its true form, so that people will be able to hear the man as he speaks even though they are petrified. But if I displayed before you the Stygian lakes and the riverbank that resounds with fire, if I permitted you to look upon the Furies and Cerberus, shaking out his shaggy neck of snakes, and the giants, chained upon their backs, why should you be afraid, cowards, to look upon the ghosts that fear me?"

**667.** Then she opened up the chest with further wounds and filled it with seething blood. She rinsed the innards of corrupt matter and unstintingly administered moon-juice. In this was mixed whatever creature nature had produced under ill omen. Nothing was missing: not the foam of the water-fearing rabid dog, not the guts of the lynx, not the hump of the dreadful hyena, not the bone marrow of a deer pastured on snakes, not the ship-stopper [*echenais*], which detains a hull in the middle of the sea, while the east wind strains her cables, not the eyes of snakes, not the stones that murmur when incubated under a mother eagle, not the Arabian flying snake, not the viper born beside the Red Sea, guardian of the precious pearl oyster, not the slough of the still-living Libyan horned snake, not the ashes of the phoenix that settles itself upon an Eastern altar. After putting these common-or-garden and namable blights into her mixture, she added branches drenched in unspeakable spells, herbs on which her dread mouth had spat at the moment of their birth, and all the poisons she herself had contributed to the world. Then her voice, mightier than all the herbs in the bewitching of the gods of Lethe, poured out, first, mutterings that were discordant and not all of which sounded like the products of a human tongue. The voice contained the barking of dogs and the howling of wolves, the complaining cries of a scared owl and the night's screech owl, the screeching and bellowing of wild animals, and the hissing of the snake. It expressed also the dashing of waves on rocks, the sound of the woods, and the thunder of a burst cloud. So many things did the single voice comprise. Then she pronounced more clearly a second set of utterances, in a Thessalian spell, and penetrated Tartarus with her tongue. "Furies; Crimes of the Styx; Punishments [Poenae] of the guilty; Chaos, you who long to confound unnumbered worlds; Hades, Ruler in the earth, for whom the death of gods, deferred across long ages, is agonizing; Styx; Elysium, the reward of no Thessalian woman; Persephone, you who detest heaven and your mother; Hecate, the lowest manifestation of my goddess, by whose grace the ghosts and I hold converse, with silent tongue; Doorkeeper of the broad house, you who throw human guts to the cruel dog; sister-

Fates, destined to take up the threads of a life again and continue spinning; ferryman of the flaming wave, reduced to a wornout old man by all the ghosts returning for me: hear my prayers. If I invoke you with a mouth sufficiently criminal and
corrupt, if I never sing these incantations without first sating myself on human
meat, if I have repeatedly opened up breasts, with the souls still in them, and rinsed
them in warm brains, if any baby had been destined to live before it placed its head
and entrails on your dishes, obey my prayer. I do not ask for a soul lying hidden in
the cave of Tartarus and long accustomed to the dark, but one that is only just now
abandoning the light and coming down. He still hesitates at the edge of the abyss
of colorless Orcus, and, even if he does give heed to these spells [or: drink down
these herbal potions], he will still only join the other ghosts once. Let this Pompeian
ghost, until recently our soldier, prophesy everything to Pompey's son, if you are
properly honored by civil war."

719. This she said, and lifted her head and foaming mouth. She saw the shade
of the cast-out body standing beside her, in dread of the lifeless limbs and the
hated bonds of its former prison. It was terrified to enter the opened breast and the
guts and the organs smashed by the fatal wound. Ah pitiful man, from whom
death's final gift of immortality was unfairly snatched away. Erictho was taken
aback that such delays had been permitted the fates. Furious with death, she beat
the motionless body with a live snake, and she barked through the open clefts she
had driven into the earth by her incantation and ruptured the silence of the kingdom. "Tisiphone and Megaera, you who scorn my calling, do you not drive this
hapless soul through the emptiness of Erebus with your cruel whips? Any moment
now I shall call you up by your true names and make you stand as Stygian hounds
in the light of the upper world. I shall pursue you through tombs, through burials,
ever hanging on your heels, I shall drive you from barrows and keep you from all
urns. You, Hecate, decaying and colorless in appearance as you are, are in the habit
of showing yourself to the gods above only after first making up your face. I will
show you to them and forbid you to alter your hell-face. I shall blurt out, Persephone of Henna, the meal that traps you beneath the vast weight of the earth, the
agreement by which you love the somber king of the night and the corruption you
experienced that induced your mother to refuse to call you back. Upon you, Hades,
worst of the world's rulers, I shall send Titan, the Sun, bursting your caverns open,
and you will be blasted by the instantaneous light of day. Do you obey? Or will I
have to invoke him—him, whose invocation always shakes the earth and sets it
quaking, the one who looks upon the uncovered head of the Gorgon, the one who
beats the trembling Fury with her own whips, the one who occupies a Tartarus
even you cannot look down to, the one to whom you are the gods above, the one
who forswears himself by the waters of the Styx?" At once the congealed gore
warmed up, soothed the black wounds and ran into the veins and the extremities
of the limbs. As the blood struck them the organs beneath the chill breast quiv-
ered, and life, creeping anew into the innards that had forgotten it, mingled itself
with the death. Then all the dead man's limbs shook, and his sinews flexed. The
corpse did not raise itself from the ground gradually, one limb at a time. Rather, it
shot up from the earth and was upright in an instant. The eyes were laid bare, the
mouth an open grimace. His appearance was of one not yet fully alive, but of a
man still in the phase of dying. He was still pallid and stiff, and in consternation at
being brought back into the world. But his tightened mouth made no mutter. Voice
and tongue were granted him only for replying. "Tell me," said the Thessalian
woman, "what I command you, and you shall be well rewarded. For if you speak
truly to me I shall render you immune from the Thessalian crafts for as long as the

world exists. Such is the pyre on which I will burn your limbs, such is the wood with which I will burn you, to the accompaniment of a Stygian spell, that your shade will hear nothing when mages sing their incantations to it. Let your second life be as valuable as this to you: neither words nor herbs will dare to break your sleep of protracted Lethe, Oblivion, when I have given you death. Ambiguity in prediction befits Delphic tripods and prophets of the gods above. But whoever is brave enough to seek the truth from the shades and approach the oracles of hard death deserves to depart in certainty. I beg you, do not be sparing. Give things their names, give places, give forth a voice, through which the fates may converse with me." She added a spell by which she conferred knowledge of whatever she asked upon the shade. With tears falling, the gloomy corpse said: "I did not see the sad threads of the Fates, called back as I was from the bank of the silent river. But what I did happen to learn from all the shades is that the Roman ghosts are driven by wild discord, and impious arms have even broken the peace of the underworld. The Latin leaders, traveling in their various directions, have abandoned their homes in Elysium and gloomy Tartarus. These have laid open fate's preparations. The blessed dead were sad of face. I saw the Decii, the souls of son and father alike given as propitiatory sacrifices to the gods in war, Camillus and the Curii, all weeping; Sulla complaining about you, Fortune; Scipio bemoaned the fact that his luckless descendant was destined to fall in the land of Libya; Cato, the "greater" enemy of Carthage, grieves for the death of his descendant, who refuses to be a slave. You alone, Brutus, first consul after the deposition of the kings, did I see rejoicing amid the pious shades. Threatening Catiline had broken and smashed his chains and was jubilant, as were the Marii and the bare-armed Cethegi. I saw the demagogic Drusi in their joy, those who made such wild laws, and the outrageous Gracchi. Their hands, restrained by everlasting iron bonds and Dis's jail, applauded, and the host of the guilty is claiming the plains of the pious. The owner of the kingdom of the powerless opens up his colorless house. He hardens his sheer rocks and the tough steel chains, and makes ready the punishment for the victor. Have this for consolation, young man, the knowledge that the ghosts are preparing to welcome your father and his house to a place of peace and seclusion, and are reserving a spot in the bright part of the realm for the Pompeians. Do not fret about the glory of Caesar's short additional life. The hour to level all leaders will come. Hasten to your death and, proud in your lofty spirit, descend to the underworld from tombs, however small, and trample underfoot the ghosts of the Roman gods [i.e., the deified emperors]. The only issue is which tomb is to be washed by the wave of the Nile, which by that of the Tiber. For the generals the battle is just about the circumstances of burial. Do not look into your own fate. Though I say nothing, the Fates will inform you. A more reliable prophet, your father Pompey himself, will furnish you with all predictions in the fields of Sicily. He too is unsure whither to summon you and whence to warn you off, what regions and what constellations he should bid you to avoid. Pitiful people, fear Europe, Africa, and Asia! Fortune scatters your tombs over the lands of your triumphs. Wretched house, you will see no place in all the world any safer for you than Emathian Pharsalia." When he had brought his prophecy to this conclusion, he stood in silence, but with a gloomy expression that asked for death to be returned to him. Magical spells and herbs were required to make the corpse fall. Fate could not reclaim the soul for itself, having already exhausted its right to take it once. Then Erictho constructed a pyre, using an enormous amount of wood. The dead man strode into the flames. She left the young man laid out on the kindled pile of wood, deigning at last to let him die. Then she accompanied Sextus back to his father's camp. The sky was drawing on the color of dawn, but night, at Erictho's behest, held back the day and provided thick shadows, until they arrived safely back within the tents of the camp.

THIS PASSAGE FOLLOWS ON DIRECTLY FROM **96**. In that introductory material the poet had built Erictho up as terrible and grotesque, but as she enters the action here she is revealed to be a competent and reassuring professional, charmingly flattered by Sextus's approach.

This passage constitutes the most elaborate description of any necromancy in classical literature, and is also the first extant account of reanimation necromancy. Its literary antecedents are obscure. Its reanimation technique has much in common with the description of Medea's rejuvenation of Aeson in Ovid's *Metamorphoses* (**69**), but that passage is rather untypical of rejuvenation narratives (in which the client is usually hacked up and boiled in a cauldron). This raises the possibility that Ovid's narrative and Lucan's alike both remodel an earlier description of a reanimation necromancy. Its "historical" antecedents are also unclear, but there is some evidence for the manipulation of cadaverous material, in particular skulls, in association with necromancy (**158–62**). Volpilhac's suggestion (1978) that the processes to which Erictho subjects her corpse are intended to mimic Egyptian mummification has not found favor.

Erictho recommends the reanimation of a fresh corpse so that "We will not have to cope with a deathly shade, its limbs dried up by the sun, squeaking indistinctly to our hearing" (558–623). This curious expression seems to overlap the traditional notion that (detached) ghosts made a squeaking noise with the notion that the voice of a dried-up corpse might rasp like a rusty socket. It is surprising that the corpse has been jugulated (624–41). Did its voice-apparatus not need to be intact? Perhaps the forcing of speech from a jugulated corpse was greater proof of magical ability. Or perhaps the severed throat salutes the historical practice of necromancy with disembodied skulls. For a recipe for divination from a jugulated man, see **273**.

The location for the necromancy, a cave adjacent to a battlefield, shielded by a lightless, cavelike forest, could not be more apt. Lucan's uncertainty as to whether ghosts come up to the living or the living go down to the ghosts in evocation (642–41) is a knowing response to Homer and Virgil: Homer's Odysseus had called the ghosts up (**144**), but in Virgil's remodeling of the Homeric account, Aeneas had descended (*Aeneid* 6).

The bizarre list of magical ingredients (667–718) combines objects at any rate theoretically obtainable with the fantastic. The same phenomenon is found in the recipes of the Greek Magical Papyri, among which an interpretations list supplies mundane significances for fantastic terms (**156**). Erictho's employment of moon-juice alludes to the drawing-down of the moon: it was supposed to deposit a foam on plants when brought low, which could then be collected up for magical purposes (see **214–23**). The ingredients in the list from the Arabian flying snake to the phoenix consciously allude to the wonders of Egypt described by Herodotus (2.73–5).

The strange and terrible noise with which Erictho begins her spell (667–718) seems to have been completely inarticulate, unlike *voces magicae*, but like them no doubt held special meaning for the powers addressed. The threats that anticipate or constitute the second spell are of particular interest. Erictho paradoxically threatens to behave as a Fury toward the underworld powers herself with her harrying, her snakes, and her whipping; and she has indeed taken on the appearance of a Fury (see 642–41). The threat to reveal Hecate (see **275**) without her makeup, as if she is a pretentious aging woman, is comic. The threat addressed to Persephone proposes to reveal underworld mysteries. The underworld god to underworld gods is Demogorgon (for this figure see also Statius *Thebaid* 4.500–518 and *Adnotationes super Lucanum* 6.746).

This is the only account of ancient necromancy in which a distinction may be drawn between the soul and the ghost of the dead man: the narrative may or may not imply that the ghost or shade (*umbra*) that Erictho causes to materialize beside the body is distinct from the soul (*anima*) that she threatens with torture in the underworld (719–830). It is curious that Erictho should have to apply a spell to the corpse to give it knowledge: this seems an implicit denial that the dead were possessed of any wisdom as such; could not such a spell have been applied more simply to a living man? The prophecy made is one of death and doom, including that of the consulter, as often in literary scenes of necromancy. It may be significant that contact with the dead was regarded as inherently "deadening"; see **114, 157, 261**.

## 156  Banal herbal interpretations for more exotic magical ingredients

iv A.D.

*PGM* XII.401–44

Greek

Interpretations made by the priests. The sacred scribes used these. Because of the meddling of the many they engraved the plants and other things on the statues of gods, so that the many, not taking care about such things, might not meddle, in pursuit of their error. We drew the solutions from many copies, all secret. This is it:

| | |
|---|---|
| head of snake | leech |
| ball of thread of snake | wax-stone |
| blood [*haima*] of snake | hematite |
| bone of ibis | buckthorn |
| blood of hyrax-rock | This really is the blood of hyrax-rock |
| tears of baboon | juice of dill |
| dung of crocodile | Egyptian earth |
| blood of baboon | blood of gecko |
| seed of lion | seed of human |
| blood of Hephaestus | wormwood |
| hairs of baboon | seed of dill |
| seed of Hermes | dill |
| blood of Ares | purslane |
| blood from the eye | gall of tamarisk |
| blood from the shoulder | thorny plant |
| blood from the loins | camomile |
| bile of human | juice of turnip [?] |
| tail of pig | scorpion-tail [i.e. a plant] |
| bone of doctor | sandstone |
| blood of Hestia | camomile |
| eagle | wild garlic |
| blood of goose | mulberry milk |
| spice of Cronus | piglet milk |
| hairs of lion | tongue of turnip [?] |
| blood of Cronus | cedar . . . [lacuna] |

| | |
|---|---|
| seed of Helios | white hellebore |
| seed of Heracles | rocket |
| blood of a Titan | wild lettuce |
| blood from the head | lupine |
| seed of bull | egg of dung-beetle |
| heart of hawk | heart of wormwood |
| seed of Hephaestus | This means fleabane |
| seed of Ammon | houseleek |
| seed of Ares | clover |
| fat from the head | spurge |
| fat from the belly | earth-apple |
| fat from the foot | houseleek |

THIS MAGICAL PAPYRUS IS INCLUDED HERE for the light it can shed on the sort of outlandish ingredients used by Erictho in her reanimation. There is no indication in Lucan's text that we are to conceive of those ingredients in any but a literal way. But this list of interpretations suggests that exotic names of this sort were conventionally used by "Egyptian priests" for their more banal herbal ingredients. The reason for this, the introduction implies, was the protection of their art. It could also be that the readily available herbs were treated as more convenient substitutes for the exotic items to which they correspond.

## 57 An old woman of Bessa in Egypt reanimates the corpse of her dead son

iv A.D.

Heliodorus 6.12–5 (12–3 edited)

Greek

**1**12. As they [the Greek ingenue Charicleia and the Egyptian priest Calasiris] were approaching Bessa, around sunset, they came across a mass of recently slain bodies on the ground. Most of them were recognizable as Persians from their dress and equipment, but a few of them were Egyptians. . . . They came across a little old woman embracing the body of one of the Egyptians, and producing all sorts of lamentation. They decided to try to get some information from her, if they could. They sat down with her and tried to comfort her and bring her lamentation under control. As she was talked around, they asked her over whom she was grieving and what the war was, Calasiris speaking to the woman in Egyptian. She told them everything concisely. Her grief was for her son who lay there dead, and she had deliberately come to the site of the dead in the hope that someone would drive a sword through her and deliver her from life. But in the meantime she was making the customary offerings to her son as best she could in the circumstances, with tears and lamentation.

13. "But strangers, where will you go now?" [asked the old woman]. "To the village," said Calasiris. But she replied, "It isn't safe for you to mingle with the remaining men, who do not know you, at this untimely hour." "But if you were to introduce us to them," said Calasiris, "we'd have a good hope of staying safe." "I don't have time just now," replied the old woman. "For I have to perform some nocturnal rites. But if you can put up with it (and you must, whether you like it or not), stay here. Withdraw a little way to a place clear of corpses and wait through the night, and at dawn I will escort you in complete safety."

14. After the old woman had spoken Calasiris reported everything to Charicleia, and took her to one side. They picked their way over the sprawling bodies for a short distance until they found a low-lying mound. There Calasiris laid himself down, resting his head on his quiver, while Charicleia sat down, using her handbag

as a cushion. The moon was just rising and illuminating everything with its bright light, for it had been full two nights before. Calasiris fell fast asleep, as he would, being an old man and in any case worn out by traveling. But Charicleia's worries kept her awake, and so she found herself watching a scene that was impious, albeit customary for Egyptian women.

The old woman, believing that she was now free of hindrance and was not being watched, first dug a pit and then kindled a fire on one side of it. She laid out the body of her son between the two and took a ceramic bowl from an adjacent tripod. She made a libation of honey into the pit, another of milk from a second bowl, and another again of wine from a third bowl. Then she crowned with laurel and fennel a dough cake molded to resemble a man and threw it into the pit. After all that she took up a sword, worked herself up into an inspired frenzy and invoked the moon with names that sounded foreign and strange. She cut her arm open, wiped up some of the blood with a laurel branch, and threw it into the fire. She did some other strange things in addition to these and then bent over the corpse of her son and sang some incantation into his ear. She roused him and compelled him to stand upright by her witchcraft [*manganeia*].

Charicleia had been taking the scene in somewhat fearfully all along, but now she began to tremble in terror at this bizarre process. She woke Calasiris up and had him watch what was being done. They themselves could not be seen, since they were in the dark, but they could see easily what the old woman was doing in the light of the fire, and they could hear what she said because they weren't too far away, and the crone was now interrogating the corpse more loudly. She was inquiring whether her remaining son, the brother of the dead man, would return home safe and sound.

The corpse made no reply, but just nodded, allowing its mother the insecure hope that the response was favorable. But then all at once it fell headlong onto its face. The woman rolled the corpse onto its back again and would not finish with the interrogation. But she sang more powerful, as it seemed, compulsive incantations into its ears again, and there were many of them. Then, armed with her sword, she kept jumping between the fire and the pit. She managed to rouse him again. When she had uprighted him she made the same inquiries, and compelled him to reveal the divination plainly, not just by nodding, but also by speaking. While the old woman was doing this Charicleia earnestly begged Calasiris that they should approach the scene of action and make an inquiry of their own about Theagenes. He declined; it was not holy, he said, even to watch the rite, but he suffered it under the constraint of circumstance. It did not befit a prophet either to attempt or to attend such rites. Prophets derived their divination from lawful sacrifices and pure prayers, but the impure and earthly actually derived their divination from circling around corpses, just as, by accident, they were now seeing the Egyptian woman do.

**15.** Calasiris was still speaking when the corpse muttered in a deep, ugly voice as if from a crypt or a craggy cavern. "At first I spared you, mother," it said, "and I put up with you as you broke the laws of humanity, violated the decrees of the gods, and unfixed with your sorceries [*manganeiai*] what was fixed. For, so far as possible, respect for parents is preserved even among the dead. But you abolish this of your own accord. No longer are you merely dabbling in lawlessness, as at first; now you push it beyond limit. You compel a dead body not only to stand itself up and nod but even to speak. You do not care about my burial rites, and you prevent me from mixing with the other souls. You care only about yourself. Hear now these prophecies which I have long been forbearing to reveal to you. Neither will your son return safely to you nor will you yourself escape death from the sword. But, having spent your whole life in such lawless practices, you will shortly meet with the end allotted to all such people. Your other crimes aside, you did not even take care to perform these mysteries on your own, secret as they are, and guard them with silence and darkness. Rather, here you are, dancing out the fortunes of the dead before such witnesses. One of them is a prophet. This is a matter of less importance, for he has the wisdom to seal such things in silence and not bruit them abroad, and in any case he is dear to the gods. His sons are squaring up to each other for a bloody one-to-one duel, but he will appear on the scene, interrupt them, and stop them, if he hurries. What is more serious is the fact that a girl too is watching the rites you are performing over me and overhears everything. The young lady is worn out by love and is wandering over practically the whole of the earth looking for her boyfriend. After a myriad ordeals and dangers at the furthest limits of the earth she will spend her life with him in brilliant and royal condition."

This said, the corpse crumpled and fell. The crone, realizing that the strangers were the ones who had been watching her, rushed after them, just as she was, with the sword in her hand and maddened. She hurried over all the dead bodies. She suspected that they had hidden themselves among them. Her intention was to kill them if she found them, on the assumption that they were watching her sorceries [*manganeumata*] deliberately out of hostility. But as she was making her search among the corpses anger made her careless and, without realizing it, she impaled her groin on the upright shaft of a spear and died. So immediate was the just fulfilment of her son's prophecy.

THE BROAD SIMILARITIES WITH LUCAN'S ERICTHO sequence are self-evident and include the battlefield setting. This sequence, from the end of the classical tradition, plays with elements found in the *Odyssey* at its very beginning, namely, the focal pit and fire, the libations, use of grain, and use of a sword. But to these elements much has been added. This is the only certain example of the use of a voodoo doll for necromancy (but see **91** for a further problematic example and see also **71**). The use of (a small amount of) blood from her own arm is a striking innovation in a necromantic context.

The corpse's prophecies are quite vigorous. It gives responses to questions it has not even been asked. Its prophecy of death and doom is effectively self-fulfilling: the corpse's words send the witch rushing over the battlefield in such a way that she impales herself. Her reckless anger is caused by the belief that she has been victim of an evil eye (for which see **192–6**).

The rites of necromancy are here repeatedly assimilated to underworld mysteries that must not be revealed; compare **148**. It is hard to understand how such rites could be at once both impious and customary among Egyptian women. The occurrence of a full moon, an ideal occasion for necromancy, is fortunate, and the witch indeed invokes it (compare **214–33**).

The distinction made by Calasiris between high prophetic divination and low magical divination strongly parallels the distinction he has made earlier between the two varieties of Egyptian wisdom, where the lowly and earthly variety is said to use plants and incantations and to slip itself up, and is exemplified by reanimation necromancy (**56**).

## 158  The use of skulls for necromancy

158/9 A.D.

Apuleius *Apology* 34

Latin

Bear in mind that it would be as ridiculous to argue that obscenely named marine life is sought after for erotic pursuit as if you were to say that the sea-comb is sought for hair-dressing, the hawk-fish for fowling, the piglet-fish for boar-hunting, or the sea-skull for the evocation of the dead.

THE IMPLICATION OF THIS SCOFFING ARGUMENT is that it was generally believed that human skulls were indeed used for the evocation of the dead.

## 159  The oracle of Orpheus's head

ii–iii A.D.

Philostratus *Heroicus* 28 (p. 172 Kayser)

Greek

After the deed of the women, the head [of Orpheus] put into Lesbos and lived in a cranny in there, giving out prophecies in a hole in the earth.

ORPHEUS (FOR WHOM SEE **19–21, 71**) HAD BEEN dismembered by Thracian women, and his head cast into the sea. The oracle it came to occupy is also beautifully illustrated by a fifth-century Attic vase (Schmidt 1972). This shows a man having climbed down a rope into a pitlike cave and communicating with Orpheus's head, which nestles in a further cranny of its own. The oracle of Trophonius was configured in a similar way: one climbed down into a pit (by ladder) and then slid into a further hole at its base in order to communicate with Trophonius, who was, like Orpheus, at once both dead and alive (see Pausanias 9.39). The Lesbian oracle may only have had a mythical existence, but there may well have been skull-oracles of similar configuration.

## 160  Trick skull necromancy exposed

ii/iii A.D.

Hippolytus *Refutations* 4.41

Greek

They lay a skull on the ground and make it appear to speak in the following fashion. The skull is made from an ox's abdominal membrane, shaped with the help of Etruscan wax and some prepared gypsum. He folds the caul round and so makes the form of a skull. When in operation this skull appears to everyone to chatter. The method is akin to the one we laid out in the case of the boys. For an accomplice prepares the windpipe of a crane or some similar long-necked creature and secretly attaches it to the skull, and says what he wants down it. When he wants the skull to disappear, he surrounds it with coals and makes a show of burning incense. When the heat of the coals reaches the wax, it melts, and in this way the skull is believed to become invisible.

SUCH OTHER EVIDENCE AS THERE IS for pagan skull necromancy is hardly compatible with the trick outlined here, which may rather have been invented by Hippolytus or another Christian writer for the specific purpose of discrediting pagan-mage practices. If the trick worked, its effect would appear to have been much more immediate than anything experienced in traditional skull necromancy. For the use of a crane's neck as a speaking tube for trickery see **64**. For the exposure of other mage-tricks by Hippolytus see **164, 223**.

## 161  A spell for the manufacture of a ghostly assistant with a skull

iv A.D.

*PGM* IV.2006–2125

Greek

Attraction spell of Pitys. Pitys sends greetings to King Ostanes. Since you repeatedly write to me about the inquiry into skulls, I thought I should send you this technique. It is to be treasured, and it has the potential to please you greatly. First here I will give you the technique, and then afterward I shall explain about the ink. Take an ass's skin, dry it in the shade, and draw on it the figure that will be revealed and the following text, in a circle: "AAMASI NOUTHI APHTHECHEMBÔCH POUPAIEICHNERI TA LOUTHIANI

SERANOMÊGRENTI EI BIL LONOUCHICH EITA PHOR CHORTOMNOUTHI THRACH PHIBÔBI ANTERÔ POCHORTHAROCH EBOCH LESANOUACH PHEORÔBIS TRAION KÔBI IOUNIA SAPHÔBI CHIMNOUTHI ASRÔ CHNOUPHNEN PHARMI BOLCHOSÊTH EPHOUKTERÔ ABDIDANPITAAU EAE BOL SACHU ACHCHERIMA EMINTO RÔÔRIA EN AMOUN AKREMPHTHO OUTRAUNIEL LABOCH PHERACHI AMENBOL BÊCH OS-TAOUA BELTHO. I conjure you, demon of a dead man [*nekydaimôn*] by the strong and implacable god and by his holy names, to stand yourself at my side in the coming night, in the form you used to have, and tell me whether you are able to perform the (fill in blank) task. Now, now, quickly, quickly!" Then go swiftly to a place where there is a burial, or where something has been disposed of, if you do not have a burial. Spread the hide underneath at sunset. Go back home and he will by all means come to you and stand himself by you on that night. He reports to you the manner of his death and first he will tell you whether he has the strength to do anything or undertake any service for you.

Take a flax leaf and draw on it the goddess who will be revealed to you with the ink which will be revealed to you, and write this spell in a circle (and place the leaf, spread out, on the head and garland it with black ivy, and by all means he will stand himself beside you during the night, in your dreams, and will ask you what you want, with the words, "Instruct me what you wish, and I do it"): "PHOUBEL TAUTHU AI DE MINÔOURITHI SENECHÔ CHELÊTHICHITIATH MOU CHÔ ARIANTA NARACHI MASKELLI (verbal formula) AEBITHÔ ACHAIL CHAÔSOUNISOU SOUNIARTENÔPH ARCHEREPHTHOUMI BOLPHAI ARÔCHÔ ABMENTHÔ PHORPHORBA CHNOUCHIO-CHOIME. I conjure you, demon of a dead man, by the Necessity of Necessities, to come to me, (insert your name here), on today's day, on today's night and to consent to serve me. If not, expect other punishments." As soon as he agrees, get up at once, take a hieratic papyrus roll and draw on it with the black ink that will be revealed the figure that will be revealed, and write this spell in a circle and set it before him. He will immediately attract and he will do it without delay, not delaying a single day, even if you do not have any of the person's stuff [*ousia*] to control them with.

Often you will have no need of the flax leaf. In a second version of the spell the papyrus itself will be laid down after you have ordered him to serve you. He attracts people, he lays them down on a sickbed, he sends dreams, he restrains and he procures revelations in dreams too. This spell alone can do all these things. Just modify the commonplaces in accordance with your project. Most of the mages, who carried their equipment with them, laid it aside and used him for an assistant. They accomplished the things laid out here with all speed. For the technique is without all those needless extra words, but it completes the things laid out here quickly and with all ease.

**Formula:** "I say to you, demon under the earth, for whom the stuff [*ousia*] of this woman (*or* man) has been embodied on this night, travel to where she (*or* he) lives and bring her to me (insert your name here), either in the middle of the night or at any rate quickly. Accomplish the (fill in blank) deed, because it is wished and commanded of you by the holy god Osiris KMÊPHI SRÔ. Accomplish, demon, the things written here. If you do accomplish them, I shall repay you with a sacrifice, but, if you are slow about it, may I inflict upon you punishments you cannot bear. Accomplish for me the (fill in blank) deed, now, now, quickly, quickly."

**The black ink for the technique:** The skin is inscribed with blood from the heart of a sacrificed ass, with which a bronzesmith's soot is mixed. The flax leaf is inscribed with hawk's blood, with which a goldsmith's soot is mixed. The hieratic papyrus roll is inscribed with eel's blood, with which acacia is mixed. Do these things as prescribed, and may you know, when you have completed them, what a powerful nature this technique encompasses, for in all convenience it treats the assistant as its equipment. Protect yourself with whatever form of phylactery you like.

**Here is the figure drawn on the skin:** A humanoid figure, with the head of a lion, wearing a belt, brandishing a staff in the right hand, on which there is to be a snake. An asp is to be wound around the whole of his left arm, and the lion's mouth is to breathe forth fire.

**This is the figure on the flax leaf:** Three-headed Hecate, with six hands, holding torches in her hands. The head on the right as you look at her is to be that of an ox, the head on the left that of a dog, the one in the middle that of a maiden. She is to have sandals on her feet.

**The figure on the papyrus roll:** Osiris dressed in the way in which Egyptians reveal him.

THIS SPELL FOR THE MANUFACTURE OF a ghostly assistant for a range of purposes, including necromancy and erotic attraction, is cast in the form of a letter between magical greats, doubtless to lend it authority. (This effect is somewhat undermined by the discussion of variant source-papyri in the third paragraph.) The recipient, Ostanes, is the familiar great Persian mage (see **45**). Pitys combines Thessalian and Egyptian elements, as do the reanimation sequences of Zatchlas (**105**) and Erictho (**155**). We subsequently learn that king Pitys is a Thessalian king (at line 2140). But he also refracts the Egyptian prophet Bitys, or Bitos, who discovered, Khamwas-like (see **46**), eschatological hieroglyphics written by Thoth-Hermes (i.e., "Hermetic" texts) in a sanctuary at Sais and translated them on a tablet for the pharaoh Ammon (Iamblichus *On the Mysteries* 8.5 and 10.7; Zosimus *On Apparatus and Furnaces* Greek fragments 230–5 Jackson); see also **46, 53**.

The manipulation of the skull is followed by an encounter with the ghost in question during sleep; dreams are once again shown to be the principal vehicle for the experiencing of ghosts in antiquity. The ghost of the dead man is conjured to "stand" beside the practitioner before speaking: compare the preliminary making-to-stand in the other reanimation narratives (**105, 155, 157**). The ghost will begin by describing its death, a thing ghosts were always ready to do (see **114, 144**). The carrot-and-stick approach to the dead man, with rewards and punishments offered side by side, recalls Erictho's approach to her ghost (**155**). A protective phylactery was advisable, not least because contact with the dead was inherently dangerous. An amulet or ring would probably have been used, like the one Lucian's Eucrates uses to protect himself against a manifestation of Hecate (**275**). For another recipe for something like skull necromancy in the Greek magical papyri, see **273**; see also **162**.

The erotic-attraction elements of the spell lay out the ideal scenario found in many such spells: the beloved is to be dragged through the streets in the middle of the night until she hammers at the practitioner's door, maddened with lust; see the discussion before **197**. The ass is the creature of Seth-Typhon; compare **163, 173**.

## 162   A restraining seal for unsuitable skulls

iv A.D.

PGM IV.2125–39

Greek

**Restraining seal** for unsuitable skulls, and, in addition, to prevent them saying or doing anything at all. Seal the mouth of the skull with dirt from Osiris's temple doors and from a barrow. Take iron from a fetter, hammer it in its cold state to make a ring, on which a headless lion is to be engraved. Instead of a head it is to have a crown of Isis, and it is to trample a skeleton underfoot, so that its right foot will tread on the skeleton's skull. In the middle of this draw a cat with gleaming eyes holding a gorgon head, and these names in a circle: IADÔR INBA NICHAIOPLÊX BRITH.

THE CIRCUMSTANCES THAT WOULD LEAD ONE to make this spell are unclear. If a skull had proven to be incapable of or misleading in divination, why not just stop using it? Perhaps certain skulls, once activated, would continue to interrupt one's sleep of their own accord with useless information. Ghosts were inferior to iron (see **244**), and the metal's fetter-origin would enhance its binding abilities. For the magical significance of iron worked cold, see **173**. The imagery of the decapitation of the lion and the crushing of the skull on the seal are largely self-explanatory. For rings see **249–50, 253, 262, 266, 272, 274–6**.

## FURTHER VARIETIES OF DIVINATION: LECANOMANCY LYCHNOMANCY, AND OTHER MEANS

The Greek magical papyri include a large number of recipes for lecanomancy, or "bowl-divination," and lychnomancy, or "lamp-divination." These constitute subcategories of a general technique of divination called "scrying" in English, in which meaning is derived from the observation, typically, of flashing lights. In lecanomancy the flashes are observed in the surface of a liquid, or in the bowl's polished surface (perhaps images may also be seen in the clouding of mixed liquids); in lychnomancy flashes are observed in the flickering of a lamp (perhaps images may also also be seen in its shadowing); in catoptromancy, or mirror-divination, flashes are observed on the surface of a mirror (perhaps images may also be seen in distorted reflections); in crystallomancy, or gem-divination, flashes are observed in gems. The observations of such flashes were often carried out by boys in a state of hypnosis, or indeed hypnotized by the flashes themselves; see **133–8**. Some spells give self-observation or boy-observation as alternatives

## 163 A recipe for bowl-divination (lecanomancy)

iv A.D.

PGM IV.222–60

Greek

Divination by lecanomancy and necromancy. Whenever you want to make a divination about things, take a bronze vessel, a pan or a dish, of whatever sort you like, and put water in it. If you are invoking the heavenly gods, use Zeus's rain-water; if you are invoking the underworld gods, use sea-water; if you are invoking Osiris or Sarapis, river-water; if you are invoking the dead, spring-water. Hold the vessel on your lap. Pour into it the oil of unripe olives, and bending over the vessel yourself proclaim the spell written out hereafter and call on the god you want. Ask him about the subject you want, and he will answer you and tell you about everything. When he has spoken to you, dismiss him with the dismissal spell. When you use this spell you will be amazed.

The spell spoken over the vessel: "AMOUN AUANTOU LAIMOUTAU RIPTOU MANTAUI IMANTOU LANTOU LAPTOUMI ANCHÔMACH ARAPTOUMI. Come here to me, god (insert his name), manifest yourself before me this very hour and do not alarm my eyes. Come here to me, god (insert his name), pay heed to me, because this is the wish and the command of ACHCHÔR ACHCHÔR ACHACHACH PTOUMI CHACHCHÔ CHARACHÔCH CHAPTOUMÊ CHÔRACHARACHÔCH APTOUMI MÊCHÔCHAPTOU CHARACHPTOU CHACHCHÔ CHARACHÔ PTENACHÔCHEU" (there are a hundred letters here).

You are well aware, greatest king and ruler of mages, that this is the primary name of Typhon, before whom tremble the earth, the depth of the sea, Hades, heaven, the sun, the moon, the bright host of stars, and the entire universe. This is the name that, when spoken, forcibly compels gods and demons to itself. This is the name of one hundred letters. Later, when you have made your summons, the one summoned will manifest himself, a god or a dead man, and he will answer all the questions you put to him. Whenever you have learned what you want, dismiss the god with the powerful name of a hundred letters, saying, "Be off, master, for this is the wish and the command given you by the great god (insert his name)." Say the name, and he will go. Let not this recipe, greatest king, pass beyond yourself; guard it and do not share it with anyone else.

There is also the phylactery itself, which you wear while you stand and while you perform the rite: inscribe the name of one hundred letters onto a silver lamella with a bronze stylus, string it on a thong of ass-leather, and wear it.

This is a self-contained portion of a longer recipe (154–285). The sources of water used are to be derived from the realm associated with the sort of power one wishes to invoke. The prayer claims power for itself by using the true name of Seth-Typhon (associated with the ass, the hide of which animal is used in the manufacture of the phylactery); compare **173**. For the role of ultimate compeller of other gods see **155**. For the manifestations of gods or of dead men as alternatives to each other, compare **43, 53**. As often, the recipe includes a means for the dismissal of the power summoned; one would be particularly anxious to separate oneself from the deadening company of a ghost. It was advisable to be protected also during the course of the encounter; hence the protective amulet using a silver lamella (compare **248–77**). For lecanomancy in other excerpts see **43, 47, 53, 64, 135, 164**.

## 164　A lecanomancy trick exposed

ii/iii A.D.

Hippolytus *Refutations* 4.35

Greek

Nor will I keep quiet about the knavish trick behind their lecanomancy. They prepare in advance a closed chamber and paint its ceiling with blue. For the show itself they bring in some blue vessels and lift them up. A bowl filled with water is placed on the ground in the middle. This gives back a blue reflection from the "sky." The floor has a hole secretly cut in it. The bowl sits on this. It has a glass bottom, but the rest of it is stone. Underneath there is a secret chamber. The accomplices retreat into this and put on whatever costumes of gods and demons the mage wants them to show and then display them. When the dupe sees them, he is amazed by the mage's trick and thenceforth believes everything the mage will tell him.

As with the skull trick exposed by Hippolytus (**160**; see further **223**), this similarly elaborate trick does not appear compatible with the mechanics of pagan lecanomancy in other sources, and may be a Christian fantasy concocted to discredit. As with the skull trick, the effect of this one, if it worked, would be far more immediate than anything experienced through normal lecanomantic practice.

## 165　The Thessalian Pamphile divines the weather from her lamp

Later ii A.D.

Apuleius
*Metamorphoses* 2.11

Latin

It was evening now and Pamphile was staring into her lamp. "What heavy rain," she said, "there'll be tomorrow." Her husband asked her how she knew it, and she replied that her lamp had predicted it to her. Milo laughed at her claim. "We're keeping a profound Sibyl in that lamp of yours, who observes all the business of the heaven and the sun himself from her lampstand watch-tower." 12. At this I interjected, "This," I said, "is the first time I have seen this variety of divination. It is hardly surprising if this little flame of yours, for all that it is modest and manmade, nonetheless remains mindful of that greater heavenly fire, as if of its own parent, and can consequently know by divine presentiment what that fire is going to do at the top of the ether and declare it to us."

LUCID LITERARY DESCRIPTIONS OF LYCHNOMANCY ARE rare; it is unclear how many would have agreed with Lucius's explanation of the working of the technique. For Pamphile, see **107**; for more on lychnomancy see **55, 134, 166**; for magical lamps in other contexts see **211, 243, 245, 273**; for lamps in a more vague association with ghostly manifestations see **105, 115–6**.

## 166 Recipe for lamp-divination (lychnomancy)

iv/v A.D.

*PGM* I.262–347

Greek

**Invocation of Apollo.** Take a twig of laurel with seven leaves on it. Hold it in your right hand and call on the heavenly gods and the chthonic demons. Inscribe on the laurel branch the seven protective characters. These are the characters: [but in fact *eight* characters are supplied]. Inscribe the first character on the first leaf, the second character similarly again on the second leaf, until you have used up the seven leaves and the seven characters. Make sure you do not let a leaf drop off and expose yourself to harm. For this is the greatest phylactery of the body. By means of it all are subjected. The sea and the rocks shudder at it and the demons steer clear of the characters' divine power—the power that you are going to possess. For this is the greatest phylactery for the procedure, so you need not panic. This is the procedure. Take a nonred lamp, and insert a wick made from a rag of linen, and pour in rose oil and oil of spikenard. Put on a prophet's robe, hold an ebony staff in your left hand and the phylactery in your right one, that is, the laurel twig. Keep to hand the head of a wolf, so that you can mount the lamp on the head of the wolf. Set up an altar of unbaked brick beside the head and the lamp, so that you may sacrifice to the god. The divine spirit enters the lamp at once. The sacrifice consists of a wolf's-eye spice, storax, cassia, balsam, and every valuable spice. Make a libation of wine, honey, milk, and rain-water. Make seven flat cakes and seven round cakes. You are going to make all these cakes beside the lamp, wearing your costume and abstaining from all pollution, all fish-eating, and all sex, so that you may induce the greatest desire for yourself in the god. These are the names which you are going to write on the linen rag and insert into the nonred lamp for a wick:

ABERAMENTHŌOULERTHEX ANAX ETHRENLUOÔ THNEMA RAIBAI AEMINNAE BARÔTHER RETHÔBAB EANIMEA.

Whenever you have completed all the preceding rites, summon the god with the incantation:

Mighty Apollo, come with Paean, prophesy to me about the things I ask you, lord. Master, leave Mount Parnassus and Delphic Pytho as my sacred mouth voices secret words, first angel of the god, great Zeus, IAO, and you MICHAÊL, possessor of the heavenly world, and I call upon you, archangel GABRIÊL. Come here to me from Olympus, ABRASAX, you who delight in the rising of the sun, may you come to me propitious, you who watch the sun setting from its rising, ADÔNAI. All nature trembles before you, father of the universe, PAKERBÊTH. I adjure the head of God, which is Olympus. I adjure the seal of God, which is sight. I adjure the right hand, which you held over the universe, I adjure the mixing bowl of God with its wealth, I adjure the eternal God, AIÔN of all things, I adjure nature that grows of its own accord, the strongest ADÔNAIOS, I adjure the setting and the rising ELÔAIOS. I adjure these sacred and divine names. I adjure all these so that they may send me the divine spirit and so that it may accomplish everything I have in my mind and heart. Hear me, blessed one, I call upon you, the leader of heaven and earth, of chaos and Hades, where there live. . . . [lacuna] Send this demon at my sacred incantations, driven by commands through the night, by your compulsion. This comes from his corpse/tent [*skênos*]. Let him speak the truth and tell me everything I wish in my mind, propitious, gentle, and without hostile intent towards me. Do not be angry with sacred incantations, but keep watch over my entire body, so that it comes into the light intact. For it was you who ordained the learning of these things among men. I invoke your name, which is numerically equivalent to the Fates, ACHAIPHÔ THÔTHÔ AIÊ IAÊIA AIÊ AIÊ IAÔ THÔTHÔ PHIACHA.

Whenever he comes, ask him about the things you want, about divination, about initiation, about dream-sending, about the seeking of revelation through dreams, about dream interpretation, about disease-infliction, about everything in magical expertise. Strew a throne and couch with linen sheets, but stand to make the aforementioned sacrifice. After your enquiry, if you wish to dismiss the god himself, transfer the afore-mentioned ebony staff, which you are holding in your left hand, to your right hand, and the laurel twig, which you are holding in your right hand, to your left hand. Extinguish the flame of the lamp. Use the same sacrifice and say:

"Be propitious to me, forefather, born first, self-produced, I adjure the fire that first shone in the abyss, I adjure your power, the greatest for all, I adjure the god that destroys one even until one is within Hades, so that you may go off to your own ship and not do me harm, but be continually friendly toward me."

APOLLO WAS THE GREEK GOD PRIMARILY associated with prophecy and divination, as most famously at his shrine at Delphi; the laurel was sacred to him. Since the rite will bring one into close contact with powers, it is advisable to use a phylactery. As often for acts of divination, one is bidden keep oneself pure (compare **53, 148**). Jewish influence can be seen in the invocation. Again a special set of instructions for dismissal is included. The incantation, beginning with "Mighty Apollo . . ." is in verse, mostly poor hexameters. The lines from "Hear me, blessed one . . ." partly correspond with incantations in *PGM* IV and VIII, and these are reconstructed by Preisendanz into an original magical hymn to Helios, "Hymn 4" (Preisendanz and Henrichs 1973–74 ii pp.239–40).

## 167   The Homer oracle

iii/iv A.D.

*PGM* VII.1–148 (part)

Greek

1.1.1. But they have terrible woes on account of their accursed stomach [Homer *Odyssey* 15.344]

1.1.2. Neither to throw down anchor-stones nor to fasten stern cables [Homer *Odyssey* 9.137]

1.1.3. Men being struck with a sword, and the water was running red with blood [Homer *Iliad* 21.21]

ONE FRAMES AN ENQUIRY AND THROWS a die three times. A supposedly prophetic verse of Homer is supplied for each of the 216 possible combinations up to 6.6.6. The sequence of the results is also significant: thus, separate verses are given for 1.1.2, 1.2.1, and 2.1.1. The first three combinations are given here, *exempli gratia*. The lines appear to have been selected at random. The oracle attests the magical power attributed to the Homeric texts, which make a number of appearances in the Greek magical papyri. This was a result, no doubt, not only of the ancient and classic nature of Homeric poems, but also of their inclusion of paradigmatic magical episodes (**72–5, 144–5**). Elsewhere we find a line of Homer used as an anger-restraining spell ("Will you have the heart to lift your huge spear against Zeus?" *Iliad* 8.424, *PGM* IV.467–8), and a group of three disparate verses used as an amulet described as an "assistant" (**273**).

# 10
## Curses

### BINDING CURSES: LAW, COMPETITION, AND TRADE

Binding curses are primarily known from their use in curse tablets (in Greek *katadesmoi*, in Latin *defixiones*). Their properties may be summarized as follows:

- Some 1,600, the majority in Greek, survive from all periods of antiquity from ca. 500 B.C. onward.
- They are found throughout the Graeco-Roman world, from Egypt to Britain.
- They seek, often explicitly, to "bind" or "restrain" their victims.
- The desired restraint or confusion of the victim is often reflected in or induced by the use of reversed, twisted, or jumbled forms of writing, conventions, or imagery.
- They are often inscribed on lead, which is then rolled or folded and nailed, in additional symbolic acts of twisting and restraint.
- In their imagery and application they have much in common with "voodoo dolls," which are already found in the archaic period (for which see **236–47**).
- Their curses are to be enacted by ghosts and/or underworld powers.
- To this end they are typically deposited in graves, in "underground" bodies of water, such as springs or wells, or in chthonic sanctuaries. They can also be deposited in the victim's home or workplace.
- The majority of curses, where their subject can be discerned, fall into one of the following categories: legal; choral or athletic competition; trade (**168–84**); love and sex (**197–213**); and prayers for justice (**185–91**).
- The curses are often made between rivals in a "competitive context," as Faraone (1991a) has observed.
- The earlier tablets tend to be concise. The later ones are usually much more prolix and enhanced with various paraphernalia: *voces magicae*, vowel patterns, palindromes, appeals to protracted lists of syncretized gods or demons and images.

For professionals selling binding curses cheap see **14**. There are numerous references to binding magic also in the passages collected at **91–107**.

## 168 A legal, tongue-binding, lead curse tablet from Selinus

Late vi/ early v B.C.

Lopez Jimeno 1991, no. 3

Greek

**A.** The tongue of Eucles and the tongue of Aristophanis and the tongue of Angeilis and the tongue of Alciphron and the tongue of Hagestratos. The tongues of the advocates of Eucles and Aristophanis. The tongue of . . .[lacuna]

**B.** and the tongue of Oinotheos and the tongue of . . .[lacuna]

ONE OF THE VERY EARLIEST TO survive, this curse tablet was discovered adjacent to a cemetery. It is typical of the earlier curses in that, despite being repetitive, it is brief and lacks ornament. It focuses tightly on naming the intended victims and on singling out for binding of that part of them which is particularly threatening to the curse-maker. For further legal curses see **47, 237, 273**. See also **267** for an amulet for protection in a lawsuit, and **278–300** for magic and the law.

## 169 An Attic lead binding-curse tablet against legal opponents and against other binding curses

Early iv B.C.

Jordan 1999, no. 1

Greek

**A.** If anyone put a binding spell [*katedêsen*] on me, be it man or woman, slave or free, alien or citizen, from my household or from outside it, be it out of envy toward my work or my actions, if anyone put a binding spell on me before Hermes, be it Hermes *Eriounios* or Hermes Restrainer or Hermes Trickster, or before some other power, I bind in return [*antikatadesmeuô*] all my enemies.

**B.** I bind [*katadesmeuô*] my opponent in court Dion and Granicos.

THE REMAINDER OF SIDE B IS partly legible but uninterpretable. This relatively early tablet shows itself to be part of a developed magical "arms race." How does one defend oneself against secretly made curses? By putting a reciprocal curse on the makers; compare **269–70**. This tablet partly belongs in the prayers-for-justice category of curse tablets (**185–91**): it is retributive, it cannot name its victim(s), and it is conditional. This tablet also offers an early example of the use of the highly stylized "exhaustive dichotomies" in curse tablets. The notion that Hermes is the most likely restrainer, but that he might perform the act of restraint in his various different aspects, is intriguing.

## 170 A legal lead curse tablet addressed to the ghost Pasianax, from Megara or Arcadia

ii–i B.C.

Voutiras 1998, 65–6 (*DT* 43–4)

Greek

**A.** Whenever you, O Pasianax, read this text—but neither will you, O Pasianax, ever read this text, nor will Neophanes ever bring a case against Agasibolos. But just as you, O Pasianax, lie here ineffectual, so too may Neophanes become ineffectual and nothing.

**B.** Whenever you, O Pasianax, read this text—but neither will you ever read this, nor will Acestor or Timandridas ever bring a case against Eratomenes. But just as you lie here ineffectual and nothing, so may Acestor and Timandridas be ineffectual and nothing.

THIS FASCINATING TEXT EXPLOITS CONTRADICTORY notions about ghosts. On the one hand the curse depends for its activation on the ghost's vigor; on the other it depends on the ghost's ineffectualness for its "sympathetic" spell; compare **177**. The contrivedly "twisted" nature of the thought is remarkable too. Had the curse-maker known Pasianax in life? Or read his name from his tombstone? It has been suggested that Pasianax, which means "Lord to all," is not the real name of the dead man but the epithet of a powerful underworld demon with which his ghost is identified (Voutiras 1999).

## 171   The Erinyes attempt to bind Orestes before his murder trial

458 B.C.

Aeschylus *Eumenides*
306, 327–33

Greek

**306. Chorus of Erinyes:** You will hear this hymn of ours that will bind you.

**327–33 Chorus of Erinyes:** This is our song over our sacrificial victim [Orestes]: insanity, mind-ruining derangement, a hymn of the Erinyes to bind the mind, unaccompanied by the lyre, a withering for mortals.

THIS BINDING SONG IS SUNG BY the Erinyes in Aeschylus's tragedy as they prepare to prosecute Orestes before the Areopagus. Lines 327–33 are repeated at 341–6. See Faraone (1985).

## 172   The advocate Curio supposedly has his tongue bound by Cicero's client

46 B.C.

Cicero *Brutus* 217

Latin

When I had rounded off the case for the defense on behalf of Cotta's Titinia in a very important private suit, he [Curio] was speaking against me on behalf of Servius Naevius. All of a sudden he forgot his entire case and said that this had been caused by Titinia's spells/poisons [*veneficia*] and incantations.

## 173   A "Sethian" circus-competition curse tablet from Rome

Late iv A.D.

Wünsch 1898, no. 16;
*DT* 155 [text]; *CT* no.
13, side A

Greek

EULAMÔN, restrain, OUSIRI OUSIRI APHI OUSIRI MNE PHRI, [lacuna] . . . and archangels, in the name of the underworld one, so that, just as I entrust to you this impious and lawless and accursed Cardelus, whom his mother Fulgentia bore, so may you bring him to a bed of punishment, to be punished with an evil death, and to die within five days. Quickly! Quickly!

Spell: You, Phrygian goddess, nymph goddess, Eidonea [i.e., ADÔNAI?] NEOI EKATOIKOUSE, I invoke you by your [lacuna] . . . so that you may help me and restrain and hold in check Cardelus and bring him to a bed of punishment, to be punished with an evil death, to come to an evil condition, him whom his mother Fulgentia bore. And you, holy EULAMON, and holy Characters, and holy assistants, those on the right and those on the left, and holy Symphonia [?]. These things have been written on this (EULAMÔN, restrain, OUSIRI OUSIRI API OUSIRI MNE PHRI) tablet made from a cold-water pipe, so that, just as I entrust to you this impious and accursed and ill-fated Cardelus, whom his mother Fulgentia bore, bound, tied up, and restrained, Cardelus whom his mother Fulgentia bore, so that you may so restrain him and bring him to a bed of punishment, to be punished and to die an evil death, Cardelus whom his mother Fulgentia bore, within five days, because I invoke you by the power that renews itself under the earth, the one that restrains the [zodiacal] circles and OIMENÊBENCHUCH BACHUCH BACHACHUCH BAZACHUCH BACHAZACHUCH BACHAXICHUCH BADÊTOPHÔTH PHTHÔSIRÔ. I invoke you, holy angels. [The text continues, repetitively, on side B.]

THIS TEXT DERIVES FROM A BATCH of around fifty-six curse tablets that were rolled up, transfixed with nails, sealed in terracotta sarcophagi, and deposited in tombs on the Via Appia. The tablets in the batch address themselves to the restraint of circus charioteers; these were the focus of great passions in antiquity, and support for the different teams, identified by colors, could even take on political dimensions.

This tablet from the end of the ancient world is at heart comparable to that from its beginning reproduced at **168**, in that both aim to achieve an act of binding. But the late tablet not only massively expands its text but also incorporates into it a varied panoply of devices. The most striking is the use of strings

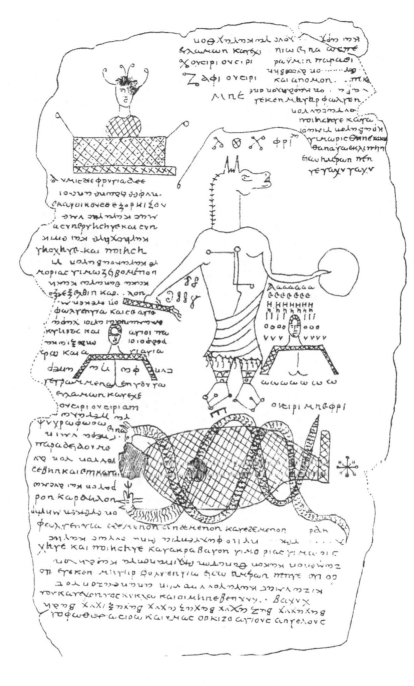

Figure 10.1.
"Sethian" curse
tablet from Rome.
Wünsch 1898, no.
16 (*DT,* no. 155;
Gager 1992, no.
13). Wünsch's line
drawing.

of *voces magicae*, demonic names not immediately meaningful (they are conventionally printed in capitalized form in modern translations; see **174**). Behind these names one can find the divine powers of a number of cultures: Judaeo-Christian (Adonai, archangels); Egyptian (Osiris, Phri = Ra, etc.); Greek (Symphonia, if the reading is correct). Eulamon is a popular demon in the later tablets, but his origin remains obscure. As often in later tablets, the victim is identified by maternal lineage, a social inversion (from the usual patronymic) to match such tablets' many linguistic inversions. The hectoring "quickly, quickly" is a common formulaic feature of the later tablets.

The tablet is visually interesting (see figure 10.1). Alternate lines of its text are written upside down, so that it "snakes." It is also richly illustrated with an appropriately horse-headed demon (misinterpreted by the first editor, Wünsch, as Seth-Typhon, hence the batch's designation) holding a whip and a chariot-wheel (?), a pair of charioteers in their bound chariots (or perhaps the named assistant demons) on right and left, a mummy around which twisting snakes entwine, and a bound and nailed man in a bound and nailed coffin. There are also vowel patterns and "characters," meaningless (?) letter-like symbols, the latter also being explicitly appealed to.

Gods or demons are appealed to for the enactment of the curse, but the curse is deposited with a dead man. Is the ghost is to take the message to the demons, or is it to act alongside them, or is it to be made to act by them? Cardelus is subjected to slander—he is "impious," "lawless" and "accursed"—in order to encourage the demons to act against him; compare **211**. A recipe among the Greek Magical Papyri similarly instructs one to make a lead tablet from a cold-water pipe (*PGM* VII.396–404); its association with underground water will have brought it into contact with ghosts; see also **162**. For amulets to bring victory in competition, including that in the circus, see **271–2**.

## 174   *Voces magicae*: The "Ephesian letters" explained

Ca. 200 A.D.

Clement of Alexandria
*Stromateis* 6.45

Greek

Androcydes the Pythagorean says that the well-known so-called Ephesian letters are organized in allegory. *Askion*, he says, means "darkness," for it has no shadows [*skiai*]; *kataskion* means "light," since it illumines the shadow [*kataugazei . . . skian*]; *lix* is an ancient word for "earth," *tetrax* for "year," because of the four [*tetra-* = "four"] seasons; *damnameneus* is the sun, because it conquers [*damazôn*]; *aisia* means "the true voice." The allegory means that the divine world has been arranged, such as darkness for light and sun for the year and earth for every sort of generation.

THE "EPHESIAN LETTERS" ARE THE OLDEST known series of *voces magicae*, words of power, used in magical incantations and curses. Found on curse tablets only from the first century A.D., they are known to have been in circulation since the fifth century B.C. *Voces magicae* are not immediately meaningful in Greek, although anything can become meaningful enough if used repeatedly in specialized contexts or if regarded as a demonic name, as such words often were; to know something's name, especially its secret one, is ipso facto to exercise power over it. Clement here takes the rather different approach of attempting to render the words meaningful partly through forced false etymologies and partly through allegorization. A great many of the *voces magicae* in the Greek magical papyri can be understood as (often garbled) Egyptian or Hebrew names, words, or phrases.

## 175 A sorcerer offers Augustine a binding curse for a poetry competition

Ca. 400 A.D.

Augustine *Confessions* 4.2

Latin

I recall that once, when I had decided to enter a competition for producing a poem for the theatre, some diviner [*haruspex*] sent to ask how much I would be willing to pay him for victory. But I despised and abominated those disgusting rites, and replied that I would not permit even a fly to be killed, even if the victory crown were to be made of everlasting gold. For he was planning to kill animals in his sacrificial rites, and seemed to intend to petition for the aid of demons with these offerings.

THE ASSOCIATION OF CURSE-TABLET MANUFACTURE with divination, and probably also with shabby hucksterism, recalls Plato's amalgam, **14–7**.

## 176 Attic lead trade curse tablet against shopkeepers

iv B.C.

*DTA*, no. 87a

Greek

I bind [*katadô*] Callias, the local shopkeeper/innkeeper, and his wife Thraitta, and the shop/inn of the bald man, and the shop/inn of Anthemion, which is adjacent to . . . [lacuna] and Philon the shopkeeper/innkeeper. Of all these people I bind their soul, work, hands, feet, and shops/inns. I bind Sosimenes (and[?]) his brother, and Carpos his slave, the linen-seller, and Glycanthis, whom they call "Gentle" [*Malthake*], and Agathon the shopkeeper/innkeeper, the slave of Sosimenes, of all these people I bind their soul, work, life, hands, and feet. I bind Cittos, my neighbor, the hemp-worker, the Craft of Cittos, his work, his soul, his mind, and the tongue of Cittos. I bind Mania the shopkeeper/innkeeper at the spring and the shop/inn of Aristander the Eleusinian, their work and mind. Soul, hands, tongue, feet, mind: I bind all these in graves . . . [lacuna] before Hermes the Restrainer.

IN THIS FINE EXAMPLE OF A trade curse the people bound are evidently not all of the same trade. If the curse-maker also had a shop or inn, his motivation may simply have been the desire to do better than his neighboring shopkeepers, whatever their trade. Or perhaps the curse was made by a customer who had felt himself swindled by these various establishments. The range of body parts specified for binding appears to be an all-purpose generalized list. Appeal is made to Hermes, escort of souls to the underworld, to enact or take part in the binding.

## 177 Attic lead trade curse tablet against pimps, bawds (?), and prostitutes

iv B.C.

Jordan 1999, no. 2 (*DT* 52)

Greek

Cercis, Blastos, Nicander, Glycera. I bind (*katadô*) Cercis and the speech and actions of Cercis and his/her tongue before bachelors and whenever they read this, only then may Cercis have the power to speak.

I bind Theon, himself and his girls and his trade and his work-opportunities and his work and his speech and his deeds. Underworld Hermes, perform this act of restraint and keep reading this so long as these people live.

THE SECOND PORTION OF THIS TEXT seems to restrain a pimp and his girls. His speech is presumably bound because he uses this to entice customers. The first portion of the text presumably has a similar purpose; the gender of Cercis is disputed. The binding is to be enacted by underworld Hermes and, in some way, the ghosts of bachelors. The latter are used because untimely dead and so appropriately restless; compare **110, 112**. These ghosts too are exploited in contradictory ways, as was that of Pasianax (170): on the one hand they are to be vigorous enough to participate in the act of binding; on the other their inability even to read is used sympathetically to silence Cercis's tongue.

## 178  A traditional quasi-trade curse against potters

v B.C.

[Homer] *Epigram* 14

Greek

If you pay me, potters, I will sing. Come here to me, Athene, and shield the kiln with your hand. May the cups and all the dishes be well completed, may they fire beautifully, may they bring in a good price and be sold in large quantities in the marketplace and the streets. May the potters make good profits, and grant me that I should, consequently, sing to them. But if you potters turn yourselves to shameless behavior and make me false promises, then I shall call on the destroyers of kilns, Basher, Smasher too, and Over-fire, Shatterer and Under-fire, provider of many ills for this craft. Lay waste to the furnace and the workshop, may the entire kiln be confounded and may the potters wail at length. Just as the jaw of the horse grinds, may the kiln also grind all the pots within it and turn them into fragments. Come here to me too, daughter of Helios, Circe of the many drugs [*polupharmakê*]. Cast your wild spells and damage these men and their works. Let Chiron also bring here to me the host of centaurs, both those who escaped from the hands of Heracles and those who were killed. May they smash these works up, and destroy the kiln. May the potters themselves witness these terrible deeds and lament. But I will rejoice as I look upon their ill-fated craft. If any of them peep into the kiln, may his entire face be scorched by the fire, so that they may all learn to treat people fairly.

IN THIS VIGOROUS POEM THE SINGER threatens potters with the invocation of a range of demons embodying the various disasters that can befall pots in the firing process. Although a (conditional) curse between tradesmen, it is not made between men of the same trade, as was often the case. In calling also on Circe (for whom see **72, 144**) the singer associates his cursing activity with the witch tradition.

## 179  Lead curse tablet against the gates of Rome

iii A.D.

*SEG* 14: no. 615, Guarducci 1978, 251–4 (incorporating revisions from Jordan 1985c, no. 129)

Greek

Restrain Artemidoros the doctor of the Third Praetorian Cohort. The brother of the dead Demetrios is his servant, who now wants to go out to his own fatherland. Therefore do not let him [i.e., do not let Artemidoros stop me], but restrain the Italian land, knock out the gates of the Romans. Restrain Artemidorus the son of Artemidoros the doctor. Eulamon, Laimeila, Omelieus, Axeieus, Areieus and Lathos and Thambos, restrain!

THIS CURSE TABLET IS NOTEWORTHY IN two respects. First, it is the most ambitious of extant tablets in its attempt to bind the whole of Italy and the city of Rome in particular, within which the maker is confined. Second, the curse-maker curiously exploits the ghost of his own dead brother for the task. We presume, therefore, that a ghost, perhaps in any case restless, was not subjected to undue suffering by being made to enact curses. What prevented the curse-maker from leaving Rome as he wished? Slavery is the most obvious answer.

## 180 Thanks given for the deliverance of the government of Tuder from a slave's curse

i A.D.

CIL 11.2.4639

Latin

In return for the salvation of the town and of the order of the town senate, to Jupiter best and greatest, the guardian and the preserver, because he, by his power, brought forth the names of the town senators which had been attached [*defixa*] to tombs by the unutterable crime of a most wicked public slave, and he liberated and freed the town and the citizens from the fear of dangers. Lucius Cancrius Primigenius, the freedman of Clemens, member of the board of six, both Augustan and Flavian, the first member of the order to be honored in this way, fulfilled his vow.

THIS UNIQUE INSCRIPTION GIVES THANKS TO Jupiter for the fact that curse tablets against the town as a whole and its senatorial class in particular had been discovered at the tombs where they had been deposited. Discovery permitted deactivation; see **190**, with commentary. It is remarkable that the cheap and easy mechanism of curse tablets could be held capable of inverting the town's social structure; compare **238, 278**.

## 181 Germanicus is killed with binding spells

Ca. 120 A.D.

Tacitus *Annals* 2.69, 2.74, 3.7

Latin

**2.69.** Germanicus's conviction that he had been poisoned/put under a spell [*veneni*] by Piso aggravated the disease. They dug up the floor and the walls and found remains of human bodies in them, spells and binding curses [*devotiones*], and the name of Germanicus inscribed on lead tablets, ashes half-burned and smeared with gore and the other evil devices by which it is believed that souls are devoted to the infernal powers. It was also complained that men sent by Piso were prying into the disease's deleterious effects.

**2.74.** Sentius sent to the city a woman renowned for poisoning/ witchcraft [*veneficia*] in that province [Syria] and beloved of Plancina [Piso's wife]. She was called Martina. This was at the behest of Vitellius, Veranius, and the others who were preparing charges and a case [against Piso and Plancina], as if against people already arraigned as defendants.

**3.7.** The complaint was repeatedly made that Piso was in the meantime drifting around the pleasant parts of Asia and Achaea and making arrogant and cunning delays to give himself the opportunity to make away with proofs of his crimes. For it was bruited abroad that the infamous poisoner/witch Martina, who had been dispatched, as I said, by Cnaeus Sentius, had died suddenly at Brundisium, and that poison/drugs had been found in the knot of her hair, with no indications of suicide found on her body.

GERMANICUS, WHO DIED AT ANTIOCH IN 19 A.D., was the nephew and adopted son of the emperor Tiberius. It is noteworthy that in this instance, where the lead curse tablets are deposited in the home of the victim rather than in the realm of the dead, they are nonetheless associated with cadaverous material so as to enlist a ghost for their activation. For the Syrian witch, compare **51–2**. In this narrative the equivocation in the Latin word *venenum* between "poison" and "spell" is particularly evident.

## 182  A curse tablet against Silvanus from Cirta in Numidia, using a maternal lineage formula

iv A.D.

DT 300, with Jordan 1976

Latin

May he be seized so that you may render him without feeling, without memory, without the ability to perform rites, without marrow, may he be. . . .[lacuna] I commit to you Silvanus, whom a womb bore, so that you may take him and restrain him, his deeds and his concerns. . . .[lacuna] I commit him to you, so that you may render him dead, so that you may deposit him in Tartarus.

THIS TEXT IS ACCOMPANIED BY AN image of a demon with hairy goat's feet, armed with two nooses and a hook, and with genitals hanging. The context of the curse is unclear. Its principal interest lies in its use of the abbreviated formula *qpvulva* to mean "whom a womb bore." The identification of maternal lineage was evidently felt to be so important that it gave rise to this paradoxical, nonidentifying formula for use when the mother's identity was unknown to the curser. The formula's abbreviated nature suggests that it had, furthermore, become commonplace.

## 183  A lead curse tablet from Rome to spare Politoria from the workhouse

iv A.D.

Wünsch 1909 (CT 78)

Greek

A. PHANOIBIKUX PETRIADÊ KRATARNADÊ, restrain, lord angels, Clodia Valeria Sophrone from getting hold of Politoria.
    B. ARTHU LAILAM SEMISILAM BACHUCH BACHAXICHUCH MENEBACICHUCH ABRASAX, restrain, lord gods, the boss of the workhouse, Clodia Valeria Sophrone, and let her not take Politoria to the workhouse [*ergastill[o]n*], to see lifelessness [*apsychia*].

THIS TABLET IS PRIMARILY OF INTEREST for the social-historical insight it provides. Politoria seems to be a slave-girl, or perhaps an indebted free woman. This is one of the relatively few examples of a nonerotic curse tablet where the maker can be positively identified as female. Politoria makes appeal to both Judaeo-Christian powers and to *voces magicae*.

## 184  A description of the feeling of being subject to binding magic

iii A.D.

Porphyry *Life of Plotinus* 10

Greek

Olympius of Alexandria was one of those who pretended to be a philosopher. He had briefly been a pupil of Ammonius. He had a contemptuous attitude toward Plotinus because of his own desire to be the first. His attacks culminated in an attempt to use magic [*mageusas*] to sun-scorch [*astrobolêsai*] him. But when he perceived that the assault was rebounding on himself, he told his friends that Plotinus's soul was so powerful that it could beat back attacks against him and turn them on those who were trying to harm him. However, Plotinus perceived Olympius's attack and said that at that moment his body felt drawn tight as if by purse strings, with his limbs being crushed together. After repeatedly exposing himself to harm as opposed to inflicting it on Plotinus, Olympius gave up.

ALTHOUGH IT IS NOT EXPLICITLY SAID that Olympius used binding magic as such, this is the implication of Porphyry's description of his sensations while under attack. For other descriptions of the physical experience of being subject to a binding spell see **94, 247**.

## PRAYERS FOR JUSTICE

The most distinctive subcategory of curse tablets is that of "prayers for justice," which most often seek the restitution of or revenge for stolen goods. These tablets can overlap with other curse tablets in all respects (see **169**), but they need not use or imply a binding formula, nor need they name their victim, who is in any case normally unidentifiable. They are usually addressed to gods or goddesses.

**185** **A pewter prayer for justice from Bath seeking restoration of a stolen cloak**

iii A.D.

*Tab. Sulis* no. 62

Latin

I, [. . .]eocorotis, have lost my *laena*-cloak, *pallium*-cloak, *sagum*-cloak (and) my tunic. I have given <it to> Sulis, so that the thief may deliver it in his beak within nine days, whether free or slave man, whether free or slave woman, whether boy or girl. <Let him> deliver the horse-blanket, <whether slave or free man, whether> slave or free woman, whether boy <or girl> in his beak.

THIS IS ONE OF THE HUNDRED or so curse tablets excavated from the sacred spring of Sulis Minerva at Bath (see figures 10.2 and 10.3). They are all made of pewter, lead alloyed with tin. Typically the tablets seek redress for thefts of items in the baths, and cloak-snatching was indeed regarded as the characteristic crime of the bathhouse. Note the frenzied overdefinition of the lost item. As often, the curse-maker has given the stolen object to the goddess, so that the crime is transformed from mere theft into sacrilege. The injury then is to the goddess, and she at least has the power to find the culprit and avenge herself. It is uncertain what became of the goods if recovered: were they in fact given to the goddess, so that the former owner had the satisfaction only of revenge? Or could he borrow them back from her or redeem them in some way? The exhaustive dichotomies are typical of the curse tablets. The graphically expressed wish that the thief should be made to bring the stolen goods back in his "beak" is striking.

Figures 10.2 and 10.3. An unrolled curse tablet (*Tab. Sulis* no. 9a.) and some rolled curse tablets from Bath. Photograph © Mr. R. Wilkins, Institute of Archaeology, Oxford, whose kind help I gratefully acknowledge.

## 186    A pewter prayer-for-justice tablet from Bath seeking restoration of a stolen bowl

iii A.D.

*Tab. Sulis* no. 44

Latin

The one who has stolen my bronze bowl is accursed. I give the person to the temple of Sulis, whether woman or man, whether slave or free, whether boy or girl, and may the man who did this pour his own blood into the very bowl. I give you that thief who stole the item itself, for the god to find, whether woman or man, whether slave or free, whether boy or girl.

HERE IT IS NOT THE STOLEN item as such that is given to the goddess but the thief himself. For all its formulaic nature, the curse-maker individualizes the tablet with the bitter wish that the thief use the bowl he has stolen to catch up his own spilt blood as if in a sacrifice. Once again exhaustive dichotomies are used.

## 187    A lead prayer-for-justice curse tablet from Lydney Park in Gloucestershire, and an associated ring from Silchester

Later iv A.D.

*DT* 106 (*RIB* 306)

Latin

**Lydney Park tablet:** To the god Nodens. Silvianus has lost his ring. He has given half its value to Nodens. Do not allow good health among those who possess the name of Senicianus until he brings it right to the temple of Nodens.

**Silchester ring:** Venus [seal]; Senicianus, may you live in God! [loop].

THESE REMARKABLE FINDS WERE MADE SOME thirty miles apart. The hearer of Silvianus's petition is a Romano-Celtic pagan god; the tablet was found in his temple. The Silchester ring seems to have been a pagan one, initially saluting Venus (an erotic amulet?—compare **229, 248–53**), which was then recustomized with a Christian inscription for one Senicianus. It is tempting to think that this is the pagan Silvianus's ring, stolen by the Christian Senicianus. We can only speculate as to how Silvianus may have known the thief's name but not his specific identity. Here it is just half the value of the stolen goods that is dedicated to the god.

## 188    A lead prayer-for-justice curse tablet against Epaphroditus, addressed to Demeter

ii B.C.–ii A.D.

Homolle 1901

Greek

Lady Demeter, my queen, I am your suppliant. I fall before you as your slave. One Epaphroditus has lured away my slaves. He has taught them evil ways. He has put ideas into their heads, he has given them advice, he has seduced them. He has laughed at me, he has given them wings to waste time in the marketplace. He gave them the idea of running away. He himself bewitched my slave-girl, so that he could take her to wife against my will. For this reason he bewitched her to run away along with the others. Lady Demeter, being the victim of these things, and being on my own, I take refuge with you. May I find you propitious, and grant that I should find justice. Grant that the one that has done such things to me should find no peace in body or mind anywhere, whether still or moving. May he not be served by slaves or slave-girls, by small people or a large person. May he fail to accomplish his aims. May a binding-curse [*katadesmos*] seize hold of his house and hold it fast. May no child cry [?]. May he not lay a happy table. May no dog bark. May no cockerel crow. May he not harvest after he has sown. . . . May neither the land nor the sea bear fruit for him. May he not have blessed joy, and may he himself perish miserably, and all that is with him.

Lady Demeter, I beseech you as the victim of injustices. Help me, goddess, and make a just choice, so as to bring the most terrible things and even harsher terrible things on those who contrived such things and laughed at us and inflicted grief on both myself and my wife Epictesis. Queen, heed us in our plight and punish those who are glad to see us in such a condition.

THE DATE OF THIS, THE MOST expansive of prayers-for-justice curses, is uncertain. The prayer is addressed to Demeter and would originally have been deposited in a sanctuary of hers. This chthonic goddess was also the recipient of regular curse tablets. The protracted narrative is vivid and heartfelt; the curser wishes to convey fully the extent to which he has been the victim of a concerted campaign of harassment. Note that Epaphroditus is himself accused of having used erotic magic to lure away the slave-girl. In expressing the wish "May a binding curse seize hold of his house," the tablet oddly seems to distance the act of binding from itself.

## 189  A recipe from the Greek magical papyri for the revelation of a thief

iv A.D.

PGM V.70–95

Greek

Take a *chelbei* plant and some bugloss, filter them, burn the filtered material and mix it well with juice, then use this mixture to write "CHOO" [Coptic, "hand over"?] on a wall. Take some Christ's-thorn wood, carve a hammer out of it, and strike the eye with it while reciting this spell: "I conjure you by the sacred names. Hand over the thief that lifted whatever it was, CHALCHACK CHALKOUM CHIAM CHARCHROUM ZBAR BÊRI ZBARKOM CHRÊ KARIOB PHARIBOU, and by the terrifying names, A EE ÊÊÊ IIII OOOOO UUU-UUU ÔÔÔÔÔÔÔ. [Two vowel triangles with an illustration of an eye between them and a vowel series underneath follow.] Hand over the thief that stole whatever it was. May the thief's eye be struck as vigorously as I strike the eye with this hammer, and may it become inflamed, until it reveals him." Strike with the hammer while reciting this.

THIS RECIPE FROM THE GREEK MAGICAL PAPYRI IS, strictly speaking, not a prayer for justice as such but a rite to reveal the identity of the thief, albeit in a somewhat punitive fashion. A drawing on the papyrus may indicate that the Sun is to be considered one of the addressees of this petition, which also makes use of *voces magicae* and vowel series.

## 190  Artemisie's prayer for justice for her daughter's deprivation of burial

iv B.C.

PGM XL

Greek

O master Oserapis and gods sitting with Oserapis, I, Artemisie here, the daughter of Amasis, pray to you, against the father of my daughter, because he deprived her of her funeral gifts and her tomb. So if he did wrong to me and my children likewise—and in fact he did do wrong to me and my children likewise—may Oserapis and the gods grant that he should receive no tomb from his children, and that he should not bury his own parents. So long as my clamor for help lies here, may he be destroyed miserably on land and sea, himself and his descendants, by Oserapis and the gods that sit in attendance on him, and may he not find Oserapis propitious, nor the gods that sit with Oserapis.

Artemisie deposited this supplication, supplicating Oserapis and the gods that sit with Oserapis to give justice. And so long as this supplication lies here, may the father of my little girl find the gods in no way propitious. If anyone picks up this text and wrongs Artemisie, may the god punish him [text becomes lacunose] . . .

unless Artemisie orders . . . just as . . . insufficient . . . stood by and saw . . . me alive . . . stood by and saw . . .

THIS DISTINCTIVE PRAYER FOR JUSTICE WAS deposited in the main temple of Oserapis in the Serapeum at Memphis. It is the oldest of the Greek Magical Papyri and one of the earliest Greek papyri of any kind. Artemisie's daughter had died untimely and had, furthermore, been left unburied or inadequately buried. Her ghost will accordingly be restless; compare **110, 112**. Artemisie prays that the same fate should befall the child's father; it is unclear whether the father is her husband, but it would seem that the couple is estranged. Removal from its place of deposition will deactivate the curse; hence an additional curse against anyone who does remove it, unless they should have Artemisie's consent. For deactivation see also **180, 197, 204, 209, 238, 246**.

## 191  A Megarian lead prayer for justice appeals to Hecate

i/ii A.D.

*DT* 41 (*CT* no. 85)

Greek

A. ZÔAPHER TON THALASSOSÊ-MON ["sea-sign"?] SEKNTÊPAPHO-NOCHAI the little child Panaitios, whose name is written [text becomes lacumose] . . . CECHAIAM . . . we register them . . . EKAIPÊN . . . and we devote them to evil. Althaea, Kore, OREOBAZAGRA, Hecate the tail-eating, Moon. ITHIBI . . . ME . . . we devote these people to evil, body, spirit, soul, intellect, reflection, perception, life, with Hecataean words and Hebraic oaths . . . justice . . . Earth, Hecate . . . under the command of the holy names and the Hebraic oaths, hair, head, brain, face, ears, eyebrows, nostrils . . . jaws, teeth . . . soul groan, health . . . blood, burn flesh . . . groan at what (s)he suffers . . .

B. I adjure . . . the triple-named Moon . . . middle of the night, whenever . . . nurtured and the divine . . . running through heaven, strong-handed, observable, blue-robed . . . by land and by sea, Enodia . . . we deposit these people with you . . . we register them for punishments, penalties, and revenge . . . the body. A thing devoted to evil [*anathema*].

THIS PRAYER FOR JUSTICE ADDRESSED (untypically) to Hecate exhibits strong Jewish influence. This is found not only in explicit references to Hebraic oaths but also in the use of the Septuagint terms *anathema* and *anathematizô*, denoting the Judaeo-Christian concept of devotion to evil. There is also a touch of Egyptian imagery in the assimilation of Hecate to an *ouroboros*.

## THE EVIL EYE

<hr/>

## 192  A disquisition on the mechanics of the evil eye

Early ii A.D.

Plutarch *Moralia* 680c–683b (*Table Talk* problem 7, edited)

Greek

Problem: On those said to evil-eye [*katabaskainein*].

[**Mestrius Florus speaks:**] For we know of people who do severe harm to children by looking at them, influencing their development in this weak and tender stage, and turning them to the bad. Those with sturdier and full-grown bodies are less susceptible to this. And yet Phylarchus [*FGH* 81 F79] says that the Thibians, who long ago lived in the area of Pontus, were deadly not just to children but also to adults. Those on the receiving end of a look, a breath, or an utterance from them wasted away and fell sick. This was the experience, as it seems, of those people who used to import mixed-race slaves [translation based on the reading *migadas*] from them.

[Plutarch speaks:] It is likely that this [the streaming of emanations from the body] should occur above all through the eyes. For vision is mercurial and conveyed by a medium that gives off a fiery radiance. It diffuses an amazing power. Hence, men experience and effect a great deal through it.

[Plutarch speaks:] Envy [phthonos] similarly naturally penetrates the soul and fills the body up with evil, which artists make good attempts to portray when painting an envious face. So when people consumed by envy rest their eyes on persons, and these eyes, being situated adjacently to the soul, draw evil from it and attack the persons as if with poisoned/bewitched [pepharmagmena] missiles, it is not at all unexpected or unbelievable, I think, if they influence the persons they look at. For dog-bites are more severe if the animals bite in anger, and they say that people's sperm takes hold better when a couple feel desire. All in all, the emotions of the soul intensify and invigorate the powers of the body. That is why people think that the category of "anti-evil-eye" amulets/talismans [probaskania] help against envy, because they draw off the gaze by their bizarreness, so that it rests less upon those that are affected by it.

[Scolarus speaks:] If we consider true what many say about those subject to the evil eye, you are well aware, I believe, that they suppose that friends and relatives, even fathers, according to some, have an evil eye [baskanos], with the result that their wives will not show them their children or let the children be looked upon by such people for any length of time. Given this, how can the evil eye still be considered the work of envy? And what, by Zeus, will you say about those people who are said to evil-eye [katabaskainein] themselves? For you have heard of that. But at any rate you have read:

> Beautiful once, beautiful were the locks of Eutelidas. But that destructive man looked into the river's eddy and evil-eyed [baskainen] himself. At once he was seized by an unseemly sickness . . . [Euphorion F175 Powell]

It is said that Eutelidas thought himself beautiful and was undone by looking at himself. As a result of this he fell sick and lost his health together with his bloom. See if you have the inventiveness to account for such a strange phenomenon.

[Plutarch speaks:] All emotions, dwelling in souls for an extended period, effect evil conditions in them. When these evil conditions have become ingrained, they are set in motion by any chance cause and often direct the emotions against family and friends. . . . It is only to be expected that people should look more upon their family and those they love. That is why they also damage them more. . . . Self-evil-eyeing is usually caused by emanations from water or some other reflective surfaces. These emanations bounce back upon the lookers so that people are harmed by the same mechanism by which they themselves harmed others. Often perhaps this is what is happening with children, while those who look upon them are wrongly accused.

[Gaius speaks:] Democritus says that the envious emit images [eidôla], not altogether without their own realization and impulse, and that they are full of the wickedness and evil-eyeing [baskania] that derives from their projectors. Together with this wickedness and evil-eyeing these images mold themselves to, remain with, and take up residence with the evil-eye victims and damage and blight their body and mind.

FOR ALL THE IMPORTANCE OF ACTUAL eyes in the difficult concept of the "evil eye," the normal ancient terms for it do not incorporate an eye-word (Greek *baskania*, Latin *fascinatio*). Despite its latter-day rationalization, Plutarch's discussion usefully lays out the beliefs that underpinned the concept:

- The evil eye was primarily generated by the emotion of envy (Greek *phthonos*, Latin *invidia*). The archetypal evil-eye-ers of mythology were the envious and envied Telchines (**22–3**). Sorcery is often associated with envy. This underpins many of the curse tablets (**168–84**; see Faraone 1991a). Sorcerers are sometimes portrayed as enjoying competitive, envious relationships with each other; see **295**.

- It was probably, even before such scientific rationalization, primarily conceived of as a blighting ray that was projected from the eye.

- However, it could also work through speech (**195**) and breath.

- It could be deliberately projected, as is magnificently illustrated by Medea's use of it to destroy Talos (**70**).

- It could also be inadvertently projected, tragically against one's own loved ones.

- It often acted against fertility. People, animals (**194**), or plants were particularly vulnerable to its blight in their developing stages (the occasion of the initial envy), especially those of promise. Hence, children and crops were its primary victims.

- It was particularly associated with: (1) a selection of remote, marginal races; (2) fathers. See **193** for both.

- It could be defended against with protective amulets. Note that the Telchines were metalworkers (**22–3**). A surviving intaglio depicts a disembodied eye pierced by a dagger (Delatte and Derchain 1964 pp.72–3).

From further sources we also learn:

- It was also particularly associated with people, especially women, with double pupils (**102, 193**).

- It was particularly associated with delivery by a sidelong look (**196**).

- It could blight rites of magic, and so sorcerers, living as they did in a world of envy and slander, particularly feared it: compare **157, 169, 211, 300**.

- It could blight developing love affairs (**195**).

- It could be averted by spitting (**193**); see **148**.

- It could be averted by the phallus, and in particular by phallus amulets (**193**).

- It could be averted by the skin of the hyena (**47**).

## 193 Remote races associated with the evil eye; the phallus protects babies and triumphing generals from it

i A.D.

Pliny *Natural History* 7.16–8, 28.39

Latin

**7.16–8.** Isigonus and Nymphodorus report that in the same part of Africa [i.e., adjacent to the Nasamones] there are certain families of evil-eye-ers [*effascinantes*], at whose praise meadows perish, trees dry up, and children die. Isigonus adds that there are people of a similar kind among the Triballians and the Illyrians, who evil-eye also with looking and kill those they direct their gaze toward for a longer time, particularly when they have anger in their eyes. Adults are more prone to experiencing this evil. It is somewhat noteworthy that they have two pupils in each individual eye. Apollonites adverts women of this sort too in Scythia, who are called the Bitiae, and Phylarchus also the race of the Thibians and many others of a similar nature in Pontus. These, he reports, are distinguished by having a double pupil in one eye and the shape of a horse in the other. Moreover, these same people cannot be drowned, not even when weighed down by clothes. Damon speaks of the not dissimilar race of the Pharnaces in Ethiopia, whose sweat draws corruption out of bodies to which it is applied. Our own Cicero too guarantees that all women everywhere blight by looking if they have double pupils. Indeed when nature had produced in men the wild practice of eating human innards, she also decided to produce poisons [*venena*] throughout the body and actually in the eyes of some people, lest there should be some evil somewhere that was not in man.

**28.39.** If we believe this, we should also hold that the due course of action, if a stranger arrives or a sleeping infant is looked upon, is that its nurse should spit on it three times. However, Fascinus too gives due divine protection to the child, guardian similarly of generals as he is, not just of infants. In Roman religion the cult of this god is maintained by the Vestal Virgins. He also protects the chariots of generals from envy [*invidia*] as they parade in triumph, hanging underneath them, like a doctor. A similar spoken medicine bids the generals look behind them, so that Fortune, the executioner of fame, may be propitiated behind him.

THE ROLE OF ENVY IN THE evil eye is again made clear. *Fascinus* was the phallus-deity, embodied in phallus effigies, and he had the power to avert the action of the evil eye. For the protective power of the phallus, compare the "herms" of Attica and the phallic god Priapus, whom Horace portrays as averting the witches Canidia and Sagana (**91**). Pliny refers to the custom of hanging phallus effigies around the necks of babies. The phallus and spitting alike could afford protection from the evil eye; the two methods are combined in a Roman mosaic portraying a phallus ejaculating into a disembodied eye (Bernand 1991, 102). See **47** for more of Pliny on the evil eye.

## 194   The evil eye reduces Menalcas's sheep to emaciation

Ca. 38 B.C.

Virgil *Eclogue* 3.103

Latin

Yet for these [sheep]—and love is not the cause—they scarcely stick to their bones. Some eye or other is evil-eye-ing [*oculus . . . fascinat*] my tender lambs.

THE EMACIATION OF THE SHEPHERD'S flock is caused by envy.

## 195   Catullus and Lesbia protect their kissing from the evil eye

55 B.C.

Catullus 5, 7

Latin

**5.** Let us live and love, my Lesbia. And let us consider all the grumblings of the moralizing old men to be worth no more than a penny. Suns can set and rise again, but after our brief light has gone down just once there is only one uninterrupted night to sleep through. Give me a thousand kisses, give me a hundred, then another thousand, then a second hundred, and then yet another thousand, and then a hundred. Then, when we have made many thousands of them, we will go bankrupt, so that we don't know how many of them there were, and so that no wicked person may cast the evil eye upon us [*malus invidere*], once he knows how many kisses there were.

**7.** You ask me, Lesbia, how many of your kisses are enough or more than enough for me: as great as the number of grains of Libyan sand that lie in asaphoetida-producing Cyrene, between the oracle of sweltering Jupiter [i.e., Ammon] and the sacred tomb of old Battus; or, as many as the stars that look down in the silence of the night on people's secret loves. That's how many kisses from you are enough and more than enough for maddened Catullus, so many that busy-bodies cannot count them all, nor an evil tongue evil-eye them [*mala fascinare lingua*].

EXACT KNOWLEDGE OF THE NUMBER OF kisses that pass between Catullus and Lesbia will permit the envious to blight their relationship.

### 196　The evil eye bewitches with an envious sidelong look

Ca. 19 B.C.

Horace *Epistles*
1.14.37–8

Latin

There is no one there [on my farm] to put a limit to my pleasures with sidelong look [*obliquo oculo*], nor to poison/bewitch [*venenat*] me with a bite of concealed hatred.

CONTEXT DICTATES THAT THE EVIL EYE proceeds from envy, the implication, in any case, of the "sidelong look."

# 11
## Erotic Magic

Erotic magic was usually the primary concern of the literary witch (66–107). It is also the principal concern of the Greek Magical Papyri from Egypt, formularies and actual curses alike, the majority of which were written in the third and fourth centuries A.D. The literature and documentation of erotic magic are dominated by the attraction mode. Erotic spells typically envisage and attempt to effect a vignette in which a magical messenger is sent to the beloved where her (or his) sleep is disturbed by it with dreams or with wakefulness. She is then viscerally dragged, raving, through the streets (the context is usually implicitly urban), sometimes even made to take wing, until she arrives at the her admirer's door and frenziedly beats on it. A neat synoptic example of the vignette is found in **244**.

## SEPARATION CURSES

Erotic curse tablets, which are found from the fourth century B.C. onward, can be broadly classified into two groups: those of separation and those of attraction. The separation spells align more naturally with other categories of binding spell, seeking, as they do, to enact an obvious type of restraint. Until recently it was thought that binding spells of attraction were a relatively late development and one originating in Roman North Africa. However, the new discovery of a late-fourth-century attraction-curse tablet from Acanthus in Macedon (**205**) indicates that they are hardly less ancient than curses of the separation variety.

### 197 Phila's (?) lead separation-curse tablet against Dionysophon, from Pella in Macedonia

iv B.C.

Voutiras 1998, 8

Greek

I register [katagraphô] the rite and the marriage of Thetima and Dionysophon, and those of all other women, widows, and maidens alike, but especially that of Thetima, and I deposit this spell with Macron and the demons. If I were ever to dig up, unroll, and read this tablet again, then may Dionysophon marry, but not before. May he take no woman other than me, and let me grow old beside Dionysophon, and no other woman. I am a suppliant woman before you. Take pity on <Phil-[?]>a, dear demons. . . . [lacuna] I have no friends or family and I am all alone. But guard this text for me, so that these things don't come to pass and so that the evil Thetima is destroyed in a fittingly evil fashion. . . . [lacuna] [M]ay I become fortunate and blessed.

THIS SEPARATION CURSE, RECENTLY DISCOVERED where it was deposited, rolled, in the tomb of (we presume) Macron, is a poignant example. The curse-maker named herself, but the name is lost. The common Macedonian name Phila fits the spaces and traces well enough. Phila's expression of her loneliness, or at any rate isolation, does not appear formulaic, and her unusual supplicatory appeal to the ghosts for pity is touching. Under the circumstances Phila may have set her cap at Dionysophon for social and financial reasons as much as for sexual or romantic ones, but we can be sure that marriage is her goal. The underlying agenda of attraction is clear here, with the restraint of the potential marriage not merely of Thetima, who is perceived as a particular threat, but also of the potential marriages of other categories of marriageable women, exhaustively articulated. The restraining idiom used here is a common one, namely, "registration" or "indictment," a quasi-legal term, before the underworld powers (*katagraphô*). Although Thetima and the other women are the tablet's victims, the explicit restraint is not put on them themselves but on the abstract entities of their potential marriages. For good measure, the final line seeks Thetima's death too, unusually for the early tablets. We learn that the exhumation and unraveling of the tablet will deactivate it, but Phila does not seem to contemplate this seriously; for deactivation see **190**.

## 198   An Attic lead separation-curse tablet curtails Aristocydes's sex life

iv B.C.

*DTA*, 78

Greek

(I bind) Aristocydes and the women who show off to him. He is never to marry/have sex with [*gameô*] another woman or with a girl/boy [*pais*].

THE TABLET SEEMS TO BE WRITTEN from a woman's point of view, and so Aristocydes's current partner may well be the curse-maker. The distinction between women and girls as potential objects of marriage is curious, so it may be preferable to take the common-gendered *pais* as meaning "boy"; in this case, we have an early example of the word *gameô*, the normal term for "marry," being used in a cruder and more general sense. Both readings are interesting: on the one the curse-maker indirectly expresses a wish to marry to Aristocydes; on the other she aspires to sexual fidelity from him.

## 199   A binding curse addressed to the ghost of Theonnastos to separate Zoilos from Antheira; lead curse tablet from Boeotia

iii/ii B.C.

Ziebarth 1934, no. 23 (*DT* 95)

Greek

A. Just as you, Theonnastos, have no power in your hands, feet, or body to do, organize, love . . . [text is lacunose] so too may Zoilos stay powerless to have sex with Antheira and may Antheira stay powerless to have sex with Zoilos in the same way . . . Hermes too . . . the reciprocal affection and the bed and the chattering and the love of Antheira and Zoilos and . . . their dealings with each other. Just as this lead too is in a place divided from men, so may Zoilos be divided from Antheira, her body and her touch and her kisses and the sex of Zoilos and Antheira and . . . fear of Zoilos . . . I inscribe also this spell of ineffectualness and seal it.

B. . . . such a kind of . . . but caught . . . and may you not catch, god, Antheira and Zoilos . . . this night and . . . not be with each other and . . . Timocles the same . . . wrap people and tie them up . . . binding spell [*katadesmon*] . . . so too Zoilos . . . even if completes . . . this binding spell and . . . again let be . . . chattering . . . forgotten . . . just as this lead has been buried, completely buried and . . . so too may you bury for Zoilos his work, his organizing, his love, and everything else.

THE TEXT (SIDE A OF WHICH IS written in concentric circles) is partly damaged and partly indecipherable. As with the Pasianax curse (170), this one works in part by constructing a "sympathetic" analogy between the ghost or corpse of the grave of deposition and the condition desired for the victim.

## 200 The sexual allure of Zois is restrained; lead curse tablet from Boeotia

Undated

Ziebarth 1934, no. 22
(*DT* 86)

Greek

A. I deposit Zois the Eretrian, the wife of Cabeiras, with Earth and Hermes, her eating, her drinking, her sleep, her laughter, her "intercourse," her lyre-playing, her "entrance," her pleasure, her little buttocks, her mind, her eyes . . .

B. <I deposit with> Hermes her wicked parading-around, her words, her deeds, her evil talk, and her . . .

THE CURSE-MAKER HERE PRESUMABLY WISHES to supplant the frustratingly alluring Zois in her husband's affections. The words in quotation marks translate apparent double-entendres. The restraint of a person's eating, drinking, and sleeping in erotic context is more often associated with attempts to make a lover of them.

## 201 The pursuit of Philoxenus the lyre-player: Papyrus homosexual separation (and attraction?) curse from Oxyrhynchus in Egypt

iii–iv A.D.

*PGM* LXVI

Greek

CHAÔR CHTHÔR CHARABA CHOLBAS CHTHRUTHUR CHORBATH CHTHAMNÔ CHTHODUCHRA CHUCHCHUCH CHÔAR—as far as the bottom.

I adjure you by the great names. Throw Philoxenos the lyre-player into a fight with Gennadios, his friend. Throw the elder Pelagios into a fight with Philoxenos the lyre-player.

THERE IS NOTHING EXPLICITLY SEXUAL IN the text itself, but it is accompanied by two poorly drawn male figures with erections. Rather than fighting, these seem to reach out to each other, which may imply an attraction element in addition to the separation one. The syntax of the text is very poor, with accusatives and genitives confused.

## 202 A lotion to avert women from sex

i A.D.

Pliny *Natural History* 28.256

Latin

If the loins of a woman are smeared with the blood of a tick from a wild black bull, she is made to find sex repulsive, as Osthanes says, and love too, if she drinks the urine of the billy-goat, with nard mixed in to disguise the disgusting taste.

FOR THE GREAT MAGE OSTHANES AND his lore see 45; for more from Pliny on magical uses of the tick see his *Natural History* 30.82–4.

## 203 The empress Faustina is delivered from her love for a gladiator by bathing in his blood

Ca. 320 A.D.

Capitolinus (SHA)
*Marcus Aurelius* 19

Latin

Some men say (and it could well be true) that Commodus Antoninus, his [Marcus Aurelius's] son and heir, was not born of him, but from an adulterous liaison, and they weave the following sort of tale together from common gossip. They say that Faustina, the daughter of Antoninus Pius and the wife of Marcus Aurelius, was once fired with love for a gladiator when she saw him passing by in a troupe. She suffered from a protracted sickness over this and eventually confessed her love to her husband. Marcus referred the matter to the Chaldaeans. Their counsel was that the gladiator should be killed and that Faustina should bathe herself in his blood, then sleep with her husband in this condition. This was duly done, and she was delivered of her love, but her son Commodus was a gladiator, not an emperor. After he had come to the throne he presented almost a thousand gladiatorial shows before the Roman people, as will be explained in his life.

AS WITH THE TICK RECIPE (202), smeared blood ends sexual desire. For Chaldaeans compare 49–50.

## ATTRACTION CURSES

▬▬▬▬▬▬▬     For further sources for attraction magic see 47, 72, 76–82, 89–92, 104, 107, 158, 161, 188, 239–40, 244, 273, 299.

### 204   Saint Hilarion exorcises a demon sent into a virgin by curse tablets buried under her threshold

iv–v A.D.

Jerome *Life of St. Hilarion the Hermit* 21, PL 23, 38–9

Latin

In that same town of Gaza a young man fell desperately in love with a virgin of God who lived nearby. He repeatedly touched her, joked with her, nodded at her, whispered to her, and did other things like this, the sort of things that tend to herald the destruction of virginity. But he got nowhere. So he journeyed to Memphis, so that, after disclosing his wound, he might return armed with magical techniques to use against the virgin. Accordingly, after a year of instruction by the priests of Asclepius, who do not cure souls but ruin them, he came back bursting for the fornication he had anticipated in his mind. He inscribed some verbal monstrosities and monstrous forms on plates of Cyprian bronze and buried them under the threshold of the girl's house. At once the virgin went mad. She cast off her veil, she swung her hair around, she gnashed her teeth, she shouted out the young man's name. The enormity of her love had transformed itself into frenzy. So her parents brought her to the monastery and handed her over to the old man. At once the demon howled and confessed, "I was the victim of force and kidnapped against my will. How well I used to deceive men with dreams in Memphis! O the tortures and torments I suffer! You compel me to come out, but I am held in bonds under the threshold. I cannot come out unless the young man that holds me dismisses me." Then the old man replied, "Great is your strength, if you are held fast by a little thread and metal plates. Tell me why you dared to enter the girl of God." "To save that virgin," came the reply. "You, save her, you betrayer of chastity? Why did you not rather enter into the man that was trying to send you?" "What?" he replied, "enter into him when he was already occupied by my love-demon colleague?" The saint would not let the symbols or the young man be hunted down before he had exorcised the virgin, lest the demon should be thought to have been detached and expelled by incantations, or he should himself be thought to have put faith in what the demon said. He affirmed that demons were deceitful and clever at pretence. When the virgin had been put back on the road to sanity he told her off for acting in such a way as to allow the demon to enter her.

THIS CHRISTIAN NARRATIVE, FOR ALL ITS imaginativeness, offers an insight into the circumstances in which erotic-attraction curses might have been used, and into their supposed effects. For Asclepius in an Egyptian magical context and the keen young man's quest for an ultimate revelation see 53. For exorcism see 127–32. The demon's attitude of courtesy toward his professional colleague is intriguing, if not to be construed merely as part of its dissimulation. For the possibility of deactivating curse tablets, which, despite what the demon says, could presumably have been done by anyone once the tablets had been found, compare 190.

## 205  An early lead attraction-curse tablet from Acanthus in Macedonia

Late iv or early iii B.C.

Jordan 1999, no. 3

Greek

**A.** Pausanias binds [*katadei*] Sime, daughter of Amphitritus (may no one except Pausanias undo this spell) until she does for Pausanias everything Pausanias wants. May she not be able to lay hands on a sacrificial victim of Athene, nor may Aphrodite look kindly upon her, before Sime holds Pausanias tight.

**B.** Of Melissa of Apollonia. Pausanias binds [*katadei*] Aenis. May she not be able to lay hands on a sacrificial victim or achieve any other good thing before Aenis looks kindly upon Pausanias. May no one except Pausanias undo this spell.

THIS CURSE TEXT, FOUND IN A cemetery, is remarkable for a number of reasons. As an erotic curse of the attraction variety it precedes other such ones by three hundred years. It exploits the language and ideas of the prayers-for-justice curse category in conditionally debarring the beloved from propitiating the gods until she does what the curse-maker wishes. The withholding of Aphrodite's kind regard denies sex to Sime, or at any rate pleasure in it; the withholding of Athene's perhaps frustrates her weaving. Pausanias comes close to identifying himself with the goddesses: he and they alike require "propitiation" (*hilaskomai*). Pausanias is hedging his bets. He seeks to attract at least two women on the same tablet. The seeming sentence-fragment "Of Melissa of Apollonia" is puzzling: it may be a run-over from side A and may constitute the maternal lineage of Sime; it may be a run-over from the bottom of its own side, B, and constitute the maternal lineage of Pausanias; it may be a vestigial or abortive attempt to attract a third woman; or, less plausibly, it has been suggested that the phrase constitutes the signature of the witch who made the tablet for Pausanias.

## 206  Ammonion pursues Theodotis; a lead tablet of both separation and attraction from Egypt

ii A.D.

*Suppl. Mag.* 38

Greek

I bind [*katadesmeuô*] you, Theodotis, daughter of Eus, to the snake's tail, the crocodile's mouth, the ram's horns, the asp's poison, the cat's whiskers, the god's appendage, so that you may never be able to have sex with another man, not be screwed or be buggered or give oral sex, nor do anything that brings you pleasure with another man, unless I alone, Ammonion, the son of Hermitaris, am the man. For I alone am LAMPSOURÊ OTHIKALAK AIPHNÔSABAÔ STÊSEÔN UELLAPHONTA SANKISTÊ CHPHURIS egg. Accomplish this erotic binding-spell [*philtrokatadesmos*], this one that Isis used, so that Theodotis the daughter of Eus may no longer submit to penetration by a man other than me alone, Ammonion, the son of Hermitaris, dragged in slavery, driven crazy, taking to the air in search of Ammonion, the son of Hermitaris, and that she may apply her thigh to my thigh, her genitals to my genitals, for sex with me for the entire span of her life. These are the images: [A series of pictures and ten characters follow. The recognizable pictures depict a god with a scepter, a snake, a crocodile, and a couple kissing. A further picture may represent a penis entering a vagina.]

THE EXACT PROVENANCE OF THIS TABLET is unknown. Its most striking feature is its use of very explicit and direct sexual language, which perhaps constitutes a verbal enactment of Ammonion's desires in regard to Theodotis (and one of the illustrations may similarly constitute a pictorial enactment). Varieties of sexual congress are listed in the "exhaustive dichotomies" mode so often found in the tablets. For all the curse's apparent concentration on immediate sexual gratification, its final line suggests its author, unless very cruel, wishes to construct a long-term relationship with Theodotis. The objects to which the author binds Theodotis, and which at least partly correspond with the illustrations on the tablet, are aspects of familiar Egyptian gods; such imagery seems to belong to spells of threatening. The author makes two strong claims to authority: first, he identifies himself with a *voces-magicae* demon; second, he identifies his spell with one used by the goddess Isis herself, and does so in the form of a brief paradigmatic tale, or *historiola* (for which see 260–1).

## 207 Theon pursues Euphemia; papyrus attraction curse from Egypt

v A.D.

*Suppl. Mag.* 45

Greek

I bind [*desmeuô*] you with unbreakable bonds of underworld Fate and stern Necessity, because I adjure you, demons, who lie here, feed here and reside here, and the youths here, dead before their time. I adjure you by the invincible god IAÔ BARBATHIAÔ BRIMIAÔ CHERMARI. Wake up, demons who lie here, and seek out Euphemia, to whom Dorothea gave birth, for Theon, to whom Proechia gave birth. May she not be able to find sleep the whole night long, but bring her until she comes before his feet, lusting after him with a crazed lust, with love and with sexual congress. For I have bound her brain, her hands, her upper belly, her vulva, and her heart so that she loves me, Theon. If you ignore me and do not quickly accomplish what I tell you, the sun does not set beneath the earth, and neither Hades nor the universe exist. If you bring Euphemia, to whom Dorothea gave birth, to me, Theon, to whom Proechia gave birth, I will give you Osiris NOPHRIÔTH, brother of Isis. He draws up cold water and will give your souls peace. But if you do not accomplish for me what I tell you, EÔNEBUÔTH will incinerate you. I adjure you, demons who lie here, IEÔ II-IIAIA ÊIA IAÔ IAÊ IAÔ ALILAMPS. I send you, in the land of dogs [i.e., the cemetery], a deposit. Bind Euphemia so that she loves me, Theon. I adjure you by the inscription of the gods, I adjure you by those in the inner shrine, I adjure you by the names of the god that oversees all, IA IA IA IÔ IÔ IE IE IE OUÔA ADÔNAI. I adjure you by the god that finds pleasure in *purity* and by the blood that the great god IO-THATH took. I adjure you by the god that sits on the four points of the winds. Do not ignore me, but carry out quickly the orders that come to you from ACHRAM-MACHAMARI BOULOMENTHOREB GENIOMOUTHIG DÊMOGENÊD ENKUKLIE ZÊNOBIÔTHIZ ÊSKÔTHÔRÊ THÔTHOUTHÔTH IAEOUÔI KORKOUNOÔK LOULOENÊL MOROTHOÊPNAM NERXIARXIN XONOPHOÊNAX ORNEOPHAO PUROBORUP REROUTOÊR SESENMENOURES TAUROPOLIT UPEPHENOURU PHIMEMAMEPH CHENNEOPHEOCH PSUCHOPOMPOIAPS ÔRION, true one. Let me not be compelled to say the same things again IÔÊ IÔÊ. Bring Euphemia, to whom Dorothea gave birth, to Theon, to whom Proechia gave birth, loving me with lust, longing, affection, and sexual congress, crazed with lust. Burn her limbs, her liver, her woman's body, until she comes to me, loving me and not ignoring me. Because I adjure you by stern Necessity MASKELLI MASKELLÔ PHNOUKENTABAÔTH ORE-OBAZAGRA RÊXICHTHÔN HIPPOCHTHÔN PURICHTHÔN PURIPÊGANUX LEPETAN LEPETAN MANTOUNOBOÊL. So bind [*katadêsate*] Euphemia for me, for me, Theon, with love and lust and longing for ten months from today, which is the twenty-fifth of Hathyr [November 21], of the second taxation-year. Again I adjure you by your king, so that you don't ignore me. And again I adjure you by the one who occupies the air. And again I adjure you by the seven thrones ACHLAL LALAPHENOURPHEN BALEÔ BOLBEÔ BLOBEÔCH BOLBESRÔ UUPHTHÔ and by the god impervious to prayer, CHMOUÔR ABRASAX IPSENTHANCHOUCHAINCHOUCHEÔCH. Seize Euphemia and bring her to me, to me Theon, loving me and crazed with lust. And bind her with unbreakable bonds, strong and adamantine ones, so that she loves me, Theon, and do not allow her to eat, drink, find sleep, joke, or laugh, but make her leap up out of every place and every house and abandon her father, mother, brothers, and sisters, until she comes to me, Theon, loving me, lusting after me with a divine, unstoppable lust and a mad love. If she holds another man in her embrace, let her cast him off, forget him, and hate him, but let her feel love, warmth, and affection for me, give me her property, and do nothing against my wishes. Holy names, here, and powers, here, enforce this spell and bring it to fruition, now, now, quickly, quickly.

THIS TEXT WAS FOUND SEALED IN a clay pot together with a *symplegma*, a pair of dolls in embrace (for which see **239** and **245** with commentaries). These dolls are ca. seven centimeters high, and were further fused by melting. The female doll is made of a wax a lighter brown than the male one. As often, the spell is addressed to restless ghosts, here the untimely dead; compare **110**, **112**. The carrot-and-stick approach, blending threats and promises of reward to the dead, is again adopted. And again the spell is dominated by the vignette of the frenzied woman being dragged through the streets. The word *purity* is an Egyptian one written in Greek letters.

## 208    Attraction of a woman with a mussel shell and a bathhouse furnace

iii or iv A.D.

PGM VII.467–77

Greek

Take a mussel shell from the sea and paint the figure of Typhon shown below on it, with myrrh ink, together with his names, in a circle, and cast it into the furnace of a bathhouse. When you cast the shell, recite these names written in a circle and add, "Bring me (insert her name), whom (insert her mother's name) bore, today, from this hour, burning in her soul and her heart, quickly, quickly, now, now." The figure to use is hereafter. On reciting the spell, preface it with this: "This is the god of compulsion ÔKÊSÊ EÊRINIAREMIN ENTÊNTAIN PHOOU TÔNKTÔ MNÊ SIETHÔN OSIRI ENABÔTH PHANOU LAMPSOUÔR IEOU IÔ IÔ AI ÊI EI AI EI AÔ, bring (insert her name), the daughter of [insert her mother's name], to me, and so on." This is the figure: [no figure is included in the manuscript].

THIS RECIPE EXPLOITS THE HEAT of the bathhouse to instill the heat of desire. Seth-Typhon is one of the most popular underworld powers in the Greek Magical Papyri (compare **173**).

## 209    Attraction of a woman with a model dog and sleeplessness

iv A.D.

PGM IV.2943–66

Greek

**Attraction spell by sleeplessness.** Take the eyes from a bat and let it go alive. Take a bit of raw dough or unmelted wax. Make a little model of a dog. Insert the right eye of the bat into the right eye of the little dog, and its left eye similarly into the left. Take a needle, thread the stuff [*ousia*] through the needle, and pull it through the eyes of the little dog, so as to leave the stuff showing. Put it into a new drinking cup and attach a papyrus label to it. Seal it with a personal ring with a motif of crocodiles head-to-tail. Deposit it where three roads meet, marking the place, so that you can find it again if you want to take it up. This is the spell written on the label: "I adjure you by Hecate, three times over, PHOR-PHORBA BAIBÔ PHÔBÔRBA, so that (insert her name) may lose the spark in her eye and lie awake with nothing in her mind, but me alone (insert your name). I adjure you by the Persephone, who became Goddess of the Three-Ways, who is the real mother . . . [lacuna] . . . (the people you wish) PHORBEA BRIMÔ NÊRÊATO DAMÔN BRIMÔN SEDNA DARDAR, goddess seeing all, IOPE. Make (insert her name) sleepless and love me forever.

THIS RECIPE OFFERS US ANOTHER FAMILIAR vignette of erotic magic: the beloved made to toss and turn without sleep (like a restless ghost?) until she gratifies her lover. Dogs feature in a variety of ways in erotic attraction spells. Here the model dog stands for Hecate, who presided over crossroads. By contrast, in the recipe at **246** the model dog represents not Hecate but Cerberus. The eyes of a bat are significant because they are open all night long. The difficulty and unpleasantness of removing the eyes from a live bat no doubt enhanced the efficacy of the magic. It seems to be assumed by the recipe that in this instance the role of the victim's "stuff" will be taken by hair. The spell provides for its own deactivation, for which compare **190**.

## 210   Heraeis pursues Sarapias; a lesbian papyrus attraction curse from Egypt

ii A.D.

*PGM* XXXII

Greek

I adjure you, Euangelos, by Anubis, Hermes, and the remaining powers of the underworld, to bring and bind [*katadêsai*] Sarapias, to whom Helen gave birth, to Heraeis, to whom Thermoutharin gave birth, now, now, quickly, quickly. Draw her by her soul and heart to Sarapias, to whom Helen gave birth with her own womb, MAEI OTE ELBOSATOK ALAOUBETO OEIO AEN. Bring and bind the soul and heart of Sarapias, to whom Helen gave birth, to Heraeis, to whom Thermoutharin gave birth with her womb, now, now, quickly, quickly.

IDENTIFIABLE LESBIAN EROTIC-ATTRACTION CURSES ARE relatively rare. One other is known, the extensive *Supplementum Magicum* no. 42 from Hermoupolis in Egypt, also in Greek, in which Sophia pursues Gorgonia (iii–iv A.D.). In such a lesbian context the use of maternal lineage may take on added significance.

## 211   Attraction of an ungovernable woman with lamps and slander

iii or iv A.D.

*PGM* VII.593–619

Greek

Attraction spell for an ungovernable woman. Take a lamp, not a red one, with seven wicks and make wicks from the tackle of a shipwreck. With myrrh write on the first wick, IAÔ; on the second ADÔNAI; on the third SABAÔTH; on the fourth PAGOURÊ; on the fifth MARMOROUTH; on the sixth IAEÔ; on the seventh MICHAÊL. Put oil in the lamp and place it in a window with a southerly aspect. Let there be seeds of wormwood on the lamp (around its opening) and recite this spell: "I invoke you, the rulers, the great gods, those who shine like a glow-worm at this hour, today, because of the impious (insert her name). For she has said, 'IAÔ has no sinews; ADÔNAI was forcibly thrown on the dung-heap; SABAÔTH let out three cries.' (Insert her name) has said, 'PAGOURÊ is a hermaphrodite.' (Insert her name) has said, 'MARMOROUTH is eunuch.' (Insert her name) has said, 'IAEÔ was not entrusted with the ark of the covenant.' (Insert her name) has said, 'MICHAÊL is a hermaphrodite.' It is not me who is saying this, master, but the impious (insert her name). So bring her to me, aflame, distressed and incapable of sleep, until she comes to me." Say it seven times over. If the first lamp [wick] sputters, you are to know that she has been taken by the demon; if the second one, she has come out; if the third, she is walking; if the fourth, she has come; if the fifth, she has come to the gate; if the sixth, she has come to the terrace; if the seventh, she has come to the house. The spell brings people even from across the sea. To that end, put the lamp in a bit of water outside. Under the lamp there should be a barge made from papyrus. Recite the spell six times over.

THE WOMAN ENVISAGED AS "UNGOVERNABLE" IS presumably so only insofar as she has hitherto refused to gratify the user of the recipe. Jewish influence is again apparent in the *voces magicae*. Shipwrecks are valuable sources of magical supplies, associated as they are with masses of unburied dead (see **107**), and this is presumably the source of the demon that will bring the woman. Once again, the recipe makes much of the vignette of the victim being dragged through the streets to her lover's door. Her designation as "impious" is an act of slander-magic: she is abused so that the demons will be readier to act against her; compare **173, 234**. Note the recipe's anxiety to protect its user from the suspicion of endorsing the slander. For the magical use of lamps see **165–6**, with commentaries.

## 212   "Vulva key": Attraction of a woman with a penis lotion

iv A.D.

*PGM* XXXVI.283–94

Greek

Vulva key. Take a crow's egg, the juice of the crow's foot plant, the bile of an electric ray from the river, work them together with honey, and say the spell whenever you work them and anoint your genitals with them. The spoken spell is this: "I say to you, womb of (insert her name), gape open and receive the seed of (insert your name) and the uncontrolled seed of IARPHE ARPHE (write this). Let (insert her name) love me all her life, as Isis loved Osiris, and let her stay chaste for me as Penelope did for Odysseus. You, womb, remember me for the entirety of my life, because I am AKARNACHTHAS." Say these things as you work the substances, and whenever you anoint your genitals, and so have sex with the woman you want. She will love only you, and no one but you will copulate with her.

A MAN IS TO ATTRACT A WOMAN by smearing his genitals with a lotion; compare **202–3**. The spell seems to aim at the construction of a lasting relationship, and to incorporate a separation element. The citings of the paradigms of Isis and Penelope constitute mini-*historiolas*; see **260–1**. For another method of enhancing male sexual prowess see **254**.

## 213   Attraction of a woman with an apple

v A.D.

*Suppl. Mag.* 72.1–14

Greek

Extract from spells from <a collection [?]> in a sacred book ascribed to Hermes, found in Heliopolis, in the inner shrine [aduton], written in Egyptian letters and translated into Greek ones.

Spell using an apple. Say it three times over. I will pelt with apples . . . [lacuna] I will give this spell which is ever apt for eating for mortal men and immortal gods. Whichever woman I give the apple to, whichever woman I throw the apple at and hit with it, may she put off everything else and become crazy with love for me. Whether she takes it in her hand and eats it, or puts it away in her dress, may she not stop loving me. Cyprus-born Aphrodite, bring this spell to fruition.

FURTHER LOVE SPELLS FOLLOW ON THE papyrus, and finally a spell against headache. The introduction, which constructs authority for the book, makes claims comparable to those found elsewhere in the magical papyri, and should in particular be compared with the tales of magical Egyptian books in inner shrines (*aduta*) at **46, 53–4**. But, despite such claims, the first spell in the series could not be more Graeco-Roman. There are numerous attestations in Greek and Roman culture of "apple spells," in which one seduces one's beloved by throwing soft fruit at her; once the target accepts the fruit or eats it, she is secured. This phenomenon underlies the myths of Acontius and Cydippe and Hippomenes and Atalanta, where again apples are used, and perhaps even that of Hades and Persephone, where pomegranate seeds are used (see Faraone 1999a).

## DRAWING DOWN THE MOON

The drawing-down of the moon was one of the most familiar commonplaces of literary magic in the Graeco-Roman world, and it was associated above all with the performance of erotic magic by witches. For further references to the drawing-down of the moon see **13–4, 45, 65–6, 68–9, 89–92, 94, 96–104, 106, 155, 157,** and especially **244**; compare figure 11.1. We may summarize the principal features of the topos:

- The drawing-down of the moon is *the* characteristic activity of Thessalian witches. Statius *Thebaid* 3.558–9 refers to it in passing as "the Thessalian crime."
- It is drawn down for the purpose of erotic attraction magic.
- It is either made to turn pale or to turn blood-red when subject to drawing.

Figure 11.1.  Naked witches bind (?) and draw down the moon, addressing it, "Hear me, Lady Moon." Line drawing of vase now lost, from Roscher 1884–1937, "Mondgöttin" (2.2.3165–6).

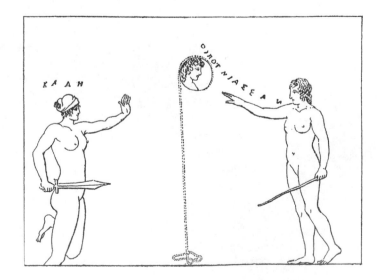

- The drawing-down can be counteracted by the clashing of bronze cymbals.
- When brought down to the earth it deposits its foam on plants as "moon-juice" (*virus lunare*). This can then be collected and used in a love potion.
- The control of the moon in this way is sometimes contextualized against the witches' wider ability to control the sun and stars and consequently time itself.
- The Thessalian women pay a terrible price for the drawing-down of the moon: they must lose either children or an eye.
- The poetic conceit that the moon, like the sun, rides in a horse-drawn chariot, is frequent.

The origin of the notion that the moon could be drawn down remains obscure. Plutarch gives the hint that it was a way of thinking about lunar eclipses, and many follow him in this belief. The moon does indeed turn blood-red during a full lunar eclipse, as it reflects only the sunlight refracted red through the earth's atmosphere.

## 214   A scheme to use a Thessalian witch to avoid interest payments

423 B.C.

Aristophanes *Clouds*
746-57

Greek

**Strepsiades:** Dear litte Socratikins!

**Socrates:** What is it, old man?

**Strepisades:** I have a plan for getting rid of my interest-payments.

**Socrates:** Explain it.

**Strepsiades:** Tell me now . . .

**Socrates:** Yes?

**Strepsides:** What if I bought a Thessalian witch [*pharmakis*] and drew down the moon by night and then shut it up in a round helmet-crest case, like a mirror, and then kept it under guard?

**Socrates:** How would that help you?

**Strepsiades:** Because if the moon were never to rise again, I wouldn't have to pay any interest.

**Socrates:** Why not?

**Strepsiades:** Because interest is payable by the month.

**Socrates:** Well done!

THE EXCHANGE IMPLIES THAT THE drawing-down of the moon was associated with Thessalian witches above all. We need not assume that the bumpkin Strepsiades' comically literal interpretation of the witches' drawing-down of the moon was widespread. It is unlikely that Thessalian women were available for sale as slaves in classical Athens.

## 215   Even Thessalian girls can draw down the moon

iv B.C.

Sosiphanes of Syracuse
*Meleager, TrGF* 92 F1

Greek

With magical [*magois*] incantations every Thessalian girl is a drawer-down [*kataibatis*] of a false moon rom the ether.

THE ABILITY TO BRING DOWN THE moon is here presented as so basic to Thessalian womanhood that even girls can do it, although the phenomenon is also presented as trickery. This is a relatively early application to a female witch of a term with the *mag-* root.

### 216   Thessalian witches are undone by drawing down the moon

Earlier iv B.C.

Plato *Gorgias* 513a

Greek

See whether this is to your advantage and to mine, so that we may not, my good friend, suffer the fate commonly ascribed to those women that draw down the moon, the Thessalians. Our choice of this power in the city will come at the price of what we hold dearest.

PLATO ASSOCIATES THE DRAWING-DOWN OF the moon with Thessalian witches in particular. For the damage done to oneself in drawing down the moon see **217**. For the notion that sorcerers undo themselves in the course of their magical activities see also **56**.

### 217   The price paid by Thessalian women for drawing down the moon

ii A.D. (Zenobius); Byzantine (scholium)

Zenobius *Epitome* 404, with scholium, at *CPG*, 1:83

Greek

Zenobius: "The drawing-down of the moon is on your own head." Thessalian women drawing down the moon are said to be deprived of their eyes and their children. The proverb is applied to those who bring trouble upon themselves.
    Scholium: Asclepiades says that the Thessalian women learned how the moon moved and advertised that they could draw it down, but only at the cost of damaging themselves. For they either had to sacrifice some of their children or lose one of their eyes. So it is said of those bringing trouble upon themselves. Duris says that an astrologer predicting eclipses of the moon did not come off well.

EVIDENTLY THIS IS WHAT PLATO HAD in mind. For the association of the drawing-down of the moon with eclipses see **218**.

### 218   Aglaonice exploits a predicted eclipse to claim the ability to draw down the moon

Early ii A.D.

*Moralia* 145cd (*Coniugalia praecepta*)

Greek

If someone undertakes to draw down the moon, she [a woman who understands mathematics] will laugh at the ignorance and stupidity of the women she takes in, for she will be not unfamiliar with astronomy, and will have heard of Aglaonice the daughter of the Thessalian Hegetor. She knew all about total eclipses of the moon, and, able as she was to predict the occasions on which the moon is overtaken by the shadow, she used to trick the women and make them believe that she was drawing down the moon herself.

THE STORY OF AGLAONICE PERHAPS PRESUPPOSES that the notion that witches could draw down the moon was a way of thinking about eclipses. Plutarch repeats the tale at *Moralia* 416f–17a.

### 219   The drawing-down of the moon with a magic wheel

Ca. 94 A.D.

Martial 9.29.9

Latin

[Philaenis is dead.] Which woman now will know how to draw down the moon with a Thessalian wheel [*rhombus*]?

HERE THE DRAWING-DOWN OF THE moon is associated with the use of the *rhombus*, for which see **226–7**.

### 220   Incantations turn the moon blood-red and draw it down

16 B.C.

Ovid *Amores* 2.1.23–8

Latin

Incantations draw down the horns of the bloody moon and call back the snowy horses of the departing sun. By an incantation snakes are burst and their jaws broken off, and waters turn around and flow back to their sources. Doors have yielded before incantations, and the bar, fixed into the post, has been overcome by an incantation, though made of oak.

INCANTATIONS ARE HERE SAID NOT ONLY to draw the moon down but to turn it blood-red. *Carmen*, the word translated here as "incantation," can more mundanely mean simply "song" or "poem." Ovid plans to use his elegies to persuade his beloved Corinna to unbar her door to him, and exploits the equivocation in *carmen* to magnify the power of his craft. Particularly worthy of note is the assimilation between the lover's persuasive song sung against the shut door of the beloved, the *paraclausithyrum*, and the spells to open lovers' doors in the Greek magical papyri (e.g., *PGM* XII.270–350, *PGM* XIII.1–343 at 320, *PGM* XIII.734–1077 at 1044, *PGM* XXXVII.312–20). For the delaying of the sun in its course see **96**; for snake-bursting see **49**.

## 221 The moon blushes red when drawn down; cymbals are clashed to help it

8 A.D.

Ovid *Metamorphoses*
4.329–33 (edited)

Latin

A blush suffused the boy's face. . . . This is the color . . . of the moon when it blushes beneath its gleam and bronze cymbals are clashed in a vain attempt to help it.

## 222 The moon, drawn down, is skimmed of its foam

ii A.D.

Apuleius *Metamorphoses* 1.3

Latin

Yes, that lie of yours is as true as if someone wanted to say that by magical muttering fast rivers are turned back, the sea is bound down and slowed, the winds are deprived of their life-breath, the sun is checked in its course, the moon is skimmed of its foam, stars are uprooted, daylight is removed, and night is held in place.

THIS PASSAGE IS NOT OUT OF place among those grouped at **97–103**. Here it is of interest for indicating that when drawn down the moon was skimmed of its foam. It was held to deposit this foam on plants, from which it could be collected as "moon-juice" (*virus lunare*) and used for magical purposes, for which compare **155**.

## 223 The trick of drawing down the moon exposed

ii/iii A.D.

Hippolytus *Refutations* 4.37

Greek

They exhibit the moon and the stars on the ceiling in the following fashion. They fix a mirror to the central part of the ceiling and place a bowl of water directly beneath it in the middle of the floor. Then they put a dimly shining lamp in the middle of the room, suspended above the bowl. In this way the mage makes a moon appear in the mirror from the reflection of the bowl. Also, the mage often suspends a drum from a height and cloaks it with a cover. This is kept covered by an accomplice, so that it should not be seen before the right time. The mage places a lamp behind it. When he gives the agreed signal to his accomplice, the accomplice removes part of the cover, just enough to mimic the phase of the moon at that point. The mage paints the translucent parts of the drum with cinnabar and gum. With a greater degree of preparation, the mage removes the neck and base from a round bottle, puts a lamp inside and covers it with some equipment in such a way that the shape of the moon shines through. . . . One of the accomplices secretly takes up position on high, behind a screen. After receiving the agreed signal, he lowers the apparatus from its suspended position, so that the moon appears to be descending from heaven. A similar trick with a pot is done in wooded places. Tricks can be done with a pot indoors too. An altar is set up and the pot is positioned behind it with a dimly shining lamp. When several lamps are shining, this remains un-detectable. Now when the enchanter [*epaoidos*] calls on the moon, he gives the order to extinguish the lamps, but to leave one dim one. Then the light from the pot reflects onto the ceiling and shows an image of the moon to the audience. The pot is kept covered until the time comes for displaying its moon-shaped image on the roof.

As USUAL, HIPPOLYTUS'S INGENIOUS EXPOSÉ PROBABLY tells us more about his agenda to discredit pagan rites than it does about actual pagan practice; compare **160, 164**. The drum is evidently painted with red cinnabar to produce the blushing effect conventionally associated with the moon's drawing-down.

## IUNX AND RHOMBOS

The exact nature of the lover-drawing erotic-magical implements denoted by these terms, and whether they were one or two, is the subject of continuing controversy: see the contrasting views in *A Guide to Further Reading* 11.4. Many ancient sources treat the two terms as synonymous, but Theocritus's Simaetha poem, **89**, leads some modern scholars to argue for an original distinction between the two. The *iunx* was a whistling wheel, usually made of metal, which was spun between the hands on a loop of thread passed through two central eyes. Several vase illustrations of this wheel, sometimes in the hands of Eros himself, survive (for some of which see Gow 1934). It took its name from the bird *iunx*, the wryneck, which can spin its head round while keeping its body stationary; this dance of warning was construed in antiquity as a highly erotic mating dance. Analogy may also have been drawn between the *iunx*'s call and the whistling of the wheel. Pindar supplies an aetiological myth for the wheel in accordance with which an actual bird was attached to it. If the term *rhombos* (Latin *rhombus*) did not (always) denote the same thing, then it perhaps denoted a "bull-roarer," a rhomboid block of wood or metal with a string tied to one end, which is then spun in the air over one's head. For the *iunx* and *rhombos* see further **52, 90, 102**.

**224  Aphrodite gives Jason a *iunx* to seduce Medea**

Earlier v B.C.

Pindar *Pythian* 4.211–50

Greek

Then they came to the river Phasis where they fought the black-faced Colchians before Aeetes himself. The Cyprus-born lady of the sharpest arrows yoked fast the variegated wryneck [*iunx*] from Olympus to a four-spoked wheel and brought this bird of madness to men for the first time. She taught the wise son of Aeson prayers and spells, so that he could remove Medea's shame before her parents, and so that desirable Greece might set her ablaze in her heart and drive her with the whip of Persuasion. At once she showed him how to succeed in the contests set him by her father. She blended drugs [*pharmakôsaisa*] with olive oil as a protection against harsh pains and gave them to him to anoint himself with. They agreed to be joined together with each other in sweet marriage.

PINDAR IS A VALUABE SOURCE BECAUSE of his earliness. Here even the goddess Aphrodite turns to magical paraphernalia to bring about her desires (compare her use of her "saltire" at **248**). It is paradoxical that Jason should win for himself the aid of Medea, the archetypal witch, by subjecting her to erotic magic. For Medea see **66–71**, especially **68** for her invincibility lotion.

## 225   The *iunx* of Nico is dedicated to Aphrodite

Hellenistic

*Hellenistic Epigrams*
Anonymous 35 Gow
and Page

Greek

This wryneck [*iunx*] of Nico, which knows how to draw a man from across the sea and girls from their bowers, decorated with gold, inset with translucent amethyst, is dedicated as a dear gift to you, Cyprian, tied through its middle with a gentle thread of purple wool, a gift of guest-friendship from a Larissaean witch [*pharmakis*].

THIS POEM IDENTIFIES THE *IUNX* WITH a (birdless) spinning wheel. For the twisting of colored thread see **254**.

## 226   A list of erotic magical equipment

i B.C.

Laevius F27 Morel (at
Apuleius *Apology*
30.13)

Latin

They pull out love potions from everywhere. That famous *antipathes* is sought, as are little wheels, wrynecks [*iunges*], ribbons, root tendrils, herbs, shoots, enticing double-tailed lizards, the sweet charms of whinnying creatures.

PLINY TELLS THAT *ANTIPATHES* WAS A black coral protective against witchcraft (*Natural History* 37.145). The distinction between wheels and wrynecks here is unclear, although the second term could denote the birds themselves, which did have their own use in erotic magic (see **229**). For lizards in erotic magic compare **89** and, more generally, **247**. The "sweet charms of whinnying creatures" are *hippomanes*, for which see **230–2**.

## 227   Ancient scholarly identification of *iunx* and *rhombos*

Ca. v A.D.

Psendo-Acro on Horace
*Epodes* 17.7

Latin

The *turbo* ["wheel"] is an instrument of evil sorcery [*maleficium*]. By its whirling people are compelled into love, by a certain craft. It is called *iunx* in Greek. By *turbo* he means *rhuthmos* [Greek], which the Greeks call a *rhombos*.

FOR THE TEXT THIS ELUCIDATES SEE **94**. This ancient scholar evidently considered *iunx* and *rhombos* to be one and the same.

## 228   The natural history of the wryneck

Later iv A.D.

Aristotle *History of Animals* 504a

Greek

Some [birds] have two toes in front and two behind, such as the one called the wryneck [*iunx*]. This bird is a little bigger than the chaffinch, and it is mottled. The arrangement of its toes is unique and it has a tongue like those of snakes. For it can stick its tongue out to the breadth of four fingers and pull it back in again. Also, it twists its neck round back to front, while the remainder of its body stays motionless, like snakes. Its claws are large, like those of green woodpeckers. It makes a high-pitched noise.

IN FACT THE DANCE IS ONE of warning.

## 229   A lapis lazuli ring enclosing a wryneck's eye bestows sexual favor and legal success

iv A.D.

*Cyranides* 1.10.39–42
(Waegeman 1987,
kappa)

Greek

If someone wears the right eye [of the *kinaidios* bird] underneath an unblemished lapis lazuli, on which Aphrodite has been engraved, the man who wears this will be desired. His words will please men and he will win every lawsuit. The left eye too does the same when worn by a woman.

THE *KINAIDIOS*, "SEXUALLY PROFLIGATE," IS AN alternative name for the *iunx* bird. For the "alphabetic" amulets of the first book of *Cyranides* see **253, 255, 276**. Images of Aphrodite are particularly associated with blue stones, and lapis lazuli was sacred to her. The association of male with right and female with (inferior) left was pervasive in antiquity. As often, spells to bestow favor and success generally are rooted in the promotion of erotic attractiveness.

## HIPPOMANES

The favorite love-potion ingredient of *hippomanes*, or "horse-madness," was applied to four distinct substances:

- An herb; see **89, 230**.
- A growth on the forehead of the newborn foal; see **231**.
- A discharge secreted by the mare; see **230–1**.
- Stallion's semen; see **232**.

For further references to *hippomanes* see **89–90, 96, 101–2**.

---

**230**  *Hippomanes* **is caused by mares' wind-pregnancies, and exploited by wicked stepmothers**

29 B.C. (Virgil);
iv A.D. (Servius)

Virgil *Georgics*
3.274–83, with Servius
*ad loc.*

Latin

Virgil. Often, without any coupling, mares become pregnant by the wind (a remarkable thing to relate). Then they flee across rocks and crags and through low-lying valleys, neither in the direction of your rising point, East Wind, nor, Sun, in the direction of yours, but in the direction of the north wind and the northwest wind, or in the direction of the place from which the darkest south wind is born and from which it brings gloom to the sky with rain and cold. Only then does the secretion that shepherds correctly term *hippomanes* drip slowly from their genitals, *hippomanes*, which wicked stepmothers have often collected and blended with herbs and words far from harmless.

**Servius ad loc.** He knows that Hesiod [F350 Merkelbach-West] says that there is a certain herb that is called *hippomanes*, namely, "the madness of the horse." If horses eat it, they shake with frenzy.

VIRGIL EVIDENTLY TAKES HIS LORE FROM Aristotle (**231**). For a wicked stepmother who might have been tempted to use *hippomanes*, obviously on her stepson, see **83**. The Hesiodic fragment preserved by the commentator is our earliest reference to *hippomanes*.

---

**231**  **The natural history of** *hippomanes*

Later iv B.C.

Aristotle *History of Animals* 572a, 577a, 605a

Greek

572a. The female most eager for coupling is the mare, followed by the cow. Mares become "horse-mad" [*hippomainousin*]. Hence the term deriving from this particular creature is applied abusively to women who recklessly abandon themselves to their sexual urges. At this time mares are said to be impregnated by the wind. So in Crete they don't remove the stallions from the mares. For, whenever the mares are wind-impregnated, they run away from other horses. (In pigs the phenomenon is called "boor-ing.") They run neither east nor west, but north or south. Whenever the condition comes upon them, they will not allow anyone to come near, until they fail through exhaustion, or they reach the sea. Then they make a discharge. They call this *hippomanes* ["horse–madness"], just like the growth on the foal they produce. This is like the *kapria* [i.e., in pigs], and women who concern themselves with spells seek after it strenuously. In the mating season the mares huddle closer to each other than before, they flick their tail frequently, and their neighing takes on a different tone from its usual one. A substance resembling semen flows from their genitals, but much thinner than male seed. Some call this *hippomanes*, as opposed to the thing that grows on foals. They say it is difficult to get hold of, because it only flows in small quantities.

**577a.** Whenever the mare gives birth, she at once gobbles down the afterbirth, and eats the growth from the head of her foals, and this is called *hippomanes*. In size it is a little smaller than a dried fig. It is flat, round, and black in appearance. If someone takes this before the mare, but she smells it, the smell drives her mad. Hence witches [*pharmakides*] seek after it and collect it.

**605a.** The so-called *hippomanes* grows, as it is said, on foals, and the mares devour it as the lick them clean. It has been somewhat mythologized by women and those who concern themselves with spells.

HERE ARISTOTLE SUPPLIES A RANGE OF identifications for *hippomanes*, all of which can be found refracted in various references to its magical exploitation in the Latin poets.

## 232 A range of erotic equine products

i A.D.

Pliny *Natural History* 28.261

Latin

Gall of the wild boar, smeared on, promotes copulation, and likewise the devouring of pig's marrow, or an ointment made from ass's suet mixed with the fat of a gander, and similarly the fluid, described by Virgil too, from a horse's copulation, and a horse's testicles, dried so that they may be ground up and put in a potion, or the right testicle of an ass drunk in wine in a suitable dose or attached to a bracelet, or the foam from the same creature after sex in a red rag and shut up in silver, as Osthanes tells.

PLINY LOCATES THE POETS' MUCH-LOVED *hippomanes* here in the context of a wider range of sex-promoting equine products. These may have been favored for erotic purposes because the male animals of the species were held to have large penises. For erotic stimulants, see **212**. For Osthanes see **45**.

## ABORTION AND CONTRACEPTION

For the supposed magical infliction of sterility or miscarriage with or without the will of the potential mother see **47, 57, 79, 82, 96, 279**. For a contraceptive amulet see **255**. For a complementary variety of spell, a fertility spell to counteract barrenness in a woman, see **47**, again; for spells to promote fertility (perhaps) in men see **212, 254**.

## 233 Apphia burns a sapphire to procure an abortion: a confession inscription from Maeonia in Asia Minor

Ca. 150–250 A.D.

Petzl 1994, no. 59

Greek

Syntyche, the wife of Theogenes, dedicated this stele to Men Axiottenos, of the cult founded by Artemidorus. Her husband Theogenes found a sapphire gem. The stone was kept in her house, but then stolen. As she searched for it and was being interrogated over it, she prayed to Men Axiottenos to give her satisfaction about it. It was discovered burned and destroyed, wrapped up in a linen shirt and put back by the thief in the place where it had been kept when it was still undamaged. Thus the god manifested himself on the thirty-first day and deflowered Apphia, the daughter of Glycon, who was a virgin and who had stolen the stone and done this. Syntyche completely concealed the power of the god, because the virgin's mother had asked her to keep quiet. The god took revenge for this, because Syntyche had not publicized and exalted the god. Therefore he made her set up in his sanctuary this account of the revenge he took on her child of thirteen years, Heraclides, because Syntyche held the things of man in higher regard than the things of the god. It is Syntyche the daughter of Apollonius and Meltine who has published this act of vengeance.

THE EVENTS UNDERLYING THIS CONFUSING NARRATIVE may have been as follows. The virgin girl Apphia, on finding herself pregnant, stole the precious sapphire from Syntyche, her mother's friend, in order to burn it to procure menstruation and thereby an abortion. The *Orphic Lithica* (485–91) and *Damigeron* (20) explain that a woman may induce menstruation by squatting over burning lignite stone (*gagatês*) and fumigating her vagina with it. Syntyche published a "prayer for justice" (see **185–91**) to the god Men in which she asked him to make the (presumably hitherto unidentified) thief return the stone. Apphia had burned the stone as soon as she had taken it, and then waited for her periods to return. After a further thirty-one days without one, it became apparent that the magic had not worked, and that the game was up. The pregnancy was confessed, the theft with it, and the stone, albeit in its ruined state, was duly returned. The god had done what was asked of him, and it was accordingly Syntyche's duty to add to his praise by publishing this demonstration of his efficacy. She declined to do so, however, out of respect for her friend, Apphia's mother, who wished to conceal her daughter's theft and, doubtless more so, the fall from virtue that had occasioned it. But, angry at Syntyche's betrayal, Men killed her son Heraclides. This more terrible demonstration of Men's power forced Syntyche to erect the confession text translated here after all. Whether Apphia had realized it or not, Men had manifested himself to her or within her in prompting her to return the stone. Such contact conveniently afforded a new defense of her honor, now that the news of her defloration and pregnancy had to come out: she had been impregnated by the god himself. And the real father? Syntyche's son Heraclides is an obvious candidate. At thirteen he will have been very close in age to Apphia, a girl who was old enough to be fertile but not to be married. Their mothers' friendship will have given them access to each other. And who was in a better position to alert Apphia to the existence of Syntyche's stone, or to get it for her?

## 234  An abortifacient spell or curse

iii A.D.

*PGM* LXII.76–106, (reedited by Aubert 1989, 428)

Greek

[A complex arrangement of *voces magicae* and vowel series heads the recipe. Some of the *voces magicae* are written within a figure described as "heart-shaped," which represents a womb.] "Let the vagina and womb of [insert her name] be open, and may she be bloodied night and day." Write these things in sheep's blood and recite the spell laid out above during the night . . . [lacuna] she did unprovoked wrong, and bury it near flowing water or near . . . [lacuna] scratch it on a strip of papyrus . . .

THE FLOWING WATER WILL SYMPATHETICALLY persuade the blood to flow, as will the writing of the text in blood. The spell uses slander magic ("she did unprovoked wrong"); see **211**.

## 235  A contraceptive amulet

iv–v A.D.

*PGM* XXIIa. 11–4

Greek

This Homeric verse, if carried together with a magnetic stone, or even just recited, prevents one from conceiving: "You should have been without offspring and should have perished unmarried" [Homer *Iliad* 3.40]. Write this on a new tablet and tie it around with the hairs of a mule.

MULE HAIRS ARE EVIDENTLY TO BE used because the animal is paradigmatically sterile. For the magical significance of the text of Homer compare **167**. The verse is to be worn as an amulet; compare **273**.

# 12
## *Voodoo Dolls and Magical Images*

"Voodoo dolls," or *kolossoi*, were already thriving in the early archaic period, prior to the development of binding-curse tablets, to which they were closely related in use and deposition, at the end of it. Indeed they had no doubt been in use before literacy returned to Greece. Like the tablets too, they were used throughout antiquity, wherever Graeco-Roman culture was to be found; for a useful catalogue of the thirty-eight archaeological finds of individual dolls or doll-groups, see Faraone 1991b.

Voodoo dolls attempted in a (primarily) plastic medium what binding-curse tablets attempted in a verbal-and-plastic one. Hence the restraint of the victim was achieved through his or her representation as bound or twisted or even decapitated in his or her corresponding doll. For an explanation, acceptable to modern understanding, as to how these dolls may in fact have "worked" upon their victims see 16, with commentary. Dolls were made from a wide range of materials: lead, bronze, and clay ones survive; in addition to these, wax, wool, and dough ones are mentioned in the literary sources.

Similar dolls were also used for laying ghosts, where they provided new bodies for them (124). It is tempting to believe that this was their original function. The hobbling of the dolls could have here performed a function similar to of *maschalismos* (122). Then, perhaps, the opportunity was taken, while laying ghosts, to ask them to take (aspects of) the living with them, to deaden them. As such a practice developed, the dolls will have become construed as representing the curse victim rather than the ghost.

For further literary accounts of erotic voodoo dolls see 67, 89–91, 94, 98–9, 207.

## 236 The melting of dolls in the Cyrenean foundation decree

iv B.C. (vi B.C.?)

Meiggs and Lewis 1969, no. 5, lines 40–51

Greek

Oaths were sworn to this agreement both by those who remained in Thera and those who sailed to settle. And they called down curses on those who should foreswear themselves and fail to abide by their oath, be they among those settling in Libya or those remaining behind in Thera. They molded wax dolls [*kolossoi*] and burned them while calling down the curse, all having come together, men, women, boys, and girls. They prayed that the one who did not abide by these oaths but foreswore himself should melt and dissolve just like the dolls, he himself, his descendants, and his property, but that those that did abide by these oaths, whether among those sailing to Libya or those remaining behind in Thera, should have many good things, both they themselves and their descendants.

THIS FAMOUS INSCRIPTION RECORDS A fourth-century recreation of an oath supposedly sworn upon the foundation of the colony of Cyrene from Thera in ca. 630 B.C. The story is told by Herodotus (4.150–8): Thera was driven to dispatch the settlers because afflicted by famine, hence the importance of everyone abiding by the agreement. Here wax voodoo dolls are used in a distinctive and, in Greek terms, exceptional fashion to enact a conditional curse. It has been argued that such a rite has significant Near Eastern antecedents (Faraone 1993a). The curse exploits the sympathetic principle.

### 237 The Mnesimachos doll and its coffin from the Athenian Ceramicus cemetery

Ca. 400 B.C.

Trumpf 1958

Greek

Inside coffin lid: Barburtides, Xophugos, Nicomachos, Oenocles, Mnesimachos, Chamaios, Tesonides, Charisander, Democles, and any other advocate or witness they have on their side.

Right leg of doll: Mnesimachos

THIS DISTINCTIVE COMBINATION OF VOODOO DOLL and curse tablet (see figure 12.1) was found in the grave in the Athenian Ceramicus cemetery where it was deposited ca. 400 B.C., alongside the remains of body from which parts had been removed, doubtless for further magical operations (see **96, 107, 181**, with commentaries). The little lead doll, six centimeters tall, has its arms folded in what is no doubt supposed to be a bound pose, and enlarged genitals. It was enclosed within an oval coffin made from lead tablets. Holes in the coffin suggest that nails were once driven through it. The inside of the lid is inscribed with a fairly standard legal binding curse (see **168–72**), and one of the names included here, Mnesimachos, is also inscribed on the right leg of the doll itself, seemingly identifying it with that person in particular. It is especially intriguing that both Nicomachos and Mnesimachos were legal opponents of the great orator Lysias. It could well be that this curse was made by someone very close to him.

### 238 Clarian Apollo tells that Artemis will melt an evil mage's wax dolls to deliver Sardis (?) from plague

Ca. 165 A.D.

Graf 1992

Greek

"[Approach] Artemis of the fair quiver, born from the same stock as I am, for she is the leader of the whole city, nurse of your family, increaser of men, giver of fruits. Bring in her image, shining with gold, from Ephesus, and set it up in a temple, with joy in your hearts. She will ward off your sufferings and dismiss the man-destroying spells/poisons [*pharmaka*] of the plague, melting the wax-molded dolls by night with the flames of her fire-bearing torches, the evil tokens of the mage's craft. But when you have carried out my instructions for the goddess, worship the arrow-pouring goddess, invincible, straight-shooting, the glorious girl who watches over you. Girls and boys together, celebrate the maiden in dances and feasts everywhere above the salty lands of Maeonian Hermus, garlanding yourselves with broad myrtle, after summoning chaste Artemis from the land of Ephesus, so that she may help you forever, in her undefiled state. If you do not accomplish these rites, then you will suffer the punishment of fire." This oracle was given by Apollo.

THE INSCRIPTION RECORDING THIS REMARKABLE RESPONSE was found in Ephesus; it was perhaps given to Sardis, and the prescribed rites were perhaps to be performed in the sanctuary of Artemis at Koloe. The Apollo in question is probably that of Clarus, and the plague in question the great plague of 165

Figure 12.1. The Mnesimachos voodoo doll and its "coffin" case from the Ceramicus cemetery. Athens, Ceramicus Museum, case 33 (Faraone 1991c, no. 5; Gager 1992, no. 19. Photograph © Deutsches archäologisches Institut Athen (neg. Ker 5879) and Hellenic Republic Ministry of Culture Archaeological Receipts Fund. The help of Mr. H. R. Goette and Mr. P. Massouras is gratefully acknowledged.

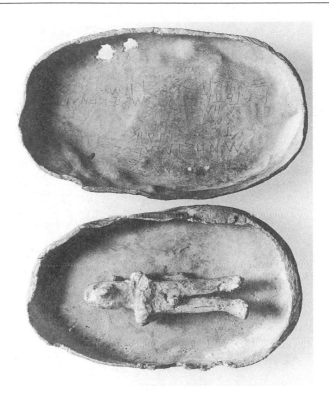

A.D., on which Clarian Apollo gave responses to many different cities. Artemis here provides a valuable mechanism for the deactivation of curse equipment in a case where it cannot be found and retrieved; compare **190**, with commentary. In other contexts, by contrast, wax dolls are burned in the course of their activation; see **89–90, 236**. The configuration of the goddess who will purge the plague interestingly resembles Hecate herself, with her (here highly useful) raised torches; compare **275**. For binding-magical attacks against an entire city, compare **179–80, 278**.

## 239 Attraction curse recipe using a pair of voodoo dolls

iv A.D.

PGM IV.296–466

Greek

Amazing binding love spell (philtrokatadesmos). Take some wax or some clay from a potter's wheel and mold two figures, male and female. Arm the male one like Ares, brandishing a sword in his left hand and striking the female's neck on her right side. Put the female doll's hands behind her back and make her kneel. You will fasten the stuff [ousia] on her head or on her neck. Inscribe the doll of the woman being attracted: on her head, "ISEÊ IAÔ ITHI OUNE BRIDÔ LÔTHIÔN NEBOUTOSOUALÊTH"; on her right ear, "OUER MÊCHAN"; on her left ear, "LIBABA ÔIMATHOTHO"; on her face, "AMOUNABREÔ"; over her right eye, "ÔRORMOTHIO AÊTH"; over the other one, "CHOBOUE"; on her right collarbone, "ADETA MEROU"; on her right arm, "ENE PSA ENESGAPH"; on the other one, "MELCHIOU MELCHIEDIA"; on her hands, "MELCHAMELCHOU AÊL"; on her breast, the name of the woman being attracted, with her metronymic; over her heart, "BALAMIN THÔOUTH"; under her stomach, "AOBÊS AÔBAR"; on her vulva, "BLICHIANEOI OUÔIA"; on her bottom, "PISSADARA"; on the soles of her feet, on the right one, "ELÔ"; on the other one, "ELÔAIOE." Take thirteen bronze needles and insert one of them into the brain while saying, "I pierce your brain (insert her name)"; insert two into her ears, two more into her eyes, one into her mouth, two below her rib cage, one into her hands, two into her vulva and anus, and two into the soles of her feet, while on each occasion saying once, "I pierce the (insert name of part) of (insert her name), so that she may think of no one, except me alone, (insert your name)." Take a lead tablet, inscribe the same spell on it, and say it through. Bind the tablet to the figures with the warp from a loom, in which you have made 365 knots while saying, as you know how to, "Abrasax, constrain her." Lay it as the sun sets beside the grave of one untimely dead or dead by violence, and lay flowers of the season there with it. The inscribed and recited spell is this:

"I deposit with you this binding-curse [*katadesmos*], chthonic gods and Pluto; UESEMIGADON; Maiden Persephone Ereschigal and Adonis the BARBARITHA; underworld Hermes THÔOUTH PHÔKENTAZEPSEU AERCHTHATHOU MISONKTAI KALBANACHAMBRÊ; powerful Anubis PSIRINTH, holder of the keys to Hades; gods and demons of the underworld; untimely dead, male and female; lads and maidens; year on year, month on month, day on day, hour on hour. I adjure all demons in this place to assist this demon. Rouse yourself for me, whoever you are, whether male or female, and take yourself off to every district, every block, and every house. Bring her and bind her. Bring her (insert her name), the daughter of (insert her mother's name), whose stuff you have, in love with me, (insert your name), whom (insert your mother's name) bore. Let her not fornicate, let her not be buggered, and let her not do anything that brings pleasure with another man, unless with me alone, (insert your name), so that (insert her name) is not able either to drink or to eat, or hold out, or to endure it, or be calm, so that (insert her name) is not able to find sleep without me, (insert your name), because I adjure you in the name that inspires fear and trembling, the name at the sound of which the earth will be opened up, the name at the sound of which the frightening demons will be frightened, the name at the sound of which the rocks are shattered. I adjure you, ghost-demon [*nekudaimôn*], whether male or female, by BARBARITHA CHENMBRA BAROU-CHAMBRA and by ABRAT ABRASAX SESENGEN BARPHARRANGÊS and by the honored AÔIA MARI and by MARMAREÔTH MARMARAUÔTH MARMARÔTH MARECHTHANA AMARZA MARIBEÔTH. Do not ignore my commands and my names, ghost-demon, but just rouse yourself from the rest that encompasses you, whoever you are, whether male or female, and take yourself off to every district, every block, and every house, and bring me (insert her name), prevent her eating and drinking and do not let (insert her name) have sex that brings pleasure with any other man, not even her own husband, except with me alone, (insert your name), but drag (insert her name) by her hair, by her guts, by her soul, to me, (insert your name), every hour of time, by night and by day, until she comes to me, (insert your name), and let her stay inseparably by my side. Make her, bind her for the full extent of my life and compel (insert her name) to serve me, (insert your name), and let her not prance away from me for an hour of time. If you achieve this for me, I shall give you rest at once. For I am BARBAR ADÔNAI, the concealer of the stars, the ruler of bright-shining heaven, the lord of the universe ATHTHOUIN IATHOUIN SELBIOUÔTH AÔTH SARBATHIOUTH IATHTHIERATH ADÔNAI IA ROURA BIA BI BIOTHÊ ATHÔTH SABAÔTH ÊA NIAPHA AMARACHTHI SATAMA ZAUATH-THEIÊ SERPHÔ IALADA IALÊ SBÊSI IATHTHA MARADTHA ACHILTHTHEE CHOÔÔ OÊ ÊACHÔ KANSAOSA ALKMOURI THUR THAÔOS SIECHÊ. I am THÔTH OSÔMAI. Bring her, bind (insert her name), loving me, lusting after me, longing for me, (insert your name; add the commonplaces), because I adjure you, demon of the dead, by the fearsome, great IAEÔ BAPHRENEMOUN OTHI LARIKRIPHIA EUEAI PHIRKI-RALITHON UOMEN ER PHABÔEAI, so that you may bring me (insert her name) and glue her head to my head, fasten her lips to my lips, glue her stomach to my stomach, draw her thigh to my thigh, integrate her black with my black, and let (insert her name) satisfy her sexual desires with me, (insert your name), for all the time of eternity."

Then inscribe the characters in a heart-shape as set out hereafter on another part of the tablet:

[Various magical figures follow, including characters, a large seven-line trapezoid palindrome, vowel series, and *voces magicae*.]

This is the prayer for the rite. Speak it to the setting sun, with the stuff from the tomb: "(I appeal to you,) Sun of the golden locks, riding on the breezes of the winds that roam through the air, manipulating the tireless flame of fire, wheeling around the great pole in ethereal cycles, generating everything yourself, and then breaking it down again. For all the elements are derived from you. They are arranged in accordance with your laws, and they nurture the entire universe with its four turning points over the cycle of a year. Hear me, blessed one. For I call on you, the ruler of heaven, of earth, chaos, and Hades, where the demons of men who formerly saw the light live. Now I beseech you, blessed, indestructible one, lord of the universe. If you go into the recesses of the earth, to the place of the dead, send this demon, from whose corpse I hold this fragment in my hands, to me in the middle hours of the night, coming in accordance with commands and under your compulsion, so that it may accomplish for me everything I wish for in my heart, gentle, propitious, and not hostile toward me. And may you not be angry at my powerful incantations. For it was you who made these arrangements among men, so that they should discover the spinnings of the Fates [*Moirai*], following your counsel. I invoke your name, which is numerically equivalent to those of the Fates themselves ACHAIPHÔ THÔTHÔ PHIACHA AIÊ ÊIA IAÊ ÊIA THÔTHÔ PHIACHA. Be propitious to me, primal god, scion of the universe, self-engendered, fire-bringing, gold-shining, bringer of light to mortals, lord of the universe, demon of tireless fire, indestructible, gold-circled, sending a pure light to the earth from your rays. Send the demon I asked for to (insert her name; add the commonplaces)."

Another version of the spell gives this name: ACHAI PHÔTHÔTHÔ AIÊ ÊIA IAÊ ÊIÔ THÔ THÔ PHIACHA. Another version again gives: ACHAI PHÔTHÔTHÔ AIÊ IÊA ÊAI IAÊ AÊI ÊIA ÔTHÔTHÔ PHIACHA.

THIS RECIPE FROM THE GREEK MAGICAL PAPYRI is remarkable for its correspondences with a discovered curse-papyrus-and-voodoo-doll assemblage, **239**. Although this version of the recipe was written out after the manufacture of the assemblage, the *PGM* IV papyrus is thought to recycle material from the second century A.D. Whereas the assemblage contains only a female doll, the pair of dolls prescribed here bear a striking similarity to those placed by Horace into the hands of his witch Canidia, where a woolen doll is made to subject a wax one, kneeling before it, **91**. Some voodoo-doll pairs survive, but not in this configuration; rather, they embrace or are bound to each other tightly (`"symplegmata"`; compare **207**). We may assume that rituals of the general sort outlined here lay behind the deposition of many of the voodoo dolls found.

The prescribed tablet and doll are to be deposited with a ghost, as usual.

The other ghosts of the untimely dead in the vicinity are also called on to aid the chosen one in its task of binding (compare **110, 112**). The ghost is presented with both carrot and stick: torture by underworld terrors if it does not oblige; peace if it does. This is precisely the approach taken by Lucan's Erictho in her necromancy spell (**155**). The recipe-user is to claim authority by identifying himself with the power designated by the *voces magicae*.

The purpose of the spell is explicitly attraction (see **204–13**), but it also contains strong elements of separation from hypothetical competitors. As often in attraction curses, the woman is restrained from food, drink, and sleep until she gratifies her lover; in this way the binding power of the tablet is put to more flexible ends. In his flying around to find and fetch the beloved woman the ghost plays a role similar to that of the animated Eros doll in **244**. As usual the woman is to be dragged through the streets to the door of the curse-maker; here the dragging language is literally visceral (see the discussion before **197**). The multiple piercings of the female doll with pins seem to enact the desired sexual penetration of the beloved, as does the sexually explicit language. But the recipe also seems to envisage the construction of a permanent relationship.

The prayer to the Sun accompanying the rite is in hexameters. The Sun (the Greek Helios associated with the Egyptian Horus) is a power commonly exploited by the Greek magical papyri, although it is initially surprising to see it appealed to in association with the manipulation of underworld beings such as ghosts (see however, **105**).

## 240  Lead erotic curse tablet against Ptolemais, accompanying the Louvre voodoo doll from Antinoupolis in Egypt

iii or iv A.D.

*Suppl. Mag.* 47

Greek

I deposit this binding-spell [*katadesmos*] with you, underworld gods, Pluto and Kore-Persephone-Erschigal and Adonis, a.k.a. BARBARITHA, and underworld Hermes-Thoth PHÔKENSEPSEU EREKTATHOU MISONKTAIK and Anubis PSÊRIPHTHA, holder of the keys to the underworld, and with you, underworld demons, gods, untimely dead, male and female, lads and maidens, year on year, month on month, day on day, hour on hour, night on night. I adjure all you demons in this place to assist this demon Antinous. Rouse youself for me and take yourself off to every district, every block, every house, and bind Ptolemais, to whom Aias gave birth, Ptolemais the daughter of Horigenes, so that she may not be screwed and may not be buggered and may not do anything that brings pleasure for a male companion, except for me alone, Sarapammon, to whom Area gave birth. Do not permit her to eat, drink, hold out, go out, or find sleep apart from me, Sarapammon, to whom Area gave birth. I adjure you ghost-demon [*nekudaimôn*] Antinous, in the name that brings fear and trembling, the name at the sound of which the earth will open up, the name at the sound of which demons are seized with fear and terror, the name at the sound of which rivers and rocks are broken. I adjure you, ghost-demon Antinous, by BARBARATHAM CHELOUMBRA BARRUCH ADÔNAI and by ABRASAX and by IAÔ PAKEPTÔTH PAKEBRAÔTH SABARBAPHAEI and by MARMAROUÔTH and by MARMARACHTHA MAMAZAGAR. Do not ignore me, ghost-demon Antinous, but rouse yourself for me and take yourself off to every district, every block, every house and bring me Ptolemais, to whom Aias gave birth, Ptolemais, the daughter of Horigenes. Restrain her food, her drink, until she comes to me, Sarapammon, to whom Area gave birth, and do not permit her to be penetrated by any man other than me alone, Sarapammon. Drag her by the hair, by the guts, until she no longer disdains me, Sarapammon, to whom Area gave birth, and until I have her, Ptolemais, to whom Aias gave birth, Ptolemais the daughter of Horigenes, subservient to me for the full extent of my life, loving me, lusting after me, telling me what she has in her mind. If you do this, I will give you release.

THE TABLET WAS FOUND ENCLOSED IN a jar with a distinctive voodoo doll now known as the Louvre doll after the museum in which it resides (Louvre no. E27145). The correspondence between this assemblage and the recipe in **239** is remarkable and testifies to the wide circulation and relatively conservative reproduction of such recipes in Roman Egypt. The doll closely resembles the female one prescribed for manufacture in it: it clearly portrays a woman; it is made of unbaked clay; her feet and hands are bound behind her, so that she is a kneeling posture; she is transfixed by thirteen needles in the parts prescribed by the recipe above. However, contrary to the recipe, the doll is uninscribed (but there may well be inscriptions on a papyrus strip enclosed within the clay, as is known from other Egyptian dolls).

A range of restless ghosts is called on to help, as in the recipe, but that of Antinous is singled out as the principal agent. If the assemblage does indeed derive from Antinoopolis (which is not entirely certain), then it is likely that the ghost addressed is that of the emperor Hadrian's favorite of that name. He had died young and was buried in the city, formerly Ptolemais, which was renamed for him. The circumstances of his death and the rumors that attended it rendered his ghost particularly appropriate for magical exploitation: see **241**.

## 241   Hadrian sacrifices Antinous for necromancy

ii–iii A.D.

Dio Cassius 69.11

Greek

In Egypt too he rebuilt the city named for Antinous. Antinous was from the city of Bithynium in Bithynia, also known as Claudioupolis. He had been his catamite, and died in Egypt, either after falling into the Nile, as Hadrian writes, or after being sacrificed, as the truth is. Hadrian was generally very meddlesome, as I said, and used divinations and sorceries [*manganeiai*] of all kinds. And so he gave honor to Antinous in this way, either because of his desire for him or because he had gone to his death voluntarily (for he needed a willing soul for his project). He founded a city in the place of his death and named it after him. And he dedicated statues of him over almost the entirety of the known world, or, rather, sacred images of him.

THIS TALE, RELATING TO 130 A.D., explains how it could have been believed that the ghost of Antinous was spectacularly restless in Antinoupolis. For boy-sacrifice see **133–7**. Antinous's statues survive in vast numbers.

## 242   Apuleius's magical Hermes doll

158 A.D.

Apuleius *Apology* 61, 63–4

Latin

61. After reading Pudentilla's letters, they have also made the accusation about the manufacture of a certain statuette. They say that I had this made by a secret process from a most choice wood, to use for destructive magic and that, although it is a horrid, foul thing in the form of a skeleton, I worship it devotedly and address it by the Greek term *basileus*, "king." Unless I am mistaken, I follow their tracks in due order and reweave the complete web of their slander, taking it point by point.

How can the manufacture of this statuette have been secret, as you say, when you yourselves are so familiar with the craftsman who made it that you served a summons on him to present himself in court. See! Here is Cornelius Saturninus the craftsman. Among his own people he is praised for his craft and admired for his character. When you were carefully interrogating him a little earlier, Maximus, he went through everything that happened in a reliable and truthful fashion. He said that I had seen in his shop many geometrical forms he had made out of boxwood with delicacy and skill. Enticed by his craftsmanship I had asked him to make some mechanical devices for me, together with an effigy of a god of his choosing, to whom I could pray in accordance with my custom, and to carve it from any material, so long as it was wooden. So at first he embarked on making one from boxwood. But in the meantime, when I was in the country, my stepson Sicinius Pontianus, who wanted it made for me, secured an ebony casket from that most respectable of ladies, Capitolina, and brought it to him, and urged him to make it rather from this material, which was so much rarer and so much more durable. This gift would, he said, bring me especial delight. Following these instructions he made the statuette as best he could from the casket. And so he fixed the tiny pieces of the casket together into a solid block and was able to make a little Mercury from them.

**63.** You concocted a third lie, to the effect that the figure made was an emaciated or altogether disemboweled one of a dreadful corpse, a terrible form resembling an evil ghost. But if you had discovered such a glaring proof of magic, why did you not require me to display it by summons? Was it so that you could be free to make up lies about it if it wasn't here? But you have lost the opportunity to pursue this deception by a fortunate custom of mine. For I'm in the habit of taking with me wherever I go an effigy of one of the gods, stored in my book box. I worship it on feast days with incense, unmixed wine, and sometimes with an animal sacrifice. So when, before, I heard the utterly outrageous lie being repeated that it was a skeleton, I told someone to run and fetch the little Mercury that Saturninus made for me at Oea from my lodging. Give him to them: let them see it, let them hold it, let them inspect it. There you have the figure that scallywag called a skeleton. Do you hear the protests of everyone here? Do you hear their condemnation of your lies? Do you not now feel wholly ashamed for so many slanders? Is this a skeleton? Is this an evil ghost? Is this what you kept calling an evil little demon [*daemonium*]? If this effigy a magical one or common-or-garden religious one?

Take it please, Maximus, and look at it. It is good that a sacred object should be entrusted to hands so pure and pious. Look, see how attractive its form is, and how full of a wrestler's vitality. See how happy the god's face is, how attractively the down spreads over his cheeks, how one can see a curly lock of hair peeping out from under the shade of the felt cap on his head, how charmingly his little pair of wings project over the sides of his head, how pleasingly, finally, his cloak is drawn around his shoulders. Anyone who dares to call this a skeleton must never see any effigies of the gods, or must ignore them all. In short, anyone who thinks this is a ghost is himself a necromancer [*larvans*].

**64.** But in return for your lies, Aemilianus, may that god who goes to and fro between the gods above and those below bring upon you the ill will of both groups and continually confront your vision with manifestations of the dead, all the shades [*umbrae*] there are, all the specters [*lemures*], all the ghosts [*manium*], all the ghouls [*larvae/larbae*], all the apparitions of the night, all the fears of graves, all the terrors of tombs . . . not that you are far removed from these things, in view of your age and your deserts.

But we disciples of Plato know nothing except that which is happy, joyful, lofty, divine, and heavenly. Indeed, in its enthusiasm for the heights this school has mapped out the regions higher than heaven itself and has stood upon the outermost surface of the universe. Maximus knows that I'm speaking the truth, because he has assiduously read the phrases "place above the heavens" and "surface of the heavens" in the *Phaedrus* [247c]. Maximus too knows very well—to reply to the charge about the name—who it is that is called *basileus*, "king," not by me first, but by Plato: "all things depend on the king of all things, and he is the cause of all things." That king is the cause, reason, and first origin of nature, the ultimate sire of the soul, the everlasting preserver of living things, the continual builder of the universe, but a builder without labor, a preserver without concern, a sire without propagation. He cannot be encompassed in space or time and he remains unchanging. Few can therefore conceive of him, and no one can convey him in speech. See! I go out of my way to incur further the suspicion that I practice magic: I give you no answer, Aemilianus, when you ask me whom I worship as *basileus*. Even if the proconsul himself were to ask me what my god is . . . silence!

APULEIUS DENIES MAGICAL PRACTICES, BUT THE superficial plausibility of the accusations made against him is often manifest; see **134, 299**. Here the prosecution has alleged that Apuleius cherishes a sinister doll for magical purposes. Apuleius rebuts the accusation, yet much of what is said in defense can be seen to strengthen the prosecution case, especially in view of the papyrus recipe using a Hermes voodoo doll in **243**.

- The jokes in sections 63–4 indicate that the prosecution had accused Apuleius of using his doll to manipulate ghosts, one of the usual functions of voodoo dolls. By Apuleius's own account, the doll represented Hermes/Mercury, and, as he concedes, this god was the escort of souls between the upper and lower worlds and a figure of central importance for ghost manipulation. For Apuleius on ghosts, see **105, 111, 114**.

- Elsewhere in this speech Apuleius speaks of the use of an image of Hermes in magical divination and of Pythagoras's behest that Hermes statuettes be made of exceptional varieties of wood (42–3: **134**).

- The papyrus recipe reproduced at **243** provides for the manufacture of a Hermes doll for magical purposes, albeit specifically to promote trade.

- The wood from which the doll was made was ebony; hence it was black, the color of night, of death, and of some ghosts. To ancient eyes, then, the doll would indeed have resembled a corpse, if not actually a skeleton.

- The doll was fitted together from separate plates. Perhaps, therefore, it incorporated a compartment into which papyrus strips inscribed with a magical texts could be inserted, as with the Hermes doll in the *PGM* IV recipe at **243**. See also **66**.

- Apuleius presents his offerings of animal sacrifice and wine to his Hermes doll as simple piety; but the *PGM* IV recipe prescribes offerings of chicken-sacrifice and wine similarly to its Hermes doll for its magical ends.

- The Greek magical papyri apply the term *basileus* to some of the powers they invoke.

## 243　Recipe for the promotion of trade with a Hermes doll

iv A.D.

*PGM* IV.2359–72

Greek

**Spell to promote trade.** Take some tawny wax and the juice of the plants *aeria* and ground ivy, blend them together, and mold a hollow figure of Hermes, brandishing a herald's staff in his left hand and a pouch in his right. Write the following names on a strip of hieratic papyrus, and you will see trade without end: "CHAIOCHEN OUTIBILMEMNOUOTH ATRAUICH. Give means and trade to this place, because PSENTEBETH dwells in it." Insert this into the model and seal up the hole with wax of the same sort. Stow it away in a wall where it won't be seen. Garland him outside and sacrifice a cock to him, with a libation of Egyptian wine. Light a nonred lamp for him.

THIS RECIPE MAKES APULEIUS'S ATTEMPT TO differentiate his handling of his Hermes doll from magic (**242**) look rather thin. In addition to being the escort of souls, Hermes was also the divine patron of trade. This recipe is immediately followed in the formulary by a similar one for enhancing trade with a wax model of a begging man (2373–2440). For magical lamps see **165-6**, with commentary.

## 244　A Hyperborean mage evocates a ghost, draws down the moon, and sends an animated Eros doll to enact an attraction spell

ii A.D.

Lucian *Philopseudes* 13–5

Greek

**13.** "You jest," said Cleodemus, "but I myself used to be even more cynical than you about such things, for I thought that there was no way they could happen, yet when I first saw the foreign visitor fly—he came from the Hyperborean people, as he said—I came to believe and I was overcome, despite having held out for so long. For what was I supposed to do when I saw him traveling through the air in the middle of the day, walking on water, and strolling through fire at a leisurely pace?"

"You saw these things," I said, "the Hyperborean man flying or walking on water?"

"Yes indeed," he said. "He had on brogue shoes of the sort that those people wear. Is there any need to recite his minor miracles, sending eros-dolls to get people, bringing demons up from the underworld, reanimating moldy corpses, summoning Hecate herself before him to assist him, large as life, and calling down the moon? **14.** I'll just tell you what I saw him do in the house of Glaucias, son of Alexicles.

"Just after his father had died and Glaucias had taken over his estate, he became enamored of Chrysis, the wife of Demeas. He had hired me to teach him reason, and if this love had not occupied him, he would by now know all the Peripatetic teachings. For when he was just eighteen he was solving logical conundrums and had pursued the lectures on *Physics* right to the end. However, he did not know what to do about his love, and he let me in on the whole thing. As you would expect, since I was his teacher, I introduced that Hyperborean mage to him. The terms were a four-mina downpayment—an initial payment was needed to fund the purchase of the sacrificial victims—and then a further sixteen minas, if he got Chrysis. The mage waited for the moon to start waxing, for this is the time at which rites of this kind are usually performed. Then he dug a pit in the court within the house and at around midnight called up for us, to begin with, Alexicles, the father of Glaucias, who had died seven months earlier. The old man was angry about the love and lost his temper, but even so in the end gave him permission to pursue the affair. After that he brought up Hecate and she brought Cerberus along, and he drew down the moon. It exhibited itself in a range of different guises and kept changing its appearance. First it displayed the form of a woman, next it became a magnificent ox, and then showed itself as a puppy. Eventually, the Hyperborean fashioned an eros-doll from clay and said to it, 'Off you go, and bring Chrysis.' The clay flew aloft, and soon there she was knocking on the door. She came in and embraced Glaucias as absolutely insane with love, and she slept with him until we heard the cocks crowing. Then the moon flew back up into the heavens, Hecate dove back down under the earth, and the other manifestations disappeared. We sent Chrysis off home round about dawn. **15.** If you'd seen this, Tychiades, you would not have doubted that there is much that is effective in incantations."

"Indeed," I said, "I would believe it, if I had seen it, but as is, you must forgive me, if I do not have your keen vision. But as a matter of fact I know the Chrysis whereof you speak. She is a lustful woman and very easy. I don't know why you needed the clay ambassador to send against her, the mage from the Hyperboreans and the moon herself: for twenty drachmas you could have brought her to the Hyperboreans! That is the spell to which the woman really surrenders. Her condition is diametrically opposed to that of ghosts. For if they hear the clash of bronze or iron, they're off – this is your story – but she actually heads straight for the noise, if there's a sound of silver somewhere. For the rest, I am curious about the mage. He had the power to attract the love of the richest women, and get them to give him whole talents, and yet he was so penny-pinching that he was prepared to make Glaucias alluring for a mere four minas."

THIS TALE IS A RICH ONE for a number of themes. The sorcerer is a "mage" but also a Hyperborean, a member of the marvelous and mythical race from the extreme north, and so salutes the shaman tradition as represented by Abaris and Aristeas (**5–7**). And like the shamans he can himself fly through the air, as can his animated Eros-doll. The animation of this doll to fetch a woman, the tale's central theme, is shown to be strongly and strikingly rooted in actual magical practice by the recipe from a papyrus formulary from two centuries later, reproduced in **245**.

It is initially curious that the father's ghost should be called up at all here (for evocation and reanimation see **144–62**). Was it thought that it might be so outraged by the affair that it would return to cause trouble unless propitiated first? This would have been an unusual cause of restlessness. The presence of the ghost in these erotic-attraction rites may be best explained with reference to another recipe in the Greek magical papyri, reproduced in **246**, in which a ghost is evocated to activate a doll, this time in the shape of a dog, for the attraction of a woman. It is noteworthy that both the underworld "dog" powers, Hecate and Cerberus, are present in Lucian's tale, and that the drawn-down moon's transformations also end in the shape of a puppy. The comparison of Lucian's tale with these recipes gives an important insight into the relationship that an imaginative and fantastical narrative of this sort could have with practical magic. With the flying Eros-doll compare also the flying ghost of the erotic-magical recipe at **239**.

The account of the drawing-down of the moon, an unusual rite for a male practitioner, is one of the most graphic. For her Protean form-changing see **115**. The moon and Hecate alike were aspects of Artemis, and Lucian here makes a symmetrical association between the calling-up of the one and the drawing-down of the other (for Hecate see **275**). The full moon was also a particularly suitable time for necromancy; see **148, 157**.

For voodoo dolls made of clay or earth see **240**. We have the vignette familiar in erotic magic of the beloved woman being dragged in a state of frenzy through the streets until she hammers at her lover's door (see discussion before **197**). In the papyrus recipes the woman is often said in this context to "fly" to her lover; but here it is the (winged) Eros doll that flies to fetch her.

As usual in the *Philopseudes*, a more cynical alternative explanation is offered for the wonderful events narrated. Here it is the lustful and venal nature of Chrysis, whose name, "Goldie," would not be inappropriate to a courtesan. This explanation plays knowingly with ghost-lore and in so doing provides us with a helpfully explicit statement of the notion that ghosts are averted by clashing metal; see **144** and, for the more general aversive power of jangling metal, **221**.

Tychiades's cynical response also exploits a version of a seemingly commonplace retort to the claims of beggarly practitioners of magic: if their powers are so great, how come they are themselves so poor? Compare **19, 300**. However, at the fee stated, this mage was not particularly cheap. If we conjecture, by default, that the sacrificial victims used were a pair of sheep, and that these accounted for most of the downpayment, the fee was equivalent in value to ten sheep. This would have represented a considerable sum, albeit not a fortune.

The natural alliance that Cleodemus perceives between "philosophy" and "magic" would have perturbed both Plato (**14–7**) and Apuleius (**299**). But Iamblichus the philosopher himself summoned up two Eroses (Eunapius *Lives of the Philosophers*, p.459 Boissonade).

## 245 A recipe for the animation of an Eros doll to fetch a woman

iv A.D.

*PGM* XII.14–95

Greek

Eros-assistant; rite of Eros. The consecration and preparation. He carries out the following functions: dream-sending and wakefulness, and he delivers one from an evil demon, if you use him properly and in holy fashion. For he has the power to do everything. Take some Etruscan wax and blend with it every kind of aromatic herb, and make an Eros eight fingers high, carrying a torch, and with a broad base to receive offerings. Let his left hand brandish a bow and arrow. Make a Psyche in similar fashion to the Eros. When you have done all this, consecrate the doll for three days. You will lay before the Eros all kinds of fresh fruits, together with seven sacrificial cakes, seven pine cones, every kind of dried fruit, seven nonred lamps and three small two-handed swords, tablets, bows, fruits of the date palm, and a bowl of honey-wine mixture. When you have done this and set these things before the Eros, as laid out, you will put the Eros on a table covered in fruit with seven lamps burning with white oil and all the things prescribed, so as to persuade this amazing Eros. On the first day, when you have put him on the table and arranged it as prescribed—I record its form in full detail for you, so that you may understand it and have no further questions—make a pure altar, namely, take two unbaked bricks and make four horns from them, on which you put the fronds of fruit. Also on the first day, take seven creatures and throttle them: one cock, a quail, a wren, a pigeon, a turtle-dove, and two chicks that happen to fall into your hands. Do not make burnt sacrifices of these creatures, but you will hold them in your hand and throttle them, while offering them up to Eros, until each of the creatures is choked and their breath passes into him. Then place the choked creatures on the altar with all sorts of aromatic herbs. On the second day throttle a male chick before Eros and burn it in holocaust, and on the third day put another chick on the altar. Perform the rite on your own and devour the chick. Let no one else be with you. If you do this in holy and pure fashion, you will get everything.

The first formula spoken with the sacrifice: "I call on you, on your beautiful bed, in your desirable house. Do a service for me and at all times carry whatever message I give you, to whatever place I send you, taking upon yourself the form of whatever god (or goddess) men and women revere, saying at once everything that is prescribed for you or spoken to you and deposited with you.

"Fire caught up with the greatest ghosts and heaven gulped down the sun-circle of the sacred scarab, called PHÔREI, without realizing it. The scarab, the winged ruler of middle heaven, was beheaded and torn apart. They destroyed his best and most glorious qualities. They shut him up and changed the lord of heaven. In this way you will serve me, against the men and women I want.

"Come here to me, master of heaven, shining over the known world, and do service for me either against men or against women, great and small, and at any one time compel them to do all the things I prescribe.

"Come here to me, master of beauty, and rouse up men and women for me, compel them by your always strong and forceful power to do all the things prescribed and uttered by me EISAPHSANTA PHOUREI ARNAI SUSUN PHREÔ RIÔBAIOSOI you are ATEPHTHO AÔREL ADÔNAI. Fill them with fear and trembling, terrify them, disturb their minds through fear of you, and do all the things written out for (insert your name). If you ignore me, the circle of the sun will burn up, and there will be darkness over the whole known world. The scarab will come down until you do for me everything I write or say, compliantly. Now, now, quickly, quickly."

Second spell, said over the sacrifice: "I adjure you, the possessor of the universe, who made the four foundations, who mixed the four winds. You are the lightning-sender; you are the thunderer; you are the shaker; you are the one who overturned everything and built it up again. Make all men and all women turn to lust for me, (insert your name, whether male or female), from whatever hour I ask you in this touch-charm [parapsimon], by command of the highest god, IAÔ ADÔNEAI ABLANATHANALBA. You are the one who embraces the Graces on the peak, LAMPSRÊ; you are the one with Compulsion in your right hand, BELTEPIACH; you are the one who releases and binds, SEMESIELAMPEKRIPH. Heed me from today and for all time."

The spell over the same sacrifice: "I call on you, gods in heaven, on the land, in the air, and on the earth, and I adjure you by the possessor of the foundations to accomplish this task for me, (insert your name), and to give me grace, a sweet tongue, and attractiveness for all men and all women in the world, so that they may be subjected to me for whatever I wish, because I am a slave of the highest god, the possessor of the universe and the all-ruler, MARMARIÔTH LASIMIÔLÊTH ARAAS [lacunas follow] . . . S . . . SÊBARBAÔTH NOÔ AÔI ÔIÊR (ornament/spice [reading disputed]). AAAAA ÊÊÊÊÊÊÊ ÔÔÔÔÔÔÔ. I command Eros, said to be in charge of these instructions, because I am god of all gods, IAÔN SABAÔTH ADÔNAI ABRASAX IARABBAI THÔURIÔ THANAKERMÊPH PANCHONAPS."

These spells should be performed and spoken over the three days, so that you render the rite perfect. Whenever you send the Eros after what you desire, just say this next spell, lifting from the table the Eros and the things set before him, and write about the things you desire on a little tablet.

The spell written on the little tablet: "You are the infant, the living god, the one with the beauty . . . SAMMÔTH SABAÔTH TABAÔTH SORPHÊ SEOURPHOUTH MOUI SI SRÔ SALAMA GÔUTH ETHEIMÊOUS OUSEIRI ESEIÊ E PHTHA NOUTH SATHAÊ Isis ACHTHI EPHANOUN BIBIOU BIBIOU SPHÊ SPHÊ ASÊÊAÊI. Go to every district and every house to which I send you, to (insert a male name), the son of (insert mother's name) (or (insert a female name), the daughter of (insert mother's name)), taking on the form of the god (or goddess) the person reveres, compel him to perform this task. (Write everything you want on the tablet with the spell.) Rouse yourself, and be terrible. I adjure you by the sacred and honored name, to which all the world is subject, PASICHTHÔN IBARBOU THARAKTITHEANÔ BABOUTHA KÔCHED AMÊN. Let this act take place, now, now . . . of the Red Sea, the one who shakes together the winds of the quarters, the one who sits on the lotus and lights up the entire known world. For you sit in the form of a crocodile. In the southern parts you are a winged snake. For this is how you are in truth. IÔIÔ BARBAR ADÔNAI KOMBALIÔPS THÔB IARMIÔOUTH. Come here to me, heed me, and address my need for action, greatest HARAMÔSI MOUCHA LINOUCHA snatcher ADÔNEAI. I am the one whom you met beneath the sacred mountain and you gave me knowledge of your greatest name. I will guard this name in holy fashion and impart it to no one, except to my fellow initiates into the sacred rites, IARBATHATRA MNÊPSIBAÔ CHNÊMEÔPS. Go and assist me in my need and work with me."

This recipe, two centuries later though it is, reveals some of the magical practices of the sort that underpinned Lucian's Glaucias narrative, **244**. Here too an Eros doll is animated to fetch a woman to the house of the practitioner, among other things. The infliction of wakefulness and the dream-sending advertised in the introduction are one with the Eros doll's act of fetching; for a literary account of an erotic dream-sending see **55**. The infliction of wakefulness is the common means of torturing the beloved until she comes. As becomes clear in the final paragraph, the Eros doll will also compel the woman to love by manifesting itself to her as a dream, in the guise of an appropriate god. Dreams were commonly regarded as winged in antiquity, like Eros himself. The throttling of the birds before the Eros in such a way that their breath passes into it seems to be a means of transferring their flying souls into it.

The Eros doll is to be made as one of a male-female pair (for which see **207, 239**), although his mate Psyche is soon forgotten in the recipe. For Eros and Psyche see **249** and, above all, Apuleius *Metamorphoses* books 4–6.

The incantations include claims to authority, and in particular the claim to have been instructed in arcane wisdom and initiated by Eros in an underground chamber (see **1–2, 53–4**). They also incorporate familiar varieties of threat for noncompliance. There are some Jewish touches (ADÔNAI, Amen) amid the heavily Egyptianizing prayers. For magical lamps see **165–6**, with commentaries.

## 246   Attraction of a woman with a model dog and a restless ghost

iv A.D.

*PGM* IV.1872–1927

Greek

Don't teach this spell to anyone, for it is exceedingly powerful and unsurpassable. It works against everyone, on the very day of its use. It binds completely and it is quite exceedingly powerful. This is it. Take four ounces of wax, eight ounces of *agnus castus* fruit, four drachmas of manna. Grind these substances down separately, mix them with pitch and more wax, and make a model of a dog, eight fingers in length, with its mouth agape. Insert into the dog's mouth a piece of skull from a man dead by violence and write the following characters on its flanks: [nine characters follow]. You will then set the dog on a tripod. Let the dog hold its right paw aloft. Inscribe on a strip these names and what you want: IAÔ ASTÔ IÔPHÊ. You will put the strip on the tripod, set the dog up on top of the strip, and repeat these names over and over. After you have uttered the spell the dog whistles <or barks [Preisendanz's supplement]>. And if it whistles, she is not coming. Say the spell over it again, and if it barks, it is bringing her. Then open the door and you will find the woman you want at your door. Have a censer by the side of the dog and put frankincense on it as you say the spell. This is the spell: "Bark-dog, I adjure you, Cerberus, by those who have hanged themselves, by the dead, and by the dead by violence. Bring me, (insert your name), the son of (insert your mother's name), (insert her name), the daughter of (insert her mother's name). I adjure you, Cerberus, by the sacred head of the underworld gods. Bring me (insert her name), the daughter of (insert her mother's name) ZOUCH ZOUKI TO PARU UPHÊBARMÔ ENÔR SEKEMI KRIOUDASEPHÊ TRIBEPSI. Bring me (insert her name), the daughter of (insert her mother's name), bring her to me, (insert your name), now, now, quickly, quickly." You will also recite the spell for all things. You will do this in a level, pure place.

THE RECIPES OF THE GREEK MAGICAL papyri often vaunt themselves, as here. The plea for secrecy also helps to project the recipe as revealed mysteries. The dog model evidently constitutes an embodiment of Cerberus; for the role of dogs in erotic magic compare **209**. The general association between the manufacture of a model, the manipulation of a ghost, and the bringing of a woman through the streets is found in Lucian's tale of Glaucias, **244**. The ghosts exploited here belong to familiar restless categories: the dead by violence and suicides (see **110, 112**).

## 247 A chameleon voodoo doll in Libanius's lecture room binds his tongue

iv A.D.

Libanius 1.243–50

Greek

**243.** Those old headaches, which had been produced by the thunder, had been in abeyance for sixteen years, but they now began to afflict me again, and more intensely. They began immediately after the great festival [of the New Year], which is held in common by the subjects of the Romans, and I was frightened of collapsing while I sat before the boys, or while lying on my couch. Every day was agonizing. I was grateful to the nights for bringing me sleep, but when day came it brought the pain with it, with the result that I even prayed to the gods and asked for death before any other beneficence, and I could not believe that the disease would not destroy my mind. **244.** As I write now, this has yet to happen, but I cannot be confident about the future. And the gods are to thank for the fact that this has not yet happened to me. For they had a diviner forbid me to open a vein and let blood, even though I was very keen to do so. The doctor said that, if this had been done, the letting of the blood would have caused a violent discharge, my head would by all means have been weakened, and it would have brought me low. **245.** While in this state I had a dream, which went like this: I thought I saw some people sacrifice two children and put one of the two dead bodies in the temple of Zeus, behind the door. I became angry at this outrage against Zeus, but some people told me that this would only be until evening, and that when this time came the body would be given over to burial. This dream seemed to reveal spells [*pharmaka*] and trickery [*manganeumata*] and war against me by sorcerers [*goêtes*]. **246.** This had the due effect of inducing those fears and the desire for nothing but death. This it was that formed the subject of my conversations with my companions at any one time, and of my prayers to the gods. If someone made mention of a trip to the baths, he was my enemy, likewise if he made mention of dinner, and I fled from books containing the works of the ancients, and from the writing and developing of speeches. My ability to speak had been destroyed, even though the young men emphatically asked to hear me. For whenever I applied myself to it, I would be distracted, like a little boat in a contrary wind. There they were, expecting a lecture, but I could only be silent. The doctors told me to look for a cure somewhere else, since they had no appropriate drugs/spells [*pharmaka*] in their craft. **247.** They and others decided that the same cause was responsible for the pain I was experiencing in my ankle-joints, a double dose, which was something I had not had before, in both winter and summer. The ailment brought its investigators to say that I would die in the course of the next day. Other cities actually thought I had died, and they asked our many ambassadors whether this was actually the case. **248.** Anyway, some of my friends were pushing me and each other to take action against the people who were believed to have contrived my affliction. But I did not feel the same way about it myself and I reined them in. I told them that they should pray rather than have people dragged off for dark schemes. **249.** However, a chameleon, of uncertain origin, was discovered in the classroom. It had been there a long time, and had been dead for many months. We saw that its head had been placed between its hind feet. Of its forefeet, one was nowhere to be seen, and the other was closing its mouth to keep it silent. **250.** Not even after a revelation of this magnitude did I associate a name with this discovery, but it seemed to me that the people who had this on their conscience were overtaken by fear and that they backed off, and that I regained my mobility. It was an improvement in my fortune that the things which had been buried were now lying on the ground for anyone who wanted to see.

The chameleon had been mutilated in a fashion broadly comparable to that of some surviving human-shaped dolls. The mutilations are particularly appropriate to the binding of speech: the lizard is beheaded and, further to this, its mouth is stopped up. The missing forelimb was doubtless the "right arm" with which an orator would gesticulate; compare **105**. Curse tablets and voodoo dolls alike need not be deposited in graves; as here, they can be deposited in a place of special significance for the victim. Perhaps some human cadaverous material was associated with it, in order to engage a ghost; or perhaps the dead chameleon itself afforded the services of its own ghost. This narrative gives one an impression of what it felt like physically to be subject to a binding curse; compare **184**. For more Libanius see **300**.

# 13
## *Amulets*

Amulets were the most pervasive of magical tools in antiquity. At the simplest level, they were a protective or empowering magical bond: the basic Greek term for amulet, *periamma* (or *periapton*), literally means "object tied around." Amulets consisting of little more than tied threads or material are to be found in **248, 254, 256**. From the imperial period a number of extended amulet texts survive, usually inscribed on silver lamellas or papyrus strips that were rolled up, like curse tablets, and then worn in a bronze tube or fabric pouch around the neck. From this period also survive vast numbers of intaglios, engraved gemstones that could be used in rings or in clothing, some of which include brief inscribed texts. For excerpts bearing upon amulets elsewhere see **21, 47, 131, 193**. For rings elsewhere see **127**.

## EROTIC AMULETS

### 248 Hera deceitfully borrows Aphrodite's "embroidered band" to seduce Zeus

vii B.C. or earlier

Homer *Iliad* 14 197–222

Greek

Lady Hera addressed Aphrodite with cunning in her mind: "Now give me love and desire, with which you subdue all the immortals and mortal men too. For I am going to go to see the boundaries of the bountiful earth and Oceanus, the sire of the gods, and mother Tethys, who reared and nurtured me in their house, after they had taken me over from Rheia, when far-sounding Zeus forced Cronus beneath the land and the unharvested sea. I am going to go and see them, and to settle their unresolved disputes. For they have been avoiding sex and love with each other for a long time now, since anger fell upon their hearts. If I could talk the couple's dear hearts round, and bring them to go to bed and unite with each other in love, they would evermore call me dear and revere me."

Laughter-loving Aphrodite replied to her: "It is neither possible nor seemly to deny your request, for you sleep in the arms of the greatest god, Zeus."

So she spoke, and she took her variegated embroidered band [*kestos himas*] from her breast, in which she had wrought all charms. In it there was love, in it there was desire, in it there was sweet intimacy, which steals the wits of even the sensible. She put it into Hera's hands and spoke to her, addressing her by name: "Take this variegated band now, in which all things have been wrought, and tie it across your bosom. I can tell you that you will not come back without effecting the thing you desire in your heart."

APHRODITE'S EMBROIDERED BAND FUNCTIONS AS A love amulet. Hera tricks Aphrodite into letting her borrow it. Her real purpose is to use it to seduce her husband, Zeus, in which she is successful. It is unclear what Aphrodite understands as she lends Hera the band. Does she think she will simply pass it on to Tethys, who will use it to seduce Oceanus? Or does she think that Hera will herself wear it and use the charm's effects simply to make herself more agreeable and persuasive in her peace-making? The band is almost certainly to be understood here as the "saltire" Aphrodite is sometimes depicted as wearing in statuary (e.g., *LIMC* nos. 779, 1083). This consists of a pair of straps worn over the upper torso and crossed over the breasts, like a "cross-your-heart" bra. They emphasize the shape and prominence of the breasts beneath a loose-fitting *peplos*-dress. The function of such a band as an erotic charm is therefore self-evident. Embroidery often carried magical connotations, as, more widely, did the twisting-together of threads of different colors (**90, 254**). The *Cyranides* (1.10.49–100; for this work see **253**) obscurely describes two broad types of "embroidered band" of Aphrodite, of which the second may include the saltire. The text prescribes a series of intaglios to be fitted to the band, but, as can be seen from **254**, bands of thread could be powerful in themselves.

## 249 A green jasper intaglio with Eros and Psyche for erotic attraction

OBV.: Eros. "As you me, so I you."
REV.: Iao.

Period of Roman empire

Delatte and Derchain 1964, no. 324

Greek

THE OBVERSE LEGENDS RELATE TO AN illustration of a naked, winged Eros setting a torch to the feet of a naked, winged Psyche, who is tied to a tree. The reverse of the gem portrays a cock-headed anguipede ("snake-foot"), with the legend "Iao"; this demon, similarly portrayed elsewhere, evidently powers the spell. The gem instills in a woman the burning erotic desire that she herself instills in the wearer. For another example of the projection of the mythical couple Eros and Psyche onto lover and beloved in a magical context see **245**.

One of the recipes among the formularies of the Greek magical papyri, *PGM* IV. 1716–1870, "The Sword of Dardanus," prescribes the manufacture of an intaglio from a magnetic stone for erotic attraction, the imagery of which partly coincides with this one and with that of the intaglio given in **250**. On the obverse Aphrodite, touching her hair (compare **253**), sits astride Psyche, and Eros burns Psyche's feet with a torch. On the reverse Eros and Psyche embrace each other.

## 250 A green jasper intaglio with copulating couple for erotic attraction, from Tarsus in Cilicia

OBV.: Grace. Desires.
REV.: Reciprocated love of my soul.

Period of Roman empire

Delatte and Derchain 1964, no. 329

Greek

BOTH SIDES OF THE INTAGLIO PORTRAY a naked couple (Eros and Psyche?) in sexual congress on a bed; on the obverse the woman sits astride the man in the "riding" position: see figures 13.1 and 13.2. The imagery partly corresponds with that of the intaglio prescribed in the "Sword of Dardanus" recipe (see **249**).

Figure 13.1. Graeco-Egyptian erotic-magical green jasper intaglio with copulating couple (Eros and Psyche?); (a) obverse; (b) reverse. Paris, Bibliothèque nationale cat. no. 2208 (Delatte and Derchain 1964, no. 329). Photograph © Bibliothèque nationale de France.

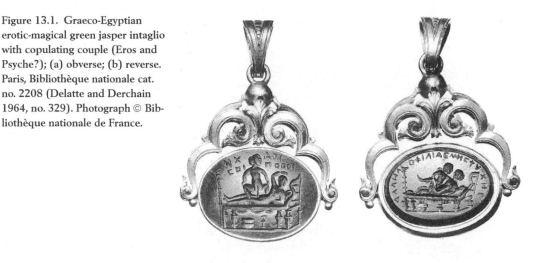

## 251 Erotic (?) demon-redirecting amulet, gold lamella, from Orsova in Romania

Demon hanging over me in this place, go and do your hanging at Julia Cyrilla's house, for me, now, now.

ii A.D.

Kotansky 1994, no. 24

Latin

THIS LAMELLA WAS FOUND IN A building identified as a workshop. It also includes some signs on its left side that are difficult to decipher. They may be vowels and a crude drawing of the demon. Kotansky compares the Demotic recipe *PDM* xiv 1070–7, where one inscribes a reed leaf and sleeps on it to receive dreams oneself but also to send dreams to fetch a woman. So perhaps this amulet was made by a man who wanted to exploit a dream demon that was visiting him to improve his love life.

## 252 Amulet bestowing the favor of Aphrodite and sexual success on a woman, gold lamella, from Thessaloniki

ON PAOCHOI. The name of Aphrodite: PAITH PHTHA PHÔZA PAIPHÔUTH LAEILAPS CHERSUBAÔ MITHRÊI. Make grace, success for her with all people [*anthrôpoi*] and women, and especially before the man before whom she herself wishes it.

ii A.D.

Kotansky 1994, no. 40

Greek

THIS AMULET SEEMS TO BESTOW AT once both general success in relationships and sexual success with the man of the wearer's desires. It draws its power from the invocation of Aphrodite's secret name. The *voces magicae* of which this consists can be seen to make use of the names of Ptah and Mithras and the Greek word for "hurricane," *lailaps*.

## 253 An opal-stone amulet bestows sexual attraction and general favor

Aphrodite, binding up the hair and the locks on her head, is engraved on the all-gold *euanthês* stone [i.e., blue opal

iv A.D.

*Cyranides* 1.4.45–51; Waegeman 1987, epsilon

Greek

(?)]. The root of the plant [i.e., rocket, *euzômos*] is put underneath the stone, together with the tongue of a nightingale [i.e., *euboê*]. When you have set the stone in its ring, wear it. You will be loved by all men, famous and sweet-tongued, not only to people, but also to gods and demons, and every beast will flee before you.

THE *CYRANIDES* DISCUSSES THE MAGICAL POWERS of animals, plants, and stones. The text as we know it was compiled by a number of hands across a number of centuries but built around an original core composed by Harpocration of Alexandria in the fourth century A.D., now forming its first book. Harpocration's prologue tells that his work conveys revelations of Hermes Trismegistus, the god of Hermeticism, which he had found as a traveler in Mesopotamia inscribed on an iron stele amid three ruined towers near Babylon. The stele had been retrieved from a Syrian lake, and its text was translated from the Syriac for him by an old Syrian companion (compare broadly, **46, 53**). This first book addresses the sympathetic, unifying forces of the universe as manifested in the four elements of air, earth, water, and fire. These elements are embodied in, respectively, birds, plants, fish, and stones. It is the Greek alphabet (not any found in Mesopotamia!) that provides the key to the connections between the different elements. Each of the book's twenty-four chapters, one for each letter, discusses the powers of a representative of each of the four elements, the names of which all begin with this letter. The chapters prescribe the assembly of amulets using items from among those so collated.

The amulet prescribed here derives from the epsilon chapter; it does not use the representative of the sea element, the sea urchin (*echinos ichthuoeidês*). For the erotic or more generally charming power of Aphrodite touching her hair compare **249**; it may be significant that she is associated with an act of "binding," and that this in turn is associated with hair, commonly used as "stuff" or *ousia*, in binding spells. *Cyranides* tells that the *euanthês* stone was sacred to Aphrodite; she was particularly associated with blue stones. Rocket was considered aphrodisiac. The significance of the nightingale's sweet tongue is self-evident. For another Aphrodite amulet in *Cyranides* see **229**.

## 254   A old woman activates a twisted-thread antiimpotence amulet

Ca. 66 A.D.

Petronius *Satyricon* 131

Greek

I strolled about a bit and had sat down in the same place as the day before, but Chrysis soon came along, dragging a little old woman after her. After saying hello she asked, "Well, my proud man, have you begun to feel better?" The old woman produced a cord from the folds of her dress, twisted together from threads of different color, and she tied it around my neck. Then she mixed some dust up with spit, took it up on her middle finger, and drew a sign on my forehead, despite my objections. . . . When she had completed the spell she bade me spit three times over and drop some pebbles down my robe three times over. She had kept these stones, which she had charmed, wrapped up in purple. She applied her hands and began to test the vigor of my loins. Sooner than you could say it, the muscles jumped to the command, and the old woman's hands were filled with the great upheaval. She was overjoyed and said, "Do you see, my Chrysis, what a hare [*leporem*] this thing is that I have started for others to chase?"

THIS NARRATIVE FEATURES THE SIMPLEST OF amulets, a mere band of thread; for magical threads twisted from three colors see **90, 248**; for magical threads more generally see **89, 96, 102–3, 107, 225**, and Pliny *Natural History* 28.48 (a knotted-thread amulet tied around the groin). For witches in the Latin novels, see **104–7**. For aversive spitting compare **193**. The old woman's final question may include a pun. *Leporem*, "hare," from *lepus*, almost coincides with *lepôrem*, "charm, attractiveness."

**255 A recipe for a contraceptive amulet** A contraceptive spell: Take a bean with an insect in it, and fasten it around yourself as a amulet.

ii/iii B.C.

*PGM* LXIII.24–5

Greek

THE BEAN IS PERHAPS TO BE construed as "pregnant" with the bug, a life-form inside a life-form, and so blocks further pregnancy in the woman with whom it is associated. For magical contraception see **235**.

## HEALING AND EXORCISTIC AMULETS

For further sources for healing magic see **13, 47, 51**, with commentary.

**256 Odysseus's wound is healed with a binding and an incantation** The boar gored him first above the knee, and by charging him sideways tore off a great deal of flesh with its tusk, but it did not penetrate all the way to the bone. Odysseus aimed at its right shoulder and struck it there. The point of his shining spear went right through. It fell down in the dirt with a bellow, and its life flew away. The dear sons of Autolycus busied themselves with the leg. They skilfully bound [*dêsan*] the wound of the blameless, godlike Odysseus, and they staunched the black blood with an incantation. Then they soon came back to the house of their dear father.

vii B.C. or earlier

Homer *Odyssey* 19.449–58

Greek

THE USE OF THE INCANTATION HERE suggests that the binding of Odysseus's thigh may have had an amuletic significance as well as a practical one.

**257 Asclepius's healing technology** People came to Asclepius afflicted with nature's sores, or with limbs wounded by gray bronze or a stone flung from afar, or with their frame racked by summer fever or by winter cold. He would free them and deliver them from their respective agonies. Some he tended with gentle incantations. Others he tended with mild drugs [*pharmaka*]: either they drank them, or he fastened them all around their limbs. Others again he set back upon their feet with surgery.

Earlier v B.C.

Pindar *Pythian* 3.47–53

Greek

IN THIS IMPORTANT EARLY SUMMARY OF the healing god's techniques there is no differentiation between what we might regard as "magical" and "medical." The term *pharmaka* appears to be applied equally to ingested drugs and externally applied amulets.

**258 A cure for fracture and dislocation with a binding and an incantation** If you have a dislocation of any sort, it will be healed by this incantation. Take a green reed four or five feet long, split it down the middle, and have two men apply it to your hips. Begin the incantation, *motas vaeta daries dardares astataries dissunapiter*, until they come together. Wave a knife over them. When they have met and are touching each other, take the reed in your hand and cut it short on both right and left sides. Bind the reed-pieces to your dislocation or fracture and it will heal. Even so, use the incantation on a daily basis. Or, for a dislocation, you can use this one: *huat haut haut istasis tarsis ardannabou dannaustra*.

Ca. 160 B.C.

Cato *De agri cultura* 160

Latin

THE COMBINATION OF MAGICO-MEDICAL BINDING and incantation is similar to that in **256**. The terms of the incantations resist interpretation and are best considered *voces magicae*.

## 259  An amulet is attached to the dying Pericles

Early ii A.D.

Plutarch *Pericles* 38

Greek

At that time, as it seems, the plague attacked Pericles, not violently, as happened to others, or vigorously, but by gradual degrees. It progressed through various phases over its course and bit by bit exhausted his body and subverted his high-minded soul. At any rate Theophrastus has inquired in his *Ethics* [L21 Fortenbaugh] whether one's character is molded by one's fortunes and relinquishes virtue under the compulsion of bodily suffering. He has told the story that when Pericles was sick he drew attention to the amulet that had been fastened round his neck by the women to one of his friends who came to visit him, so implying that he was in a very bad way if he was allowing himself to be subjected to this stupidity.

THE BELIEF IS IMPLIED THAT WOMEN in particular were devoted to amulets. A similar tale is told of Bion of Borysthenes (Diogenes Laertius 4.54).

## 260  The historiola of Antaura the female migraine demon; a migraine amulet, silver lamella, from Altenburg in Austria

i/ii A.D.

Kotansky 1994, no. 13

Greek

For half-of-the-head. Antaura came up out of the sea, she shouted out like a deer, she cried aloud like an ox. Ephesian Artemis meets her: "Antaura, where are you taking yourself?" "Into the half-of-the-head." "You certainly will not go into the . . ."

THIS IS ONE OF FOUR LAMELLAE found in a third-century A.D. stone coffin at Altenburg, Roman Carnuntum. The vivid Greek term for migraine, *hêmikranon*, "half-of-the-head," lies at the root of our own word's etymology. The etymology of Antaura's personal name suggests that she is visualized as a wind. The text, incompletely preserved, supplies us with the most distinctive use of a *historiola* in ancient magical documents. The paradigmatic tale of Artemis's dismissal of Antaura as she makes her way into a victim's head deters her and her fellow migraine demons from attempting to enter the wearer's head. The verbal exchange in direct speech is striking. A group of remarkably similar *historiolas* survive in some Byzantine prayers, with the role of Artemis assumed by Christ and Michael. One even preserves the derivative name "Abra" (pronounced "Avra") for the demon (in modern Greek Antaura would be pronounced "Andavra"). The course of the Byzantine prayers suggest that in the lost portion of the ancient *historiola* Artemis went on to divert Antaura into the head of a bull in the mountains. Kotansky concludes that the amulet had been passed down within a family of sufferers: the lamella is significantly older than the coffin in which it was found; it is not, at any rate in its preserved section, customized for one named wearer; and migraine is hereditary. For other *historiolas* see **206, 261**.

## 261  Antiheadache incantation, with *historiola*, attributed to the Thessalian Philinna; papyrus recipe

i B.C.

*PGM* XX.13–9

Greek

Incantation of the Thessalian Philinna to combat headache. "Flee, pain in the head, vanish and flee under a rock. Wolves flee, single-hoofed horses . . . with blows . . ."

THIS FRAGMENTARY RECIPE, FROM ONE OF the older texts in the corpus of Greek Magical Papyri, derives its authority from a Thessalian witch; compare **96-107**. There was a famous Thessalian Philinna, the wife of Philip II and mother of Philip Arrhidaeus, although she is not otherwise associated with witchcraft. Olympias, however, a rival wife of Philip and mother of Alexander the Great, was strongly associated with magic (**55**) and in particular was said to have turned Philip Arrhidaeus's mind feeble with drugs as part of her rivalry with Philinna (87). The incantation was presumably intended for writing out onto an amulet but could also simply have been uttered. As amulets sometimes do, it makes use of a *historiola*, "Wolves flee . . . ," for which see 260.

## 262 A hematite intaglio delivers Priscus from liver pain

Period of Roman empire

Delatte and Derchain 1964, no. 461

Greek

OBV.: I call on you, Lord, I KAITHBRUTHIBUA PHIAÊMETHÔR SPHÔI IEPHÊMIN ENROUCHAN ANEMESÊRINTHRA name [characters] IMÊN.
REV.: BALALOU SÊMINASTHENSIE, deliver Priscus from pain in the liver.

THIS UNILLUSTRATED HEMATITE INTAGLIO USES Judaeo-Christian language.

## 263 Jewish exorcism of hysteria from the ("wandering") womb, gold lamella, from Beirut

i B.C./i A.D.

Kotansky 1994, no. 51

Greek

I adjure [*exorcizô*] you, womb of (insert your name), to whom (insert your mother's name) gave birth—so that you may never leave your place—in the name of the Lord God, living and invincible, to remain in place within (insert your name), to whom (insert your mother's name) gave birth.

THE TEXT OF THIS GOLD LAMELLA, found in a golden tube (see figure 13.2), combines Jewish divine apparatus with Greek medical theory. The Greeks commonly regarded the womb (*hystera*) as the chief cause of sickness in women (hence *hysteria*), as it detached itself from its location and wandered around the torso interfering with other organs (see Aretaeus of Cappadocia *On the Causes and Symptoms of Acute Diseases* 2 for a graphic description of the phenomenon and remedies for it). Accordingly, this protective amulet promotes a woman's health by fixing her womb in its place. The use of blank formulas here suggests either that the amulet has been designed to serve any number of women, or that the maker has misinterpreted a recipe and failed to realize that she (?) should have incorporated her own name. The term used for the blank formulas here is not the usual *hê deina* but *ipsa*, the Latin word "she herself," transcribed in Greek letters. (It remains possible that *Ipsa* is

Figure 13.2. Exorcistic amulet; bronze capsule and inscribed gold lamella; 7(a) capsule; (b) lamella, obverse; (c) lamella, reverse. Paris, Bibliothèque nationale cat. no. Froehner 287; Kotansky 1994, no. 51. Photograph © Bibliothèque nationale de France.

after all an actual proper name shared by mother and daughter.) The use of the maternal lineage seems particularly thematically appropriate here.

### 264  Papyrus Abrasax amulet protects Sophia-Priscilla from illness, ghosts, and demons

iv A.D.

*Suppl. Mag.* 13 (PGM LXXXIX)

Greek

SÔ SÔ ABRASAX [character] ABRASAX. I am ABRASAX ABRASI CHÔ OU. Come to the aid of little Sophia, a.k.a. Priscilla. Restrain and render ineffectual the attacker of little Sophia, a.k.a. Priscilla, whether it is shivering, restrain it, whether it is a ghost, restrain it, whether it is a demon, restrain it. SÔ SÔ ABRASAX ABRASAX, I am ABRASAX ABRASI CHÔ OU. Restrain and render ineffectual the things that attack little Sophia, a.k.a. Priscilla, on this very day, whether it is shivering, restrain it, whether it is a demon, render it ineffectual.

THE NAMES SOPHIA AND PRISCILLA IMPLY that the wearer of this amulet was Christian, for all the amulet's identification with pagan powers for its authority. The description of Sophia-Priscilla as "little" suggests that the amulet was made by parents for their child.

### 265  Spirit-repelling amulet for a woman, gold lamella, from Rome

Period of Roman empire

Kotansky 1994, no. 25

Greek

Drive off from R———ia any spirit that is wicked, evil-doing, and destructive. PTA NEBR AN THABIASA.

AS WITH EXORCISM NARRATIVES (**127–32**), the Jewish influence on exorcistic amulets is often clear and can be seen here in the phraseology "spirit . . . wicked." The first three *voces magicae*, however, may be construed as "Ptah entirely beautiful" in Egyptian. The name of the woman to be protected could not be satisfactorily deciphered before the text was lost.

### 266  A Nemesis-stone ring exorcises and averts demons

iv A.D.

*Cyranides* 1.13.16–29; Waegeman 1987, nu

Greek

The Nemesis-stone is a stone taken from the altar of Nemesis. Nemesis is engraved on the stone standing with her foot on a wheel. Her form is that of a maiden, brandishing a cubit ruler in her left hand, and a staff in her right. You will enclose under the stone the wing-tip of a duck [*nêssa*] and a small piece of the plant [i.e., mullein, *nekua*, literally "death plant"].

If you apply this ring to a possessed man, the demon will at once confess himself and flee. It also cures moonstruck people if worn round the neck. It averts manifestations of demons in dreams, the terrors that afflict children and nightmares. The wearer must avoid everything abominable.

When worn this ring indicates the number of years of your lifetime, together with the manner and place of your death. The wearer must avoid everything wicked.

THE REPRESENTATIVE OF THE WATER ELEMENT not used by this n-amulet is *naukratês ichthus*, the "ship-stopping fish," also known as the *echeneis* (compare **155**). Nemesis is a suitable goddess to invoke against malicious demons because she punishes those who exceed the measure, hence her cubit ruler. Her wheel is usually construed as the Wheel of Fortune. As the "death plant," mullein self-evidently lends itself to the prediction of death, a sort of prediction particularly associated with necromancy (e.g., **157**). For necromantic rings see *PGM* V.213–303 and XII.270–350 and **275**. The plant seems to be used to protect against demons, presumably demons of the dead (*nekudai-*

*mones*) in the first instance, on the "fighting fire with fire" principle (for which see Faraone 1992c). For the self-confession of an exorcised demon see **127–32** and note the use of the ring in **127**.

## PROTECTIVE AND LUCKY AMULETS

### 267  Amulet protecting Rufina from a lawsuit, silver lamella, from Amisos in Pontus

i B.C./i A.D.

Kotansky 1994, no. 36

Greek

I am the great god sitting in heaven, the mobile sphere of the entire universe, Arsenophrephres, the secure name MIARSAU, like the good demon BARICHAA KMÊPHI, the king over kings, ABRIAÔTH ALARPHÖTH OI SÉTHTH, the one that is. Let the evil manifest itself no more. Send away, send away the lawsuit from Rufina. And if anyone wrongs me in the future, turn them away. Let no poison/drug/spell [*pharmakon*] harm me, the king of kings, NARBIAÔN TÔ ORTHIARÊ. I am king over this place in the name of Mousa.

THIS AMULET WAS CUSTOM MADE, AS they often were, for a particular, named individual: Rufina. It protects her in the first instance from a specific lawsuit, but it is also endowed with more general protective powers for the future and the power to defend her against poisonous/magical attacks. For the use of magic as a defense against magic see **269**, with commentary. Rufina or her amulet claims authority through self-identification with the divine. The great king of Pontus, Mithridates VI Eupator (120–63 B.C.), at one time resident at Amisos, exercises a considerable influence on this text. He is saluted in the phrase "king of kings," a title accorded him in an Augustan-period inscription. And, like the "king of kings" here, he was invulnerable to poison; the notion of a "*pharmakon* of Mithridates," supposedly the antidote with which he had protected himself, subsequently flourished in antiquity. Mousa Orsobaris was Mithridates's daughter.

### 268  An amulet to protect fields from hailstones, bronze lamella, from Avignon in France

ii A.D.

Kotansky 1994, no. 11 A

Greek

THÔSOUDERKUÔ vineyard NOUMIXÔNTHEI. Divert from this place all hailstones and all snow and everything that damages the place. This is the command of the god ÔAMOUTHA. You too help in this, ABRASAX IAÊ IAÔ.

THIS TEXT WAS FOUND CLOSE TO another one, Kotansky 1994, 11 B. That one is less well preserved but is identical, such as it is, save that at the end it also records the name "Julius Pervincus." The farmer Julius Pervincus would have set such amulets up around his fields or inserted them into them.

### 269  Amulet against sorcery and demons, silver lamella, from Beroea in Syria

ii/iii A.D.

Kotansky 1994, no. 46

Greek

[Among characters] BOTÊZ . . . EUU . . . DÔ . . . ES. Deliver Juliana from all witchcraft/poisoning [*pharmakia*] and all suffering and all active attack and the manifestation of demons, night and day, now, now, quickly, quickly, at once, at once, at once.

ALMOST CERTAINLY *PHARMAKIA* HERE IS TO be understood as witchcraft, and the amulet seeks to use magical defense against magical attack. For magical defenses against magic compare **47, 169, 184, 188, 270, 273, 300**.

## 270  A recipe for an amulet against spells

iv A.D.

PGM XXXVI.256–64;
CT no. 130

Greek

Take a triangular potsherd from the place where three roads meet. Take it up in your left hand, inscribe it with myrrh ink, and conceal it: "ASTRAÊLOS CHRAÊLOS, ruin every spell that is cast against me, (insert your name), because I adjure you by the great and terrifying names, the names the winds shudder at, the names at the sound of which the rocks shatter [seven characters]."

HERE AGAIN IS AN AMULET DESIGNED to protect against magical attack; compare **269**. Crossroads were sacred to Hecate. The *voces magicae* are Jewish.

## 271  Victory charm, gold lamella, from Rome

i B.C./i A.D.

Kotansky 1994, no. 28

Greek

Lord Sarapis, always at work, grant me victory over the names below.

THIS AMULET'S FUNCTION SEEMS SIMILAR TO that of a competition curse-tablet (compare **173**), and it was indeed found inside the mouth of a skull, in a terracotta urn, in a crypt near the tombs of the Scipios. However, Jordan suggests rather that the amulet was put in the corpse's mouth to serve as a coin to pay Charon to ferry the dead man across the underworld river (compare **148**). No names, it seems, were ever "written below." A recipe has perhaps been crudely followed, with specific names omitted to give the amulet wider usefulness.

## 272  A marble intaglio bestows favor on Candidus for a circus race

Period of Roman
empire

Delatte and Derchain
1964, no. 468

Greek

Favor to Candidus!

THE SIMPLE TEXT OF THIS MARBLE intaglio is accompanied by drawings of a whip and a victor's crown, which indicate is context and function; see **173**.

## 273  A multipurpose amulet consisting of three verses of Homer

iv A.D.

PGM IV.2145–2240

Greek

Three lines of Homer as an assistant.

"So speaking, he drove the uncloven-hoofed horses through the ditch" [Homer *Iliad* 10.564]

"And men gasping amid the dreadful slaughter" [Homer *Iliad* 10.521]

"And they themselves washed off all their sweat in the sea" [Homer *Iliad* 10.572]

If a runaway slave wears these lines inscribed on an iron tablet, he will never be discovered. Similarly, put the same lamella around someone who is just about to die, as an amulet, and you will learn everything that you ask. If anyone thinks he has become the victim of a binding spell, let him proclaim the lines while sprinkling seawater [lacuna] . . . against enchantments. An athlete who wears the tablet remains unbeaten, and so does the charioteer who wears the tablet together with lodestone. Similarly in the courtroom. A single-combat gladiator should wear them. Attach it to a condemned and jugulated man, recite the lines into his ear, and he will tell you everything you want. Place the tablet into his wound and you will do well with those above you or your masters or other people. You will be respected and trusted. It also dismisses demons and wild beasts. Everyone will be frightened of you, you will be unwounded in war, ask and you shall receive, you will acquire grace, you will be transformed. Whatever woman or man you have dealings with, you will be loved by them. You will be respected, blessed. Bequests will be made to you. You will be lucky. You will get the better of drugs/spells [*pharamaka*] used against you. You will undo binding spells and you will defeat your enemies.

This is the spell that is recited when you dip the tablet: "(Insert name), leave the sweet light and perform for me any service I need, whenever I summon you (add the commonplaces), because I adjure you by the underworld gods, GONGU-LORUNCHE OMBROLIGMATE THOÊRUSÊRIS. Serve me in the end for which I summon you." Speak the spell that works over all.

Consecration of the tablet. Go into a pure house and set up a table. On this there should be some clean linen and seasonal flowers. Sacrifice a white cockerel. Beside it should be placed seven round cakes, seven flat cakes, and seven lamps. Make a libation of milk, honey, wine, and olive oil. This is the spell spoken when you consecrate the tablet: "Come to me, master ruling above the earth and beneath the earth, watching the west and the east, and looking to the south and the north, master of all things, Eternity [Aion] of Eternities. You are the ruler of the universe, Ra, Pan AR PENCHNOUBI BRINTATÊNÔPHRI BRISKULMA AROUZARBA MESENKRIPHI NIPTOUMI CHMOUMAÔPHI IA IOU IUÔ AII OUÔ AEÊIOUÔ BAUBÔ BAUBÔ PHORBA PHORBA OREOBAZAGRA ÔUOILLA ER." Say the spell over Compulsion: "MASKELLI (spell) IARCHTHA ECHTHABA CHOIX IABOUCH IABÔCH." This is the basic rite. Here are its applications.

For divination. Write the following text on a laurel leaf in myrrh-ink mixed with the blood of a man dead-by-violence and place it under the tablet: "ABRAA, you are the revealer of everything, MARIAPHRAX."

For smashing chariots. Sacrifice lone-growing garlic and snake's slough and inscribe a tin tablet: "NEBOUTOSOUALÊTH BEU ERBÊTH PAKERBÊTH and ÔNOUPH. Defeat (insert his name) and his men." Bury the tablet in the tomb of a man dead-before-his-time for three days. He will be active as he lies there.

For restraining spells. Make an inscription on a shell from the sea from the ink mentioned hereafter and add some Typhon's blood. Bury it in the tomb of a man dead-before-his time when the moon is opposite the sun. The lines inscribed are the three and the following: "IÔ BOLCHOSÊTH IAKOUB IAI IÔ PATATHNAX ERBÊTH IÔ PAKERBÊTH." The tablet is to be hung [i.e., around the neck], as in the first instructions.

For spells to bring favor and love-spells. Write on a golden tablet: "MURI MURI NES MACHESNÔN." Place it underneath the iron tablet for three days to prepare it, then take it up and wear it in pure fashion.

For spells of attraction. Sacrifice roses and sumac. Take myrtle leaves and inscribe them with the ink: "STHENEPIÔ ARRÔRIPHRASIS UUUU IIII, bring (insert her name) for (insert your name)." Say the spell and place her stuff [*ousia*] under the tablet. Add some single-stem wormwood into the myrrh-ink. The tablet should be hung on a woolen string. Take it from the places where the wool-workers do their business.

FOR HOMER-MAGIC SEE ALSO **167**. Here the unrelated lines have a variety of functions in amuletic form. They enable prophecy in association with both the dead (compare **158–62**) and the dying. The dying were held to enjoy prophetic abilities, not just for their kinship with those already dead but more particularly because their souls were in the process of being released from the body and hence into a state of purer percipience; compare **133**. The various properties attributed to the lines can all be found, separately, in other amulets, thus: protection against binding-spells and other magic, **269**; victory in competition, **271–2** (and compare **173**); grace and erotic attraction, **248–55**; protection in court, **267** (and compare **168–72**). For the dead-by-violence see **110, 112**. For magical lamps see **165–6**, with commentaries. For purifications in advance of magical rites see **53, 148**.

## 274   Invisibility is conferred by the ring of Gyges

Mid–iv B.C.

Plato *Republic* 359d–60b

Greek

[Gyges] was a shepherd and servant of the current ruler of Lydia. One day there was a great deal of rain and an earthquake, and part of the ground was broken open. A chasm appeared at the point where he was pasturing his flocks. According to myth, he saw it, was amazed, and descended into it. Among the wonderful things he saw was a hollow bronze horse with doors in it. He peeped through these and saw a dead body inside of seemingly greater than human size. The corpse had no adornment except for a gold ring on its hand, which Gyges removed before leaving. The shepherds were gathering as usual to make their monthly reports on their flocks to the king. Gyges came too, wearing the ring. He sat with the others, and by chance turned the ring's bezel toward himself, into the inside of his hand. Upon this he became invisible to those sitting beside him, and they spoke of him as if he had left. He was amazed, and feeling over the ring again he turned the bezel back to the outside, and once he had turned it he became visible. He reflected on this and experimented with the ring, to see if this power emanated from it, and he discovered that he became invisible when he turned the bezel to the inside, but reappeared when he turned it to the outside. On realizing this he at once contrived to become one of the messengers sent to the king. He came to him, seduced his wife, and with her help attacked the king, killed him, and took the crown.

THIS PASSAGE ILLUMINATES A POSSIBLE MEANS of directly accessing and activating powers already conferred on a ring; for the method compare **275**. For another ring of invisibility see **276**, and for another means to magical invisibility see **277**. For invisible witches see **72, 106**.

## 275   An Arab's ring protects against a manifestation of Hecate

ii A.D.

Lucian *Philopseudes* 17, 22–4 (edited)

Greek

22. "Listen to this then," said Eucrates, "—and I have witnesses to it—something I saw five years ago. It happened to be around harvest time in the year. I was on the farm at midday. I left the workers to their grape-picking and went off on my own into the wood. I had something on my mind I wanted to mull over. Once I was under the tree canopy, there came, first of all, a barking of dogs, and I guessed that my son Mnason was at sport and running to hounds, as so often, and that he had come into the forest with his comrades. But that was not it. Soon, there was an earthquake and, simultaneously, a shout like thunder. I saw a fearsome woman approaching me, almost half a stadium's length high. In her left hand she held a torch and in her right a sword twenty cubits long. Below the waist she had snake-feet; above it she resembled a Gorgon, so far as concerns the look in her eyes and her terrible appearance, I mean. Instead of hair, writhing snakes fell down in curls around her neck, and some of them coiled over her shoulders. See, my friends," he said, "how my hair stands on end at my mere telling of the story." As he spoke he showed Eucrates the hairs on his forearm, supposedly bristling from fear.

23. Ion, Dinomachus, and Cleodemus and their fellows gaped at him in rapt attention, old men being led along by the nose, virtually doing obeisance before such

an implausible colossus, a woman the height of half a stadium's length, a giant bogie. In the meantime I reflected that men of this sort associated with the young to teach them wisdom, and were admired by many, but that it was only their white hair and their beards that distinguished them from babies. In fact, babies were less gullible than they were. **24.** Thus Dinomachus asked, "Tell me, Eucrates, how big were the goddess's dogs?"

"They were taller than Indian elephants," came the reply, "similarly black and shaggy, with dirty, matted hair. Anyway, when I saw her, I came to a halt and at the same time turned back the seal-ring that the Arab had given me to the inside of my finger. Hecate stamped on the ground with her snake foot and created a huge chasm, as deep as Tartarus. Presently, she jumped into it and was gone. I steeled myself and bent over it, after taking hold of a tree that was growing near the hole, in case I got vertigo and fell into it headlong. Then I saw everything in Hades, Pyriphlegethon, the lake, Cerberus, and the dead, whom I could see so clearly that I even recognized some of them. I got a good view of my father, still dressed in the clothes in which we had buried him. . . . As soon as I had seen everything to my satisfaction, the chasm came together and closed itself."

HERE WE HAVE A CLEAR AND simple example of a seal-ring being used as a phylactery against the horrors of the underworld. Its method of activation corresponds to that of the ring of Gyges (**274**). An early attestation of such protective rings is provided by Aristophanes *Wealth* 883–4 (388 B.C.), where we find the joking notion that one may wear a ring, bought for no more than a drachma, inscribed with the phrase "against the bite of a vexatious litigant" to protect one against the same. Compare **267** for legal protection, but the joke assumes a practice of wearing rings to protect against insect, animal, or snake bites. Arabs do not often feature as a magical race in classical literature, although their location between and beyond Egypt and the Orient qualifies them well for the role. For further tales from Lucian's *Philopseudes* see **54, 115, 244, 49**.

For Hecate see also **13, 66–9, 71, 88–90, 91–2, 97, 155, 161, 238, 244, 270**. For all its parodic nature, the graphic description of the goddess here generally conforms with her visualization in other magical contexts. Gorgons aside, with her harrying torches and whips she resembles those other underworld stalwarts, the Furies. For the sometimes gigantic size of apparitions compare **59** and Pliny *Letters* 7.27 (a massive woman). As often, Hecate's approach is preceded by the howling of her dogs (or her own dog-head); compare **89**. Dark and cavelike woods are a suitable environment for underworld encounters. For the underworld rivers compare **144**. For the notion that the dead in the underworld still wear the clothes in which they are buried compare **150**.

## 276 An onyx ring confers invisibility

iv A.D.

*Cyranides* 1.15.33–7
(Waegeman 1987,
omicron)

Greek

Engrave a quail [*ortyx*] on the onyx-stone, and the sea perch [*orphos*] under its feet. Put beneath the stone some of the preparation for the lamp, and no one will see you, not even if you carry something off. Anoint your face with some of the preparation and wear the ring, and no one will see you, whoever you are or whatever you are doing.

THE O-PLANT OMITTED FROM THIS AMULET is the oleander (*onothursis*). The amulet seems to depend in part for its power on a sympathy of names: the sea perch (*orphos*) is used to shroud one in darkness (*orphnê*).

## 277   Recipe for an invisibility lotion

iv–v A.D.

*PGM* I.222–32

Greek

Necessary spell for inducing invisibility. Take some fat or an eye of a long-eared owl and a scarab's dung-ball and some sage oil. Rub them down to form a smooth paste, smear it all over your body, and say to Helios: "I adjure you by your great name, BORKÊ PHOIOUR IÔ ZIZIA APARXEOUCH THUTHÊ LAILAM AAAAAA IIIII ÔÔÔÔ IEÔ IEÔ IEÔ IEÔ IEÔ IEÔ IEÔ NAUNAX AIAI AEÔ AEÔ ÊAÔ." Dilute it and say further: "Make me invisible, lord Helios, AEÔ ÔAÊ EIÊ ÊAÔ, before every person until sunset, IÔ IÔÔ PHRIX RIZÔ EÔA."

One could become invisible using lotions as well as amulets, as this recipe indicates: see Apollonius of Rhodes, **68**, where, at Medea's behest, Jason smears a lotion over his body to become invincible.

# 14
## *Magic and the Law*

## LEGISLATION AGAINST MAGIC AND ITS REPRESSION

Greek legislation against magic is hard to find. The two most explicit examples of it follow. Both address harmful magic rather than magic per se. While we have a considerable amount of information about classical Athenian law as a whole, even here the evidence for legislation against magic is thin. The concubine of Philoneos was prosecuted and executed for murder, plain and simple, not magic (**77**). The witch Theoris was perhaps prosecuted and executed for impiety (**85–6**). It has recently been suggested that harmful magic could also have been prosecuted at Athens under a "public prosecution for damage" (*dikê blabês*; Gordon 1999a, 250).

For further associations between magic and the law see the trial of Piso, **181**; the fictitious legal cases at **43, 78–9, 84, 125**; the "ideal" laws against magic proposed by Plato, **15–6**; the use of curse tablets in legal contexts, **168–72**; and the use of amulets in legal contexts, **267**.

## 278   Dirae Teiorum: The curses of the Teian state

After 479 B.C.

Meiggs and Lewis 1969, no. 30

Greek

1. If anyone makes harmful spells/poisions [*pharmaka dēlētēria*] against the Teian state or against individuals of it, he is to die, himself and his family with him.

2. If anyone obstructs the importation of corn into Teian territory by any means, be it by land or sea, or thrusts it back once it has been imported, he is to die, himself and his family with him.

3 . . .

4 If anyone rebels against a Teian examiner or chief executive, he is to die, himself and his family with him.

5 If anyone hereafter, being chief executive in Teos or in Teian territory . . . kills . . . betrays the city and territory of the Teians or the men on the island or in Teian waters or hereafter betrays the fort in Aroe or robs on the highway or harbors highway robbers or commits piracy or deliberately harbors pirates engaged in the plunder of Teian land or waters or deliberately conspires with Greeks or barbarians to damage the Teian state, he is to die, himself and his family with him.

6 If anyone in office does not perform this curse at the statue of Dynamis when the games are convened at the Anthesteria or the festival of Heracles or that of Zeus, he is to be the object of the curse.

7 If anyone breaks the inscription on which this curse has been written, or chips off the letters, or rubs them smooth, he is to die, himself and his family with him.

THIS FASCINATING INSCRIPTION IN MANY WAYS resembles inscribed law codes of the classical period, but, as can be seen from clauses 6 and 7, it is rather a series of curses called down by the state in defense of itself. These curses may well, however, have coincided with laws. The most interesting clause is the first one, which seeks to protect the state and its individuals against the practice of harmful *pharmaka*. Since the state as a whole is envisaged as a potential victim, *pharmaka* must here refer to, or include reference to, spells, not merely poison. For magical attacks against an entire city compare **104, 179–80, 238**. As usual in the Greek world, the state takes measures against only harmful magic, not magic in general.

## 279   Sacred law of private cult from Philadelphia in Lydia

i B.C.

*Syl.*³, no. 985

Greek

With good fortune. The instructions given to Dionysius in his sleep are here recorded for health and common safety and the greatest glory. Access to his house is granted to men and women, slave and free. For in this house altars have been constructed for Zeus the Kindly, and Hestia his consort, and the other Savior gods, and Prosperity, and Wealth, and Virtue, and Health, and Good Fortune, and Good Daimon, and Memory, and the Graces, and Victory. Zeus gave Dionysius instructions for the performance of expiations and purifications and sacrifices in accordance both with tradition and with current practice. Upon entering this house men and women, free and slave, must swear an oath by all the gods not to use trickery against men or women, not to devise or perform a wicked spell [*pharmakon*] against people, nor wicked charms [*epôidai*], nor a love charm [*philtron*], nor an abortifacient, nor a contraceptive, nor themselves to commit robbery/rape or murder, nor to incite another person to do so, nor to be an accessory after the fact to these crimes. They must swear without fraud to be a friend of this house, and if any of these people does anything or plots anything, they must swear neither to allow it nor to keep quiet about it, but to reveal it and to try to prevent it. A man who has a wife of his own must swear not to corrupt another man's woman, free or slave, or a boy or a virgin, and not to incite another man to do it. But if he knows of someone who has done this, he must make such a person known, the man and the woman, and not conceal the matter or keep quiet about it. Any man or woman who does any of the things written above may not enter this house. For cults of great gods are established in it and they watch over these things and will not put up with people who transgress their rules. A free woman must be chaste and not know the bed of or intercourse with a man other than those of her own husband. If she does, such a woman is not to be considered chaste, but defiled and completely polluted and unworthy to worship this god, whose rites have been established here, nor is she to participate in sacrifices nor . . . intervene in nor see the mysteries being performed. If she does any of these things after this inscription of the instructions, she will have evil curses from the gods for neglecting these instructions. For the god does not want these things to be done in any way, but he wants people to follow the rules. The gods will be propitious to those who do follow the instructions and will always give them all the good things that gods give to the people they love. But if people transgress these rules, they will hate them and inflict severe punishments on them. The policing of these rules has been entrusted to Agdistis, the holiest guardian and the mistress of this house. May she predispose the minds of men and women, free and slave, to abide by the rules written here. Let all the men and women who have confidence in themselves lay hold of this inscription, on which the god's instructions have been written, at the monthly and at the annual sacrifices, so that it may be made apparent which people are abiding by the rules and which are not. Savior Zeus, please receive this text with propitious and friendly mind and [lacunas follow] . . . reward us well with health, safety, peace, security on land and sea . . . likewise.

IN THESE RULES FOR A PRIVATE cult members are required to avoid wicked spells and incantations, alongside adultery, murder, and robbery or rape, but they are not asked to avoid spells and incantations in general. More specifically, they are required to avoid love charms, which are, accordingly, classified as wicked. In all probability the immediately following prohibitions, against abortifacients and contraceptives, are also to be classified with wicked spells and incantations. Certainly they were often to be found in magical contexts (see **233–5**).

## 280 Interdiction against evil incantations and crop-charming (excantatio cultorum) in Rome's archaic law code

A. Whoever has sung an evil incantation [*malum carmen*] . . .

B. It is illegal for anyone to charm away another man's crops.

451 B.C.

*Twelve Tables* 8; (fragments at Ernout 1957,119)

Latin

NO INDICATION OF THE PRESCRIBED PENALTIES is preserved in these two fragments from Rome's ancient law code, the *Twelve Tables*. The law explicitly against an *evil* incantation suggests, as, for example, does the work of Cato (see **258**), that beneficial incantations were not prohibited in the earlier Republic. For crop-charming see **90, 281, 299**. In general Roman law was much more interested in the repression of magic, subcategories thereof, and allied phenomena than was Greek, as can be seen from **281–98**.

## 281 Cresimus and the crop-charming

i A.D.

Pliny *Natural History* 18.41–3, including Piso F33

Latin

41. I cannot keep myself from relating a case from antiquity, from which it can be understood that it was the custom to refer to the people even on matters of farming, and how men of that time used to be defended. The freedman C. Furius Cresimus produced from his rather tiny farm crops which were far more plentiful than his neighbors did on their vast estates. He was the victim of enormous envy, as people believed that he had charmed away the others' crops through sorcery [*veneficiis*]. 42. The curule aedile Spurius Albinus indicted him for this, and he feared condemnation when the tribes had to go to vote. So he took all his agricultural material into the forum and took along his slaves, strong as they were and, as Piso says, well looked after and well clothed, and his well-made tools, his stout mattocks, his heavy plowshares, and his well-fed oxen. 43. Then he said: "These, Romans, are my spells, but I cannot also show you or bring into the forum the nights I work into or completely through, or my sweat." And so he was unanimously acquitted. Indeed, farming depends on toil, not the expenditure of money, and for that reason our ancestors said that the master's eye was the most fertilizing thing in a field.

THIS TALE, APOCRYPHAL AND MORALIZING AS it evidently is, provides an example of how it was envisaged that the law against crop-charming might be put into use. Its historical setting is the first half of the second century B.C.; the annalist Calpurnius Piso wrote in the later second century B.C. Graf (1997b,

61–88) interestingly compares this tale with the charges that Apuleius had to confront after winning the hand of the prize rich widow of Oea (**299**), to conclude that successful newcomers to communities were particularly likely to attract accusations of magic. For the association between envy and the accusation of magic see **22–3, 300**; see also **192–6**.

## 282    A senatorial decree attempts to contain Bacchic rites

186 B.C.

*Senatus Consultum de Bacchanalibus* (at Ernout 1957, 58–60; *ILS* 18)

Latin

The consuls Quintus Marcius, son of Lucius, and Spurius Postumius, son of Lucius, put a motion before the senate on the seventh day of October in the temple of Bellona. Present at the recording were: Marcus Claudius, the son of Marcus, Lucius Valerius, the son of Publius, and Quintus Minucius, the son of Gaius. They resolved that an edict about Bacchanals [Bacchic shrines] be given to the allies:

Let none of them aspire to maintain a Bacchanal. If there are any who say they must have one, they should approach the city praetor in Rome. When it has heard what they have to say our senate will rule on these matters, provided that not less than a hundred senators are present when the subject is debated. Let no man, be he a citizen, of Latin status or one of the allies, aspire to approach the women Bacchants, unless they have approached the city praetor, and he has given permission on the basis of a senatorial decree, provided that not less than a hundred senators are present when the matter is debated. They resolved this.

No man is to be a priest. Neither man nor any woman is to be a master, nor is any of them to aspire to hold money in common, nor is any of them to aspire to make a man or a woman a master or an acting master. Nor are they to aspire henceforth to exchange oaths between themselves, or vows, agreements, or promises, nor is anyone to aspire to exchange pledges. No one is to aspire to perform rites either in secret, or in public, or in private, or outside the city, unless he has approached the city praetor, and he has given permission on the basis of a senatorial decree, provided that not less than a hundred senators are present when the matter is debated. They resolved this.

No one is to aspire to perform rites when there are more than five people present in total, men or women, nor are more than two men and more than three women to aspire to participate in the rites, unless on the basis of a decree of the city praetor and the senate, in accordance with the preceding provisions.

So that you will proclaim this decree in assemblies over not less than three weekly market days, and be aware of the senatorial decree, this was the senatorial decree: if there are any people who contravene the decree written heretofore, they resolved that they are to be prosecuted on a capital charge. The senate also resolved that you should inscribe this decree on a bronze plaque, and that you should have it fixed up wherever it can be read most easily. And they resolved that you should ensure the removal of any Bacchanals that there are, apart from anything sacred in them, within ten days of your receipt of this text. In the Teuranian territory.

THIS INSCRIPTION ON A BRONZE TABLET from Bruttium (an important document for the archaic Latin language) is one among many copies that would have been set up all over Italy in response to the senate's decree. The crisis that gave rise to the decree is narrated in some detail by Livy (39.8–14). It supposedly began when a Greek "petty sacrificer and diviner" (*sacrificulus et vates*) had introduced his initiations and secret and nocturnal rites into

Etruria. This figure is broadly akin to that of Plato's "sorcerer amalgam" (14–7). The petty sacrificer's cult spread quickly to Rome and with it came, we are told, human sacrifice, criminality, drunkenness, and promiscuous sex of all varieties. The Romans were to continue to associate together magic, foreign cults, and conspiracies to overthrow the state; the best explanation of this perceived association is found at 286. As can be seen, the decree did not seek to abolish Bacchic worship entirely, but it did seek to contain it very strictly. It is noteworthy that shortly after this decree, in 184 and 180 B.C., if we believe Livy, some five thousand people were executed in Italy for *venefi-cia* (Livy 39.41 and 40.43). For bacchants see 66, 87.

## 283 Cornelius Hispalus expels Chaldaeans and a Jewish sect in 139 B.C.

Ca. 26 A.D.

Valerius Maximus 1.3.3

Latin

In the consulships of M. Pompilius Laenas and L. Calpurnius [139 B.C.] Cn. Cornelius Hispalus the praetor for resident aliens issued a decree ordering the Chaldaeans to depart from the city and from Italy within ten days, because they were profiteering by fogging up weak and foolish minds with their lies and bogus readings of the stars. He also compelled the Jews who had been trying to corrupt Roman morality with their cult of Jupiter Sabazius to return home.

HERE WE SEE THE ROMAN TENDENCY to identify astrology with foreign cults, and an early example of Rome's frequent expulsions of Chaldaeans (for whom compare 49–50), further examples of which follow at 286, 291–2, 294.

## 284 Pseudo-Paulus's opinions on Sulla's law of 81 B.C. against assassins and sorcerers (Lex Cornelia de sicariis et veneficis)

Late iii A.D.

Paulus *Sententiae* 5.23.14–9

Latin

If they give someone a love potion or an abortifacient, even if they do not do it deceitfully, nonetheless, because it sets a bad example, the lower classes are relegated to the mines, the upper ones to an island, with a portion of their property forfeit. But if either a woman or a man dies as a result of this, they pay the ultimate penalty. Those who perform or direct the performance of impious or nocturnal rites, in order to bewitch, bind, or tie [*obcantarent, defigerent, obligarent*] a person, are either crucified or thrown to the beasts. Those who sacrifice a human being, make offerings of human blood, or pollute a sanctuary or temple, are thrown to the beasts or, if they are of the upper classes, executed. It is resolved to subject those who know the craft of magic to the ultimate punishment, that is, to throw them to the beasts or crucify them. Actual mages, however, are burned alive. No one may have books on the craft of magic in his house. If they are found in someone's house, they are burned in public and their owner has his property confiscated; upper classes are deported to an island, lower classes are executed. Even the mere knowledge of this craft, let alone its pursuit as a trade, is forbidden. If a man dies as a result of a drug given to him as a cure or a palliative, the one that gave it him is relegated to an island, if he is of the upper class, but executed if of the lower one.

THIS DISCUSSION OF ROME'S PRINCIPAL LAW against magic reflects many of the beliefs about the nature of the practice of magic in Roman literature; see 91–107. Justinian's *Digest* (285) indicates that it outlawed the selling, buying, possession, and administering of harmful drugs. The position that knowledge of magic is hardly less culpable than its actual practice reveals the precariousness of Apuleius's defence, **299**. For the burning-alive of the soothsayers compare **295** and Heliodorus *Aethiopica* 8.9.

## 285   A commentary on Sulla's law of 81 B.C.

530 A.D.

*Digest of Justinian* 48.8.2 (Mommsen *et al.* 1985, 4:818–21)

Latin

Marcianus *Institutes* 14. In the fifth chapter of that same Cornelian law on assassins and poisoners/ sorcerers [*venefici*] punishment is prescribed for the person who has made, sold, or kept poisons/drugs [*venenum*] for killing. This law's punishment is also given to the person who has sold evil drugs [*medicamenta*] to the public or who keeps them for killing. The addition of the phrase "of an evil drug [*venenum*]" shows that there are nonevil drugs. Therefore the term is a general one and embraces the drug that is prepared for healing as much as it does the one that is prepared for killing, as well as the drug termed "aphrodisiac." The only sort of drug meant in this law is one kept for killing. But the punishment of exile has been ordained by a decree of the senate for a woman who gives a drug [*medicamentum*] to aid conception that causes the death of the woman that consumes it. Even though she may have had no evil intent, she acted on a bad example. Another decree of the senate ordained that unguent dealers [*pigmentarii*] should be subject to punishment under the same law if they rashly give someone hemlock, salamanders, aconite, pine-caterpillars, bubrostis insect, mandrake, or Spanish fly-beetle (except, in this case, for purification [? text uncertain]) . . . The penalty of the Cornelian law on assassins and poisoners/sorcerers is deportation to an island and confiscation of all property. But today people are usually given capital punishment, unless they belong to too high a class to be subject to the punishment prescribed by the law. The lower classes are usually either crucified or thrown to the beasts, but the upper classes are deported to an island.

CICERO'S ALLUSIVE REFERENCES TO THE CORNELIAN law (*Pro Cluentio* 148) also indicate that it outlawed the selling, buying, possession, and administering of harmful drugs.

## 286   Agrippa expels the astrologers and the sorcerers from Rome in 33 B.C., and accounts for his policy

ii–iii A.D.

Dio Cassius 49.43.5, 52.36.1–2

Greek

49.43.5. [33 B.C.] Agrippa did this, and he also drove the astrologers [*astrologoi*] and the sorcerers [*goêtes*] out of the city.

52.36.1-2. [29 B.C.; Agrippa speaks to Augustus:] You should hate and punish those who introduce foreign elements into our religion, not just for the sake of the gods (for if a man despises the gods, he could hardly have respect for anyone else), but because men of this sort, by importing new powers [*daimonia*], persuade many people to take up foreign customs, and from this are born conspiracies and gatherings and secret clubs, which are the last thing a monarchy needs. Do not then permit people to be atheists or sorcerers [*goêtes*]. We need prophecy [*mantikê*], and by all means you must appoint soothsayers [i.e., *haruspices*, entrail-diviners] and augurs, with whom people who want to consult on some other matter will consort. But it is proper that there should be no mages [*mageutai*] whatsoever. For such men often incite many to revolution, either by telling the truth, or, as more often, by telling lies. And no few of those who pretend to practice philosophy do the same. Just because you have had good experiences with Areius and Athenodorus, fine and upright men, you should not think that all the others who claim to practice philosophy are the same as they are. For the men who hide behind such a front do untold damage to societies and individuals alike.

THE IDENTIFICATION OF THE PRACTICE OF magic with the forces of revolution seems remarkable and barely credible, but it is clear from repeated subsequent imperial persecution of magicians that the Roman emperors tended to think in this way; see also **282**. But the capacity of even the most elementary magical practices to invert social structure has been noted: see **180**, with commentary. The truths and lies with which mages incite revolution are doubtless in the first instance predictions of the imminent death of the emperor; see **136**, **291–2**, **294**, **289**, **296**, **298**. Sorcerers and diviners had been associated with revolutionary threats against the state in the age of the Republic, as shown in **282**. In the age of the empire, the state had become identified with the emperor, and the threat now tended to be seen as focused on his person. Agrippa's association of philosophers with magicians would not have pleased Apuleius, who made it his task to dissociate the two, **299**; see also **14–7**. The events in **291** constitute a reenactment of Agrippa's measures here.

## 287 The emperor Augustus burns the books of the prophets in 31 B.C.

Early ii A.D.

Suetonius *Augustus* 31

Latin

After he had at long last taken on the office of chief priest [*pontifex maximus*] on the death of Lepidus (for he had not had the heart to deprive him of it during his lifetime), he gathered together from all quarters over two thousand books of prophetic writings in Greek and Latin, commonly held to be anonymous or penned by insufficiently suitable authors, and burned them. He just preserved the Sibylline books, but in the case of these too he chose some and rejected others. He buried them in two gilded boxes under the pedestal of Palatine Apollo.

THE PASSAGE RELATES TO 31 B.C. For the burning of magical books compare **293**. For the symbolic importance of books in ancient magic see **46**. If this text is taken at face value, it suggests that magical books could be hugely expensive, unless the number of books burned was vast.

## 288 Augustus expels Anaxilaus of Larissa in 28 B.C.

iii–iv A.D.

Eusebius *Chronicle of Jerome* at 28 B.C., (Helm p. 163)

Latin

28 B.C. Anaxilaus of Larissa, the Pythagorean and mage, is expelled by Augustus from the city and from Italy.

THE CHRONICLE PRESERVES THE FORMAL LANGUAGE of expulsion decrees in the phrase "from the city and from Italy." For Anaxilaus of Larissa see **45**, with commentary.

## 289 Augustus bans divination to individuals and on the subject of death in 11 A.D.

ii–iii A.D.

Dio Cassius 56.23

Greek

It was forbidden that diviners [*manteis*] should give divinations to individuals or to give any divination on the subject of death, not even if other people were present. And yet so little did Augustus care about any of this that he displayed the configuration of the stars under which he was born in a public notice for all to see. Even so, he made this ban.

## 290   Tiberius bans divination to individuals

Early ii A.D.

Suetonius *Tiberius* 63.1

Latin

There are many indications here not merely of the extent to which he was loathed and hated, but also of the extent to which he lived in a state of terror and was the object of abuse. He forbade the consultation of soothsayers [*haruspices*] in secret and without witnesses. He actually tried to dismantle oracles near the city, but desisted for fear of the power of the Lots of Praeneste, for these were sealed into a chest and brought to Rome, but he could not find them in it until it was restored to the temple.

TIBERIUS HERE REENACTS AUGUSTUS'S BAN ON divination to individuals, **286**. We learn form Pseudo-Paulus *Sententiae* 5.21.3 that he also specifically banned divination for the date of the emperor's death.

## 291   The condemnation of Libo Drusus for magical practices against the emperor Tiberius in 16 A.D.

Ca. 120 A.D.

Tacitus *Annals* 2.27–32
(edited)

Latin

**27.** At about the same time Libo Drusus, from the family of the Scribonii, was indicted for revolutionary activity. I will give particular attention to the beginning of this case, as well as its course and conclusion, because it witnessed the first invention of a phenomenon that was to eat into the state over so many years. Firmius Catus, a senator and very close friend to Libo, directed this young man, improvident as he was and easily engaged by stupidities, toward the predictions of the Chaldaeans, the rites of the mages, and even the interpreters of dreams. He drew it to his attention that Pompey was his great-grandfather, that Scribonia, who had at one point been Augustus's wife, was his great-aunt, that the Caesars were his cousins, and that his house was full of ancestral masks. He persuaded him into excess and into debt and shared his debaucheries and his overspending, so as to entrap him with plenty of evidence. **28.** When he had found enough witnesses and slaves who were also in the know, he asked for an audience with the emperor. . . . Although Tiberius could have put a stop to everything Libo was saying and doing, he preferred just to bear them in mind, until a certain Junius, whom Libo had asked to call up underworld ghosts with incantations, reported this evidence to Fulcinius Trio.

**30.** In addition to Trio and Catus, Fonteius Agrippa and Caius Vibius had now presented themselves as accusers and they competed for the privilege of making the big formal oration against the defendant, until Vibius declared that he would deal with the charges one at a time, since they could not agree among themselves and Libo was in any case without an advocate. He produced some crazy evidence from Libo's papers. Libo had taken divination to discover whether he would acquire sufficient wealth to be able to pave the Via Appia with money all the way to Brundisium. They included other empty follies of this sort—occasions for pity, if you looked on them with kindliness. But the accuser contended that in one paper written in the hand of Libo sinister or secret marks had been added to the names of the imperial family or senators. Libo denied the charge, but his slaves recognized his hand.

**31.** Libo directed two sword-blows to his stomach.

**32.** The senate also decreed that astrologers [*mathematici*] be expelled from Italy. One of them, Lucius Pituanius, was thrown from the Tarpeian rock, while the consuls executed Publius Marcius in the traditional fashion outside the Esquiline gate, to the accompaniment of the trumpet.

BY YOKING TOGETHER THE CALLING UP of the dead and the writing of strange marks, that is, no doubt, "characters," against the names of the imperial family, the prosecutors were able to insinuate that Libo Drusus was attempting to curse the emperor to death. Here again, as often in Roman legal and historical sources, magic is closely identified with divination: Libo is accused of associating with the Chaldaeans and of inquiring into his future wealth; in the wake of the affair astrologers are banished. But they were lucky. We are told that one hundred and thirty sorcerers (*venenarii* and *malefici*) were executed under Tiberius, and that eighty-five of these were women (*Chronicle of the Year* 354 A.D. at *MGH* 9 p. 145). It may have been supposed that Libo's inquiries were directed specifically to the occasion of the emperor's death, which the Roman emperors found intolerable; see **286**, with commentary. In 25 A.D. Claudia Pulchra was to be similarly accused of, among other things, magic (*veneficia*) and binding curses (*devotiones*) against the emperor (Tacitus *Annals* 4.52).

## 292  Nero punishes divination for the date of his death and expels astrologers from Italy in 52 A.D.

Ca. 120 A.D.

Tacitus *Annals* 12.52

Latin

In the consulships of Faustus Sulla and Salvius Otho [52 A.D.] Furius Scribonianus was sent into exile on the ground that he had consulted Chaldaeans and looked into the death of the emperor. His mother Vibia was also implicated in the charge, because she found it hard to bear her previously decreed fate of exile. Camillus, the father of Scribonianus, had instigated a rebellion in Dalmatia. Caesar brought the matter up to demonstrate his clemency in preserving this enemy family a second time. But he did not live long in exile. Stories are told in accordance with personal belief: some say that he died by chance, others that he was killed with poison. There was a cruel but pointless decree of the senate expelling astrologers [*mathematici*] from Italy.

FOR NERO'S PERSONAL USE OF MAGES, compare **45, 126**.

## 293  Paul's Ephesian converts burn their magical books

Late i A.D.

Acts 19.17–9

Greek

This became known to all the Jews and Greeks living in Ephesus, and fear fell upon them all, and they exalted the name of Jesus Christ. Many of those converted to belief came and confessed their practices openly. Numbers of those who had practiced sorcery [*ta perierga*] collected their books and burned them in front of everybody. They reckoned up their value and discovered it to be fifty thousand pieces of silver. In this way the word of the Lord powerfully increased and grew strengthened.

THERE WERE SOME THINGS ON WHICH the pagan Roman state and the early Christians could agree; compare **287**.

## 294  Vitellius, emperor in 69 A.D., expels the Chaldaeans and they pray for his death

Early ii A.D.

Suetonius *Vitellius* 14

Latin

To no one was he [Vitellius] more hostile than to lampoon-writers and astrologers [*mathematici*]. Whenever an accusation was laid against one of them he would have him executed without hearing the trial. He was furious because when he had issued the edict in which he ordered the astrologers to depart from the city and from Italy by October 1, a handbill was circulated that said, "And the Chaldaeans say, for the good of the state, may Vitellius Germanicus cease to exist before that same day."

HERE THE ASSOCIATION BETWEEN THE DIVINATION of the date of an emperor's death, the magical infliction of that death, and revolution becomes particularly clear; see **286**, with commentary.

## 295   Witches are burned at the stake

ii A.D.

Hadrian of Tyre at Polemon *Declamationes* pp. 44–5 Hinck

Greek

Premise: A woman has been convicted of witchcraft [*pharmakeia*] but could not be burned. Another woman undertook to burn her and and contrived to do so. Hadrian the rhetorician argues that this woman too should be burned.

The defense claims that the law punishes not women who have merely acquired the craft but only those that have used it for ill. But it is easy to learn the truth of the matter from the text of the law itself. For it does not speak of "a woman who has performed witchcraft [*pharmakeusasa*]" but of "a witch [*pharmakis*]." It is obvious that in using the noun "craft" [*technê*] in its prescription of punishment the law hates the capacity in itself to perform witchcraft. Crimes that depend on impulse are proven only by action, but crimes that depend on an acquired craft, as do those of witchcraft, are betrayed before the deed by intent. One must suspect the desires of people who have learned crafts from which the capacity to do harm may be acquired. One must not wait until suffering is inflicted before seeking to take measures against those with the capacity to inflict the damage suffered, but one must hold the capacity to inflict suffering in suspicion before actually suffering anything. In short, the sorcerer [*pharmakeus*] is an admitted brigand offering a craft of injury, he is plotting perfected, the promise of lawlessness and vigorous impiety. We keep in check most of those creatures who share your craft, woman, despite having suffered no injury from them first, but simply because we hate their power, because each of them too has a natural poison. If your actual actions have remained undetected through your concealment of your capacity, nonetheless, now that your capacity to do harm has been detected, you will pay the penalty on the basis that you have acted, even if until now you have been able to conceal yourself. What is one to say of you? If you hated the craft, you would not have been learning it. Since you have knowledge of it, you acted out of envy, not out of hatred. One punishes what one shuns, but one is jealous of what one shares with others. And indeed brigand kills brigand in anger over booty, and the tyrant is killed by the man that wants to rule alone. This is the sort of consideration that underlies your impulsive act. You think you have made yourself sole queen of witchcraft [*pharmakeia*] by doing away with the woman who shared your craft.

THIS IS A RHETORICAL EXERCISE BASED on an absurd hypothesis, as is **125**. The law in question is a vague construct, but the central notion that sorcerers might be burned accords well enough with **284**. This passage is particularly useful for illustrating the atmosphere of competitive envy that was held to obtain between sorcerers; see **22–3, 192–6, 300**.

## 296   The prefect of Egypt writes to district governors telling them to suppress divination in 198/9 A.D., under the emperor Septimius Severus

198/9 A.D.

*P. Yale* inv. 299, as edited by Rea (1977)

Greek

Since I met many people who thought that they had been deceived by forms of divination, I at once came to consider it necessary to declare here to all that they were banned from this precarious meddling, so that no danger should attend their folly. So, let no one pretend to know that which is beyond human understanding through oracles or writings bestowed under the influence of the divine, or through processions of images or sorcery [*manganeia*] of this sort. Nor let him make professions about that which is obscure in the future. Nor let him give himself over to those who make inquiry into this, nor let him give any answer at all. If anyone is discovered to be abiding in this trade, let him realize that he will be given over to the ultimate penalty. Let each of you take care to publish a copy of this letter on a white board in the regional capitals and in every village in clear and legible letters. Let him make detailed inquiries, and if he finds anyone acting in contravention of the ban, let him send him in bonds for my judgment. Nor will the situation be without risk for you, if I learn hereafter that such people are being overlooked in the districts under you, but you will be subject to the same punishment as those being sheltered. For each of those people, even if he makes bold undertakings contrary to what has been forbidden, is all the same just one man. But the one who does not everywhere keep them down has himself become a cause of danger to many.

The seventh year of the emperors Lucius Septimius Severus Pius Pertinax Arabicus Adiabenicus Parthicus Maximus and Marcus Aurelius Antoninus, Augusti. [lacuna]

THE PREFECT IN QUESTION WAS PROBABLY Q. Aemilianus Saturninus. This edict ostensibly bans not only the use of magical divination but also the use of established "religious" oracles of the Delphic type.

## 297 Law of the emperor Constantius II, 357 A.D., on sorcerers (malefici), astrologers (mathematici), and others

iv A.D.

Ammianus Marcellinus 19.12.14

Latin

For if anyone wore an amulet on his neck to cure the quartan ague or some other disease, or was accused on the evidence of those who wished him ill of having passed by a tomb in the evening, supposedly collecting the horrible contents of graves and the empty illusions of ghosts that wander about in these places, he was condemned on a capital charge and executed.

THIS WAS, SUPPOSEDLY, THE EFFECT OF the Christian Constantius's severe laws as set out at *Theodosian code* 9.16.4–6. For healing amulets see **256–6**. For ghosts hovering around their graves see **109**.

## 298 A necromantic divination for a successor to Valens (ruled 364–78 A.D.) results in mass exterminations

v A.D.

Socrates *Ecclesiastical History* 4.19

Greek

At about the same time an avenging demon exploited the emperor's cruelty. For it persuaded some meddlesome people to perform necromancy to discover who should be emperor after Valens. They pursued their magical sorcery [*magik . . . manganeia*] and the demon gave them a reply which was far from clear but obscure, as usual. It indicated four letters, *Th, E, O,* and *D,* and said that the name of the emperor to succeed Valens began with them, and that it was a compound name. Rumor of what had taken place came to the emperor's hearing. He would not leave knowledge of the future to God or considered action to the fine manager of all things. He abandoned the Christian precepts he aspired to adhere to and began to slaughter many he suspected would be emperor. Accordingly there were killed Theodoruses, Theodotuses, Theodosiuses, Theoduluses, and all those that had names similar to these. Among these victims even a Theodosiolus, a distinguished scion of Spanish nobility, was killed. Because of the prevailing fear many changed their names and disowned the ones that their own parents had bestowed upon them as too dangerous.

THE TALE IS TOLD AT GREATER length and with some variation at Ammianus Marcellinus 29.1. These measures accord, in broad terms, with the laws ascribed to Valens and others in the *Theodosian Code*, 9.16.7–10. For imperial attitudes to the divination of their death, see **286**, with commentary. For necromancy see **144–62**.

## APULEIUS AND LIBANIUS IN COURT

For another legal speech on a magical theme, see **125,** a rhetorical exercise like Libanius's.

### 299    Apuleius on the difficulties of bringing and rebutting charges of magical practice; its Persian origins

158/9 A.D.

Apuleius *Apology* 2,
25–7, 47, 80, 90–1
(edited)

Latin

**2.** Aemilianus . . . chose to base his accusation solely on the calumny of magic, which lends itself more easily to defamation than to proof.

**25.** For if, as I read in many authors, a "mage" in the Persian tongue is a "priest" in ours, then what crime is there in being a priest, in having due knowledge of, familiarity with, and experience of ceremonial rules, the proper conduct of rites and sacred law? If in fact magic is as Plato expounds it when he relates the disciplines in which the Persians instruct an adolescent prince . . . I remember the very words of the divine man. Recall them with me, Maximus: "When the boy is fourteen they hand him over to men they call the royal pedagogues. They are chosen as ostensibly the four best Persians of their generation: the wisest, the most just, the most self-controlled, and the bravest. One of them teaches the magic of Zoroaster the son of Oromazes. This is the worship of the gods. He also teaches him kingship." [*Alcibiades* 121e–122a.]

**26.** [The education of Persian princes in magic.] Do you hear this, you who so rashly bring accusations against the art of magic, that it is welcomed by the gods, and is well versed in the worship and cultivation of them? It is a pious craft, with knowledge of the divine. It has enjoyed distinction since the time of its founders, Zoroaster and Oromazes. It is a high priestess of the heavenly gods. Magic is among the basic elements of royal education and the Persians do not casually permit just anyone to be a mage, any more than they do to be a king. Plato again, in another bit of dialogue, this time about a certain Zalmoxis of Thracian race, a man of a similar craft, put it like this: "beautiful words are charms" [*Charmides* 157a]. But if this is the case, why am I not to be allowed to know the good words of Zalmoxis or the sacred rites over which Zoroaster presided?

But if the prosecution think, as ordinary people do, that a mage is properly a man who converses with the immortal gods and has the power to perform all the miracles he likes through the power of incantations, then I am completely amazed that they have not been frightened to lay an accusation against someone they admit to have such great power. For one cannot protect oneself against such a secret and divine power as one can against other things. A man who brings a case against a cutthroat arrives with an escort. A man who accuses a poisoner is more vigilant about what he eats. A man who charges a thief guards his belongings. But if a man brings a mage of the sort of which they speak to trial for a capital offense, with what escort, with what vigilance, with what guards is he to avert undetectable and ineluctable destruction? By none, of course. Hence, no one who believes that a crime of this sort is being committed is going to make an accusation of it.

**27.** But accusations of this sort are cast against philosophers because of a general misconception among the ignorant. So some of them think that people who investigate the basic constituents of bodies are irreligious and they therefore say that they deny the gods, for example, Anaxagoras, Leucippus, Democritus, Epicurus, and other advocates of materialism. Others commonly call those people mages who map out the workings of universal providence with particular care and worship the gods with particular zeal, as if they knew how to do the things they know to be done. This was once the case with Epimenides, Orpheus, Pythagoras, and Ostanes. The *Purifications* of Empedocles fell under similar suspicion, as did Socrates' "little demon" [*daimonion*] and Plato's "idea of goodness." Accordingly, I congratulate myself for being numbered among so many great men.

But as to the stupid and disingenuous allegations cast against me by the prosecution in their attempt to prove their case, I fear that you may think they constitute proper charges simply for being cast against me. "Why," he says, "did you look for certain varieties of fish?" As if a philosopher is not allowed to do for understanding what a roué is permitted to do for his gullet! "Why did a free woman marry you after thirteen years of widowhood?" As if the fact that she had not married for so many years were not more amazing! "Why did she write certain reflections in a letter before marrying you?" As if anyone ought to account for another person's opinion! "But in fact, although older, she did not scorn the young man." So this in itself is the proof that there was no need of magic to make a widowed woman wish to marry a bachelor, although his senior. And he has more of the same: "Apuleius has a thing at home that he worships solemnly." As if it is not a greater crime to have nothing to worship! "A boy collapsed before Apuleius." What if a young man, what, for that matter, if an old man had collapsed before me either stricken by a bodily disease or losing his footing on something slippery? Are these your proofs of my magic—the fall of a boy, the marriage of a woman, and shopping for fish?

**47.** And why were you insisting that such a large band of slaves present themselves in court? You have laid an accusation of magic based on the evidence of fifteen slaves. So, fifteen slaves know something, and yet it remains secret. Or is it not secret, and yet still magical? You have to admit one of these alternatives: either the activity in which I had no fear in involving so many witnesses was not illicit, or, if it was illicit, I cannot have involved so many accomplices. This magic of yours, so far as I hear, has long been a matter for the law and was outlawed already in antiquity by the Twelve Tables because, incredibly, of the charming-away of crops. So magic is no less secret than it is foul and horrible. Usually one remains awake through the night to practice it, buries it in darkness, performs it apart from witnesses, and mutters its incantations. Few free men are admitted to the rites, let alone slaves. And you want fifteen slaves to have been involved? Was it a wedding, or some other packed celebration, or a seasonal banquet? Fifteen slaves take part in a magical rite, as if an elected board-of-fifteen for ritual performance? Would I have included this number of men in the activity if there were more of them than needed to know? Fifteen free men constitute a district, as many slaves constitute a household, as many chained slaves a prison-house. Did I need this crowd to help me, so that they could hold the purificatory victims for hour upon hour? But you have named no victims other than hens! Or were they there to count the grains of incense? Or to knock Thallus over?

**80.** What's your case then? That she was sane or insane when she wrote [i.e., that she had been maddened by my love magic]? Sane, will you say? In that case she had not been the victim of magical practices. Insane, will you reply? In that case she did not know what she wrote, and so cannot be believed. Rather, if she had been insane, she would not have known that she was insane. For just as it is absurd to say that one is silent, because one at once ceases to be silent by the very fact of saying that one is silent, and invalidates the thing claimed with the claim itself, so it is more self-contradictory still to say "I am mad." This cannot be true, unless the person who says it knows what he is saying. And of course a man who knows what insanity is is sane, for insanity cannot know itself, any more than blindness can see itself. Therefore Pudentilla was in possession of her faculties, if she did not regard herself to be so. I can take this line of reasoning further, should I wish, but that's enough dialectic.

**90.** I come now to the central point of the accusation, the motive itself for the use of evil magic. Let Aemilianus and Rufinus tell me for what profit I had enticed Pudentilla into marriage with incantations and spells [*venena*], even if I was the greatest of mages. . . .

Consider how confident I am in my own innocence, and how much I despise you. If you find one reason, however tiny, for me to have pursued marriage with Pudentilla for some advantage, if you prove there was some profit in it for me, however modest, then let me be Carmendas or Damigeron or Moses or Iohannes or Apollobex or even Dardanus or any other famous mage since Zoroaster and Ostanes.

**91.** Look, please, Maximus, what an uproar they have created, because I have told off a few mages by name. What can I do with such philistines, such savages? Am I to tell you again that I have read these names and many others besides in public libraries in the works of the most distinguished authors? Or am I to argue that the knowledge of names is one thing, participation in the craft wholly another, and that one should not make a confession of guilt out of a component of education or a retentive memory. Or, what is preferable by far, Claudius Maximus, should I rely on your education and your full learning and not deign to reply to the allegations of these stupid and insensitive people? This will be the better course of action. I won't give a fig for what they think. I shall proceed with the argument on which I had embarked, that I had no reason to entice Pudentilla into marriage with spells [*venecifia*]. The prosecution has made a point of denigrating the woman's appearance and age, and made them a reason to find fault with me. They claim that it was for greed that I conceived a desire for a woman of this kind and that I snatched a huge and healthy dowry from her at our first embrace.

Apuleius's lengthy speech of defense against various accusations of having practiced magic nowhere specifies the law under which he is charged. It is usually assumed that it was the catch-all *Lex Cornelia de sicariis and veneficis*, introduced by Sulla in 81 B.C. (see **285**). Apuleius had arrived in the North African town of Oea and persuaded its most desirable rich widow, Pudentilla, to marry him, to the chagrin of her family, who wished to retain control of her money. It was the family who brought him to trial, primarily on the ground that he had used erotic magic to seduce Pudentilla, but the case was built up with many further allegations of magical practice, such as those relating to his Hermes doll (**242**, mentioned also here at 27) and his treatment of Thallus (**134**; 47 is drawn from the argumentation relating to Thallus; and see 27 again); see also **158**.

The prosecution evidently made much of the fact that Pudentilla was older than Apuleius, although the exact extent of the age-gap between them remains obscure. According to the stereotype represented in Apuleius's own *Metamorphoses*, one might rather have expected the suspicion of erotic magic to have fallen upon the older woman who is able to entice the younger man into her affections (**104, 107**).

As noted in the commentaries on **134** and **242**, Apuleius's defense is not always convincing. Of particular interest here are some of the sophistic points made about the bringing of legal proceedings against magic. First is Apuleius's point that there are no circumstances under which a charge of magic should be brought in the first place (**26**): if a charge is false, it should not be brought for that reason alone; but if a charge is true, then the accuser will fall victim to the magician's terrible power, which is inevitably greater than that of the court. The corollary is that charges of magic are only brought by people who believe them to be untrue. Second is his argument about the use of witnesses in accusations of magic: magical practice is by nature secretive, so the more witnesses there are to a specific rite, the less likely it is to have taken place (**47**; compare **2**)! Third is the point that one can not sanely declare that one had been turned mad by magical means (**80**). These arguments had no doubt originated hundreds of years before in the golden age of Greek rhetoric; for rhetoric as itself magical see **12**.

As Apuleius repeatedly makes clear (**27, 91**), his accusers hold the knowledge of magic he employs to defend himself against their charges as proof of involvement in it. The superficial plausibility of this inference aside, it should be noted that in Pseudo-Paulus's opinion on the Cornelian law it is opined that those who exhibit mere knowledge of the craft of magic, despite not practicing it, should be executed, **285**. It is noteworthy too that the study of arcane books in itself played an important role in popular beliefs about the training of magicians; see **46**, with commentary. In Libanius's fictitious prosecution of a mage (**300**) he expresses the concern that, for all that he is the prosecutor, the knowledge of magical practices he must evince in making his case may give the impression that he is himself a mage. Apuleius's broad defense is that he pursues knowledge of all things with the disinterest of the philosopher, and indeed he professes himself more interested in defending the reputation of philosophy itself than his own from the taint of magic (for which compare **286**). Yet he is awkwardly aware that the tradition of philosophy draws its roots from figures in the shaman tradition who are difficult to distinguish in kind from the founder-mages: behind Plato and Socrates were Orpheus, Pythagoras, Zalmoxis, Epimenides, and Empedocles (**26–7**), for whom see **1–9**.

Apuleius distinguishes supposedly true magic from popular misconceptions about it. He locates the origin of true magic among the Persian mages (**25–6**), as do Pliny (**45**) and Tertullian (**112**). He emphasizes that for them it is a matter of pious religion. The practice of true magic, then, ought anyway to be no crime at all. It is helpful to have the popular and supposedly false definition of magic laid out for us, namely, as converse with the gods and the performance of miracles through incantations. Apuleius's canon of traditional magical figures (**90**) is comparable to that developed by Pliny. Carmendas is otherwise unknown. Damigeron gave his name to a treatise on the magical properties of stones (for which see Halleux and Schamp 1985). Moses was famed as a Jewish magician, and a formulary calling itself his supposed *Eighth Book* is reproduced in one of the most important Greek Magical Papyri

(*PGM* XIII). The Jewish name Iohannes is often found confused with that of Iannes, an Egyptian magician who opposed Moses. Apollobex is doubtless to be identified with Pliny's Apollobeches; see **45** also for Dardanus and the famous mages Ostanes and Zoroaster. The name Oromazes (26) refracts the name of the Persian god Ahura Mazda. Apuleius here helps us to understand a conceptual link between the original, "scientific" Democritus and the magical Pseudo-Democritus of Bolus of Mendes (27).

## 300   A rhetorical exercise against a lying mage

iv A.D.

Libanius *Declamatio* 41

Greek

Plague attacked the city. The god prophesied the cessation of the plague if the people would sacrifice a child of one of the citizens. The lot fell upon the son of the mage. The mage promises to stop the plague, if they leave his son alone. The question is debated.

**1.** It is no great surprise to me, citizens, that this man should try to snatch back his own son by every available means. But it is indeed surprising that you should sit and listen to arguments of the sort he is making when your city is sick. If you were sensible and really wanted to stop the plague immediately, all you would have to do is submit to the god's instructions, neither making nor listening to any further debate. But since you have forsaken the salvation of the city in favor of protracted debates, and since one man has achieved so much influence over you that he can make you question whether you should neglect the manifest road to recovery and wait instead for something that is not going to happen, how can you not reasonably be thought to have taken leave of your senses? **2.** I thought that you should have cast this fellow out immediately after his opening words and consulted no other speaker after him, but simply done the job of the people. But since you gave so much time to this man's lies and asked somehow or other for someone to advise you about the one subject on which there is no need for advice, I have come forward, since I do not intend to allow the mage to be thought better than Apollo.

**3.** It is easy not just for me but for everyone to prove that this man is a charlatan, since there was nothing plausible in these promises of his. Two aspects above all,citizens, of the mage's speech-making annoy me. The first is that many citizens, bewitched in the course of his speech (and he is responsible for this too) are now dying as the plague continues to take its course. The second is the prospect that the god will not be so willing to give us his help in the same way in the future. For when he sees us placing our hope elsewhere and listening to discussions about other solutions after the great one that he has offered us, I would not be surprised if he were to take away a significant part of the friendliness and support he has displayed for this city. **4.** Therefore we should hold this man in the strongest contempt and punish him for depriving us of such an important outcome while promising and claiming that he will deliver it to us. And I think it reasonable that the mage's supporters should also meet with your anger (it's obvious why they like him so much), since they put the well-being of a man of this sort ahead of that of the city.

**5.** Some of the others are at a loss and have been repeatedly asking themselves what is the origin and cause of this terrible and unbearable disease that is emptying our city. Indeed I have heard some people complaining to one another in the marketplace, "For what wrongdoing are we paying this penalty? Have not the temples, sacrifices, sacred enclosures, and altars been maintained for the gods' honor according to our ancient customs? Do we not sacrifice? Do we not make libations? Do we not perform rituals? Do we not celebrate festivals? Do we not honor the gods before battle? Do we not bring them dedications after victories? Do we not observe our treaties? Do we not abide by our oaths? Do we not treat out neighbors justly? So why are we sick?" **6.** This is what the others are saying, but I never considered it surprising that we are suffering as we are. This is not because I have condemned the city's morality or because I share with you the guilty awareness of some impiety or cruelty. May I never be misread the city so! Rather, it is because I see that this man refuses to make a living from the land or the sea or any other reasonable trade but pursues this base craft and claims to know the gods and their secrets beyond other men, and to know in what they delight and by what they are drawn and to what gifts they respond. **7.** In short, by calling himself the comrade and friend of the gods and by promising to solve every difficulty through them, this accursed man has overturned many houses, hiring himself out in disputes between citizens, rolling around tombs and inflicting deaths from them on men who do him no wrong, disturbing the dead and preventing the ghosts from resting in their accustomed places. **8.** And many used this one hireling to destroy people who have offended them, while he was even securing for himself immunity from punishment for the misfortunes in which he had already involved so many. Perceptive and discerning people advised silence on the ground that it was not safe to antagonize a man who drew his strength from tombs. Indeed I myself too know what I will now suffer, but I have taken my stand because I place the safety of the community before my own. This struggle was not with the mage alone. All those grateful people for whom he had performed services also were ready to do or suffer everything on his behalf. See how even now they shrink from nothing.

**9.** The gods have witnessed these deeds. They hate them and they pity those who have fallen foul of this man. So they have sent their anger upon us all, as often happens in this world. Our noble poets were familiar with the phenomenon, and they know what they are about when they sing, "Often even the entire city of an evil man is made to suffer" [Hesiod *Works and Days* 240]. This brings earthquakes on cities, this brings tidal waves, this brings rains beyond measure, this brings famine, this brings our present condition. But the source of the affliction is also the source of succor. For now that many have died, and medicine has been of no avail, we know to where we should look: to the one who has delivered no few cities of these and many other disasters, the god at Delphi. I feared—yes, I feared, citizens—that we would be denied an oracle for our failure to expel this man from the city. But the god is greater in his beneficence than I expected. He has given a lucid and straightforward response, and not one of the sort often received from Delphi that permits some to interpret it in one way and others to interpret it in the opposite one. Rather, he said distinctly that if the child of one of the citizens were sacrificed by the people, he would stay the disease. **11.** On hearing this our sacred ambassadors turned back and ran through night and day alike in their haste, while we sat here, trembling in anticipation of the message with which they would return. When we saw them coming, many of us poured around them before they could enter and asked them if they had heard anything to give the city some respite. On their assurance of good news we thought there should be no delay, but we all ran to the assembly and the clerk read out the oracle. **12.** Thereupon it was decided that we should not make a decree that so-and-so, the son of so-and-so . . . and so on, for that would ill befit our democracy, I think, but the occasion called for the lot, and in this way equality was preserved. The fathers were assembled and the names of their children were inscribed on the lots, and the procedure was duly carried out. The lot fell on the son of this perpetrator of so many terrible crimes. This was greeted with applause, as you know, because we had the prospect of being delivered from two evils, the pestilence and this wicked offspring. **13.** If justice had been served, the sacrifice would have been made right away, and the plague would have been on its way and the city would now be making a second set of sacrifices in thanksgiving for its deliverance. As for this man, he would not be grieving too hard as being the recipient of a public honor, and if this were not possible, he would even so be pretending it was the case. But as things are he makes war on the god, he despises you. He prolongs the disease by speaking and says, "Pay no attention to Apollo, but listen to me. For I will bring an end to the pestilence. What need is there to sacrifice my son?" This is what the sorcerer [goês] says, and you suffer him to do so. **14.** You accursed man, do you say this now and dare to admit that that you refused to help us although it was in your power? This is no reason for his son to live. Rather, it is a reason for this man to be sacrificed along with his son. It is just, is it not, that the boy should comply with the oracle and that the father should pay the penalty for standing by and pitilessly watching the city perish so pitifully and refusing to come to its aid, although he had it in his power, as he himself admits?

**15.** But this accusation is not worth making, for neither did he have such power then nor does he have it now. He is just being evasive and trying to lead you astray and he is consistently wicked. First of all, he does not permit you to abide by your decisions. Come now, what did you resolve at that time when you took counsel for the deliverance of the city? Did you not resolve to leave all individuals out of consideration since they were of less import than the interests of the state, and to take refuge in the source of succor that is powerful enough to overcome any disaster, namely the god in Delphi? **16.** You didn't make a great many speeches about the matter—I would not say you did—but one man spoke briefly, no one opposed him, and the people took their vote. Sacred ambassadors were chosen, they went there, the consulted the oracle and asked what would put an end to the disease. They listened, they returned, they reported back: "We have the means to escape the plague." Shall we now undo our resolutions? Are we not ashamed at this change of heart that brings the greatest reproaches upon man and city alike? One can not be acquitted of the charge of folly in such circumstances, for it is impossible to succeed in doing the right thing when confronted by incompatible alternatives: you must admit that one or other course of action is wrong. **17.** I find it amazing that we despise tyrants, because they make the people weak, but are going to be grateful to this man who makes himself more powerful than the ratified decisions of the people. If someone had repealed the decree passed about bribery or the decree about the requirement to come to the aid of one's neighbors, or the one about sending to them for help, it would be terrible and we would be furious. **18.** What do you mean, then? Is it in vain that we assemble, listen to orators, weigh up what they say, vote, ratify the judgment we like, and go home again? Will we now take it lightly that our resolution to oppose the pestilence with the oracle is being frustrated? **19.** If he were attempting what he is doing now before the sacred ambassadors had set out, even so it would be arrogance, and his words would not have been preferred to the hopes offered by Delphi. But now that they have gone there and consulted the oracle and received the information they sought, shall we scoff at all they achieved and stand in awe of this idea of the mage's instead? And if it was to another god that someone had taken us, this would not have been free of blame either, albeit a lesser offence than the present one, but still subject to criticism. But as it is, approaching as we are a mere mortal after a god, shall we do no wrong? **20.** And this is to say nothing of the fact that we went to the oracle, nor of the fact that it is one of the most trusted, nor of the fact that it is there above all that truth is found, but everyone knows that the Delphic oracle surpasses all others in its location, its renown, and its truthfulness on all subjects. Even the kings of the barbarians knew this and brought the finest treasures they had and dedicated them there. It was this oracle that founded most of the Greek cities, it was this oracle that came to the aid of the Greek race in the greatest difficulties. **21.** And it is not for the first time that its power is being tested, but this man, the enemy of the gods, thinks he can impress us as more awe-inspiring than long centuries, vast experience, and public testimony. Nor indeed is the proposed method of the cure a novel one, but already other men have been delivered from disasters by similar measures. These sacrifices have not been hidden from view, but even the children could tell you these things and relate the people who performed the sacrifices, the people who have been sacrificed, and for what reasons. So what is there to persuade us to prefer the mage to the god and the message that comes from him?

**22.** So even if absolutely everything yielded before this man's craft, it would be incredibly foolish to condemn our recent resolutions as a fit of madness and to dishonor the god who has done no dishonor to the city. It is easy to see that he lies and cheats and falls far short of his claims. For to which of you, citizens, is it plausible that this man, a citizen seeing such destruction of his fellows, and such a risk that none of us will be left, as well as burial customs thrown into chaos because of the numbers of the dead, would have held himself back and declined to reveal himself, and would have given up the opportunity to have himself declared the savior of the city? Why did you not demonstrate this power, since you are prepared to contend with the gods today? Did you think that to do so would have been disreputable? On the contrary, one could not begin to express the repute of such an action. Or do you say that you were not offered the profit you desired? But you would have been denied nothing you demanded, whatever it was. **23.** Each of the other public benefactors became enviable after receiving a single reward, but we would have gathered everything together and given it to you, food, tax-immunity, vast quantities of land, heaps of money, statues all over the city, in the colonnades, in the gymnasia, in the temples. In all probability someone would have proposed a decree that you should be drunk to and be hymned among the gods. So why did you choose to punish yourself along with the city, begrudging so many benefits to yourself and salvation to the city, when you could have profited so greatly, along with the city? Who is so unnatural as to avoid such things as opposed to actively seeking them? Who would not pray to die after having been able to do this, in the knowledge of the sorts of epitaphs he would receive for such achievements? But you would have been able to enjoy such rewards even in your own lifetime. **24.** Indeed, this man could be more powerful than pestilence and famine. He would therefore have freed cities of famines by summoning the rain that was failing to appear, and checking it when it came in excess and by persuading the seasons to do no harm to the earth. And of course a man who was powerful in these respects could also easily rout enemies without recourse to arms, horses, or generals. So how many trophies have you set up in honor of victories over opponents? **25.** Yet, if you did have the power, these things too would have been done. Rather than being willing to congratulate others for their outstanding achievements in war, you would be wanting to be among the garlanded yourself, and indeed to receive greater praise than is accorded to military heroism, insofar as you would be driving off the enemy without a sound and without trouble. I often saw this man haggling with merchants about money, sometimes demanding it, at other times giving thanks for receiving it. Yet why did he have to trouble the rich when he had the power to be one of those giving money out? **26.** Why has your craft not opened up for you all the treasuries and why has it not joined everything which currently lies buried in the earth to your estate? "Because," comes the response, "Men have different areas of expertise. I know my own field rather well. I didn't approach you or make my proposition before because of these envious [*phthonountas*] people who slander my craft, but now I have been left with no choice." **27.** My own view is that there is absolutely no need to inform people, as they would surely know already, that someone might have come and made a name for himself among them by extinguishing epidemics. And I also have something to say about his reference to slander. Who would not have endured a few words of abuse if he was going to confute the sycophants who were doling it out? Why would you not have choked off those maligning [*baskainontas*] your power, if you demonstrated that you had acquired it for the common good of the city? I would now be the first to stand up and declare them the pestilences and the enemies of the city, and I would be demanding that they be punished. But you were not afraid of envy [*phthonos*]. Why? Because you knew that you possessed no power great enough to incur it. For this reason you approved of our trip to consult the god.

**28.** Do not consider everything these men claim they can do to be possible for them, citizens. Consider some to be so, others not to be so, and some to be highly possible, others minimally so. It isn't the case that people like this fellow here usually deliver us from a catastrophic situation, but rather that they devise and set it up in the first place. This is the reason they belong among the hated rather than the honored. For they have made no one fortunate, but many wretched. **29.** Why is it so? The more evil of the demons, whose nature it is to do bad, take delight in their activities and they help them achieve these terrible things which destroy people. With the help of these demons they set friends at variance, they start wars within families, they scatter wealth, they inflict poverty, they strike out eyes, they twist back tongues, they make people dumb, they bind feet, they disable hands, they make bodies waste away, they do much in addition to these things. This man knows well how they are able to do these things and what they do and say to achieve them, but I have not learned how, and I hope never to do so. Anyway, these are the deeds of their fellowship and this is the work of this fine craft. **30.** So let him call himself the friend of evil demons—I don't deny it—but he is the enemy of the powers from whom come good things for men and deliverances from evils precisely because of this friendship with the other powers. For the same man cannot have influence with both groups, but a man who does harm through the agency of the one group deprives himself of the opportunity to give help through the agency of the others. They harm one or two men, and if they are exceptionally powerful, a whole house or a city. What enables them to inflict damage is their own wicked nature and the fact that they get away with it; their magical skill and spells [*pharmaka*] are of no consequence.

**31.** Why need I proceed with the proof that this man has no power to do good, when I can demonstrate this from the present situation? Can a man who is not even able to divert the lot deliver an entire city from disease? Can a man who is unable to help his son in the hour of need triumph over the plague? Were you not frightened that the lot might fall to him? Why do you tremble now that it has done so? You were frightened that the lot might fall to him? So why didn't you ensure that it didn't fall to him? Didn't you expect it to do so? Where then is this amazing mage? **32.** Forget all this. I, with all these people here, now take hold of your son and we are going to sacrifice him. Overcome us, save his body, snatch him from our hands, make the lad disappear in a cloud, make us think we have him when we don't. Do you see how you are at a loss and, confounded, have no response to offer?

**33.** What proof that you will eradicate the plague do you offer us in support of your insistence that we give up the only thing in which we have any confidence and wait about for developments in which we can place no trust whatever? "The proof," he says, "is that if I had not been firmly persuaded that I would be up to the task, I would not have made my offer. What further advantage is there in taking my son to the slaughter?" **34.** Only this, first of all, mage, that he is not dying today. And you, as seems likely, will ask also for the following day, a third, a fourth, then ten and twice as many again, while you claim that you can provide one of the elements contributing to the cure but are not yet able to provide the other, and that it is the element that has yet to materialize that is the more powerful. And you will chatter on about the moon and the days of the month and you will in general find one cause of delay after another. And to do nothing, but to speak continually of what you are going to do is itself sufficient to buy time. **35.** This one consequence is no small profit to this man, but a second one, equally great, or even greater, is that many of the citizens should die in these days before the boy selected by the lot. For he thinks that will bring no mean consolation to the child and to himself and he believes that the effects of the pestilence will alleviate his disaster if it continues to rage unchecked. **36.** What if he says that it is necessary to circumambulate the territory by night, and that no one else should be present, just his boy, who alone is able to participate in such purifications, and that everything will have been done in vain without these concessions? What if he compels you with these arguments to hand the boy, on whom the salvation of the city depends, over to him, and then absconds off to our enemies? What will we do then? Tell me. Shall we turn to another victim? Who will submit? Will we find anyone? **37.** If the resentful god vitiates the enterprise, shall we send, by Zeus, to him and ask about the disease and seek a cure again? He will say "You are the silliest of men. You found a ready source of help. You had the sacrificial offering in your hands. You had it in your power to bring an end to the pestilence, but instead you held a debate after receiving my oracles. Why then do you dissemble? You have men who are better than me: why don't you rid yourself of your troubles by following their advice?" What shall we do then? We shall blame, by Zeus, those who helped this man and we shall say that we should not have been dissuaded by this man's tears. But we shall perish all the same. **38.** Isn't it our terrible bad luck if through the mage's prevarications we miss the deliverance now being offered us and subsequently fail to receive another in its place? The terrible consequences are not limited just to this immediate situation, but the god will refuse to help us in the future when called in upon another disaster. For why should he? To retrieve pious men from dangers? Our present behavior is indeed a fine demonstration of piety! In this way to accept this man's case today renders Apollo hostile to us once and for all, and there is no small fear lest something else be added to the disease and that this should be incurable for the city now that hope from Delphi has been cut off for us.

**39.** Moreover, citizens, there is yet another point from which you could learn that no attention should be paid to this man. I question him before you. Will you overcome your adversary by sacrificing a second boy in some secret corner? Who is this to be? Where will you get him from? Who will give him to you, given that the oracle names no one? How much more just is it that the one to die should be the one chosen by the lot? **40.** Or will you find a cure for the disease in another way? But the oracle says this is the only way. If more ways were available, the god would not have concealed the abundance of routes to healing, nor would he have shown himself to be inferior to these doctors who compete in the listing of all manners of cures, but he would have told off for us all the courses of action we could take to escape the pestilence—this course or that course, or, by Zeus, another one again, or indeed the very one that has now been prophesied to us. But see how the god leaves everything else aside and says that help depends on this one boy alone, to catch out, I think, these very people, as if the actual origin of the pestilence lies with them, with the father giving directions and leading the attack and the son complying and trying to copy him. **41.** "So why," he says, "does he not slaughter me?" Because he considers the death of your child more terrible for you than your own death. Grief over the death of a loved one while one yet lives oneself is more grievous for all men. "Why then," he says, "did the god not explicitly tell you to sacrifice my son?" Because he knew that in that case you would slander the oracle: "Citizens, this response has been organized from here. It is the work of those who envy me, of those who cannot endure my repute. This was not the response of the god, but of the Delphians who will do anything for money." **42.** This was the reason that he did not utter your name directly, but brought about the same result through the use of the lot. Or do you believe that the lot was not performed in a way that reflected the choice and decision of the god? So why do you make trouble and quarrel and behave like some impious archer of old, who, the poets tell us, raised his bow against the god? You too now compete against the oracle, but the difference is that the archer was a lone madman, whereas you want to turn the whole city mad. Citizens, are these the actions of prudent men? Does anyone deliberate about oracular responses when what is needed is to proceed with the task? Does anyone hold onto the disease when he is able to get rid of it and give ear to the words of men after hearing divine oracles? Does anyone want to go home and see his family sick when he could see them healthy? **43.** And what will you say to those in their beds, those around the wells, those in bad condition, those who are feverish? They certainly learned of the god's response and they are surprised, as you might expect, that they have not yet been freed of the disease. What will you say to them, still sick as they are? Will you tell them about the mage and the offer he makes and that he will perhaps achieve something? How will you then bear the laments of the sick? You will be shown to have valued the son of the mage more highly than your own children.

**44.** I see the majority of you dressed in black, citizens, one of you for your brother, another for a wife, another for a child, another for all of these. Do you want those who are not yet raising the lament to suffer the same things and greater sufferings to be inflicted on those who have already been stricken? Don't, I beg you by the many graves already dug, but take pity on those who are sick now and those who will soon be so. For the evil will come, it will come, I say, step by step, upon all of us, if it is not stayed with the sword. The mage will not be experiencing any uncommonly strange or pitiable grief as he goes in search of his own son in the company of most other fathers, nor would it be right for him to say to us, "Preserve my son, but abandon your own." For this is what he is asking for, even if his words avoid it. **45.** None of this would be necessary, if he were truly capable of fulfilling his claims and promises. For what was there to prevent him, tell me, before he said anything, before he made any promises, from attaching the cure to the lot, and from turning a chance for making speeches into one to rid our city of the plague, and so prevent our sacrificing as there would no longer be any compelling need for it? **46.** "But it was not possible to bring about a cure so promptly, only over a period of time." Therefore, even if you are going to dismiss the pestilence in this way—let us make allowance for the possibility, however silly it seems—you do not give a fair exchange. For where is the equality in on the one hand seeing our children healthy here and now and on the other attaining this goal only after many of them have died? Why should we put up with our fellow-citizen expressing his dissent in this way if he will be of some use to the city through his son? **47.** Each of these men, if he had seen his own son seized on by the lot, would probably not even have cried. Indeed, he might even have some pleasure mingled in with his grief, if he could be making such a contribution to the city. But this man is contentious and refuses to undertake his liturgy and abuses the gods and all but demolishes their temples. The gods, who have conferred the greatest benefits upon us, would be lying idle, while this man, who has devoted his life to wicked spells, like some tyrant, claims that the safety of the community should give place to his own pleasures. **48.** Why? Because of his many trophies of war, captured prisoners, ships, harbors, and territories? And yet even if he had achieved all this, not even in this case would it be reasonable of him to ask for the annihilation of the city in return. If you would not have bestowed such an honor upon generals, victorious heroes, or those who have saved us from the greatest dangers, why will you grant it to the sorcerer [goês]? **49.** You cannot endure the sacrifice of your son? If he had grown to manhood and taken up arms and fallen fighting on behalf of his city, would you not have endured it even then? Well, the other fathers used to bury with pride their sons who died in this way. And there have been times when a general too has taken his sons into battle and brought them back dead, without blaming himself or the city or the boys themselves. But you would be advising your own sons to stay at home and expose themselves to indictment for avoiding military service rather than to the possibility of wounds. If the oracle had called for high-mindedness on the part of a father, this man would in all probability have jumped up before everyone else and given his son freely, this man who does not even endure the lot.

**50.** If you were not a mage, I would be consoling you with the same words I would address to any other father. "My dear friend," I would say, "believe that your son is dying in the context of the plague, only before he actually contracts it Count how many boys of the same age as him we buried yesterday. What if his life after this point was even less agreeable than his present death? He departs crowned and to the accompaniment of libation and prayers and leaving a glorious reputation behind him." **51.** I would have run through these commonplaces and many similar ones too, if you were just like other men, but as it is, just listen to the words of consolation your craft enables me to utter for you. Why are you frightened, mage? Why do you weep? You will have your son even after his sacrifice. He will hear you when you call, he will appear, he will converse with you, he will spend the nights with you, and indeed he will do your bidding more eagerly than the other ghosts. So you have no need to be upset when you yourself are profiting personally along with the city.

LIBANIUS (314–CA. 393 A.D.) OF ANTIOCH WAS A pagan rhetorician of great distinction. He corresponded with emperors (he was a supporter of Julian the Apostate) and taught many men, both pagan and Christian, who were to become distinguished in turn, including John Chrysostom, Gregory of Nazianz, and Ammianus Marcellinus. For an excerpt from his autobiography see **247**. This speech is a rhetorical exercise, its premise set out in the prefatory note. It is Classical and traditional not only in style but also in the magical commonplaces it recycles.

The principal axis of the speech is the antithesis between the respectable, authoritative, powerful, and benign divine, as embodied in the Apollo of Delphi, and the disreputable, fraudulent, ineffectual, malevolent, and impious mage. The Delphic oracle was famously obscure but is here portrayed as a model of simple and transparent clarity in contrast to the mage's deceitful obfuscations (9, 15, 20). The mage claims to be the companion of the gods and, in the familiar fashion of ancient magicians, to be able to compel them (6, 7, 13); in reality, he is their enemy (9, 21–2).

The projection of the mage has much in common with projections in the classical authors (10–7). Libanius similarly uses the terms mage (*magos*, throughout) and "sorcerer" (*goês*, 13, 48) interchangeably. The mage is similarly too accused repeatedly of lying and chalatanry (2, 3, 4, 15, 22, 27, 28, 45), although much of the speech inconsistently assumes that he does indeed possess the genuine ability to contrive malicious effects. The commonplace identification between magic and rhetoric is much in evidence. The mage is said to bewitch the citizens with his words (3), and a distinction is repeatedly drawn between the simple instructions of the oracle with the resolution that followed and the wordy and obfuscating debate about it initiated by the mage (e.g., 16; compare 12, with commentary). Indeed it seems that the mage's true power lies in his ability to bamboozle with words; he is a tyrant overthrowing the will of the people (17–8, 38). The mage is accused of acting for his own personal ends rather than for the general good of the city (4, 14, 22, 27, 44, 47–8, 51), in marked contrast to the speaker, who puts the welfare of the city before his personal safety (8, 15). The mage is abused also as a hireling and beggarly (6–8, 25–6). This attitude stems in part from the old snobbery against *banausoi*, those who depended on the patronage of others for their livelihood, as opposed to the supposedly self-sufficient farmers or fishermen. The old Platonic theme that mages trouble the rich for their trade is rehearsed (25; compare 14).

The mage is attributed with, or is said to claim for himself, a range of powers. The speech is founded on the premise that the mage can bring about purifications to deliver the city from pestilence and famine (see especially 24, 27, 36). In this respect he recalls Epimenides of Cnossus (5, 9). Also like Epimenides, the mage could aspire to control of the weather and to controlling victory in wars (24).

Particular attention is drawn to his necromantic activities. Tombs constitute the main source of his strength (8; compare 108–14). The strange phrase in which he is said to "roll around tombs" reflects both the notion that he morbidly makes cemeteries his haunts and the circular, purificatory movements made around graves in ghost-laying (36; see 30). He uses the ghosts to inflict death and curses (7; compare 114). He can use his powers to divide friends and families, inflict poverty, blind, render dumb, bind limbs, and make bodies waste away (29). Much of this can be understood in terms of the familiar binding curses (see 168–84, 237, 239–40). In the witty and sarcastic final chapter it is implied that the mage can call up ghosts with ease, have conversations with them, and have them do his bidding (51). The association here of necromancy with consolation for the death of a son is reminiscent of Crantor of Soli's tale of Elysius of Terina, 149. Necromancy constitutes the most obvious basis for the claim that the mage can predict the future (31). The mage is also attributed with boy-sacrifice in the furtherance of his magical activities, presumably to manufacture ghosts to do his bidding (39; compare **133-8**). This is not a little awkward in context, given that the mage's prime concern is obviously to prevent a boy-sacrifice.

The speaker must tread a fine line. He must show himself familiar enough with the mage's magical techniques in order to make a case against him, but without giving the appearance that he is himself a magical adept (29). Apuleius faced the same difficulty when defending himself against the accusation of the practice of magic: How could he argue in technical detail against the charge of having performed magic without ipso facto demonstrating the knowledge of a magical expert (**299**; compare **286**)?

When considering the mage's powers genuine, Libanius ascribes their source to his alliance with evil demons. Good powers are the enemies of such demons, and so the mage excludes himself from the possibility of doing good; for these demons compare **43, 112**. Hence his magic can only be used for bad ends (28–30). These words would not have been uncomfortable for the Christians in his audience.

One of the most interesting aspects of this speech is the insight it gives into sorcerers' explanations as to why their powers do not work, or why they should forbear to use them. Slander, so often found in the company of magic, is a prime consideration: to be seen to be exercising magical powers can lead to ill repute and the slander of the envious (*phthonos, baskainontas*, 22, 26–7, 41). These terms themselves have magical overtones and therefore imply that the mage holds his scope of activity to be limited by his rivals (compare **192–6, 295**). Accordingly, the mage himself is also portrayed as a proponent of slander (41, 47). The aura of competitive malice that surrounded the profession of the ancient mage may often have hindered trade in individual cases. But at a broader level it supported the profession by furnishing it with a justification in its own terms for its presumably frequent failures. So too the aura of charlatanry that clung to the profession as a whole paradoxically implied the possibility of a genuine magic. When spells are failing one can also appeal to the need for the magical process to be extended over a prolonged period (46) or the need to wait for significant days of the month on which to accomplish the magic (34). For the attribution of this type of excuse-manufacturing to mages see **45**. Procrastination through argument is itself also a useful tool (34). The mage has not been able to use his powers to enrich himself because sorcerers are very specialized in their abilities, and wealth-creation is not his field (25–6); compare the mockery Philip the *Orpheotelestês* supposedly incurred for his penury (19) and so too that leveled at Lucan's Hyperborean mage (**244**).

The old notion that plague might descend on a community because of the unjust behavior of one man within it is rightly referred back to Hesiod (5–6, 9, 12, 40, 44). Underneath the idea that a communal pestilence sent from the gods can be expunged by the expulsion or sacrifice of an individual lies the custom of scapegoating (*pharmakeia*); compare **58**.

# Bibliographies

## TEXT LIST

*Note*: where texts belong to one of the major series, notably Oxford Classical Texts, Teubner, or Budé, this is indicated.

**Aelian Fragments**: D. Domingo-Forasté. 1994. *Claudii Aeliani Epistulae et Fragmenta*. Teubner Stuttgart. ***Varia historia***: N.G. Wilson, ed. 1997. *Aelian. Historical Miscellany*. Loeb Classical Library. Cambridge.

**Aeschines**: V. Martin, and G. de Budé, eds. 1927–28. *Éschine. Discours*. 2 vols. Paris.

**Aeschylus** *Aichmalotides, Psychagogoi*: *TrGF*. **Persians**: Broadhead 1960.

**Aesop** *Fables*: B.E. Perry, 1952. *Aesopica: A series of texts relating to Aesop or ascribed to him or closely connected with the literary tradition that bears his name*. Urbana, Ill.

**Aetius** book 6: A. Olivieri, ed. 1950. *Aetii Amideni libri medicinales v–viii*. Berlin.

**Antiphon** 1: M. Gagarin, ed. 1996. *Antiphon. The Speeches*. Cambridge.

**[Apollodorus of Athens]** *Bibliotheca* and **Epitome**: J.G. Frazer. 1921. *Apollodorus. The Library*. Loeb Classical Library. 2 vols. Cambridge, Mass.

**Apollonius** *Historiae mirabiles*: A. Giannini, ed. 1965. *Paradoxographorum Graecorum reliquiae*. Milan.

**Apollonius of Rhodes** book 3: R.L. Hunter, ed. 1989. *Apollonius of Rhodes. Argonautica Book III*. Cambridge Greek and Latin Classics. Cambridge. Book 4: H. Fraenkel, ed. 1961. *Apollonii Rhodii Argonautica*. Oxford Classical Texts. Oxford.

**Apuleius** *Apology*: V. Hunink, ed. 1997. *Apuleius of Madauros. Pro se de Magia (Apologia)*. 2 vols. Amsterdam. ***Metamorphoses*** (i.e., ***Golden Ass***): D.S. Robertson, and P. Valette, eds. 1940–45. *Apulée. Les Métamorphoses*. Budé. 3 vols. Paris. ***De deo Socratis***: J. Beaujeu, ed. 1973. *Apulée. Opuscules philosophiques*. Budé. Paris.

**Aristophanes** *Clouds*: K.J. Dover, ed. 1968. *Aristophanes. Clouds*. Oxford. ***Wasps***: D.M. MacDowell, ed. 1971. *Aristophanes. Wasps*. Oxford.

**Aristophanes Scholia**: W.J.W. Koster, and D. Holwerda, eds. 1978. *Scholia in Vespas, Pacem, Aves et Lysistratam*. Part 2 fascicle 1. Groningen.

**Aristotle Fragments**: V. Rose, ed. 1886. *Aristotelis qui ferebantur librorum fragmenta*. Teubner. Leipzig. **[Aristotle]** *Magna moralia*: F. Susemihl, ed. 1935. *Aristotle*. Vol. 18. Loeb Classical Library. Cambridge, Mass.

**Arnobius** *Adversus nationes*: C. Marchesi, ed. 1934. *Arnobii Adversus Nationes. Libri vii*. Turin.

**Athenaeus** *Deipnosophistai*: G. Kaibel, ed. 1887–90. *Athenaei Naucratitae Deipnosophistarum Libri xv* . Teubner. 3 vols. Leipzig.

**Augustine** *City of God* and **Confessions**: *PL*, 32–46.

**Basil of Caesarea** *Letters*: Y. Courtonne, ed. 1957–66. *Saint Basile. Lettres*. Budé. 3 vols. Paris.

**Bekker** *Anecdota Graeca*: I. Bekker, ed. 1814–21. *Anecdota Graeca*. 3 vols. Berlin.

**[Callisthenes]** *Alexander Romance*: W. Kroll. 1926. Reprinted 1958. *Historia Alexandri Magni*. Berlin.

**Capitolinus:** D. Magie, ed. 1922–23. *Scriptores Historiae Augustae*. 2 vols. Loeb Classical Library. Cambridge, Mass.

**Cato *De agri cultura*:** A. Ernout, 1957. *Recueil de textes latins archaiques* Paris.

**Catullus:** D.F.S. Thomson, 1997. *Catullus. Edited with a textual and interpretative commentary*. Toronto.

**Cicero *Tusculan Disputations 1*:** A.E. Douglas, ed. 1985. *Cicero: Tusculan Disputations I*. Warminster. **On Divination:** W. Ax, ed. 1938. *Cicero. De divinatione, de Fato, Timaeus*. Leipzig.

**Claudian:** J.B. Hall, ed. 1985. *Claudianus. Carmina*. Teubner. Leipzig.

**Clearchus of Soli:** F. Wehrli, ed. 1948. *Die Schule des Aristoteles. Texte und Kommentar. Klearchos*. Basel.

**Clement of Alexandria *Protrepticus and Stromata*:** O. Stählin, ed. 1905–36. Teubner. 4 vols. Berlin.

**[Clement of Rome] *Recognitions*:** *PG*, 2: 19–646.

***Cyranides*:** D. Kaimakis, ed. 1976. *Die Kyraniden*. Meisenheim, am Glan, with emendations noted by Prof. David Bain *per litteras*.

**Demosthenes:** S.H. Butcher, and W. Rennie, eds. 1907–55. *Demosthenis orationes*. Oxford Classical Texts. 3 vols. Oxford.

***Derveni Papyrus*:** A. Laks, and G.W. Most, eds. 1997. *Studies on the Derveni papyrus*. Oxford.

***Digest of Justinian*:** T. Mommsen, P. Krueger, and A. Watson, eds. 1985. *Digesta. English and Latin*. 4 vols. Philadelphia.

**Dio Cassius:** U.P. Boissevain, ed. 1895–1901. *Cassii Dionis Cocceiani historiarum romanarum quae supersunt*. Teubner. 3 vols. Berlin.

**Diodorus:** F. Vogel and K.T. Fischer, eds. 1890–1906. *Diodori Bibliotheca Historica* Teubner. 5 vols. Leipzig.

**Diogenes Laertius:** H.S. Long, ed. 1964. *Diogenis Laertii Vitae Philosophorum*. Oxford Classical Texts. 2 vols. Oxford.

**Donatus:** P. Wessner, ed. 1902–8 *Aeli Donati quod fertur Commentum Terenti*. 3 vols. Teubner. Leipzig.

**Empedocles Fragments:** M.R. Wright, ed. 1995. *Empedocles. The extant fragments*. 2nd ed. Bristol.

**Euripides *Alcestis*:** A.M. Dale, ed. 1954. *Euripides. Alcestis*. Oxford. **Andromache:** P.T. Stevens, ed. 1971. *Euripides. Andromache*. Oxford. **Hippolytus:** W.S. Barrett, ed. 1964. *Euripides. Hippolytos*. Oxford. **Medea:** D.L. Page, ed. 1938. *Euripides. Medea*. **Orestes:** M.L. West, ed. 1987. *Euripides. Orestes*. Warminster. Oxford. **Scholia:** E. Schwartz, ed. 1887–91. *Scholia in Euripidem*. 2 vols. Berlin.

**Eusebius *Against Hierocles*:** C.L. Kayser, ed. 1870. *Flavii Philostrati opera* vol. 1. Teubner. Leipzig. ***Chronicle of Jerome*:** R. Helm. 1984. *Eusebius Werke. Siebenter Band. Die Chronik des Hieronymus*. Berlin.

**Gorgias *Encomium of Helen*:** D.M. MacDowell, ed. 1982. *Gorgias, Encomium of Helen*. Bristol.

**Heliodorus *Aethiopica*:** R.M. Rattenbury, T.W. Lumb, and J. Maillon, eds. 1960. *Héliodore. Les Éthiopiques (Théagène et Chariclée)*. Budé. 3 vols. Paris.

**Hesychius:** M. Schmidt, ed. 1861. *Hesychii Alexandrini Lexicon*. 4 vols. Halle. Reprinted Amsterdam, 1965.

**Heraclitus:** M. Marcovich, ed. 1967. *Heraclitus*. Meridia, Venezuela.

**Herodotus:** H.B. Rosén, ed. 1987–97. *Herodoti Historiae*. Teubner. 2 vols. Leipzig.

**Hippocrates *On the Sacred Disease:*** H. Grensemann, ed. 1968. *Die hippokratische Schrift "Über die heilige Krankheit."* Berlin.

**Hippolytus *Refutations*:** M. Marcovich, ed. 1986. *Refutatio omnium haeresium*. Berlin.

**Homer *Iliad*:** T.W. Allen, ed. 1931. *Homeri Ilias*. Oxford Classical Texts. 2 vols. Oxford. **Odyssey:** P. von der Muehll, ed. 1962. *Homeri Odyssea*. Basel. **[Homer] *Epigrams*.** In [Herodotus] *Vita Homeri*. T.W. Allen, ed. 1912. *Homeri opera*. Vol. 5. Oxford Classical Texts. Oxford.

Horace: D.R. Shackleton-Bailey, ed. 1985. *Horatius. Opera*. Teubner. Stuttgart.

Hyginus *Fabulae*: H.I. Rose, ed. 1933. *Hygini Fabulae*. Leyden.

Iamblichus (novelist): *see* Photius.

Iamblichus (philosopher): L. Deubner, and U. Klein, eds. 1975. *Iamblichi de vita Pythagorica liber*. Teubner. Stuttgart.

Josephus *Jewish Antiquities*: B. Niese, ed. 1888–92. *Flavii Josephi Opera*. 3 vols. Berlin.

Julius Africanus *Kestoi*: J.-R. Vieillefond, ed. 1970. *Les "Cestes" de Julius Africanus. Étude sur l'ensemble des fragments avec édition, traduction et commentaires*. Paris.

Justin Martyr *Apologies*: E.J. Goodspeed, ed. 1915. *Die ältesten Apologeten*. Göttingen.

Libanius: R. Förster, ed.1903–22. *Libanii opera*. Teubner. 11 vols. Leipzig. Reprinted Hildesheim, 1963.

Lucan *Pharsalia*: A.E. Housman, ed. 1926. *Lucani Belli civilis libri x*. Oxford.

Lucian: M. MacLeod, ed. 1972–87. *Luciani opera*. Oxford Classical Texts. 4 vols. Oxford.

Maximus of Tyre *Dissertationes*: M.B. Trapp, ed. 1994. *Maximus Tyrius. Dissertationes*. Teubner. Stuttgart.

Menander: A. Körte, and A. Thierfelder, eds. 1959. *Menandri quae supersunt*. 2nd ed. Teubner. Leipzig.

New Testament: British and Foreign Bible Society ed. 1954. *Η ΚΑΙΝΗ ΔΙΑΘΗΚΗ*. London.

Origen *Contra Celsum* 1: M. Borret, ed. 1967. *Origène. Contre Celse*. Vol. 1, books 1 and 2. Paris.

Orphic *Argonautica*: F. Vian, ed. 1987. *Les Argonautiques orphiques*. Budé. Paris.

Ovid *Amores, Remedia Amoris*: E.J. Kenney, ed. 1994. *P. Ovidi Nasonis Amores, Medicamina faciei femineae, Ars amatoria, Remedia Amoris*. 2nd ed. Oxford Classical Texts. Oxford. *Fasti*: E.H. Alton, D.E.W. Wormell, and E. Courtney, eds. 1978 *P. Ovidi Nasonis Fastorum Libri Sex*. Teubner. Leipzig. *Heroides*: H. Dörrie, ed. 1977. *P. Ovidii Nasonis Epistulae Heroidum*. Teubner. Berlin. *Metamorphoses*: D.E. Bosselaar, and B.A. van Proosdij, eds. 1951. *P. Ovidii Nasonis Metamorphoseon Libri i–xv*. Leiden.

*Papyri Graecae Magicae*: Preisendanz and Henrichs 1973–4, incorporating most revisions as noted in Brashear 1995. But for *PGM XXIII* (Julius Africanus *Kestoi* 18), see Vieillefond 1970.

Pausanias: F. Spiro, ed. 1903. *Pausaniae Graeciae descriptio*. Teubner. 3 vols. Leipzig.

Petronius *Cena Trimalchionis*: M.S. Smith, ed. 1975. *Petronii Arbitri Cena Trimalchionis*. Oxford. Other fragments of the *Satyricon*: A. Ernout, ed. 1931. *Pétrone. Le Satiricon*. Budé. Paris.

Philostratus *Life of Apollonius of Tyana*: L. de Lannay, ed. 1977. *Flavii Philostrati Heroicus*. Teubner. Berlin..

Phlegon of Tralles *Mirabilia*: A. Giannini, ed. 1965. *Paradoxographorum Graecorum reliquiae*. Milan.

Photius *Bibliotheka*: R. Henry, ed., 1959–77. *Photius. Bibliothèque*. Budé. 8 vols. Paris.

Pindar: A. Turyn, ed. 1952. *Pindari Carmina cum fragmentis*. Oxford.

Plato: J. Burnet, ed. 1900. *Platonis opera*. Oxford Classical Texts. 5 vols. Oxford. Scholia: W.C. Greene, ed. 1938. *Scholia Platonica*. Haverford, Pa.

Plautus *Mostellaria:* A. Ernout, ed. 1938. *Plaute. Tome v. Mostellaria—Persa—Poenulus*. Budé. Paris. *Amphitruo*: W.B. Sedgwick, ed. 1960. *Plautus. Amphitruo*. Manchester.

Pliny [the Elder] *Natural History*: J. Beauleu, et al., eds. 1947–85. *Pline l'ancien. Histoire naturelle*. Sundry volumes. Budé. Paris.

Pliny [the Younger] *Letters*: R.A.B. Mynors, ed. 1963. *C. Plini Caecili Secundi Epistularum Libri Decem*. Oxford Classical Texts. Oxford.

Plutarch *Moralia*: H. Wegehaupt, et al., eds. 1935–. *Plutarchi Moralia*. Teubner. Leipzig. *Lives*: K. Ziegler, ed. 1964–71. *Plutarchi vitae parallelae*. Teubner. 3rd/4th eds. 4 vols. Leipzig.

Polemon *Declamationes*: H. Hinck, ed. 1873. *Polemonis declamationes quae extant duae*. Teubner. Leipzig.

Porphyrio: G. Meyer, ed. 1874. *Pomponii Porphyrionis commentarii in Q. Horatium Flaccum*. Teubner. Leipzig.

Porphyry *Life of Pythagoras*: E. des Places, ed. 1982. *Porphyre. Vie de Pythagore. Lettre à Marcella*. Budé. Paris. *Life of Plotinus*: P. Henry, and H.-R. Schwyzer, eds. 1964. *Plotini opera*. Vol. 1. Oxford Classical Texts. Oxford.

Proclus *Commentary on Plato's Republic*: W. Kroll, ed. 1899–1901. *In Platonis rem publicam commentarii*. 2 vols. Teubner. Leipzig.

Propertius: A. Barber, ed. 1960. *Properti carmina*. 2nd ed. Oxford Classical Texts. Oxford.

Python: *TrGF*.

[Quintilian] *Declamationes maiores*: L. Håkanson, ed. 1982. *Declamationes XIX maiores Quintiliano falso ascriptae*. Teubner. Stuttgart.

Selinus *Lex sacra:* Jameson, Jordan, and Kotansky 1993.

Seneca *Medea*: C.D.N. Costa. 1973. *Seneca. Medea*. Oxford. *Oedipus*: O. Zwierlein, ed. 1986. *L. Annaei Senecae Tragoediae*. Oxford Classical Texts. Oxford.

Socrates *Ecclesiastical History*: W. Bright, ed. 1893. *Socrates. Ecclesiastical History*. Oxford.

Sophocles: H. Lloyd-Jones, and N.G. Wilson, eds. 1990. *Sophoclis Fabulae*. Oxford Classical Texts. **Fragments**: *TrGF*.

Sophron: G. Kaibel, ed. 1899. *Comicorum Graecorum fragmenta*. Vol. 1.1. Berlin. K.T. Kock. 1880–88. *Comicorum Atticorum Fragmenta*. 2 vols. Leipzig.

Statius *Thebaid*: D.E. Hill, ed. 1983. *P. Papini Stati Thebaidos libri xii*. Leiden.

Stephanus of Byzantium: A. Meineke, ed. 1849. *Stephan von Byzanz. Ethnika*. Berlin.

Strabo: H.L. Jones, ed. 1917–32. *Strabo. Geography*. Loeb Classical Library. 8 vols. Cambridge, Mass.

Suda: A. Adler, ed. 1931. *Suidae Lexicon*. Teubner. 4 vols. Leizpig.

Suetonius: M.C. Ihm, ed. 1908. *Suetoni Tranquilli opera*. Vol. 1. *De vita Caesarum libri vii*. Stuttgart.

*Supplementum Magicum*: Daniel and Maltomini 1990–92.

Synesius of Cyrene: N. Terzaghi, ed. 1944. *Synesii Cyrenensis Opuscula*. Scriptores Graeci et Latini Consilio Academiae Lynceorum Editi. Rome.

Tacitus *Annals* 1–6: S. Borzsak, ed. 1992. *Tacitus Annales i–vi*. Teubner. Leipzig. *Annals* 11–6: K. Wellesley, ed. 1986. *Tacitus Annales xi–xvi*. Teubner. Leipzig.

Tertullian *De anima*: J.H. Waszink, ed. 1947. *Quinti Septimi Florentis Tertulliani De Anima*. Amsterdam.

Theocritus: A.S.F. Gow, ed. 1950. *Theocritus, edited with a translation and commentary*. 2 vols. Cambridge.

*Theodosian Code*: T. Mommsen, and P.M. Meyer, eds. 1905. *Theodosiani libri xvi cvm Constitutionibus Simmondianis*. Berlin.

Theophrastus *Characters*: J. Rusten, ed. 1993. In *Theophrastus, Characters; Herodas, Mimes; Cercidas and the Choliambic poets*. Loeb Classical Library. Cambridge, Mass.

Thessalus of Tralles: H.-V. Friedrich, ed. 1968. *Thessalos von Tralles. Griechisch und lateinisch*. Meisenheim am Glan, Germany.

Thucydides: H.S. Jones, and J.E. Powell, eds. *Thucydidis Historiae*. Oxford Classical Texts. 2 vols. Oxford.

Tibullus: G. Luck, ed. 1988. *Albii Tibulli allorumque carmina*. Teubner. Stuttgart.

Valerius Flaccus *Argonautica*: E. Courtney, ed.1970. *C. Valerius Flaccus. Argonauticon*. Teubner. Leipzig.

Virgil. *Eclogues*: R. Coleman, ed. 1977. *Vergil. Eclogues*. Cambridge Greek and Latin Classics. Cambridge. *Aeneid* and *Georgics*: A.B. Mynors, *Vergili opera*. Oxford Classical Texts. Oxford. [Virgil] *Dirae*: F.R.D. Goodyear. 1971. "The 'Dirae.'" *PCPS* 17: 30–43.

Xenophon *Memorabilia*: E.C. Marchant, ed. 1921. *Xenophontis opera omnia*. Vol. 2. Oxford Classical Texts. Oxford.

**Zosimus book 1:** F. Paschoud, ed.1971. *Zosime. Histoire nouvelle.* Vol. 1, books 1 and 2. Budé. Paris.

## A GUIDE TO FURTHER READING

The series of texts translated in this book give rise to some complex issues of interpretation, some of which have been merely touched upon in the accompanying commentaries. It is therefore only appropriate to offer some guidance on further reading for those who wish to pursue it. The following lists of items, cited in author-plus-date style, refer to the general bibliography of "works cited" that follows. I trust that the economy of this system will mitigate its initial opaqueness. The numbers under which these bibliographies are organized correspond to the relevant chapters.

### 1. Documents and General Books

*1. Defixiones: Standard Corpora and Lists*

Audollent 1904; Besnier 1920; Daniel and Maltomini 1990–92; Gager 1992; Jordan 1985b; Kagarow 1929; Lopez Jimeno 1991; Solin 1968; Tomlin 1988; Wünsch 1897, 1898; Ziebarth 1934.

*2. Greek magical papyri: Standard Corpora, Commentaries and Translations*

Betz 1992; Daniel and Maltomini 1990–92; Meyer and Smith 1994; Preisendanz and Henrichs 1973–74 (important update, Brashear 1995).

*3. Voodoo Dolls: Standard List*

Faraone 1991b.

*4. Amulets and Intaglios. Standard Corpora and Ancient Texts*

Bonner 1950; Delatte and Derchaine 1964; Halleux and Schamp 1985; Kaimakis 1976; Kotansky 1994.

*5. Ancient Literary Texts Bearing upon Magic Translated*

Luck 1985.

*6. General Volumes on Ancient Magic*

Annequin 1973; Bernand 1991; Caro Baroja 1964; De Jong 1921; Dickie 2001; Fahz 1904; Faraone 1992, 1999; Faraone and Obbink 1991; Flint et al. 1999; Graf 1997; *Helios* 1994; Hopfner 1921-24; Jordan et al. 1999; Lowe 1929; Luck 1962; Massoneau 1934; Meyer and Mirecki 1995; Moreau and Turpin 2000; Rabinowitz 1998; Tavenner 1916; Tupet 1976; Xella 1976.

*7. Some Important General Articles*

Eitrem 1941; Le Glay 1977; Tupet 1986.

*8. The Definition of Magic in Ancient Context and the Magic/religion Debate*

Bernand 1991; Braarvig 1999; Deubner 1922; Dickie 2001: 18–46; Faraone and Obbink 1991; Garosi 1976; Goode 1949, 1999; Graf 1995, 1997a: 1–19, 206–23; Hammond 1970; Segal 1981; Thomassen 1999; Tupet 1976: vii–xv; Versnel 1991b.

*9. Magic and Christianity*

Aune 1980; Barb 1963; Brown 1970; Flint 1999; Merlan 1954; Smelik 1979; Smith 1978.

*10. Anthropological Perspectives on Ancient Magic*

Evans-Pritchard 1937; Graf 1997a; Tambiah 1973, 1995; Thomas 1973; Ward 1980.

*11. Bibliography for Ancient Magic*

Moreau and Turpin 2000: iv.

## 2. Greek Sorcerers

*1. Shamans and Pythagoreans*

Bolton 1962; Burkert 1962, 1972: 97–116, 1979: 78–98; Dodds 1951; Eliade 1964, 1972; Flintermann 1995; Inwood 1992; Kingsley 1995; Lévy 1926; Luck 1999: 117–19; Mellor 1968; Meuli 1935, 1975; Parker 1983: 281–307; Philip 1966; Schibli 1990; Tavenner 1916: 1–5; Van der Waerden 1979; Vrugt-Lentz 1960: 15–31; Wright 1981; Zhmud 1997. See section 4.1 and 4.2 for neo-Pythagoreans.

*2. Goetes, Agurtai, etc.*

Annequin 1973: 93–5; Bernand 1991; Bowie 1993: 112–24; Burkert 1962, 1983b, 1992: 55–73; De Romilly 1975: 23–44; Dickie 2001: 47–78; Graf 1994, 1997b: 20–60, 89–117; Johnston 1999a: 82–123, 1999b; Luck 1999: 102–10; Motte 2000; Parker 1983: 207–34; Tavenner 1916: 1–5.

*3. Semnai Goddesses, Eumenides, and Erinyes*

Brown 1984, Henrichs 1984, 1991, 1994, Johnston 1994, 1999a: 25–87; Laks and Most 1997; Lardinois 1992; Lloyd-Jones 1990.

*4. Magic and Rhetoric*

De Romilly 1975; Gellrich 1993–94; MacDowell 1982; Motte 2000; Segal 1962.

*5. Orphism and Orpheotelestai*

Alderink 1981; Athanassikis 1977; Bernand 1991: 381–97; Böhme 1970; Borgeaud 1991; Bowra 1952; Bremmer 1991; Burkert 1975, 1976, 1982, 1987; Clark 1979: 95–124; Deonna 1925; Detienne 1971; Di Fabio 1993; Di Marco 1993; Dronke 1962; Eisler 1925; Foti and Pugliese Caratelli 1974; Graf 1974, 1983, 1987, 1991b, 1993; Guthrie 1952; Heath 1994; Johnston and McNiven 1996; Kern 1920, 1922; Laks and Most 1997; Lee 1965; Linforth 1941; Lobeck 1829; Masaracchia 1993; Meyer 1987; Nock 1927; Parker 1995; Robbins 1982; Robert 1917; Romanelli 1975; Schmidt 1972, 1975, 1981, 1991; Schuchhardt 1964; Segal 1964; Tsantsanoglou and Parassoglou 1987; West 1975, 1983; Zhmud 1992, Zuntz 1971. See also Section 2.1.

*6. Telchines, Dactyls, and Hephaestus*

Delcourt 1957; Detienne and Vernant 1978; Faraone 1987, and 1992c; *LIMC*, s.v. "Hephaestus."

*7. Evocators*

Burkert 1962; Cavaignac 1959; Christidis et al. 1999; Ganschinietz 1929; Henrichs 1991; Johnston 1999a: 82–123; Kramer et al. 1980; Lloyd-Jones 1981; Rusten 1982.

*8. Hermes as Conductor of Souls*

Eitrem, 1909; Höfer 1884–1937; Kerenyi 1976; Raingeard 1934–35.

*9. Ventriloquism and the Witch of En-dor*

Grotanelli 1987; Rabinowitz 1998: 125–35; Schmidt 1995; Smelik 1979; Tropper 1989.

## 3. Alien Sorcerers

*1. Persian Magi, Babylonian Chaldaeans, and Egyptians Priests in the Graeco-Roman Tradition*

Beagon 1992: 102–13; Benveniste 1938; Bernand 1991; Bi(c)kerman and Tadmor 1978, Bidez and Cumont 1938; Boulogne 2000; Bremmer 1999; Burkert 1983b, 1992, Cumont 1933; Dickie 1999, 2001: 96–123; Diouf 2000; Ernout 1957; Gordon 1987a; Graf 1997b: 20–117; Hallock 1969; Nock 1972: 1:308–30; Xella 1976. See sections 3.4 and 9.3.

*2. Magical Lore*

Dickie 1999; Wellmann 1928.

*3. Snake-blasting*

Tupet 1986: 2617–26.

*4. Magic in Mesopotamia*

Abusch 1974, 1987, 1989; Bayliss 1973; Biggs 1967; Bottéro 1987 90, 1992, 2000; Caplice 1970; Caquot 1968; Castellino 1953; Contenau 1940; Dietrich and Loretz 1990; Ebeling 1925; Egger 1948; Elat 1982; Faraone 1993a; Finkel 1983–84; Galter 1993; Goetze and Sturtevant 1938; Meier 1937; Pritchard 1955; Reiner 1966, 1987; Scurlock 1988, 1995; Tropper 1989; Tsukimoto 1985.

*5. Magic in Egypt*

Aufrère 2000, Borghouts 1978; Lichtheim 1973–80; Pinch 1994; Raven 1983; Ritner 1993.

*6. Astrology*

Barton 1994; Bouché-Leclercq 1879; Gordon 1997; Luck 1985: 307–58; Maury 1877; Olivieri et al. 1898–1936.

## 4. The Rivals of Jesus

*1. Apollonius of Tyana*

Anderson 1986, 1994; Annequin 1973: 116–22; Bernard 1977; Bowie 1978; Dzielska 1986; Luck 1999: 130–7.

*2. Alexander of Abonouteichos*

Annequin 1973: 101–6; Babelon 1900; Caster 1938, 1973; Cumont 1922; De Faye 1925; Nock 1928; Robert 1981; Victor 1997; Weinreich 1921.

*3. Simon Magus*

Amann 1941; Arai 1977; Beyschlag 1974; Bremmer 1998, 2000; Cerfaux 1954; Daniélou 1974; Edwards 1997; Foerster 1972: 1: 27–32; Grant 1964; Heintz 1997; Luck 1999: 125–30; Rudolph 1977; Salles-Dabadie 1962; Simonetti 1970.

*4. Jesus as Mage*

Aune 1980: 1523–49; Cotter 1999; Luck 1999: 124–5; Smith 1978.

**5. Medea and Circe**

*1. Medea*

Belloni 1981; Bernand 1991: 198–200: Clauss and Johnston 1997; Halm-Tisserant 1993; Moreau 1994; Moreau and Turpin 2000: 2: 245–333; Parry 1992; Tupet 1976.

*2. Circe*

Karsai 2000; Marinatos1995; Paetz 1970; Page 1972: 49–69; Segal 1968; West 1997: 405–12; Wildhaber 1951.

**6. Witches in Greek Literature**

*1. Deianeira*

Davies 1989, 1991; Easterling 1982; Errondonea 1927; Faraone 1994; Herzig 1940; Holt 1981.

*2. Love Potions, Poisons, and Pharmacology*

Derrida 1981(with care); Faraone 1999a: 110–32; Graf 1997b: 46–9; Pailler 1987; Scarborough 1991; Tupet 1976: 56–91.

*3. Thessalian Witches*

Dickie 2001: 79–95; Grégoire 1949; Hill 1973.

*4. Theocritus's Simaetha*

Dover 1969; Fantuzzi and Maltomini 1996; Faraone 1995; Gow 1952; Graf 1997b: 176–90; Gwyn Griffiths 1979; Pralon 2000; Schweizer 1937; Segal 1973; Sutphen 1902; Tupet 1976: 151–3.

*5. Virgil's Amaryllis (?)*

Coleman 1977; Faraone 1989; Richter 1970; Tupet 1976: 223–32.

**7. Witches in Latin Literature**

*1. Ancient Witches, Mainly in Latin Literature*

Annequin 1973: 86–90; Bernand 1991; Caro Baroja 1964; Dickie 2001: 162–201 Fahz 1904; Lowe 1929; Luck 1962, 1999: 121–3; Myers 1996; Novara 2000; Rabinowitz

1998; Scobie 1978, 1983; Segal 2000; Tavenner 1916: 33–7; Tupet 1976; Ward 1981; Xella 1976.

### 2. *Horace's Canidia*

Freudenburg 1995; Ingallina 1974; Mankin 1995; Manning 1970; Tupet 1976: 284–329; Watson 1993.

### 3. *Lucan's Erictho*

Ahl 1969, 1976; Baldini-Moscadi 1976; Bourgery 1928; Braund 1989; Dick 1963; Eitrem 1941; Fahz 1904; Fauth 1975; Gordon 1987a, 1987b; Graf 1997b: 190–204; Grenade 1950; Johnson 1987; Korenjak 1996; Longo 1989; Marastoni 1979; Martindale 1977, 1980; Masters 1992; Morford 1967; O'Higgins 1988; Paratore 1974, 1992: 44–66; Rose 1913; Schotes 1969: 50–99; Tupet 1988; Verberne 1988; Viansino 1995; Volpilhac 1978.

### 4. *Apuleius and His* Metamorphoses

Fick 1985; Griffiths 1975; Gwyn Griffiths 1975; Harrison 2000; Hijmans and van der Paardt 1978; Hijmans et al. 1977–95; Hoevels 1979; Kenney 1990; Molt 1938; Sandy 1997; Scobie 1975, 1978, 1983; Tavenner 1916: 40–5; Van der Paardt 1971. See section 14.3 for Apuleius's *Apology*.

## 8. Ghosts

### 1. *General Works on Ghosts*

Bonner 1932; Bremmer 1983; Callois 1937; Dingwall 1930; Felton 1999; Harrison 1922; Hickman 1938; Jacoby 1944; Magdelain 1976; Mende 1913; Otto 1923; Preisendanz 1935; Rohde 1925; Rose 1948; Russel 1981; Stanford 1940; Winkler 1980; Zintzen 1976. See section 9.2 for the ghost of Darius.

### 2. Aoroi, Biaiothanatoi, Agamoi, Ataphoi *(with tombstone curses)*

Bernand 1991: 131–55, 363–79; Cumont 1945, 1949; Delcourt 1939; Eitrem 1933; Johnston 1999a; Kraggerud 1999, Lattimore 1962, Nock 1950; Reiner 1938; Strubbe 1991; Vrugt-Lentz 1960; Waszink 1947, 1954; Wide 1909.

### 3. *Attacking Ghosts, Bogies, and Vampires*

Brown 1991; Dodds 1973; Drexler 1884–1937; Hatch 1908; Jobbé-Duval 1924; Johnston 1995, 1999a.

### 4. *Haunted Houses and Ghost Stories*

Bevan 1926; Collison-Morley 1912; Dingwall 1930; Felton 1999; Kytzler 1989; Lateiner 1990; Nardi 1960; Römer 1987; Russel 1981; Sherwin-White 1966; Wendland 1911.

### 5. *Phlegon of Tralles*

Giannini 1965; Hansen 1980, 1989, 1996.

### 6. *Ghost-laying*

Garland 1989; Jameson et al. 1993; Kittredge 1885; Parker 1983, 1984; Reiner 1984; Schäfer 1957; Stukey 1937; Sussman 1987.

### 7. Exorcism of Ghosts and Demons from People

Bonner 1943, 1944; Edwards 1989; Kotansky 1995; Oesterreich 1930; Smith 1965; Thraede 1967.

### 8. Jewish Magic

Fox 1913–14; Kotansky 1995; Margalioth 1966; Morgan 1983; Naveh and Shaked 1985, 1993; Smith 1978. See section 2.7 for the witch of En-dor.

### 9. Exploitation of Boys

Abt 1908: 160–6, 184–5; Hopfner 1926; Hughes 1991.

### 10. Werewolves

Burkert 1983: 83–134; Buxton 1987; Cook 1914–40: 1:63:99; Eckels 1937; Gernet 1981: 125–39; Hughes 1991; Johnston 1991: 181–2; Jost 1985: 258–67; Mainoldi 1984; Schuster 1930; Smith 1894; Tupet 1976: 73–8, 1986: 2647–52; Villeneuve 1963.

### 11. General Works on Death in the Ancient World

Andronikos 1968; Antonaccio 1995; Bernstein 1993; Bickel 1925; Brelich 1958; Bremmer 1983, 1994; Garland 1985; Gnoli and Vernant 1982; Knight 1970; Kurtz and Boardman 1971; Larson 1995; Lattimore 1962; Moore 1963; Morris 1989; O'Hara 1990; Sourvinou-Inwood 1995; Toynbee 1971; Vermeule 1979.

## 9. Necromancy

### 1. General Works on Necromancy and Evocation

Bernand 1991: 259–82; Bouché-Leclercq 1879; Collard 1949; Deubner 1900; Donnadieu and Vilatte 1996; Fahz 1904: 110–21; Ganschinietz 1919; Halliday 1913: 235–45; Headlam 1902; Jouan 1981; Kalitsounakis 1953–4; Liedloff 1884; S. West, 1983.

### 2. Julius Africanus

Vieillefond 1970; Thee 1984.

### 3. Aeschylus's Necromancy of Darius

Alexanderson 1967; Belloni 1982, 1988; Bi(c)kerman 1978; Bidez 1937; Broadhead 1960; Citti 1962; Eitrem 1928; Haldane 1972; Hall 1989, 1996; Headlam 1902; Lawson 1934; Moritz 1979; Rose 1950; Scazzoso 1952; Taplin 1977.

### 4. The Heracleia Pontica Nekuomanteion

Hoepfner 1966, 1972.

### 5. The Tainaron Nekuomanteion

Bölte 1932; Cooper 1988; Cummer 1978; Günther 1988; Moschou 1975a, 1975b; Papachatzis 1976; Schumacher 1993.

### 6. The Acheron Nekuomanteion: The Site

Baatz 1979, 1982, 1999; Dakaris 1963, 1973, 1993; Dalègre 1983; Eitrem 1945; Ekschmitt 1998; Huxley 1958; Mouselimis 1987; Müller 1987; Tsouvara-Souli 1983; Van Straten 1982; Will 1953; Wiseman 1998.

### 7. The Acheron Nekuomanteion: Periander and Melissa

Loraux 1993; Salmon 1984; Stern 1989.

### 8. The Avernus Nekuomanteion

Amalfitano 1986; Amalfitano et al. 1990; Ameling 1986; Austin 1977; Bonner 1937; Brooks 1953; Castagnoli 1977; Clark 1979; Corssen 1913; De Caro and Greco 1981; Eitrem 1945; Frederiksen 1984; Gigante 1986; Giuliani 1976; Gotoff 1985; Hardie 1969, 1977; Highbarger 1940; Kerrigan 1980; Kresic 1968; McKay 1972; Maiuri 1963; Martin 1984; Monti 1980; Norden 1916; Pagano et al. 1982; Paget 1967a, 1967b, 1967c; Parke and McGing 1988; Phillips 1953; Préaux 1960; Pugliese Caratelli 1986; Quiter 1984; Tarrant 1982.

### 9. Reanimation and Talking Heads

Bruce 1913; Deonna 1925; Doerig 1991; Nagy 1990; Robert 1917; Schmidt 1972. See section 7.3.

### 10. Lecanomancy, Lychnomancy, and Magical Divination

Böhm 1916; Delatte 1932; Eitrem 1991, forthcoming; Ganschinietz 1925; Graf 1999; McCarty 1989; Riess 1896.

## 10. Curses

### 1. Curses and Curse-tablets

Annequin 1973: 21–5; Aupert and Jordan 1991; Bernand 1991: 107–30; Bevilacqua 1997; Bonner and Youtic 1937; Braarvig 1999; Brashear 1979; Bravo 1987; Calder 1963; Chaniotis 1992; Curbera 1999; Curbera and Jordan 1998; Dubois 1995; Dunant 1978; Elderkin 1937; Engelmann 1975; Faraone 1985, 1989b, 1991a, 1999a; Fox 1912a, 1912b; Garcia Ruiz 1967; Gáspár 1990; Giordano 1999; Gordon 1999; Graf 1997: 118–74; Guarducci 1978; Humphrey et al. 1972–73; Jameson et al. 1993; Johnston 1999a: 71–80, 1999b; Jordan 1976, 1977, 1980b, 1985a, 1985c, 1988a, 1988b, 1988c, 1989, 1999; Kagarow 1929; Kakridis 1929; Levi della Vida 1933; Lopez Jimeno 1991; Massart 1959; Masson 1972; Massoneau 1934: 101–18; Milne 1966; Moraux 1960; Ogden 1999; Parker 1983: 191–206; Preisendanz 1972; Robert 1978; Sergent 2000, Thomassen 1999; Tupet 1986: 2601–6; Van Rengen 1984; Versnel 1985, 1991a, 1998, 1999; Voutiras 1996, 1998, 1999; Willemsen 1990; Winkler 1990, 1991; Wortmann 1968; Wünsch 1902; Youtie and Bonner 1937.

### 2. Bath and British Defixiones

Bathurst 1879; Bonner 1932; Goodchild 1953; Jordan 1990; Tomlin 1988; Turner 1963; Wright 1958.

### 3. Greek Magical Papyri

Betz 1980, 1981, 1982, 1991; Brashear 1992, 1995, Ciraolo 1995; Daniel 1991; Eitrem 1925; Fowden 1986: 186–72; Frankfurter 1994; Gager 1987, 1992; Graf 1991;

Griffith and Thompson, 1904; Johnston 2000; Martinez 1991; Merkelbach et al. 1990–; Nock 1925, 1929, 1972: i 176–94; Winkler 1990, 1991.

*4. Ephesia Grammata*

McCown 1923; Preisendanz 1962.

*5. The Evil Eye*

Bernand 1991: 85–105; Dickie 1990, 1991, 1995; Dunbabin and Dickie 1983; Dundes 1981; Elsworthy 1895; Geffcken 1930; Jahn 1855; Johnston 1999; Kötting 1954; Limberis 1991; Moreau 1976; Schlesier 1994; Schmidt 1913; Tupet 1976: 178–81, 1986: 2606–10; Vernsel 1999; Yatromanolakis1988.

## 11. Erotic Magic

*1. Erotic Magic: General Material*

Bernand 1991: 161–83, 285–310; Boll 1910; Bonner 1932; Cairns 1989; Daniel 1975; Dickie 2000; Du Bourguet 1975; Fahz 1904: 121–43; Faraone 1992a, 1992b, 1996, 1999a, 1999b, forthcoming-a; Gager 1992: 78–115; Graf 1997b: 175–90; McCartney 1925; Maltomini 1979; Martinez 1991a, 1991b, 1995; Massoneau 1934: 86–90; Pérez 2000; Petropoulos 1993, 1988; Segal 1974; Tavenner 1942; Tupet 1976: 56–91, 1986: 2626-47; Versnel 1994; West 1994; Winkler 1990, 1991.

*2. Ritual Slander*

Eitrem 1924.

*3. Apple Spells*

Bonner 1932; Brazda 1977; Faraone 1999a: 69–77; Foster 1899; McCartney 1925; Myers 1938; Trumpf 1960.

*4. Drawing Down the Moon*

Gordon 1999a: 223–4; Hill 1973; Mugler 1959; Préaux 1973; Tupet 1976, 92–103.

*5. Iunx and Rhombos*

Bury 1886; De la Genière 1958; Faraone 1993b; Gow 1934, 1952; Graf 1997b: 179–80; Johnston 1995; Nelson 1940; Pirenne-Delforge 1993; Segal 1973; Tavenner 1933; Tupet 1976: 50–5; Vermeule 1979.

*6. Hippomanes*

Stadler 1913; Tupet 1976: 79–81, 1986: 2653–7.

*7. Abortion Magic*

Aubert 1989; Chaniotis 1990; Petzl 1994; Petzl and Malay 1987.

## 12. Voodoo Dolls and Magical Images

*1. Voodoo dolls*

Bonner 1932; Desborough et al. 1970; Dickie 1996; Dugas 1915; Faraone 1989a, 1991b, 1992c, 1993a; Graf 1992; Jones 1985; Knigge 1991; Mariani 1910; Ogden 1999: 71–9; Reiner 1988; Schlörb-Vierneisel 1964; Trumpf 1958.

2. *Lucian as a Source for Magic*

Anderson 1976a, 1976b; Betz 1961; Herzig 1940; Luck 1999: 140–8; Radermacher 1979; Schwartz 1951, 1965.

## 13. Amulets

### 1. *Amulets*

Annequin 1973: 25–9; Barb 1950, 1966; Blanchet 1923; Bonner 1942; Frankfurter 1995; Jordan 1985b, 1988a, 1991; Kotansky 1991, 1995; Lancellotti 2000; Ogden 1999: 51–4; Perdrizet 1922; Renehan 1992, Robert, 1981, Sande 1999, Schwartz 1981; Seyrig 1935; Smith 1979; Tavenner 1916: 76–123; Waegeman 1987.

### 2. *Aphrodite's Girdle*

Bonner 1949; Brenk 1977; Faraone1999 a: 97–110.

### 3. *Further Healing Magic*

Annequin 1973: 49–54; Edelstein et al. 1945; Friedrich 1968; Grégoire et al. 1949; Kerenyi 1959; Lanata 1967; Martini 1977; Massoneau 1934· 72–6; Weinreich 1909.

### 4. *Hecate*

Annequin 1973: 83–6; Clay 1984; Graf 1985: 257–9; Heckenbach 1912; Johnston 1990, 1991, 1999a: 203–49; Jordan 1980a; Kraus 1960; *LIMC*, s.v. "Hekate"; Massoneau 1934: 58 60; Nouveau Piobb 1061; Rabinowitz 1998. 17–72, Roshier 1886–90, s.v. "Hekate"; Sauzeau 2000; Tupet 1976: 14–17.

## 14. Magic and the Law

### 1. *Legislation against Magic*

Beckmann 1923; Clerc 1995; Gordon 1999a: 243–66; Graf 1997b· 36–60; Hunink 1997; Kippenberg 1997; Massoneau 1934: 136–261; Parassoglou 1976; Pharr 1932; Phillips 1991; Rea 1977; Tavenner 1916: 12–17; Ward 1981; Xella 1976.

### 2. *Excantatio Cultorum*

Graf 1997: 62–5; Heim 1892; Tupet 1976: 181–7, 1986: 2610–7.

### 3. *Apuleius and His* Apology

Abt 1908; Annequin 1973: 106–16; Butler 1909; Butler and Owen 1914; Fantham 1995; Graf 1997b: 61–88; Hijmans 1994; Hunink 1997; Méthy 2000; Valette 1908, 1924.

### 4. *Libanius*

Festugière 1959; Petit 1956.

## WORKS CITED

Abel, E. 1881. *Orphei Lithica*. Berlin.

Abt, A. 1908. *Die Apologie des Apuleius von Madaura und die antike Zauberei*. RGVV 4.2. Giessen, Germany. Reprint, 1967.

Abusch, I.T. 1974. "Mesopotamian anti-witchcraft literature; texts and studies. Part 1:

The nature of the *Maqlû*, its character, divisions and calendrical setting." *JNES* 33: 251–62

———.1987. *Babylonian witchcraft: Case studies*. Atlanta.

———. 1989. "The demonic image of the witch in standard Babylonian literature: The reworking of popular conceptions by learned exorcists." In *Religion, science and magic: In concert and conflict*, edited by E. Frerichs, J. Neusner, and P.V.M. Flesher 27–58. New York.

Ahl, F.M. 1969. "Appius Claudius and Sextus Pompey in Lucan." *C&M* 30: 331–46.

——— 1976. *Lucan. An introduction*. Ithaca.

Alderink, L.J. 1981. *Creation and salvation in ancient Orphism*. Chico, Calif.

Alexanderson, B. 1967. "Darius in the *Persians*." *Eranos* 65: 1–11.

Amalfitano, P., G. Camodeca, and M. Medri. 1990. *I campi Flegrei. Un itinerario archeologico*. Venice.

Amalfitano, P., ed. 1986. *Il destino della Sibilla. Mito, scienza e storia dei Campi Flegrei*. Naples.

Amann, É. 1941. "Simon le magicien." In *Dictionnaire de théologie catholique*, edited by A. Vacant, et al., 14: 2, cols. 2130–40. Paris.

Ameling, W. 1986. "Baiae, Odysseus und Marc Aurel." *Hermes* 114: 380–2.

Anderson, G. 1976a. *Lucian: Theme and variation in the second sophistic*. Leiden.

———. 1976b. *Studies in Lucian's comic fiction*. Leiden.

———. 1986. *Philostratus: Biography and belles-lettres in the third century* A.D. London.

———. 1994. *Sage, saint and sophist*. London.

Andronikos, M. 1968. *Totenkult*. Archeologia Homerica iii.W. Göttingen.

Annequin, J. 1973. *Recherches sur l'action magique et ses représentations (Ier et IIème siècles après J.-C.)*. Besançon. Reviewed by A.-M. Tupet. 1973. *REL* 51: 448–51

Antonaccio, C.M. 1995. *An archaeology of ancestors. Tomb cult and hero cult in early Greece*. Lanham, Md.

Arai, S. 1977. "Simionianische Gnosis und die Exegese über die Seele." In *Gnosis and Gnosticism*, edited by M. Krause, Nag Hammadi Studies 8, 185–203. Leiden.

Athanassikis, A.N. 1977. *The Orphic hymns. Text, translation and notes*. Atlanta.

Aubert, J.-J. 1989. "Threatened wombs: Aspects of ancient uterine magic." *GRBS* 30: 421–49.

Audollent, A. 1904. *Defixionum tabellae*. Paris.

Aufrère, S.H. 2000. "Quelques aspects du dernier Nectanébo et les échos de la magie égyptienne dans le *Roman d'Alexandre*." In Moreau and Turpin 2000, 1: 95–118.

Aune, D.E. 1980. "Magic in early Christianity." *ANRW* 2.23.2: 1507–57.

Aupert, P., and D.R. Jordan, 1981. "Magical inscriptions on talc tablets from Amathous." *AJA* 85: 184.

Austin, R.G. 1977. *Vergil* Aeneid *vi*. Edited with an introduction and commentary. Oxford.

Baatz, D. 1979. "Teile hellenistischer Geschütze aus Griechenland." *Archäologischer Anzeiger* 94: 68–75

———.1982. "Hellenistische Katapulte aus Ephyra (Epirus)." *AM* 97: 211–33.

———.1999. "Wehrhaftes Wohnen. Ein befestigter hellenistischer Adelsitz bei Ephyra (Nord griechenland)." *Antike Welt* 30, 2: 151–5.

Babelon, E. 1900. "Le faux prophète Alexandre d'Abonotichos." *Revue numismatique*, 4th series, 4: 1–30.

Baehrens, A. 1879–86. *Poetae Latini minores*. 5 vols. Teubner. Leipzig.

Baldini-Moscadi, L. 1976. "Osservazioni sull' episodio magico del VI libro della *Farsaglia* di Lucano." *SIFC* 48: 140–99.

Barb, A.A. 1950. "The Eagle Stone." *JWCI* 13: 316–8.

———. 1957. "Abrasax-Studien." In *Hommages à W. Deonna*. Collection Latomus 28, 67–86.

———. 1963. "The survival of the magic arts." In *The conflict between paganism and Christianity in the fourth century*, edited by A. Momigliano, 100–125. Oxford.

———. 1966. "Antaura the Mermaid and the Devil's grandmother." *JWCI* 29: 1–23.

Barton, T. 1994. *Ancient astrology.* London.

Bathurst, W.H. 1879. *Roman antiquities at Lydney Park, Gloucestershire.* London.

Bayliss, M. 1973. "The cult of dead kin in Assyria and Babylonia." *Iraq* 35: 115–25.

Beagon, M. 1992. *Roman nature,* 102–13. Oxford.

Beckmann, F. 1923. *Zauberei und Recht in Roms Frühzeit.* Osnabrück.

Belloni, L. 1981. "Medea πολυφάρμακος." CCC 2: 117–33.

———. 1982. "L'ombra di Dareio nei Persiani di Eschilo: la regalità degli Achaemenidi e il pubblico di Atene." *Orpheus* 3: 185–99.

———. 1988. *Eschilo. I Persiani.* Milan.

Benveniste, E. 1938. *Les mages dans l'ancien Iran.* Paris.

Bérard, C. 1974. *Anodoi: essai sur l'imagerie des passages chthoniens.* Neuchâtel.

Bernand, A. 1991. *Sorciers grecs.* Paris.

Bernard, J.-L. 1977. *Apollonius de Tyane et Jésus.* Paris.

Bernardakis, G.N., ed 1888–96. *Plutarchi Chaeronensis Moralia.* 7 vols. Teubner. Leipzig.

Bernstein, A.E. 1993. *The formation of Hell: Death and retribution in the ancient and early Christian worlds.* London.

Berthelot, M., and C.E. Ruelle. 1887–88. *Collection des alchimistes grecs.* 3 vols. Paris.

Besnier, M. 1920. "Récents travaux sur les *defixionum tabellae latines* 1904–1914." *RP* 44: 5 30.

Betz, H.D. 1961. *Lukian von Samosata und das Neue Testament.* Berlin.

———. 1980. "Fragments from a catabasis ritual in a Greek magical papyrus." *History of Religions* 19: 287–95.

———. 1981. "The Delphic maxim 'Know Yourself' in the Greek magical papyri." *History of Religions* 19: 287–95.

———. 1982. "The formation of authoritative tradition in the Greek Magical Papyri." In *Self-definition in the Graeco-Roman world.* Vol. 3. *Jewish and Christian self-definition,* edited by B.F. Meyer, and E.P. Sanders, 162–171. Philadelphia..

———. 1991. "Magic and mystery in the Greek magical papyri." In Faraone and Obbink 1991, 244–59.

———, ed. 1992). *The Greek magical papyri in translation, including the demotic spells.* 2nd ed. Chicago. (1st ed. 1986.) Translation, with additions, of Preisendanz and Heinrichs 1973–74; incorporates Greek papyri under *PGM* (with upper-case Roman numerals) and demotic papyri under *PDM* (with lower-case Roman numerals).

Bevan, E. 1926. "Classical ghosts." *Quarterly Review* 246: 60–74.

Bevilacqua, G. 1997. "Un incantesimo per odio in una *defixio* di Roma." *ZPE* 117: 291–3.

Beyschlag, K. 1974. *Simon Magus und die christliche Gnosis.* Tübingen.

Bickel, E. 1925. *Homersicher Seelenglaube.* Berlin.

Bi(c)kerman, E.J., and H. Tadmor. 1978. "Darius I, Pseudo-Smerdis and the magi." *Athenaeum* 59: 239–61

Bidez, J. 1937. "À propos des *Perses* d'Éschyle." *Bulletin de l'académie royale de Belgique. Classe des lettres* 206–35.

Bidez, J., and F. Cumont. 1938. *Les mages hellénisés.* 2 vols. Paris.

Biggs, R.D. 1967. *SA.ZI.GA: Ancient Mesopotamian potency incantations.* Locust Valley, N.Y.

Blanchet, M. 1923. "Venus et Mars sur les intailles magiques et autres." *CRAI:* 220–34.

Boissonade, J.F. 1849. *Eunapii Vitae Sophistarum.* Paris.

Böhm, F. 1916. "Hydromanteia." *RE,* 10: 79–86.

Böhme, R. 1970. *Orpheus. Das Alter der Kitharöden.* Bern.

Bölte, F. 1932. "Tainaron." *RE,* 4a: 2030–46.

Boll, F. 1910. *Griechischer Liebeszauber aus Aegypten.* Sitzungsberichte der Heidelberger Akademie der Wissenschaften, no. 2. Heidelberg.

Bolton, J.D.P. 1962. *Aristeas of Proconessus*. Oxford.

Bonnechère, P. 1990. "Les oracles de Béotie." *Kernos* 3: 53–65.

Bonnechère, P. and M. 1989. "Trophonius à Lébadée. Histoire d'un oracle." *Études classiques* 57: 289–302.

Bonner, C.A. 1932. "Hades and the pomegranate seed (*Hymn to Demeter* 372–374)." *CR* 52: 3–4.

———. 1932a. "Demons of the bath." In *Studies presented to F.Ll. Griffith*, 10–20. London.

———. 1932b. "Witchcraft in the lecture room of Libanius." *TAPA* 63: 34–44.

———. 1937. "The Sibyl and bottle imps." In *Studies presented to Kirsopp Lake*, 1–8. London.

———. 1942. "Two studies in syncretistic amulets." *Proceedings of the American Philosophical Society* 85: 466–71.

———. 1943. "The technique of exorcism." *HTR* 39–43.

———. 1944. "The violence of departing demons." *HTR* 334–6.

———. 1949. "*Kestos himas* and the saltire of Aphrodite." *AJP* 70: 1–6.

———. 1950. *Studies in magical amulets, chiefly Graeco-Egyptian*. Ann Arbor.

Bonner, C.A., and H.C. Youtie, 1937. "Two curse-tablets from Beisan." *TAPA* 68: 43–77. Reprinted in Youtie, *Scriptiunculae posteriores*, 2: 269-303. Bonn.

Borgeaud, P., ed., Rudhardt, J., hon. 1991. *Orphisme et Orphée*. Geneva.

Borghouts, J.F. 1978. *Ancient Egyptian magical texts*. Nisaba 9. Leiden.

Bottéro, J. 1987–90. "Magie A. In Mesoptamien." in *Reallexicon für Assyriologie* 7: 200–234.

———. 1992. *Mesopotamia. Writing, reasoning and the gods*. Chicago. Trans. of 1987. *Mésopotamie. L'écriture, la raison et les dieux*. Paris.

———. 2000. "Magie, exoricisme et religion en Mésopotamie." In Moreau and Turpin 2000, 1: 63–76.

Bouché-Leclercq, A. 1879. *Histoire de la divination dans l'antiquité*. 4 vols. Paris.

Boulogne, J. 2000. "Plutarque et les mages." In Moreau and Turpin. 2000, 2: 59–78.

Bourgery, A. 1928. "Lucain et la magie." *REL* 6: 299–313.

Bowie, A.M. 1993. *Aristophanes: Myth, ritual and comedy*. Cambridge.

Bowie, E.L. 1978. "Apollonius of Tyana: Tradition and reality." *ANRW* 2.16.2: 1652–99.

Bowra, C.M. 1952. "Orpheus and Eurydice." *CQ* 46: 113–26.

Braarvig, J. 1999. "Magic: Reconsidering the grand dichotomy." In Jordan, Montgomery, and Thomassen 1999, 21–54.

Brashear, W.M. 1979. "Ein Berliner Zauberpapyrus." *ZPE* 33: 261–78.

———. 1992a. "Ein neues Zauberensemble in München." *Studien zur Altägyptischen Kultur* 19: 79–109.

———. 1992b. "Magical papyri: Magic in bookform." In *Das Buch als magisches und als Repräsentationsobjekt*, edited by P. Ganz, 25–59. Wiesbaden.

———. 1995. "The Greek Magical Papyri: An Introduction and Survey with an Annotated Bibliography." *ANRW* 2.18.5: 3380–3684.

Braund, S.H. 1989. "Lucan 6.715." *CQ* 39: 275–6.

Bravo, B. 1987. "Une tablette magique d'Olbia pontique, les morts les héros et les démons." In *Poikilia: études offerts à Jean-Pierre Vernant*, 185–218. Paris.

Brazda, M.K. 1977. "*Zur Bedeutung des Apfels in der antiken Kultur*." Diss., Bonn University.

Brelich, A. 1958. *Gli eroi greci*, 46–59. Rome.

Bremmer, J.N. 1983. *The early Greek concept of the soul*. Princeton.

———. 1991. "Orpheus: From guru to gay." In Borgeaud 1991, 13–30.

———. 1994. "The soul, death and the afterlife in early and classical Greece." In *Hidden futures: Death and immortality in ancient Egypt, Anatolia, the classical, biblical and Arabic-Islamic world*, edited by J.-M. Bremer, [sic], T.P.J. van den Hout, and R. Peters, 91–106. Amsterdam.

———. 1999. "The birth of the term magic." *ZPE* 126: 1–12.

———. 2000. "La confrontation entre l'apôtre Pierre et Simon le magicien." In Moreau and Turpin 2000, 1: 219–34.

———, ed.1998. *The Apocryphal Acts of Peter*. Leuven, Netherlands.

Brenk, F.E. 1977. "Aphrodite's girdle: No way to treat a lady." *Classical Bulletin* 54: 17–20.

Broadhead, H.D. 1960. *The Persae of Aeschylus*. Edited with an introduction and commentary. Cambridge.

Brooks, R.A. 1953. "'Discolor aura': Reflections on the golden bough." *AJP* 74: 260–80.

Brown, A.L. 1984. "Eumenides in Greek tragedy." CQ 34: 260–81.

Brown, C.G. 1991. "Empousa, Dionysus and the mysteries: Aristophanes *Frogs* 285ff." CQ 41: 41–50.

Brown, P. 1970. "Sorcery, demons and the rise of Christianity: From late antiquity into the middle ages." In *Witchcraft confessions and accusations*, edited by M. Douglas, 7–46. London. Reprinted in 1972. *Religion and society in the age of St. Augustine*, 119–46. New York.

Bruce, D.J. 1913. "Human automata in classical tradition and mediaeval romance." *Modern Philology* 10:511–26.

Bücheler, F., ed. 1895–97. *Carmina Latina epigraphica*. Leipzig.

Burkert, W. 1962. "Goes. Zum griechischen Schamanismus." *RhM* 105: 36–55.

———. 1972. *Lore and science in ancient Pythagoreanism*. Cambridge, Mass.

———. 1975. "Le laminette auree: da Orfeo a Lampone." In Romanelli 1975, 81–104.

———. 1976. *Orphism and Bacchic mysteries: New evidence and old problems of interpretation*. Center for Hermeneutical Studies in Hellenistic and Modern Culture, colloquy 28. Berkeley.

———. 1979. *Structure and history in Greek mythology and ritual*. Berkeley.

———. 1982. "Craft versus sect: the problems of Orphics and Pythagoreans." In *Self-definition in the Graeco-Roman World*. Vol. 3. *Jewish and Christian self-definition*, edited by B.E. Meyer and E.P. Sanders, 1–22. London.

———. 1983a. *Homo necans*. Berkeley.

———. 1983b. "Itinerant diviners and magicians. A neglected element in cultural contacts." In *The Greek renaissance of the eighth century B.C.: Tradition and innovation*, edited by R. Hägg, 115–119. Stockholm.

———. 1987. *Ancient mystery cults*. Cambridge, Mass.

———. 1992. *The orientalising revolution: Near eastern influence on Greek culture in the early archaic age*. Cambridge, Mass.

Bury, J.B. 1886. "*Iunx* in Greek magic." *JHS* 7: 157–9.

Butler, H.E. 1909. *The Apologia and the Florida of Apuleius of Madaura*. Oxford. English translation.

Butler, H.E., and A.S. Owen. 1914. *Apulei apologia sive Pro se se magia liber*. Oxford.

Buxton, R.W.B. 1987. "Wolves and werewolves in Greek thought." In *Interpretations of Greek mythology*, edited by J. Bremmer, 60–79. London.

Cairns, F. 1998. "Asclepiades and the *hetairai*." *Eikasmos* 9: 1–21.

Calder, W.M., III. 1963. "The great defixio from Selinus." *Philologus* 197: 163–72.

Callois, R. 1937. "Les démons de midi." *Revue de l'histoire des religions* 115 (1937): 142–73, 116 (1937): 54–83, 143–86.

Caplice, R. 1970. "Namburbi texts in the British Museum iv." *Orientalia* 39: 134–41.

Caquot, A. 1968. "La divination dans l'ancien Israel." In *La divination*, edited by A. Caquot and M. Leibovici. 2 vols., 1: 83–113. Paris.

Caro Baroja, J. 1964. *The world of witches*. Chicago. Translation of 1961. *Las brujas y su mondo: con varias ilustraciones*. Madrid.

Castagnoli, F. 1977. "Topgrafia dei Campi Flegrei." In *I Campi Flegrei dell' archeologia e nella storia. Atti dei convegni Lincei*, no. 33, 41–77 Rome.

Castellino, G. 1953. "Rituals and prayers against 'appearing ghosts.'" *Orientalia* 22: 240–74

Caster, M. 1938. *Études sur Alexandre ou le faux prophète de Lucien*. Paris.

————. 1973. *Lucien et la pensée religieuse de son temps*. Paris.

Cavaignac, E. 1959. "Pythagore et Socrate." *RP* 33: 246–8.

Cerfaux, L. 1954. "La gnose Simonienne." In *Recueil L. Cerfaux*, 191–258. Gembloux.

Chaniotis, A. 1990. "Drei kleinasiatische Inschriften zur griechischen Religion." *Epigraphica Anatolica* 15: 127–34.

————. 1992. "Watching a lawsuit: A new curse tablet from southern Russia." *GRBS* 33: 69–73.

Christidis, A.-P., et al. 1999. "Magic in the oracular tablets from Dodona." In Jordan, Montgomery, and Thomassen 1999, 67–72.

Ciraolo, L.J. 1995. "Supernatural assistants in the Greek magical papyri." In Meyer and Mirecki 1995, 279–98.

Citti, V. 1962. *Il languaggio religioso e liturgico nelle tragedie di Eschilo*. Bologna.

Clark, R.J. 1979. *Virgil and the wisdom tradition*. Amsterdam.

Clauss, J.J., and S.I. Johnston, eds. 1997. *Medea*. Princeton.

Clay, J.S. 1984. "The Hekate of the *Theogony*." *GRBS* 25: 37.

Clerk, J.B. 1995. *Homines magici. Étude sur la sorcellerie et la magie dans la société romaine impériale*. Berne.

Coleman, R. 1977. *Vergil. Eclogues*. Cambridge.

Collard, M., 1949. "La nécromancie dans l'antiquité." Thesis, University of Liège.

Collison-Morley, L. 1912. *Greek and Roman ghost stories*. Oxford.

Contenau, G. 1940. *La divination chez les Assyriens et Babyloniens*. Paris.

Cook, A.B. 1914–40. *Zeus: A study in ancient religion*. Cambridge.

Cooper, F.A. 1988. "The quarries of Mount Taygetos in the Peloponnesos, Greece." In *Classical marble: Geochemistry, technology, trade*, edited by N. Herz, and M. Waelkens, 65–76. Dordrecht.

Cooper, J.S. 1992. "The fate of mankind: death and afterlife in ancient Mesopotamia." In *Death and the afterlife: Perspectives of world religions*, edited by H. Obayashi, 19–34. New York.

Copenhaver, B.P. 1992. *Hermetica: The Greek Corpus Hermeticum and the Latin Asclepius in a new English translation, with notes and an introduction*. Cambridge.

Corssen, P. 1913. "Die Sibylle im sechsten Buch der Aeneis." *Sokrates*, N.F., 1: 1–16.

Cotter, W. 1999. *Miracles in Greco-Roman antiquity: A sourcebook for the study of New Testament miracle stories*. London.

Cummer, W. 1978. "The sanctuary of Poseidon at Tainaron, Lakonia." *AM* 93: 35–43, plates 17–8.

Cumont, F. 1922. "Alexandre d'Abonotique et le néopythagoreanisme." *RHR* 83: 202–10.

————. 1933. "L' iniziazione di Nerone da parte di Tiridate d' Armenia." *Rivista di filologia classica* 11: 145–54.

————. 1945. "Virgile et les morts prématurés." *Publication de l'ENS, section des lettres* 2: 123–152.

————. 1949. *Lux perpetua*. Paris.

Curbera, J. 1999. "Maternal lineage in Greek magical texts." In Jordan, Montgomery, and Thomassen 1999, 195–204.

Curbera, J.B., and D.R. Jordan. 1998. "A curse tablet from the 'Industrial District' southwest of the Athenian agora." *Hesperia* 67: 215–8.

Dakaris, S.I. 1963. "Das Taubenorakel von Dodona und das Totenorakel bei Ephyra." *Antike Kunst* Beiheft 1: 35–55.

————. 1973. "The oracle of the dead on the Acheron." In *Temples and sanctuaries of ancient Greece*, edited by E. Melas, 139–49. London.

————. 1993. *The nekyomanteion of the Acheron*. Ministry of Culture, Archaeological Receipts Fund. Athens.

Dalègre, J. 1983. "Un sanctuaire des morts, le Nekuomanteion de l'Achéron en Épire." *Connaissance hellénique* 6: 49–51.

Daniel, R. 1975. "Two love charms." *ZPE* 19: 249–64.

————. 1991. *Two Greek Magical Papyri in the National Museum of Antiquities in Leiden*. Papyrologica Coloniensia 19. Opladen.

Daniel, R.W., and F. Maltomini, eds. 1990–92. *Supplementum Magicum*. Papyrologica Coloniensia. Vols. 16.1 and 16.2. 2 vols. Cologne. Numeration is continuous between volumes.

Daniélou, J. 1974. *La teologia del giudeo-cristianesimo*. Bologna.

Davies, M. 1989. "Deianeira and Medea: A footnote to the prehistory of two myths." *Mnemosyne* 42: 469–72.

————. 1991. *Sophocles. Trachiniae*. Oxford.

De Caro, S., and A. Greco, 1981. *Campania*. Guide archeologiche Laterza no. 10. Rome.

De Faye, E. 1925. "Alexandre d'Abonotique a-t-il été un charlatan ou un fondateur de religion?" *Revue d'histoire et de philosophie religieuses* 5: 201–7.

De Jong, K.H.E. 1921. *De magie biy Grieken en Romeinen*. Haarlem. Rev. ed. 1948.

De la Genière, J. 1958. "Une roue à oiseau du Cabinet des Medailles." *REA* 60: 27–55.

Delatte, A. 1927. *Anecdota Atheniensia*. Tome I. *Textes grecs inédits relatifs à l'histoire des réligions*. Liège.

————. 1932. *La catoptromancie grecque et ses dérivés*. Liège.

Delatte, A., and P. Derchain, 1964. *Les intailles magiques gréco-égyptiennes*. Paris.

Delcourt, M. 1939. "Le suicide par vengeance dans la Grèce ancienne." *RHR* 119: 154–71.

————.1957. *Héphaistos, ou la légende du magicien*. Liège.

Deonna, W. 1925. "Orphée et l'oracle de la tête coupée." *REG* 38: 44-69.

De Romilly, J. 1975. *Magic and rhetoric in ancient Greece*. Cambridge, Mass.

Derrida, J. 1981. *Dissemination*. Chicago. Translation of 1972. *La dissémination*. Paris. Use with care.

Desborough, V.R., R.V. Nicholls, and M. Popham. 1970. "A Euboean centaur." *BSA* 65: 21–30, plates 7–11.

Des Places, E. 1971. *Oracles chaldaïques*. Paris. Text and French translation.

Detienne, M. 1971. "Orphée au miel." *QUCC* 12: 7–23. English translation in 1981. *Myth, religion and society*, edited by R.L. Gordon, 95–110. Cambridge,.

Detienne, M., and J.-P. Vernant, 1978. *Cunning intelligence in Greek culture and society*. Hassocks. Translation of 1974. *Les ruses d'intelligence: la Metis des grecs*. Paris.

Deubner, L. 1900. *De incubatione*. Leipzig.

————. 1922. *Magie und Religion*. Fribourg-en-Brisgau.

Dick, B.F. 1963. "The technique of prophecy in Lucan." *TAPA* 94: 37–49.

Dickie, M.W. 1990. "Talos bewitched: Magic, atomic theory and paradoxography in Apollonius' *Argonautica* 4.1638–88." *Papers of the Leeds International Latin Seminar* 6: 267–96.

————. 1991. "Heliodorus and Plutarch on the evil eye." *CP* 86: 17–29.

————. 1995. "The Fathers of the Church and the evil eye." In Maguire 1995, 9–34.

————. 1996. "What is a *kolossos* and how were *kolossoi* made in the Hellenistic period?" *GRBS* 37: 237–57.

————. 1999. "The learned magician and the collection and transmission of magical lore." In Jordan, Montgomery, and Thomassen 1999, 163–94.

————. 2000. "Who practiced love-magic in Classical antiquity and in the Late Roman world?" *CQ* 50: 563–83.

————. 2001. *Magic and magicians in the Graeco-Roman world*. London.

Dietrich, M., and O. Loretz. 1990. *Mantik in Ugarit, Keil-alphabetische Texte der Opferschau—Omensammkungen—Nekromantie*. Münster.

Di Fabio, A. 1993. "La catabasi di Orfeo in Ermesianatte di Colofone: metamorfosi di un mito." In Masaracchia 1993, 199–210.

Di Marco, M. 1993. "Dioniso ed Orfeo nelle Bassaridi di Eschilo." In Masaracchia 1993, 101–53.

Dingwall, E. 1930. *Ghosts and spirits in the ancient world*. London.

Diouf, E. 2000. "Magie et droit chez Pline l'Ancien." In Moreau and Turpin 2000, 3: 71–84.

Dodds, E.R. 1951. *The Greeks and the irrational*. Berkeley.

———. 1963. "New light on the 'Chaldaean oracles.'" *HTR* 54: 263–73.

———. 1973. "Supernormal phenomena in classical antiquity." In *The ancient concept of progress and other essays on Greek literature and belief*, 156–210. Oxford.

Doerig, J. 1991. "La tête qui chante." In Borgeaud 1991, 61–4.

Donnadieu, M.-P., and S. Vilatte. 1996. "Genèse de la nécromancie hellénique: de l'instant de la mort à la prédiction du futur (la Nekuia de l'Odysée, Ephyra, Perachora)." *Dialogues d'histoire ancienne* 22, 2: 53–92.

Dover, K.J. 1969. *Theocritus: Select poems*. Edited with an introduction and commentary. London.

Drexler, J. 1884–1937. "Meridianus daemon." In Roscher 1884–1937, 2: 2832–6.

Dronke, P. 1962. "The return of Eurydice." *C&M* 23: 198–215.

Dubois, L. 1995. "Un tablette de malédiction de Pella. S'agit-il du premier texte macédonien?" *REG* 108: 190–7.

Du Bourguet, P. 1975. "Ensemble magique de la période romaine en Égypte." *Revue du Louvre* 25, 255–7.

Dugas, C. 1915. "Figurines d'' envoûtement trouvées à Délos." *BCH* 39: 413–23.

Dunant, C. 1978. "Sus aux voleurs!" *Museum Helveticum* 35: 241–4.

Dunbabin, K.M.D., and M.W. Dickie. 1983. "Invidia rumpantur pectora." *JbAC* 26: 737.

Dundes, A., ed. 1981. *The evil eye*. New York.

Dzielska, M. 1986. *Apollonius of Tyana in legend and history*. Rome.

Easterling, P.E., ed. 1982. *Sophocles. Trachiniae*. Cambridge.

Ebeling, E. 1925. *Liebeszauber im Alten Orient*. Mitteilungen der Altorientalischen Gesellschaft 1.1. Leipzig.

Eckels, R.P. 1937. "Greek wolf-lore." Ph. D. Diss., University of Pennsylvania.

Edelstein, E.J. and L. 1945. *Asclepius: A collection and interpretation of the testimonies*. 2 vols. Baltimore.

Edwards, M.J. 1989. "Three exorcisms in the *New Testament* world." *Eranos* 87: 117–26.

———. 1997. "Simon Magus, the bad Samaritan." In *Portraits*, edited by M. Edwards and S. Swain, 69–91. Oxford.

Egger, R. 1948. "Liebeszauber." *JOAI* 37: 112–20.

Eisler, R. 1925. *Orphisch-dionysische Mysteriengedanken in der christliche Antike*. Leipzig.

Eitrem, S. 1909. *Hermes und die Toten*. Christiania Videnskabs-Selskabs Forhandlinger for 1909, no. 5. Kristiania, Norway.

———. 1924. "Die rituelle *diabolê*." *SO* 2: 33–61.

———. 1925. *Papyri Osloenses*. Fasc. 1. *Magical Papyri*. Oslo.

———. 1928. "The necromancy of in the *Persae* of Aeschylus." *SO* 6: 1–16.

———. 1933. "Das Ende Didos in Vergils *Aeneis*." *Festskrift H. Koht*, 29–41. Oslo.

———. 1941. "La magie comme motif littéraire chez les grecs et les romains." *SO* 21: 39–83.

———. 1945. "La Sibylle de Cumes et Virgile." *SO* 24: 88–120.

———. 1991. "Dreams and divination in magical ritual." In Faraone and Obbink 1991, 175–87

———. Forthcoming. *Magie und Mantik der Griechen und Römer*.

Ekschmitt, W. 1998. "Das Totenorakel von Ephyra." *Antike Welt* 29, 3: 225–30.

Elat, M. 1982. "Mesopotamische Kriegsritualen." *BO* 39: 5–25.

Elderkin, G.W. 1937. "Two curse inscriptions." *Hesperia* 6: 382–95.

Eliade, M. 1964. *Shamanism*. London.

———. 1972. *Zalmoxis, the vanishing god*. Chicago.

Elsworthy, F.T. 1895. *The evil eye*. London.

Engelmann, H. 1975. *The Delian Aretology of Sarapis*. Études préliminaire aux religions orientales dans l'Empire romain 44. Leiden.

Ernout, A. 1957. "La magie chez Pline l'Ancien." *Latomus* 16: 628–42.

Errondonea, J., 1927. "Deianeira vere DEI-ANEIRA."*Mnemosyne* 55: 145–64.

Evans-Pritchard, E.E. 1937. *Witchcraft, oracles and magic among the Azande.* Oxford. See also M. Douglas. 1980. *Evans-Pritchard*, 49–61. Glasgow.

Fahz, L. 1904. *De poetarum romanorum doctrina magica* RGVV 2.3. Giessen, Germany.

Fantham, E. 1995. "Aemilia Pudentilla, or a wealthy widow's choice." In *Women in antiquity: New assessments*, edited by R. Hawley, and B. Levick, 220–32. London.

Fantuzzi, M., and F. Maltomini. 1996. "Ancora magi in Teocrito (vii 103–14)." *ZPE* 114: 27–9.

Faraone, C.A. 1985. "Aeschylus' *hymnos desmios* (*Eum.* 306) and Attic judicial curses." *JHS* 105: 150–4.

———. 1987. "Hephaestus the magician and near-eastern parallels to Alcinous' watch-dogs." *GRBS* 28: 257–80.

———. 1989a. "Clay hardens and wax melts. Magical role-reversal in Virgil's eighth *Eclogue.*" *Classical Philology* 84: 294–300.

———. 1989b. "An accusation of magic in classical Athens (Ar. *Wasps* 946–48)." *TAPA* 119: 149–60.

———. 1991a. "The agonistic context of early Greek binding spells." In Faraone and Obbink 1991, 3–32.

———. 1991b. "Binding and burying the forces of evil: The defensive use of 'voodoo' dolls in ancient Greece." *CA* 10: 165–205.

———. 1992a. "Aristophanes *Amphiaraus* Frag. 29 (Kassel-Austin): Oracular response or erotic incantation?" *CQ* 42: 320–7.

———. 1992b. "Sex and power: Male-targeting aphrodisiacs in the Greek magical tradition." *Helios* 19: 92–103.

———. 1992c. *Talismans and Trojan horses: Guardian statues in Greek myth and ritual.* Oxford.

———. 1993a. "Molten wax, spilt wine, and mutilated animals: Near eastern and early Greek oath ceremonies." *JHS* 113: 60–80.

———. 1993b. "The wheel, the whip, and other implements of torture: Erotic magic in Pindar *Pythian* 4:213–19." *CJ* 89: 1–19.

———. 1994. "Deianeira's mistake and the demise of Heracles: Erotic magic in Sophocles' *Trachiniae.*" *Helios* 21, 2: 115–35.

———. 1995. "The "performative future' in three Hellenistic incantations and Theocritus' *Second Idyll.*" *CP* 90: 1–15.

———. 1996. "Taking Nestor's cup seriously: conditional curses and erotic magic in the earliest Greek hexameters." *CA* 15: 77–112.

———. 1999a. *Ancient Greek love magic.* Cambridge, Mass.

———. 1999b. "The construction of gender in ancient Greek love magic." In Jordan, Montgomery, and Thomassen 1999, 279–82. Summary of Faraone 1999a.

———. Forthcoming-a "The ethnic origins of a Roman era *philtrokatadesmos* (*PGM* IV 296–343)."

———. Forthcoming-b *Incantation as a poetic genre in ancient Greece.*

Faraone, C.A., and D. Obbink, eds. 1991. *Magika hiera: Ancient Greek magic and religion.* New York.

Fauth, W. 1975. "Die Bedeutung der Nekromantie-Szene in Lucans *Pharsalia.*" *RhM* 118: 325–44.

Felton, D. 1999. *Haunted Greece and Rome. Ghost stories from classical antiquity.* Austin.

Festugière, A.J. 1944–45. *La révélation d'Hermès Trismégiste.* 4 vols. Paris.

———. 1959. *Antioche païenne et chrétienne.* Paris.

Fick, N. 1985. "La magie dans les métamorphoses d'Apulée." *REL* 63: 132–47.

Finkel, I.C. 1983–84. "Necromancy in ancient Mesopotamia." *AfO* 29–30: 1–17.

Flint, V. 1999. "The demonisation of magic and sorcery in Late Antiquity" In Flint et al. 1999, 277–348.

Flint, V., R.L. Gordon, G. Luck, and D. Ogden. 1999. *The Athlone history of magic and witchcraft in Europe.* vol. 2. London.

Flintermann, J.P. 1995. *Power, Paideia and Pythagoreanism*. Amsterdam.

Foerster, W. 1972. *Gnosis*. Oxford.

Fortenbaugh, W.V., ed. 1992. *Theophrastus of Eresus: Sources for his life, writings, thought and influence*. Leiden.

Fossum, E. 1989. "Samaritan sects and movements." In *The Samaritans*, edited by. A.D. Crown, 293–389. Tübingen.

Foster, B.O. 1899. "Notes on the symbolism of the apple in classical antiquity." *HSCP* 10: 39–55.

Foti, G., and G. Pugliese Caratelli, 1974. "Un sepolcro di Hipponion e un nuovo testo orfico." *PP* 29: 91–126.

Fowden, G. 1986. *The Egyptian Hermes: A historical approach to the late pagan mind*. Cambridge.

Fox, W.S. 1912a. *The Johns Hopkins Tabellae Defixionum*. Baltimore.

———. 1912b. "Submerged tabellae defixionum." *AJP* 33: 301–10.

———. 1913–14. "Old Testament Parallels to *Tabellae Defixionum*." *American Journal of Semitic Languages* 30: 111–24.

Frankfurter, D. 1994. "The magic of writing and the writing of magic: The power of the word in Egyptian and Greek traditions." *Helios* 21, 2: 189–221.

———. 1995. "Narrating power: The theory and practice of the magical historiola in ritual spells." In Meyer and Mirecki 1995, 457–76.

Frazer, J.G. 1921. *Apollodorus. The Library*. Loeb Classical Library. 2 vols. Cambridge Mass.

Frederiksen, M.W. 1984. *Campania*. British School at Rome monograph. London.

Freudenburg, K. 1995. "Canidia at the feast of Nasidienus (Hor. *S.* 2.8.95)." *TAPA* 125: 207–19.

Friedrich, H.-V. 1968. *Thessalos von Tralles. Griechisch und lateinisch*. Meisenheim, am Glan, Germany.

Furley, W.D. 1993. "Besprechung unde Behandlung: Zur Form und Funktion von *Epoidai* in der griechischen Zaubermedizin." In *Philanthropia kai Eusebeia: Festschrift für A. Dihle zum 70. Geburstag*, edited by G.W. Most, H. Petersmann, and A.M. Ritter, 80–104. Göttingen.

Gager, J.G. 1972. *Moses in Greco-Roman paganism*. Nashville.

———. 1987. Review of Betz 1986/1992. *Journal of Religion* 67: 80–6.

———. 1992. *Curse tablets and binding spells from the ancient world*. Oxford.

———. 1994. "Moses the magician." *Helios* 21, 2: 179–88.

Galter, H., ed. 1993. *Die Rolle der Astronomie in den Kulturen Mesopotamiens*. Graz.

Ganschinietz/Ganszyniec, R. 1919. "Katabasis." *RE*, 10: 2359–449.

———. 1921. "Katoptromanteia." *RE*, 11. 1: 27–9.

———. 1925. "Lekanomanteia" *RE*, 12: 1879–89.

———. 1929. "De antiquorum psychagogia." *Eos* 32: 557–8.

Garcia Ruiz, E. 1967. "Estudio linguistico de las defixiones latinas no incluidas el corpus de Audollent." *Emerita* 35: 55–89.

Garland, R. 1985. *The Greek way of death*. London.

———. 1989. "The well-ordered corpse: An investigation into the motives behind Greek funerary legislation." *BICS* 36: 1–15.

Garosi, R. 1976. "Indagini sulla formazione del concetto di magia nella cultura romana." In Xella 1976, 13–93.

Gáspár, D. 1990. "Eine griechische Fluchtafel aus Savaria." *Tyche* 5: 13–6.

Geffcken, J. 1930. "Baskanos Daimon." In *Charisteria: Alois Rzach zum achtzigsten Geburstag dargebracht*, 36–40. Reichenberg, Germany.

Gellrich, M. 1993–94. "Socratic magic: Enchantment, irony and persuasion in Plato's dialogues." *CW* 87: 275–307.

Gernet, L. 1981. *The anthropology of ancient Greece*. Baltimore.

Giannini, A. 1965. *Paradoxographorum graecorum reliquiae*. Milan.

Gigante, M. 1986. "Momenti e motivi dell' antica civiltà Flegrea." In Amalfitano 1986, 65–141.

Giordano, M. 1999. *La parola efficace. Maledizioni, giuramenti e benedizioni nella grecia arcaica*. Pisa.

Giuliani, C.F. 1976. "Note sull' architettura nei Campi Flegrei." In *I Campi Flegrei nell' archeologia e nella storia. Convegno internazionale, Roma*, 365–75. Rome.

Gnoli, G., and J.-P. Vernant, eds. 1982. *La mort, les morts dans les sociétés anciennes*. Cambridge.

Goetze, A., and E.H. Sturtevant, 1938. *The Hittite ritual of Tunnawi*. New Haven.

Goodchild, R.G. 1953. "The ring and the curse." *Antiquity* 27: 100–102.

Goode, W.J. 1949. "Magic and religion: A continuum." *Ethnos* 14: 172–82.

Gordon, R. 1987a. "Aelian's peony: The location of magic in the Graeco-Roman tradition." *Comparative Criticism* 9: 59–95.

———. 1987b. "Lucan's Erictho." In *Homo viator: Classical essays for John Bramble*. edited by M. Whitby, P. Hardie, and M. Whitby, 231–41. Bristol.

———. 1997. "*Quaedam veritatis umbrae:* Hellenistic magic and astrology." In *Conventional values of the Hellenistic world*, edited by R.T. Engberg-Pedersen, and L. Hannested, 128–52. Odense.

———. 1999a. "Imagining Greek and Roman magic." In Flint et al. 1999, 159–275.

———. 1999b. "'What's in a list?' Listing in Greek and Graeco-Roman malign magical texts." In Jordan, Montgomery, and Thomassen 1999, 239–78.

Gotoff, H.C. 1985. "The difficulty of the ascent from Avernus." *CP* 80: 35–40.

Gow, A.S.F. 1934. "IYNX, RHOMBOS, rhombus, turbo." *JHS* 54: 1–13.

———. 1952. *Theocritus*. Edited with an introduction, translation, and commentary. 2 vols. Cambridge.

Gow, A.S.F., and D.L. Page. 1965. *The Greek Anthology: Hellenistic Epigrams*. 2 vols. Cambridge.

Gow, A.S.F., and A.F. Scholfield 1953. *Nicander. The poems and poetical fragments*. Cambridge.

Graf, F. 1974. *Eleusis und die orphische Dichtung Athens in vorhellenistischer Zeit*. RGVV 33. Berlin.

———. 1985. *Nordionische Kulte. Religionsgeschichtliche unde epigraphische Untersuchungen zu den Kulten von Chios, Erythrai, Klazomenai und Phokaia*. Rome.

———. 1987. "Orpheus, a poet among men." In *Reflections of Greek mythology*, edited by J.N. Bremmer, 80–106. London.

———. 1991a. "Prayer in magical and religious ritual." In Faraone and Obbink 1991, 188–213.

———. 1991b. "Textes orphiques et rituel bacchique. À propos des lamelles de Pélinna." In Borgeaud 1991, 87–102.

———. 1992. "An oracle against pestilence from a western Anatolian town." *ZPE* 92: 267–79.

———. 1993. "Dionysian and Orphic eschatology: New texts and old questions." In *Masks of Dionysus*, edited by T. Carpenter, and C. Faraone, 239–58. Ithaca.

———. 1994. "The magician's initiation." *Helios* 21, 2: 161–77.

———. 1995. "Excluding the charming: The development of the Greek concept of magic." In Meyer and Mirecki 1995, 29–42.

———. 1997a. "How to cope with a difficult life: A view of ancient magic." In *Envisioning magic: A Princeton seminar and symposium*, edited by P. Schäfer, and H.G. Kippenburg, 93–114. Leiden.

———. 1997b. *Magic in the ancient world*. Cambridge, Mass. Translation of 1996. *Gottesnähe und Schadenzauber: Die Magie in der griechisch-römischen Antike*. Munich; in turn a (slight) expansion of 1994. *La magie dans l'antiquité gréco-romaine*. Paris.

———. 1999. "Magic and divination." In Jordan, Montgomery, and Thomassen 1999, 283–99.

Grant, R. 1964. *La gnose et les origines christiennes*, 63–82. Paris.

Grégoire, H. 1949. "Thraces et Thessaliens, maîtres de religion et de magie." In *Homages à Joseph Bidez et à Franz Cumont*, honn. J. Bidez, and F. Cumont, 375–8. Brussels.

Grègoire, H., R. Goossens, and M. Mathieu. 1949. *Asklèpios, Apollon, Smintheus et Rudra. Études sur le dieu à la taupe et la dieu au rat dans la Grèce et dans l'Inde*. Brussels.

Grenade, P. 1950. "Le mythe de Pompée et les Pompéiens sous les Césars." *REA* 52: 28–63.

Griffith, F.L., and H. Thompson, eds. 1904. *The Leyden papyrus: An Egyptian magical book*. Reprint 1994. New York.

Griffiths, F.T. 1979. "Poetry as *pharmakon* in Theocritus' *Idyll* 2." In *Arktouros: Hellenic Studies presented to Bernard M.W. Knox on the occasion of his sixty-fifth birthday*, edited by G.W. Bowersock, W. Burkert, and M.C.J. Putnam, 81–8. Berlin.

Grotanelli, C. 1987. "Messaggi dagli inferi nella Bibbia ebraica: la necromante di En-dor." In *Archeologia dell' Inferno*. edited by P. Xella, 191–207. Verona.

Guarducci, M. 1978. *Epigrafia greca*. vol. 4. Rome.

Günther, K. 1988. "Der Poseidontempel auf Tainaron." *Antike Welt* 19. 2: 58–60.

Guthrie, W.C.K. 1952. *Orpheus and Greek religion*. 2nd ed. London.

Gwyn Griffiths, J. 1975. *Apuleius of Madauros. The Isis-Book*. Leiden.

Haavio, M. 1958. "Der Seelenvogel." *Studia Fennica* 8: 61–81.

Haldane, J.A. 1972. "'Barbaric cries' (Aesch. *Pers*. 633–79)." *CQ* 22: 42–50.

Hall, E. 1989. *Inventing the barbarian. Greek self-definition through tragedy*. Oxford.

———. 1996. *Aeschylus: Persians* Edited with an introduction, translation, and commentary. Warminster.

Halleux, R. 1981. *Les alchimistes grecs*. Vol. 1. Paris.

Halleux, R., and J. Schamp. 1985. *Les lapidaires grecs*. Paris.

Halliday, W.R. 1913. *Greek divination*, 235–45. London.

Hallock, R.T. 1969. *Persepolis fortification tablets*. Chicago.

Halm-Tisserant, M. 1993. *Cannibalisme et immortalité*. Paris.

Hammond, D. 1970. "Magic: A problem in semantics." *American Anthropologist* 72: 1349–56.

Hansen, W.F. 1980. "An ancient Greek ghost story." In *Folklore on two continents: Essays in honor of Linda Dégh*, edited by N. Burlakoff and C. Lindahl, 71–7. Bloomington.

———. 1989. "Contextualizing the story of Philinnion." *Midwestern Folklore* 15: 101–8.

———. 1996. *Phlegon of Tralles' Book of Marvels*. Exeter.

Hardie, C. 1969. "The Great Antrum at Baiae." *PBSR* 37: 14–33.

———. 1977. Appendix in *Vergil Aeneid vi*, edited by R.G. Austin with an introduction and commentary, 279–86. Oxford.

Harrison, J.E. 1922. *Prolegomena to the study of Greek religion*. Cambridge.

Harrison, S.J. 2000. *Apuleius. A Latin sophist*. Oxford.

Hatch, W.H.P. 1908. "The use of ἀλιτήριος, ἀλιτρός, ἀραῖος, ἐναγής, ἐνθύμιος, παλαμναῖος and προστρόπαιος: A study in Greek lexicography." *HSCP* 19: 157–86.

Headlam, W. 1902. "Ghost-raising, magic and the underworld." *CR* 16: 52–61.

Heath, J. 1994. "The failure of Orpheus." *TAPA* 124: 163–86.

Heckenbach, J. 1912. "Hekate." *RE*, 7: 2769–82.

Heim, R. 1892. *Incantamenta magica graeca latina*. Leipzig.

Heintz, F. 1997. *Simon "Le magicien": Actes 8, 5–25 et l'accusation de magie contre les prophètes thaumaturges dans l'antiquité*. Paris.

*Helios* 21, 2. 1994. Special issue. *Exploring the shadows: ancient literature and the supernatural*. Edited by S.I. Johnston.

Henrichs, A. 1984. "The Eumenides and the wineless libation in the Derveni papyrus." In *Atti del xvii congresso internazionale di papirologia*, 2: 255–68. Naples.

———. 1991. "Namenlosigkeit und Euphemismus: zur Ambivalenz der Chthonischen Mächte im attischen Drama." In *Fragmenta dramatica: Beiträge zur Interpretation der griechischen Tragikerfragmente und ihrer Wirkungsgeschichte*, edited by H. Hoffmann, 161–201. Göttingen.

————. 1994. "Anonynity and polarity: Unknown gods and nameless altars at the Areopagus." *ICS* 19: 27–58.

Herzig, O., 1940. "Lukian als Quelle für die antike Zauberei." Diss., University of Tübingen.

Hickman, R. 1938. *Ghostly etiquette on the classical stage*. Iowa Studies in Classical Philology 7. Cedar Rapids.

Highbarger, E.L. 1940. *The gates of dreams. An archaeological examination of Vergil, Aeneid VI, 893–899*. Baltimore.

Hijmans, B.L., Jr. 1994. "Apuleius orator: 'Pro se de magia' and 'Florida.'" *ANRW* 2. 34.2: 1708–84.

Hijmans, B.L., Jr., and R.T. van der Paardt, eds. 1978. *Aspects of Apuleius' Golden Ass*. Groningen, Netherlands.

Hijmans, B.L., Jr., et al., eds. 1977–95. *Apuleius Madaurensis Metamorphoses*. 4 vols. Groningen.

Hill, D.E. 1973. "The Thessalian trick." *RhM* 116: 221–38.

Höfer, O. 1884–1937. "Psychopompos." In Roscher 1884–1937, 3:2, cols. 3256–8.

Hoepfner, W. 1966. *Forschungen an der Nordküste Kleinasiens ii.1: Herakleia Pontike— Eregli: eine baugeschichtliche Untersuchung*. Ergänzungsbände zu den Tituli Asiae Minoris, nr. 1. Vienna.

————. 1972. "Topographische Forschungen." In *Forschungen an der Nordküste Kleinasiens i*, edited by D. Asheri, W. Hoepfner, and A. Erichsen, Ergänzungsbände zu den Tituli Asiae Minoris, nr. 5, 37–46, plans 4–5, plates 1–3. Vienna.

Hoevels, F.E. 1979. *Märchen und Magie in den Metamorphosen des Apuleius von Madaura*. Amsterdam.

Holt, P. 1981. "Disease, desire and Deinaneira: A note on the symbolism of the *Trachiniai*." *Helios* 8: 63–73.

Homolle, T. 1901. "Inscriptions d'Amorgos." *BCH* 25: 412–56.

Hopfner, T., 1921–24. *Griechisch-ägyptischer Offenbarungszauber*. Studien zur Paläographie und Papyruskunde. 2 vols. Frankfurt.

————. 1926. "Die Kindermedien in den griechisch-ägyptischen Zauberpapyri." In *Recueil N.P. Kondakov*, hon. N.P. Kondakov, 65–74. Prague.

Hughes, D.D. 1991. *Human sacrifice in ancient Greece*. London.

Humphrey, J.H., F.B. Sear, and M. Vickers, 1972–73. "Aspects of the circus at Lepcis Magna." *Libya Antiqua* 9–10, 25–97, plates 18–37.

Hunink, V. 1997. *Apuleius of Madauros. Pro se de magia*. 2 vols. Edited with a commentary. Amsterdam.

Huxley, G.L. 1958. "Odysseus and the Thesprotian oracle of the dead." *PP* 13: 245–8.

Ingallina, S. 1974. *Orazio e la magia*. Palermo.

Inwood, B. 1992. *The poem of Empedocles*. Toronto.

Jacoby, F. 1944. "GENESIA: A forgotten festival of the dead." *CQ* 38: 65–75.

Jackson, H.M. 1978. *Zosimos of Panopolis, On the Letter Omega*. Missoula, Montana.

Jahn, O. 1855. "Über en Aberglauben des bösen Blicks bei den Alten" *ASG* 7: 28–110.

Jameson, M.H., D.R. Jordan, and R.D. Kotansky. 1993. *A lex sacra from Selinus. GRBS* supplement. Durham, N.C.

Jobbé-Duval, E. 1924. *Les morts malfaisants, "larvae, lemures," d'après le droit et les croyances populaires des Romains*. Paris.

Johnson, W.R. 1987. *Momentary monsters. Lucan and his heroes*. 19–33. Ithaca.

Johnston, S.I. 1990. *Hekate Soteira: A study of Hekate's roles in the Chaldaean oracles and related literature*. Atlanta.

————. 1991. "Crossroads." *ZPE* 88: 213–20.

————. 1994. "Penelope and the Erinyes: *Odyssey* 20.61–82." *Helios* 21,2: 137–59.

————. 1995a. "Defining the dreadful: Remarks on the Greek child-killing demon." In Meyer and Mirecki 1995, 361–87.

————. 1995b. "The song of the *Iynx*: Magic and rhetoric in *Pythian* 4." *TAPA* 125: 177–206.

————. 1999a. *Restless dead*. Berkeley.

————. 1999b. "Songs for the ghosts: Magical solutions to deadly problems." In Jordan, Montgomery, and Thomassen 1999, 83–102. Summary of part of Johnston 1999a.

————. 2000. "Le sacrifice dans le papyrus magiques grecs." In Moreau and Turpin 2000, 2: 19–36.

Johnston, S.I., and T.J. McNiven, 1996. "Dionysus and the underworld in Toledo." *MH* 53: 23–36.

Jones, C.P. 1985. "Neryllinus." *CP* 80: 40–5.

Jordan, D.R. 1976. "*CIL* viii 19525 (B).2: QPVULVA = Q(UEM) P(EPERIT) VULVA." *Philologus* 120: 127–32.

————. 1977. "A ghost-name ENEMERESEPTA." *ZPE* 24: 147–9.

————. 1980a. "Hekatika" *Glotta* 83: 62–5.

————. 1980b. "Two inscribed lead tablets from a well in the Athenian Kerameikos." *AM* 95: 225–39.

————. 1985a. "Defixiones from a well near the southwest corner of the Athenian agora." *Hesperia* 54: 205–55.

————. 1985b. "The inscribed gold tablet from the Vigna Codini." *AJA* 89: 162–7.

————. 1985c. "A survey of Greek defixiones not included in the special corpora." *Greek, Roman and Byzantine Studies* 26: 151–97.

————. 1988a. "A love charm with verses." *ZPE* 72: 245–59.

————. 1988b. "New archaeological evidence for the practice of magic in classical Athens." In *Praktika tou xii diethnous synedriou klasikês archaiologias 1983–4*. Vol. 4. 273–7. Athens.

————. 1988c. "New defixiones from Carthage." in *The circus and a Byzantine cemetary at Carthage*, vol. 1, edited by J.H. Humphrey, 117–40, including, at 134–40, appendix, by A. Rosenberg, "The conservation of lead curse tablets." Ann Arbor.

————. 1989. "New evidence for the activity of scribes in Roman Athens." In *Abstracts of the American philological association—120th annual meeting (Baltimore)*, 55. Atlanta.

————. 1990. Review of Tomlin 1988. *JRA* 3: 439–40.

————. 1991. "A new reading of a phylactery from Beirut." *ZPE* 88: 61–9.

————. 1999. "Three curse tablets." In Jordan, Montgomery, and Thomassen 1999, 115–24.

Jordan, D.R., H. Montgomery, and E. Thomassen, eds. 1999. *The world of ancient magic*. Papers from the Norwegian Institute at Athens 4. Bergen.

Jost, M. 1985. *Sanctuaires et cultes d'Arcadie*, 258–67. Paris.

Jouan, F. 1981. "L'évocation des morts dans la tragédie grecque." *RHR* 198: 403–21.

Kagarow, E.G. 1929. *Griechische Fluchtafeln*. Eus Supplement 4. Leopoli, Poland.

Kaimakis, D. 1976. *Die Kyraniden*. Meisenheim am Glan, Germany.

Kakridis, J.T. 1929. "*Ἀραί*." Athens.

Kalitsounakis, I. 1953–54. Ἡ ἐν τῇ ἀρχαίᾳ φιλολογίᾳ ψυχομαντεία τῶν ἀποθνησκόντων." *Arch. Ephem*. Part 3, 146–56.

Karsai, G. 2000. "La magie dans l'*Odyssée*: Circé." In Moreau and Turpin 2000, 2: 185–98.

Kees, H. 1923. "Seth." *RE* 2. Reihe ii.a cols. 1896–1922. Stuttgart.

Kenney, E.J. 1990. *Apuleius. Cupid and Psyche*. Cambridge.

Kerenyi, K. 1959. *Asklepios. Archetypal image of the physician's existence*. New York. Translation of 1947. *Der göttliche Arzt: Studien über Askelpios unde seine Kultstätten*. Basel.

————. 1976. *Hermes, guide of souls*. Woodstock, Conn. Translation of 1944. *Hermes der Seelenführer*. Zürich.

Kern, O. 1920. *Orpheus*. Berlin.

————. 1922. *Orphicorum fragmenta*. Berlin.

Kerrigan, M.B. 1980. "A theme by the CA painter: Necromancy at lake Avernus." *Archaeology News* 9: 21–32.

Kingsley, P. 1995. *Ancient philosophy, mystery and magic: Empedocles and the Pythagorean tradition.* Oxford.

Kippenberg, H.G. 1997. "Magic in Roman civil discourse: Why rituals could be illegal." In *Envisioning magic: A Princeton seminar and symposium,* edited by P. Schäfer, and H.G. Kippenberg. Studies in the History of Religions 75, 137–63. Leyden.

Kittredge, G. 1885. "Arm-pitting among the Greeks." *AJP* 6: 151–69.

Klotsche, E.H. 1918. "The supernatural in the tragedies of Euripides as illustrated in prayers, curses, oaths, oracles, prophecies, dreams and visions." *University Studies of the University of Nebraska* 18: 55–106.

Knigge, U. 1991. *The Athenian Kerameikos.* Athens. Translation of 1988. *Der athenische Kerameikos.* Athens,

Knight, J.F. 1970. *Elysion: On ancient Greek and Roman beliefs concerning a life after death.* New York.

Korenjak, M. 1996. *Die Ericthoszene in Lukans* Pharsalia: *Einleitung, Text, Übersetzung, Kommentar.* Frankfurt.

Kotansky, R. 1991. "Incantations and prayers for salvation on inscribed Greek amulets." In Faraone and Obbink 1991, 107–37.

———. 1994. *The Greek magical amulets. The inscribed gold, silver, copper and bronze lamellae.* Part 1. *Published texts of known provenance.* Papyrologica Coloniensia Vol. 22. 1. Opladen.

———. 1995. "Greek exorcistic amulets." In Meyer and Mirecki 1995, 243–78.

Kötting, B. 1954. "Böser Blick." *RAC* 2: 473–82.

Kraggerud, E. 1999. "Samson Eitrem and the death of Dido: a literary reappraisal of a magical scene." In Jordan, Montgomery, and Thomassen 1999, 103–12.

Kramer, B., M. Erler, D. Hagedorn, and R. Hübner, eds. 1980. *Kölner Papyri 3.* Papyrologica Coloniensia Vol. 8. Opladen.

Kraus, T. 1960. *Hekate. Studien zu Wesen und Bild der Göttin in Kleinasien und Griechenland.* Heidelberg.

Krauss, F.B. 1930. *An interpretation of the omens, portents and prodigies recorded by Livy, Tacitus and Suetonius.* Philadelphia.

Kresic, S. 1968. "Le rameau d'or chez Virgile." *EMC/CV* 12: 92–102.

Kurtz, D.C., and J. Boardman. 1971. *Greek burial customs.* London.

Kytzler, B. 1989. *Geister, Gräber unde Gespenster: antike Spuksgeschichten.* Leipzig.

Laks, A., and G.W. Most, ed. 1997. *Studies on the Derveni papyrus.* Oxford.

Lanata, G. 1967. *Medicina magica e religione popolare in Grecia fino all' età di Ippocrate.* Filologia e critica 3. Rome.

Lancellotti, M.G. 2000. "Problèmes méthodologiques dans la constitution d'un corpus des gemmes magiques." In Moreau and Turpin 2000, 2: 153–66.

Lardinois, A. 1992. "Greek myths for Athenian rituals: Religion and politics in Aeschylus' *Eumenides* and Sophocles' *Oedipus Coloneus.*" *GRBS* 33: 313–27.

Larson, J. 1995. *Greek heroine cults.* Madison, Wisc.

Lateiner, D. 1990. "Deceptions and delusions in Herodotus." *Classical Antiquity* 9, 2: 230–46.

Lattimore, R. 1962. *Themes in Greek and Latin epitaphs.* Urbana, Illinois.

Lawson, J.C. 1934. "The evocation of Darius (Aesch. *Persae* 607–93)." *CQ* 28: 79–89.

Lee, M.O. 1965. "Orpheus and Eurydice: Myth, legend and folklore." *C&M* 26: 402–12.

Le Glay, M. 1977. "Magie et sorcellerie à Rome au dernier siècle de la république." In *Mélanges Jacques Heurgon,* 525–50. Paris.

Leutsch, E.L. von, and F.G. Schneidewin, eds. 1834–51. *Corpus Paroemiographorum Graecorum.* 2 vols. Göttingen.

Levi della Vida, G. 1933. "Sulla tabella devotionis punica." *RSO* 14: 312–3.

Lévy, I. 1926. *Recherches sur les sources de la légende de Pythagore.* Paris.

Lewy, H. 1978. *Chaldaean oracles and theurgy.* 3rd ed. Paris.

*Lexicon Iconographicum Mythologiae Graecae.* 1981–. Zurich.

Lichtheim, M. 1973–80. *Ancient Egyptian literature.* 3 vols. Berkeley.

Liedloff, C. 1884. *"De tempestatis, necyomanteae, inferorum descriptionibus quae apud poetas Romanos primi post Chr. saeculi leguntur."* Diss., University of Leipzig.

Limberis, V. 1991. "The eyes infected by evil: Basil of Caesarea's Homily *On Envy.*" *HTR* 84: 163–84.

Linforth, I.M. 1941. *The arts of Orpheus.* Berkeley.

Lloyd-Jones, H. 1981. "Notes on P. Köln iii 125 (Aeschylus, *Psychagogoi?*)." *ZPE* 42: 21–2.

———. 1990. "Erinyes, Semnai Theai, Eumenides." In *Owls to Athens: Essays on classical subjects presented to Sir Kenneth Dover,* edited by E.M. Craik, 203–11. Oxford.

Lobeck, C.A. 1829. *Aglaophamus sive de theologiae mysticae graecorum causis.* 3 vols. Continuous pagination. Königsberg.

Longo, V. 1989. "Oniromanzia e negromanzia nel *Bellum Civile* di Lucano." *Atti dell' Accademia Ligure di Scienze e Lettere* 45: 331–42.

Lopez Jimeno, M.d. A. 1991. *Las tabellae defixionis de la Sicilia griega.* Amsterdam.

Loraux, N. 1993. "Melissa, moglie e figlia di tiranni." In *Grecia al femminile,* edited by N. Loraux, 3–37. Rome.

Lowe, J.E. 1929. *Magic in Greek and Latin literature.* Oxford.

Luck, G. 1962. *Hexen und Zauberei in der römischen Dichtung.* Zurich.

———. 1985. *Arcana mundi. Magic and the occult in the Greek and Roman worlds.* Baltimore.

———. 1999. "Witches and sorcerers in Classical literature." in Flint et al. 1999, 91–158.

McCartney, E.S. 1925. "How the apple became a token of love." *TAPA* 56: 70–81.

McCarty, T. 1989. "The shape of the mirror: Metaphorical catoptrics in classical literature." *Arethusa* 22: 161–95.

McCown, C.C. 1923. "The Ephesia grammata in popular belief." *TAPA* 54: 128–40.

MacDowell, D.M. 1982. *Gorgias: Encomium of Helen.* Edited with an introduction, translation, and commentary. Bristol.

McKay, A.G. 1972. *The Phlegraean fields: Ancient Campania.* Vol. 1. London.

Magdelain, A. 1976. "Le *pomerium* archaique et le *mundus.*" *REL* 54: 71–109.

Maguire, H., ed. 1995. *Byzantine magic.* Washington, D.C.

Majercik, R. 1989. *The Chaldaean oracles: Text, translation and commentary.* Studies in Greek and Roman Religion 5. Leiden.

Mainoldi, C. 1984. *L'image du loup et du chien dans la Grèce ancienne d'Homère à Platon.* Paris.

Maiuri, A.G. 1963. *I campi Flegrèi. Dal sepolcro di Virgilio all' antro di Cuma.* 4th ed. Rome. English translation of an earlier edition: 1958. *The Phlegraean fields.* Rome.

Maltomini, F. 1979. Review of "Eroticism in the Greek magical papyri: Selected studies," by D.F. Moke, Ph.D. diss.. University of Minnesota 1975 *Aegyptus* 59: 273–84.

Mankin, D. 1995. *Horace. Epodes.* Cambridge.

Manning, C.E. 1970. "Canidia in the *Epodes* of Horace." *Mnemosyne* 23: 393–401.

Marastoni, A. 1979. "Sull' episodio Lucaneo della Thessala vates (6, 413–830)." In *Studi di poesia Latina in onore di Antonio Traglia,* hon. A. Traglia. 2 vols. Continuous pagination, 2: 777–88. Rome.

Margalioth, M. 1966. *Sepher ha-Razim.* Jerusalem.

Mariani, L. 1910. "Osservazioni intorno alle statuette plumbee sovanesi." *Ausonia* 4, 1: 39–47.

Marinatos, N. 1995. "Circe and liminality: Ritual background and narrative structure." In *Homer's world: Fiction, tradition and reality,* edited by Ø. Andersen, and M. Dickie, 133–40. Bergen.

Martin, P.M. 1984. *La Campanie antique des origines à l'éruption de Vésuve.* Paris.

Martindale, C.A. 1977. "Three notes on Lucan vi." *Mnemosyne* 30: 375–87.

———. 1980. "Lucan's Nekuia." In *Studies in Latin literature and Roman history,* edited by C. Deroux, Collection Latomus 168. 367–77. Brussels.

Martinez, D.G. 1991a. *A Greek love charm from Egypt (P. Mich. 757).* American Studies in Papyrology 30. Michigan Papyri. Vol. 16. Atlanta.

———. 1991b. "T. Köln inv. and erotic *damazein*." *ZPE* 83: 235–6.

———. 1995. "'May she neither eat nor drink': love magic and vows of abstinence." In Meyer, and Mirecki 1995, 335–60.

Martini, M.C. 1977. *Piante medicamentose e rituali magico-religiosi in Plinio*. Rome.

Masaracchia, A., ed. 1993. *Orfeo e l'orfismo*. Rome.

Massart, A. 1959. "À propos des 'listes' dans les textes funéraires et magiques." *Analecta Biblica* 12: 227–46.

Masson, O. 1972. "La grande imprécation de Sélinonte (SEG XVI, 573)." *BCH* 96: 375–88.

Massoneau, E. 1934. *La magie dans l'antiquité romaine*. Paris. Reedited version of 1933. *Le crime de la magie dans le droit romain*. Paris.

Masters, J. 1992. *Poetry and civil war in Lucan's Bellum Civile*, 179–215. Cambridge.

Maury, A. 1877. *La magie et l'astrologie dans l'antiquité et au moyen age*. 4th ed. Paris.

Meier, G. 1937. *Die assyrische Beschwörungs Sammlung Maqlu*. Archiv fur Orient-forschung, beiheft 2. Berlin.

Meiggs, R., and D. Lewis, eds. 1969. *A selection of Greek historical inscriptions to the end of the fifth century B.C.* Oxford.

Mellor, C. 1968. *L'Hyperborée et les Hyperboréens*. Mémoire de maîtrise, Faculté des Lettres et Sciences humaines de Paris. Paris.

Mende, H. 1913. "De animarum in poesi epica et dramatica ascensu." Diss. University of Breslau.

Merkelbach, R., and M.L. West, eds. 1967. *Fragmenta Hesiodea*. Oxford.

Merkelbach, R., et al. 1990–. *Abrasax. Ausgewählte Papyri religiösen und magischen Inhalts*. Abhandlungen der Rheinisch-Westfälischen Akademie der Wissenschaften. Sonderreihe Papyrologica Coloniensia. 4+ vols., Opladen.

Merlan, P. 1954. "Plotinus and magic." *Isis* 44: 341–8. Reprinted in his 1976 *Kleine Schriften*, 388–95. Berlin.

Méthy, N. 2000. "Magie, religion et philosophie au second siècle de notre ère. À propos du dieu-roi d'Apulée." in Moreau and Turpin. 2000, 3: 85–108.

Meuli, K. 1935. "Scythica." *Hermes* 70: 121–76.

———. 1975. *Gesammelte Schriften*. Basle.

Meyer, M., ed. 1987. *The ancient mysteries: A sourcebook*. San Francisco.

Meyer, M., and P. Mirecki, eds. 1995. *Ritual power in the ancient world*. Leiden.

Meyer, M., and R. Smith, eds. 1994. *Ancient Christian magic: Coptic texts of ritual power*. San Francisco.

Milne, M.J. 1966. "The poem entitled 'Kiln.'" In *The techniques of Attic painted pottery*, edited by J.V. Noble. 102–13 (appendix 3). London.

Molt, M. 1938. *Ad Apulei Madaurensis Metamorphoseon librum primum commentarius exegeticus*. Groningen.

Mommsen, T., P. Krüger, and A. Watson, eds. 1985. *The digest of Justinian*. 4 vols. Philadelphia.

Monti, A. 1980. *The Campi Phlegraei: Vulcano-Solftara*. Venice.

Moore, C.H. 1963. *Ancient beliefs in the immortality of the soul*. New York.

Moraux, P. 1960. *Un défixion judiciaire au Musée d'Instanbul*. Brussels.

Moreau, A. 1976. "L' oeuil maléfique dans l'oeuvre d'Éschyle." *REA* 88: 50–64.

———. 1994. *Le mythe de Jason et Médée. Le va-nu-pied et la sorcière*. Paris.

Moreau, A., and J.-C. Turpin, eds. 2000. *La magie*. 4 vols. Montpellier.

Morel, W., and C. Büchner. 1982. *Fragmenta Poetarum Latinorum Epicorum et Lyricorum praeter Ennium et Lucilium*. 2nd ed. Teubner. Leipzig.

Morford, M.P.O. 1967. *The poet Lucan. Studies in rhetorical epic*, 59–74. Oxford.

Morgan, M.A., ed. 1983. *Sepher ha-Razim. The book of mysteries*. Chico, Calif.

Moritz, H.E. 1979. "Refrain in Aeschylus: Literary adaptation and traditional form." *CP* 74: 187–213.

Morris, I. 1989. "Attitudes towards death in archaic Greece." *CA* 8: 296–320.

Moschou, L. 1975a. "Τοπογραφικὰ Μάνης" *AAA* 8: 160–77.

——. 1975b. "Τοπογραφικὰ Μάνης' *Πελοποννησιακά*" Supplement vol. 6. Acts of the First International Congress of Peloponnesian Studies. Sparta.

Motte, A. 2000. "À propos de la magie chez Platon: l'antithèse sophiste-philosophe vue sous l'angle de la pharmacie et de la sorcellerie." In Moreau and Turpin, 2000, 2: 267–92.

Mouselimis, S.G. 1987. ὁ αρχαῖος Ἅδης καὶ τὸ νεκυομαντεῖο τῆς Ἐφύρας. Ioannina, Greece.

Müller, D. 1987. *Topographischer Bildkommentar zu den Historien Herodots: Griechenland*. Tübingen.

Mugler, C. 1959. "Sur l'origine et le sens de l'expression *kathairein ten selenen.*" *REA* 61: 48–56.

Myers, J.L. 1938. "Persephone and the pomegranate (*H. Dem.* 372–4)." *CR* 52: 51–2.

Myers, S.K. 1996. "The poet and the procuress: The *lena* in Latin love elegy." *JRS* 86: 1–21.

Nagy, J.F. 1990. "Hierarchy, heroes and heads: Indo-European structures in Greek myth." In *Approaches to Greek myth*, edited by L. Edmunds,. 200–238. Baltimore.

Nardi, E. 1960. *Case "infestate da spirit" e diritto Romano e moderno*. Milan.

Naveh, J., and S. Shaked, 1985. *Amulets and magic bowls. Aramaic incantations from late antiquity*. Jerusalem. 2nd ed., with additions and corrections, 1987.

——. 1993. *Magic spells and formulae. Aramaic incantations of late antiquity*. Jerusalem. Texts in continuous series with Naveh and Shaked 1985.

Nelson, G.W. 1940. "A Greek votive iynx-wheel in Boston." *AJA* 44: 443–4.

Nock, A.D. 1925. "Magical notes 1: The sword of Dardanus." *JEA* 11: 154–158. Reprinted in Nock 1972.

——. 1927. "The Lyra of Orpheus." *CR* 41: 169–71.

——. 1928. "Alexander of Abonouteichos." *CQ* 22: 160–2.

——. 1929. "The Greek magical papyri." *Aegyptus* 15: 219–35. Reprinted in Nock 1972.

——. 1950. "Tertullian and the *Ahori.*" *VC* 4: 129–41. Reprinted in Nock 1972.

——. 1972. *Essays on religion and the ancient world*. Edited by Z. Stewart. 2 vols. Oxford.

Norden, E. 1916. *P. Vergilius Maro Aeneis Buch VI*. 2nd ed. Leipzig.

Novara, A. 2000. "Magie, amour et humour chez Properce." In Moreau and Turpin 2000, 3: 15–44.

Nouveau-Piobb, M.F. 1961. *Hécate, la déesse magique des âmes*. Paris.

Oesterreich, T.K. 1930. *Possession, demonical and other: Among primitive races in antiquity, the Middle Ages and modern times*. London. Translation of 1921. *Die Besessenheit*. Langsalza, Germany.

Ogden, D. 1999. "Binding spells." In Flint et al. 1999,1–90.

O'Hara, J. 1990. *Death and the optimistic prophecy in Vergil's* Aeneid. Princeton.

O'Higgins, D. 1988. "Lucan as vates." *CA* 7: 208–26.

Olivieri, A., et al., eds. 1898–1936. *Catalogus codicum astrologorum graecorum*. 12 vols. Brussels.

Otto, W.F. 1923. *Die Manen oder Von den Urformen des Totenglaubens*. Berlin.

Paetz, B. 1970. *Kirke und Odysseus*. Berlin.

Pagano, M., M. Reddé, and J.-M. Roddaz. 1982. "Recherches archéologiques et historiques sur la zone du lac d'Averne." *MÉFRA* 94: 271–323.

Page, D.L. 1942. *Greek literary papyri*. Vol. 1. Loeb Classical Library. Cambridge, Mass.

——. 1972. *Folktales in Homer's Odyssey*, 49–69. Berkeley.

Paget, R.F. 1967a. "The Great Antrum at Baiae." *Vergilius* 13: 42–50.

——. 1967b. "The Great Antrum at Baiae: A preliminary report." *PBSR* 35: 102–12, plates 27–28.

——. 1967c. *In the footsteps of Orpheus: The finding and identification of the lost entrance to Hades, the oracle of the dead, the river Styx and the infernal regions of the Greeks*. London.

Pailler, J.-M. 1987. "Les matrones romaines et les empoisonnements criminels sous la République." *CRAI* 111–28.

Papachatzis, N.D. 1976. "Ποσειδῶν Ταινάριος." *Arch. Eph.* 102–25.

Parassoglou, G. 1976. "Circular from a prefect: Sileat omnibus perpetuo divinandi curiositas." In *Collecteanea papyrologica. Texts published in honor of H.C. Youtie*, edited by A.E. Hanson, hon. H.C. Youtie, 1: 262–74. Bonn.

Paratore, E. 1974. "Seneca e Lucano, Medea ed Erictho." in *Hispania Romana*. Accademia nazionale dei Lincei, 169–81. Rome. Reprinted in 1976. *Romanae litterae*, edited by E. Paratore, 585–95. Rome.

———. 1992. *Lucano.* 55–66. Rome.

Parke, H.W., and B.C. McGing, 1988. *Sibyls and Sibylline prophecy in classical antiquity.* London.

Parker, R.C.T. 1983. *Miasma.* Oxford.

———. 1984. "A note on φόνος, θυσία, and μασχαλισμός." *LCM* 9: 138.

———. 1995. "Early Orphism." In *The Greek world*, edited by A. Powell, 483–510. London.

Parry, H. 1992. *Thelxis: Magic and imagination in Greek myth and poetry.* Lanham, Md.

Pauly, A.F., G. Wissowa, and W. Kroll, 1893–. eds. *Real-Encyclopädie der klassischen Altertumswissenschaft.* Multiple volumes and series. Stuttgart.

Perdrizet, P. 1922. *Negotium perambulans in tenebris.* Publications de la faculté des lettres de Strasbourg 6. Strasburg.

Pérez, B. 2000. "La magie d'Éros." in Moreau and Turpin. 2000, 1: 293–306.

Peter, H., ed. 1883. *Historicorum Romanorum Fragmenta.* Teubner. Leipzig.

Petit, P. 1956. *Libanius et la vie municipale à Antioche au IVe siècle.* Paris.

Petrakos, V.C. 1968. *Ὁ Ὠρωπὸς καὶ τὸ ἱερὸ τοῦ Ἀμφιαράου.* Athens.

———. 1974. *The Amphiareion of Oropus.* Athens.

Petropoulos, J.C.B. 1988. "The erotic magical papyri." *Proceedings of the eighteenth international congress of papyrology*, 2:215–22. Athens.

———. 1993. "Sappho sorceress: Another look at frag. 1 (L.-P.)." *ZPE* 97: 43–56.

Petzl, G. 1994. "Die Beichtinschriften Westkleinasiens." *Epigraphica Anatolica* 22. Article occupies entire volume.

Petzl, G., and H. Malay. 1987. "A new confession-inscription from the Katakekaumene." *GRBS* 28: 459–72.

Pharr, C. 1932. "The interdiction of magic in Roman law." *TAPA* 63: 269–95.

Philip, J.A. 1966. *Pythagoras and early Pythagoreanism.* Toronto.

Phillips, C.R., III, 1991. "*Nullum crimen sine lege*: Socioreligious sanctions on magic." In Faraone and Obbink 1991, 260–76.

Phillips, E.D. 1953. "Odysseus in Italy." *JHS* 73: 53–67.

Pinch, G. 1994. *Magic in ancient Egypt.* London.

Pirenne-Delforge, V. 1993. "L'iynge dans le discours mythique et les procédures magiques." *Kernos* 6: 277–89.

Powell, U.E. 1925. *Collecteanea Alexandrina.* Oxford.

Pralon, D. 2000. "Théocrite, *La magicienne*." In Moreau and Turpin 2000, 1:307–26.

Préaux, C. 1973. *La lune dans la pensée grecque.* Academie royale de Belgique, mémoire de la classe des lettres, fasc. 4. Brussels.

Préaux, J.G. 1960. "Virgile et les rameau d'or." *Latomus* 45: 151–67.

Preisendanz, K. 1926. *Akephalos. Der kopflose Gott.* Leipzig.

———. 1935. "Nekydaimon." *RE*, 16.2: 2240–66.

———. 1962. "Ephesia Grammata." *RAC* 5: 515–20.

———. 1972. "Fluchtafel (Defixion)." *RAC* 8: 1–29.

Preisendanz, K., and A. Henrichs, 1973–74. *Papyri Graecae Magicae. Die griechischen Zauberpapyri.* 2nd ed. 2 vols. Stuttgart. Revisions to the readings of these papyri and new editorial suggestions, often crucial, are catalogued in Brashear 1995.

Pritchard, J.B. 1955. *Ancient near eastern texts relating to the Old Testament.* 2nd ed. Princeton.

Procopé-Walter, A. 1933. "Iao und Set (zu den figurae magicae in den Zauberpapyri)." *ARW* 30: 34–69.

Pugliese Carratelli, G. 1986. "Vitalità dell' immagine storica dei Campi Flegrei." In Amalfitano 1986, 11–9.

Quiter, R. 1984. *Aeneas und die Sibylle.* Meisenheim am Glan, Germany.

Rabinowitz, J. 1998. *The rotting goddess: The origin of the witch in classical antiquity.* New York.

Radermacher, L. 1979. "Aus Lucians Lügenfreund." In *Festschrift Theodor Gomperz dargebracht zum siebzigsten Geburtstage am 29. März 1902*, edited by M. Schwind, 197–207. Vienna. Reprint.

Radke, G. 1939. "Trophonius." *RE*, 2. Reihe 7a, 678–95.

Raingeard, P. 1934–35. *Hermès psychagogue.* Rennes-Paris.

Raven, M.J. 1983. "Wax in Egyptian magic and symbolism." *OMRL* 64: 7–47.

Rea, J. 1977. "A new version of *P.Yale* inv. 299." *ZPE* 27: 150–6.

Reiner, E. 1938. *Die rituelle Totenklage der Griechen.* Tübinger Beiträge zur Altertumswissenschaft 30. Tübingen.

Reiner, E. 1966. "La magie babylonienne." In *Le monde du sorcier.* Sources orientales 7, 69–98. Paris.

———. 1987. "Magic figurines, amulets and talismans," In *Monsters and demons in the ancient and medieval worlds*, edited by A.E. Farkas, et al., 27–36. Mainz.

Renehan, R. 1992. "The staunching of Odysseus' blood: The healing power of magic." *AJP* 113: 1–4.

Richter, A. 1970. *Virgile, La huitième bucolique.* Paris.

Riese, A., and F. Bücheler, eds. 1894–1926. *Anthologia Latina.* 2 vols., 5 parts and supplement. Teubner. Leipzig.

Riess, E. 1896. "Astragalomanteia." *RE*, 2: 1793.

Ritner, R.K. 1993. *The mechanics of ancient Egyptian magical practice.* Chicago.

Robbins, E.R. 1982. "Famous Orpheus." In *Orpheus: The metamorphoses of a myth*, edited by J. Warden, 3–23. Toronto.

Robert, C. 1917. "Das orakelnde Haupt des Orpheus." *Jahrbuch des kaiserlich deutschen archäologischen Instituts* 32: 146–7.

Robert, L. 1978. "Malédictions funéraires grecques." *CRAI* 241–89.

———. 1981a. "Amulettes grecques." *Journal des Savants* 3–44.

———. 1981b. "Le serpent Glycon d'Abônouteichos à Athènes et Artémis d'Ephèse à Rome." *CRAI* 513–35. Reprinted in 1989. *Opera minora selecta.* Amsterdam.

Roesch, P. 1976. "Lebadeia." In *Princeton encylcopedia of classical sites*, edited by R. Stillwell, Princeton.

———. 1982. *Études béotiennes.* Paris.

———. 1984. "L'Amphiareion d'Oropos." In *Temples et sanctuaires*, edited by G. Roux, 173–84. Lyon.

Rohde, E. 1925. *Psyche. The cult of souls and belief in immortality among the Greeks.* London.

Romanelli, P. 1975. *Orfismo in Magna Grecia.* Atti del quattordicesimo convegno di studi sulla Magna Grecia. Naples.

Römer, F. 1987. "Vom Spuk zur Politik: Der Gespensterbrief des Jüngeren Plinius." *Wiener humanistische Blätter* 29: 26–36.

Roscher, W.H. 1884–1937. *Ausfürliches Lexicon der griechischen und römischen Mythologie.* Leipzig.

Rose, H.J. 1913. "18. The witch scene in Lucan (*Pharsalia*, VI, 419 sqq.)." *TAPA* 44: 50–3.

———. 1948. "Keres and Lemures." *HTR* 41: 217–28.

———. 1950. "Ghost ritual in Aeschylus." *HTR* 43: 257–80.

Rudolph, K. 1977. "Simon Magus–Magus oder Gnosticus? Zur Stand der Debatte." *Theologische Rundschau* 42: 279–359.

Russel, W.M.S., 1981. "Greek and Roman Ghosts." In *The folkore of ghosts*, edited by H.R.E. Davidson, and W.M.S. Russel, 193–213. Cambridge.

Rusten, J.S. 1982. "The Aeschylean Avernus." *ZPE* 45: 33–38.

Saffrey, H.D. 1990. *Recherches sur le néoplatonisme après Plotin*. Paris.

Salles-Dabadie, J.M.A. 1962. *Recherches sur Simon le Magicien*. Paris.

Salmon, J.B. 1984. *Wealthy Corinth*. Oxford.

Sande, S. 1999. "Famous persons as bringers of good luck." In Jordan, Montgomery, and Thomassen 1999, 227–38.

Sandy, G. 1997. *The Greek world of Apuleius. Apuleius and the Second Sophistic*. Leiden.

Sauzeau, P. 2000. "Hékatè, archère, magicienne et empoisonneuse." In Moreau and Turpin 2000, 2: 199–222.

Scarborough, J. 1991. "The pharmacology of sacred plants, herbs and roots." In Faraone and Obbink 1991, 138–74.

Scazzoso, P. 1952. "Il rito regale dell'evocazione di Dario nei *Persiani* di Eschilo." *Dioniso* 15: 287–95.

Schachter, A. 1967. "A Boeotian cult type." *BICS* 14. 1–16.

———. 1981–94. *Cults of Boiotia*. BICS Supplements. 4 vols. London.

Schäfer, J. 1957. "Das Eidolon des Leonidas." In *Charites: Festschrift E. Langlotz*, edited by K. Schauenberg, 223–33. Bonn.

Schibli, H. 1990. *Pherekydes of Syros*. Oxford.

Schlesier, R. 1994. "Zauber und Neid: zum Problem des bösen Blicks in der antiken griechsichen Tradition." In *Tradition und Translation: Festschrift C. Colpe*, C. Elsas, et al., 96–112. Berlin.

Schlörb-Vierneisel, B.1964. "Zwei klassische Kindergräber im Kerameikos." *AM* 79: 85–113.

Schmidt, B. 1913. "Der böse Blick und ähnlicher Zauber im neugriechischen Volksglauben." *NJKlA* 31: 574–613.

Schmidt, B.B. 1995. "The 'witch' of En-Dor, 1 Samuel 28, and Near Eastern necromancy." In Meyer and Mirecki 1995, 111–29.

Schmidt, M. 1972. "Ein neues Zeugnis zum Mythos vom Orpheushaupt." *Antike Kunst* 15: 128–37.

———. 1975. "Orfeo e orfismo nella pittura vascolare italiota." In Romanelli 1975, 105–38.

———. 1981. "Aietes." *LIMC* i.1 (Zurich) 353–5.

———. 1991. "Bermerkungen zu Orpheus in Unterwelts-und Thrakerdarstellungen." In Borgeaud 1991, 31–50.

Schotes, H.-A. 1969. *Stoische Physik, Psychologie und Theologie bei Lucan*, 50–99. Bonn.

Schuchhardt, W.H. 1964. *Das Orpheusrelief*. Stuttgart.

Schumacher, R.W.M. 1993. "Three related sanctuaries of Poseidon: Geraistos, Kalaureia and Tainaron." In *Greek sanctuaries: New approaches*, edited by N. Marinatos, and R. Hägg,. 62–87. London.

Schuster, M. 1930. "Der Werwolf und die Hexen." *WS* 48: 149–78.

Schwartz, J. 1951. *Lucien de Samosate. Philopseudès et De morte Peregrini*. Paris.

———. 1965. *Biographie de Lucien de Samosate*. Collection Latomus. Vol. 83. Brussels.

———. 1981. "Papyri Graecae Magicae und magische Gemmen." In *Die orientalischem Religionen im Römerreich*, edited by M.J. Vermasseren, EPRO 93, 485–509. Leiden.

Schweizer, H. 1937. *Aberglaube und Zauberei bei Theokrit*. Basel.

Scobie, A.S. 1975. *Apuleius Metamorphoses I: A commentary*. Meisenheim, am Glan Germany.

———. 1978. "Strigiform witches in Roman and other cultures." *Fabula* 19: 74–101.

———. 1983. *Apuleius and folklore*. London.

Scurlock, J.A. 1988. "Magical means of dealing with ghosts in ancient Mesopotamia." Ph.D. diss., University of Chicago.

———. 1995. "Magical uses of ancient Mesopotamian festivals of the dead." In Meyer and Mirecki 1995, 93–107.

Segal, A.F. 1981. "Hellenistic magic: Some questions of definition." In *Studies in gnosti-*

*cism and hellenistic religions presented to Gilles Quispel*, edited by R. van den Broek, and M.J. Vermasseren, EPRO 91. 349–75. Leiden.

Segal, C.P. 1962. "Gorgias and the psychology of *logos*." *HSCP* 66: 99–155.

——. 1968. "Circean temptations." *TAPA* 99: 419–42.

——. 1973. "Simaetha and the *Iunx* (Theocritus *Idyll* ii)." *QUCC* 17: 32–43.

——. 1974. "Eros and incantation: Sappho and oral poetry." *Arethusa* 7: 139–60.

——. 1990. "Dionysus and the gold tablets from Pelinna." *GRBS* 31: 411–19.

——. 2000. "*Tantum medicamina possunt*: la magie dans les *Métamorphoses* d'Ovide." In Moreau and Turpin 2000, 3: 45–70.

Seppilli, A. 1971. *Poesia e magia*. 2nd ed. Turin.

Sergent, B. 2000. "Maponos. La malédiction." In Moreau and Turpin 2000, 1:197–218.

Seyrig, H. 1935. "Amulette et sortilèges d'Antioche." *Berytus* 2: 48–50.

Shackleton-Bailey, D.R., ed. 1982. *Anthologia Latina* 1.1 Teubner. Stuttgart.

Sherwin-White, A.N. 1966. *The letters of Pliny: A historical and social commentary*. Oxford.

Simonetti. M. 1970. *Testi gnostici cristiani*, 1–3. Bari.

Smelik, K.A.D. 1979. "The witch of Endor: I Samuel 28 in Rabbinic and Christian exegesis till 800 A.D." *VC* 33: 160–78.

Smith, K.F. 1894. "An historical study of the werewolf in literature." *Publications of the Modern Language Association of America* 9,1: 1–42.

Smith, M. 1978. *Jesus the magician*. San Francisco.

——. 1979. "Relations between magical papyri and the magical gems." *Papyrologica Bruxellensia* 18: 129–36.

Smith, W.D. 1965. "So-called possession in pre-Christian Greece." *TAPA* 96: 403–26.

Solin, H. 1968. *Eine neue Fluchtafel aus Ostia*. Commentationes humanarum literarum. Societas scientiarum Fenica 42.3. Helsinki. See especially "Eine Übersicht über lateinische Fluchtafeln, die sich nicht bei Audollent und Besnier finden," 23–31.

Solmsen, F., and E. Fraenkel, eds. 1966. *Inscriptiones Graecae ad inlustrandas dialectos selectae*. Stuttgart.

Sourvinou-Inwood, C. 1995. *"Reading" Greek death*. Oxford.

Stadler, H. 1913. "Hippomanes." *RE*, 8.2: 1879–82.

Stanford, W.B. 1940. "Ghosts and apparitions in Homer, Aeschylus and Shakespeare." *Hermathena* 56: 84–92.

Stephens, S.A., and J.J. Winkler. 1995. *Ancient Greek novels. The fragments*. Princeton.

Stern, J. 1989. "Demythologisation in Herodotus." *Eranos* 87: 13–20.

Strubbe, J.H.M. 1991. "'Cursed be he that moves my bones.'" In Faraone and Obbink 1991, 33–59.

Stukey, H.J. 1937. "The Cyrenean *hikesioi*." *CP* 32: 32–43.

Sutphen, M. 1902. "Magic in Theocritus and Vergil." In *Studies in honor of Basil L. Gildersleeve*. 315–27. Baltimore.

Sussman, L.A. 1987. *The major declamations ascribed to Quintilian*. Studien zur klassischen Philologie, band 27. Frankfurt.

Tambiah, S.J. 1973. "Form and meaning of magical acts: A point of view." In *Modes of thought*, edited by R. Horton, and R. Finnegan, 199–229. London.

——. 1995. *Culture, thought and social action*. Cambridge.

Taplin, O.P. 1977. *The stagecraft of Aeschylus*. Oxford.

Tarrant, R.J. 1982. "Aeneas and the Gates of Sleep." *CP* 77: 51–5.

Tavenner, E. 1916. *Studies in magic from Latin literature*. New York.

——. 1933. "Iynx and Rhombus." *TAPA* 64: 109–27.

——. 1942. "The use of fire in Greek and Roman love magic." In *Studies in honor of F.W. Shipley*, 17–37. St. Louis.

Thee, F.C.R. 1984. *Julius Africanus and the early Christian view of magic*. Tübingen.

Thomas, K. 1971. *Religion and the decline of magic*. London.

Thomassen, E.1999. "Is magic a subclass of ritual?" In Jordan, Montgomery, and Thomassen 1999, 55–66.

Thraede, K. 1967. "Exorzismus." *RAC* 7: 44–117.

Tomlin, R.S.O. 1988. "The curse tablets." In *The temple of Sulis Minerva at Bath*. Vol. 2. *The finds from the sacred spring*, edited by B. Cunliffe. Oxford University Committee for Archaeology monograph no. 16, 59–277. Oxford. Also published separately (but preserving original pagination) as *Tabellae Sulis: Roman inscribed tablets of tin and lead from the sacred spring at Bath* (fascicle 1 of monograph no. 16). Full list of non-Bath British curse tablets, 60–1.

Toynbee, J.M.C. 1971. *Death and burial in the Roman world*. London.

Tropper, J. 1989. *Nekromantie: Totenbefragung im Alten Orient und Alten Testament*. Alter Orient und Altes Testament 223. Neukirchen-Vluyn, Germany.

Trumpf, J. 1958. "Fluchtafel und Rachepuppe." *AM* 73: 94–102.

———. 1960. "Kydonische Äpfel" *Hermes* 88: 14–22.

Tsantsanoglou, K., and G.M. Parassoglou, 1987. "Two gold lamellae from Thessaly." *Hellenika* 38: 3–16.

Tsukimoto, A. 1985. *Untersuchungen zur Totenpflege (kispum) im alten Mesopotamien* AOAT Alter Orient und Altes Testament 216. Neukirchen-Vluyn, Germany.

Tupet, A.-M. 1976. *La magie dans la poésie latine*. Vol. 1. *Des origins à la fin du règne d'Auguste*. Paris.

———. 1986. "Rites magiques dans l'antiquité romaine." *ANRW* 2:16.3: 2591–2675.

———. 1988. "La scène de magie dans la Pharsale: Essai de problématique." In *Hommages II. Le Bonniec*, edited by D. Porte, and J.-P. Néraudau, 419–27. Brussels.

Turner, E.G. 1963. "A curse tablet from Nottinghamshire." *JRS* 53: 122–4.

Valette, P. 1908. *L'Apologie d'Apulée*. Paris.

———, ed. 1924. *Apulée, Apologie. Florides*. Paris.

Vallas, E., and N. Pharaklas, 1969. "Περὶ τοῦ μαντείου τοῦ Τροφωνίου ἐν Λεβαδείᾳ." *AAA* 2: 228–33.

Van der Paardt, R.T. 1971. *Apuleius. The Metamorphoses III*. Amsterdam.

Van der Waerden, B.L. 1979. *Die Pythagoreer*. Munich.

Van Lieshout, R.G.A. 1980. *Greeks on dreams*. Utrecht.

Van Rengen, W. 1984. "Deux défixions contre les bleus à Apamée (VIe siècle apr. J.-C.)." In *Apamée de Syrie. Bilan des recherches archéologiques 1973–79*, edited by J. Balty, 213–34. Paris.

Van Straten, F.T. 1982. "Twee orakels in Epirus. Het orakel van Zeus in Dodona en het nekyomanteion aan de Acheron." *Lampas* 15: 195–230.

Vatin, C. 1971. "Le règlement de Lébadée sur la consultation de l'oracle de Trophonios." In *Inscriptions de Grèce centrale*, edited by F. Salviat, and C. Vatin. 81–94. Paris.

Verberne, J. 1988. "Lucanus en Vergilius." *Lampas* 21, 1: 25–33.

Vermeule, E. 1979. *Aspects of death in early Greek art and poetry*. Berkeley.

Versnel, H.S. 1985. "'May he not be able to sacrifice . . .': Concerning a curious formula in Greek and Latin curses." *ZPE* 58: 247–69.

———. 1991a. "Beyond cursing: The appeal to justice in judicial prayers." In Faraone and Obbink 1991, 60–106.

———. 1991b. "Some reflections on the relationship magic-religion," *Numen* 38: 177–97.

———. 1994. "Πεπρημένος: The Cnidian curse tablets and ordeals of fire." In *Ancient Greek cult practices from the epigraphic evidence: Proceedings of the second international seminar on ancient Greek cult*, edited by R. Hägg, 145–154. Stockholm.

———. 1996. "Die Poetik der Zauberspruche." In *Die Macht des Wortes*, T. Schabert, and R. Brague, 233–97. Munich.

———. 1998. "And any other part of the entire body that there may be . . . : An essay on anatomical curses." In *Ansichten griechischer Rituale: Geburtstags-Symposium für Walter Burkert*, edited by F. Graf, 217–67. Stuttgart.

———. 1999. "Κόλασαι τοὺς ἡμᾶς τοιούτους ἡδέως βλέποντες 'Punish those who rejoice in our misery': On curse texts and *Schadenfreude*." In Jordan, Montgomery, and Thomassen 1999, 125–62.

Viansino, G. 1995. *Marco Anneo Lucano. La guerra civile (Farsaglia). Libri VI–X*. Mondadori editions. Verona.

Victor, U. 1997. *Lukian von Samosata. Alexandros oder der Lügenprophet*. Leiden.

Vieillefond, J.-R. 1970. *Les "Cestes" de Julius Africanus. Étude sur l'ensemble des fragments avec édition, traduction et commentaires*. Florence.

Villeneuve, R. 1963. *Loups-garous et vampires*. Paris.

Volpilhac, J. 1978. "Lucain et l'Égypte dans la scène de nécromancie de la *Pharsale* vi.413–830 à la lumière des papyri grecs magiques." *REL* 56: 272–88.

Voutiras, E. 1996. "À propos d''une tablette de malédiction de Pella." *REG* 109: 678–82.

———. 1998. *Διονυσοφῶντος γάμοι: Marital life and magic in fourth-century Pella*. Amsterdam.

———. 1999. "Euphemistic names for the powers of the nether world." in Jordan, Montgomery, and Thomassen 1999, 73–82.

Vrugt-Lentz, J.T. 1960. *Mors immatura*. Groningen.

Waegeman, M. 1987. *Amulet and Alphabet: Magical amulets in the first book of Cyranides*. Amsterdam.

Ward, J.O. 1980. "Witchcraft and sorcery in the later Roman Empire and early Middle Ages: An anthropological comment." *Prudentia* 12: 93–108.

———. 1981. "Women, witchcraft and social patterning in the later Roman law codes." *Prudentia* 13: 99–118.

Waszink, E. 1968. "The location of the oracle of Trophonius at Lebadeia." *Bulletin van de Vereeniging tot Bervorderung der Kennis van de Antike Beschavung* 43: 23–30.

Waszink, J.H. 1947. *Quinti Septimi Florentis Tertulliani De Anima*. Edited with an introduction and commentary. Amsterdam.

———. 1954. "Biothanati." *RAC* 2: 391–4.

Watson, L.C. 1991. *Arae: The curse poetry of antiquity*. Leeds.

———. 1993. "Horace *Epode* 5: Theme and purpose." In *Tria Lustra. Essays and notes presented to John Pinsent*, edited by H.D. Jocelyn, and H. Hurt, Liverpool Classical Papers no. 3. 269–82. Liverpool.

Weicker, G. 1902. *Der Seelenvogel*. Leipzig.

Weinreich, O. 1909. *Antike Heiligungswunder: Untersuchungen zum Wunderglauben der Griechen under Römer RGVV* 8.1. Giessen, Germany.

———. 1921. "Alexander der Lügenprophet unde seiner Stellung in der Religiosität des zweiten Jahrhunderts nach Christus." *Neue Jahrbuch für das klassische Altertum* 47: 129–51.

Wellmann, M. 1928. *Die Physika des Bolos' Demokritos und die Magier Anaxilaos aus Larissa*. Abhandlunger der preussischen Akademie der Wissenschaften. Philologische-historische Klasse, no. 7. Berlin.

Wendland, P. 1911. "Antike Gesiter- und Gespenstergeschichten." In *Festschrift zur Jahrhundertfeier der Universität zu Breslau, im Namen der schlesischen Gesellschaft für Volkskunde*, edited by T. Siebs. Breslau.

West, M.L. 1975. "Zum neuen Goldplättchen aus Hipponion." *ZPE* 18: 229–36.

———. 1983. *The Orphic poems*. Oxford.

———. 1997. *The East Face of Helicon. West Asiatic elements in Greek poetry and myth*. Oxford.

West, S. 1983, "P. Mich. 3378: A voice from the grave?" *ZPE* 51: 55–8.

———. 1994. "Nestor's bewitching cup." *ZPE* 101: 9–15.

Wide, S. 1909. "*Aôroi biaiothanatoi*." *Archiv für Religionswissenschaft* 12: 224–33.

Wildhaber, R. 1951. "Kirke und die Schweine." in *Festschrift K. Meuli*, 233–6. Basel.

Will, E. 1953. "Sur la nature de la mantique pratiquée à l'Héraion de Perachora." *Revue de l'histoire des réligions* 143: 145–69.

Willemsen, F. 1990. "Die Fluchtalfeln." In *Die Eckterasse und der Gräberstrasse des Kerameikos*, edited by W.K. Kovacsovics. Kerameikos 14, 142–151. Berlin.

Winkler, J.J. 1980. "Lollianos and the desperadoes." *JHS* 100: 155–81.

———. 1990. *The constraints of desire*. New York.

———. 1991. "The constraints of Eros." In Faraone and Obbink 1991:214–43. Also published in Winkler 1990:71–98.

Wiseman, J. 1998. "Rethinking the 'Halls of Hades.'" *Archaeology* 51, 3: 12–8.

Wortmann, D. 1968. "Neue magische Texte." *BJ* 168: 56–111.

Wright, M.R. 1981. *Empedocles: The extant fragments*. Yale.

Wright, R.P. 1958. "Roman Britain in 1957. Part 2. Inscriptions." *JRS* 48: 150–5.

Wünsch, R. 1897. *Defixionum tabellae [Atticae]*, IG iii.3 Appendix. Guide no. 63. Berlin. "Atticae" is not part of the published title of this volume but is conventionally added to distinguish it from Audollent 1904.

———. 1898. *Sethianische Verfluchungstafeln aus Rom*. Leipzig.

———. 1902. "The limestone inscriptions of Tell Sandahannah." In *Excavations in Paluestine during the years 1898–1900*, edited by F.J. Bliss, and R.A.S. Macalister, 158–87. London.

Wünsch, R. 1909. "Deisidaimoniaka." *ARW* 12: 37–41.

Xella, P., ed. 1976. *Magia. Studi di storia delle religioni in memoria di R. Garosi*. Rome.

Yatromanolakis, Y. 1988. "*Baskanos eros*: Love and the evil eye in Heliodorus' *Aethiopica*." In *The Greek novel, A.D. 1–1985*, edited by R. Beaton, 194–204. London.

Youtie, H.C., and C. Bonner, 1937. "Two curse tablets from Beisan." *TAPA* 68: 43–77.

Zhmud, L. 1992. "Orphism and graffiti from Olbia." *Hermes* 120: 159–68.

———. 1997. *Wissenschaft, Philosophie und Religion im frühen Pythagoreismus*. Berlin.

Ziebarth, E. 1934. "Neue Verfluchungstafeln aus Attika, Boiotien und Euboia." *Sitzungberichte der preussischen Akademie der Wissenschaften. Philologisch-historische Klasse* 1022–34, plates 1–3.

Zintzen, C. 1976. "Geister (Dämonen)." *RAC* 9: 640–67.

Zuntz, G. 1971. *Persephone*. Oxford.

# Index of Source Passages

Please note that these indices direct to source-passages, not to page numbers.

# General Index

Note also the cross-references provided in the commentaries to the source-passages. For ancient authors, the source-passage index should also be consulted.